A Concise History of Chinese Philosophy

Main Currents of Philosophical Thought from Mythology to Mao

Jiefu Xiao
Professor of Chinese Philosophy, Wuhan University

Jinquan Li
Professor of Chinese Philosophy, Zhongshan University

Long River Press
San Francisco

Published in the United States of America by
Sinomedia International Group
Long River Press
360 Swift Avenue, Suite 48
South San Francisco, CA 94080

A portion of this book was originally published by Foreign Languages Press
24 Baiwanzhuang Road, Beijing 100037, China
Translated from the Chinese by Zhang Siqi

Editorial team: Ted Chan, Jane Lael, Chris Robyn
Text design: Linda Ronan
Cover design: Tiffany Cha

Library of Congress Control Number: 2011937586

Contents

Introduction

The study of Chinese philosophy has long suffered from problems of undefined breadth and scope. As a result, the history of Chinese philosophy is often mixed with elements of intellectual and even cultural history, including politics, ethics, jurisprudence, religion, and education. In ancient China, there emerged treatises and books which served as commentary on the academic thought of past ages. This volume refers directly to these original texts, most of which are unknown outside China. Some of the more popular works include *Under Heaven* by Zhuang Zhou (c. 369-286 BC), *A Treatise on the Major Ideas of the Six Schools* by Sima Tan (d. 110 BC), and *Academic Cases of the Song and Yuan Dynasties* and *Academic Cases of Ming Confucians*, both edited by Huang Zongxi (1610-1695). These works, since they summarize and analyze the sources and courses of various schools of thought from different ideological angles under the influence of the demands of different historical periods, are of great value for present-day research in the field of the history of philosophy.

In the West, modern philosophy emerged several centuries ago by casting off religious dogma. Contact with the West led to a similar tendency in China, where independent thought had long been fettered by the Confucian orthodoxy. The pioneers of the study of ancient Chinese philosophy and its history were Zhang Taiyan (1869-1936), Liu Shipei (1884-1919), Liang Qichao (1873-1929) and other scholars. By the mid 20th-century, *An Outline History of Chinese Philosophy (Part One)* by Hu Shi (1891-1962), and *A History of Chinese Philosophy* by Feng Youlan (1895-1990) were published. Since the 1930s the works of Xiao Gongquan (1897-1981), Fan Shoukang (1894-1983), Tang Junyi (1909-1978), Qian Mu (1895-1990), Lu Zhenyu (1900-1980), Du Guoyang

(1889-1961), and Hou Wailu (1903-1987) have enabled the theory of historical materialism and the characteristics of the development of the history of Chinese philosophy to become a true academic discipline.

During the Spring and Autumn (770-476 BC) and Warring States (475-221 BC) periods of Chinese history, the emperors of the Zhou Dynasty were virtually powerless, and a number of states contended for hegemony. Parallel to this in the field of ideas arose the "hundred schools of thought". Confucius, Mencius and Xunzi belonged to the Confucian School; Laozi and Zhuangzi to the Taoist school; Mozi founded the Mohist School; Shang Yang and Han Fei belonged to the Legalist School; Hui Shi and Gongsun Long were leading members of the School of Logicians; and Zou Yan represented the Yin-Yang School. At the same time, there appeared some works of philosophy, such as *Lu's Spring and Autumn Annals* and *Commentaries on the Changes* (also known as *The Ten Wings of the Book of Changes*). This was a Golden Age in the history of Chinese philosophy. In this book the thoughts of these schools are the first focus of our research.

The second focus is the early philosophy of enlightenment, which emerged in the period which saw the transition from the Ming to the Qing dynasties (from the Longqing and Wanli reign periods of the Ming Dynasty to Jiaqing reign period of the Qing Dynasty, namely, from the mid-16th to the early 19th centuries). This was a special historical phase for China in the history of both its social and intellectual development. In the middle period of the Ming Dynasty, after the centuries-old feudal society reached its last phase, new capitalist economic relations began to sprout. Meanwhile, since the decaying relations of production of feudalism and its superstructure obstructed and even destroyed the growth of the new productive force in many ways, various social contradictions became more acute than ever before. During this period the development of philosophical thought, which was promoted by the movement of social contradictions, formed an important stage in the history of Chinese philosophy.

In this system, political organizations and economic structures were closely linked with patriarchal relations. By the reign of Yu the Great, founder of the Xia Dynasty, patriarchal rule characterized by the concept of regarding "the whole country as one own family" had been established. The Shang Dynasty has left at least 200 names of clans.* Among the inscriptions on bones and tortoise shells dating from Shang times, there are the characters *shi* (示) and *zong* (宗) — both indicating patriarchal clan descent. Furthermore, *shi* is divided into two, namely, the major *shi* (大示) and the minor *shi* (小示), the former signifying the direct line, and the latter signifying the collateral line.

During the reign of King Wuding (before 1250 BC), "the right of primogeniture limited to the eldest legitimate son" was established. This limited the right of inheritance to the eldest son born of the legal wife, as distinguished from concubines. This indicates the strengthening of the patriarchal clan system in the Shang Dynasty. The Zhou clan had formerly been a small tribal alliance whose territory extended not much more than 100 *li* (one *li* equals about 500 meters) before it toppled the Shang Dynasty, and its rule was exerted by means of patriarchal relations as before. The Lord of Zhou allowed the heads of the patriarchal clans of varying sizes to rule the different clans. "These in turn gathered the families of the other small clans and administered the slaves owned by their subordinates, so that all of them might be ruled by the Lord of Zhou and follow the commands of the Zhou court." (*The Zuo Commentary·Duke Ding, 4th Year*).

Under the patriarchal system, it was considered that a ruler "inherited his subjects and territory." Zhou the Son of Heaven was the "lord of all under Heaven" and thus supreme ruler of the whole country and at the same time the paramount patriarch. He divided up and apportioned the field, appointed officials and decided their emolument, all according to patriarchal ranking. Between the Son of Heaven, dukes and princes, high ministers and officials, and low-ranking rulers there was a dual relationship: Politically they were members of a hierarchy of duties and responsibilities, but at the same time, they were connected by a blood relationship as the major branch of clan to the minor ones. The latter relations reinforced the rigidity of the system. As for the ruled, blood relations alone fixed their status. "Among the peasants, craftsmen and traders there was no ranking of high and low, but a difference of closeness in relations." (*The Zuo Commentary·Duke Huan, 2nd Year*) In this way,

* Cf. Ding Shan, *Clans and Clan Systems Witnessed from the Inscriptions on Bones and Tortoise Shells,* in Chinese, Beijing: Zhunghwa Book Company, 1988.

the patriarchal clans safeguarded the power of the supreme ruler, and the law of the land was supplemented by family regulations. A sentimental veil of genetic connection was used to adjust the relationship between the monarch and his courtiers, the superior and the inferior, and the antagonisms and contradictions between the ruling class and the ruled, the conqueror and the conquered were obscured. As a result, a pyramidal system of strata and privileges was established, and landholding was based on bloodline, with the clans, be they of the direct line or of a collateral line, inheriting their shares. This was the patriarchal slave society which was being perfected in the Zhou Dynasty. From that time on, this peculiar system exerted a significant impact on Chinese history.

In the Warring States Period the social contradictions were extremely intense and complicated as well. Two social forces are fundamental: one attempting to establish and consolidate the feudal system, the other attempting to maintain the slavery system. In politics, there was a concentrated manifestation of this contradiction, namely, in various states there were political and institutional reforms and struggles to seize power. Early in the first stage of the Warring States Period, the feudal lords began to strive for hegemony in order that the state might become rich and militarily powerful. Political reform aimed at feudalization was carried out in varying degrees in the States of Wei, Han, Zhao, Qi, Chu, Yan, Zheng and Song. A great upsurge in political reform swept across all the states. Comparatively backward both in politics and economy, the state of Qin began to carry out political reform after all the others, but its reform was thorough and on going. Duke Xiao of Qin appointed Shang Yang as his "Left Prime Minister," a senior official in charge of government affairs. In 359 BC and 350 BC, respectively, Shang Yang issued political reform decrees, which made Qin the most powerful of all the states. The success of political reform laid a basis for Qin to unify the whole of China.

In addition, there were new developments in the natural sciences and in technology. In astronomy, there appeared two experts. One was called Gan De, who was a scholar of the State of Qi (or, as some believe, of the State of Chu) The other was called Shi Shen, a scholar of the State of Wei. They made the first star charts in the world. Later these charts were incorporated into one book called *The Star Classics of Messieurs Gan and Shi*. In mathematics, scientists discovered how to calculate volume and the functions of fractions. In physics, magnetism and the compass were discovered, a type of clepsydra, an ancient time-measuring device worked by a flow of water, was invented and the technique of making fire using a concave mirror of bronze to concentrate the sun's rays was discovered. In mechanics, the principles of the pulley and the lever were widely applied. The *Mozi* and the *Book of Diverse Crafts* contain records of investigations of time and space, geometry, optics, acoustics and mechanics. Medicine too made great strides. Bian Que (c. 407-310 BC) was a famous doctor of that period.

In the Warring States Period, the great social changes and development of science inevitably stimulated philosophical thought. Since some states carried out political reform before others, there was an unbalanced development among them both politically and economically. At this time scholars of all the states took a great interest in political theory. Their debates covered topics such as the relationship between Heaven and Man, the connection between the past and the present, the significance of the rites and the laws, and metaphysical and objective being. This was a philosophical reflection of the objective reality of the Warring States Period in which all the states underwent great social upheavals and class struggles. It was also a theoretical reflection of the intellectual ferment that started in the late Spring and Autumn Period. It was said that "Philosophers arose like a swarm of bees," and "A myriad schools of thoughts contended for attention." The main schools of thought were the School of Positive and Negative Forces, the Confucian School, the Mohist School, the Legalist School and the Logicians School.

The main bone of contention between these schools may be summed up as the relationship between Heaven and Man. The first question is whether or not the world is possessed of unity and whether or not the law of the world is objective. The second is whether or not man is possessed of the initiative to know and to transform the objective world. If the the answer is affirmative, what is the relation between man and the objective world? The Taoists of Jixia inherited and transformed the thought of the *Laozi*, and adopted the theory of "the vital *qi* of yin and yang" so as to demonstrate the unity and law of the materialist world. What is more, by advocating "the Way that can only be followed with tranquility," they persisted in the principle of the theory of reflection.

This may be called the logical starting point of the philosophical controversy which was unfolded in this period.

Both Mencius (c. 372-289 BC) and Zhuangzi (c. 369-286 BC), from different angles expounded, and in fact exaggerated, the initiative of man's subjective spirit. Mencius laid stress on the moral conscience, advocating, "One should satisfy the design of one's bodily organization and exert one's nature." Zhuangzi sought freedom of spirit, which he claimed should be totally absolute. These two thinkers, facing objective necessity, inescapably fell into self-contradiction, and finally into fatalism. As we know, Mencius fell into fatalism time and again; even so, some of his propositions in fact surpassed the limitation of his own cognition. For example, he advocated "innate knowledge and instinctive ability," and "man is able to know his own nature and to know Heaven." Therefore, man can "stand in the universe alongside Heaven and Earth." By advocating that "the function of the mind" is rational thinking, he surpassed the narrow empiricism of the Mohist school of thought. Hui Shi (c. 370-310 BC) proposed "the uniformity of the same and the different." Gongsun Long (c. 320-250 BC) proposed "the separation of the qualities of hardness and whiteness from the object itself."

In this way, these philosophers achieved the logical cognition of the difference and identity of things, and the relativity and absoluteness of human knowledge. Zhuangzi came to know that man's knowledge is limited and truth is relative, so he opposed dogmatism but he fell into relativism and agnosticism. The later Mohists combined their knowledge with scientific experiments, and they noticed the affinity between the perceptive and the rational, the relative and the absolute. Based on these ideas, they overcame various wrong tendencies in the debates on the relationship between name and reality.

These developments laid the theoretical groundwork for later scholars, such as Xun Kuang (c. 298-238 BC) and Han Fei (c. 280-233 BC). The former's contribution lies in his critical summary of the various schools of thoughts in the Warring States Period by "dispelling blindness," and by adopting their theories into his own philosophical system he formed several theoretical links interrelated with one another. For example, he affirmed that "Heaven" was nothing but Nature, saying, "The course of Nature is constant." And he made an analysis of the "difference between Heaven and man," saying, "The cause of things" is knowable.

He emphasized that the mankind was "able to live in groups," "man has its own government," therefore he was able to draw a correct conclusion. For example, he says, "The mandate of Heaven can be controlled." He stated, "One who concentrates on the Way will treat things in all their combinations as one thing." Xun Kuang had his own epistemological dialectics, that is, "The mind knows its own emptiness, unity and stillness."

This is a return to the proposition about "the Way that can only be followed with tranquility," which had been put forth by the Taoists of Jixia, but Xun Kuang's proposition is at a level of theoretical thinking much higher than theirs. Xun Kuang made a correct explanation of man's subjective initiative, of the objective law of both Nature and society, and of the relations between the two sides. Han Fei followed in Xun Kuang's footsteps, and went on to assert, "The Way corresponds to the principles." From the *yinkuo*, a device for straightening surfaces or line, he constructed the "Way of the *yinkuo*," that is, using man-made instruments or tools man can remold Nature. So he says, "If you follow the Way, there is nothing that you cannot accomplish." The Mohists had taught that "the name must be in accordance with reality, and this must be tested by man's actions," while Xun Kuang proposed that "learning reaches its terminus when it is fully put into practice." On the basis of these two ideas, Han Fei proposed that the criterion for testing truth was "investigation and checking" real situations. The theories of these men logically marked the high point of the development of pre-Qin Dynasty philosophy.

In 221 BC, the State of Qin unified China, after conquering the other six major Warring States. This was not only a political unification, but a cultural one as well, as the First Emperor of the Qin Dynasty (221-206 BC) unified the administrative, transportation and writing systems of the empire. The Qin Dynasty was the first absolutist feudal empire in Chinese history, which then entered a new era. Historians divide feudal China into two major stages. The earlier stage includes, successively, the Qin-Han Period, the Three Kingdoms, the Western and Eastern Jin Dynasties, the Northern and Southern Dynasties and the Sui-Tang Period. China saw rapid social, political, and culture development in this period, and all these dynasties showed some common features.

The intersection between the Ming and Qing dynasties refers to the period from the Longwan reign period of the Ming to the Qianlong and Jiaqing reign periods of the Qing, namely, from the middle 16th century to the early 19th century. It is a special stage of development both in the history of Chinese society and the history of Chinese ideas. At this stage, the ideological trends in line with the enlightenment, which arose time and time again, followed a historical road full of twists and turns, presenting an era of Renaissance with Chinese characteristics.

The philosophical thought of the enlightenment thinkers at the turn of the Ming and Qing dynasties sprang from the struggle against the Neo-Confucianism of the Song-Ming period. Its development followed an innate logical progress. First of all, in Wang Shouren's doctrine of the mind some self-denying factors emerged, which led to doubts about and denial of feudal dogmatism. Li Zhi rejects "taking the Confucian standard of right and wrong for our own standard," and his doctrine of "childlike innocence" grows out of such self-denying factors. Secondly, from different aspects Fang Yizhi, Huang Zongxi and other scholars all cast off the bonds of the Neo-Confucianism of the Song-Ming period, and opened up a new road for pursuing scholarship, which included the following key points: "In geography and measuring is the universal law," "To be a Confucian of sound scholarship you must read history," "The past should be quoted in order to plan for the present," and "It is necessary to have ability in order to rule the country." Finally, Wang Fuzhi summed up the new achievements in philosophy by comprehensively sublimating the doctrines of the two Cheng brothers, Zhu Xi, Lu Jiuyuan and Wang Yangming, and critically summarizing the Neo-Confucianism of the Song-Ming period. This was the logical terminal of the development of the philosophy of the previous stage of Chinese feudal society. A short time after that, Yan Yuan laid stress on "Learning through practice," while Dai Zhen laid stress on "Knowing through your mind." Their common tendency was to persist in learning based on "realistic things" and the "principle of things," and to place particular emphasis on a metaphysical method focused on inductive inference. This foreshadowed the transformation of Chinese philosophy into philosophical thought in a new form, characterized by metaphysical methodology.

The philosophical trends of the early enlightenment period, in the 17th and 18th centuries, were products of the special historical conditions of the last stage of Chinese feudal society. The social foundation can be traced to the renovation party of the landlord class in the last stage of feudal society. As for the motive force of development, it was the large-scale peasant wars, arising from the serious social crises of the time. During this period, the feudal system still wielded formidable ruling power, although the germs of capitalism had already appeared and the early movement of urban dwellers had mounted the stage of history. Therefore, the ideas of the thinkers of the early enlightenment period were inevitably subject to the class limitations of the times. New shoots were mixed with old dregs. In their struggle against feudal absolutism and its reactionary ideology, the thinkers boldly criticized the old world, but were unable to discover an old one. Although they were brave enough to reveal the social contradictions and the age-old malpractices in the last stage of feudal society, their design for the ideal society had to be hidden under a cloak of "the purport of the six Confucian classics" or "the laws of the three remote dynasties." The entanglement between new thoughts and the old tradition created a queer situation of multiple contradictions between originality and outmoded rules, content and form, the living and the dead. In general, the trends of the early enlightenment moved forward by undulating along an axis. This axis was basically parallel to another axis along which the germination of Chinese capitalism developed in a zigzag manner, and class struggle unfolded wave after wave.

The First Opium War erupted in 1840, and the resultant period of "Unequal Treaties" marked a watershed between two historical epochs. After the Treaty of Nanking in 1842, China entered the stage of being a semi-colonial, semi-feudal society, and the country's early modern history began. From then on, Chinese society underwent a series of unprecedentedly rapid changes, and in the economic structure, class relationships, social struggles, cultural thoughts and suchlike important aspects there appeared many new features, completely different from those of the traditional society. The period of early modern history refers to the 110-year-span from 1840 to 1949, when the People's Republic of China was established. The May 4th Movement of 1919 further divides this period into two stages, one being that of the old democratic revolution, the other being that of the new democratic revolution.

Because the Reform Movement of 1898 and the Revolution of 1911 failed to accomplish the task of wiping out the old feudal culture, the New Culture Movement was initiated. Under the slogan of democracy and science, the New Culture Movement waged a fierce attack against the old feudal culture. Just at that juncture, the First World

War broke out, bringing with it the October Revolution. In these great historical events, all the inner contradictions of Western capitalism were thoroughly exposed. Those who had advocated Western learning became divided, and a controversy over Eastern and Western cultures emerged. At the time of the heated controversy between the "faction of wholesale Westernization" and the "faction of Eastern Culture," some advanced intellectuals turned their eyes from the Western world of capitalist countries to the Soviet Russia of socialism led by Vladimir Lenin. They came to see that only Marxism was the truth that could save the country and the people, and that only the road of the October Revolution was the road to the liberation of China. They began to think profoundly over both traditional Chinese culture and Western capitalist culture. From that time on, Marxism began to develop in China and was integrated into concrete practice.

Chinese philosophy in modern times has developed upon a foundation of the social struggles of the period; it has unfolded against a background of collisions between the ancient and modern cultures of both China and the West. These cultural characteristics became interchangeable and merged and separated in the curvilinear ebb and flow of history.

PART I

Pre-Dynastic Through Early Feudal China

(Mythology to Qin Dynasty)

1.

Philosophy and Divine Right in the Xia, Shang, and Zhou Cultures

The concepts of the Mandate of Heaven (divine rule) and the right of rulers, adhered to by the ruling classes of the slave-owning Xia and Shang dynasties, were preceded by the animism and totemism of primitive society. Hunter-gatherer communities worshipped natural forces; they vaguely formed the concept that such forces were wielded by supernatural beings. As clans and tribes formed, each took a certain animal with an imposing nature as its totem. At the same time, important discoveries were made—how to make fire; how to fish, hunt, and raise livestock—and agriculture and herbal medicine were introduced.

In primitive society, members of a clan owned property collectively. As this was mirrored in their concept of religion, all members had an equal right to communicate with the gods. The subsequent concept and expression of private property rights created polarization between rich and poor, and the new aristocracy began to monopolize the right to communicate with the gods. As a result, the concept of God on High—corresponding to emperor on earth—came into being: the Mandate of Heaven. Emperor Yao created a policy of "cutting off communication between Heaven and Earth" and assigned special officials to mediate between man and God. As a result, the consciousness of democracy and social equality contained in the primitive religion withered away.

During the reigns of the first five rulers of China—the Yellow Emperor, and Emperors Zhuanxu, Ku, Yao and Shun—Chinese society was dominated by the patriarchal system. When slavery became the economic base of society in the Xia Dynasty, the ruler became supreme. "There was not a foot of ground which he did not possess, and there was not one person who was not his subject." (*Mencius·Gongsun Chou, Part I*)

As for the tribes, no matter how remote their territory, they "dared not but come to pay / Homage under his way. / Such was the rule of Shang." (*Book of Poetry·Hymns of Shang·Hymn to King Wuding*) The dynastic rulers owned all land, all slaves. They had the right, bestowed on them by Heaven, to quash rebellion, and to grant titles and territories to their subjects. This intensification and centralization of power was reflected in the sphere of religion as a shift from polytheism to monotheism. The Yin Dynasty rulers were thought to merge with God on High after death.

In Chinese folklore, many myths and legends reflect the yearning of primitive man to overcome the forces of Nature. Pan Gu, creator of the universe, separated heaven and earth; goddess Nuwa created human beings and patched holes in the sky; Kuafu overtook the fleeting rays of the sun; the beauty Chang'e flew to the moon and became the Moon Goddess; Jingwei, a mythical bird said to be the reincarnated drowned daughter of the mythical emperor Yandi, filled the sea with pebbles; and the Foolish Old Man removed mountains blocking his way.

As primitive man gained experience, he learned it was important to understand, not conquer, Nature. In this era arose the story of Yu the Great, who "harnessed the rivers and leveled the land." According to geological research, the melting of retreating glaciers at the end of the Ice Age resulted in massive floods, remembered in the folklore of many civilizations. In China, the Huaxia tribal confederacy in the valley of the Yellow River was afflicted by this disaster.

"In the 13th year of King Wen of Zhou, the Viscount of Ji said, 'I have heard that in the flood time when Gun dammed up the flood, he threw into disorder the arrangement of the five elements: water, fire, wood, metal, and earth. This angered God, who withheld from Gun the nine great principles of how to manage a country, bringing ruin to the realm. Gun's son, Yu the Great, took up his father's unfinished work, and made a great contribution to the welfare of mankind. So God gave him the nine great principles, and order was restored to the country.'" (*Book of History·The Books of Zhou: The Great Norm*)

The legend indicates "five elements" theory started in the great campaign to deal with the floods at the end of the Ice Age. The Viscount of Ji called the five elements the first of the nine great principles. He expounded this theory as follows:

> "The first of the five elements is water; the second is fire; the third is wood; the fourth is metal; and the fifth is earth. Water, which flows downward, has the Nature of moisture. Fire, which rises upward, has the Nature of burning. Wood can be crooked or straight. Metal can be changed in its form according to man's will. And earth can be used to grow grain." (*Book of History·The Books of Zhou: The Great Norm*)

Five element theory is the first summary, based on rudimentary observation of natural phenomena, of the way Nature works, and of the relationship between man and Nature.

We notice first that this theory contains the germination of the concept of difference. Water, fire, wood, metal, and earth are compared with one another. Once this is emphasized, the mind naturally makes the connection with the principle of opposites, or, as it is referred to here, contradiction.

Second, the theory contains the germination of the concept of relationship. Gun's harnessing of the rivers is a good example. Because he was unable to grasp the different natures of water and earth, he tried to stop water with earth (by building dams), and failed. Yu drew a lesson from this, knowing that "water, which flows downward, has the nature of moisture." Yu grasped the objective nature of water and "let high places be high, and low places be low, so that rivers flowed, and backed-up water was expelled." (*Conversations of the States·Conversations of Zhou*)

Third, the theory contains the germination of man's dynamic role. For example, as Yu knew that the property of water was to flow downward, and that it "had the nature of moisture," he ordered Yi, a minister, "to distribute rice seeds among the people, so that they might grow paddy rice in the low-lying damp land," (*Records of the Historian·Primary Chronicle of the Xia Dynasty*)—hence the development of paddy rice.

When Shun learned the property of fire, namely, that it "rises upward and has the nature of burning," he ordered Yi to use fire to consume the forests and vegetation on the mountains and in the marshes, so that the birds and beasts fled and hid." (*Mencius·Duke Wen of Teng, Part I*) This gave birth to the slash-and-burn method of farming. When people ascertained that the property of wood was to be able "to be crooked and straight," they developed methods of transportation. "To travel on land, people employed vehicles; by water, boats; on the muddy moors, sledges; and in mountainous areas, sedan chairs." (*Records of the Historian·Primary Chronicle of the Xia Dynasty*)

When people got to know the property of metal, namely, that "metal can be changed in its form according to the man's will," they immediately made good use of it. As we know, metal (here, bronze) needs a smelting process to produce it, since it is different from water, fire, and other materials, which can be taken directly from Nature. The Viscount of Ji generalized the properties of metal with the two Chinese characters 从 (follow) 革 (change). Literally, these two characters mean that metal "follows man's will to change it." For the first time in the long course of the history of philosophy, a simple generalization about the "dynamic role of man's own will" was made. In short, the primitive theory of the five elements formed when China was first crossing the threshold of civilization. A marked advance from the era of religious superstition, five-element theory exerted a far-reaching influence on the development of Chinese philosophy.

In the last years of the Yin Dynasty, the tyranny of King Zhou exacerbated social contradictions. Yet among the ruling class were those who dared to look squarely at reality with a premonition of social crisis: the Viscount of Ji, the Viscount of Wei, Bi Gan, and others. In the *Book of History· Viscount of Wei*, we can read their comments and opinions:

"Now the subjects of Yin even dare to steal the sacrificial offerings and utensils dedicated to the gods and spirits of Heaven and Earth. As they are bold enough to steal the sacrificial offerings from the temples, what else might they do? If the gods lose their authority, what authority can the king wield?"

When the tyrant King Zhou burned himself to death, and his dynasty came to an end, the Viscount of Ji saw that a ruler must keep in contact with the world outside the court, consulting first with his ministers, then with the common people. He must also pay attention to the "five businesses": appearance, speech, observation, hearing, and thinking: "Appearance should show respect. Speech should be reasonable. Observation should be clear. Hearing should be extensive. And thinking should be sensible" (*Book of History· The Books of Zhou: The Great Norm*).

Ji's ideology is characterized by the materialist theory of reflection—a form of self examination directed at understanding one's actions and the laws that govern them. The content of this reflection is determined by objective activity, what comes in via the senses. Ultimately, reflection yields conscious awareness of how things are done and of the objective world of human culture. In this sense, reflection is a method of philosophy.

This awareness was an important landmark in the history of Chinese epistemology. The *Book of Changes* (*I Ching, Yi Jing*) has long been held to encapsulate the philosophical thought of the early part of the Western Zhou Dynasty. The main body of the book is made up of permutations and combinations of the Eight Diagrams, different patterns of groups of six solid and broken lines. According to legend, Fuxi first drew the Eight Diagrams. If so, the date of the book is much earlier than that of King Wen of the Zhou Dynasty.

A book about divination, in its patterns, numbers, inferences, and evolutions, The *Book of Changes* is a rational kernel. In its inquiries about good or bad fortune, predictions are based on a summary of people's experiences observing the opposing movements of Nature and human society. First, the book contains the view that there is opposition in all things. The title of the *Book of Changes* has been explained as follows: "The sun (日) above and the moon (月) below make the character 'change' (易; 勿 is an alternative form of 月), and symbolizes the unity of yin and yang." The two characters yin and yang do not appear in The *Book of Changes*, but do appear in the *Commentaries on Changes* (*The Ten Wings of the Book of Changes*).

The concept of positive and negative became known very early in Chinese history. For instance, people came to know that a field with a sunny exposure promised a good harvest, while a shady field did not. "The hill and plain, broad and long he surveyed. The streams and springs, light and shade, he surveyed." (*Book of Poetry·Epics·Duke Liu*) From social phenomena, filled with contradictions and opposites, political commentators formed their ideas. "Explain how to administer the way of morality, how to rule over the country, and how to regulate yin and yang." (*Book of History·The Books of Zhou: The Establishment of Offices in the Zhou Dynasty*)

By means of various permutations and combinations, diagrammatic patterns were formed, as were categories such as Stagnation and Peace, Severance and Return, Decrease and Increase, Creative and Receptive. As for the connotations of the two signs, in modern times some scholars think they represent the external male and female genitals; others think they are signs for odd and even numbers invented by diviners in ancient times, later said to represent the concepts of yin and yang.

Second, the book contains the concept of change and development. As its title shows, the book is concerned with changes, that is, it acknowledges that all things change all the time.

> "In the first or lowest line, undivided, we see its subject as a dragon lying hidden in the deep. It is not the time for activity. In the second line, undivided, we see a dragon appearing in a field. It will be advantageous to meet with a great man. In the third line, undivided, we see a superior man active and vigilant all day, and in the evening careful and apprehensive. The position is dangerous, but there will be no mistake. In the fourth line, undivided, we see a dragon looking as if it were leaping up, but still in the deep. There will be no mistake. In the fifth line, undivided, we see a dragon on the wing in the sky. It will be advantageous to meet with a great man. In the sixth and topmost line, undivided, we see a dragon exceeding the proper limits. There will be occasion for repentance. The lines of this hexagram are all strong and undivided from the use of the number nine. If the host of dragons thus appearing were to divest themselves of their heads, there would be good fortune." (Hexagram No. 1, Qian — The Creative)

The dragon, a divine creature able to fly and change its shape, is here used as a metaphor. From "lying hidden in the deep" to "appearing in a field," from "leaping up" to "flying in the sky," the developmental process of change is symbolized. The victory of the "small State of Zhou" over the "big country of Yin" is reflected, too. But the unknown author of *The Book of Changes* did not just blindly hope for the best; he knew there would be frustrations along the way. "The dragon exceeds the proper limits. There will be occasion for repentance" means that the subject of these changes is in a predicament.

Third, the book contains the germination of the transformation of opposites. Reversals and zigzags, which occur in the changing and developmental process, are observed in the *Book of Changes*.

The aphorism used in everday China even today, "Extreme adversity marks the beginning of fortune," is sourced from the *Book of Changes*. The hexagram "Tai" does not mean only gains and no losses; it means great gains with few losses, hence a favorable hexagram. The hexagram "Pi" means having few gains with no great gains, hence unfavorable. But gains and losses, like flat and hilly terrain, constantly shift and can transform into each other. After adversity comes fortune; difficult may become easy; dangerous may become safe. When people do not do a good job, smooth may become difficult; stable may become dangerous. Here the book reminds people to be mentally prepared, that is, though enjoying security one should ever be prepared for danger; in peaceful and prosperous times one should never forget upheavals and rebellions. In this respect, primitive dialectics radiates with eternal light.

Fourth, the book deals with the relationship between the transformation of a contradiction and the subjective initiative of man. The author of the *Book of Changes* knew that while opposites may transform into each other, the conditions and results of the transformation have much to do with man's efforts. As success or failure of a business is closely related to man's efforts, the author was careful to sum up experiences in this aspect. For instance, the hexagram Modesty asks people to be modest instead of arrogant. "The superior man adds humility to humility." Once he turns the corner, he will find himself "in every way at an advantage." (Hexagram No. 15, Qian — Modesty)

There is a distinction between the *Book of Changes* and the primitive theory of the five elements. The former understands the initiative spirit of man better than the latter. By the time the *Book of Changes* came into being, the level of dialectics of Chinese thinkers had risen.

The *Book of Changes* mirrors the social changes of the transition from Yin to Zhou. The conquest of the mighty State of Yin by the small tribal group of Zhou illustrates the dialectical principle of how the new replaces the old:

> "Yin neglected moral administration, and that is why it prematurely lost the blessing of Heaven." (*Book of History· The Books of Zhou: The Announcement of Zhaogong*)

> "Heaven never ignores human feelings. It takes account of virtue. There is no eternal sovereign in the people's hearts; what they cherish is the benevolent sovereign." (*Book of History· Pseudo-Ancient Text· Caizhong*)

The lesson of the loss of the Mandate of Heaven by Yin and its passing to Zhou provided scholars with important ideological materials for discussing philosophical problems such as the relationship between Heaven and man, humans and gods, force and fate.

From the reign of King Li (877–841 BC), the relative stability of Western Zhou society was disturbed, and a period of turbulence set in. The ruler was slandered openly, and the concepts of the Mandate of Heaven and the divine right of rulers were questioned. A number of the era's poems, called "the disguised songs and odes," are valuable materials for studying the history of Chinese philosophy.

The Spring and Autumn Period of the Western Zhou Dynasty marked the beginning of the collapse of slave society, and the consequent rise of class contradictions, here exposed in these poems:

"Chop, chop! We cut down the elms,
And pile them on the river bank,
By the waters clear and rippling.
Those who neither sow nor reap,
How then do they have three hundred sheaves?
They neither hunt nor gather.
But precious badgers hang in their yards.
How wonderful to be a lord,
And not have to work for food!"
—*Book of Poetry· Folksongs of Wei· The Woodcutter's Song*

In this series of metaphors for the drastic changes taking place in society, opposites began to transform into their antitheses:

"Bad omen. The moon and sun don't keep their proper way.
In the states evil's done; the good are kept away.
An eclipse of the moon is no uncommon thing,
That of the sun at noon will dire disaster bring.
Lightning flashes, thunder rolls; there's neither peace nor rest.
Streams bubble from underground; crags fall from the mountain-crest.
The heights become deep vales; deep vales turn into heights.
Men of this time bewail; what to do in such a plight?"

—*Book of Poetry·Odes·President Huangfu*

These poems cast doubt on the Mandate of Heaven and the authority of the Son of Heaven, the emperor. This is the first movement of ideological emancipation in the history of Chinese philosophy. Some poets blamed earthly troubles on Heaven itself.

"Heaven is unfair!
…
Heaven is pitiless!
…
Heaven is unjust!"

—*Book of Poetry·Odes·To Grand Master Yin*

"God's influence spreads over the people here below.
God's terror strikes so fast; he deals them blow on blow."

—*Book of Poetry·Epics·Warnings*

"Heaven on high is not kind for long,
Spreading famine far and wide.
Heaven is unfair, punishing the innocent,
And smiling on the guilty ones."

—*Book of Poetry·Odes·Untimely Rain*

In these poems, there appears no concept of Heaven having moral attributes. It became natural to focus on society as the source of fortune both good and bad. In the history of epistemology in China, this shows a progression from theism via skepticism to atheism.

"My woe was brought upon me by my unkind lord."

—*Book of Poetry·Folksongs of Bei·The Degraded Queen*

The parasitical aristocracy was sometimes referred to as scavenging birds or rats:

"O yellow bird, hear me please.
Don't settle on the trees.
Don't eat my paddy grain.
…
O yellow bird, hear me please.
Don't perch on the mulberry trees.
Don't eat my sorghum grain.
…
O yellow bird, hear me please.
Don't settle on the trees.
Don't eat my millet grain."

—*Book of Poetry·Odes·Yellow Birds*

Two progressive views emerged: "Harmony is the true producer of things," and "Yin and yang move in a regular order." Shi Bo and Yang Bofu are representatives of these propositions, by which they further probed into and explained opposing phenomena in both Nature and human society, and attacked the theories of the Mandate of Heaven and the divine right of rulers.

Another important theory in early Chinese philosophy is that of the five elements. The primitive theory of the five elements emerged in the efforts to harness Nature, specifically rivers. In this extract, by generalizing the categories of harmony and identity, Shi Bo puts forth two aspects of a philosophical world outlook.

Duke Huan of Zheng asked Shi Bo: "Is the Zhou Dynasty going to decline?" Shi Bo answered, "Probably it will decline." Shi Bo explained that it asked only for identity, instead of harmony. "Things harmonious with one another may truly produce milliards of things; things simply identical to one another find it hard to last long.

Heaven made myriad things by mixing earth with metal, wood, water, and fire. A single sound cannot appeal to people's ears. One color cannot form intricate patterns. One flavor cannot make food delicious. A single thing cannot be used to make a comparison. How can a king stress identity and ignore harmony? (*Conversations of the States·Conversations of Zheng*).

By generalizing the categories of harmony and identity, Shi Bo puts forth two aspects of a philosophical world outlook.

First is the problem of the origin of the world. For the first time, Shi Bo used an abstract philosophical proposition to expound on the relationship between "things" and the "five elements." By "thing," he meant the numerous material objects in the macro world that differ from one another in thousands of ways. He talked about earth, metal, wood, water and fire, regarded as basic elements that when combined produce all things. This is a materialist point of view.

Second is the problem of relations among opposites. Shi Bo strictly differentiated the categories of "harmony" and "identity," and opposed stressing identity at the expense of harmony. What does "identity" mean? It means one element balancing another so that the unity of a contradiction may be reached. For instance, music pleasing to the ear is the result of "harmonizing the six tones," delicious dishes are the result of "harmonizing the five flavors," the milliard things are the result of "mixing the five materials" and "combining them in dozens of ways."

Therefore, a wise king should be good at "coordinating some things with other things." To govern a country in this way, a "harmonious and pleasing family-like situation" may be brought about. A king may then "carefully choose courtiers who dare to criticize," so that he may hear different opinions unpleasant to the ear. In ancient times "to cut off," that is, to remove people with different views, was regarded as a sure recipe for disaster.

Shi Bo advocated "coordinating some things with other things." This means he opposed metaphysics, which stresses absolutely the identical. It also means that he admitted the existence of opposites, so that contradictions old and new might be kept in balance. This ideology echoes the conflict between the rising forces of feudalism and the established forces of slavery during the changeover from the Western to Eastern Zhou dynasties.

Besides the five elements there is the conceptual pair of yin and yang, which

emerged at an ancient date. But yin and yang used as philosophical concepts are a semiotic matter that arose in a later age. Bo Yangfu, a scholar of the last phase of the Western Zhou, explained earthquakes with the theory of yin-yang:

> In the second year of King You of Zhou (780 BC), an earthquake struck the three valleys of Western Zhou. Bo Yangfu commented, "The Zhou Dynasty is going to decline. The vital forces of Heaven and Earth must not lose their order. When they are out of order, someone must have put them out of order. When yang is subdued, it cannot come out. It is yin that enforces such subjection on yang. The earthquake shows that yang has been suppressed by yin. When yang loses its normal position and lies under yin, the river sources become stopped up. When the river sources are stopped up, the country is doomed to perish. When the vital forces of water and earth are unimpeded, the people have the means to live. When water and earth have no place to develop their vital forces, the people are short of materials, and become poor. In such a situation, how can the country avoid extinction?" (*Conversations of the States·Conversations of Zhou, Part I*)

This political treatise discusses social issues brought about by natural catastrophes. In Bo's opinion, three things are worth noticing:

First, what fills the world is not the "five materials" that "the people use all alike; not one can be dispensed with." (*Zuo Commentary·Duke Xiang 27th Year*) What fills the world are the two vital forces of yin and yang, always in motion and contradictory to each other. Here we see that Bo extracted the two vital forces from the five materials or elements.

Second, the two vital forces exist in a process of continual contest: yin wants to emerge, but is suppressed by yang; yang wants to emerge, but is suppressed by yin. When the latter tendency of opposites surpasses a certain degree, an earthquake erupts. By analogy, "political earthquakes" are the result of the social contradictions of his time, and the rule of the aristocratic slave-owners faced general collapse. Thus the doctrine of yin-yang became a theoretical weapon.

In its origin, the doctrine of yin-yang was tinged with simple materialism and naive dialectics. But by the Spring and Autumn Period, the doctrine of yin-yang was in widespread use, as was five elements theory.

2.

The Spring and Autumn Period: Atheism, Dialectics, and the Art of War

In the Spring and Autumn Period, social productivity developed, and the feudal system emerged in advanced states, gradually replacing slavery. The ideological underpinnings of the old slave-owning society—belief in the Mandate of Heaven and the divine right of rulers—were increasingly shaken, and an atheistic tendency arose in the field of philosophy, with Ji Liang, Shi Xiao, Shu Xing, Zi Chan, and others as its proponents.

Ji Liang, a senior official of the State of Sui, lived in the early years of the Spring and Autumn Period. Although he did not deny the existence of gods, he carried forward progressive ideas from the early years of the Western Zhou, such as "What the people desire, Heaven should comply with." (*Book of History·Pseudo-Ancient Text·The Great Declaration*) Ji put forth a new proposition that the common people are the masters of the deities. Therefore, what the ancient sages and rulers did first was to build the wealth of the common people and unite with them." (*Spring and Autumn Annals*)

The proposition that "What the people desire, Heaven should comply with" still contains the implication that Heaven is the force that controls man's destiny. But in Ji Liang's opinion, the common people are the principal drivers, their rulers subordinate. In this breakthrough concept we see the people becoming a stronger force.

Forty years later, a supernatural phenomenon was reported at Shen in the State of Guo. The Duke of Guo offered a sacrifice and asked the local deity to give him more territory. Shi Xiao, a high priest, said, "Alas! The State of Guo will perish. I have heard that when a state is about to flourish, its ruler receives his lessons from the people; and when it is about to perish, he receives his lessons from the gods. The gods are wise, correct, and impartial. But their course is regulated by the feelings of men. The State of Guo is lacking in virtue; how can it obtain any increase of territory?" (*Spring and Autumn Annals*)

In Shi Xiao's opinion, the gods carry out their function according man's good or bad behavior. Compared with Ji Liang, Shi Xiao puts more responsibility on man's role.

Since Ji Liang and Shi Xiao acknowledge the existence of supernatural beings, they are not atheists in the true sense of the word, but do foreshadow the emergence of atheistic thought in later ages.

The *Book of Songs* expresses the viewpoint that the cause of the sufferings and miseries of human beings are not to be sought in Heaven far above, but in society here below. The idea that Heaven and Man should be divided into two categories had already germinated, and in the Spring and Autumn Period it developed further.

In the 16th year of the reign of Duke Xi of the State of Lu, five boulders, likely meterorites, fell from the sky in the State of Song. In the same month, six fish hawks flew backwards over the Song capital. Shu Xing, a historiographer of the Zhou court, was there on business. Duke Xiang of Song asked him what these strange phenomena portended. Shu Xing later told a friend: "The duke asked the wrong question. The phenomena were merely connected with the problem of yin and yang, and had nothing to do with predicting good or evil fortune, which are dictated by the actions of human beings themselves. My answer was a forced one, because I did not dare to disappoint the duke." (*Spring and Autumn Annals*)

Following the trend of thought of Shu Xing, Zi Chan (c. 580–522 BC), a minister of the State of Zheng, proposed that the ways of Heaven and the ways of man should be clearly separated from each other. One year, Mars appeared at dusk. On the seventh day there was wind. Later, the wind became stronger and stronger, and the capitals of the States of Song, Wei, Chen, and Zheng all caught fire. Pi Zao, an official of Zheng, urged a full-scale ritual to placate the gods. Zi Chan, prime minister, did not agree.

"Zi Chan said, 'The way of Heaven is far, far away, but the way of man is near, near by. They have nothing to do with each other. How can we know the relations between them? How can Pi Zao know the way of Heaven?' Zi Chan would not consent to the ritual, and there was no repeat of the calamity." (*Spring and Autumn Annals*)

The idea of separating Heaven and Man put forth by Shu Xing, Zi Chan, and others did not deny that gods, spirits, and other strange beings existed behind natural phenomena. But in opposing the prevailing superstition that celestial phenomena explained human affairs, it played a progressive role.

In the last phase of the Spring and Autumn Period, productivity increased and society underwent profound changes. Accordingly, naive dialectics as a way to understand Nature and social conditions progressed further. Both Yan Ying of the State of Qi and Shi Mo of the State of Jin contributed to this development. Shi Mo's comparatively profound understanding resulted in conclusions that reveal a universal law.

In the last years of the Western Zhou Dynasty, Shi Bo put forth the idea that all things come from the harmony of some things different in nature, not from a simple collection of things of the same kind. Based on this view, Yan Ying held that "harmony" and "identity" are two diametrically opposed categories. He pointed out that miscellaneous and even opposite things "benefit each another" and "complete each other."

Yan Ying expounded on "harmony" and "identity" in a conversation with the ruler of the State of Qi, who thought the relationship between himself and his minister Liang Qiuju was in harmony. Yan Ying disagreed, saying, "Liang Qiuju is only in agreement with you. How can he be said to be in harmony with you? Harmony and identity are different." Achieving harmony is like cooking, he said. People use water, fire, vinegar, soy sauce, salt, and plums to cook fish and meat over a wood fire. Only by mixing different ingredients can the cook adjust the taste properly.

So it is with political affairs. He said, "Were you to season water with water—who would care to taste it? Were a lute to play only one note—who would listen? Liang Qiuju is a yes-man. Whatever the ruler approves, he also approves. Whenever the ruler says 'no,' he says 'no.' One should not always be in agreement with the ruler." (*Spring and Autumn Annals*)

When Yan Ying analyzed the difference between "identity" and "harmony," he held that, as a general rule, contradictions exist: clear and opaque, large and small, long and short, fast and slow, soft and hard, high and low, compact and diffuse, solemnity and joy, male and female, yes and no. They oppose each other, yet may complete each other. There is identity among contradictions; the opposites rely on each other and are linked to each other. This is Yan Ying's cognition of the dialectical relationship of the unity of things.

While Yan Ying's view emphasizes the aspect of opposites completing each other and forming unity, it ignores the aspect of change and transformation. When his theory was applied to political affairs, the intent was to harmonize social contradictions, not to change or transform them.

Yan Ying denied the dominating role of gods and spirits in bringing order and disorder to state affairs. In his opinion, only the ruler's administration brought about order or disorder, and he emphasized that "standards" were needed to ensure good government."

The *Spring and Autumn Annals* records how the powerful Ji overthrew Duke Zhao, ruler of the State of Lu. The duke fled into exile in the State of Jin, and in 510 BC died there. Zhao Yang, a ranking Jin official, made the following inquiry of the historian Shi Mo:

"Ji expelled the ruler. The people obeyed Ji, and the other feudal lords submitted to his authority. When Zhao died outside the state, no one went to incriminate him. What was the reason for this?" It seemed to be a very strange incident. To such a question, Shi Mo gave a brilliant answer.

> "Things are produced in twos, in threes, in fives, and in pairs complementary to each other. Hence there are three celestial bodies (sun, moon, and stars) in Heaven. There are five elements on earth. The human body has left and right sides, and limbs in pairs. Emperors have their dukes, princes have their ministers, all complementary to each other. Heaven produced Ji to assist the rulers of Lu. The people obeyed him. Was it not right in this case? The rulers of Lu have, one after another, been gadding about and self-indulgent. Ji clansmen have, one after another, been diligent and conscientious in

their positions. The people have forgotten their ruler. Who is to pity him?

The altars are not always maintained in a state. Rulers and ministers do not always retain appropriate positions. This has been so since ancient times. Hence *The Book of Songs* says, 'High banks become valleys, / Deep valleys become heights.' Descendants of three previous emperors have become commoners. Among the diagrams in *The Book of Changes* is Da Zhuang—the Power of the Great, a trigram of thunder mounted upon that of Heaven, showing the regular way of Heaven." (*Spring and Autumn Annals*)

Implied in Da Zhuang is that change is brought about through great effort.

In Shi Mo's opinion, the reason why all things that exist have their own process of development lies in the internal contradictory nature of the things themselves, because each and everything is a unity of opposites. Things are "produced in twos, in thress, in fives and in pairs complementary to each other." When Shi Mo mentions "two," it is not a simple number. It means that in the process of growth there are always two sides, contradictory and yet complementary, with one side guiding, the other following. This is true of Nature, the human body, and all human relationships. For example, a man has a wife, a king has ministers, a lord has officials, and in all cases the latter assists the former—"All are complementary to each other."

Shi Mo cites the relationship between the ruler of Lu and the Ji clan as an example of the principle of the transformation of opposites. The ruler of Lu was the main aspect of a contradiction, while the Ji clan served as his subordinate part, as if they had been a pair. When Duke Zhao lost the support of his people because of his incompetence and corruption, the Ji clan, through their diligence in state affairs generation after generation, gained the people's support and were eventually favored by them over Duke Zhao.

Shi Mo's view of contradiction is different from that of Yan Ying, in that Mo emphasized the absoluteness of the struggle between the aspects of a contradiction and the inevitability of their transformation. As court historian for Jin, he found that stable periods in history mask the constant struggle between opposites underneath the surface.

But when contradictions between old and newly emerging forces appear in a society, the struggle inevitably becomes violent. From gradual and quantitative change to sudden and qualitative change, society itself changes, resulting in the two sides of a contradiction switching positions.

More or less contemporary with Shi Mo was the great strategist Sun Wu. The *Sunzi* (*The Art of War*), a military treatise handed down from ancient times, is believed to be his work. Sun Wu is regarded as the first Chinese military strategist, his book the earliest Chinese work of military science. But the book's importance, not confined to its contribution to military science, contains an abundance of thought concerning materialism and dialectics.

The naive materialism in *Sunzi* lies principally in its cognitive line, which urges people to follow the principle of reflective theory, as materialism does, to solve practical problems met in warfare. The main ideas are as follows:

First, one starts from objective practice to set the principles and tactics for pursuing war. From the first chapter:

> "The art of war is governed by five constant factors: Moral law, Heaven, Earth, the Commander, and Method and Discipline. ... These five headings should be familiar to every general. He who knows them will be victorious; he who knows them not will fail. Therefore, in your deliberations, when seeking to determine the military conditions, let them be made on the basis of a comparison, in this way: First, which of the two sovereigns is imbued with moral law? Second, which of the two generals has the most ability? Third, with whom lie the advantages derived from Heaven and Earth? Fourth, on which side is discipline most rigorously enforced? Fifth, which army is stronger? Sixth, on which side are officers and men more highly trained? Seventh, in which army is there greater constancy of both reward and punishment? By means of these seven considerations I can forecast victory or defeat." (*Sunzi·Chapter I: Laying Plans*; hereinafter when quoted only chapter number and title appear)

Sun Wu discusses Method and Discipline carefully. He divides the problem into seven aspects, including weapons and equipment, training of soldiers, and rewards and punishment. In his opinion, objective conditions are the basic factors that decide the outcome. But victory or defeat also depends on commanders. Sun Wu points out:

> "It is a rule in war that when our force is ten to the enemy's one, we surround him; when five to one, we attack him; when twice as numerous, we divide him into two; when equally matched, we offer battle; when slightly inferior in number, we avoid him; when we are quite unequal in every way, we flee from him." (*Chapter III: Attack by Stratagem*)

Second, "When you know the enemy and know yourself, you need not fear the result of a hundred battles." What enables the wise sovereign and the good general to strike and conquer, and to achieve things beyond the reach of ordinary men, is foreknowledge.

> "Hence, when you know the enemy and know yourself, you need not fear the result of a hundred battles. When you know yourself but not the enemy, for every victory gained you will also suffer a defeat. When you know neither the enemy nor yourself, you will lose every battle." (*Chapter III. Attack by Stratagem*)

War is always carried out in perplexing, complicated, and fast-changing conditions; hostile forces may use camouflage and feint. Sun Wu points out that one must see through false appearances when examining the enemy's situation, and cites examples from battle experience:

> "Humble words and increased preparations are signs that the enemy is about to advance. Violent language and driving forward as if to attack are signs that he will retreat when battle is joined. When the light chariots come out first and take up a position on the wings, it is a sign that the enemy is preparing for battle. Peace proposals unaccompanied by a sworn covenant indicate a plot. When there is much running about and soldiers fall into rank, the critical moment has come. When some are seen advancing and some retreating, it is a lure." (*Chapter IX: The Army on the March*)

Materialistic cognition is embodied as the guiding principle of war. Victory is established on the basis of a correct grasp of the objective situation.

There is an abundance of military dialectics in *Sunzi*.

First, as war is organically connected with other things, it is necessary to observe all problems in a balanced way, and to observe them from positive and negative perspectives:

> "As regards military method, we have Measurement, Estimation of Quantity, Calculation, Balancing of Chances, and Victory." (*Chapter IV: Tactical Dispositions*)

Measurement refers to the size of the land surface involved. Estimation of Quantity refers to available resources. Calculation refers to the number of officers and men available. Balancing refers to the comparison between the opposing military forces. Victory refers to the final triumph.

Commanders should observe a problem from both sides, advantageous and disadvantageous: .

> "Only one who is thoroughly acquainted with the evils of war can thoroughly understand the profitable way of carrying it on." (*Chapter II: Waging War*)

> "Hence, in the wise leader's plans, considerations of advantage and disadvantage will be blended. When in the midst of difficulties we are always ready to seize an advantage, we may extricate ourselves from misfortune." (*Chapter VIII: Variation of Tactics*)

To be prepared everywhere means to not be prepared anywhere:

> "Should the enemy strengthen his vanguard, he will weaken his rear; should he strengthen his rear, he will weaken his vanguard; should he strengthen his left, he will weaken his right; should he strengthen his right, he will weaken his left. Were he to send reinforcements everywhere, he will everywhere be weak." (*Chapter VI: Weak and Strong Points*)

Advantage and disadvantage dwell in one and the same thing, so the commander should pay heed in order to turn disadvantage into advantage.

Second, by analyzing the contradictory movement and its transformation in war, Sun Wu emphasizes that it is necessary to adopt flexible tactics to meet the circumstances.

He puts forward a series of antithetical categories to grasp the movement of war: the enemy and ourselves, invading force and defender, superior forces and inferior, strength and weakness, attack and defense, advance and retreat, win and defeat, indirect and direct, weak points and strong, stillness and motion, courage and fear, order and disorder, ease and harassment. Yet each side may turn into its opposite.

> "Simulated disorder postulates perfect discipline; simulated fear postulates courage; simulated weakness postulates strength." (*Chapter V: Energy*)

> "Place your army in deadly peril, and it will survive; plunge it into desperate straits, and it will come off in safety. For it is precisely when a force has fallen into harm's way that it is capable of striking a blow for victory." (*Chapter XI: The Nine Varieties of Ground*)

Deadly peril and desperate straits are disadvantageous conditions; nevertheless, an army in such conditions may come off victorious when a commander acts correctly.

> "Military tactics are like water; for water in its natural course runs away from high places and hastens downwards. So in war, the correct way is to avoid what is strong and strike what is weak. Water shapes its course according to the nature of the ground over which it flows; the soldier works out his victory in relation to the foe he is facing. Therefore, just as water retains no constant shape, so in warfare there are no constant conditions. He who modifies his tactics in relation to an opponent and is thereby victorious may be called a Heaven-born captain." (*Chapter VI: Weak Points and Strong*)

A wise commander will change tactics endlessly, responding to battle situations that change from minute to minute. He must make use of borh direct and inrect methods, the former being conventional tactics used when two armies directly confront one another on the battlefield and the latter being flexible tactics used, for example, in a raid.

> "In all fighting, the direct method may be used for joining battle, but the indirect method is necessary to secure victory..... In battle, there are no more than two methods of attack—the direct and the indirect. It is like moving in a circle—one never comes to an end. Who can exhaust the possibilities of their combination?" (*Chapter V: Energy*)

A true soldier must not unvaryingly adhere to any established practice, as this will lead to failure.

Sun Wu notes that it is necessary to make a good study of the features of the enemy:

> "Five dangerous faults may afflict a general: Recklessness, which leads to destruction; cowardice, which leads to capture; a hasty temper, which can be provoked by insults; a delicacy of honor, which is sensitive to shame; and over-solicitude for his men, which may expose him to worry and trouble." (*Chapter VIII: Variation of Tactics*)

With such information, one may aim at his weak points or make good use of his strong points.

Third, on the basis of acknowledging the material conditions, particular stress is laid on how to give full play to the commander's ability:

> "The clever combatant looks to the effect of combined energy, and does not require too much from individuals." (*Chapter V: Energy*)

A ruler cannot make excessive demands in disregard of possible conditions. At the same time, subjective blind actions are incorrect:

> "No ruler should put troops in the field merely to gratify his own spleen, and no general should fight a battle simply out of pique. When it is to your advantage, make a forward move; when not, stay where you are." (*Chapter XII: The Attack by Fire*)

Sun Wu cautions, "One may know how to conquer without being able to do it." (*Chapter IV: Tactical Dispositions*) Because both sides are eager to take the initiative, when the enemy leaves no chance for us to make use of our initiative, even when we have made careful calculations, it will be hard for us to win, as has occurred many times. Therefore, whether victory can be achieved or not depends on our own concrete conditions and those of the enemy. That is to say, we must take all possibilities into account when we desire to avoid the mistakes of subjectivism and mechanicism.

We can see that while the *Sunzi* is primarily a book on military science, it is solidly based on the principles of naive materialism and naive dialectics. As such, it is an important document in the history of the development of Chinese philosophy.

Moreover, strategies from *Sunzi,* the world's oldest and most successful book on military strategy, are used around the globe to guide transactions of war, peace, business, sales, and negotiations. Those doing business with China in the modern world are advised to study it.

3.

Fate, Benevolence, and Cognitive Theory in the Philosophy of Confucius

Kong Qiu (551–479 BC) with the literary name Zhongni, was generally called Master Kong, Kong Fuzi, later Latinized as Confucius. His ancestors were a noble family of the State of Song before they settled in Zouyi (present-day Qufu, Shandong Province). As a scion of aristocrats, Confucius was familiar with ritual affairs. He acted as a funeral attendant in his youth. He served briefly as head of the forestry department, then as minister of justice of his home State of Lu. In middle age he began to gather disciples and formed a school. After a period of traveling around various states with his disciples seeking in vain a ruler who would put his political and ethical ideas into practice, he returned to Lu and devoted himself to collecting and editing the classics. He is credited with putting into their accepted form the *Book of Songs*, the *Book of History*, the *Book of Rites,* and the *Book of Music*, and he wrote the *Spring and Autumn Annals.* The *Analects* is a collection of his discourses recorded and collated by his disciples, and is the main source for research into Confucian thought.

Confucian thought embodies the ideological features of the period when Chinese society was moving from the slavery system to the feudal system in the last phase of the Spring and Autumn Period. Generally speaking, Confucius tended to be conservative in political thought. He proclaimed, "When good government prevails in the empire, ceremonies, music, and punitive military expeditions proceed from the emperor.

When bad government prevails in the empire, ceremonies, music, and punitive military expeditions proceed from the princes." (*Analects*, 16: 2; book title is omitted hereinafter)

Therefore, he advocated that the rites of the Western Zhou Dynasty be restored, so that the government would not be in the hands of the great officers and there would be no discussions of state affairs among the common people. He maintained that only the Son of Heaven had the right to deal with administration; political power should never fall into the hands of the great officers; and common people had no right to participate in the administration, or to even express an opinion on state affairs. Nevertheless, he recognized that times were changing. Knowing it was impossible to return to the heyday of the Zhou Dynasty, he advocated "change without disorder."

Confucius was honored as a "sage" throughout the history of Chinese feudal society. He is still respected today as an educator and expert on the ancient classics, especially the six he expounded on to his disciples.

In the *Analects* there is a passage: "The subjects of which the Master seldom spoke were profitableness, the appointments of Heaven, and perfect virtue." (9: 1) In the Chinese original, the key words are *yu ming yu ren*. Here the character *yu* is a verb, meaning to follow, to uphold, and to approve. Fate and benevolence are the core points of his world outlook.

Confucius inherited the tradition of calling the supreme dominator of the universe and human society "Heaven" and the blind alien force governing social life "fate." Sometimes he used "Heaven-fate" as one concept, treated as a dominating force that plays its role mysteriously. Sometimes he separated "Heaven" from "fate," although one has much to do with the other. Hence, there are differences in their connotation.

In Confucian theory, "Heaven" is sometimes used as a deity that has its own will and is able to reward or punish. For example:

> "He who offends against Heaven has none to whom he can pray." (3:13)

> "But there is Heaven that knows me!" (14: 35)

> "Heaven produced the virtue that is in me. Huan Tui—what can he do to me?" (7: 23)

"While Heaven does not let the cause of truth perish, what can the people of Kuang do to me?" (9: 5)

In the first two quotations, we sense Confucius' disappointed sigh. In the other two, he shows his confidence in morality, and acknowledges that Heaven bestowed knowledge of ethics upon him. There are, however, times when Confucius is equivocal as to the functions of Heaven:

"The Master said, 'Does heaven speak? The four seasons pursue their courses, and all things are continually being produced, but does Heaven say anything?'" (17: 19)

Some scholars explain: although Heaven does not actually speak, it possesses a sort of personal will that manipulates seasonal changes and the growth of all Nature. Others say that Heaven has no personal will, and is nothing but Nature, which is in a state of continuous change.

Confucius appears to be reconciling the ancient concept of Heaven as a deity and the new concept of Heaven as simply the prime mover of natural forces—a problem that emerged during the changeover from a slave-owning to a feudal society.

As for the relationship between Heaven and man, Confucius inherited and developed the idea of "requiting Heaven with virtue" formed in the early years of the Western Zhou Dynasty. He warns rulers:

"When there is distress and want within the four seas, your Heavenly blessings will come to a perpetual end." (20: 1)

Regarding himself as the heir to the moral and cultural tradition started by King Wen,

Confucius devoted himself to restoring the flourishing age of the Zhou Dynasty, but failed to turn the tide of social change. He thought, then, that there must be some supernatural force dominating everything, and called it "fate."

"If my principles are to advance, it is so determined by fate. If they are to fail, it is likewise determined by fate." (14: 36)

"Without recognizing fate, it is impossible to be a superior man." (20: 3)

Therefore, as a superior man, Confucius could do nothing but accept fate. Here he discusses "fate" only, and leaves "Heaven" aside. When his disciple Ran Boniu fell ill, Heaven could not protect him, and he died. Confucius sighed, "Fate is killing him. Alas!" The Confucian esteem of Heaven finally developed into fatalism, an idealist category of philosophy.

Confucius did his best to explain the social changes taking place in his day in a conservative—not dynamic—way. He simply called on the people of different classes to rest content with their lot in life.

Confucius' separation of "fate" from "Heaven," and his stress on the primacy of "fate" were attacked by Mo Di (c. 476–390 BC), who wrote a chapter in his book titled "Attack on Fatalism."

From the above discussion, we can see that Confucian fatalism, with which he either esteems the Mandate of Heaven or urges people to follow the Mandate of Heaven, belongs to the philosophical category of objective idealism. But when he adds "benevolence" to his theory, he sets a fine example of affirming man's subjective conscientious spirit.

The Confucian theory of benevolence is an *a priori* category of morality. The benevolence advocated by Confucius is possessed of an *a priori* attribute, although it belongs to the category of morality:

> "Superior men, and yet not always virtuous, there have been, alas! But there never has been a mean man who at the same time was virtuous." (14: 6)

In the slavery society of China, "superior man" and "mean man" denoted members of the ruling class and the ruled. But in the last years of the Spring and Autumn Period, the slave-owning class became divided. Some slave owners changed over to the feudal mode of production, behavior running counter to the "code of the Duke of Zhou." In other words, respect for status began to break down. Confucius condemned these people as malevolent, although they belonged to the class of "superior men."

Confucius denied that the lower classes, the "mean men," could be benevolent. Logically speaking, all "superior men" should be benevolent.

But as this was not the case, Confucius turned to the theory of subjective consciousness, acknowledging conscious choice.

> "Is benevolence a thing remote? I wish to be benevolent. Lo and behold! Benevolence is at hand." (7: 30)

> "The practice of benevolence comes from a man himself; how can it come from the others?" (12: 1)

Here we see the Confucian idea of benevolence. To reach a kind of ideal world of the spirit, one must start from subjective desire. In fact, Confucian benevolence is nothing but the moral principle of slave-owning society, the self-awakening of the class-consciousness of the slave owners. In this way, human subjectivity and inborn morality are combined in one. "The practice of benevolence comes from a man himself."

The Confucian concept of benevolence emphasizes man's subjective spirit, affirming that by human effort one can achieve anything. In a relative way, it weakens the role of Heaven, fate, ghosts, and spirits upon human affairs. Confucius held a skeptical attitude towards the existence of ghosts and spirits, and prudently kept himself away from them. In the *Analects*, we find:

> "The subjects on which the Master did not touch were extraordinary things, feats of strength, disorder, and spiritual beings." (7: 21)

> "Ji Lu asked about serving the spirits of the dead. The Master said, 'While you are not able to serve men, how can you serve their spirits?' Ji Lu added, 'I venture to ask about death.' The Master answered, 'While you do not know life, how can you know about death?'" (11: 12)

> "To devote oneself earnestly to the duties due from men, and, while respecting spiritual beings, to keep aloof from them, may be called wisdom." (6: 22)

To safeguard the old system governed by rites, Confucius endeavored to develop man's subjective spirit. Yet he never escaped from the contradiction that through "benevolence" the world could be put right, even "benevolence" was helpless when "fate" intervened.

Although in the Confucian theory of knowledge there exists a dichotomy of both acquired and inborn knowledge, Confucius focuses more on acquired knowledge. Nevertheless, he puts forth a cognitive theory that puts equal value on learning and thinking.

To safeguard the old system of rites, Confucius attempted to demonstrate that the stratified relationship between superior and inferior was rational.

> "Those born with knowledge are the highest class of men. Those who learn and get possession of it are the next highest. Those who learn after they meet with difficulties are another yet lower class. As to those who meet with difficulties and yet do not learn—they are the lowest of people." (16: 9)

> "Only the wise men of the highest class and the stupid ones of the lowest class cannot be changed." (17: 3)

> "To those whose talents are above mediocrity, the highest matters may be introduced. To those who are below mediocrity, the highest matters may not be introduced." (6: 21)

Those "born with knowledge" refer to people whose knowledge does not come from experience or practice, the upper class. People of the lowest class are fit only to obey orders. Therefore, Confucius says, "The common people may be made to follow a path of action, but they cannot be made to understand it." (8: 9) And, "When a man of high station is well instructed, he loves men; when a man of low station is well instructed, he is easily ruled." (17: 4)

This idealistic apriorism resulted from Confucius' conservative standpoint, which resisted the concurrent social changes.

Confucius was realistic enough to acknowledge that those who "know from birth" are few and far between. He himself said, "I am not one born in possession of knowledge; I am one fond of antiquity, and earnest in seeking it." (7: 20) He knew clearly that his achievement came from diligent study. "In a hamlet of ten families, there may be found one as honorable and sincere as I am, but not so fond of learning." (5: 28) Confucius kept in close contact with common people and dabbled in professions disdained by those of noble origin. He spent most of his life teaching people who were only capable of acquiring knowledge, not born with it. He hoped all his disciples could "excel in learning and become officials." He valued lifelong education. "Is it not pleasant to learn with a constant perseverance and application?" (1: 1) He was able to sum up his experiences and the lessons therein:

> "When you know a thing, to assert that you know it, and when you do not know a thing, to allow that you do not know it—this is knowledge." (2: 17)
>
> "When I walk with two others, they may serve as my teachers. I will select their good qualities and follow them, their bad qualities and avoid them." (7: 22)
>
> "There are those who act without knowing why. I do not do so. Hearing much and selecting what is good and following it, seeing much and keeping it in memory—this is the second sort of knowledge." (7: 28)

Confucius points out that it is necessary to pay attention to thinking. "Learning without thought is labor lost; thought without learning is perilous." (2: 15) Also, "I have been the whole day without eating, and the whole night without sleeping—occupied with thinking. It was of no use. The better plan is to learn." (15: 31)

Confucius insisted that his students master practical skills needed for serving society, although he hoped they would also attain official rank and all that went with it. He therefore urged his students to "be able to recite the three hundred *Songs*,"[1] so they might "be sent to any quarter on a mission."

Confucius' focus on "knowing by learning" is a valuable proposition in the history of epistemology. But his theory of apriorism that made the "naturally wise" the only people fit to rule had a harmful effect on generations to come.

The dizzying changes that took place in the era Confucius lived caused him to urge people to stick to the unchangeable in a rapidly changing society. The *Doctrine of the Mean* reflects his search for the unchanging essence of things.

The general features of the *Doctrine of the Mean* are as follows: Confucius acknowledges contradictions and recognizes the harmony between them. The constant way does not change, but some adaptation to changing circumstances is necessary.

> "There was Shun. He was indeed wise. Shun loved to question others, and to study their words, though they might be shallow. He concealed what was bad in them, and displayed what was good. He took hold of the two extremes, determined the Mean, and employed it in his government." (*Doctrine of the Mean·Chapter 6*)

The mythical ruler Shun is lauded for using the contradictions to yield practical solutions.

In Confucius' opinion, the superior man is perfectly impartial, for he can serve as a mediator among different people. The mean man goes against the Golden Mean and gangs up with other scoundrels for selfish interests, even defying his superiors. Confucius sees the difficulty of class conflict, and says, "Perfect is the virtue that is according to the Constant Mean! Rare for a long time has been its practice among the people." (6:29)

To Confucius, the Golden Mean is the highest virtue. This is the Confucian theory of the harmony of contradictions.

In the last phase of the Spring and Autumn Period, Confucius saw that social changes were so great that some Zhou Dynasty rules and regulations had to be eliminated and others added. He said, "The Yin Dynasty followed the regulations of the Xia. The Zhou Dynasty followed the regulations of the Yin. Other rulers may follow the rites of Zhou, but though it be at the distance of a hundred ages, its affairs may still be known." (2:23) On the one hand, Confucius affirms the traditional ritual systems; on the other, he thinks that later ages may revise them. Herein lies the heart of the matter: what degree of revision is permissible?

When discussing the principle of administration, he says, "Govern the people by moral force, and keep order among them by ritual." (2: 3) When discussing the way of learning, he says, "The superior man studying all learning and keeping himself under the restraint of the rules of propriety may thus likewise not overstep what is right." (6: 27) Only by taking tight hold of constancy can one adapt to an ever-changing situation. The doctrine of the Golden Mean as the guideline for compromise and conciliation is a metaphysical view of the development of history.

In the doctrine of the Golden Mean, which denies the mutual transformation of opposites, Confucius clung to a desire to sustain traditional rites in politics. But in the field of education he broke through this limitation time and again.

> "When a man cherishes his old knowledge and continually acquires new, he may be a teacher of others." (2: 11)

> "A youth should be regarded with respect. How do we know that his future will not be equal to our present?" (9: 23)

Confucius advocated the heuristic method of education, which is in accordance with dialectical thought. "The Master said, 'I do not open up the truth to one who is not eager to acquire knowledge, nor assist one not anxious to explain himself. When I have presented one corner of a subject to any one, and he cannot from it learn the other three, I do not repeat my lesson.'" (7: 9) By advocating "inferring other things from one fact," Confucius gives a good reply to the question of how to acquire knowledge. He opposes mechanical memorizing; instead he assists the students' logical thinking and trains them to apply reasoning.

While Confucian thought is basically conservative, Confucius realized that by holding fast to the "Way," one might not be able to adjust to changing circumstances. He regarded adaptability in tactics and adaptation to circumstances as the highest level of personal accomplishment.

Confucius lived in the last phase of the Spring and Autumn Period, when the new was emerging but had not matured, when the old was dying but had not passed away. He founded the Confucian school, which gained an honored reputation from its early years. It was the first to educate anyone who wished to learn, not just aristocrats. The curriculum was marked by a high level of ideology and dealt with important problems of philosophy.

The world outlook and methodology of Confucius is marked both by the traditional influence of esteem for the Mandate of Heaven—and the political demand to follow the Golden Mean. "Be fond of antiquity and be earnest in seeking knowledge!" is his attitude to learning. "One unity pervades all things" is his ideological system. With these strong points, Confucius greatly surpassed many contemporary thinkers. Confucius' work is an important link in the philosophy of pre-Qin China, and he was the first to emphasize rational self-awakening.

Still, Confucian philosophy is filled with contradictions, such as that between his focus on rational thinking and his focus on bringing into play man's subjective initiative. However, Confucius also displays the essence of consistency. With his doctrine of practical reason centered on the category of "benevolence," he wanted superior men to exercise their own free will as "benevolence" in practice. But his doctrine of "benevolence" was an innovation in the history of philosophy. The theory, its ethical and moral contents deeply rooted in traditional patriarchal relations, had a profound influence on later ages. His view of "taking hold of the two extremes and determining the Mean" establishes a particular pattern of metaphysics: people should start by acknowledging the contradictions that already exist, then harmonize them. Harmony is a most precious aspect. This "Doctrine of the Mean" exerted a powerful influence on later ages.

As for Confucian educational thought, theoretically it is related to his rational epistemology and to his view of contradiction marked by balancing and determining the mean. Since the practical needs of education at that time spurred him to collate and edit a large number of ancient books and records, and to get people to study them, he became highly knowledgeable about the historical documents that have been passed down to posterity as the Confucian Canon. Confucius was honored throughout the history of feudalism in China as a paragon of virtue and learning, and "the model teacher for all ages." No other Chinese thinker has ever attained this exalted status.

4.

Ideological Contradictions: The Mohist School

Mo Di (c. 476–390 BC), a thinker of the pre-Qin period and founder of Mohism, was a native of the State of Lu. He called himself a "contemptible wretch," but many called him, reverently, "Mozi," Master Mo. Learned and gifted in many ways, he had been a craftsman before serving as a senior official in the State of Song. In the history of Chinese philosophy, Master Mo represents individual small producers in the early stage of the Warring States Period.

By tradition, in his early years Mo Di was educated in Confucianism. Later, he founded the Mohist school of thought in opposition to Confucian political views. He "abandoned the ritual ways of the Zhou Dynasty to adopt the politics of the Xia Dynasty." (*Huainanzi·Chapter XXI: The Essential Outline*)

The Mohist school was formed of a very strictly organized ascetic group whose members were imbued with religion. Most came from lower classes occupied in productive labor. Living a simple and frugal life, they observed the diverse regulations of the group. Later, Mohists appeared in various states, where they engaged in political activities. They preached Mohist political views and Mo Di's ideological line, and put them into practice. As Mencius said, "The words of Yang Zhu and Mo Di fill the empire. When you listen to people's discourses, you will find they have adopted the views of Yang or of Mo." (*Mencius*, 6: 9)

In *Lu's Spring and Autumn Annals*, we may also read the following comment: "Although Confucius and Master Mo passed away long ago, their followers are increasing in number, and soon will fill the whole country." (*Chapter 4: Appropriate Infection*) Although their views were diametrically opposed, both schools were "renowned schools of thought" at the time. When Mo Di passed away, his followers elected one of their own to be the "Great Apostle." The Mohist school later split into three branches, called the Later Mohists.

The *Mozi* was written and edited by disciples of Mo Di on the basis of his discourses. Only twenty-four of an extant fify-three chapters that directly record his discourse are considered authentic and reliable for research.

Mo Di's philosophy embodies a concentrated reflection of itself in the aspect of epistemology. He was the first pre-Qin thinker to apply empiricism to oppose apriorism. To him, man's knowledge originates in objective reality as perceived through his sense organs: "The way to find out whether anything exists or not is to depend on the testimony of the eyes and ears of the multitude. When some have heard it or some have seen it, then we have to say it exists. When no one has heard it and no one has seen it, then we have to say it does not exist." (Mozi·*Chapter 31: On Ghosts*; hereafter only chapter number and title appear.)

Individual subjective impressions are excluded; the standard is what the common people see with their own eyes and hear with their own ears—the materialist theory of perception.

Following such a cognitive line, Mo Di denies the Confucian apriorism marked by "One is born with knowledge." In Mo Di's opinion, the cognitive ability of a sage is indeed higher than that of the average people, but this is not because he is born with knowledge, but because he is able to "use the eyes and ears of other people to help himself see and hear." Confucius focuses on "fate," whereas Mo Di passes judgment according to the common people's perception. Mo Di refutes the fatalism advocated by Confucius, but is by no means a narrow empiricist. In his cognitive method he puts forth the concept of "plan":

> "There is an ancient saying that when one is not successful in making plans, then predict the future by the past, and learn about the absent from what is present. When one plans like this, one can be intelligent." (*Chapter 18: Condemnation of Offensive War (II)*)

Here, Mo Di tells us how to reason, that is, one ought to proceed from points known to deduce points unknown. This belongs to the sphere of rational knowledge. But Mo Di fails to take it as an inevitable stage in the development of perceptive knowledge, the only shortcoming in his theory of the origin of knowledge.

Confucius taught the rectification of names, citing the following basic relationships in life: father to son, elder brother to younger, husband to wife, elder to younger, ruler to subject.

With each name came fixed responsibilities and duties, which when carried out properly maintained both social order and righteous government—rectifying the name with the behavior, and pinpointing Confucius' discomfort with social upheaval and change.

Criticizing Confucius' theory of "rectification of names" as reversing the order of name and fact, Mo Di recommends "Naming things on the basis of facts."

> "Master Gong Meng said, 'The gentleman has to be ancient in attire and in speech before he can be magnanimous." Mo Di said, 'In ancient times, minister Fei Zhong and King Zhou of the Shang Dynasty were the terrors of the world, while Baron Ji and Baron Wei were the sages of the world. They all spoke the same language, but two were benevolent and two not. Later, Duke Dan of Zhou was the sage of the world, while Guan Shu was the villain. The duke and Guan Shu wore the same type of clothes, but one was benevolent and the other not. Therefore, whether or not one is benevolent lies not in the clothes he wears nor the words he speaks.'" (*Chapter 48: Gong Meng*)

To assess presence or absence of benevolence, a required behavior from ruler to subject, we ought not pay attention to superficial phenomena such as speech and dress, but to the actual situation. "For the interests of the people all over the world, the sage must promote what is beneficial and abolish what is harmful." (*Chapter 16: Universal Love (III)*)

Now we cannot help asking: How can we know that a thing is truly worthy of its name but not the other way round? As a reply to this question, Mo Di said, "Examine analogical things to know the cause." For example, as far as war is concerned, there are diverse kinds. When the cause of starting a war is the desire for plunder, such a war is called "aggression." When the cause of starting a war is to prevent aggression, to save the country and the people, such a war is called "eradication." Mo Di opposes aggression, but he agrees with the "war to eradicate."

"Analogy" here means that similar things may be known by analogy or by comparison. "Cause" here refers to the cause of things or the purpose of action. "Reason" here is a large concept that includes the above two, namely, "analogy" and "cause." It refers to the basis on which people accept or reject a thing, and distinguishes between right and wrong.

Mo Di left us two famous statements: "Name things on the basis of fact" and "Examine analogical things to know the reason." Both are materialist propositions.

Mo Di maintained that standard criteria must be used to test whether or not man's cognition is correct:

"Some standard of judgment must be established. To expound a doctrine without regard to the standard is like determining the directions of sunrise and sunset on a revolving potter's wheel. In this way, the distinction of right and wrong and benefit and harm cannot be clearly known." (*Chapter 35: Anti-Fatalism (I)*)

Mo Di proposed testing any theory or mode of cognition via "the three tests."

> The three tests of a doctrine are "basis, verifiability, and applicability. . . . It should be based on the deeds of the ancient sage-kings. It is to be verified by the senses of hearing and sight of the common people. It is to be applied by adopting it in government and observing its benefits to the country and the people."(*Chapter 35: Anti-Fatalism (I)*)

To examine the indirect experience of ancient people from the historical records and to use this as the basis for reasoning is a cognitive line of materialism.

The most fundamental test is the second, to use the direct perceptive experiences of the broad masses as the basis for reasoning, is characteristic of a materialist theory of reflection. Finally,

to examine a certain view in the practical process of its application, its social effect is a materialist standard.

Thus, the subjective ideas of individuals are totally excluded, and the theory of such unity is a naive, materialist, and empirical theory of truth—an important contribution to the history of epistemology.

But the method of "the three tests" is not strictly logical. To regard experience as the basis on which people test their knowing is not scientific. Moreover, the method of the "three tests" is somewhat tinged with metaphysics. Man's knowing develops throughout life. If one regards the chronicles of the deeds of the ancient sage-kings as a foundation of cognition, copies them word for word, or imitates them indiscriminately as rigid dogma, one falls into the trap of mechanical materialism. Meanwhile, "the actual experience of the eyes and ears of the people" varies with changes in real-life conditions. And in a society characterized by divisions among the people, there exists no unified standard of advantages and disadvantages for the people as a whole.

In the history of Chinese philosophy, Mo Di was the first to postulate the necessity of and criteria for testing the accuracy of cognition, an important development in the epistemology of materialism.

The thought of "elevating strength" and "attacking fatalism" is the concentrated manifestation of the militant spirit of materialism in Mo Di's doctrine. Confucius preached that Heaven foreordains all that happens, such as poverty and riches, high and humble station, long and short life, disorder and order. All are determined by fate. Confucius emphasizes, "Without recognizing the ordinances of Heaven, it is impossible to be a superior man." (*Analects*, 20: 3)

Mo Di denied the objectivity of "fate." As he points out, neither "the people below" nor "the sage-kings above" have ever seen "fate as an object" or heard "fate as a voice." "In ancient times, the confusion of Jie was reduced to order by Tang, and that of Zhou by King Wu. Under Tang and Wu, it was orderly; under Jie and Zhou it was disorderly. Hence, peace and danger, order and disorder all depend on the government of the superior. How can it be said that everything is governed by fate? So, assertions about fate are quite false." (*Chapter 37: Anti-Fatalism (III)*)

First, "to attack fatalism" by "elevating strength" manifests the people's yearning to break the bonds of fatalism by their own efforts, and shows that Mo Di has deepened his knowledge of himself. He provided later scholars such as Han Fei (c. 280–233 BC) and Xun Kuang (c. 313–

238 BC) with material for their ideas of "controlling the Mandate of Heaven and making use of it."

Second, Mo Di analyzes the social roots of predestination and the harm it may bring about. "The wicked kings of the Three Dynasties (Xia, Shang, and Zhou) did not control the lust of their ears and eyes, and did not retain the passions of their hearts. . . . They oppressed the common people. As result, the people had no affinity for their superiors, and the country became a heap of ruins, the common people writhing in agony." (*Chapter 36: Anti-Fatalism (II)*) According to Mo Di, it was the rulers who invented "fate," by which they deceived themselves and others:

> "For fatalism is an invention of wicked kings and the practice of miserable men. It is not a doctrine of the magnanimous. Therefore, those who practice magnanimity and righteousness must examine and vigorously refute it." (*Chapter 37: Anti-Fatalism (III)*)

Fate was a theory invented to fool the masses, according to Mo Di. Those whose family's social stratum had been high and had fallen, resigned themselves to their lot. Mo Di commented, "The fatalists say: when fate decrees that a man shall be wealthy, he will be wealthy. When it decrees poverty, he shall be poor. When fate decrees that the population shall be large, it will be large. When it decrees that it shall be small, it will be small. For those who believe in fate, there will be no room for "great strength" to play its role in times of calamity What is the use of making a strong effort against fate?" (*Chapter 35: Anti-Fatalism (I)*)

Mo Di's analysis of the social effect and the social sources from which the doctrine of "fate" originates is pertinent. In place of "fate," he advocates belief in "strong efforts to display man's talent." This puts responsibility for social development and the human condition back in its proper place at the forefront of social reality.From start to finish, Mo Di, as a representative of the small producers, was unable to rid himself of the traditional idea of the Celestial God. Although he denies the existence of "fate," he substitutes for it the Will of Heaven, and acknowledges the existence of "ghosts and spirits." However, his concept of the Will of Heaven is not the same as the traditional Mandate of Heaven, which legitimized the rule of monarchs and the aristocratic class.

"Similarly with the Will of Heaven, Master Mo will measure the jurisdiction and government of the lords in the empire on the one hand, and the doctrines and teachings of the multitudes in the empire on the other. If some conduct is observed to be in accordance with the Will of Heaven, it is called good conduct; if it is opposition to the Will of Heaven it is called bad conduct. . . . With this as the model and with this as the standard, whether the lords and ministers are magnanimous or not can be measured as easily as distinguishing black from white." (*Chapter 27: Will of Heaven (II)*)

"Hence Master Mo established the Will of Heaven as his standard, just as the wheelwright uses his compasses and the carpenter uses his square as their standards." (*Chapter 28: Will of Heaven (III)*)

The Will of Heaven has been turned into a supreme umpire that allows of no exception, and has the function of both rewarding and punishing human beings for their deeds. Mo Di says, "Those who obey the Will of Heaven will surely obtain rewards; those who oppose the Will of Heaven will surely incur punishment." (*Chapter 26: Will of Heaven (I)*) In this respect, there are abundant historical instances. "The ancient sage-kings Yu, Tang, Wen, and Wu of the three dynasties were those who obeyed the Will of Heaven, and obtained rewards. The wicked kings Jie, Zhou, You, and Li of the three dynasties opposed the Will of Heaven, and incurred punishment." (*Ibid*)

It is clear that the Will of Heaven is the deified supreme principle, governing the behavior even of the emperor, the Son of Heaven. Mo Di invoked the Will of Heaven in his lifelong quest to rectify the world so that the people would practice universal love, abolish war, adopt the policy of "non-attack," and realize the political goal of "agreement with the superior."

Mo Di holds that it is necessary to "beware of ghosts." "In the distribution of rewards by ghosts and spirits, no man is too insignificant to be rewarded for his virtue. And in the meting out of punishment by ghosts and spirits, no man is too great to be punished." (*Chapter 31: On Ghosts (III)*) Here the political demands of the common people dressed in religious garb. The theory of "ghosts and spirits" and the "Will of Heaven" as advocated here differs from the superstitious belief in the Mandate of

Heaven and the claim by the ruling class that ghosts and spirits reward and punish at random.

In Mo Di's ideological system, ideas such as "elevating strength" and "anti-fatalism" contradict other ideas such as the "Will of Heaven" and "ghosts and spirits"—a reflection of the double disposition of the small producers, who were both progressive and backward in that period. They wanted to continue to live and work in peace, so they nursed strong dissatisfaction toward the exploitation, oppression, and religious fraud imposed on them by "tyrant kings" and "despotic rule." Though eager to change their circumstances by their own strength, they were fettered by traditional ideas of subservience to the aristocracy and religious superstition. So they put their trust in the "Will of Heaven" and "ghosts and spirits" to rein in the excesses of their rulers. Mo Di lived when social productivity was seriously harmed by continuous internecine warfare as the various states battled for dominance. "The hungry could not be fed, the cold could not be clothed, and the laborers could have no rest." (*Chapter 32: Condemnation of Music (II)*)

He said, "it is highly necessary to promote benefit for the world and to remove harm from the world." To do this, ten tasks had to be pursued, which are given in the *Mozi*:

> "Master Mo replied. Upon entering a country, one should locate the need and work on that. When a country is in confusion, teach the doctrines of the Exaltation of the Virtuous and Identification with the Superior. When a country is mired in poverty, teach the doctrines of Economy of Expenditures and Simplicity in Funerals. When a country is indulging in music and wine, teach the doctrines of Condemnation of Music and Anti-fatalism. When a country is insolent and has no propriety, teach its people to revere Heaven and worship the spirits. When a country is engaged in conquest and oppression, teach the doctrines of Universal Love and Condemnation of Offensive War." (*Chapter 49: Lu's Question*)

The ten tasks are the following: 1. Elevate the worthy to government positions. 2. Be in agreement with superiors. 3. Condemn elaborate funerals. 4. Condemn unnecessary expenses. 5. Condemn wasteful musical activities. 6. Wage war on fatalism. 7. Bring about universal love.

8. Condemn wars. 9. Acknowledge the will of Heaven. And,10. Shun ghosts.

Moreover, it is necessary to treat the states differently, for their concrete conditions are different. Mo Di perceives that in society there are differences caused by social class and various objective contradictions. He calls these contradictions "particularity." "Particularity" here is the mere consideration of one's own interests. He says, "The Will of Heaven abominates the large state which attacks small states, the strong who plunder the weak, the clever who deceive the stupid, and the honored who disdain the humble." (*Chapter 27: Will of Heaven (II)*)

How can we eliminate this? Mo Di says, "It should be replaced by the way of universal love and mutual benefit." (*Chapter 15: Universal Love (II)*) "It is to regard other people's countries as one's own, . . . other people's households as one's own, . . . other people's person as one's own." (*Ibid*) Simply speaking, this means, "To consider for the sake of others is just as for one's own sake." (*Chapter 16: Universal Love (III)*)

To substitute the hierarchical version of love with "universal love" is a criticism of the traditional patriarchal system and of progressive significance.

In Mo Di's period, "many a state cannot be rich but be poor, the population cannot be large but be small, and the society cannot be orderly but be chaotic." Why? Because "the princes and dukes who are in power cannot elevate the worthy to government positions," according to their merit. (*Chapter 8: Elevating the Worthy to Government Positions (I)*)

> "In ancient times, sage-kings governed this way. They gave the virtuous appropriate ranks, and elevated the worthy to government positions. The capable people were raised and promoted, although some had been peasants, merchants, and laborers. They were entrusted with important affairs and endowed with the power to decide by themselves." (*Chapter 8: Elevating the Worthy to Government Positions (I)*)

> "No officials are everlastingly honorable. No common people are eternally humble. When one is capable, he must be raised and promoted. When one is incapable, he must be removed from his office." (*Ibid*)

But "to elevate the worthy to government positions" is by no means the ultimate purpose of Mo Di. He advocates it because he wants all people to "agree with the superior." "There is great disorder in the empire because the empire lacks an administrative chief." (*Chapter 11: Agreement with the Superior (I)*) And he points out the reason of disorder further. In the beginning when man was created, there was no ruler. People existed as individuals. As they existed as individuals, there was no unified concept of right for everybody, which became the root of social chaos. Therefore Mo Di advocates agreement with the superior: everybody is willing to "agree with the superior instead of following the below." (*Chapter 11: Agreement with the Superior (I)*) One should submit oneself to direction from above; one must not chime in with others who live below. "One must say yes when his superior says yes, one must say no when his superior says no." (*Ibid*)

What is the standard of "the agreement with the superior"? Mo Di says, "The common people in the whole empire must agree with the emperor, the son of Heaven." (*Ibid*) "When order prevails in the empire, the emperor further unifies all concepts of right as one in the empire and makes it agree with Heaven." (*Chapter 13: Agreement with the Superior (III)*) "The will of Heaven," then, is the general standard of "the agreement with the superior."

As stated above, the so-called "will of Heaven" is nothing but the will of the small producers. "The agreement with the superior" is the ideological standard of the small producers represented by Mo Di. Politically speaking, there is a positive aspect in the idea as it expresses their hope for a stable, unified political situation. Nevertheless, the unified politics Mo Di hopes for is like this: "To administer a country is just like to manage a household, to order about the common people in the whole country is just like to boss one man around." (*Ibid*) Mo Di, since he always thinks about how to extinguish the "particularity" with the "universality" and to melt "differences" into "agreement," finally falls into the abyss of metaphysics.

In Mo Di's opinion, lack of mutual love is the root of all evil deeds. "Because of want of mutual love, all the calamities, usurpation, hatred, and animosity in the world have arisen." (*Chapter 15: Universal Love*) Hence, he advocates "universal love" as the solution:

> "When feudal lords love one another, they will not fight in the fields. When heads of families love one another, they will not usurp one another. When individuals love one another, they will not injure one another. When ruler and minister love each other, they will be kind and loyal. When father and son love each other, they will be affectionate and filial. When brothers love each other, they will be peaceful and harmonious. When all the people in the world love one another, the strong will not overcome the weak, the many will not oppress the few, the strong will not insult the poor, the honored will not despise the humble, and the cunning will not deceive the ignorant." (*Chapter 15: Universal Love*)

In a class society this fanciful idea can never be realized for it does not correspond with reality.

"The feudal lords love their own countries, they do not love other people's countries at all. Therefore they attack the other people's countries to benefit their own. All the chaotic things in the world lie right here." (*Chapter 14: Universal Love (II)*) Based on this, Mo Di condemns war, describing its crimes "The feudal lords attacked the sinless countries, crossed the boundary of the other countries, cut off growing crops, cut down trees, and destroyed the cities. . . . They cruelly killed people by hundreds and thousands." (*Chapter 19: The Condemnation of War (III)*) But Mo Di saw only one side of the problem; namely, a war might cause destruction. He failed to see that in the early stage of the Warring States Period, it was the only route history could take. It was necessary to use military force to annex territories of the feudal lords. Of course, such a view of wars runs against historical dialectics.

When Mo Di saw the social harms caused by the Confucian school that advocated "elaborate funerals," "extended mourning," and "beating gongs and drums at the funeral," he put forth two views: one condemning wasteful musical activities, the other condemning unnecessary expenses. He denounced the followers of Confucianism: "Complicating the rites and music, they made people wallow in luxury and leisure. Pretending to be sad in extended mourning, they insulted the kinsmen who passed way." (*Chapter 39: Attack on Confucianism (II)*) Mo Di vehemently assailed an institution left by the slavery system: to bury the living with the dead. "As for the institution of burying the living with the dead, in case of an emperor's death, several hundred people are to be immolated. In case of the death of a general or a minister, several dozens of people are to be immolated." (*Chapter 25: The Condemnation of Elaborate Funerals (III)*)

But he once again fell into the abyss of one-sidedness of metaphysics for he condemned the wasteful musical activities without any discrimination. For instance, in the society the poetic and musical creation is indispensable, so also is the case with the cultural and entertaining activities, which the laboring people engage themselves in the productive process. This is because these musical activities are absolutely necessary to the promotion of the spiritual civilization and of the economic development. To condemn the musical activities without discrimination and to label them as wasteful pursuits, this reflects the narrow-mindedness of the small producers.

As Xun Kuang (c. 313–238 BC) once pointed out in the *Xunzi*, "Master Mo had insight into 'uniformity,' but none into 'individuation.'" (*Chapter 17: Discourse on Nature*) In Xun Kuang's opinion, the unified feudal country was established solely on the basis of the social estate system. "Where the classes of society are equally ranked, there is no proper arrangement of society; where authority is evenly distributed, there is no unity; and where everyone is of like status, none would be willing to serve the other." (*Chapter 9: On the Regulations of a King*) If absolute equality prevails in a society, it is impossible to carry out government decrees.

The doctrine of Mo Di had great influence when the Mohist school of thought was in its prime. The gradual establishment of the political power of landlords as a rising class led to the doctrine being suppressed. And some political views, for their supra-class nature, were absolutely impossible to realize in the historical conditions then. Master Mo's doctrine fell into oblivion.

Some rational factors contained in the philosophy of the Mohist school of thought were inherited and developed by the later Mohists and the materialist philosophers who later appeared on the academic arena of China. As for the mystical elements contained in the doctrine of the Mohist school of thought, some idealist theists used it to create their system of teleology, such as the divine right of kings. In this sense, the influence of the Mohist school of thought lasted, and we find its influence even after the dynasties of Qin and Han.

5.

Daoism: The Way to Nature in the Philosophy of Laozi

The Taoist school, with Laozi as its founder, was a leading school of thought in pre-Qin days, alongside the Yin-Yang, Confucian, and Mohist schools. But who was Laozi? In his *Records of the Historian*, Sima Qian mentions three names: Laodan, Lao Laizi, and Dan. Any one of these may have been the author of the Taoist classic the *Tao Te Ching*. Laodan and Lao Laizi were contemporaries of Confucius, while Dan was a court historian of the Zhou Dynasty during the Warring States Period.

According to the *Records of the Historian·Biographies of Laozi and Han Fei*, Laodan was born in Kuxian County in the State of Chu (present-day Luxian County, Henan Province), Li was his family name, Er his given name. He is reverently referred to as Laozi, "Master Lao." He served at one time as the official librarian at the Eastern Zhou court, and Confucius once consulted him on the rites of Zhou. In his later years he lived as a hermit, "writing a book of five thousand characters discussing virtue," popularly known as the *Laozi*. A rhymed philosophical work (two parts, 81 chapters), it has since the Han Dynasty been called the *Tao Te Ching (The Canon of Tao and Te,* or *The Classic of the Way and Virtue)*. Textual criticism by scholars of the Song Dynasty and modern times holds that it is probably a record of Laozi's thought and speech edited by his followers after their master's death. Here we discuss the *Laozi* as the systematic formulation of the thought of the Taoist school formed during the last years of the Spring and Autumn Period and the early years of the Warring States Period.

The philosopher Han Feizi wrote the earliest annotated works on the *Laozi*, the "Jie Lao" (*Explanation of the Laozi*) and "Yu Lao" (*Elucidation of the Laozi with Parables*). From the Han Dynasty to modern times, the number of annotated editions of the *Laozi* is topped only by those of *The Analects* of Confucius. There are translations of the work in many languages.

In 1973 in Tomb 2 at Mawangdui, Changsha, two handwritten copies of the *Laozi* were unearthed, the most ancient copies extant. Not divided into chapters, they start with Part II of the various versions circulating today, namely, *Te Jing (The Canon of Te)* comes first, and *Tao Jing (The Canon of Tao)* second, following the same order as the "Jie Lao."

From the last years of the Spring and Autumn Period onwards, on the philosophical front, thinkers of different schools engaged in heated arguments on what was called the "Way of Heaven." The *Laozi* initiated this controversy. The "Way" is the supreme substance, the origin of all things in the world, and contains within it the law of their change and movement. The "Way" is also the norm that human society must observe, and the general term for the origin, essence, and law of all things. Thus, a philosophical system was set up, with the "Way" as its kernel.

The "Way" originally meant a road for people to pass along. Later it came to mean the "right way," then the law and norm by extension. In the Spring and Autumn Period, people used it to express the law of the movement of Nature and celestial phenomena as well as the norm of human behavior—the "Way of Heaven" and "Way of Man." It is the *Laozi* that first takes the "way" to refer to the supreme substance, the general origin of all things in the world, and gives it a systematic demonstration in the philosophical sense.

What is the exact connotation of the "Way" in the *Laozi*? There has been controversy about this for a long time. The *Laozi* is full of references such as "Yet within it is an image," "Yet within it is a substance," "Yet within it is an essence. This essence is quite genuine." (*Laozi·Chapter 21;* hereinafter only chapter number appears) These sayings refer to a substance with a material attribute. On the other hand, it says, "And returns to that which is without substance," "This is called the shape that has no shape, the image that is without substance." (*Chapter 14*)

Nevertheless, the "Way" as the supreme origin of all things in the universe has been categorized after all, and the constitution of the universe has been explained with a general term. This is a deepening of cognition as compared with the view of primitive materialism. For instance, the theory of the Five Elements explains the universe as being made up of combinations of water, fire, earth, wood, and metal. The theory of the eight trigrams explains the universe as being made up of combinations of heaven, earth, wind, thunder, water, fire, mountain, and marsh. Therefore, the world outlook in the *Laozi*, with the Way as the supreme substance, was a breakthrough.

But the *Laozi* tries to abstract a unified "Way" from the variety and complicity of concrete material objects, for example, "The Way is forever nameless," (*Chapter 32*) The reasoning is from the concrete to the abstract, from the particular to the general, and from material objects to the origin. So the abstraction of the "Way" breaks away from the realistic world and becomes "nothing," or the "dim," which "cannot be asked the reason why it is so." So the "Way" has been rendered empty and is the "nothing" from which the myriad creatures are derived.

The mode of producing of all things in the universe, as expounded in the *Laozi*, and the role the "Way" plays in such a process are exemplified as follows:

> The Way produced the One.
> The One produced the two.
> The two produced the three.
> And the three produced the ten thousand things.
> The ten thousand things carry the yin and embrace the yang, and through the blending of the material force (qi) they achieve harmony.
> —*Chapter 42*

> Therefore the Way is great.
> Heaven is great.
> Earth is great,
> And the king is also great.
> There are four great things in the universe, and the king is one of them.

Man models himself after Earth.
Earth models itself after Heaven.
Heaven models itself after the Way.
And the Way models itself after Nature.
—*Chapter 25*

The *Laozi* states that the Way produces the myriad things, and that the Way models itself after Nature—a refutation of previous claims that Heaven, and its ruler the Lord on High, had a "will" of its own. It downplays the idea of the "Mandate of Heaven" revered by Confucius and the "Will of Heaven" preached by Mo Di. The dominating roles of the Lord on High, ghosts, and spirits are not admitted in the *Laozi,* not to mention the Creator. "If the Way is employed to rule the empire, spiritual beings will lose their supernatural power." (*Chapter 60*) And the "Way" "seems to have existed before the gods." (*Chapter 4*) Thus, in the face of the "Way," the Lord on High, ghosts, and spirits have no authority at all, and the book is tinged with atheism.

Moreover, the dominating role of the "Way" is different from the dominating role of personified Heaven and the Lord on High, as conceived of in other systems of philosophy.

The Way is the storehouse of all things.
It is the good man's treasure and the bad man's refuge.
—*Chapter 62*

The great Way flows everywhere.
It may go left or right.
All things depend on it for life, and it does not turn away from them.
It accomplishes its task, but does not claim credit for it.
It clothes and feeds all things, but does not claim to be master over them.
Always without desires, it may be called The Small.
All things come to it and it does not master them; it may be called The Great.
—*Chapter34*

In the sentence "The Way is the storehouse of all things," in Text A and Text B of the *Laozi* unearthed from Mawangdui, the character for "storehouse (奥)" is 注, which is interchangeable with主. Wang Bi's commentary says, "奥, just as 暖, refers to a refuge one can get and be protected in," it also means to dominate. This indicates that the "Way" governs the destiny of all things; and man cannot depart from it, whether his behavior be good or bad. Nevertheless, although all things grow by depending on the Way, it does not interfere with or manipulate them, nor does it glory in its success and greatness. This is the key to understanding the success and greatness of the "Way." The dominating function of the "Way" is just to let all things follow their own course, and it does nothing itself. The "Way" is only a functioning law that exists universally and obeys Nature. As compared with the clumsy theism of previous philosophies, the level of theoretical thinking has been raised in the *Laozi*, although there remains a touch of the mysterious.

We cannot say that there is no contradiction in the philosophical thought of the *Laozi*. For example, references to "Heaven" make it assume the attributes of the deity in man's person:

> Who knows why Heaven dislikes what it dislikes?
> Even the sage considers it a difficult question.
> The Way of Heaven does not compare, and yet it skillfully
> achieves victory.
> It does not speak, and yet it skillfully responds to things.
> It comes to you without your invitation.
> It is not anxious about things, and yet it plans well.
> Heaven's net is indeed vast.
> Though its meshes are wide, it misses nothing.
> —*Chapter 73*

The epistemology of the *Laozi* is correlated with its world outlook. The "Way" is the supreme substance and the origin of all things in the universe and is therefore the object of cognition. The pursuit of concrete things is called "pursuit of learning." Only what leads people to knowledge of the Way can be called "pursuit of the Way." The two are opposed to one another. "The pursuit of learning is to increase day after day. The pursuit of the Way is to decrease day after day." (*Chapter*

48) This is the starting point and return of the *Laozi*, which opposes striving as a way to know about concrete things, preaching distrust of the sense organs and negating perceptual knowledge.

It holds that understanding the "Way of Heaven is not available via perceptive experiences." One may know the world without going out of doors.

> One may see the Way of Heaven without looking through the
>   windows.
> The further one goes, the less one knows.
> Therefore, the sage knows without going about,
> Understands without seeing,
> And accomplishes without action.
>   —*Chapter 47*

This postulation in the *Laozi* is different from the Confucian apriorism that the sage knows everything from birth. The *Laozi* holds that the fundamental task of cognition is to grasp the "Way." Since the 'Way" has neither form nor name, it cannot be grasped by the sense organs and it cannot be known by rational thinking, but only by a special method, namely, to observe calmly:

> Attain complete vacuity,
> Maintain steadfast quietude.
> All things come into being,
> And I watch them return.
> All things flourish,
> But each one returns to its root.
> This returning to its root means tranquility.
> It is called returning to its destiny.
> To know the eternal is called enlightenment.
> Not to know the eternal is to rashly bring about disaster.
>   —*Chapter 16*

Stop interacting.
Shut the doors (of cunning and desires).
Blunt the sharpness.
Untie the tangles.
Soften the light.
Become one with the dusty world.
This is called profound identification.
—*Chapter 56*

To know the "Way," it is necessary to use a directly introspective method. One must "purify one's profound insight." (Cf. *Chapter 10*. In the Mawangdui texts copied on silk, the character 览, insight, is written as监, i.e., 鉴, mirror) A person must make his heart completely clean, and exclude all outside interference. When the heart is like a mirror, which is clear, deep, and serene, completely free from dust, all things will present themselves in it naturally.

In *Heshanggong's Interpretation of the Laozi,* "profound insight" is explained thusly: "One may know all things as if one has watched them with one's heart, which is in a profound and dark place." This mysterious method involves getting to know the "Way" through "profound insight" first, then attaining a comprehensive view of all things through "calm observation." It is an attempt to pursue a kind of rational intuition so as to reach absolute identity between subject and object, namely, to reach the realm of "profound identification." The limitations and superficiality of perceptive cognition have already been noticed in the *Laozi,* and so also is the case with the relativity and restriction of rational cognition. This is an advance in epistemology, but it results in the advocacy of the pursuit of a mysterious intuition, rejecting the perceptual and the rational, and leading the approach to cognition onto another wrong path.

Later, the Taoist school of Jixia talked about "the Way of calmness as its cause." (*Guanzi·Chapter 36: Xinshu (I)*) Xun Kuang developed this, saying, "The empty, the one, and the calm, these constitute the great pure brightness." (*Xunzi·Chapter 21: Dispelling Blindness*), as did Han Fei, saying, "Being open-minded, keeping calm, and standing at the back, he has never used his own subjective desire." (*Han Feizi·Chapter 8: Publicizing the Monarchical Power*) The cognitive method embodied in these propositions is the continuation and transformation of the "calm observation" and "profound insight" expounded in the *Laozi.* In the *Laozi* there is an epistemological aspect that agrees with the development of man's cognition by denying the postulates of Confucius and Mozi. Nevertheless, Laozi once again falls into mysticism in that perspective experiences are denied in the book, and he has not yet grasped the dialectical relationship between perceptual knowledge and rational knowledge in the book.

Early on, the *Laozi* holds that in both society and Nature are a large number of contradictions. It presents a series of contradictory concepts—big and small, high and low, front and back, life and death, difficult and easy, advance and retreat, ancient and present, start and finish, positive and negative, long and short, wise and foolish, beautiful and ugly, direct and indirect, old and new, good and bad, strong and weak, hard and soft, rise and fall, give and take, victory and failure, being and nonbeing, increase and decrease, advantage and disadvantage, yin and yang, wax and wane, calmness and agitation, open and closed, showy and substantial, submission and integration, bent and straight, female and male, noble and base, honor and disgrace, good luck and ill luck, calamity and happiness, and so on. In the presentation of a large number of contradictory concepts, the universality and objectivity of contradictions are brought to light.

The *Laozi* not only notices contradictions, but the contradictions are by no means isolated; the two parts of a contradiction are in a unity of opposites, interrelated and interdependent: When the people of the world all know beauty as beauty,

There arises the recognition of ugliness.
When they all know the good as good,
There arises the recognition of evil.
Therefore:
Being and nonbeing produce each other;
Difficult and easy complete each other;
Long and short mutually shape each other;
High and low mutually fill each other;
Sound and voice harmonize with each other;
Front and back follow each other.
It is constantly so.

—*Chapter 2*

The factors in any contradiction are both opposite and complementary to each other.,Each side takes the opposite for the premise of its own existence but they are in one and the same unity.

To yield is to be preserved whole.
To be bent is to become straight.
To be empty is to be full.
To be worn out is to be renewed.
To have little is to possess.
To have plenty is to be perplexed.
—*Chapter 22*

Such extensive statements on contradictions and the unity of opposites clearly reflect a grasp of dialectical thinking. Besides,

the two sides of any contradiction change into the opposite: "Reversion is the action of the Way." (*Chapter 40*):

He who hoards most will lose heavily.
—*Chapter 44*

After things reach their prime, they begin to grow old.
—*Chapter 55*

When the army is strong, it will not win.
When a tree is stiff, it will break.
—*Chapter 76*

Calamity is that upon which happiness depends.
Happiness is that in which calamity is latent.
—*Chapter 58*

Moreover, negation is the mechanism for dialectical development as things turn into their opposites. It follows that "Weakness is the function of the Way." (*Chapter 40*) and "The softest things in the world overcome the hardest things in the world." (*Chapter 43*)

A tree as big as a man's embrace grows from a tiny shoot.
A tower of nine stories begins with a heap of earth.
A journey of ten thousand *li* starts from where one stands.
—*Chapter 64*

Prepare for the difficult while it is still easy.
Deal with the big while it is still small.
Difficult undertakings have always started with what is easy,
And great undertakings have always started with what is small.
—*Chapter 63*

The *Laozi* applies dialectics to the process of quantitative development. The *Laozi* occupies an important place in the history of Chinese philosophy for containing clear dialectical ideas.

"Conversion is the action of the Way." By this proposition, the *Laozi* puts forth a view about the transformation of contradictions. For example,

When man is born, he is tender and weak.
At death, he is stiff and hard.
All things, grass as well as trees, are tender and supple while alive.
When dead, they are withered and dried.
Therefore, the stiff and the hard are companions of death.
The tender and the weak are companions of life.
Therefore when the army is strong, it will not win.
When a tree is stiff, it will break.
The strong and the great are inferior,
While the tender and the weak are superior.
—*Chapter 76*

However, Laozi falls into the trap of metaphysics by trying to interfere with the dialectical process, by "returning to the root" and striving to "know the eternal." (*Chapter 16*) He advocates "blunting the sharpness," "untying the tangles" "softening the light" to "become one with the dusty world." Thus he acknowledges a world that is called "profound identification," where there are neither contradictions nor struggles. (*Chapter 56*)

The naive dialectics finally draws to a metaphysical conclusion. As reflected in the *Laozi's* view of society and history, ideological maintenance through conservation, restoration, and retrogression is formed. This is summed up in a description of "a small country with few people."

> Let there be a small country with few people.
> Let there be ten times and a hundred times as many utensils,
> But let them not be used.
> Let the people value their lives highly and not migrate far.
> Even if there are ships and carriages, none will ride in them.
> display them.
> Let the people again knot cords and use them (in place of writing).
> Let them relish their food, beautify their clothing,
> Be content with their homes, and delight in their customs.
> Though neighboring communities overlook one another and,
> The crowing of cocks and the barking of dogs can be heard,
> Yet the people there may grow old and die without ever visiting one another.
> —*Chapter 80*

There can be no contradictions in such an ideal society. People forever live in a small closed world, where things are isolated from one another and each provides for itself. The author of the *Laozi* has gone much farther than did Confucius, who "believed in and loved the ancients" and wanted to restore the Western Zhou Dynasty. Laozi dreamed of going back to primitive times.

Laozi opposed the development of material civilization, culture, and knowledge. For instance, he says, "The more sharp weapons the people have, the more troubled the state will be. The more cunning and skill a man possesses, the more vicious things will appear." (*Chapter 57*) And he goes so far as to say, "When knowledge and wisdom appeared, there emerged great hypocrisy." (*Chapter 18*)

With the development of human society, and especially since the human race entered the era of civilization, the covetous desires of the ruling classes have become the lever of historical development. The *Laozi* says "The Way of man" is to "reduce the insufficient to offer to the excessive." (*Chapter 77*) "The people starve because the ruler eats too much tax-grain." "The people take death lightly because their ruler strives for life too vigorously." (*Chapter 75*) And there is a warning to oppressive rulers: "The people are not afraid of death. Why, then, threaten them with death?" (*Chapter 74*) The *Laozi* blames the evils of the time on the development of social productivity, of science and technology, and of even human knowledge.

The *Laozi* opposes the development of society and advocates the restoration of old customs. The ruler should "cause his people to be without knowledge or desire," so that they will not rise up in revolt. At the same time, the ruler should curb his lust for power. So it urges the ruler "to retreat and stand on the defensive," and it advocates being "modest and in a low position." It says, "It is precisely because he does not compete that the world cannot compete with him." (*Chapter 66*) Only by so doing can a ruler become "the lord of the land" and "the monarch of the empire."

Therefore in the *Laozi·Chapter 3,* the statement "By acting without action, all things will be in order" is in fact an art of political maneuver. Later, Ban Gu (32–92) had a comment on the Taoist school, saying, "They have taken hold of the essence. By living a simple life with few worries they can defend themselves. For they are in a low place and appear to be weak, and can control themselves. This is the art of political maneuver of the man who desires to proclaim himself emperor." (*History of Han·Bibliography*) Ban Gu did notice the political message in the *Laozi.*

The philosophy of the *Laozi* is a summation of Chinese philosophical development in the era of slavery, just as that period was passing from the historical stage—at the intersection of the Spring and Autumn, and Warring States periods.

The *Laozi* departs from the old religious way of thinking that considered Heaven as the supreme ruler of all things in the universe. Expressions such as the "Mandate of Heaven" and the "Will of Heaven" do not appear in the book, which also ignores the theories of the Five Elements and the *Book of Changes*. In epistemology, the *Laozi* puts "calm observation" and "profound insight" as the fundamental route to understanding the "Way," different from Confucius' apriorism and Mo Di's empiricism. The *Laozi* surpasses these both in the depth of speculation, suggesting a new channel of epistemological inquiry and marking the historical formation of ancient Chinese dialectical contradictions.

In the *Laozi,* "Heaven"—as a traditional personalized divinity, together with the Lord on High, ghosts, and gods, previously considered to dominate the world and human society—has lost its splendor. But the book takes the road of natural fatalism and denies the subjective initiative of man, maintaining that the Way models itself after Nature and that each thing returns to its root and its destiny. By claiming that the "Way" produces all things and all things return to the "Way," it contradicts its dialectical view of development. Its critical spearhead is blunted by the noumenon of the "Way," which moves in circles and returns to tranquility.

Since the philosophy of the *Laozi* possesses a specific duality, in later ages the philosophers of different tendencies absorbed the author's philosophical thought from different angles. Philosophers such as Han Fei, Wang Anshi, and Wang Fuzhi made a further development of Laozi's naive dialectical thought by means of expounding and annotating his book. The Jixia Taoist School gradually transformed the "Way" of the *Laozi* by placing it in the materialist dimension. Other philosophers such as Zhuang Zhou pushed it to the extreme of idealism, and led dialectics to relativism and sophism. Wang Bi developed the "Way" in the direction of idealist ontology, making it the theoretical basis of his metaphysics in the Wei and Jin dynasties. In short, the *Laozi* had an important influence upon the development of Chinese philosophy.

6.

Mencius and the Confucian Tradition

Mencius is the Latinized form of Meng Ke (c. 372–289 BC). Born in the small State of Zou (present-day Zouxian County, Shandong Province), tradition has it that he was a descendent of the Mengsun family, State of Lu. In his youth Mencius was a pupil of Zisi, grandson of Confucius, for whom he had deep respect and admiration. In his own words, "What I wish to do is learn to be like Confucius." (*Mencius·Gongsun Chou (I)*: hereafter only chapter title appears) Like Confucius, he spent many years traveling with his disciples among the various states, disseminating his theories of benevolent government. He had to contend with rival thinkers who advocated military force and harsh rule as the way to build up a powerful and prosperous state. We quote historian Sima Qian: "After the State of Qin appointed Shang Yang prime minister, it became rich and militarily powerful. When the States of Wei and Chu listened to the advice of Wu Qi, they conquered their enemies. Sun Wu, Tian Ji, and the like helped kings Wei and Xuan of the State of Qi to force other feudal lords to submit to Qi." (*Records of the Historian·Biographies of Meng Ke and Xun Qing*)

But Mencius opposed the use of violence, and felt ashamed to talk about material gain. As a result, he failed to find a patron among the feudal lords. In his later years he retired to his native place and devoted himself to teaching. "He wrote prefaces to the *Book of Poetry* and to the *Book of History*. He explained the sayings of Confucius, and wrote the *Mencius* in seven volumes." (*Ibid*) He engaged in political and academic activities all his life. As his doings and sayings contributed a great deal to the development of Confucianism, he is revered as second only to Confucius himself as a pioneer of Confucianism.

Mencius formed the political concepts of the "kingly way" and the "mighty way." The former entailed using virtue to command submission, while the so-called "mighty way" meant using force. Virtuous rulers were to be honored, those who relied on force were to be despised. The "kingly way" demanded that the ruler treat his people with kindheartedness, which in turn would earn him their ardent support. Such a ruler would eventually reach the great goal of unifying China.

To carry out benevolent rule, it was first necessary to guarantee the common people's livelihood. To this end, he proposed keeping the traditional slave society "well-field system." Arable land in square plots was divided into nine sections. Slave-farmers cultivated the outer eight sections for themselves, the central one for their masters. Mencius set great store by careful regulation of farmland, telling nobles and rulers: "When the boundaries have been defined correctly, the division of the fields and the regulation of allowances may be determined by you, sitting at your ease." (*Teng Wen Gong (I)*).

Not only did Mencius stress the importance of ensuring people's livelihood, he claimed that the welfare of the people led to stable politics: "The people are more important than the ruler. When the people are protected, the ruler can sit at ease on the throne." This "people-first" idea has had a profound influence throughout Chinese history.

In philosophy, Mencius focuses on self-examination. He explains society, history, and the relationship between Heaven and man with the human mind and human nature as his central concerns. He gives full play to man's subjective initiative in an idealistic way, laying the foundation for the development of subjective idealism in Chinese thought.

As recorded in the text, the theory of the original goodness of human nature occupies an extremely important role in the philosophical thought of Mencius.

Confucius had said, "By nature, men are alike; by practice, they get to be wide apart." (*Analects*, 17:3) That is, people's original natures are similar, but circumstances and habits make them differ in virtue and wisdom. In the Warring States Period (475 BC–221 BC), the different ideological and moral characters of people were exposed to the full. This motivated thinkers to explore the original nature of man and the relationship between human nature and reality as a means of solving social problems, a key issue in the contention between the "hundred schools of thought"—and an important research task for Chinese philosophy for the next 2,000-plus years.

According to Mencius, in man's consciousness there is an *a priori* germination of goodness, a feature that differentiates man from beast. When a person sees a child about to fall into a well, he or she will rush to save the child. Mencius regarded such "kindheartedness" as the germination of basic moral concepts such as benevolence, righteousness, propriety, wisdom, and so on. He says:

> "The feeling of commiseration is the initial principle of benevolence. The feeling of shame and dislike is the initial principle of righteousness. The feeling of modesty and complaisance is the initial principle of propriety. The feeling of approval and disapproval is the initial principle of knowledge. Men have these four principles just as they have their four limbs" (*Gongsun Chou (I)*)

Mencius put forth the concept of "intuitive knowledge and intuitive ability." He says, "The ability possessed by men without having been acquired by learning is intuitive ability; the knowledge possessed by them without exercise of thought is intuitive knowledge. Babes in arms all love their parents. Filial affection for parents is the working of benevolence. Respect for elders is the working of righteousness. There is no other reason for those feelings—they belong to all under Heaven." (*Jin Xin (I)*)

Although man's innate nature is good, this does not mean that everybody is able to bring his or her nature of goodness into full play. Mencius cites the example of water, which always flows downwards; this is the innate nature of water. But when you strike water you may cause it to leap up, even over your forehead, and, by damming and leading it, you may force it to flow uphill. These are not innate movements of nature. An external force caused those movements. Next he adds, "In good years the children of the people are mostly good, while in bad years most of them abandon themselves to evil. It is not owing to their natural inclinations conferred by Heaven that they are thus different. The abandonment is owing to the circumstances in which they allow their minds to be ensnared and drowned in evil." (*Gao Zi (I)*) When he explains why some people are "not good," Mencius acknowledges the influence of objective circumstances.Mencius puts forth a set of idealistic methods to cultivate man's original nature and improve man's character.

Mencius says, "To nourish the heart there is nothing better than to make the desires few." (*Jin Xin (II)*) Mencius summed up the causes of the social evils and chaos that abounded in his time into two categories, "seeking fame and wealth" and "having many desires." He says as follows:

> "Benevolence is man's mind, and righteousness is man's path. How lamentable it is to neglect the path and not pursue it, to lose this mind and not know to seek it again. When men's fowls and dogs are lost, they seek them, but when they lose their minds, they do not know how to seek them. The great end of learning is nothing else but to seek the lost mind." (*Gao Zi (I)*)

Mencius exaggerates the function of "mind," in which he focuses on thinking at the expense of input via the sense organs: "The senses of hearing and seeing do not think, and are obscured by external things. When one thing comes into contact with another, as a matter of course it is led astray. The function of the heart is to think. By thinking, it gets the right view of things; by neglecting to think, it fails to do so." (*Gao Zi (I)*)

"The function of the heart is to think." This is a great contribution to epistemology in the history of Chinese philosophy. However, rational reality is one-sidedly emphasized, and as a result Mencius fails to appreciate that rational cognition relies upon perceptual cognition. This inevitably leads him to idealism. Mencius not only sets the perceptual against the rational, he also thinks that only great men can understand the thinking function of the mind. As for the "little men," since they only seek material things that satisfy their sense organs, it is rather hard for them to keep their inborn goodness. He says, "Those who labor with their minds govern others; those who labor with their strength are governed by others." (*Teng Wen Gong (I)*)

This theory of the original goodness of human nature was applied to the elucidation of feudal moral principles and ethics. It was also used as the theoretical basis of Mencius' doctrine of benevolent government. He explains, "All men have a mind that cannot bear to see the sufferings of others. The ancient kings had this commiserating mind, and they, as a matter of course, had likewise a commiserating government." (*Gongsun Chou (I)*)

Mencius spent his whole life doing his best to persuade the rulers of various states "to extend benevolence" to the common people and "to practice the kingly way."

He inherited the thought of the Mandate of Heaven from Confucius. His idealist system was a combination of three strands: the heavenly way, inborn goodness, and benevolent government. In his opinion, "Heaven" is the dominator of all things on earth, and therefore possesses moral attributes. "Sincerity is the way of Heaven." (*Li Lou (I)*) "Sincerity" is a mysterious concept whose significance is the most genuine "goodness." "Sincerity" is the way of Heaven, which decides man's life in this world according to the principles of morality. Meanwhile, Mencius' idea of "regarding the people as the foundation" adds a new element to the traditional view of the Mandate of Heaven, as may be seen in the following elements of his thought.

First let us consider his thought of "abdicating and handing over the crown to another person." Mencius thinks that a ruler does not pass his throne on to one of his descendants via free will. "The emperor cannot give the empire to another." (*Wan Zhang (I)*) In Mencius' opinion, Heaven bestowed the throne on a new ruler. "Heaven does not speak. Its will is manifested in the personal conduct of human beings, and human conduct of affairs." (*Ibid*) If a new emperor can win support from the people and rule the empire well, he is in fact a lawful emperor, as these attributes are evidence that Heaven bestowed power on him. Mencius quotes a passage from *The Great Declaration, Book of History*, which asserts, "Heaven sees according as my people see. Heaven hears according as my people hear." "Heaven" observes and deals with national affairs through the eyes and ears of the people. Mencius' exposition of the authority of Heaven reflects more or less the wishes of the people. He also said, "If an individual obtains the empire, there must be in him virtue equal to that of Shun or Yu. Moreover, there must be the presenting of him to Heaven by the preceding emperor. It was on this account that Confucius did not obtain the empire." (*Wan Zhang (I)*) The idea that any private individual, were he to have enough virtue, could become an emperor was a revolutionary proposition in that period. But such a person had to be recommended to Heaven by the incumbent ruler: Mencius believed in the stability of monarchical rule.

Mencius explains the intention of Heaven with two statements: "The people on the land under Heaven obeyed him," and "The people reposed under him"—unifying the "the will of the people" and "the will of Heaven." Within the theory of the Mandate of Heaven, his idea of regarding the people as the foundation is reflected. Such an idea, of course, belongs to the rational factor of his thought, though it is contained in a heap of irrational ideas.

Regarding the formation and development of human ability and wisdom, Mencius says:

> "Thus, when Heaven is about to confer a great office on any man, it first exercises his mind with suffering, and his sinews and bones with toil. It exposes his body to hunger, and subjects him to extreme poverty. It confounds his undertakings. By all these methods it stimulates his mind, hardens his nature, and supplies his deficiencies." (*Gao Zi (II)*)

"That which is done without man's doing is from Heaven. That which happens without man's causing it to happen is from fate." (*Wan Zhang (I)*) This fatalist outlook, a spiritual fetter on thought, was a brake on social progress in China for hundreds of years.

With regard to the relationship between Heaven and man, the moral attributes of Heaven are contained in "human nature," the laws of Heaven originate in the morality of people in this world, and the virtues of Heaven lie in the human mind. Human mind and "Heavenly mind" communicate with each other. In this way he transforms the cardinal guides and constant virtues of feudalism into the laws of Heaven—and puts forth a cognitive line that asks people to think, to know their nature, and to know Heaven, as "man is an integral part of Nature."

In epistemology, Mencius' thought is characterized by two aspects: one, his subjective starting point, from which he regards cognition as the probing into one's own inner world, and two, the attachment of undue importance to the rational by neglecting the perceptual. He contends:

> "He who has exhausted all his mental constitution (to think) knows his nature. Knowing his nature, he knows Heaven." (*Jin Xin (I)*)

By self-awakening and enlargement of the "principle of goodness" in their inner life, people may understand the inborn nature of man, for it embodies the moral attributes of Heaven.

In short, cognition does not mean a route from outside objects to the senses, and then to thought; instead, man's cognition starts from the probe into one's own inner life and inborn nature; after a series of introspective activities like this, it finally reaches the goal of "knowing Heaven, which is the supreme realm of human life and the consummation of cognition.

The significance of human life lies in self-perfection of the spirit. Heaven, human mind, and human nature are originally integral. All that Heaven contains lies at the same time in the human mind. "Heaven" as the objective spirit has thus been transformed into the subjective "mind." Therefore, Mencius responds:

> "All things are already complete in us. There is no greater delight than to be conscious of sincerity upon self-examination. When one acts with vigor on the law of reciprocity when seeking the realization of perfect virtue, nothing can be closer than one's approximation to it." (*Jin Xin (I)*)

By "all things," in the main, Mencius means the feudal cardinal guides and constant virtues. He regards feudal morality as an attribute of Heaven, the essence of man, and *a priori* content of thought. In Mencius' opinion, to understand this principle is beyond the understanding of the average person. Only those who "have foresight" can possess such a moral self-awakening.

Mencius was the first Chinese philosopher to scrutinize the then-prevalent idea that heroes create history. First, he made a distinction between the "foresighted" and the "hind-sighted." "Those who are first informed should instruct those who are later in being informed, and those who first apprehend principles should instruct those who are slower in doing so." (*Wan Zhang (II)*) The "foresighted" have the right to lead, and even to rule the "hind-sighted." This is, according to Mencius, the will of Heaven—and also his inheritance and development of the theory that "The highest are the wise and the lowest are the stupid," as put forth by Confucius.

Second, heroes make history because they possess moral qualities higher than those of average people. Only "the noble and honorable" can understand the principle that the function of the mind is to think. Only they can cultivate themselves in line with the "cardinal principle." And only they can benefit society.

Mencius puts the heroic conception of history into a system of historic cycles. "It is a rule that a true imperial sovereign should arise in the course of 500 years, and that during that time there should be men illustrious in their generation." (*Gongsun Chou (II)*) Following are his grounds of argument: "From Yao and Shun down to Tang some 500 years elapsed. . . . From Tang to King Wen some 500 years elapsed. . . . From King Wen to Confucius some 500 years elapsed." (*Jin Xin (II)*) Mencius postulates a cyclical theory of the empire progressing from disorder to order and back again every 500 years. In his opinion, only when the true "kingly persons" and "natural geniuses" appear can disorder be turned into order. Speaking of his era, he says, "From the commencement of the Zhou Dynasty up till now, more than 700 years have elapsed. Judging numerically, the date is past for heroic figures to appear. Examining the character of the present time, we might expect the rise of such individuals. But Heaven does not yet wish that the empire should enjoy tranquility and good order. If it wished that, who is there besides me to bring it about?" (*Gongsun Chou (II)*)

Mencius considered himself to be the successor of Confucius and the defender of that sage's philosophy. Determined to "rectify the human mind and extinguish heretical ideas," he waged a vigorous offensive against the doctrines of the various other schools of thought. In the controversy, by developing the thought of Confucius and of Zisi, he promoted Confucianism of Zou and Lu to be "a renowned school" when a hundred schools of thought were contending for attention. Xunzi once denounced the thought of Mencius, saying, "He studied the deeds of the former kings a little, but he did not grasp their system of thought." And Sima Qian criticized Mencius, saying, "Mencius was an impracticable person, and his ideas are inapplicable in practical affairs." Sang Hongyang once laughed at him, too, saying, "Mencius sticks to the old ways. He knows nothing of worldly affairs." Nevertheless, Mencius' ideas became an integral part of the Confucian school of thought in the period that saw the Han Dynasty replace the Qin. It exerted a great influence upon the development of philosophy in the long centuries of feudal society in China.

7.

Zhuangzi's Development of Daoist Philosophy

Master Zhuang, or Zhuangzi, (c. 369–286 BC) was born in the region of Meng in the State of Song during the Warring States Period. His personal name was Zhou, his courtesy name Zixiu. His masterpiece, called *Zhuangzi*, is noted for its use of parables to express his philosophical ideals. In his *An Outline History of the Chinese Literature*, Lu Xun (1881–1936) speaks highly of Master Zhuang as an intelligent writer for his artistic expressions, saying, "His writings are as free and natural as the vast ocean, and his style appears in all its glory, unique, extraordinary, and variable." Master Zhuang was as important to the Taoist school of thought as Mencius was to the Confucian school, and his name was often combined with that of his predecessor, Laozi, as Laozhuang. Master Zhuang's writings have had a profound influence on Chinese philosophy, literature, arts, and politics for more than 2,000 years.

According to legend, Zhuang Zhou came from a poor family, and in his early years did menial jobs like weaving straw sandals. Later, he obtained a minor post looking after the royal lacquer trees. But he soon retired to live as a hermit and expound his philosophical thoughts.

According to Sima Qian's *Records of the Historian*, King Wei of the State of Chu heard of Zhuang Zhou, and was so impressed with his thought that he invited him to become his prime minister for a salary of 1,000 pieces of gold. Zhuang Zhou, however, declined:"A thousand pieces of gold are valuable indeed, and that of prime minister is of course an honorable position. But have you never seen an ox being prepared for sacrifice? After being fattened up for several years, it is decked with embroidered trappings and led to the altar. Would it not willingly then change places with some uncared-for piglet? Go away at once! Defile me not! I would rather disport myself to my own enjoyment in the mire like a small fish than be slave to the ruler of a state. I will never take office. Thus I shall remain free to follow my own inclinations."

He refused to hold any public office, and lived as a hermit for the rest of his life.

In the *History of Han·Catalogue of Biographical History, Political Literature and Local Records,* the *Zhuangzi* is recorded as having 52 chapters. The extant version of 33 chapters was compiled by Guo Xiang (252–312) of the Jin Dynasty. Of these 33 chapters, seven chapters are called the *Inner Chapters*, 15 the *Outer Chapters*, and 11 the *Miscellaneous Chapters*. Other versions of the work have different arrangements of chapters.

Master Zhuang inherited and developed Laozi's concept of the "Way." In Master Zhuang's view, the Way is the most real and substantial entity of all, though without form and impalpable. Master Zhuang says, "It is its own source and its own root, existing since time immemorial, before Heaven and Earth came into existence." Such is the Way, not only "did it come into existence before Heaven and Earth," but also "it begot Heaven and Earth." (*Zhuangzi·The Great Teacher*, hereafter only chapter title appears)

Zhuangzi stretches the dialectical relationship between the limited and the limitless. In the chapter *On the Uniformity of All Things*, he stresses that there is no end to the discussion of the beginning or "ultimate cause" of the universe, and he recommends a completely skeptical attitude toward the objective existence of the materialist world.

Zhuang Zhou calls things "the limited" and the Way "the limitless." All visible things exist relatively in time and space, whereas the Way is the absolute existence that transcends time and space. The Way depends on nothing—"It is its own source and its own root." It existed before Heaven and Earth separated from each other. It existed before time and exists beyond space.Master Zhuang severs the dialectical relationship between the limited and the limitless. He puts the Way outside time and space, and beyond everything. Therefore, he denies the materialist unity of the objective world.

The world outlook of Master Zhuang is in general idealistic. But there are some rational elements in his idea of the Heavenly way that follows Nature and does nothing. There is a vivid description of the wind in *On the Uniformity of All Things*: "At times it is inactive, but once it becomes active, angry howls are emitted from ten thousand crevices." A gentle breeze produces a faint response and a strong wind produces a gigantic response. Whether to blow or to cease blowing totally depends on themselves. Suddently, they begin to blow and abruptly they stop. Behind them there is neither the role of spiritual dominator nor that of creator.

As regards life and death, Master Zhuang thinks that both life and death arc natural phenomena, just as are the four seasons, which happen successively. He says, "Life is the succession to death, and death is the beginning of life. No one knows exactly the regular patterns for both. The birth of a man is the convergence of the vital force that in turn forms life. The breaking-up of the vital force causes death. If life and death are closely related to each other, why then should I worry about death? Therefore, all things in the world are encompassed in the same circle of life and death. Thus, beauty can be considered as something miraculous, while ugliness can be considered obnoxious. Something obnoxious can be transformed into something miraculous, and something miraculous can be transformed into something obnoxious. So it is said, 'Everything in the world is attributed to the same vital force.' Therefore, the scholar places high value on the unification of all things in the vital force." (*Knowledge Travels North*)

Master Zhuang sees that the convergence of the vital force is to its breaking-up what the emergence of things is to their extinction. This view shows a tinge of naive materialism, and may be called "the transformation of the vital force." Nevertheless, Master Zhuang does not acknowledge that the "vital force" is the origin of all things. In relation to spirit and form, he only acknowledges that "When one's body decays, his soul decays with it." (*On the Uniformity of All Things*) In his idealist system of thought, these naive ideas occupy a secondary position.

Relativism is the core of the philosophical thought of Master Zhuang, and can be traced to the development of the negative factors hidden in Laozi's naive dialectics. Laozi lays more stress on the mutual transformation of opposites than does Master Zhuang. But he fails to give adeqiate attention to the conditions in which a contradiction may be transformed. That is to say, the dialectic thought of Laozi contains a possibility of developing into relativism. And Master Zhuang develops such a possibility into an integral theory of relativism. First of all, the relativism advocated by Master Zhuang manifests itself in denying the differences in the properties of objective things. In his opinion, if things are examined from the high plane of the noumenon of the Way, they are all in a process of continuous transformation, so their properties, even their existence, are relative and temporary. As such, they are far from possessing stability or differences in quality. He cited an example, saying, "So let us consider the blade of grass and the pillar, the leper, and the beautiful Xishi, and all sorts of strange things and fantastic phenomena—they are all one from the viewpoint of the Way." (*On the Uniformity of All Things*) That is, there are various differences of quality such as the spacious, the deceitful, the strange, the coquettish, and so on. And the difference is as great as that between a thin blade of grass and the pillars of a house, and between the ugly person in the legend and the beautiful concubine of the King of Wu. Yet judged from the lofty height of the Way, they can all be unified as one existence.

Master Zhuang says, "There is in the world nothing greater than the tips of the down of a bird in autumn, while Mount Tai is tiny. There is no one who lives longer than a dead baby, while Peng Zu, who lived over 700 years, died young." (*On the Uniformity of All Things*) This is another case in which the size and duration of life are treated within the reference system of Nature. Master Zhuang quoted Confucius, saying, "If we look at things with regard to their differences, the liver and the gall bladder are as different as the State of Chu and the State of Yue. However, if we look at things with regard to their likeness, everything in the world is one." (*Signs of Complete Integrity*) Master Zhuang points out, "From the viewpoint of distinction, if we say that something is large because it is relatively large, then everything can be said to be large. If we say that something is small because it is relatively small, then everything can be said to be small. Once you know why heaven and earth are like grains of millet and why a tiny piece of down is like a hill, you will understand the distinction between large and small." (*Autumn Floods*)

Hence, relativity does not originate from things proper; it depends on human cognition and on the angle from which man observes them. It is the subject that endows the object with relativity. When they are looked at from the angle of the Way, the differences, contradictions, and properties of things all become illusions, and are changing all the time. Based on this, Master Zhuang draws a conclusion that all things are in uniformity. In his opinion, there is neither the truly right nor the truly wrong, so there is simply no use discussing the difference. The conception of right and wrong originates in human prejudice, which he calls the "fixed idea." He says, "If you try to tell what is right and what is wrong when you do not have your own fixed idea, it is as if you set out for the State of Yue today and arrived there yesterday." (*On the Uniformity of All Things*) The "fixed idea" as Master Zhuang calls it, or "prejudice" as we usually term it, includes in fact all people's opinions and arguments.

He says, "When clear distinction between right and wrong appeared, the Way was injured." (*Ibid*) "The Way is obscured when concealed by minor achievements. Speech is obscured when concealed by flowery words. Hence the dissension between Confucianism and Mohism—each approves what the other disapproves and disapproves what the other approves." (*Ibid*) The Later Mohist School generalized the viewpoint of Master Zhuang into the proposition "All words are paradoxical."

Starting with relativism, Master Zhuang inevitably heads for skepticism and agnosticism. In *On the Uniformity of All Things* there is an interesting story illustrating the viewpoint that debate cannot result in telling what is right from what is wrong. No matter which side wins the debate, it is impossible to know the right from the wrong. As for the debaters, is there really one side that is right, and the other wrong? Perhaps both are right. Perhaps both are wrong. It is beyond our knowledge. Yet a third party will take a stance on one side or the other. By limiting the judgment of right and wrong to the sphere of subjectivity, Master Zhuang denies the objective criterion of truth. As a result, not only does prolonged debate fail to make a matter any more clear, but also one can never make a clear statement of what one wants to say. The later Mohists agreed, saying, "Debate has no winners."

In *On the Uniformity of All Things*, Master Zhuang says, "Taking a lot of trouble to unify things without knowing that things are in fact already in uniformity is illustrated by the fable 'Three in the morning.' Once upon a time, there was a monkey-keeper who fed the monkeys with acorns. When he said that he would give them three bushels of acorns in the morning and four bushels of acorns in the evening, the monkeys thought they were being cheated, and were angry. However, when he said that he would give them four bushels of acorns in the morning and three bushels of acorns in the evening, all the monkeys were pleased. In fact, the total number of acorns remained the same, but there was an abrupt change from anger to pleasure. In our daily life, quite a few people take a great deal of trouble to square accounts in every detail. How do they differ from the monkeys?

In Master Zhuang's opinion, only when people are without senses and thought can they meet the requirements of the Way. A parable reads: "The ruler of the South Sea was called Helter, the ruler of the North Sea was called Skelter, and the ruler of the Central Region was called Chaos. Helter and Skelter often met each other in the land of Chaos, who treated them very well. They wanted to repay his kindness, saying, 'Every man has seven apertures with which to hear, to see, to eat, and to breathe, but Chaos alone has none of them. Let's try and bore some for him.' They bored one aperture each day, and on the seventh day Chaos died." (*The Philosopher King*) Helter and Skelter wanted to give Chaos sense organs with which to acquire knowledge. The result was that they destroyed him.

Master Zhuang maintains that the distinction between right and wrong should be totally ignored, and knowledge abolished. This is in accordance with his doctrine of the Heavenly Way, and his life philosophy of nihilism and world-weariness.

Starting with idealism and relativism, he also takes a skeptical attitude towards man's cognitive ability and the reliability of knowledge. He says, "Knowledge has to be based on something, but that something is unstable." (*The Great Teacher*) That is, human cognition needs a certain condition and foundation, such as the target to be known and the ability to know the target, and so on. But it seems to Master Zhuang that all such foundations are illusory, so it is impossible to distinguish between knowledge and ignorance, and it is impossible to demonstrate them either. He sighs, "As I see it, the principles of benevolence and righteousness, the standards of right and wrong, all these things are so complicated that I can hardly tell which is which." (*On the Uniformity of All Things*) The practice of benevolence and righteousness may bring about either benefit or loss. What benefits me may be a loss to somebody else, and what the other party regards as right may be wrong in my view. Therefore, the controversy between the Confucians and the Mohists can never be resolved.

Master Zhuang criticized subjectivism and arbitrariness with relativism, making a great contribution to the philosophical concept of everything in the world being relative. This brilliant idea contains some factors of dialectics. But dialectics rejects anything absolute. It is precisely because Master Zhuang takes relativism for the basis of the theory of knowledge that he one-sidedly exaggerates the relativity of things and knowledge. He is then side-tracked into skepticism, agnosticism, and subjective idealism.

Xunzi made a frank comment on him, "Master Zhuang was blinded by Nature and was insensible to men." (*Xunzi·Dispelling Blindness*).

In Zhuang's opinion, man can do nothing but submit to Nature, which is beyond human interference. "If you do not put out the torch when the sun or the moon is shining, isn't it hard to see the torch light? If you continue to water the fields when timely rains are falling, isn't it a waste of labor?" (*Wandering in Absolute Freedom*) Man appears tiny, even superfluous, in the face of Nature. In the same vein, he says, "Life and death are destined, just like the eternal succession of day and night—a natural course of events. Men do not have the power to control it, and this is true of everything in the world." (*The Great Teacher*)

> Master Zhuang not only thinks that man cannot conquer Nature, but also emphasizes that fate plays a dominating role: "Life and death, gain and loss, failure and success, wealth and poverty, worthiness and worthlessness, praise and blame, hunger and thirst, cold and heat—all are transformations that follow the natural order." (*Signs of Complete Integrity*) Furthermore, he says, "Don't destroy the inborn nature Heaven has given you with enforced behavior. Don't destroy the destined lot Fate has given you with painstaking affections." (*Autumn Floods*)

On the one hand, Master Zhuang demands that people submit themselves to the arrangements of fate: "It is the first of all human virtues to cultivate one's mind and make it unmoved by sadness or joy, and content with the inevitable." (*The Human World*) On the other, he believes that some day he may free himself from reality to pursue absolute spiritual liberty. Since he sets necessity against liberty in an absolute way, his fantasy sometimes transcends reality. "While seeking communication with the infinity of Heaven and Earth, he was totally free and alone. He neither showed disdain for anything nor questioned whether anything was right or wrong, but harmonized with worldly affairs. . . . Above, he traveled with Heaven and Earth. Below, he befriended those who disregarded life and death and those who ignored the beginning and the end." (*The Human World*)

How can one reach the realm of being "independent of anything"? In Master Zhuang's opinion, the most fundamental way is to "care for no self." That is, spiritually one must be above natural and social restrictions in any form, extinguish the opposition between the outside world and oneself, forget society, forget oneself — forget everything. In his view, it is not objective necessity that binds human liberty, but human thought.

In the chapter titled "Wandering in Absolute Freedom" Master Zhuang says, "The perfect man cares for no self. The holy man cares for no merit. The sage cares for no name." Because of "caring for no self," there is no need to render meritorious service and to pursue a distinguished career. Thus one will not fuss over praise or blame. This is the mysterious realm in which the Way and the self have already become one. Only the "true man" extolled by Master Zhuang can reach such a realm:

> "The true man in ancient times knew neither the joy of life nor the sorrow of death. He was not elated when he was born. He was not reluctant when he died. Casually he went to another world. Casually he came back to this world again. He did not forget the origin of his life. He did not explore the final destiny of his life either. He was pleased to accept whatever came into his life. He gave no thought to life and death, and regarded the latter as returning to Nature. This is what is meant by not impairing the Way with the mind and not assisting Heaven with human efforts. This is what the true man is like." (*The Great Teacher*)

In their formation some "true men" are ugly and even disfigured, but in spirit all are flawless. He makes a comment on this, saying, "For men with ample virtue, their physical defects can be forgotten." (*Signs of Complete Integrity*) He also says, "Rather than praise King Yao and denounce King Jie, it would be better for the people to forget both of them and integrate themselves with the Way." (*The Great Teacher*)

This is the so-called "sitting and forgetting" or "mental fasting," namely, by forgetting everything, inwardly one feels nothing of one's own existence and outwardly one knows nothing of Heaven and Earth. To illustrate this idea, he cites the parable of how Yan Hui told Confucius about his "progress." First Yan Hui forgot benevolence and righteousness. Several days afterwards, he forgot the ceremonies and music. And at last he could "forget everything while sitting down." At this, Confucius was astonished, and he asked Yan Hui what he meant by "sitting down and forgetting everything." Yan Hui said, "I cast off my limbs and trunk, give up my hearing and sight, leave my physical form and deprive myself of my mind. In this way, I can identify with the great Way. This is the so-called 'sitting and forgetting'." (*The Great Teacher*)

Once reasoning is excluded, the mind is void and tranquil, so it may be integrated with the Way. Once the inner spirit becomes one with the Way, it is possible to reach the spiritual realm "as fresh as dawn," when the sun rises in the morning, and everything is clear and bright. So also is man's mental state. Once all considerations are excluded from our mind, we feel extremely calm, and peace rules everywhere. At this instant, the Way and the self are one, and we may suddenly see everything in a clear light. Master Zhuang says, "After he had a clean mind as fresh as dawn, he was able to discern the independent Way." (*The Great Teacher*) Because the "Way" has no opposite, it is modified as "independent." At this instant, man and the Way belong to one and the same body, so he may go wherever the Way goes, and he may coexist with what changes constantly. He says, "Heaven and Earth and I came into existence at the same time. All things in the world and I are one uniformity." (*On the Uniformity of All Things*)

Although Master Zhuang tries his best to transcend reality spiritually, in fact, he cannot divorce himself from society. Therefore, he forms a life philosophy as follows. "He neither showed disdain for anything nor questioned right and wrong, but harmonized with worldly affairs."

(*The Human World*) In the chaotic times in which Master Zhuang lived, the Warring States Period, life was precarious for all, high as well as low. Safety was to be sought in keeping aloof from worldly affairs. He cites the example of the huge gnarled and knotted tree which survives simply because its wood is no good for the carpenter, whereas trees with excellent qualities are cut down in their prime. He says, "The perfect man is free from praise or blame, appears and disappears at will as the snake and dragon do, and changes to adapt himself to the changing times with no desire to stick to anything. He goes up and down in perfect harmony with Nature, wandering freely in the Way, which is the origin of everything. He is the master of everything who is not mastered by anything. How then can he have any trouble? " (*Ibid*)

As regards his view of history, Master Zhuang advocates going back to the primitive world of chaos, in which man was not separated from the beasts and birds. In the chapter titled "The Hooves of Horses," he says, "Therefore, in ancient times, when perfect virtue prevailed, the people lived together with the birds and animals, and mixed with everything in the world. How did they know the distinction between superior men and inferior men? All ignorant, they did not lose their virtue. All desire-less, they were in as natural a state of simplicity as rough timber, which kept intact their inborn nature." Here, he mentions "simplicity." What is simplicity? "Discard the sages and wisdom, and the great robbers will be curbed. Destroy the jades and pearls, and the petty robbers will not appear. Break the tallies and seals, and the people will be simple and natural. Crush the weights and scales, and the people will no longer quarrel. Abolish all the sagely laws, and the people will be able to listen to reason." (*Break Open the Boxes*) This total negation of civilization is a form of extreme nihilism.

Judging from Master Zhuang's attitude to reality and life, his advocacy of idealism and relativism, his denial of cultural achievements and his doctrine of returning to the ancients, we have to say that the social role of his thought is a negative one. However, his criticism of the prevailing hypocrisy that preached benevolence, righteousness, ceremonies, and laws, since it exposed the avarice and arrogance of the ruling class of his time and the seamy side of society, exerted a powerful influence upon later trends of thought in China.

8.

The Cognitive Line: Natural Philosophy and Logical Theory

Different schools of thought in the Warring States Period debated a philosophical controversy about the relationship between concept and objective being—an important bone of contention between the "hundred schools of thought."

In the Warring States Period, ceremonial observances withered, and music became decadent. In the *Xunzi*, the author comments on current affairs, saying, "Since the feudal lords employ different principles of government and the hundred schools of thought offer different explanations, of necessity some will be right and others wrong, some will produce order and others disorder." (*Xunzi·Book 21: Dispelling Blindness*) "Strange propositions have sprung up, names and realities have become confused." (*Xunzi·Book 22: On the Correct Use of Names*) As the phenomenon became more and more conspicuous, all schools of thought plunged into the controversy.

In those years, the rulers were eager to make use of scholars to advise them. For example, according to the *Records of the Historian* by Sima Qian, in the reigns of King Wei and King Xuan of the State of Qi, an academy was set up in the capital, housing a big group of "persuasive talkers" who "never held a public office but talked about state affairs animatedly." (*Records of the Historian·Book 46: The Hereditary House of Tian Wan Posthumously Titled Jingzhong*)

Nevertheless, most of the so-called persuasive talkers, those who went around urging rulers to adopt their views during the Warring States Period, including Mencius, Gongsun Yan, Su Qin, and Zhang Yi, concentrated their debates on politics, so their debating activities have little to do with the history of philosophy.

But some people belonged to another category. At first they focused their attention on examining the relationship between names and actuality; then they formulated concepts and classified them; then they researched problems in logic such as judgment and reasoning. At first, they were called "debaters," then the School of Names, or the Logicians. Hui Shi and Gongsun Long were their two leading representatives.

Hui Shi (c. 370–318 BC), a native of the State of Song, rose to prominence as the prime minister of the State of Wei, a position he held for fifteen years. He pursued a balance-of-power strategy by organizing a "vertical (north–south) alliance of states" to check the growing power of the State of Qin.

As a philosopher, Hui Shi expounded the so-called ten propositions, all paradoxes, extant in the *Zhuangzi·The Human World*. They are as follows:

1. The greatest has nothing beyond itself; it is called the great unit. The smallest has nothing within itself; it is called the small unit.
2. That which has no thickness cannot have any volume, and yet in extent it may cover 1,000 *li*.
3. Heaven is as low as Earth; mountains and marshes are on the same level.
4. When the sun is at noon, it is setting; when there is life, there is death.
5. A great similarity is different from a small similarity; this is called the lesser similarity-and-difference. All things are similar to one another and different from one another; this is called the great similarity-and-difference.
6. The south has no limit and yet has a limit.
7. One goes to the State of Yue today and arrives there yesterday.
8. Joint links can be separated.
9. I know the center of the world: it is the north of the State of Yan (in the north) and south of the State of Yue (in the south).

10. Love all things extensively. Heaven and Earth form one body.

Of these paradoxes, the first, fifth, and tenth are fundamental propositions that embody the thought of Hui Shi. The first is concerned with his world outlook and ontology, the fifth with his epistemology and methodology, and the tenth is his final conclusion. The others are illustrations or concrete cases of application.

The first proposition brings people into contact with the size of the universe, the macrocosm infinitely great ("great unit") and the microcosm infinitely small ("small unit)."

The fifth proposition comments on similarities/differences great and small. The duality in Hui Shi's idea of "the uniformity of the similar and the different," shows a trace of dialectical thinking. His concept is a definition of the relationships between species and genus. For example, dogs and sheep belong to the same genus of beast; this is the similarity. But they belong to two species; this is the difference. When emphasis is placed only on the similarity, it is possible to conclude that "a dog may be a sheep," as some debaters did.

The tenth proposition reads, "Love all things extensively. Heaven and earth form one body." This is the summation of Hui Shi's thought. He divides "unit" into two, namely, the "great unit" and the "small unit." And then, after a process of "the uniformity of the similar and the different," all things return to the state of "unit." Thus he could say, "Heaven and Earth form one body." As for "Love all things extensively," this is a logical conclusion. Hui Shi's basic thought is to make uniform what is different and stress the similarity.

Today, when we study the thought of Hui Shi, we run into a special difficulty: he makes inductive and deductive inferences about concepts in an exaggerated way, and makes inferences divorced from objective facts. Master Xun, a philosopher of a later age, said, "Hui Shi was blinded by propositions and insensible to realities." (*Xunzi· Chapter 21: Dispelling Blindness*)

Gongsun Long (c. 320–250 BC), a native of the State of Zhao, was at one time attached to the household of its Prince, Ping Yuan. There are six chapters in the extant version of the *Gongsun Longzi* (*Book of Master Gongsun Long*). The first is a biography written by someone of a later generation, but the other five chapters are believed to be by Gongsun Long himself, and are the basic materials for research into his doctrine.

Those who maintain that the philosophy of Gongsun Long belongs to the category of materialism cite two passages, both in *Chapter 6: On Names and Actuality*:

> "Heaven, Earth, and their products are all things. When things possess the characteristics of things without exceeding them, there is actuality. When actuality fulfills its function as actuality, without wanting, there is order. To be out of order is to fall into disorder. To remain in order is to be correct."

> "When the name is rectified, then 'this' and 'that' are restricted. When the designation 'that' is not restricted to that, then the 'that' will not do. When the designation 'this' is not restricted to this, then the 'this' will not do." (*Chapter 6: On Names and Actuality*)

That name and actuality must be in accordance to each other is a fundamentally correct idea. But how can the accordance be reached? In *Chapter 6: On Names and Actuality*, he says, "To rectify is to rectify actuality, and to rectify actuality is to rectify the name corresponding to it."

This contradicts his proposition that "A name is what designates an actuality." Although he acknowledges that a name comes from an actuality, he over-emphasizes the independent existence of concepts and names once they appear.

Gongsun Long's well-known viewpoint that "A white horse is not a horse" is expressed in *Chapter 2: On the White Horse*:

> "Because horse denotes the form and white denotes the color, what denotes the color does not denote the form. Therefore, we say that a white horse is not a horse."

> "Ask for a horse, and either a yellow horse or a black one may answer. Ask for a white horse, and neither the yellow horse nor the black one may answer. . . . Now, the yellow horse and the black horse remain the same. And yet they answer to a horse but not to a white horse. Obviously, therefore, a white horse is not a horse."

> "Horses of course have color. Therefore, there are white horses. If horses had no color, there would be simply horses. Therefore, whiteness is different from horse. A white horse means a horse combined with whiteness. Thus, in one case it is a horse and in the other it is a white horse. Therefore, we say that a white horse is not a horse." (*Chapter 2: On the White Horse*)

He conscientiously persists in formal logic but draws an absurd conclusion. In this world, there cannot be a single horse that is with form but without color. Such a horse is an abstract concept.

To emphasize the differences among and the independence of concepts, Gongsun Long designed this dialog:

> A: "Is it correct that hardness, whiteness, and stone are three separate things?"
> B: "No."
> A: "Is it correct that they are two separate things?"
> B: "Yes."
> A: "Why?"
> B: "When whiteness but not hardness is perceived, we have a case of two. When hardness but not whiteness is perceived, we have a case of two."
> ...
> B: "When seeing does not perceive hardness but whiteness, there is no hardness to speak of.
> When touching perceives not whiteness but hardness, there is no whiteness to speak of."
> ...
> B: "Whether one perceives the whiteness of the stone or perceives the hardness of the stone depends on whether one sees or not. Seeing and not seeing are separate from each other.

Neither one pervades the other. And therefore they are separate. To be separated means to be hidden." (*Chapter 5: On Hardness and Whiteness*)

And here lies the epistemologically serious defect in Gongsun Long's philosophy. He regards the various attributes of the unity of a thing as absolutely isolated. He regards the roles that the different human sense organs play as absolutely separate, and denies that the human senses may act upon one another. This is of course a metaphysical viewpoint.

Also, when he discusses the relationship between names and actuality, he starts his discussion from the materialist theory of reflection. But when he finishes his theory of rectifying names, he ends with idealism. He started the debate because "he felt deep hatred for the chaotic situation of the relationship between names and actuality." (*Chapter 1: Biography*) And, "As for the kings of old, they examined names and actuality, and were careful in their designations." (*Chapter 6: On Names and Actuality*)

That Gongsun Long thinks attributes of a thing are detached from one another, and may even exist after they are detached from that very thing, leads him into sophistry. In reproof, Han Fei says, "When words about hardness and the whiteness, or about ungenerous treatment are in vogue, the laws and decrees are extinguished." (*Han Feizi·Chapter 41: Asking the Causes of the Debate*) It is thus clear that the rise of such a debate is by no means accidental.

To sum up, although both Hui Shi and Gongsun Long belong to the school of the Logicians, they emphasize different points in the debate on the relationship between names and actuality, and on similarity and difference—and both go to extremes to develop their theories. In the view of the scholars of this school, all differences are relative. Contrary to Hui Xi›s thought, to Gongsun Long, all differences are absolute. Neither appreciates the dialectical tension between the absolute and the relative. Both make the mistake of one-sidedness, although on different sides.

The Later Mohists were Mo Di's disciples and the subsequent generations of their students. Six chapters of the extant version of the *Mozi*, thought to be written by them, are known collectively as *Mohist Debate*. (Hereafter only the numbers and titles of the quoted chapters are given.)

Most members of the Later Mohist School probably belonged to the ranks of self-employed handicraftsmen and intellectuals springing from this class. They had an extensive range of productive skills, knowledge of natural sciences, comparatively abundant social experience, and logical knowledge acquired from debating metaphysical concepts. In the *Mohist Debate,* knowledge of the natural sciences is in evidence: "Level means at the same height." "Middle means at the same length from both sides." "Circle means at the same length from any point to the center." "End means any point in an object being without volume." (*Chapter 40: Classic I*) There is data about the inverted image, similar to the principle of the camera. (*Chapter 42: The First Explanation of the Classic*) In mechanics and physiology, the Later Mohists had sound views and made great achievements in the sphere of natural sciences. They developed a theory of knowledge in line with naive materialism, and established a comparatively integrated system of logic.

The Later Mohists inherited and developed Mo Di's thought, discarding what they found unsuitable. As they focused on practical utility, they combined Mo Di's ideas of "righteousness" and "interest" in an organic way and clearly defined the two. "Righteousness is interest." (*Chapter 40: The Classic I*) "Interest is what pleases you once you have it. Harm is what displeases you once you have it." (*Ibid*) This is not only an ethical doctrine of utilitarianism, but is also a criticism of Confucius' moral teaching that benefit should be discarded to preserve the principle of righteousness.

They gave up Mo Di's idea that monarchical power should be supreme, and put forth new ideas about the ruler and the common people. "The ruler should conform to the wishes of the people." (*Chapter 42: The First Explanation of the Classic*) Their behavior must be in accordance with their social status, and the relative systems for all are rooted in the agreement they have brought about.

They deny that "righteousness" is an abstract moral concept endowed by Nature, and think that the content of "righteousness" should develop along with the times. "Yao talked about 'righteousness' in ancient times, but the word is still in use at the present time. Since the times are different, there are two connotations of the same word." (*Chapter 41: Classic II*) On this basis, they put forth the bold view that different ages should have different governments. "Emperor Yao was good at ruling the country. This is a present-day judgment on ancient affairs. Were it possible to judge present-day affairs from the angle of ancient times, obviously Emperor Yao would be incompetent to rule the country." (*Chapter 43: The Second Explanation of the Classic*) This counters Confucius' and Mencius' advocacy of "following the ancient rulers."

The Later Mohists abandoned some mystical ideas of Mo Di: they deny that Heaven, devils, and ghosts reward the virtuous and punish the wicked. "Merit means benefiting the people. Reward is what the superior bestows on the inferior. Crime means doing what is forbidden. Punishment is what the superior bestows on the inferior." (*Chapter 40: The Classic I*)

While the Later Mohists failed to reach a clear understanding that the unity of the world lies in its materiality, they accumulated knowledge of natural sciences in those years and made a materialist explanation of categories such as time, space, and movement.

On the category of time: "A long duration means to generalize all different times in an overall way." (*Chapter 40: The Classic I*) "A long duration includes the ancient times, the present times, the mornings, and the evenings." (*Chapter 42: The First Explanation of the Classic*)

On the category of space: "Universe means a generalization of all places in an overall way." (*Chapter 40: Classic I*) "Universe means all the space including the east, the west, the south, the north, and so on." (*Chapter 42: The First Explanation of the Classic*) "Limit means in a certain region there is neither room for a single demarcation line to be put in, nor for you to advance a step forward." (*Chapter 40: The Classic I*) "Limitless means that in a certain region there is yet some room for a single demarcation line to be put in." (*Chapter 42: The First Explanation of the Classic*)

On the category of movement: "Movement means to move location." (*Chapter 40: the Classic I*) "There is stoppage because there an external force obstructs." (*Chapter 40: The Classic I*) "Let's discuss walking. Whoever walks always reaches a place near by first and then reaches a place far away. Distance refers to the length of a journey. Priority refers to the duration of time." (*Chapter 43: The Second Explanation of the Classic*)

Since the Later Mohists thought that the limitless universe is made up of limited places and time intervals, shown by the mode in which things move, they put forth a proposition that "Being exists before non-being." (*Chapter 43: The Second Explanation of the Classic*). This is in contrast to the Taoist viewpoint that "Being comes from nonbeing."

The Later Mohists' principal contributions to philosophy include acknowledging that "substance" is an objective existence, so it is primary. This is the basis of their epistemology. Starting from this, they dispose of the physiological function of human cognition as well as some physiological and psychological phenomena: "Life means body and perception getting together. Sleep means consciousness lies in a state of unconsciousness." (*Chapter 40: The Classic I*) "Mental peace means there is neither selfish desire nor personal disgust in cognition." (*Chapter 40: The Classic I*) These descriptions, in accordance with scientific principles, provided scholars of later generations with valuable reference data by which they attempted to identify the relationship between the body and the spirit.

According to the Later Mohists, man is able to acquire perceptive knowledge through contact with the outside world.

On the basic activity of cognition: "To know is a kind of ability." (*Chapter 40: The Classic I*) "Men of wisdom can know things because they have the ability to know things. But all who have the ability to know things do not necessarily know things." (*Chapter 42: The First Explanation of the Classic*)

On the concrete activity of cognition: "To perceive is a kind of touching." (*Chapter 40: The Classic I*) "Perception is when people touch external things so that they may know their shapes and forms as if they saw them with their own eyes." (*Chapter 42: The First Explanation of the Classic*)

On the five senses of cognition: "Man has only five senses to know things." (*Chapter 43: The Second Explanation of the Classic*) "Man is able to know things not through the five senses of eyes, ears, nose, mouth, and heart. Man is not able to know time through the five senses." (*Chapter 41: The Classic II*) The Later Mohists claim that the "heart" has the function to recognize things, thus overcoming the narrow empiricism of Mo Di.

On perceptual knowledge: "To hear is the function of the ears." (*Chapter 40: The Classic I*) "By following the voice one has heard, one is able to perceive what people want to express. This is because man is able to recognize meaning through hearing." (*Chapter 40: The Classic I*) "To speak is the function of the mouth." (*Chapter 40: The Classic I*)

On rational knowledge: "To think is a kind of seeking activity." (*Chapter 40: The Classic I*) "Intellectuality is a kind of clear knowledge." (*Chapter 40: The Classic I*) "Intellectuality means that people's knowledge has been improved after discussion and applied to recognition. It seems that they have a brighter pair of eyes than usual." (*Chapter 42: The First Explanation of the Classic*)

The Later Mohists see the limitation of perceptual knowledge.

Their theory of knowledge proceeds from the knowledge acquired from "touching things" to the knowledge acquired by "discussing things," from perceptual knowledge to rational knowledge, and has factors of naive materialism and elements of naive dialectics.Mo Di said, "The common people must have a standard for knowing what things exist and what things do not exist. The standard is the actual experience of the eyes and ears of the common people." (*Mozi·Chapter 31: On Ghosts*) The Later Mohists do not agree, pointing out, "Whether criticism is correct or not, it does not depend on how many people hold such criticism, but on the target. What has been criticized should deserve the criticism." (*Chapter 41:The Classic II*)

Having a sure foothold in the materialist theory of knowledge, and aiming at winning victories in debates, the Later Mohists set up their own system of logic. In those years almost all schools of thought paid great attention to "assertion," namely, propositions and arguments. The Later Mohists discussed these problems in a clear way, and defined three categories of logic— cause, principle, and analogy.

:"An assertion emerges from the cause, it grows with the principles, and it calls for reasoning by analogy." (*Chapter 44: Major Choice*)"Cause is what gives rise to effect or result, so it must be determined first." (*Chapter 40: Classic I*)

Principle, sometimes called "law" or "way," "is the norm or model by which people act or make things." (*Chapter 40:The Classic I*) "Now people cannot walk when there is no way. Even when they have strong thighs and arms, they will be worn out very soon when they are not aware of the way." (*Chapter 44: Major Choice*)

On analogy: "Several things have something in common, called similar uniformity. . . . Several things have nothing in common, called dissimilar difference." (*Chapter 42:The First Explanation of the Classic)*

The three fundamental categories of ancient Chinese logic, cause, principle, and analogy are the basic forms for the reaching of a correct judgment.As for the basic content of established logical theories, the Later Mohists sum them up in the *Minor Choice* as follows:

"The purpose of debate is to distinguish between right and wrong, to examine the laws of order and disorder, to make clear where similarity and difference lie, to make a study of names and actuality, to decide gains and losses, and to free people from doubts and misgivings." (*Chapter 45: Minor Choice*)

From these six aspects, the task of logic is explained in two points: to know the truth and to serve society.

"Therefore, we are determined to seek the original form of the myriad things by analyzing and comparing the various discourses." (*Chapter 45: Minor Choice*)

The Later Mohists clarified the method of debate: When you wish to reflect reality you use concepts (names). When you wish to express your idea you use judgments (assertions). When you wish to explain the causes you use discourses (inferences). You may induce from the particular to the general according to the principle of "similarity" (to take things by similarity). You may deduce from the general to the particular according to the principle of "similarity" (to give things by similarity). And a debater should not impose his will on others. These are methods with comparatively clear forms of logical thinking.

Based on their rich accumulation of scientific, technological, and social knowledge, the Later Mohists have three major achievements to their credit. First, they persisted in the positive aspect of the cognitive line of materialism started by Mo Di. Second, they eschewed the negative aspects of Mo Di's thought, such as religious superstition and narrow empiricism. Third, they criticized idealism and sophistry in the doctrines of other schools of thought. Their outstanding advance in epistemology, and especially in logic, became an essential link in the history of the development of philosophy in pre-Qin China.

9.

The Hundred Schools of Thought

Xun Kuang (c 298–238 BC) was a native of the State of Zhao, had earned a reputation as an expert debater. As a young man, he journeyed to the capital of the State of Qi, where he delivered lectures at the local academy, and later became its president. Dismissed from this office, he retired to a small town where he spent his later years writing academic works.

Later scholars compiled his writings into the *Xunzi* (*The Book of Master Xun*). According to the traditional Chinese editing convention, it contains twenty chapters, called "volumes." Because some are divided once again, the book now contains thirty-two. Most content is thought to be Xun Kuang's authentic work.

In the Warring States Period, along with the development of agricultural production and commodity exchange, people accumulated a wealth of knowledge. Great advances were made in the natural sciences, such as astronomy, the calendar, agronomy and mathematics, and in technology as well. This provided people with the ideological and material prerequisites for a comparatively correct solution to the problem of the "relationship between heaven and man." As Xun Kuang says, "Those expert at theorizing about nature will certainly support their notions with evidence from the human condition." (*Xunzi · Chapter 23: Man's Nature Is Evil*. Hereafter, only titles and chapter numbers appear.)

Xun Kuang's work summed up the wrangles between the "hundred schools of thought" in the Warring States Period in a critical way. An outstanding materialist thinker, he ingested and digested the doctrines put forth by the pre-Qin philosophers and produced some brilliant ideas, such as "understanding the division between nature and man" and "regulating what heaven has mandated and using it."

Xun Kuang thought that "heaven" was nothing but nature, which exists objectively. The sun, moon, and stars, the mountains, rivers and plants, the wind, rain and other meteorological phenomena, and the rotation of the four seasons belong to the material world. In his words, "The myriad things share the same world, but their embodied forms are different." (*Chapter 10: On Enriching the State*) Xun Kuang calls the function of Nature "god," which exerts a subtle influence upon weather, making it cloudy, sunny, windy, rainy, and the like. And he calls material nature "heaven," formed by the "invisible" function of nature.

The myriad things in the universe are the result of the movement of the universe. "Hence, it has been said that when heaven and earth conjoin, the myriad things are begotten; when the yin and yang principles combine, transformations and transmutations are produced." (*Chapter 19: Discourse on Ritual Principles*) All the phenomena in the world are regarded as "the modification of the relation of heaven and earth or a transmutation of yin and yang." (*Chapter 17: Discourse on Nature*) This is a cosmogony of naive materialism and dialectical thought.

In the history of epistemology in China, Xun Kuang was the first to burst the theological dike surrounding the mandate of heaven, and explain "god" and "heaven" from the angle of materialism. This theory laid a solid foundation for the development of materialism and dialectical thought in subsequent ages.

Xun Kuang points out, "Heaven possesses a constant way; Earth has an invariable size." (*Chapter 17: Discourse on Nature*) Both "a constant way" and "an invariable size" refer to the laws and rules innate in nature:

> "The course of nature is constant: it does not survive because of the actions of a ruler as sage as Yao; it does not perish because of the actions of a ruler as brutal as Jie. When you respond to the constancy of nature's course with good government, there will be good fortune; when you respond to it with disorder, there will be misfortune." (*Chapter 17: Discourse on Nature*)

By explaining natural phenomena with objective laws, Xun Kuang negates the traditional religious and superstitious explanations, and his materialism surpasses that of his forerunners. Starting from the principle of recognizing objec inion, the roots of social order and disorder can only be sought in society:

> "When you strengthen the basic undertakings and moderate expenditures, nature cannot impoverish you. When your nourishment is complete and your movements accord with the seasons, nature cannot afflict you with illness. When you conform to the way and are not of two minds, nature cannot bring about calamities. . . . But when you ignore the basic undertakings and spend extravagantly, nature cannot enrich you. When your nourishment lacks essential elements and your movement accords with unusual events, nature cannot make you whole. When you turn your back on the way and behave with foolish recklessness, nature cannot bring good fortune. . . . Accordingly, when you understand the division between nature and mankind, you can properly be called a 'whole person.'" (*Chapter 17: Discourse on Nature*)

This "understanding of the division between nature and man" is a leap forward in the theory of the relationship between heaven and man since the question first surfaced in pre-Qin times.

In Xun Kuang's opinion, man should give full play to his subjective initiative, so as to control, transform, and conquer nature and make it serve man. He says as follows:

> "How can glorifying Heaven and contemplating it be as good as tending its creatures and regulating them? How can obeying heaven and singing hymns of praise to it be better than regulating what heaven has mandated and using it? How can anxiously watching for the season and waiting for what it brings be as good as responding to the season and exploiting it? How can depending on things to increase naturally be better than developing their natural capacities so as to transform them? How can contemplating things and expecting them to serve you be as good as administering them so that you do not miss the opportunities they present? How can brood-

ing over the origins of things be better than assisting what perfects them? Accordingly if you cast aside the concerns proper to man to speculate about what belongs to heaven, you will miss the essential nature of the myriad things." (*Chapter 17: Discourse on Nature*)

Avowing that "Heaven and man are separate from each other," Xun Kuang puts forth the proposition that "When the physical form becomes whole, the spirit is born." For the first time in the history of Chinese philosophy, a materialist explanation of the relationship between the spirit and the body is offered.

According to Xun Kuang, the epistemological activities of man are carried out through the functions of the human body. "As a general principle, the faculty of knowing belongs to the inborn nature of man. That things are knowable is a part of the natural principle of the order of things." (*Chapter 21: Dispelling Blindness*) "The means of knowing within man is called awareness." (*Chapter 22: On the Correct Use of Names*). "Awareness tallying with the facts is called knowledge." (*Ibid*) "The means of being able that is within man is called ability." (*Ibid*)

Knowledge starts with the senses. Xun Kuang divides the cognizing process of man into two stages. In the first stage, "Man should use his natural organs." Nevertheless, a sensation having just been obtained by a natural organ cannot form a correct cognition before the sensation itself undergoes the second stage, the stage of "collecting knowledge"—acquiring rational knowledge on the basis of perceptual knowledge: "The heart (mind) that dwells within the central cavity is used to control the five faculties. It is called 'the lord provided by nature.'" (*Chapter 17: Discourse on Nature*) "The mind is the lord of the body and master of the spiritual intelligence." (*Chapter 21: Dispelling Blindness*)

Xun Kuang's negation of ghosts and gods reveals the epistemological root cause of how empiricism deteriorates into idealism, just as Mo Di did when he talked about the will of heaven and the necessity of avoiding ghosts: "As a general rule, when men think there are ghosts, it is certain to be an occasion when they are startled or confused. These are occasions when these men take what does not exist for what does, and what does exist for what does not, and they settle the matter on the basis of their own experience." (*Chapter 21: Dispelling Blindness*)

In the process of summing up the contention of the "hundred

schools of thought," Xun Kuang points out that it is important "to dispel blindness," and to oppose one-sidedness and subjectivity. He says, "It is a common flaw in men to be blinded by some small point of the truth, and to shut their minds to the great ordering principle." (*Chapter 21: Dispelling Blindness*)

Only by "knowing the Way," can man dispel blindness. But how can the objective Way be known by the subjective "mind"? Master Xun makes a dialectical analysis:

"What does a person use to know the Way? I say it is the mind. How does the mind know? I say by its emptiness, unity, and stillness." (*Chapter 21: Dispelling Blindness*)

"The mind never stops storing; nonetheless, it possesses what is called emptiness. The mind never lacks duality; nonetheless, it possesses what is called unity. The mind never stops moving; nonetheless it possesses what is called stillness." (*Chapter 21: Dispelling Blindness*)

In Xun Kuang's view, only when the dialectical relationship of the above-mentioned three aspects is settled correctly can the state of "emptiness, unity, and stillness," or "great pure understanding," be finally attained:

> "Emptiness, unity, and stillness are called the Great Pure Understanding. Each of the myriad things has a form that is perceptible. Each being perceived can be assigned its proper place. Having been assigned its proper place, each will not lose its proper position. Although a person sits in his own house, he can perceive all within the four seas. Although he lives in the present, he can put in its proper place what is remote in space and distant in time. By penetrating into and inspecting the myriad things, he gets to know their essential qualities. By examining and testing order and disorder, he is fully conversant with their inner laws. By laying out the warp and woof of heaven and earth, he tailors the functions of the myriad things. By regulating and distinguishing according to the Great Ordering Principle, he encompasses everything in space and time. . . . How indeed could he have obsessions?" (*Chapter 21: Dispelling Blindness*)

Xun Kuang's cognitive method of "emptiness, unity, and stillness" brings into bold relief the entirety and motility of man's cognitive activity. It is also a theoretical result of actively transforming and developing the thought of Lao Dan, who advocates a mysterious epistemology of "calm observation" and "profound insight," and Master Guan, who advocates the "Way that can only be followed with tranquility."

While persisting in the materialist theory of knowledge, Xun Kuang emphasizes that it is necessary to study hard and accumulate knowledge gradually: "Not having heard something is not as good as having heard it. Having heard it is not as good as having seen it. Having seen it is not as good as knowing it. Knowing it is not as good as putting it into practice. Learning reaches its climax when it is fully put into practice." (*Chapter 8: The Teachings of the Ru*)

Xun Kuang also asserts that correct cognition must stand any test. As a general principle, what is to be prized in the presentation of a thesis is consistency in the structure of the argument advanced to support it, and evidence that shows facts accord with reality. Thus, they will sit on their mats to propound their theories, will rise up to show that they apply comprehensively, and will stand up straight to show that it is possible for the ideas they have propounded to be put into practice." (*Chapter 23: Man's Nature Is Evil*) This lays the foundation for Han Fei to urge his disciples to "compare and verify" all statements in practice.

Xun Kuang's materialist theory of knowledge agrees with the Mohist instruction to "name things on the basis of facts." By expounding the relation between name and fact dialectically, he sums up the logic and epistemology formed in pre-Qin times.

He affirms that "object" is primary and "name" secondary. "Man instituted names to refer to objects." (*Chapter 22: On the Correct Use of Names*) People use names to express or exchange their thoughts, and even to consolidate the social order.

"To make clear what is noble and what is base" refers to the rectification of names in both ethics and politics, the purpose of which is to make a clear division between high and low social strata and between close and distant relatives. Master Xun puts three groups of names under this major category: "the names of criminal law" (politics and law); "the names of titles of rank and dignity" (feudal ranks); "the names of the forms of culture" (feudal rites).

In addition to the proper naming of the status and position of ruler and ministers, father and son, it is necessary to differentiate the appellations of various positions and ranks, such as scholar, farmer, artisan, and merchant. This reflects the situation in that period, the beginning of the feudal system, when the division of labor was being deepened and becoming widespread.

What is "the basis of deeming something the same or different"? In Xun Kuang's view, all "names" should be applied to specific "objects," and therefore the cognition of "objects" should first pass through the sense organs. The naming of things must be governed by propriety and social customs as well. This is the situation in which "Names are shaped by the common practice of society."

What are "the crucial considerations for instituting names"?

> "When things are the same, we should give them the same name; when they are different, we should give them different names. When a single name is sufficient to convey our meaning, a single name is used; when it is not, we use a compound name. When the single name and the compound name do not conflict, a general name is used. Although it is a general name, it will not create inconsistencies." (*Chapter 22: On the Correct Use of Names*)

His proposition that "Man made distinctions and separations so as to institute names to refer to objects" belongs to the materialist theory of reflection.

In the same chapter, Xun Kuang points out that, "Names have no intrinsic appropriateness. Names have no intrinsic object." "The agreement becomes fixed, the custom is established." That is to say, the names, when universally acknowledged by society and people, are truly appropriate.

In the philosophical debate in pre-Qin China, human nature was another important problem. Taking the materialist stance of "eschewing the separation of man from heaven," Xun Kuang denies that there is any *a priori* basis for morality in human nature. According to him, natural elements should be divided from those caused by man. Holding that man's nature is evil, Xun Kuang provided a theoretical foundation helpful for the establishment of the feudal ethical modes and the feudal system itself.

Xun Kuang regards human nature as man's inborn natural attribute, primitive and simple. "As a general rule, 'inborn nature' embraces what is spontaneous from nature, what cannot be learned, and what requires no application to master. . . . What cannot be gained by learning and cannot be mastered by application, and yet is found in man is properly termed 'inborn nature.'" (*Chapter 23: Man's Nature Is Evil*) "When hungry, he desires something to eat, when cold, he wants warm clothing, and when weary, he desires rest." (*Chapter 23: Man's Nature Is Evil*)

Human nature is understood to be simply a kind of abstract biological demand plus instinctive psychology: "The nature of man is such that he is born with a love of profit. . . . Humans are born with feelings of envy and hatred. . . . Man is born possessing the desires of the ears and eyes, which are fond of sounds and colors. . . . When each person follows his inborn nature and indulges his natural inclinations, aggressiveness and greed are certain to emerge. This is accompanied by violation of social class distinctions, and throws the natural order into anarchy, resulting in a cruel tyranny." (*Chapter 23: Man's Nature Is Evil*) Therefore man's nature is evil. How does the "goodness" of human nature come into being? It is produced by human effort: "Human nature is evil; any good in humans is acquired by conscious exertion." (*Chapter 23: Man's Nature Is Evil*) Conscious exertion is separated from inborn nature, which embodies the opposition of the two contradictory aspects—and of the unity of conscious exertion with inborn nature, which embodies the unity of the two contradictory aspects. Thus Xun Kuang sees the dialectical relationship of the two contradictory aspects in a comprehensive way.

"The man in the street can become as wise as Yu." (*Chapter 23: Man's Nature Is Evil*) "The capacity of becoming good" can be turned into "the possibility of becoming good." This is Xun Kuang's theoretical contribution to the relationship between "inborn nature" and "conscious exertion."

Xun Kuang criticizes Mencius for his theory that man's nature is good, saying, "It shows that Mencius did not reach any real understanding of what man's inborn nature is, and that he did not investigate the division between those things that are inborn in man and those that are acquired." (*Chapter 23: Man's Nature Is Evil*) However, Xun Kuang's theory of human nature being basically evil is, after all, an abstract theory, hence idealistic. Xun Kuang blames Mencius for confusing "the division between those things that are inborn in man and those that are acquired." But he himself confounds the difference between man's natural attributes and his social ones.

Xun Kuang puts forth his theory of the origin of society in *On the Regulations for a King*: "It is necessary to make clearly defined class divisions when giving form to society." He explains:

> "In physical power they are not so good as the ox, in swiftness they do not equal the horse; yet the ox and horse can be put to their use. Why is that? I say it is because humans alone can form societies and animals cannot. Why is man able to form a society? I say it is due to the division of society into classes. How can social divisions be translated into behavior? I say it is because of humans' sense of morality and justice. Thus, when their sense of morality and justice is used to divide society into classes, concordance will result. When there is concordance between the classes, unity will result; when there is unity, great physical power will result; when there is great physical power, real strength will result; when there is real strength, all objects can be overcome." (*Chapter 9:*)

Social division is a fundamental law for the formation of a society, and "[o]f the instruments for distinguishing social classes, none is more important than ritual principles." (*Chapter 5: Central Physiognomy*) He does not mean working in cooperation with a due division of labor, on the basis of equality and mutual benefit, and on the premise of the interests of the broad masses. By "division" he means clearly marked divisions in social status, order, and degree.

> "I say that men are born with desires which, when not satisfied, cannot but lead men to seek to satisfy them. When in seeking to satisfy their desires men observe no measure and apportion things without limits, it would be impossible for them not to contend over the means to satisfy their desires. Such contention leads to disorder. Disorder leads to poverty. The ancient kings abhorred such disorder, so they established the regulations contained in ritual and moral principles to apportion things, to nurture the desires of men, and to supply the means for their satisfaction. In this way, the two of

> them—desires and goods—sustained each other over the course of time. This is the origin of ritual principles." (*Chapter 19: Discourse on Ritual Principles*)

To consolidate such a ruling order, feudal ceremony, ethics, and law, and the feudal system itself came into being.

In the Warring States Period and for a rather long time after that, thinkers of many schools of thought waged a vehement debate on the problem of change and inheritance in social and historical development. To counter Mencius' idea of "following the Former Kings," Xun Kuang proposed "following the Later Kings to unify the systems."

Nevertheless, Xun Kuang finally takes a metaphysical road, which leads to the idea that history occurs in cycles. He dreams of setting up a new, "rational" system that is exclusive of changes in an ever-changing age. The following are his views on history:

> "The beginning of heaven and earth is still present today." (*Chapter 3: Nothing Indecorous*) "That before a thousand years have passed, things undergo reversal has been a constant rule from antiquity." (*Chapter 26: Fu — Rhyme–Prose Poems*) "The ancient and the modern are one and the same. Things of the same class do not become contradictory even though a long time has elapsed, because they share an identical principle of order." (*Chapter 5: Contra Physiognomy*)

In this way, social history is rendered as a cyclic process in which there are zero qualitative changes. The Way is the supreme principle that governs human society, while "ritual and moral principles" are its concrete norms. In short, the social system of feudalism is a "rational" system with an unchangeable essence that moves in a "cycle" without beginning or end. This shows clearly that the historical view of Xun Kuang ends in the realm of metaphysics.

10.

Legalism in Pre-Qin China

Han Fei (c. 280–233 BC), born in the State of Han, was referred to respectfully as Han Feizi, or Master Han Fei. According to Sima Qian's *Records of the Historian*, Han Fei once studied under Xun Kuang and was deeply influenced by Laozi. "He delighted in the study of punishments, names, laws, and methods of government, while basing his doctrines upon the Yellow Emperor and Laozi." (*Records of the Historian·Biographies of Laozi and Han Fei*) He was involved in political struggles in his native state. In the process of studying the history and status quo of various states, he formed a progressive view of society and history and a comprehensive theory of the rule of law. He made important theoretical preparations for the State of Qin to unify China and to prepare the ground for feudalism. The extant collection of his works, the *Han Feizi*, consists of fifty-five chapters, most believed to be the work of Han Fei himself.

Pre-Qin Legalist thought finds its supreme expression in the writings of Han Fei. He inherits and develops the progressive view of society and history of the early Legalists, represented by Shang Yang (c. 390–338 BC), and takes it for the theoretical basis of his concept of the rule of law. Shang Yang sees history as a developing process. "The sages did not follow the ancient practices, and they did not stick to present particular cases, either. Had they followed the ancient practices, they would have fallen behind the times; had they stuck to present particular cases, they would have lost touch with the whole present situation." (*Book of Lord*

Shang·Chapter 7: Removing Obstacles from the Stopped-up Way, hereafter only chapter number and title appear.)

The theoretical basis on which Shan Yang carried out political reforms and innovations, and on which he opposed those who stuck to old ways, finds expression in these statements: "To administer society, one should not adopt only one method. To benefit the country, one should not follow old practices." (*Chapter 1: Reforms*) "When society changes, its affairs change. Since social affairs are ever-changing, the political measures should be changed accordingly." (*Han Feizi·Chapter 49: Five Vermin*, hereafter only the chapter number and title are given) "Indeed, customs differ between the past and the present. Old and new things are to be applied differently." (*Ibid*) All social affairs depend on the times, so the ruling measures must meet the demands of social affairs. Therefore, "When law changes with the times, it is easy to run the country well; when administrative measures fit in with the social conditions, it is easy to make contributions." (*Chapter 54: Intention and Law*)

Examining the development of history and its causes, Han Fei says, "In the distant past, people contended with one another in morality; in later times, people contended with one another in wisdom; nowadays, people are contending with one another in force." (*Chapter 49: Five Vermin*)

Legalists such as Shang Yang, Shen Buhai, Shen Dao all lived earlier than Han Fei's time. Although they advocated the ideas of "law," "method," and "power," in Han Fei's view, "All these ideas have not yet been perfected." "Shen Buhai was not good at enforcing laws he himself had made; he failed to unify them, so there appeared more wicked persons." (*Chapter 43: Enacting Laws*) As for Shang Yang's administration of the State of Qin, his focus was on "law" and he gave no consideration to "method." "He failed to adopt methods to identify those with crafty and evil intentions. What he did was nothing more than help wicked ministers and officials with the wealth of a powerful state." (*Ibid*) Han Fei sees how the three main strands of their philosophy—law, method, and power—should be connected with one another:

> "When the ruler fails to grasp the appropriate ruling methods, he will be deceived at the top level. When the ministers are beyond the law, they will rise in revolt at the lower levels. Neither can be

dispensed with, for these two are the main instruments of the monarch." (*Chapter 43: Enacting Laws*)

Han Fei inherits some ideas put forth by Xun Kuang, such as, "The course of Nature is constant" and "Understand the division between Nature and mankind." On this basis, he formulates his own view: "The Way corresponds to the principles." The "Way" is the core of Laozi's philosophical system and the supreme substance "that existed before heaven and earth." Han Fei makes a materialist transformation of the concept of the Way:

> "The Way is that by which all things become what they are. It is that with which all principles are commensurable." (*Chapter 20: Explanation of the Laozi*)

> "Such is the practical situation of the Way that it does not make anything, nor does it appear as itself in anything either. It is weak and delicate, so that it accords with the times and corresponds to the principles." (*Ibid*)

In Han Fei's opinion, that which corresponds to the "Way" are the "principles":

> "Principles are patterns according to which all things come into being. . . . Everything has its own principle different from those of others, and the Way is commensurate with all of them. Consequently, everything has to go through the process of transformation." (*Chapter 20: Explanation of the Laozi*)

> "In all cases, principle is that which distinguishes the square from the round, the short from the long, the coarse from the refined, and the hard from the brittle. Consequently, it is only after principles become definite that the Way can be realized. According to definite principles, there are existence and destruction, life and death, flowering and decline." (*Ibid*)

Han Fei was the first to expound on the category of "principle" and make a materialist explanation of the interrelationship between the "Way" and the "principles." He raised the cognition of the regularity of things so that regularity in general could be distinguished from regularity in particular.

Transforming Laozi's theory of the interrelationship between the "Way" and the "Virtue," Han Fei puts forth the idea that "Virtue is the function of the Way." (*Chapter 20: Explanation of the Laozi*) The "Way" dwells in the "Virtues," and the "Virtues" embody the "Way." The focus of Han Fei when he writes, "Virtues are what one being possesses within itself" is to study things by probing into their particularities and internal essence, which is profound cognition.

Han Fei develops Xun Kuang's the two ideas of "Beware of the separation of Heaven from Man" and "Regulate what Heaven has mandated, and use it." He advocates following the objective ways and giving full scope to the subjective initiative of man:

> "When one follows the Way and principles, one can assuredly succeed. . . . When one gives up the Way and principles, and acts rashly and blindly, one is bound to fail. A man, whether at the top level and possessed of the power and influence of the Son of Heaven, or at a lower level but as rich as Yidun, Taozhu, and Buzhu, he will lose his family, his funds, and his goods." (*Chapter 20: Explanation of the Laozi*)

> "Four things enable the enlightened ruler to make accomplishments and establish fame: timeliness of the seasons, the hearts of the people, skill and talent, and position of power. Without the timeliness of the seasons, even ten kings as sage as Yao could not grow a single ear of grain in winter. Acting against the sentiment of the people, even men of great strength could not make them exhaust their efforts." (*Chapter 28: Scholarly Honor and Official Rank*)

On the basis of respecting natural laws, Han Fei focuses on the subjective initiative of man and advocates the remaking of Nature by human efforts:

> "Mallet and forging hammer are used for leveling uneven objects, *bangqing* (a device that holds a crossbow in place) is used for correcting deformed objects. Sages formulate moral standards so that uneven behavior may be leveled and deformed behavior may be corrected." (*Chapter 35: Store of Legends and Tales, Outer Pieces (IV)*)

To explain the development of things, Han Fei uses the relationship between the Way and the principles as an analogy for that between the universal law and specific laws. He points out that either as the noumenon of things or as the universal law of the development of things, the Way cannot be created or destroyed. The ever-changing "principles," as the incarnation of the "Way," are the specific laws of things.

In the sphere of epistemology, Han Fei bases his theory on pre-Qin thinkers in many aspects, such as the subjective and the objective, knowledge and action, and the standard for checking man's knowledge. His emphasis on "investigation and checking" is an important feature.

Just like Xun Kuang, Han Fei is fully convinced that man has the capacity to know objective things. There is nobody who has no capacity to listen with his own ears, to watch with his own eyes, or to conceive with his own mind. Therefore, the "principle" of everything is available to man's cognition. "When one follows the principle when acting, success is assured." (*Chapter 20: Explanation of the Laozi*)

On the problem of the means of cognition, Han Fei emphasizes the importance of "open-mindedness and calmness":

> "As for a sage, it is necessary for him to follow the Way of Nature, to study the principles of things, to investigate and check them, and to repeat the process again and again. Being open-minded, keeping calm, and standing at the back-end, a sage never uses his own subjective desire." (*Chapter 8: Publicizing the Monarchical Power*)

This is Han Fei's development of the cognitive method of "emptiness, unity, and stillness" put forth by Xun Kuang.

Does one's knowledge accord with practice? Xun Kuang once said, "As a general principle, what is to be prized in the presentation of a thesis lies in two points: there must be consistency in the structure of the discrimination advanced to support it, and there must be evidentiary support to show that facts accord with reality." (*Xunzi· Chapter 23: Man's Nature Is Evil*) He focuses on "investigation and checking," enriching the theory of the criterion of truth in pre-Qin philosophy.

In Han Fei's view, when a ruler runs his country or examines any words, he must combine direct experiences with indirect ones so that courtiers close to him dare do no evil. "They dare not deceive their lord with false words. . . . They dare not cruelly and savagely oppress the people either" (*Chapter 14: Treacherous Courtiers Murder the Sovereign*) These are said to be important ways Prime Minister Guan Zhong administered the State of Qi and Lord Shang made Qin a powerful, prosperous state.

Another contribution Han Fei made to the theory of knowledge is his concept of "function" as the criterion of cognition. For instance, to judge whether or not a person is blind, it is necessary to ask him to look at something. To judge whether or not a person has virtues or talents, it is necessary to test him by words and deeds. Judging merely by appearance or eloquent speech, even Confucius could not tell how much ability a person had. To judge a person's ability, the only way is to put him in a certain post so that he may give full scope to his capabilities. To Han Fei, to distinguish between right and wrong, "knowledge" should be tested by "actions."

For Han Fei, the contention of the hundred schools of thought in the Spring and Autumn and Warring States periods created ideological disorder. To illustrate, he used the following parable:

> "In the State of Chu there was once a man who sold spears and shields. He praised his shields, saying, 'My shields are so solid that no spear can pierce them.' He praised his spears, saying, 'My spears are so sharp that they can pierce anything.' A passer-by asked him, 'If I throw one of your spears at one of your shields, what will happen?' The arms seller could not answer. Obviously, a shield that can withstand the impact of any spear and the spear that can pierce any shield cannot exist simultaneously. Yao and Shun cannot be praised simultaneously, just as the spear and shield cannot be praised together." (*Chapter 36: Debate (I)*)

The compound noun "*maodun*" (spear/shield) in present-day Chinese means "contradiction." Clearly it comes from this parable, in which Han Fei satirizes Confucius and Mozi who, as representatives of two entirely different schools of thought, praise Yao and Shun simultaneously. As he puts it, "Two inconsistent things cannot coexist." (*Chapter 49: Five Vermin*) He scorned the wrangling of the "hundred schools," and upheld the supremacy of the Legalist School.

Although Han Fei's concept of contradiction is different from the present-day category of contradiction in line with materialist dialectics, he does hold that contradiction is a universal phenomenon.

In his view, "As for time, the tide is sometimes full and sometimes low; as for human affairs, some bring advantages and some disadvantages; as for all things, some are growing and some dying." (*Chapter 24: Observation of Actions*) "All things cannot thrive at the same time. For this, yin and yang constitute a typical example." (*Chapter 20: Explanation of the Laozi*) As a result, the legislator must evalute advantages and harms before acting.

> "When any law is going to be made, there must be some difficulties. If it can be made after estimating the difficulties, then we make it. When any project is going to be undertaken, there must be some harm. When it can be undertaken, and when we estimate that advantages are many and harms are few, then we undertake it. In the world there can be neither laws that meet with no difficulties nor projects that bring about no harm." (*Chapter 47: Eight Situations*)

There is a famous saying: "Calamity is that upon which happiness depends; Happiness is that in which calamity is latent. Who knows when the limit will be reached?" (*Laozi·Chapter 58*) When Han Fei explains this, he clearly points out that transformation can only be done under given conditions. "A country cannot be always powerful, nor can it be weak forever. When the law enforcement personnel are powerful, the country is powerful; when the law enforcement personnel are weak, the country is weak." (*Chapter 6: A Country Must Have Law and Standards*) There is an important limitation in Han Fei's thought of naive dialectics. On the one hand, he acknowledges that "The Way . . . has no fixed mode of life," the Way "corresponds to definite principles," and the Way "grows and dies as long as time exists." That is to say, the Way is not a rigid or fixed concept. On the other hand, he pursues the "constant Way." What is the constant Way? "Only that which exists from the very beginning of the universe and neither dies nor declines until Heaven and Earth disintegrate can be called eternal." (*Chapter 20: Explanation of the Laozi*)

Han Fei's thought expresses a contradiction between the "Way" and the "principles"— hence its duality. When he feels the urgent need for political reform, he seeks "principles" that "have no fixed mode of life" and "have to go through transformations," and he acknowledges that "The way and the principles correspond to each other." When he desires to demonstrate the eternity of monarchy, as advocated by the Legalists, he pursues the constant way that "neither dies nor declines," for this is his goal.

Time and again, Han Fei combines the absoluteness and eternity of the monarchical power with the Way. And he emphasizes two points: "The Way is different from the myriad things" and "The ruler is different from all the ministers." (*Ibid*) By so doing, he inevitably enters the realm of metaphysics.

Moreover, since Han Fei frequently emphasizes the struggle of opposites, he goes to extremes in applying the opposites of a contradiction, rendering them into two sides impossible to coexist. In politics, he maintains the theory of violence. In his opinion, as long as a politician obtains the support of those who have power and influence, by violence he may solve all problems.

As for culture, Han Fei advocates that "it is necessary to take the law for education," and "it is necessary to take the government officials for teachers." In his opinion, "Two doctrines that are in nature mixed, disorderly, and contradictory to each other cannot be applied to the administration of a country." (*Chapter 50: The Renowned Schools of Confucius and Mozi*) Han Fei adopted a nihilistic attitude that totally negated China's cultural heritage, brought about extremely fateful consequences for history, and revealed the class limitation and metaphysical mistakes of his thought.

11.

Zou Yan: Commentaries on the Book of Changes

Zou Yan, a native of the State of Qi who lived in the last years of the Warring States Period, is renowned for his further systemization of the yin-yang and five-element doctrines that emerged in the first half of that era. He also represents the Yin Yang school of thought. By putting forth a cyclical theory of history, that "Five virtues succeed one after another," Zou Yan demonstrates how the Zhou Dynasty had to be replaced by a new dynasty. During or a little later than Zou Yan's lifespan, the *Commentaries on the Changes* (also known as *The Ten Wings of the Book of Changes*) emerged, written to explain the *Book of Changes*. *Commentaries on the Changes* puts forth the proposition that "The successive movement of yin and yang constitutes what is called the Way." Some aspects of the Yin Yang and Confucian schools merged in the last years of the Warring States Period. Zou Yan occupies a unique position in the history of Chinese philosophy in that he puts forth two doctrines. The first is "major and minor, two sets of nine regions." Zou Yan describes these as: The Middle Kingdom (China) is only one region of the world, which is the Sacred Land of the Red Region. The nine regions divided by Yu the Great are the nine administrative regions inside China, the minor nine regions. Outside China, there are nine other regions, the major nine, each of which has a similar topography to the Sacred Land of the Red Region. "Around each of these is a small encircling sea." Around all these is a large encircling sea, and this sea is where Heaven and Earth meet."

(*Records of the Historian·Book 74: The Biographies of Mencius and Xunzi*) While not geographically accurate, this explanation did open people's eyes to the world outside China, which spurred the Han Dynasty to send envoys to foreign lands and expand its territory.

The second doctrine is "five virtues succeeding one after another from beginning to end." The five elements (earth, water, metal, wood, fire), say Zou Yan, "not only produce but also subdue one another." In his opinion, that wood produces fire, fire produces earth, earth produces metal, metal produces water, and water produces wood expresses the formula that "The five elements produce one another." In all things there exists a relationship of unity. That water subdues fire, fire subdues metal, metal subdues wood, wood subdues earth, and earth subdues water expresses the formula that "The five elements subdue one another." In all things there exists a relationship of opposites. By these concepts he explains the regularity and stages of movement and change of all things. This view contains the ideological factors of naive materialism and dialectics.

When Zou Yan applies this theory of Nature to explain history, he says, "each of the five virtues adopts what it subdues for its application." In his opinion, every dynasty is the incarnation of a given power stemming from one of the five elements: "Each of the five virtues follows what it cannot subdue. For instance, the Yu Dynasty followed earth, the Xia Dynasty followed wood, the Yin Dynasty followed metal, and the Zhou Dynasty followed fire."

Zhou Yan's cyclical theory of history belongs in the category of metaphysics.

In Zou Yan's view, whenever a true king is going to arise, "good omens appear to the common people." This view acknowledges that Heaven has will, and contradicts the materialist viewpoint of the original doctrine of the five elements.

In the main, Zou Yan's doctrines discuss problems concerning astronomy, geography, history, and so forth. In addition to data and materials he acquired from the knowledge of astronomy, the calendar, and mathematics, he has a methodology of deduction, here commented on in *Records of the Historian:*

> "His (Zou Yan's) words were exaggerated and unorthodox. He invariably examined small objects and extended his findings from

them to larger and larger ones, to infinity. He first described the present, and then traced back to the Yellow Emperor, all of which has been recorded by scholars. Then, following the general outline of the rise and fall of the ages, he observed the times and explained the events. Thereupon, he recorded good and evil fortunes and institutions. He extended his survey backward to the time before Heaven and Earth came into existence, to what was obscure and abstruse, and on which no more inquiry was possible. He first made a list of China's famous mountains, great rivers, deep valleys, birds and animals, things produced on land and sea, and selected objects. On the basis of these, he extended his survey to what is beyond the seas, to what men are unable to see. He mentioned and cited the fact that ever since the separation of Heaven and Earth, the Five Virtues (Five Elements) have been in rotation. The reign of each virtue was quite appropriate, and corresponded to the facts." (*Records of the Historian·Book 74: The Biographies of Mencius and Xunzi*)

Zou Yan does his best to integrate the separate parts of the universe in his system, and to make a general explanation of it as a unity. His geographical doctrine and historical view are also concrete expressions of his view of the universe as a whole.

Since the Zhou Dynasty was an era of fire, its overthrow by the Qin Dynasty was regarded as the ascendancy of an era of water. When Qin perished and Han arose, Gongsun Chen, a native of the quondam State of Lu, put forth his opinion: "Since Han has overcome Qin, a period of the predominance of water has come to an end. Therefore, the Han Dynasty must be an era of earth." (*Records of the Historian·Book 28: Offering Sacrifices to Heaven and Earth on Mount Tai*)

Emperors in the dynasties after the Han acknowledged Zou Yan's doctrines. At the very beginning of the "sacred edicts," there are always the same words: "By the grace of Heaven, the Emperor on the throne decrees such-and-such." meaning the present emperor has inherited the grace of a certain "virtue" of the Five Elements.

The extant version of the *Book of Changes* includes two parts, one called "Texts," the other "Commentaries." The "Texts," from the early stage of the Zhou Dynasty, are sixty-four hexagrams of six lines each and their divinatory text. The "Commentaries," compiled by scholars of later generations, are explanations of the "Texts" and elucidation of the thought contained in the *Book of Changes*. The *Commentaries on the Changes* consists of ten treatises, called the "*Ten Wings*," which probably means that they assist the *Book of Changes* to be understood in the same way wings help a bird to fly. Later Wang Bi (AD 226–249), a scholar of the Wei Dynasty, wrote a book titled *Commentaries on the Book of Changes*, in which he took five of the ten treatises, dissected them, and mixed the relevant sentences with the "Texts" proper. This newly formed edition is still used today. *Consideration and Decision* is the explanation of the hexagram texts; *Image Explanation* explains the basic ideas contained in every hexagram and of the component-line texts; *Textual Explanation* is a discussion of the first two hexagrams, Heaven and Earth; *Appended Remarks* is the pandect of the basic thought of the *Book of Changes*; and *Expounding the Hexagrams*, *The Sequence of the Hexagrams,* and *Miscellaneous Explanations* deal with concrete problems such as the successive order of the hexagrams.

The authorship of *Commentaries on the Changes,* while traditionally ascribed to Confucius, appears to be actuallyl due to multiple people over a long period of time, by and large disciples of the Confucian school, who wrote them in the last years of the Warring States Period and during the transition between the Qin and Han dynasties. It is worth noticing that although the *Commentaries* nominally serve the purpose of explaining the *Texts*, it is also an elaboration of the author's own philosophical thought.

The author of the *Commentaries on the Changes* has something in common with Zou Yan as a representative of the Yin Yang and the Five Element schools. Both have done their best to integrate the various parts of the universe and make a general explanation of them, as a reflection of the unifying tendency of society and politics at that time.

In the *Commentaries on the Changes,* the common formulation is to juxtapose one concept with its opposite, for example, Heaven and Earth, yin and yang, the creative and the receptive. This is different from the traditional way of treating Heaven as a personified deity possessed of its own will. The book contains the following formulations with regard to the creation of the myriad things in the universe.

"First there were Heaven and Earth, and then afterwards all things were produced. What fills the space between Heaven and Earth are all those things." (*Sequence of Hexagrams*) "All material things having existence, there came male and female. From the existence of male and female came husband and wife. From husband and wife came father and son. From father and son came ruler and minister. From ruler and minister came high and low. With the existence of the distinction between high and low, afterwards came the arrangements of propriety and righteousness." (*Ibid*)

"It says in *Consideration and Decision*: Vast is the 'great and originating power' indicated by Qian! All things owe to it their beginning." (*1. Qian—The Creative*)

"It says in the *Consideration and Decision*: Complete is the 'great and originating capacity' indicated by Kun! All things owe to it their birth." (*2. Kun—Receptive, Resting in Firmness*)

"It says in the *Consideration and Decision*: Heaven and Earth exert their influences, and there ensue the transformation and production of all things." (*31. Xian—Influence*)

"When we speak of Spirit, we mean the subtle presence and operation of God with all things. . . . Thus water and fire contribute together to the one object; thunder and wind do not act contrary to each other; mountains and collections of water interchange their influences. It is in this way that they are able to change and transform, and to give completion to all things." (*Expounding the Hexagrams*)

But the cosmogony discussed in the *Commentaries* goes much farther. In another place it works out another paradigm, which contradicts its system:

"Therefore, in the system of the Changes there is the Supreme Ultimate, which produced the Two Modes. The Two Modes produced the Four Symbols that again produced the Eight Trigrams. The Eight Trigrams served to determine the good and evil issues of events, and from this determination was produced the successful prosecution of the great business of life." (*Appended Remarks (I)·Chapter 11*)

The "Supreme Ultimate" here is similar to the Absolute in the system of Western philosophy. Heaven and Earth and yin and yang produced by the Supreme Ultimate are called the Two Modes. Each of either yin or yang may be divided into two sets of major and minor, under a general appellation called the Four Symbols. When such a paradigm further unfolds, there are the Eight Trigrams, namely, heaven, earth, wind, thunder, water, fire, mountain, and swamp, the eight kinds of substantial matter. Qian stands for yang and Heaven, Kun stands for yin and Earth—the two most important trigrams. They are the parents, and all others are their children. But in the above paradigm, the Supreme Ultimate is imposed upon Heaven and Earth, or yin and yang, and a contradiction appears.

In the history of Chinese philosophy, the *Commentaries on the Changes* is first to put forth the concept of the "Supreme Ultimate." Now we cannot help asking, "What is the Supreme Ultimate?" In the Eastern Han Dynasty Xu Shen (c. 58–c. 147) wrote a note on the character *yi* (ultimate) for the *Origin of Chinese Characters*, saying, "At the very beginning, the Way was the ultimate being. Then it created and distinguished Heaven and Earth, and then it formed all things by transformation." (*Origin of Chinese Characters·Chapter 1*) It is thus clear that the "Supreme Ultimate" was what began the universe before it took the form of vital energy: "What exists before physical form is called the Way. What exists after physical form is called a concrete thing." (*Appended Remarks (I)·Chapter 12*)

These are the most important two propositions in the *Commentaries on the Changes.* Here "the Way" and "a concrete thing" are presented as a pair of antithetical categories. Following this logic, the *Changes* may cover all the principles in the universe. It may include the changes of all things, may create all things, and may predict good or ill luck for people; in short, it is no different from the philosophically abstracted God.

The trend toward unification and centralization of state power that emerged in the last years of the Warring States Period is reflected in the *Commentaries on the Changes* as follows: "The processes taking place under Heaven all come to the same issue, though by different paths; there is one result, though there might be a hundred anxious schemes." (*Appended Remarks (II)·Chapter 5*)

The character *yi* means "to change," with the implications of both change and transformation. In the *Commentaries* we find "Production and reproduction are what is called the process of change." (*Appended Remarks (I)·Chapter 5*) and "Comprehension of the changes indicated leads us to the business to be done." (*Ibid*) Moreover, "When a series of changes has run its course, another ensues. Once another series of changes starts moving, it obtains a free course. When it obtains a free course, it will continue long." (*Appended Remarks (II)·Chapter 2*) The above examples show that the implication of "change" is that things vary endlessly, and that the new supersedes the old without end.

> "The sun goes and the moon comes; the moon goes and the sun comes. The sun and moon thus take the place of each other, and their shining is the result. The cold goes and the heat comes; the heat goes and the cold comes. It is by the influence on each other of this contraction and expansion that the advantages of different conditions are produced." (*Appended Remarks (II)·Chapter 5*)

> "When change thus takes place in the proper way, occasion for repentance disappears. Heaven and Earth undergo their changes, and the four seasons complete their functions. Tang changed the appointment of the line of Xia to the throne and Wu that of the line of Shang, in accordance with the will of Heaven, and in response to the wishes of men. Great indeed is what takes place in a time of change." (*49. Ge—Revolution: Consideration and Decision*)

> "When the sun has reached the meridian height, it begins to decline. When the moon has become full, it begins to wane. The interaction of Heaven and Earth is now vigorous and abundant, now dull and scanty, growing and diminishing according to the seasons. How much more must it be so with the operations of men?" (*55. Feng—Abundance and Prosperity: Consideration and Decision*)

Of the eight trigrams, Qian and Kun are compared to father and mother, the other six their children. All sixty-four hexagrams contain a Qian (solid) line and a Kun (broken) line in different patterns. According to the *Commentaries*, the fundamental key to discovering the changes of things is the unity and interaction of the opposites Qian and Kun.

Once the two vital forces of sexual potentiality accumulated in the universe—Qian and Kun, yin and yang—touch each other, all things happen and develop. The *Commentaries* emphasizes their unity, from the angle that opposites dwell in unity. It says, "The processes taking place under Heaven all come to the same issue, though by different paths; there is one result, though there might be a hundred anxious schemes." (*Appended Remarks (II)·Chapter 5*) Here we find a difficulty. The focus on unity is emphasized, but the struggle of opposites is neglected. The origin of change and the movement of things are observed, although in a naive manner. The *Commentaries* does not attribute the agency of change to any heavenly deity.

The transformation of all things and their metaphysical end are fully dealt with in the *Commentaries on the Changes*. For instance, it puts forth a proposition that "Heaven and Earth exert their influences, and there ensue the transformation and production of all things." (*31. Xian — Influence: Consideration and Decision*) But, how do Heaven and Earth exert their influence?

> "The weak trigram is above, and the strong one below. Their two influences move and respond to each other, and thereby form a union. In the union, the repression of the one and the satisfaction of the other are reached. As for their relative positions, the male is placed below the female. All these things convey the notion of a free and successful course of fulfillment of conditions, while the advantage will depend on being firm and correct, as in marrying a young lady, and there will be good fortune." (*Ibid*)

Let's examine the hexagram "Xian." The three lines beneath form the trigram "Gen." The three lines above form the trigram "Dui." Gen is a young unmarried man, standing for the yang, strong and firm. Dui is a young unmarried woman, standing for the yin, mild and appearing weak. As far as their positions are concerned, the strong and firm partner originally ought to be above, but now it is below; the mild and weak partner originally ought to be below, but now it is above. Only by the struggle of the opposites of a contradiction can such an inverted positional relationship be changed. Only by changing such a positional relationship can mutual influence, namely sexual intercourse in the case of animals for generative propagation, be smoothly carried out. And only by successful mutual influence can all things be produced. Tang revolted and founded the Shang Dynasty, and Wu revolted and founded the Zhou Dynasty, as is affirmed by the *Commentaries on the Changes*, which used these instances to illustrate that by means of the struggle of opposites the positional change of the top and lower levels may be realized.

The *Commentaries on the Changes* also acknowledges that a reverse change may take place, saying, "Exhaustion gives rise to changes," and "the ultimate gives rise to the reverse." That is to say, in the changing process of all things, when the quantitative accumulation reaches its extreme, the hidden contradictions may change into their reverse. Some hexagramic patterns explain the principle that "the ultimate gives rise to the reverse."

> "Tai denotes things having free course. They cannot be so forever and hence it is followed by Pi, denoting being shut up and restricted. Things cannot for ever be shut up, and hence Pi is followed by Tong Ren." (*Sequence of Hexagrams*)

> "Bo denotes decay and overthrow. Things cannot be done away with forever. When decadence and overthrow have completed their work at one end, re-integration commences at the other; and hence Bo is followed by Fu." (*Ibid*)

> "Heng denotes long enduring. Things cannot long abide in the same place, hence Heng is followed by Dun. Dun denotes withdrawing. Things cannot be for ever withdrawn, hence Dun is succeeded by Da Zhuang." (*Ibid*)

Things can be neither always in a state of smooth development nor always in adversity, nor always in completion, nor always in a fixed state. But it is worth noticing that the conditions for the transformation of things are "exhaustion" and "ultimate."

But in what way do "exhaustion" and "ultimate" come into being? According to the *Commentaries,* such limits are the result of gradual accumulation:

> "The family that accumulates goodness is sure to have superabundant happiness, and the family that accumulates evil is sure to have superabundant misery. The murder of a ruler by his minister, or of his father by a son, is not the result of the events of one morning or one evening. The causes of it have gradually accumulated." (*2. Kun—Receptive, Resting in Firmness: Textual Explanation*)

"Destroy evils before they become menacing." "Be prepared for danger in times of peace." These ideas have a metaphysical tinge in the *Commentaries.* It is true that the landlord class agreed with the idea of changing the positions of the top and lower levels when it was itself engaged in the struggle to seize political power. But after it occupied the ruling position, the landlord class was determined to prevent further such transformations:

> "How great is what is symbolized by Qian!—Strong, vigorous, undeflected, correct, and in all these qualities pure, unmixed, exquisite!" (*1. Qian—The Creative: Textual Explanation*)

> "Yes, what docility marks the way of Kun! It receives the influences of Heaven, and acts at the proper time." (*2. Kun—Receptive, Resting in Firmness: Textual Explanation*) "Although the subject of this divided line has excellent qualities, he does not display them, but keeps them under restraint. 'If he engages with them in the service of the king, and is successful, he will not claim that success for himself.' This is the way of the earth, of a wife, of a minister. The way of the earth is 'not to claim the merit of achievement,' but on behalf of Heaven to bring things to their proper issue." (*Ibid*)

> "Heng denotes long continuance. The strong trigram is above, and the weak one below." (*32. Heng — Perseverance, Duration: Consideration and Decision*)

> "It says in the Minor Images: 'Such firm correctness in a wife will be fortunate.' It is hers to the end of life to follow with an unchanged mind." (*32. Heng—Perseverance, Duration: Image Explanation*)

In short, from the definite positions of Heaven and Earth and Qian and Kun, to the unchangeable social status of ruler and minister, father and son, male and female, the honorable and the humble, these antithetical relationships cannot be changed. Therefore, the dialectics in the *Commentaries on the Changes* conclude that while objects are ever-changing, the Way always remains the same. There is nothing curious at all in the so-called changes. In Nature, they refer to the winter's coming and the summer's going or the summer's coming and the winter's going. Dialectics has thus been changed into a theory of cycles.

Although many principles concerning changes are discussed in the *Commentaries on the Changes*, it cannot be said that the book exhausts all such principles. It says, "the *Book of Changes* opens up knowledge of the issues of things, accomplishes the undertakings of men, and embraces under it the way of all things under the sky. This and nothing more is what the *Book of Changes* does." All principles that govern the movement of things have already been summed up in the closed system of the way of the Changes. If so, the way of the Changes is the absolute truth, and there is no room for any development at all.

But if the way of the Changes has exhausted the truth, we cannot help asking who can thoroughly understand the secret in it? Only the great man.

> "The great man is he who is in harmony. In his attributes, he is in harmony with Heaven and Earth. In his brightness, he is in harmony with the sun and moon. In his orderly procedure, he is in harmony with the four seasons. And in his relation to what is fortunate and what is calamitous, he is in harmony with the spirit-like operations of providence. He may precede Heaven, and Heaven will not act in opposition to him. He may follow Heaven, but he will not act only as Heaven at the time would do." (*1. Qian — The Creative: Textual Explanation*)

> "In preparing things for practical use, and in inventing and making instruments for the benefit of all under the sky, there are none greater than the sages. The goal is to explore what is complex, and search out what is hidden. The goal is to hook up what lies deep, and reach to what is distant. Thereby, it is possible to determine the issues for good or ill of all events under the sky, and make all men under Heaven filled with strenuous endeavors. To achieve such goals there are no agencies greater than those of the stalks and the tortoise-shells." (*Appended Remarks (I)·Chapter 11*)

In this way, the nature of the stalks and tortoise-shells has been totally changed. In the early days, the hexagrams and component lines were applied to reflecting "the way of the changes" of objective things so that people might see in what way things could change from good to ill, and vice versa. But now, the way of changes can only be understood by the great man and the sages. Even if the great man and the sages desire to know the way of the changes, they still have to rely on the aid of the stalks and the tortoise-shells. Finally, the dialectical ideas originally contained in the *Commentaries on the Changes* end up as an esoteric mysticism characterized by a set of complex diagrams and numbers.

Part II

Philosophy in Early Feudal China: The Golden Age

(ca. 3rd Century to 9th Century A.D.)

12.

Philosophical Trends of the Qin–Han Transition

The successive Qin and Han dynasties saw the unification of China and the consolidation of the feudal system. The newly rising landlord class, however, needed an ideology to consolidate its political power. Various schools of thought dating from pre-Qin times were continuously splitting up, reorganizing, or merging, some left over from the wrangles of the "hundred schools," some harbingers of new times. Together they prepared the way for this ideology.

On the one hand, the Qin and Han rulers inherited the legacy of history and culture left by the Xia, Yin, and Zhou dynasties, and the ideological and theoretical achievements of the "hundred schools." On the other, they had to adapt to the demands of the new era, create new laws and standards, and have a relevant theoretical basis for feudalism. The proposed resolutions to these problems have philosophical significance.

For instance, on the eve of the unification of China, Lu Buwei (?–235 BC), the prime minister of the State of Qin, wrote a book titled *Lu's Spring and Autumn Annals*, a blueprint for political and ideological unification. Centered on the Taoist thought of the Yellow Emperor and Laozi, its ideology incorporated the doctrines of Confucianism, Mohism, the Logicians, the Legalists, and the Yin Yang School, but it fell out of favor with the First Emperor of Qin, and was replaced by that of the Legalists. Disputes with Confucian scholars led to their suppression, with the burning of all books not sanctioned by the Legalists and the burying alive of Confucian scholars.

Li Si and other Legalist scholars exalted the will of the monarch and insisted, "It is necessary to take the law for education, and government officials for teachers." By neglecting to accommodate the legacy of the culture, ideology, and political experience of the past, the Legalists failed to construct a suitable ideological superstructure, and the Qin Dynasty was swept away by a peasant uprising.

In the transition from the Qin to the Han dynasties, Neo-Taoism, also called "Huang-Lao Learning," spread among scholars out of office, as did Neo-Confucianism, which later provided political and philosophical theories for the newly unified empire. The early rulers of the Han Dynasty adopted an open policy as far as ideology was concerned, sought copies of destroyed books, and invited Confucian scholars to teach the their classics and to formulate state rituals. The court encouraged Neo-Taoist scholars, such as Gai Gong, Huang Sheng, and Sima Tan.

Liu Bang, first emperor of Han, had a famous debate with his counselor Lu Gu about the *Book of Poetry* and the *Book of History*. The emperor is reputed to have said, "I won the country by force of arms. Of what use are the *Book of Poetry* and the *Book of History* to me?" Lu Gu responded, "True, you won the country by force of arms, but is it possible to rule the country by force of arms? Emperor Tang of Shang and King Wu of Zhou won the country by force, but they ran the country through improved civil administration, for this is the way to ensure stability." Thereupon, the Han emperor invited Lu Gu to explain why Qin fell and Han replaced it. Lu Gu wrote twelve essays, later collected as *A New Treatise* (Cf. Sima Qian, *Records of the Historian· Book 97: Biographies of Li Sheng and Lu Gu*). The essays contain elements of Confucianism and Taoism, yet are far from outlining a clear system of ideology for the new empire.

The efforts of advanced thinkers were hampered by political intrigues in the early years of the Han Dynasty. Jealous ministers harshly criticized Jia Yi, inclined to Legalist solutions, for putting forward plans for administration reform. Emperor Wen (187–179 BC) exiled him, as the dominant trend of thought at court was Neo-Taoist. The same fate befell Chao Cuo, whose radical reform ideas in the service of Emperor Jing (163–156) led to his disgrace and execution. The guiding ideology in the early Han Dynasty was the Huang-Lao/Neo-Taoist doctrine of non-action mingled with elements of Legalism.

The early rulers of the Han Dynasty adapted themselves to the demands of realistic politics. They adopted Neo-Taoist thought "to run the country and to bring the people stability." This brought about a situation of "peace and prosperity during the reign of Emperors Wen and Jing." In the course of the struggle for influence among the Taoists, Confucians, and Legalists, each school learned from the others, gradually emerging as Neo-Taoism, Neo-Legalism, and Neo-Confucianism. Sima Qian records this transformation of political and legal ideas:

> "In the last years of the Zhou Dynasty, the State of Qin burned copies of the *Book of Poetry* and the *Book of History* and suchlike ancient classics. Books in the Bright Hall, Stone Chamber, and Gold Cabinet were lost or went missing, as did the documents engraved on the Jade Board. When the Han Dynasty was established, Xiao He sorted out laws and decrees, Han Xin rewrote military codes, Zhang Cang worked out the calendar, Shusun Tong formulated the rituals. Graceful and substantial writings appeared, and the *Book of Poetry* and the *Book of History* were gradually restored." (*Records of the Historian·Book 130: Author's Preface*)

The "non-action" thought of Huang-Lao Learning circulated both in the imperial court and among the common people, its appeal strong as all longed for peace and stability after years of warfare. The early rulers adopted the policy of "letting the common people recuperate and build up their strength."

In his book *A New Treatise*, which he dedicated to Liu Bang, the first emperor of Han, Lu Gu advises, "Govern by doing nothing that goes against Nature." He explains:

> "The Way is not greater than non-action, and action is not greater than prudence and homage. Why is this? In the remote Yu Kingdom, Emperor Shun ruled. Every day he played the five-stringed zither and sang an ode to the southern breeze. He seemed to dwell in quietude, with no idea of ruling the country, and he seemed to be indifferent to anything and to pay no atten-

tion to caring for the people. Yet, as a result, the whole country was well governed." (*A New Treatise·Chapter 4: Non-Action*)

"When a man of noble character governs a country, he seems to be a big piece of motionless wood, with no reaction to anything. The offices are quiet as if there are no functionaries there; in the townships and villages, there seem to be no gatherings of the common people. In the streets and lanes, there are no quarrels, and in the courtyards sit folks old or young, caring for nothing. Those who live near to each other have no events to discuss, and those who live far from each other have no desire to hear news. At night, no soldiers pass by the lodge as couriers. In the countryside, no officers conscript forcibly. Dogs do not bark at night, and chickens do not cluck at night. The elders eat delicious food in the hall, and able-bodied men till the farmland outside." (*A New Treatise·Chapter 8: Supreme Virtue*)

"Non-action," regarded as "positive activity" by Laozi and Lu Gu, was a direct inheritance from Laozi, the first to urge "Govern by doing nothing that goes against Nature."

In the *Records of the Historian·The Hereditary House of Prime Minister Cao*, Sima Qian describes how, soon after Cao Can became prime minister of the State of Qi, he engaged the services of Gai Gong, a famous scholar of Huang-Lao Learning. He advised a policy of "quietude and non-action" to Cao Can as the principle of administration and ideological guide. When the Han Dynasty was established, Cao Can was made prime minister, and he continued to act upon this principle. "The people all over the country praised him as an able man." Chen Ping, also "fond of Huang-Lao statecraft," succeeded Cao Can as prime minister. Huang-Lao thought also benefited from the patronage of Empress Dowager Dou, a powerful figure in the reigns of emperors Wen and Jing.

Early in the Han Dynasty, Neo-Taoism developed into a leading ideological trend. In the early years of the reign of Emperor Wu, Sima Tan (c.190–111 BC), the most erudite thinker of the time, summed up the ideological features of Neo-Taoism as follows in his masterpiece titled *On the Main Ideas of the Six Schools*:

> "Their learning follows the great order of yin and yang as two kinds of vital energy, absorbs the strong points of Confucianism and Mohism, abstracts the key points of the School of Logicians and the Legalist School, and changes as things demand. Since its main ideas are simple and concise, it is easy to grasp. Since it demands fewer actions, one may perform meritorious deeds just by keeping to it." (Quote is from Sima Qian's *Records of the Historian·Book 130: Author›s Preface.*)

According to Sima Tan, the main aspects of Neo-Taoism were three. First, it teaches how to deal with outside things. Only after one "carefully studies the practical case of all things," can one be "the master of them." Second, it teaches how to examine the relationship between names and actuality. It demands that one should be worthy of the name, and one must not lend one's ears to empty talk. Third, it transmits the pre-Qin Taoists' idea of "cherishing life" and "cultivating one's spirit." A Neo-Taoist adage is that "spirit is the basis of life, and body is the vehicle of life."

The basic works containing the doctrines of the Yellow Emperor and Laozi are the *Book of the Yellow Emperor* and the *Laozi*. According to the *History of Han·Catalogue of Bibliographical History, Political Literature and Local Records·An Outline of Philosophers*, several books under the general title of *Book of the Yellow Emperor* had been lost by the time of the Eastern Han Dynasty. But in 1973, when Tomb No. 3 of the Western Han Dynasty at Mawangdui in Changsha was excavated, silk manuscripts were discovered, including the *Huang-Lao Silk Manuscript*.

This extremely important document for the study of Neo-Taoism develops Laozi's category of the Way and takes the Way for the general law that governs Heaven, Earth, and all things. "It depends on nothing and does not change. It operates everywhere and is free from danger." (*Laozi·Chapter 25*) The silk manuscript regards the Way as an identical, eternal, and changeable entity that is the origin of all things in both creation and growth. It exists in all things, but it is invisible:

> "Before the formation of Heaven and Earth, throughout the great universal void, there existed nothing but the One. The void was the same as the One. In the primeval state of the universe in chaos

there was neither day nor night. Mysterious and subtle, the One was pervasive. Quintessential and quiescent, it was invisible. It does not depend on anything. It does not rely on myriad things either. It is formless and nameless, though great and universal. Heaven cannot cover it, nor can Earth bear it. Because of it, what is small becomes small and what is great becomes great. It not only pervades all within the Four Seas but also embraces all that exists beyond the Four Seas, for it is omnipresent throughout the universe. Dwelling in yin, it does not decay. Dwelling in yang, it does not get burned. It prescribes one single regulation without change, and yet it is fitting for all things, including those that move on legs and those that crawl like worms. Obtaining it, birds can fly, fish swim, and beasts run. Obtaining it, the myriad things can come into existence and all affairs can be completed. Everyone lives on it, but no one knows its name. Everyone makes use of it, but no one sees its form." (*On the Fundamental Way*)

Secondly, the silk manuscript emphasizes the objective necessity of the Way, time and again. "The realization of the Way follows the tendency of necessity." (*The Sixteen Classics·Section Eleven: The Basis for Military Expeditions*)

"It is the principle of Heaven and Earth that the four seasons have their regulations. It is the regulation of Heaven and Earth that the sun, the moon, and the stars have their measures. It is the Way of Heaven and Earth that there are three seasons for harvesting, namely spring, summer, and autumn, and one season for dying, namely winter. The four seasons are properly set, not deviating a hair's breadth, and without error, with constant regulation. . . . Life is followed by death." (*Constant Laws·An Outline Treatise*)

Social life, too, has objective laws proper to it. "To climax and to return, to flourish and to wane is the way of Heaven and Earth as well as the principle of human affairs." (*Constant Laws·The Four Principles*) The most fundamental law governing both the Heavenly course and human affairs is that things will develop in the opposite direction when they become extreme.

The author of the *Huang-Lao Silk Manuscript* puts forth a series of ideas in a systematic way, including "grasping the Way," "following the principles," "examining the signs of the times" and "observing the measures."

"Grasping the Way" means getting to know the universal laws of objective things. The silk manuscript emphasizes its importance:

> "Therefore, only the one who has grasped the Way in the first place understands Heaven's principles of returning on an eternal motion in cycles. Secondly, he discerns the difference between the ruler and his subordinates. Thirdly, he carefully investigates and thoroughly apprehends the beginning and the end of the myriad things, and therefore he avoids any attempt to arbitrarily dominate them. In this way, one can reach the realm in which one is able to attain the most elemental and the subtlest so as to be omnipresent and formless in emulating the Way. Only the one who has reached such a state can be considered the model sovereign under Heaven." (*Constant Laws· The Way and Laws*)

According to the manuscript›s analysis of social life at that time, the most important relationship between perversity and propriety is the "the four principles," namely, the relationships between the ruler and ministers, the worthy and the worthless, moving and resting, and life and death:

> "It is out of the Way that laws come into being. These laws are yardsticks to measure what is right and what is wrong, gains and losses, and they form the criteria for judging what is correct and what is incorrect. Therefore, he who has grasped the Way formulates laws and dares not violate them. When one conscientiously keeps oneself within the bounds of laws, one is able to understand all the important issues under Heaven without being misled." (*Constant Laws· The Way and Laws*)

The silk manuscript emphasizes that the Way begets the laws, saying the legislator must "conscientiously keep himself within the bounds of laws." This possibly addresses the shortcomings of the Legalists, who exaggerated the ruler's power. The author also advocates forming a set of unified laws and standards to be followed by everybody, with "a pure mind for the public interest and no trace of selfishness."

Particular attention should be paid to the "constant measures" that the common people must observe. Taxation either in kind or in labor must be within a certain degree. The manuscript bewails the times, saying, "The limits are transgressed and propriety is lost. What was established is arbitrarily changed, and what should be observed with constancy is heedlessly altered." (*The Sixteen Classics· The Contention of Clans*)

The *Huang-Lao Silk Manuscript* contains a contradictory view of naive dialectics: "In general, when a person discusses issues, he must reveal and elaborate the main points by means of yin and yang." (*Aphorisms*) It also puts forth the idea of "the application of the paradigm of female conduct," meaning that the soft overcomes the hard.

Contradicting opposites, such as male and female, are everlastingly combined: "The opposites nourish each other in coordinated complementarity. Being interdependent, they complete each other in accordance with proper timing." (*The Sixteen Classics· The Contention of Clans*). Therefore, we should cast away the old thing and incline toward the new, greet any changes, and be ready to enjoy the transformation of things.

The author of the silk manuscript appears to have drawn a conclusion more comprehensive than that of Han Fei concerning the changes in society. On the one hand, the inevitability and necessity of contradictory struggles is affirmed. On the other, the newborn aspect will inevitably overcome the old, as history frequently shows in the overcoming of the strong by the weak. Therefore, the tactics of struggle should in the main follow "the paradigm of female conduct."

In this way, the silk manuscript develops Lao Dan's idea that "It is important to value the soft and keep to the female." It formulates a pair of special categories—"male conduct" and "female conduct." It is characteristic of "male conduct" to be arrogant and proud, and to be haughty toward others. It is characteristic of "female conduct" to be outwardly weak, and to be modest, respectful, and frugal. It is not an advantageous thing to win victory through male conduct as the more victories one wins in that way, the more misfortune one may bring on oneself. On the other hand, even when a person fails when he keeps to female conduct, sooner or later he will be rewarded. This is because the more failures one suffers, the more virtues one may accumulate, and finally "great fortune will come."

This dialectic originated with Laozi, and touches on the tortuous nature of the process in which things advance and develop. New things grow from weak to strong, their way full of twists and turns. Therefore, the main principle of keeping to female conduct is as follows: "Obscure, respectful, frugal, modest, and simple, he preferred softness. He always stood behind others and never in front." (*The Sixteen Classics·Following the Way*) One must not initiate anything or strike first to gain the initiative. One should let one's opponent strike first, then get the better of him by making use of the objective law that the strong and weak may change into each other.

The *Huang-Lao Silk Manuscript* applies the view of contradictory transformation to the observation of social reality in a way that surpasses the pre-Qin Taoists by combining Taoist and Legalist ideas. As a practical principle for guiding politics in the early years of the Han Dynasty, it played a historical role in consolidating the rising political power of feudalism.

Jia Yi (200–168 BC), the Western Han Dynasty political commentator who fell from favor with Emperor Wen for his radical views on political reform, died at age thirty-three. Historian Sima Qian ranked Jia Yi with Qu Yuan as one of two tragic heroes "pure in ambition and noble in action, and who showed loyalty in banishment." After his death, a collection of his writings, *Jia Yi's New Book*, was made. Ban Gu recorded the most important part in "The Biography of Jia Yi," in Book 48 of his *History of Han*. Jia Yi's representative writings include essays, such as *A Discourse on Peace and Security*, *Blaming the Qin*, and *Great Policy*, and a piece of prose-verse titled *Ode to the Roc*. These are the main materials for research into his thought.

Jia Yi represented the Neo-Legalists during the transition from Qin to Han. Inheriting the doctrines of Xunzi and Han Feizi and thus influenced by both Confucianism and Legalism, Jia Yi wrote that "Stress must be laid on current affairs." His outstanding contribution to Qin-Han philosophy is his relatively comprehensive and profound philosophic analysis of the complicated contradictions in the early years of the Han Dynasty.

The Qin rulers, he maintains, had blind faith in guile and force, relying on stern laws and severe punishments. They did not express kind-heartedness and justice, and had no affinity with common people and soldiers. Moreover, they did not know the two principles that "To attack and to defend need different forces" and "To seize political power and to consolidate it needs different tactics." To Jia Yi, it was fine for the State of Qin to use "guile and force" to conquer. But once it had seized the whole country, the Qin Dynasty should have employed "kindheartedness and justice" when facing new problems of appeasing public feelings and developing production.

Jia Yi, to whom the purpose of drawing lessons from history was to observe present reality, expressed his keen observation of problems that still existed thirty years into the Han Dynasty: division and rebellion caused by princes and marquises; invasion and harassment by the Huns; and difficulties with controlling commerce and industry, changing old customs, improving the new systems, cultivating successors, setting up new laws and standards, and consolidating centralized state power. Jia Yi analyzes these problems one by one, including their history, current situation, and development trends, then puts forth principles to solve them.

From the time of the Zhou Dynasty, relatives and descendants of the ruling family were granted deeds for land, enfeoffments, in exchange for a pledge of service. The main cause of the contradiction between feudal centralization and the separatist rule of various princes and marquises was this system and its relative privileges, an inevitable source of friction between various territories and the central political power. In Jia Yi's opinion, if "the fundamental cause is not changed, disastrous and unfortunate events" caused by such a system would be unavoidable.

Further, Jia Yi advised weakening the power of the princes and marquises gradually by increasing the number of enfeoffments. In the reigns of Emperors Wen, Jing and Wu, princes and marquises revolted one after another, and had to be suppressed. Of the Hun menace, Jia Yi proposed "using three indications," "offering five inducements," and "relying on virtue to conquer the opponent."

In the meantime, the contradiction between wealthy merchants and big landlords, who were eagerly annexing the land, and farmers, who were being robbed of their land, became more acute day by day. Jia Yi proposed a stop to the annexation of land, and a halt to the increase of industrial and commercial households that occupied farmland but did not produce food, thereby provoking peasant uprisings. He recommended "valuing agriculture, for it is the root of the country, and limiting industrial and commercial business, for they are the branches only," and outlined a plan for storing up grain to ease social inequalities.

On the relationship between "the rites" and "the law," Jia Yi follows the Legalist doctrine to face contradictions squarely and to persist in ruling by law. But he takes note of the Confucian doctrine of ruling the country by "the rites" and of educating the populace in virtue.

Jia Yi's analysis also embraces the relationship among the ruler, the ministers, and the common people. To safeguard feudal rule, he defends the power of the monarch as supreme, and encourages the "moral integrity of ministers." In short, he wants to strengthen the system of order and degree to adjust and consolidate the internal unity of the ruling clique. On the other hand, he is aware of the strength of the people, having witnessed peasant uprisings, and he puts forward the proposition that "The common people are the foundation of everything":

> "As I have heard from those who are in power, the common people are the foundation of everything. The country must take the common people for the foundation, as must the ruler and the officials. The safety or otherwise of a country lies in the common people, the prestige and insult of a ruler lies in the common people, and the nobility or humiliation of individuals lies in the people." (*Jia Yi's New Book· Great Policy (I)*)

He infers a series of propositions in line with this doctrine: "The common people are the life of everything," "The common people are the function of everything," and "The common people are the motive force of everything." He draws a basic conclusion:

> "As for the common people, since they are the foundation for ten thousand generations, nobody must deceive them. It is foolish for nobles to treat scholars with negligence or embitter the common people. Nobles can be regarded as wise when they esteem scholars and love the common people. This is because it is the common peo-

ple who have the right to call a person stupid or wise." (*Jia Yi's New Book· Great Policy (I)*)

Jia Yi's dialectical view of a contradiction is in a naive form, a product of the times, formed in the early years of the Han Dynasty. Different from Confucianism and Neo-Taoism, it is more in line with the Huang-Lao Taoists.

13.

Correspondence Between Heaven and Man: Han Ideology

Dong Zhongshu (c. 179–104 BC), a native of Guangchuan (Jingxian County, Hebei Province), is the leading philosopher of the Western Han Dynasty. During the reign of Emperor Jing, he concentrated on the study of the *Spring and Autumn Annals with Commentaries by Gongyang Gao*, and once served as a professor of the imperial academy. When Emperor Wu ascended the throne, Dong Zhongshu wrote three essays on how to employ men of virtue and talent and submitted them to the emperor, who received them with favor. Dong later served as the chief minister in a provincial ruler's court at Jiangdu (Yangzhou, Jiangsu Province). When he retired, he devoted his time to writing. His prestige was such that "Whenever there were important discussions of policy at the imperial court, officials were sent to his home to ask his advice." (*History of the Han Dynasty·Biography of Dong Zhongshu*) He was "an honest and upright man." (*Records of the Historian·Biographies of Confucian Scholars*) When he studied, he could "concentrate completely on a specific problem." (*The Balanced Inquiries·Scholars and Exaggeration*) Dong epitomized the thought of Neo-Confucianism in the transition between the Qin and Han dynasties, laying a theoretical foundation for centralized state power and dictatorial rule, central features of the two dynasties.

The Qin and early Han rulers still worshiped the Five Emperors and the gods of the mountains and rivers. Mystics and Confucian scholars envisaged a Supreme God reigning above the Five Emperors and all other deities. When Emperor Wu unified China under the Han Dynasty, the worship of the "God of the Pole Star" had come into vogue, a deity said to be above all others. (Cf. *Records of the Historian·Book 28: Offering Sacrifices to Heaven and Earth on Mount Tai*).

Although centralized state power had thus been reflected in Heaven, rule by emperor as rule by divine right was still short of a full theoretical explanation. This became an urgent problem, and spilled over into the imperial examinations. Candidates were required to write an essay on how to employ men of virtue and talent. Dong›s answer provided Emperor Wu with his theory.

Dong was inspired by Zisi and Mencius, who held that to know man, one must know Heaven. In Nature there is the phenomenon of "similar things coming together, and matching ones responding to each other." Dong says, "Since they activate each other invisibly, it is thought that they do so themselves. . . . In reality, things are caused, but the cause is invisible." (*Luxuriant Dew of the Spring and Autumn Annals·Chapter 57: Things of the Same Kind Activate Each Other*, hereafter only chapter number and title appear.) To Dong, this "cause" is the Will of Heaven.

In his masterpiece *Luxuriant Dew of the Spring and Autumn Annals*, Dong makes use of scientific knowledge and combines it with theories of yin and yang and the five elements. For instance:

> "Let us discuss the vital forces (*qi*) of Heaven and Earth. When combined, they become one. When distinguished from each other, they are yin and yang. When distinguished carefully, they are the four seasons. When put in order, they are the Five Elements." (*Chapter 58: The Five Elements Produce One Another*)

> "What exists between Heaven and Earth are the vital forces of yin and yang, which serve Man as water serves fish. One force is visible, the other invisible. . . . Therefore, what exists between Heaven and Earth seems to be void, but in fact it is very substantial." (*Chapter 81: Heaven, Earth, Yin and Yang*)

> "Of all things, only the vital forces between Heaven and Earth constitute the pure essence, which enters and leaves the invisible things,

> and all things respond to it. So they are the most substantial existence." (*Chapter 77: Following the Heavenly Way*)

This cosmogony is an almost universal formulation that prevailed in the writings on natural sciences in the Han Dynasty. The vital force of Heaven and Earth is divided into yin and yang, Heaven and Earth are relatively equal to each other, and "Heaven" does not have the position of the Lord on High. But Dong transforms "Heaven," originally possessed of natural attributes, into a supernatural dominator of the universe.

> "Heaven has also the vital forces of pleasure and anger, and the mental states of sorrow and joy, as has man. When we infer them by analogy, it follows that Heaven and Man have the same motivations. Spring is the vital force of pleasure, therefore there is emergence. Autumn is the vital force of anger, therefore there is killing. Summer is the vital force of joy, therefore there is cultivation. Winter is the vital force of sorrow, therefore there is storing up. Heaven and Man are possessed of these four things in the same way." (*Chapter 49: Significance of Yin and Yang*)

Thus, Dong transforms the materialist outlook on Nature, which had been popular for a long time, into a theological teleology. Below is his philosophical generalization:

> "And therefore Heaven is in the top place, and exerts its official function upon whatever is below. It hides its form, revealing only its light. It arranges the order of all the stars, and touches the Supreme Spirit. It examines the sun and the moon, and sends down frost and dew. Because of its supreme position, Heaven is revered. Because of its official function exerted upon whatever is below, Heaven is benevolent. Because it hides its form, Heaven is divine. Because of its revelation of its light, Heaven is brilliant. Because of its arrangement of the order of all the stars, Heaven is the succession. Because it touches the Supreme Spirit, Heaven is strong. Because it examines the sun and the moon, Heaven makes the years. Because it sends down frost and dew, Heaven has the power to beget and kill. This is

> the reason an emperor must take Heaven as his mirror to make his laws." (*Chapter 78: The Behavior of Heaven and Earth*)

He reasons that in Nature the things that belong to yang are always the active guiding force, while the things that belong to yin play only the role of subordination. Therefore, "predestination helps yang, and does not help yin," and "Yang is noble, while yin is humble." (*Chapter 46: The Discernment of Heaven Is Right Here in Man*) He then goes on to apply the theory to human affairs, and draws a forced analogy, saying, "Yang is the ruler or father, and therefore the sovereign faces the south in line with the orientation of yang." (*Ibid*)

In the meantime, he describes the doctrine of the Five Elements as being analogous to the relationship between father and son. As for Earth, it is opposite to Heaven. Earth is down here; Heaven is up there. "Those who are at the lower levels should serve those who are at the upper levels, just as Earth should serve Heaven. It is the greatest loyalty to do so." (*Chapter 38: A Replay of the Five Elements*)

> "Therefore, a ruler should diligently illuminate the teachings of sages and transform the people in order to fulfill their natures. At the same time, he should appropriately adjust the laws and institutions, and differentiate the superior from the inferior in their arrangement, in order to prevent inordinate desires. If these three things are done well, what is of basic importance for government is established." (*History of the Han Dynasty·Book 56: Biography of Dong Zhongshu*)

A ruler is portrayed as a man who takes his commission from Heaven to rule the people, and the monarchical power on earth is under the guidance and protection of Heaven.

> "I have made an investigation into the interactive relation between Heaven and Man. What I have found is dreadful. When a state tends toward failure caused by losing the Way, Heaven will warn the ruler by sending disasters. When the ruler does not examine himself when disasters befall, Heaven will then send monstrosities to frighten him. When he still does not realize that he ought to make changes, the ruin of the state is inevitable. This shows that Heaven wants to pre-

vent rulers from committing misdeeds. All rulers, except those who have completely discarded the Way and caused catastrophes, will be helped and secured by Heaven." (*History of Han·Book 56: Biography of Dong Zhongshu*)

Dong finally came to the conclusion that Heaven was the Supreme God, inspired by a sentence from the *Spring and Autumn Annals with Commentary by Gongyang Gao*, namely, "You must subdue the people so as to promote the ruler, and you must subdue the ruler so as to promote Heaven." Thus, Dong completed his theological teleology.

As regards his view of development, Dong acknowledges that in all things there are contradictory opposites, but he treats them as frozen, fixed, and immutable. "As for husbands, even when they are humble and mean, they all belong to yang. As for wives, even when they are noble and dignified, they all belong to yin." (*Chapter 43: Yang Is Superior and Yin Is Inferior*) He adds, "Yang is noble and yin is base, as decided by Heaven." (*Chapter 46: The Discernment of Heaven Is Right Here in Man*)

Following the Confucian Doctrine of the Mean, Dong takes it to the extreme. Starting from the localization of a contradiction, he concludes that the "Heavenly Way is unparalleled." "With regard to the constant way of Heaven, opposite things cannot rise up as two independent existences. Therefore, I say it is the one and only way. It is the one, it is not the two, and this is the course Heaven takes. Yin and yang are opposite things. . . . They may stand side by side, but they follow different ways; they may have coitus, but they cannot substitute for each other." (*Chapter 51: The Way of Heaven Is Unparalleled*)

Dong thinks that such a situation, and such a situation alone, is the constant way of Heaven.

But how can one explain the rise and fall of dynasties? In the Zhou Dynasty, the ruling ideology postulated that "Man should play a supporting role to Heaven." A dynasty loses the Mandate of Heaven when it "loses virtue," and a new dynasty possessed of virtue takes its place. Dong put forward the theory that "the five virtues succeed one another in turn." By analogy, he applies the physical properties and actions of the Five Elements, which produce and subdue another, to the sphere of society and history. In Nature, wood subdues earth, metal subdues wood, fire subdues metal, water subdues fire, and earth subdues water.

Dong describes the Yellow Emperor, the mythical first ancestor of the Chinese race, as the representative of the virtue of earth, whose color is yellow. Emperor Yu of the Xia Dynasty substituted for the virtue of earth the virtue of wood, whose color is green. Later, Tang, the founder of the Shang Dynasty, subdued the virtue of wood of the Xia Dynasty with the virtue of metal, whose color is white. King Wen of the Zhou Dynasty subdued the virtue of metal of the Shang Dynasty with the virtue of fire, whose color is red. In this way, the development of history becomes an ever-repeating cycle of the five virtues.

While Dong acknowledges the change of institutions, he denies that history develops. And while he said, "A new ruler must change the institutions," in his opinion, "What is changed is not the Way, nor is it the principle." These changes only serve as signs that the new ruler is the recipient of the Mandate of Heaven. With regard to "the cardinal guides, ethics, principles, politics, education, customs, and cultural affairs, everything follows the old patterns." These remain unchanged. "Those who are rulers may change the institutions, but they have no means of changing the Way. The greatness of the Way originates in Heaven. So, as Heaven does not change, likewise the Way does not change." Such is Dong's metaphysical view of history.

As one of the most famous Confucian scholars of the Han Dynasty and the founder of the dynasty's orthodox theology, Dong enjoyed the reputation of being "the head of all the Confucian scholars," even in his own lifetime. His political program, centered on the Three Cardinal Guides, did a great deal to stabilize the feudal system by harnessing the enterprising spirit of the rising landlord class. His theory was also helpful for adjusting the internal and external relations of feudal political power by smoothing social and class contradictions. In the political program Dong offered to Emperor Wu of Han, he advocates strengthening of monarchical power and the rule of virtue and punishment by law, with stress laid on the rule of virtue. To form a unified guiding thought in the superstructure and to bring about an "all-round regeneration," he emphasizes "rites, music, and education." He upheld Confucianism, and advocated banning all other schools of thought. But despite his emphasis on strengthening the hand of the monarch, Dong also advises the ruler to "value the people." Further, by analyzing the intensification of contradictions between the monarch and the people, he points out that the root cause is the confrontation between the rich and the poor. In connection with this, he put forward certain progressive policies, including putting a brake on the annexation of farmland and easing the people's burdens of conscript labor and heavy taxes.

Nevertheless, the political thought of Dong was after all a theoretical weapon to maintain feudal absolutism. But, as self-negating factors began to appear in the course of the long rule of feudalism, Dong's thought lost its historical rationality, and finally became a shackle on social progress, with its focus on unchangeability and the permanent dominance of imperial power, clan power, and the authority of the husband in the feudal patriarchal system.

There is an innate tendency toward religious mysticism in Dong's philosophy. So it is not surprising that when the Western Han Dynasty reached its declining stage, Dong's philosophy started to combine with the augury-apocryphal superstition prevalent at that time. At last, an ideological counter current formed, and there appeared a large number of "apocryphal books" designed to elaborate Dong's philosophical and theological theories.

"Augural scriptures" (divinations from auspices or omens) and "apocryphal books" (books of dubious authenticity) circulated in the period of transition between the two Han dynasties. When Liu Xiu mounted the throne, in the first year (56) of the Zhongyuan reign period, he "publicized the auguries and apocrypha throughout the country" as the state philosophy. (*The History of the Eastern Han Dynasty·Chronological Biography of Emperor Guangwu (III)*) In these are social, political, and ethical thoughts and teleology marked by the correspondence of Heaven and Man. Later, Emperor Zhang of Han presided over an important conference in White Tiger Hall, where these thoughts were affirmed and documented in the book *Comprehensive Discussions at White Tiger Hall.* Treated as the theological canon authorized by the emperor, it was issued throughout the country.

On the problem of the origin of the universe and human society, *Comprehensive Discussions at White Tiger Hall* develops Dong's doctrine of yin and yang and the Five Elements so that a systematic theory of both is set up: "What is Heaven? Heaven is the stabilizer that is on high and presses down from high above to govern what are below, so it is the stabilizer of Man. Earth is the producer of the vital force and the foremother of the myriad things." (*Comprehensive Discussions a White Tiger Hall·Book 10: Heaven and Earth*). The text further elaborates:

> "First there was the Great Initial, and then there was the Great Beginning. When they took shape and became substantial there then appeared what was called the Great Simple. There was a vast piece of chaos plus chaos. . . . And then it was divided into two, one clear, the other dark. After that, the Spirit came to spread, and things acquired life. The Spirit became the sun, moon, and stars, and the Five Elements. The Five Elements produced the emotions and Nature. The emotions and Nature produced the Big Dipper. The Big Dipper produced the Divinity. The Divinity produced the Way and Virtue. The Way and Virtue produced various patterns. . . . Therefore, *A Penetration of the Laws of Qian* says, 'The Great Initial was the start of the vital force. The Great Beginning was the start of shapes and forms. The Great Simple was the start of substance.' When yang sings, yin becomes its echo. In like manner, when the husband walks, the wife follows." (*Ibid*)

In this world, the movement and change of yin and yang, life and death, and the flourishing and decaying of the myriad things are arranged by the Will of Heaven. The *Comprehensive Discussions at White Tiger Hall* preaches a series of feudal ethical dogmas such as the Three Cardinal Guides, the Six Disciplines, and the Three Obediences for women. All are the natural embodiment of Heaven and Earth, yin and yang, and the Five Elements and are possessed of their own will.

> "The Three Cardinal Guides follow Heaven, Earth, and Man. The Six Disciplines follow the Six Directions. The ruler and his ministers follow Heaven. They learn from the images of the sun and the moon. The sun and the moon rise and fall in Heaven, and they attribute their merits to Heaven. Father and son follow Earth. They learn from the images shown by the Earth, where the Five Elements

produce one another. Husband and wife follow Man. They learn from the image of Man, for human beings combine yin and yang together, and the beginning of creation is applied to Man." (*Comprehensive Discussions at White Tiger Hall·Book 8: The Three Cardinal Guides and Six Disciplines*)

"Woman is similar to man and must obey man. A woman is required to obey her father before marriage, her husband during married life, and her sons in widowhood.... Woman is obedience in that a woman is obedient to household affairs and serves men."" (*Book 10: Marriage*)

Historically speaking, the author of *Comprehensive Discussions* wholly follows Dong's doctrine of "the three orthodox systems" and of "the three first months." The only addition is the doctrine of the "three teachings." The historical substitution of one dynasty for another follows the circulation of the three teachings, namely, accomplishments, solid qualities, and rusticity.

As for the feudal patriarchy and the power to rule the people, not even the slightest change is permissible. We could say that every detail of Dong's thought of theological teleology is developed in the *Comprehensive Discussions at White Tiger Hall*. With such a development, Dong's thought of theological teleology becomes finer and more delicate, and at the same time more mystical.

14.

Wang Chong and Naïve Dialectics

Wang Chong (2–796), style named Zhongren, native of Shangyu (Shangyu County, Zhejiang Province), studied at the national college in Luoyang, capital of the Eastern Han Dynasty. (*The Balanced Discussion·Chapter 84: Autobiography*, hereafter only chapter number and title appear.) "Growing up in a very poor family with no books, he read in Luoyang bookstores. After having run his eye over a book once, he could recite the contents by heart. Gradually he had full and ready knowledge of all classes of authors." (*History of the Eastern Han Dynasty·Book 79: Biography of Wang Chong*) After serving in a succession of low-ranking official posts for many years, he retired to his hometown, where he pondered philosophical problems, wrote books, and taught. "Penniless, he could not support his family, downhearted, he could not realize his ambition." (*Chapter 84: Autobiography*) Most of Wang Chong's writings are found in *The Balanced Discussion*.

Wang Chong inherited the intellectual tradition of Sima Qian (135–86 BC) via Yang Xiong (53 BC–AD 18) and Huan Tan (40 BC–AD 32). He summed up what was known of the natural and social sciences at that time—and lifted materialist atheism to a new height. Wang restored Heaven to Nature, negating all mystical connotations regarding Heaven.

Wang refutes all ideas about the mysteriousness of Heaven, re-stipulating the category of the "vital force" in line with materialism: "Heaven and earth are Nature that contains the vital force." (*Chapter 31: Discourse on Heaven*) "When Heaven and Earth have coitus, the myriad things emerge naturally. Heaven covers everything from above, and Earth lies down here. While the vital force below ascends, the vital force above descends, and the myriad things emerge and grow by themselves between the two vital forces." (*Chapter 53: On Nature*) "Whatever has blood vessels has birth. By a thing's birth we know it must have death. Neither Heaven nor Earth had birth, so neither can have death. Neither yin nor yang had birth, so neither can have death." (*Chapter 24: The False Way*)

He denies any interaction between man and Heaven: "Man cannot move Heaven by human action. Nor can Heaven respond to human action." (*Chapter 44: Elucidation of the Rain Ceremony*) Thus, he cuts the link between Heaven and Man. Man is a product of Nature: "Man is a kind of thing, one thing of wisdom among the myriad things. Man gets his life from Heaven, and he receives the vital force from the universe; in this, he is no different from anything else." (*Chapter 77: Discerning the Evil Spirits*)

But, how can man's spiritual phenomena be explained? What is the relationship between the spirit and the body? When a man dies, does his spirit continue to exist? Wang inherits and develops the doctrine of spiritual force extant since pre-Qin times: "Man can live because of his essential forces. At death, his vital forces become extinct. What makes the vital forces possible is the blood. When a person dies, his blood becomes exhausted." (*Chapter 61: A Treatise on Death*) He regards "the spiritual force" as the vehicle of wisdom, and thus affirms that the existence of spirit (wisdom) relies on matter. Sometimes Wang identifies "the spiritual force" with "spirit." "The spirit of a man is hidden in his body, just as maize is hidden in a bag." However, it cannot "know anything without the body." Thus, Wang breaks through the limits of the traditional doctrine of the spiritual force by explicating the relationship between body, spiritual force, and consciousness as three dependent parties.

On the problem of the relations between the spiritual force and consciousness, then, he draws the conclusion that "the vital forces need the body to have consciousness." And he declares, "The dead do not become ghosts, do not possess consciousness, and cannot hurt people."

In the first century AD, Wang made a thorough criticism of the ideological trend centered on auguries (divinations from auspices or omens) and apocrypha (books of dubious authenticity)—of the theoretical basis of teleology with the correspondence of Heaven and Man as its core.

With such criticism, he set up a splendid monument in the developmental history of Chinese atheism.

Because Dong Zhongshu and other scholars exalted Confucius and the Confucian classics, the style of study in the Han Dynasty had "become more and more without foundation and pompous." Some Confucian scholars devoted their lives to the rote memorization of the Confucian classics and some stuck to textual criticism, which they were particularly good at. As for the soothsayers of the Yin Yang School, they simply concocted various "words of gods and spirits." Wang scorned such pedants, and opposed them with his key principles of materialist epistemology: "Hate and criticize the unfounded, struggle against boasting and exaggeration, be sincere and honest, and emphasize the intended effect."

Wang opposes Dong Zhongshu's cognitive line that seeks the Heavenly will by means of profound examination of names and appellations. To him, the targets of man's cognition ought to be "the affairs in the world and the things of society." (*Chapter 77: Practical Knowledge*) These include not only the spheres of astronomy, geography, politics, academics, and so on, but also the productive activities of people such as farmers and weaving women.

While Wang does not deny the differences in human abilities and wisdom, to him they are not absolute. In other words, there is no definite demarcation line between the highest, who are wise, and the lowest, who are not.

As regards the origin of knowledge, Wang vehemently opposes such Han Dynasty ideas as "sages are born with knowledge," and "gods can foretell things." To him, a person acquires knowledge only by study and using ones senses. "When one hears nothing and sees nothing, one cannot make a description of anything." (*Chapter 77: Practical Knowledge*). However, the senses are not enough, one must also use one's mind;

> A matter of right and wrong depends not only on using ones ears and eyes, but also on using one's brains. Some Mohists discuss matters purely on the grounds of what they hear and see, and do not bring their minds to bear on the matter discussed. So their opinions are inconsistent with the facts. (*Chapter 66: A Simple Funeral*)

Wang also stresses the necessity of comparative study. He says, "From one point, one may know a group of things by analogy" and "By analogy with past experiences, one may deal with future things." He advocates going deep into the internal associations of things by carefully studying relevant "omens and traces." On the one hand, Wang refutes apriorism, and on the other attacks the limitations of the Mohist school of thought.

In addition, Wang recommends the category of "intended effect" as a standard test of authenticity. "No idea is as clear as one demonstrated by proof. Although empty talk and hollow words may appear to be in accordance with a certain principle, people should not believe them." (*Chapter 66: A Simple Funeral*)

Starting from the theory that things occur by themselves as a natural process, Wang demonstrates that the myriad things and human beings were produced in a coherent process by agitation of the vital force. Everything follows the objective natural law to undergo emergence, growth, multiplication, variation, and disappearance. This reflects its self-multiplication. As for the relationship between one species and another, it causes complicated variations that can be summed up as a universal law: "The same vital forces complete each other, and different vital forces agitate each other."

Wang applies the above view to the whole of Nature. "The Five Elements harm one another, and the myriad things subdue one another." In the biosphere, such an objective law expresses itself as the struggle for existence, to select the superior and eliminate the inferior:

> "The myriad things subdue one another. As regards the way, one living thing triumphs over another, sometimes it defeats the opponent by physical strength, sometimes by powerful potentiality, sometimes by clever arts. When there is the advantage of a little powerful potentiality, when there is convenience by mouth and paws, a minor one may defeat major ones. When a major one lacks physical strength or is unable to use its horns or wings, the major one has to subject itself to the minor one." (*Chapter 14: The Potentiality of Things*)

Wang's naive dialectical thought is also expressed in his statement, "The heavenly way is non-active, while the human way is active." He says as follows:

"Man moves to realize some action, because the human way is active.... Heaven moves to endow Nature with vital force.... This is different from human behavior." (*Chapter 32: Discourse on the Sun*)

In agricultural production, man is an active force in the face of Nature. Working on Nature, man can realize his purposes. But, although the human way may assist Nature, it cannot replace the Heavenly way. It is not rational to help the shoots grow by pulling them upward. In both social life and natural phenomena, contingency plays a dominant role. By "accidental," Wang means two things. First, it refers to the various phenomena in Nature and human society. When they have some association in time and space, it is because of a coincidence. Second, the reason things occur lies in accidental factors decided by congenital endowments. "They are all possessed of material force, but some become human beings, some birds and beasts. Of humans, some are noble and some are low, some are rich and some are poor. The richest has piles of gold bricks, the poorest has to beg for food. The noblest reach the rank of marquis, the poorest serve as slaves. It is not that Heaven endows some people with more gifts and endows others with less, but that people are endowed differently by Nature." (*Chapter 5: Accidental Phenomena*)

With this theory, Wang rejects the teleology of the correspondence of Heaven and Man. This contingency, he says, comes about by necessity. "Fate" describes Nature and the objective dominant force in social life—an inexorable law independent of man's will. Once a person or a thing is endowed with vital force and attributes, it is fixed, as male and female are fixed. "Accidents and misfortunes are caused by fate. 'Fate' decides one's life span. 'Fate' decides whether one is rich or poor. From kings and dukes down to the common people, from saints and sages down to fools, any living being that has a head, a pair of eyes, or blood experiences 'fate.'" (*Chapter 3: Fate and Emolument*)

He divides a person's "fate" into two kinds, one being "the fate of life span," the other being "the fate of emolument." This is a jump from absolute contingency to absolute necessity. To explain this, he uses natural materialism, applying it to historical and social spheres. This leads Wang to mysticism, and even to the extremely absurd theory that stars, bone measurements, and physiognomy decide a person's fate.

Wang appears to confuse the essential difference between social and natural phenomena, equating necessity (fate) and contingency (accidental events) with Nature. He fails to distinguish the dialectical relationship among the three parties.

Wang inherits and further develops the progressive thought of the Mohists and the utilitarianism of the Legalists. He criticizes the Confucian view in which, he claims, morality has become empty talk. To Wang, the conditions of materialist life in a given society determine the morals and ideology of that society.

Wang also opposed the Confucian view that mankind should strive to return to a past mythical golden age. His own view of history is bound by an attachment to the dynastic cycle. However, his claims that "Heaven does not change" and "it is necessary to follow one and the same Way for a hundred dynasties" contradict his statement that "The Han Dynasty surpasses the Zhou Dynasty." What is more, he endows "the material forces" with moral attributes, with which he discusses the social movement of the whole of mankind by inference. He inevitably reaches the same goal as did Dong Zhongshu, though via different routes.

Wang concludes that an objective law independent of the sages governs the order and disorder of society, His investigation of the materialist agent of the historical dynamic leads him to realize that material life plays the major role in governing society, politics, and spiritual life. But he fails to see that the conditions of material life are decided by the internal contradictions of the social mode of production. Instead, he looks for the root causes outside society. Therefore, inescapably he walks step by step from natural fatalism toward a metaphysical view of history.

In the history of the development of Chinese philosophy, Wang Chong has an eminent place. His ideological system of materialism reflects the level of social practice and knowledge of the natural sciences of his time. Monism of the material forces is his theoretical creation. He makes a materialist demonstration of problems such as the relationship between Heaven and Man, and between body and spirit. He fills his theory of knowledge with the spirit of seeking truth from facts, a spirit manifested as factors of dialectical thinking in aspects such as his view of natural and human history. He brings the materialist thought of ancient China to a new stage.

The development of the theory of the material forces in ancient China was a long process. The start of the theory was in the Warring States Period, when the *Guanzi* (*Book of Master Guanzhong*) appeared, in which the doctrine of spiritual force is outlined. Xun Kuang developed the doctrine, and then Wang established his theory of monism of the material forces in a systematic way. Monism of the material forces is in fact a kind of world outlook that shows an active attitude toward human experience and practice. Through this empirical approach Wang opposes the dogmatism and apriorism that accompanied the theological idealism prevalent in the Han Dynasty. He exerts great efforts to refute the narrow empiricism of the Mohist School.

From his famous statement that "From one point one may know a group of things by analogy, and from the beginning one may know the end also by analogy," we can perceive that he has indeed noticed the importance of logical reasoning. Nevertheless, what he does is simply to apply formal logic to the reasoning process. Even so, his intent is but to pile up a large amount of material evidence, and nothing more. His cognitive approach, then, has not shaken off the yoke of narrow empiricism, and with his monism of the materialist forces, Wang cannot explain why the world exists as a unified whole and why there is a great variety of material phenomena.

Apart from these two questions, there remains another that he does not tackle, that is, how material forces that have no senses could produce mankind that has abundant senses. He simply divides the antithetical qualities of one thing, for instance, the general and the particular, and the ontology and phenomena, into two unrelated pieces. Later, the metaphysical scholars abandon Wang on this point, and return to Laozi's "Being comes from nonbeing." (*Laozi·Chapter 40*)

15.

The Development of Metaphysics in the Three Kingdoms Period and the Western Jin Dynasty

The philosophical movement of Metaphysics in China started in the course of political criticism by leading scholars in the last years of the Han Dynasty. From this time and during the Wei–Jin Period (220–420), the so-called "pure conversation," namely, philosophical disputes among the literati, was in vogue. These disputes, completely divorced from reality, concentrated on abstract topics to "distinguish names and analyze principles." Combining Confucianism and Taoism, northern scholars set up a new system of speculative philosophy with "the debate of being and nonbeing and of the fundamental and the incidental" as its center.

The central problem of Metaphysics was the old one of the relationship between Heaven and Man. But two new aspects emerged. One, in form, the debate got rid of the hair-splitting commentaries and notes that characterize the study of the Confucian classics in the Han dynasties. Two, in content, it discarded the teleology of "the interactive relation between Heaven and Man."

The Metaphysicists, who indulged in speculative philosophy, defined many categories, such as being and nonbeing, base and application, the fundamental and the incidental, the one and the many, and saying and meaning, as well as Nature and the Confucian ethical code. They speculated on the relationship between Heaven and Man. They gave new demonstrations of noumenon and phenomenon, motion and stillness, cognition and target, and Heavenly way and human affairs. There arose various controversies among the Metaphysicists—two emerged as central: one, that between "exalting being" and "emphasizing nonbeing," and two, that between "giving way to Nature" and "emphasizing the Confucian ethical code." Wang Bi championed the theory of "exalting nonbeing." His opponent was Pei Wei. The theory of "self-transformation" was represented by Guo Xiang. "Paganism," a revolt against Metaphysics, was represented by Ji Kang.

Metaphysics in the Wei–Jin Period revives the thought of Laozi and Master Zhuang, substituting it for the theology of auguries and apocrypha that had emerged in previous dynasties. The Metaphysicists regarded the *Laozi*, the *Zhuangzi,* and *The Book of Changes* as their classics, and by synthesizing their materials forged their own system. They transformed the theological cosmology of "the correspondence of Heaven and Man" into the ontology of the "debate on being and nonbeing, and of the fundamental and the incidental." This is an important turning point and leap forward in philosophical thinking. Ignoring traditional theological idealism and natural materialism, they employed abstract speculation to demonstrate that behind the realistic world there is an original substance that produced and dominates the phenomenal world—called "nonbeing," "the Way," or "Heavenly way of Nature."

The Metaphysicists of the Wei–Jin period transformed these categories and gave them an idealistic connotation. In addition, they demonstrated that the Taoist concept of "Nature" and the Confucian "ethical code" are identical—thus changing the ideological setup of the Han Dynasty, during which the two schools were at loggerheads. They promoted the formation of "study centered on the three works of Metaphysics" that "synthesize Confucianism and Taoism."

The development of Metaphysics underwent several stages. It emerged in the Zhengshi reign (240–248) of the Wei Dynasty, when He Yan and Wang Bi put forth the theory of "exalting nonbeing." The historical record reads as follows:

> "In the Zhengshi Reign of the Wei Dynasty, He Yan, Wang Bi, and others worshiped and followed the example of Laozi and Zhuangzi.

They set up their own theory that, without exception, Heaven, Earth, and the myriad things have "nonbeing" as the foundation of their existence. "Nonbeing" is omnipresent, and we must recognize this if we are to understand the truth of all things on earth and handle affairs successfully. With nonbeing, yin and yang may transform themselves into everything. With nonbeing, the myriad things take shape. With nonbeing, the sages cultivate the virtues. With nonbeing, scoundrels may escape the extinction of their bodies. Therefore, the function of nonbeing is immeasurably valuable." (*History of Jin·Book 43: Biography of Wang Yan*)

This "nonbeing" is also called "Nature." He Yan explains:

"By Nature is meant the Way. Essentially speaking, the Way has no name. . . . It is only because the Way has no name that all possible names in the world can be used for it." (Quotation from the author of the *Commentary on the Liezi* from He Yan's *Treatise on the Nameless*)

Wang Bi adds:

As for Nature, its omens and signs are invisible, and likewise its intention and interest are invisible. . . . It accomplishes affairs by non-action, and it teaches people by non-speech. Therefore, when it has rendered meritorious service and accomplished great causes, the common people know nothing about how it should have completed so many things." (*Commentary on the Laozi·Chapter 17*)

This emphasis on nonbeing is the first stage of the development of Metaphysics in the Wei-Jin period.

Wang Bi's theory centers on the "emphasis on nonbeing," although it affirms that "Names and teachings originate in Nature." A view held by Ji Kang, Ruan Ji, and others that "Names and teachings are not in accordance with Nature" expresses the "pagan" tendency away from Metaphysics. Yue Guang thinks that Nature is not removed from names and teachings. Pei Wei goes even farther by revising two ideas that appeared in the early stage of Metaphysics: "taking nonbeing for the fundamental" and "to uphold Nature." He wrote two treatises—the *Exalting Being* and *Emphasizing Nonbeing*. Yue Guang and Pei Wei maintain that it is necessary to unify the "emphasizing nonbeing" and the "exalting being." This is the second stage of the development of Metaphysics. "Names and teachings originate in Nature,"

On the basis of Pei Wei's thought of "exalting being," Guo Xiang says that "names and teachings" are nothing but "Nature," "self-production" is nothing but "natural non-action," and all "ranks and orders of the top, the low, the noble, and the base" are originally in accordance with "Heavenly reason and Nature"—solving the contradiction between Nature and names and teachings. This is the third stage of the development of Metaphysics in the Wei-Jin Period.

Metaphysics underwent a divergence in later ages. Part of it became enmeshed with Buddhism, and gradually became an appendage to Buddhist philosophy. The other part evolved in the direction of mysticism and evolved into Immortals Taoism.

In the transitional period between the Wei and Jin dynasties, the gentry and influential families rapidly expanded their influence. At the same time, a large number of famous literati originating from the gentry and influential families made efforts to "exercise the names and principles meticulously," and put new vigor into Metaphysics. The representatives of this school include Fu Gu, Zhong Hui, Xun Can, Pei Wei, Xiahou Xuan, and He Yan. Wang Bi was especially prominent.

Wang Bi (AD 226–249), grandnephew of Wang Can, was a leading scholar of the later part of the Han Dynasty. According to He Shao's *Biography of Wang Bi*, "He was discriminative and intelligent from childhood. While a teenager, he began to love the words of Laozi, and his turn of phrase made him a superb debater." He Yan (AD 190–249) recommended Wang Bi to Cao Shuang, a general who wielded the real power in Wei at that time. When the Sima clan gained control of Wei, Cao Shuang and He Yan were killed, and Wang Bi narrowly escaped with his life. He died of disease in autumn of the same year. In his short span of twenty-three years he wrote many important works, including the *Commentary on the Book of Changes*, *Simple Exemplification of the Principles of the Book of Changes*, *Commentary on the Laozi*, *Simple Exemplification of the Subtle*

Implications of the Laozi, and *Solving Problems of the Analects*. Wang Bi takes one proposition of the philosophy of Laozi for the starting point of his speculation: "Being comes from nonbeing." (*Laozi·Chapter 40*) In *Commentary on the Laozi*, he clarifies the purpose and main theme from the very beginning: "All beings originated from nonbeing. The time before physical forms and names appeared was the beginning of the myriad things. After forms and names appear, the Way develops them, nourishes them, and places them in peace and order; that is, it becomes their Mother. This means that the Way produces and completes things with the formless and nameless. Thus they are produced and completed, but they do not know why. Indeed, this is the mystery of mysteries." (*Commentary on the Laozi·Chapter 1*)

Here, the "nonbeing" discussed by He Yan and Wang Bi refers to a noumenon that is the basis on which all phenomena in the material world exist: vital force, material objects, sound, light, form, color, the human body, the human spirit. It is a certain kind of extremely abstracted absolute: "The Way is an application of nonbeing. There is nowhere the Way does not lead to, and there is nobody who does not follow it. So people describe it as the Way. The Way is silent and without form. The Way is without any images at all." (*Solving the Problems of the Analects*)

What properties and functions does the "nonbeing" as a noumenon possesses? As "the ancestor of the myriad things," "nonbeing" possesses no concrete properties. Man cannot hear it, see it, touch it or smell it. Precisely because of this, it can dominate both the existence, movement, and change of Heaven, Earth, and the myriad things. Why? When the dominator is any concrete thing, it must have one or other concrete attribute, it must be restricted in some way, and therefore it cannot be the grounds for the existence of a multitude of things. (Cf. *Simple Exemplification of the Subtle Implications of the Laozi*)

The guiding principle of the philosophy of "exalting nonbeing" is to take "nonbeing" (base) for the fundamental and to take "being" (application) for the incidental. Wang Bi describes the relationship between being and nonbeing as that between the many and the one, and as that between majority and minority: "The ten thousand things have ten thousand different forms but in the final analysis they are one. How did they become one? This was because of nonbeing. Because nonbeing is the one, the one may be called nonbeing." (*Commentary on the Laozi·Chapter 42*)

Wang Bi's theory of "exalting nonbeing" breaks through the framework of cosmogony formulated in the Qin and Han dynasties. It is inside things per se that people should seek the grounds of their existence and development. In Wang Bi's ontology, however, there are the ideas of worshiping "nonbeing" and of debasing "being," of elevating the "fundamental" and of belittling the "incidental"—which shows that he fails to treat the relationship between the "base" and the "application" in a proper manner.

When the view of being and nonbeing embodies itself in the view of the motional and motionless, Wang Bi takes tranquility for the fundamental, and action for the incidental. According to his logic, "nonbeing" is the absolute noumenon, and therefore has immovable, invariable, and everlasting existence; whereas "being" belongs to the relative phenomenal sphere, which is always changing: "All kinds of being originate from vacuity, and action originates from tranquility. Therefore, the myriad things are all in action, but they finally return to vacuity and tranquility, as is the ultimacy of all things." (*Commentary on the Laozi·Chapter 16*) So also is the case with human beings. People return to quietude so that they may grasp the immovable and invariant noumenon by getting out of the unending changes.

Wang Bi acknowledges that contradiction is the cause of whatever changes, and that contradictions transform into their opposites under given conditions. The agent of change is not the motive force of an outside deity. Instead, change is the result of an internal noumenon that functions all the time. As Wang Bi emphasizes, change and contradiction are relative and temporary. Essentially, such a theory is a metaphysical view of activity and quietude.

As for the theory of knowledge, Laozi has a famous statement that "The pursuit of learning is to increase day after day. The pursuit of the Way is to decrease day after day." (*Laozi·Chapter 48*) By this, he intends to urge people to "abandon sageliness and discard wisdom." (*Laozi·Chapter 19.*) Master Zhuang says that he who knows does not speak, and he who speaks does not know. So, only by transcending names and speeches can one "realize the Way." This is epistemology tinged with mysticism.

Wang Bi denies that ordinary people have the cognitive potentiality to grasp the truth, namely, the "Way," or "nonbeing." He claims that the sages have inborn and superhuman "divine" wisdom, and only the sages may "realize what nonbeing is." It is said that when the aristocratic official Pei Hui first met the youthful Wang Bi, they had the following conversation:

> "Pei Hui said to Wang Bi: 'I see that nonbeing is surely the source of the myriad things. But the sage Confucius would not say anything about it. However, Laozi discussed it time and again. Why?'" (Book 28: *History of the Three Kingdoms*) "Wang Bi answered, 'Confucius realized nonbeing, but nonbeing is beyond any description, and therefore he said nothing about nonbeing. Laozi was, of course, able to understand being, and therefore he often spoke of the insufficiency of being.'" (*Ibid*)

In Wang Bi's answer we find two points. First, he "synthesizes both Confucianism and Taoism," and he thinks that Confucius is superior to Laozi. Second, he draws a cognitive line of mysticism by upholding that "Confucius realized nonbeing." By "realization of nonbeing" he means two things, too. First, the sage possessed superhuman "divinity," and therefore he was able to realize "nonbeing" as a noumenon directly. Second, the sage "takes nonbeing for the dominator, and takes non-speech for instruction. Nonbeing and non-speech are a continuous and unbroken existence in which things acquire their true phases. What dwells in one and the same body of the Way is therefore identical with the Way." (*Commentary on the Laozi· Chapter 23*) In this way, Wang Bi makes the sage the incarnation of "nonbeing." It is obvious that in Wang Bi's view there exists a trinity: The patriarch, the sage, and the "Way" (or, the "nonbeing") are three in one.

Wang Bi started the tradition of Wei–Jin Metaphysics. Later, Xiang Xiu and Guo Xiang deepened and enlarged it. And then Dao An, Zhi Dun, and Seng Zhao, and other Buddhists grafted Metaphysics onto their own thoughts. Finally, Metaphysics and the Prajna-Madhyamika Sect of Buddhism combined into one, from which various schools of Chinese Buddhist philosophy emerged.

16.

The Confucian Canon and Metaphysics: Ideological Backlash

In the Three Kingdoms Period and in the Western Jin Dynasty, a two-wing anti-Metaphysics trend surfaced. One, a metaphysical heresy headed by Ji Kang and Ruan Ji, discussed the same problems as the famous literati within the camp of Metaphysics, but with an orientation contrary to "Confucian concepts and values" and "Nature." Two, a faction represented by Yang Quan, Ouyang Jian, and Bao Jingyan attacked Metaphysics from outside the camp of Metaphysics. Yang Quan wrote *Of the Nature of Things*, Ouyang Jian wrote *On the Fullness of Speech in Expressing Ideas*, and Bao Jingyan wrote *On the Abolition of Rulers*. Ji Kang (223–262), a native of Zhixian County in Qiao Prefecture (Suxian County, Anhui Province), was a critic of the ideological trend of Metaphysics and a famous man of letters. He served at the Wei court until power fell into the hands of the Sima clan, and he went into retirement. Together with Ruan Ji, Liu Ling, Xiang Xiu, and Shan Tao, he was one of the Wise Men of the Bamboo Grove. The Sima clan, who strongly advocated a return to Confucian values, had Ji Kang put to death. His writings are contained in the *Anthology of Ji Kang*.

Ji Kang inherited Wang Chong's materialist outlook on nature, with material force as the center. Contrary to the theory of He Yan and Wang Bi—that Heaven, Earth, and the myriad things "came into existence by nonbeing," and that it was necessary to "take nonbeing for the fundamental"—Ji Kang and Ruan Ji claimed that Heaven, Earth, and the myriad things originated in Nature and the vital force. Ruan Ji says:

> "Heaven and Earth originate in Nature, and the myriad things originate in Heaven and Earth. Nature itself is no exception, and therefore it is the name of Heaven and Earth. Since Heaven and Earth have content, the myriad things come into being." (*Treatise on How to Reach Zhuangzi*)

Similarly, Ji Kang says,

> "The vital force molds and all living creatures receive it." (*Treatise on How to Beware of Courage*) And, "The Great Simplicity has great strength and vigor, and the sun shines and the moon congeals. Heaven and Earth mold, and human relations begin." (*The Great Master's Maxim*)

"The Great Simplicity" is a term described as "the beginning of matter" in the *Apocryphal Treatise on the Changes: a Penetration of the Laws of Qian*. Both the "Great Beginning" and the "Great Start" refer to the initial state of nonbeing. The "Great Simplicity," the vast and boundless material "vital force," contains yin and yang, and is the general origin of the universe. At that time, the theory of "exalting nonbeing" advocated by Xiang Xiu and Wang Bi caused a great clamor, and Ji Kang's theory of the "vital force" suddenly came to the fore. Denying the ontology of Metaphysics, it thus became the banner of the metaphysical heresy.

On the problem of the relationship between mind and matter, Ji Kang affirms its objective reality. On the problem of name and actuality, Ji Kang points says, "it is necessary to give a name to an affair, and a thing should have its own appellation." On the problem of body and spirit, Ji Kang maintains that body and spirit depend on each other and should not depart from each other. This is a forceful criticism of Wang Bi's theory that "The spirit is what is formless." (*Commentary on the Book of Changes·Commentary on Hexagram No. 20: Guan or Contemplation*) Ji Kang opposes the various theories of predestination. He believes that man's subjective efforts are helpful for the realization of his destiny.

The philosophers of "exalting nonbeing" thought that "speech cannot express any ideas fully," because it interferes with man's consciousness. But to Ji Kang, things are discernible. As for cognition, he asserts:

> "To discern things by analogy, one must seek the principles hidden in Nature. Until the principles have been determined, ancient explanations cannot be borrowed to make them clear, yet quite a few people apply quotations from ancient arguments to their discourse. If things continue in this way, I am afraid that ingenious chronicles cannot record this rubbish any longer." (*Treatise on Why Sound Has Neither Sorrow nor Joy*)

There are other dialectical features in Ji Kang's theory of knowledge. He divides human knowledge into two forms: "knowledge by reasoning," and "knowledge by witness." (*Treatise on Keeping Good Health*) Even when one knows the principles, there are things that cannot be grasped all at once, making it necessary to observe, analyze, and synthesize. He calls this method "thinking concurrently," which is suggestive of guarding against one-sidedness.

As for how to know the truth, Ji Kang, who in this aspect is similar to Wang Chong, looks down upon Confucian scholars who "regard the rites of the Zhou Dynasty as the key," and who "take the six classics for the standard." (*Treatise on Keeping Good Health*) They are merely remaining in an old rut. Rather, it is essential to have a broad outlook and independent thinking, so as to "act as the occasion requires and be able to examine the subtle movement of any event."

Ji Kang opposed the Sima clan's ascent to power, and not purely because of his loyalty to the ruling Cao family. It is apparent from his conversations with the hermit Sun Deng and students at the imperial college that he stood on the side of the common people against the Sima clan, which represented the interests of big and influential families. He criticized the Sima clique by pointing out the contradiction between their professed Confucian virtues and their actual dastardly deeds. He also remarked that the rites, laws, and moral codes preached by the Confucian classics are against Nature and fetters on human nature, possibly the origin of evil phenomena that include hypocritical behavior and fraudulent conduct. The "Confucian codes," he says, are absolutely not a product of Nature, but are the result of the destruction of "man's natural feelings," or the product of a decaying dynasty, when "The Great Way has already been cut into pieces."

> "The six classics, in the main, were designed to suppress what emerges from within, while human nature is pleasant when its various desires are followed. To suppress what emerges from within is against human desires, and to follow the various desires is in accordance with Nature. But nothing obtained from Nature can be subdued by the six classics. To keep one's nature integrated, it is essential not to go against the rites and laws concerning human feelings. Therefore, benevolence and righteousness function to rectify things that are false, but neither is a key to cultivate one's nature. Honest and clean behavior comes from striving for interests; it does not come from Nature." (*Treatise on Rebuking the Easy Approach to Nature*)

Ji Kang dismisses the study of the six classics as being useful only for obtaining official positions and riches. He maintains that when people truly follow their original nature, they will never be willing to study the six classics or to follow Confucian ethical codes. He says, "to live a free and unrestrained life, one must oppose hypocrisy and material gains."

Yang Quan (c. 239–294) lived in Guiji Prefecture in the Kingdom of Wu in the Three Kingdoms Period. After the Jin Dynasty wiped out Wu in 280 AD, the Jin imperial court tried to appoint him to office, but he refused, lived as a hermit, and wrote books to develop his thought. Yang Quan inherited and developed the new style of study prevalent in the Jingzhou area and in regions south of the Yangtze. By imitating Yang Xiong, Yang Quan wrote the *Classic of Great Mystery* in fourteen volumes, and an important monograph of natural philosophy titled *Of the Nature of Things* in sixteen—all lost in the Song Dynasty. In the Qing Dynasty, Sun Xingyan collected the surviving fragments and edited them into the single volume *Of the Nature of Things*.

In the Han Dynasty there were three theories of the structure of the universe and Heavenly bodies. One was the theory of "canopy-heaven," as expounded in the *Mathematical Classic on the Gnomon*, a work on astronomy and mathematics written in the first century BC. It describes Heaven as a vaulted cover, Earth as a vaulted surface, with

Heaven pressing on Earth as an upper millstone presses on the lower. Another, the theory of "sphere-heaven," describes the universe as round like an egg, with Earth as the yolk. In the third, the "nocturnal theory of the universe," the sky is empty, pure, clean, and boundless, and the sun, moon, and stars float in space by means of the ether. Believing that the theories of "sphere-heaven" and "canopy-heaven" fail to give a clear explanation of the movement of the heavenly bodies., Yang Quan cleaves to the "nocturnal theory of the universe," synthesizes its positive achievements, and develops the monism of material force. In a clear and definite way he draws the conclusion that "Earth is with form, while Heaven is without a body" and "As for Heaven, it is material force alone." (*Of the Nature of Things*) Elsewhere he reiterates,

> "Since material force is vast and great, people call it the great and vast Heaven. The great and vast Heaven is material force. It is so great and vast that in it there is nothing else at all." (*Ibid*)

To Yang Quan, when the material force of yang condensed, it became the sun; when the material force of yin condensed, it became the moon. The stars come from the Milky Way, formed from essences of the steam of water and soil on Earth, which rose up into space. These brief and simple discourses synthesize the natural sciences of the era. Yang Quan's contribution lies in his demonstration that various natural phenomena are unified in the material "vital force."

In Yang Quan's view, the myriad things in Nature result from the transformation and accumulation of yin and yang as the "two basic material forces," just as a potter makes various types of pots. Everything owes its existence to "the material force," an idea diametrically opposed to Metaphysics, whose adherents maintain that "Heaven, Earth, and everything else take nonbeing for the fundamental." He regards the dissemination, accumulation, movement, and change of the material force as following the "principle of Nature," denying the agency of supernatural forces.

The critical spirit of Yang Quan's thought is in the main expressed in his persistence in the ideological tradition started by Huan Tan and Wang Chong that there is no soul. He inspires later scholars such as He Chengtian, Fan Zhen, and others who waged a theoretical struggle against Buddhism. For instance, in *A Beginner's Narrative* by Xu Jian, an important viewpoint of Yang Quan is preserved:

> "A person is born with the vital force contained in his body and he dies when the essences are exhausted. Take fire for example, when the firewood is burnt, the fire is extinguished; and when the fire is extinguished, there is no light from the fire. Therefore, after a fire is extinguishes no flame remains; and after a person dies, no soul remains." (*A Beginner's Narrative*)

Yang Quan also makes a sharp criticism of the contemporary system of office-seeking and patronage in his masterpiece *Of the Nature of Things*, saying the system produces hypocrites who "imitate the deeds of Jie the tyrant while wearing the cap of Yao the sage emperor." He criticizes the Metaphysicists, who engaged in a great controversy on the difference or similarity of Confucianism and Taoism, for only making simple things look unnecessarily mysterious.

Ouyang Jian (27–300 AD) was a native of Nanpi County, Bohai Prefecture (Cangxian County, Hebei Province). According to the "Biography of Shi Bao" in the *History of the Jin Dynasty*, he "enjoyed a good reputation at that time," but later was killed in an internal conflict within the ruling clique of the Western Jin Dynasty. Of his works, only one essay remains: *On the Fullness of Speech in Expressing Ideas*, an important attack on Metaphysics.

Ouyang Jian finds that the theoretical thinking mode of the ontology of Metaphysics—seeking the "connotation beyond the images"—is the key to Metaphysics, so he grasps the problem of criticizing it, and sets up his own theory.

First, he emphasizes the objectivity of the target of cognition. What is the target of human cognition? In Ouyang Jian's opinion, the relationship between words and ideas is in fact a relationship between the mind and things (names and actuality) or the relationship between the subject and object in human cognition. To him, there were shapes—square, round, and more—before there were names for those shapes. There were colors—black, white, and more—before there were names for those colors. The objective shapes and colors are the primary, the subjective names secondary. Furthermore, he says, "Names always change in accordance with the transformation of things. Sayings also change in accordance with the alternations of principles." (*On the Fullness of Speech in Expressing Ideas*) This lays the foundation for his theory of knowledge.

Second, he emphasizes the reliability of logical cognition. He says that all things are objective things in Nature and per se have no fixed or ready-made names. Names can have no subjective effect upon the objectively innate laws of things. Nevertheless, no one can express the innate laws of things already realized by his mind if he does not use the names appropriate to those things. Therefore, people may use names and concepts to distinguish things and to express their thoughts—a criticism of the agnosticism advocated by the Metaphysicians.

Third, he emphasizes the consistency between subject and object, which "cannot stand as two parties opposite to each other." In these two parties there is consistency on the basis of opposites, from which he draws the conclusion that "speech can express ideas fully." (*On the Fullness of Speech in Expressing Ideas*) Though Ouyang Jian's demonstration has a tendency toward over-simplification, yet he, by his own efforts, upholds the theory that "speech can express ideas fully" when the theory that "words cannot exhaust ideas" was in vogue as an ideological trend. Bao Jingyan (c. 278–342) lived in the transitional period between the Western and Eastern Jin dynasties, but little is known about his life. He once debated with Ge Hong, a scholar who later became the founder of the Golden Elixir Sect of Taoism. Some fragments of his works are preserved in *Chapter 48: Interrogating Bao* in the *Outer Chapters* of Ge Hong's masterpiece *The Master Who Embraces Simplicity*. According to Ge Hong, he "highly valued the view that in remote ages there were no rulers at all."

The Three Kingdoms and the two Jin dynasties eras were full of turmoil, except for nine years at the beginning of the Western Jin Dynasty, the "Golden Years of Taikang (280–289)." This was followed by periods of great suffering for the people—the sixteen-year "Internecine Wars among the Eight Princes" (291–306), and the "Turmoil of the Sixteen States," which lasted for more than one hundred years (304–439). There was always a ruler of the country—but no peace for the people.

Bao Jingyan, via his "theory of the abolition of rulers," attacks the irrationality of the whole system of oppression and exploitation by the ruling class, whom he describes as a "gang that cuts up the whole country with a butcher's knife." The feudal state apparatus operates by "adopting cruel tortures and setting traps." The result is that "the more you try to mitigate a disaster, the greater the disaster becomes, and the more you forbid the people to do something, the more people dare to transgress your prohibition."

In addition, Bao attempts to analyze the root cause of the irrational system. He refutes the theory of the "divine right of kings" advocated by Confucian scholars, and instead postulates that the sway of the rulers is nothing more than a system of oppression:

> "When the strong dominate the weak, the weak can do nothing but obey. When the wise defraud the foolish; the foolish can do nothing but serve the wise. Since there is obedience, the way between the ruler and the ministers comes into being. Since there is service, the people who have little power are governed. Since the relationship of subordination and service comes from competition between the strong and the weak and between the wise and the foolish, it has nothing to do with Providence." (*The Master Who Embraces Simplicity·Outer Chapters·Chapter 48: Interrogating Bao*)

While Bao Jingyan was unaware of the principle that the emergence of classes is linked with a certain stage in the development of production, he sees the relationship between strong and weak as one of exploitation and oppression. He denies the then-current argument that "common people" are born to be slaves for the "rulers."

Bao Jingyan's view of the irrationality of the system leads him to atheism, by denying rule by "divine right." He says:

> "As for Heaven and Earth, they mold things by two vital forces. Those things that find pleasure in yang rise up as flying clouds, and those things that are fond of yin fall down as rivers, and dwell in lower places. They are endowed with the soft or strong attributes that govern their natures, and they are transformed into the myriad things by following the four seasons and eight festivals. Each attaches itself to what pleases it, so in their origin there is no difference between the noble and the base." (*Ibid*)

He demonstrates that the feudal hierarchy runs against both human nature and the Heavenly way. As such, Bao directly refutes the Metaphysical theory that the Confucian ethical code accords with Nature as it comes from Nature.Bao Jingyan says, "In the remote past there were no rulers at all, and the ancient society was much better than what we have now." He envisions a utopia where "there is neither ruler nor subject." Such a society would meet the following four requirements: First, there would be neither conscript labor nor taxes, which are imposed by the imperial authority, nor annexation of land, which is done by the powerful families. Second, there would be no plundering wars or cruel punishments. Third, there would be neither laws nor discipline nor Confucian ethical codes nor empty talk. Fourth, everybody would lead a happy life, depending on his or her own labor.

17.

The Dissemination and Development of Buddhist Philosophy

In the sixth century BC, Siddhartha Gautama (c. 563–c. 483 BC), prince of Kapilavastu in the north of ancient India, founded Buddhism. Since he belonged to the Sakya family, he was called Sakyamuni, Sage of the Sakyas. He was also given the honorific title of the Buddha, the Enlightened One, or the wise man who has realized the truth. Sometime in the Eastern Han Dynasty, circa AD 65, Buddhism was introduced to China. At first there was disapproval of the new foreign religion in official circles, and the Han imperial court forbade people to become Buddhist monks or nuns. But Buddhism spread rapidly during the period of the Eastern Jin and Northern and Southern Wei dynasties (317–589) when tribes from the north settled in the Central Plains. Being Buddhists, they gave support to the spread of the religion in their areas.

Under Shi Le, the founder of Later Zhao Dynasty (319–350), and his son and successor Shi Hu, Fo Tucheng (232–348), a leading Buddhist monk, presided over the kingdom's religious affairs. Under their guidance, more than 800 temples were built. Later, Fo's disciple, the monk Dao-an (314–385), served Fu Jian (338–385), king of Former Qin. Fu Jian brought Kumarajiva (344–413), an eminent Indian Buddhist scholar famed for his encyclopedic knowledge of the scriptures, to his capital Chang'an, where he was regarded as the national mentor.

Buddhism became more and more influential in northern China.

In the Northern Wei Dynasty (386–534), more than 30,000 temples were built. There were two million monks and nuns, and more than 19,000 Buddhist scriptures were translated into Chinese. At Yungang, Maijishan, and Dunhuang, extensive grottoes were carved to house Buddhist statues and inscriptions. They are preserved to this day.

In southern China, starting in the Eastern Jin Dynasty, the ruling class embraced Buddhism, saying, "In internal affairs Buddhism is helpful for maintaining popular morale, and in external affairs it is helpful in offering amnesty and enlistment to surrendered enemy soldiers." Emperor Wen of the Song Dynasty and Emperor Wu of the Liang Dynasty were devout believers. Emperor Wu was one of the most enthusiastic advocates among the Chinese emperors, proclaiming Buddhism the state religion in 504. In the Liang Dynasty, Buddhist monasteries accumulated wealth rapidly, and it is said that about half the population lived on monastery land.

The early form of Buddhism that spread to China stressed the ideas of causality, samsara (transmigration), Naraka (Hell), and the Western paradise, but in the course of its transmission to China, superstitious ideas of ghosts and gods native to China were mixed in.

Starting in the Western Jin, a large number of sutras and treatises of Later Buddhism were translated into Chinese, most belonging to the philosophical works of Prajna-Mhyamika. Its speculative system is similar to the ontology of Metaphysics, and Chinese translators and commentators borrowed many concepts from the works of Laozi, Zhuangzi, and the Metaphysicists to explain it. As a result, Buddhist thought in China eventually merged with and supplanted Metaphysics, becoming a luxuriant plant in the garden of ancient Chinese philosophy.

In the century or so following the passing away of Sakyamuni, Indian Buddhism split into two sects, and two traditions: Theravada and Mahasanghika. From the first century of the Christian era, Mahayana (the great vehicle) evolved out of various branches of Mahasanghika, and there appeared many Mahayana scriptures. Mahayana called the sects that stuck to the original dogma Hinayana (lesser vehicle), a term tinged with depreciation. From the third to the fifth centuries of the Christian era, two sects gradually formed within Mahayana, Mhadymika and Yogacara. As a result, Buddhism developed from a simple religious form into a philosophical form imbued with speculation.

The Buddhism that spread to China in the Han and Wei dynasties included the teachings of both Mahayana and Hinayana sects.

An Shigao, the earliest translator of Buddhist scriptures in China, translated thirty-five sutras, most on Hinayana *dhadyna* (meditation). His translation exerted a great influence on the Zen Buddhism of later ages, which flourished in northern China. Lokaksema, a contemporary of An Shigao, translated twelve Mahayana sutras into Chinese, with a focus on introducing the doctrine of prajna, the achieving of ultimate knowledge.

Zhu Shixing, an eminent Buddhist monk, traveled to the Western Regions in the fifth year (260) of the Ganlu reign of the Wei Dynasty. He obtained a full edition of the Sanskrit version of the *Mahaprajnaparamita Sutra*, which was translated into Chinese by Zhu Shulan and others under the title *Fangguang Jing* (*The Scripture of the Shedding of the Light of the Buddha*). Shortly after, Dharmarksa, a great translator who lived in China as an emigrant from the Kushan Kingdom, also went to the Western Regions for further study. He had an excellent command of both Chinese and languages of various kingdoms in the Western Region. Dharmarksahe translated 159 sutras, more than 300 volumes, into Chinese, most belonging to the doctrine of prajna. From that time on, the doctrine of prajna began to gain more and more adherents.

Mahayana *prajna* first aims to demonstrate the objective aspect of things by the proposition "pratityasamutpa-sunyata," namely, "The chain of causation is empty." Second, it affirms that subjective wisdom is able to have an insight into such "sunyata" (emptiness). A new theory—"contemplation of emptiness"—appeared in their combination. While similar to that of the Metaphysicists in China at that time, the thinking routes of the two doctrines are different. In the confluence, it is hard to avoid different interpretations.

To introduce and disseminate a new doctrine, the first stage is "careful study" of the words. In China, people used nouns and concepts from the works of Laozi, Zhuangzi, and Metaphysics to explain the Buddhist sutras, which led to distortion of the original connotations. In the Eastern Jin, these interpretations resulted in the "seven sects" and six schools: *Benwu* (Sanskrit for *bhutatathata*, reality), *Xinwu* (nonbeing of mind), *Jise* (matter as such), *Shihan* (stored impression), *Huanhua* (phenomenal illusion), and *Yuanhui* (causal combination).The fundamental doctrine of the

Benwu is that the original nature of all things is empty and silent. Jizang (549–623) explains this by saying, "The monk Dao-an was the first to propagate the doctrine of original nonbeing, saying it existed before the myriad things evolved and were transformed, and that Emptiness was the beginning of all things with form. What obstructs man's mind is derived entities. When the mind finds its abode in original nonbeing, erroneous thoughts will cease. . . . When we understand this idea fully, we will realize that all elements of existence are in their original nature empty and void, tranquil, and devoid of differentiated character. Hence the name original nonbeing." (*Commentary on the Mhyamika Sastra·Chapter 2: Account of the Cause*)

The monks of the Benwu Sect explain the "contemplation of emptiness" basically within the framework of Metaphysics.

Zhi Mindu (ca. 326–342) represents the Xinwu School. Seng Zhao describes its doctrine: "Nonbeing of mind means that one should have no deliberate mind toward the myriad things. The myriad things in themselves, however, are not nonexistent." (*A Collection of Seng Zhao's Treatises*) This idea, which runs against the purport of the prajna doctrine, was ridiculed and refuted by scholars of the prajna doctrine.

Jise School's representative is Zhi Dun, (314–366). To this school, all material phenomena come from this or that cause, and nothing possesses attributes by itself (*buzise*, [it is] impossible by itself [to be] a phenomenon). Zhi explains that all things are empty in their original nature. This is slightly different from the theory of "contemplation of emptiness" that lays more stress on the aspect that "all existence is void."

The Huanhua Sect, represented by Dao-yi, affirms that the myriad things are illusions. The Shihan Sect, represented by Yu Fakai (ca. 364), affirms that everything in the world is false. The Yuanhui Sect, represented by Yu Daosui (a contemporary of Yu Fakai), affirms that the myriad things come into being because of the confluence of their conditions, and disappear with the disappearance of their conditions. All sects agree with the Jise in affirming the existence of "false phenomena" and "illusionary phenomena" from the angle of causal combination, a theory similar to the Metaphysical theory of "self-transformation."

Thus the *prajna* doctrine came to China. In the first stage it underwent a process from a careful study of words to a thorough understanding of their connotations, and in practice it merged with Metaphysics.

But the *prajna* doctrine rapidly entered upon a stage of independent development by taking Metaphysics as its medium.

In 401, Kumarajiva arrived in Chang'an. An eminent monk in the Western Regions, he had studied Hinayana in his childhood, then devoted himself to Mahayana. In Chang'an, for twelve years he was in charge of 3,000 translators, who translated more than 70 sutras in over 300 volumes. The translations are of high quality, even by today's standards. The whole of the *Mahaprajnaparamita Sutra* was retranslated into Chinese, as were the *Sdharmapundarika Sutra* (*Lotus Sutra*), *Vimalakirtinirdesa Sutra* (*The Scripture Spoken by Vimalakirti*), *Visesacintabrahmapariprccha,* and *Suramgama-samhi Sutra.* In addition, abridgments of Nagarjuna's three books—the *Mahaprajna-Dharmaraja, Mhyamika Karika* (*Treatise on the Middle Way*), and *Dvasamukha Sastra* (*The Twelve Topics Treatise*)—were produced in Chinese, as was Deva's *Sata Sastra* (*One-Hundred-Verse Treatise*). In this way, the theories of Nagarjuna and Deva were introduced to China in a comprehensive and systematic way; the translation of, introduction to, and research into the *prajna* theories of Mhymika were raised to a new level; and a group of creative scholar-monks including Seng Zhao and Zhu Daosheng were trained. Their work gave impetus to the spread of Mahayana philosophy in China.

In the first years of the Northern and Southern dynasties, Kumarajiva and his disciple Seng Zhao formed a prajna doctrine research center in the central Shaanxi plain. In addition, Huiyuan (523–592), disciple of Dao-an, formed one for research into both Mahayana and Hinayana Buddhism on Mount Lushan in south China. In the meantime, in Nanjing, Zhu Daosheng, who first studied under Huiyuan and then Kumarajiva, developed his original theory of Buddha-wisdom and Nirvana. North and south were acting in coordination with each other, and the development of Chinese philosophy moved forward full of new spirit.

Seng Zhao (385–414), native of Chang-an (now Xi'an), the most important Buddhist philosopher in the Northern and Southern dynasties period, was founder of the philosophical system of Sinicized Buddhism. Born into a poor family, he earned his living as a teenager by copying books for other people. Seng became widely acquainted with history and the classics, and was fond of the works of Laozi and Zhuangzi, then Metaphysics, and finally Prajna Mhyamika. After reading the *Vimalakir-*

tinirdesa Sutra (*The Scripture Spoken by Vimalakirti*), he became a monk. By age twenty, he enjoyed a high reputation in the Central Plains and became a disciple of Kumarajiva, together with Seng Rong, Seng Rui, and Zhu Daosheng—"the four sages." While assisting Kumarajiva, he made a profound study of the theories of Nagarjuna and Deva. Based on this, he developed the essentials of the Prajna Mhymika, and in a critical way summed up the theories of the various schools of Metaphysics and *prajna* doctrines from the Wei–Jin Period up to his own times. Finally, he established the philosophical system of Sinicized Prajna Mhymika. His fundamental works include *The Emptiness of the Unreal*, *The Immutability of Things,* and *Prajna Is Not Knowledge*, all included in the *Collection of Seng Zhao's Treatises*.

"Do not depart from the self-emptiness of the myriad things" is the fundamental thought in *The Emptiness of the Unreal*. In that text Seng Zhao writes,

> "This is to make clear that the sage, in his attitude toward the myriad things, leaves the vacuous nature of things as it is and does not need to disintegrate it before he can penetrate it," and, "The sage moves within the thousand transformations, but does not change; he travels on ten thousand paths of delusion, but always goes through. This is so because he leaves the vacuous self-nature of things vacuous." Seng Zhao criticizes all theories advocated by the seven sects and expounds his own view.

He thinks that the "emptiness" discussed in Prajna-Mhyamika is not aimed at the problem of either "being" or "nonbeing," but at the problem of either the true or the false. Because all things per se are not real, they are empty. The so-called contemplation of vacuity does not deny the phenomenal existence of "being" or "nonbeing" of objective things in a simple way. It only maintains that their phenomenal existence is not real.

> "As it is nonexistent although it seems to be existent, it is the same as being nonexistent. And as it is existent although it seems to be nonexistent, it is the same as being existent. Thus by not being existent and not being nonexistent we do not mean that there are no things, but that all things are not things in the real sense. As all things

are not things in the real sense, what is there in relation to which a thing can be so called? Therefore, the scripture (*Vimalakirtinirdesa Sutra*, namely, *Scripture Spoken by Vimalakirti*) says, 'Matter is empty by virtue of its own nature; it is not empty because it has been destroyed'." (*The Emptiness of the Unreal*)

Seng Zhao supports the claim that the existence of phenomena is neither nonexistent nor existent with the Buddhist doctrine of causality. The so-called "hetupratyaya" (primary cause and secondary cause) is nothing more than the conditions in which things exist. Here he follows Nagarjuna's thought. We cannot say that the essence of the world is neither "existent" nor "nonexistent"; we can only say that the essence of the world is "empty." The key is that nothing exists until it has a cause. Things have no self-nature, and are thus called "empty."

Finally, attacking the popular view that objective things exist both in name and in fact, Seng Zhao puts forth his theory of "false names." He presents his argument from the angle of "the emptiness of the unreal." If a thing per se is "unreal" it cannot become real by having a name given to it. Even if we know a thing by its name, the thing itself does not necessarily have the actuality corresponding to that name. Therefore, the various illusionary visions called "things" are no more than "false names" based on age-old convention.

Nevertheless, if we universally affirm that all names and words belong to the category of "false names," we shall fall into a paradox, for the statements "All things are empty in their original nature" and "since it is 'unreal' it is 'empty'" are also names and words, aren't they? Are these also "false names?" To escape from this dilemma, Seng Zhao applies the Buddhist "satya-dvaya" (two forms of statement) to his demonstration. In his opinion, "real name" is the view of "paramartha-satya" (correct dogma), and "false name" is the view of "sanivitti-satya" (common statement). According to the former, "Although there is what is real, it is not existent." According to the latter, "Although there is what is false, it is not nonexistent."

The relationship between activity and tranquility and that between constancy and change are important issues in both Metaphysics and Buddhist Prajna-Mhyamika. Buddhism affirms that the myriad things and affairs are circulating, everything is changing, and nothing is constant in the material world. It also advocates seeking the eternal, constant, clear, tranquil, perfect, and bright realm of Nirvana. Clearly, Seng Zhao knows that the absolute truth of Buddhism contradicts secular common sense. To propagate the Buddhist truth, it is necessary to solve such a contradiction from the angle of theory. In ontology, he puts forth the proposition that the myriad things are empty by their nature to dismiss the controversies between the seven schools and six sects. In a similar manner, regarding activity and tranquility, he puts forth the proposition that motion is no different from rest, and that one should not deviate from motion, but seek rest.

Seng Zhao demonstrates his theory, in the first place, by making use of the separation of the three phases of time, namely, past, present, and future.

> "When we look for past things in the past, we find that they exist in the past, but when we search for past things in the present, we find that they do not exist there. That they don't exist in the present shows that they are never to come, and that they exist in the past shows that they do not go away from it. When we turn our attention to investigate the present, we know that the present, too, does not go anywhere. This means that past things, by their very nature, exist in the past, and have never gone there from the present, and present things, by their very nature, exist in the present, and do not come here from the past. . . . Thus, it is clear that things do not come and things do not go. As there is not even a subtle sign of going or returning, what thing can there be that can move?" (*The Immutability of Things*)

In the second place, Seng Zhao continues his demonstration from angles such as the temporal point, continuation, and the relationship of continuity and discontinuity of things changing in both time and space: "As neither the past reaches the present, nor does the present reach the past, everything, according to its nature, remains in only one period of time. What thing can come and go?" (*The Immutability of Things*)

Seng Zhao reveals the relationship between material movement and time and space, expounding upon a series of contradictions concerning movement, such as the contradictions between motion and rest, change and permanence, and continuity of movement and its disconnection. His pushes forward the development of philosophical cognition.

In his treatise *On the Ignorance of Prajna*, Seng Zhao concentrates on the problem of epistemology. There are two key points in his theory of knowledge. One, he wants to demonstrate that *prajna* (wisdom) knows nothing. Two, he wants to demonstrate that *prajna* knows everything.

Prajna in Indian Buddhism is a special wisdom that has insight into truth. Seng Zhao calls "prajna" the "holy wisdom," and that as defined by ordinary people "deluding wisdom." The two have essential distinctions in targets, routes, and results. The absolute truth is the "sunya" (void), which cannot be formulated in any words, and which is neither existent nor non-existent. This is the essence or thing-in-itself of the world as maintained by Buddhism. To know such a thing-in-itself, one cannot resort to rational or logical ways of cognition. One can only rely on the mystical "illustration" (intuitive contemplation). Seng Zhao says as follows:

> "Hence the sage empties his mind, and fills it with illumination. He seeks knowledge all day long, but he thinks that he knows nothing. Therefore, he is silent and alone, and he is able to hide his light. He is open-minded, and, like a bright mirror, may reflect everything. It seems that he has stopped up the routes to his mind such as the ears and other organs, but only he knows clearly that the dark universe is indeed there." (*Prajna Is Not Knowledge*)

That is to say, only those who have "holy wisdom" can hide their wisdom and ingenuity so that they can use their silent and tranquil mind to have a far-going and direct view. Seng Zhao advocates a mystic intuition that expels sense-experience and rational cognition.

The dissemination of the *prajna* doctrine reaches its acme in Seng Zhao's comprehensive expression. This system both synthesizes the ideological data of Metaphysics centered on Laozi and Zhuangzi and digests the theoretical content of Buddhist Prajna-Mhyamika. What is more, its expression is Sinicized and it is thus incorporated into the historical development of Chinese philosophical thought.

A contemporary of Seng Zhao, Huiyuan (334–416) preached Buddhist philosophy in southern China. His teaching was a synthesis of Mahayana and Hinayana Buddhism, and the thoughts of Confucianism and Taoism. His philosophy hence exerted a much wider influence. Although he lived as a recluse on Mount Lushan for thirty years, he played an important role in propagandizing the fundamental dogma of Buddhism.

On the basis of Dao-an's theory of the original nonbeing, Huiyuan expounds on his theory that "the dharma nature does not change." He says, "The ultimate pole takes the unchangeable for Nature, and Nature's obtainment is embodied in the ultimate pole." (*The Biographies of Eminent Monks·Book 6: The Biography of Huiyuan*; quotations used hereafter come from the same source.) The so-called "ultimate pole" refers to the bhuta-tathata (reality in that manner) of Buddhist philosophy, and Huiyuan calls it dharma nature (Buddha nature). "Dharma nature" is a constant, everlasting, and unchangeable thing-in-itself. It exists as it is rather than something that has been made. Dharma nature begets everything. As an independent thing-in-itself able to beget everything, dharma nature is the Only One that resembles itself, so it is called tathata (in that manner). Tathata begets the material world while being embodied in the material world. The dharma nature of tathata expresses itself in material phenomena.

The "dharma nature of tathata" is something similar to "the principal aim" or "the fundamental" of Metaphysics. But as regards to grasping the principal aim or the fundamental, namely, the method to realize the Buddha nature, Buddhism is different from Metaphysics. In Huiyuan's view, the material world, including human beings, comes from the "dharma nature of tathata." Therefore, the human individuals in this very world must transcend secular views and reject secular life, and only by spiritual cultivation of religion can a human return to the "dharma nature of tathata."

The Sanskrit word Nirvana comes from *nirva* (be distinguished), from *nis* (out) plus *va* (blow). In Buddhism, it means perfect bliss and release from karma, a state attained by the extinction of individuality. Chinese Buddhist scholars explain it using the word *yuanji* (perfect silence), a vivid metaphor from the associative function of the two Chinese characters that make up the word. This is the supreme and ideal state in line with Buddhism. Huiyuan maintains that people should pursue the "Buddhist nature of tathata" as their final destination. Only in this way can they get rid of the implications of life and death, which fetter the mind. People should overcome material desires, and stand aloof from worldliness. Only in this way can they get rid of feelings such as love and hatred. If one has such a cultivated spirit, one may ascend to the Sukhavati (Western Paradise), having already entered the ideal state of Nirvana.

Although Huiyuan came into contact with and made a study of the prajna doctrine, he thought Nirvana should take the unchangeable for its dharma nature. Nevertheless, "the unchangeable" in Huiyuan's thought is not the same as the "Nature-void" of those who maintained the prajna doctrine in line with Mahayana. In Huiyuan's thought, the concept of "the unchangeable" is made in accordance with Hinayana, which regards the dharma nature as reality and self-nature, which does not change. Because Huiyuan thinks that the dharma nature of tathata is the unchangeable reality, on the problem of body and soul, he holds that "when a body perishes the soul remains."

Zhu Daosheng (c. 355–434), Seng Zhao's fellow student under Kumarajiva, an eminent monk of the Central Plains, later went to Nanjing to preach Buddhism. He focused on two points: the doctrine of the realization of the Buddha nature reached in Nirvana, and the attainment of Buddhahood by the immediate attainment of enlightenment. His theory contains three important propositions. First, "Good does not have its reward"; second, "There are no living things to be killed"; and third, "Every *icchantika* may become a Buddha." *Icchantika* is a Sanskrit word from *iccha* (desire) plus *antika* (near to). In Buddhism icchantika refers to unbelievers who are attached to selfish desires such as avarice. Those unbelievers are evildoers, as if the root of the *subha* (good, auspicious) is cut off from their minds. According to the old translation of the *Mahapari-Nirvana Sutra* and other scriptures, an *icchantika* can never become a Buddha. Consequently, a number of Buddhists opposed Zhu Daosheng, who was expelled from Nanjing.

Zhu Daosheng's approach was to not stick to the words of the scriptures; instead, he sought to grasp the ideological essentials. As his foundation of cognition, it enables him to be original and to have a better explanation of the old dogmas. He directly calls the thing-in-itself behind the dharmas and phenomena the "Buddha nature," the true, real, eternal and unchanging perfect, brilliant thing-in-itself. In his view, Buddha nature exists within man's "original nature." Therefore, Nirvana is by no means outside the realistic world.

In the *Mahapari-Nirvana Sutra*, the statement "All living beings have the Buddha nature" (*Taisho Shinshiu Taisokyo*, 12. 574–575) inspired Zhu Daosheng to say, "Every icchantika may become a Buddha." Shortly after he was driven out of Nanjing, a new translation of the *Mahapari-Nirvana Sutra* spread to the south, stating in black and white that "every icchantika may become Buddha." The idea gained ground that when a person departs from attachment to worldly feelings and turns his or her heart towards the Buddha nature, that person can assuredly become a Buddha by the "immediate attainment of enlightenment."

Buddhist philosophy approaches the four important concepts, namely, "faith," "awakening," "gradual attainment of enlightenment," and "immediate attainment of enlightenment," from different angles. Starting from his doctrine of the realization of the Buddha nature reached in Nirvana, Zhu first discusses the relation between "belief" and "awakening." When one has only "faith," he can never reach the goal of becoming a Buddha. "With regard to those who have realized the dharma, no boundary whatever exists any more, and groundless thoughts are discarded. They have the wonderful enlightenment that surpasses the surface of Tri-dhatu, and in a secret way their understanding of the absolute principles accords with the ideal state that is formless." (*Notes to the Vimalakirtinirdessa Sutra*)

Only through awakening can one reach the supreme state of mind.

These thoughts of Zhu Daosheng, which were afterwards inherited and brought into full play by the Chan sect of Buddhism in China, were influential on Chinese philosophy in post-Tang times.

18.

Fan Zhen the Atheist

In the period from the Eastern Jin Dynasty to the Northern and Southern Dynasties (317–589), Chinese philosophy advanced in two opposing directions—Buddhism and anti-Buddhism. The reaction against Buddhism evolved in six aspects, according to Sengyou (445–518):

First, there arose doubts about the teachings in the sutras.

Second, skepticism about the so-called three periods of the existence of an individual, namely, past, present, and future lives, gained ground.

Third, scholars started to question whether the Buddha had ever existed, for there were no reliable records of him at that time.

Fourth, it was felt by many that the late introduction of Buddhism to China, in the Han Dynasty, betrayed the shallowness of its teachings.

Fifth, some began to resent the non-Chinese trappings of Buddhism and its teachings.

Sixth, the waxing and waning of Buddhism in imperial favor—out of vogue in the Han and Wei and virtually the official state religion in the Jin—cast doubt on its supposedly universal authority (Cf. *A Collection of Expositions of Truth·Book 14*)

Fan Zhen (c. 450–515), who denied that the soul continued to exist after the body was dead, was this theory's representative philosopher. He inherited the mantle of atheism from Wang Chong, and can be regarded as one of the most important materialists and atheists in the Northern and Southern dynasties, possibly in the whole history of China. In his

Treatise on the Extinction of the Soul, he attacks the theory that the soul does not perish, the theoretical basis of Buddhism.

The problem of the relationship between matter and spirit, or body and soul, generated a long-time philosophical debate in China. As early as in the Warring States Period, the Jixia School, which upheld the doctrines of the Yellow Emperor and Laozi, regarded the body as the storehouse of essence: spirit is the finest matter that dwells in the body. Spirit may enter and leave the body all by itself. Spirit and body are separate entities. In the Eastern Han Dynasty, Huan Tan pushed this a step further with the proposition that "the spirit dwells in the body," comparing body and soul to a candle and its flame. Wang Chong inherited the concept, saying "The vital force needs the body to exert its function of perception." He regards the body as the foundation upon which spirit may play its role, that of knowing. He regards both knowledge and spirit as products of the body and maintained that no spirits wander outside it.

Before Fan Zhen, some lesser-known anti-Buddhists and leading scholars such as Sun Sheng (c. 306–378), Dai Kui (c. 330–395), and He Chengtian (370–447), denied that the soul survives when the body perishes. But all have a common shortcoming in that they fail to understand that spirit is a function and attribute of matter; they regard spirit as a special form of matter; and they treat spirit and matter as two juxtaposed substances. So they inevitably fall into a dualism in which body and spirit are disjointed. Their opponents seized on this, and waged a counter-attack. Their argument: When you claim that body and soul are like candle and flame, we can conclude that when the candle dies out, the flame can move to another.

In his *Treatise on the Extinction of the Soul*, Fan Zhen puts forth a new basic proposition that "body and soul are related." At the very beginning he states, "Soul is body, and body is soul. When the body exists, the soul exists; when the body perishes, the soul perishes." The word "related" in Fan Zhen's vocabulary has two meanings: "not separated from each other" (not to be cut apart) and "not different from each other" (not opposed to each other). Body and soul form an indivisible whole "that has different names but is one thing-in-itself." So, "when the body perishes, the soul perishes." He thus overcame the problem with comparing body and soul to a candle and its flame, routing the camp that maintained the soul does not perish with the body.

Fan Zhen draws a conclusion that contains two aspects. One is relative to the noumenon of body and soul, "they have different names but they are one thing-in-itself." The other is relative to the existing form of body and soul, that is, they are a unified whole. For the first time in the history of epistemology, someone established a monism of body and soul in line with materialism.

To the Buddhists, knowledge (spirit) is different from body. There can be no qualitative changes as things are not qualitatively different from one another. On this basis, the reason the body of a living man has a spiritual role is that knowledge or spirit exists independently of material bodies. The whole system of Buddhist theology is established on the basis of this very theory. Fan Zhen, however, through a dialectical analysis, affirms the variety of things, and claims that different materials express themselves in different functions. He says with respect to human beings:

"Now let's talk about the material of man. It is a material that has knowing ability, while the material of wood is a material that has no knowing ability." (*Treatise on the Extinction of the Soul*)

The spiritual activities of perceiving and thinking cannot depart from the physiological organs, which are material. In this way he demonstrates the monism of body and soul in line with the materialist tenet that spirit relies on matter, refuting the dualist separation of body and soul.

Fan Zhen stands at a level higher than his predecessors as he applies the relationship between "material and its function" to his demonstration that "Body and soul are relative," theoretically destroying the foundation on which Buddhist theology depends for its existence. It follows that Fan Zhen with his masterpiece occupies a position of particular importance in the developmental history of both materialism and atheism.

What is discussed above is not the total contribution Fan Zhen made to atheistic theory via *Treatise on the Extinction of the Soul*. In the field of human epistemology, Fan Zhen puts forth the pair of categories "material and function." By applying these, he solves the relationship issue between body and soul, and that between material and function, by showing how the latter is subordinate to the former—and also how different materials and their changes show that things have varieties and changes. As for the former, we see, for instance, wood and man; as for the latter, we see that a tree changes from growing to withering, a man from being alive to being dead. To Fan Zhen, the root cause is in matter per se. Compared with those of his forerunners, these ideas are highly original.

Fan Zhen's theoretical contributions are in most cases linked with his limitations. Being limited by historical conditions, his application of "material and function" and such categories is restricted to a comparatively narrow scope, focused on solving the relational problem of body and soul. His materialist monism of body and soul is mechanistic, appearing especially incompetent when he explains social phenomena. At last, he falls into determinism.

On the problem of how to treat the difference between "mortals" and "sages," he also departs from the sociality of man. He mistakenly affirms that the difference between mortals and sages is their supposedly different physiological organs. He does not understand that the thinking ability of man develops in the main through social practice, although physiology may exert some influence.

19.

Development of Buddhist Philosophy in the Sui–Tang Period

Buddhist philosophy, which spread widely in China in the period of the Eastern Jin and Northern and Southern Dynasties, enjoyed unprecedented development and prosperity in the Sui–Tang Period (581–907). Furthermore, it progressed toward systemization and Sinification.

All Buddhist sects in the Sui–Tang Period originated in the Mahayana tradition. Mahayana is divided into two schools, Madhyamika and Yogacara. Chinese Buddhism in this period not only developed the theories of the Indian sects but also continued to advance along the path of Sinicization pioneered by Seng Zhao, Huiyuan, Daosheng, and others.

Seven hundred years after the death of Sakymuni, Nagarjuna (c. 150–250) appeared in the Kingdom of Andhra in southern India. Based on new sutras, he founded Madhyamika in the Mahayana tradition, teaching that the myriad things and myriad affairs are nothing but "the sunya" (void). Great thinkers appeared in the fourth and fifth centuries in the Kingdom of Gandhara in northern India. Following the teachings of Nagarjuna and Maitreya (c. 270–350, a master of Buddhist discourse in the Mahayana tradition), Asanga, Vasubandhu, and others set up the Yogacara Sect of the Mahayana tradition. Its speculative features are the use of the analysis of names and the phases of how things come into being to demonstrate that the realistic world is an illusion of vijnana (consciousness). Both the Madhymika Sect started by Nagarjuna and the Yogacara Sect of Asanga and Vasubandhu transform Buddhism from a religion into a philosophy.

A large number of sutras and treatises on Indian Buddhism in line with the Mahayana tradition were translated into Chinese in the Eastern Jin Dynasty and later. Among the famous translators were Kumarajiva (344–413), Buddhabhadra (359–429), and Paramartha (499–569). New translations were immediately spread all over the country. Prajna studies, nirvana studies, and specialized research into the Buddhist classics and treatises thrived.

Theoretical research was in accordance with the academic atmospheres in both north and south China. Buddhism in the north tended to pay more attention to dhyana (*chan* in Chinese) and samadhi, and therefore was called "Chan Buddhism." "Analytical Buddhism" in the south focused more on the explanation of the classics and treatises and analysis of theories, for it was the melding of two ideological trends, the doctrine of prajna and Metaphysics.

By the Sui–Tang Period, the country was once again unified, and a gradual synthesis took place between southern and northern Chinese Buddhism. However, various monasteries and orders of Buddhism were attached to different social foundations, and a number of sects developed while society was undergoing upheavals in the new era.

The most successful of the Chinese Buddhist sects were the Avatamsaka (*huayan-zong*) and the Chan. Both did the most to combine Buddhist theories with traditional Chinese thought.

Buddhist philosophy in the Sui-Tang period was centered on self-consciousness—the self-contemplation of consciousness, speculation in line with relativism, and demonstration-realization in line with intuitionism. Their combination constitutes the general speculative structure of Buddhist philosophy in this era.

The ontology of Buddhist philosophy denies that the realistic world is unified in matter and that it is an objective reality. Instead, it affirms that behind the relative and realistic phenomena is an absolute "thing-in-itself" that surpasses reality. Such a "thing-in-itself" is endowed with a certain property of mysticism. "It is neither being nor nonbeing," "It is neither the constant nor the interrupted," "It is neither birth nor death," "It is neither the same nor different." Similar descriptions are numerous. Generally speaking, the final goal of Buddhism in the Sui-Tang Period is "demonstrating tathata" or "entering Nirvana."

Methodologically speaking, Buddhist philosophy in this period is characterized by unfolding speculation in line with relativism. On the one hand, it denies that the objective world is a realistic existence by saying that the myriad things do not have their own attributions. On the other, it denies that human cognitive ability is reliable by emphasizing that only by surpassing human understanding and logic can man achieve the demonstration-realization of the thing-in-itself.

This thinking method is quite different from that of Western philosophy.

The Avatamsaka (*huayan*) Sect sets forth its fundamental teachings according to the *Garland Sutra*, the abbreviation of which sounds like "*huayan*" in Chinese. In the Northern and Southern Dynasties, some masters of the dasabhumika-sastra school headed by Huiguang began to study the *Garland Sutra*, and gradually formed a research center on Mount Zhongnan. During the reign of Empress Wu, Fazang (643–712) finally completed the Avatamsaka system of philosophical thought. Studying his predecessors, he synthesized the theories of various Chinese Buddhist sects, blended the theories of the Indian Madhyamika and Yogacara schools into one, and formed a Buddhist theory perfectly in accordance with the Chinese mode of thinking.

Fazang, who once worked as a translator under the famous monk Xuanzang, gave a lecture on the *Garland Sutra* to Empress Wu Zetian (c. 627–705), who then conferred the title of "First Sage National Mentor" upon him. Fazang taught the theory of conditional causation of dharmadhatu, which centers on the relationship between "the principle and the affair."

In the Sui-Tang Period, the newly emerging sects of Buddhism all advanced their own theories on how to differentiate the Buddhist teachings, which appeared then as scriptures, classics, treatises, and a multitude of commentaries and notes. The differentiation of the teachings sheds light on the intellectual history of Buddhism in China.

Fazang puts forth his own system of differentiation, which dwells on the "five teachings" and "ten schools." He calls the Avatamsaka Sect the "Perfect Doctrine," and the other schools and sects "deviated doctrines." Furthermore, he divides the schools and sects of Buddhism into five degrees, according to stage of development:

One, the Doctrine of the Aprabuddha-Dharmas and Sravaka, namely, the doctrine of foolish laws and from hearers, refers to the schools and sects of the Hinayana tradition.

Two, the Primary Stage of the Mahayana Doctrine refers to the schools and sects of Prajna-Madhyamika, which preach that Nature is void.

Three, the Final Stage of the Mahayana Doctrine refers to the schools and sects of Yogacara, is based on the *Mahayana-Sraddhotpada-Sastra* and maintain that tathata is constant and dwells in one and the same place.

Four, the Mahayana Doctrine of Immediate Enlightenment refers to the schools and sects based on the *Vimalakirti-Nirdesa-Sutra* that claim that the identity of all things is beyond description either by words or by diagrams.

Five, the Perfect Doctrine of One Vehicle refers to Avatamsaka doctrines.

Then Fazang divides all the schools and sects into "ten schools," according to the grades of the universal truths they pursue. The first six belong to the Hinayana tradition.

One, the School of the Reality of Self and Things, which advocates that both man and the myriad things are real beings.

Two, the School of the Reality of Things and the Non-Reality of the Self.

Three, the School That Denies the Creation and Destruction of Things.

Four, the School of the Apparentness and Reality of Things.

Five, the School of the Fallacy of Phenomenal Ideas.

Six, the Truth of Fundamental Reality and School Identifying Things as Mere Names.

Seven, the School of the Non-Reality of All Things, which advocates that the myriad things are void by their own natures.

Eight, the School of the Reality of Bhutathata, teaching that tathata is constant for all eternity.

Nine, the School of the Untruthfulness of Phenomena and Perception, which advocates that it is necessary to get rid of all intentions and illusions.

Ten, the All-inclusive and Complete School of Perfect Enlightenment, the Avatamsaka School, holding that all things are in harmony with one another and there is no hindrance between things.

Fazang's classification is different from the previous one of "three periods" and "five stages," all based on historical succession. Fazang does his best to use a logical method to unify the contradictions of the various schools—and to put the development of Buddhist theories into a rational process, namely, from "small" to "big," from "the initial" to "the final," from "the gradual" to "the immediate" and from "the deviated" to "the perfect." Of all these schools and sects, the Prajna Sect focuses on "sunya (void)" and the Vijnaptimatra Sect on "sat (being)." As for the final, the immediate, and the perfect, they focus on and synthesize both the void and being. The small, the big, and the initial belong to the gradual doctrine that uses words as the means to teach people. Later, the Buddhist doctrine develops to the immediate degree, which refuses to use any words as the means to teach people. Finally, the Buddhist doctrine reaches its supreme degree in the teachings of the Avatamsaka Sect, which synthesizes the gradual and the immediate.

Zongmi, called the fifth founder of the Avatamsaka Sect, follows the reasoning of Fazang in his *Man in the Teachings of the Garland Sutra* and divides Buddhism into five classes.

One, Man-Heaven Teaching, which refers to all the Indian doctrines about causality.

Two, Hinayana, which is marked by corporeal-mental dualism.

Three, Mahayana Dharmalaksana, which affirms that "consciousness is the foundation of body" and consciousness is reality.

Four, Mahayana Teaching to Break Aspects, which maintains that "both mind and circumstances are void."

Five, Ekayana Teaching to Show Nature, the theory of the Avatamsaka Sect.

Zongmi thinks that Confucianism, Taoism, and the first four teachings of Buddhism have put forth some true views, yet all are inferior to the Avatamsaka doctrines.

The Avatamsaka Sect puts forth a concept about the "one true dharmadhatu" ("realm of things"). Within this indistinct and abstract "existence (dharmadhatu)," all things express themselves as an interrelated relationship, interdependent, mutually transformational, mutually inclusive, and mutually identifiable. As such, there are no genuine differences at all in this world. The myriad phenomena in the universe are described as a vast number of "illusions"; everything is conditionally the cause of every other thing, and all things are in perfect harmony. In Buddhist circles at that time, there were three explanations the causes of these "illusions":

One, the conditional cause relative to retribution for karma (Hinayana). All beings act. Action produces karma, and the karma of all beings forms the body, the mind, and the world.

Two, the conditional cause relative to storage consciousness (Dharmalaksana Sect Mahayana). The bija (seed) stored in alaya-vijnana (storehouse of consciousness) becomes the external circumstances, namely, the realistic world.

Three, the conditional cause relative to bhutatathata (Dharmata Sect, Mahayana). The thing-in-itself, bhutatathata, transcends the phenomenal sphere, and in some conditions produces the myriad things.

The Avatamsaka Sect preaches a doctrine of conditional cause relative to dharmadhatu, in which "all things are mixed together, and every thing is the cause of every other thing." It also maintains that "the one is the all, and the all is the one," that "all things are linked together and each thing enters every other," and that "the multitude of things overlap, layer upon layer," also called the "endless conditional cause." In other words, the world is a general illusion, a boundless network of various relationships in which there are no independent entities.

The Avatamsaka Sect regards this theory as a basic premise for solving the problem of the relationship between thing-in-itself and phenomena. The doctrine of the "four dharmadhatus" is the theoretical core of the Avatamsaka Sect. Zongmi explains it as follows:

> "As a general term, we say that the only one true dharmadhatu contains the myriad things. But the human mind may melt the myriad things, so there are four dharmadhatus. The first is the dharmadhatu of facts. Distinction characterizes this realm in which everything is clearly different from everything else. The second is the dharmadhatu of principles. Property characterizes this realm, in which there are so many things that nobody can exhaust them. The third is the dharmadhatu of no hindrance between facts and principles. Property and difference characterize this realm, in which property and difference are used to recognize it. The fourth is the dharmadhatu of

no hindrance among facts. In this realm there are differences, unification, facts, and laws. All things are in perfect harmony as their own nature demands, and all things are linked together and each thing enters each other thing." (*Notes on the Observation Door to the Dharmadhatu of the Avatamsaka Sect*)

That is to say, the myriad things in the universe originally come from what is conditionally caused by the mind of man.

The Avatamsaka Sect often uses the metaphor of "water and waves" to express the relationship between principle and fact: the universe is like a great sea in which the waves are rolling along in succession, but every wave is different from every other, and this is called the "dharmadhatu of facts." In a boundless expanse of blue water every drop is nothing but water, and this is called the "dharmadhatu of principles." Water and waves are mixed together so perfectly that one cannot tell the water from the waves, nor the waves from the water, and this is called the "dharmadhatu in which facts and the principle do not hinder each other." One wave is connected to another wave, this wave contains that wave, and vice versa, and this is called the "dharmadhatu in which all facts do not hinder one another."

All these metaphors and explanations serve only one purpose, that of solving the problem of the relationship between the noumenon and the phenomenal world. In the view of the Avatamsaka Sect, noumenon cannot be put opposite any phenomenon, nor can it be put outside any phenomenon. Noumenon and phenomenon should so coincide that they may be regarded as an identical body in which there are no differences. We can say that such a view reaches the realm in which "the base and application come from one and the same origin, and between the obvious and the obscure there is no gap at all."

"Facts do not hinder one another." In respect to the "dharmadhatu of facts," the Avatamsaka Sect put forth a series of topics, of which the most important are as follows: "The unity of all phenomena is as viewed from six characteristics." "The one and the many depend on each other and hold each other." "Different bodies are connected." "Different doors lead to one another." By seeking for the mutually containing and mutually absorbing relations among things, the Sect exerts great efforts to attribute all differences to identity.

"The unity of all phenomena is as viewed from six characteristics." According to this statement, the myriad things in the universe may be generalized into six characteristics ranked in three pairs: the general characteristics (entirety) versus the partial characteristics (parts); the identical characteristics (universals) versus the different characteristics (particulars); and the depending characteristics (interdependence) versus the destroying characteristics (respective independence). The two sides of every pair are interdependent while being opposite each other. They are treated as two sides that may be merged into one entirety, and in this entirety there are absolutely no differences. Fazang says as follows:

> "If there are no parts, there cannot be an entirety. This is because an entirety needs parts to form it. And why is this? In the final analysis, it is of parts that the entirety is made up. This may be viewed in the opposite way. When there are no parts, the entirety finds no reason to be an entirety. Therefore, we may say that the so-called parts are made up of the entirety too." (*Huayan's View of the Buddhist Schools and Sects*)

Let us return to the series of topics. "Unity of all phenomena is as viewed from six characteristics." "The one and the many lead each to other." "Things are connected with one another and things enter one another." All these statements are directed simply to this point:

"It is obvious that all dharmas are to be viewed from the mind alone. Apart from the mind, there is nothing that has its own existence. Because of this, both big and small turn round and round by following orders from the mind. Since it is so, there cannot be any hindrance when one thing enters another." (*The Aim of the Garland Sutra*)

The myriad things in the world are nothing but illusions caused by ideas that have flashed into man's mind. Although this is true, many foolish people obstinately cling to the illusion. Once such obstinacy is cut off from the human mind, the world becomes perfect, with no obstruction. The soul of man, then, will go and come in perfect freedom.

"Facts and the principle do not hinder each other." "Principle" is a category the Avatamsaka Sect postulates in opposition to the category of "facts," an old proposition of ontology from Metaphysics. In the philosophy of the Avatamsaka Sect, "facts" do not mean the real things that exist in the objective world; instead, "facts" refer to illusions that come from conditional causes according to the law that "things turn round and round following orders from the mind."

But the facts differ in thousands of ways, they are distributed in different places, and they are in different positions. Whether they all manifest the whole of the principle or each of them manifests only a part of the principle, this remains a question unresolved. In fact, this is the problem of "one principle manifesting itself as many." Fazang's solution is as follows:

> "As for facts, there are no particular facts. Whatever completely embodies the principle is a fact.... As I have said, there are neither facts nor things that are different from the principle. Therefore, facts become completely perfect only when they follow the principle. Since it is so, let a speck of dust embody the universal dharmadhatu. When the law of the whole dharmadhatu runs through all things, the function of this speck of dust is the same as that of the principle. This is because it expresses itself completely in all things." (*The Garland Sutra Shows Bodhi-Citta*)

"The principle" is a unique whole. What is manifested in every fact and phenomenon is the unique and sacred principle. As for each of the affairs, which differ in thousands of ways, it is also a perfect manifestation of the unique and sacred principle. Therefore, the principle and the facts do not hinder each other. As for facts, they do not hinder one another, either.

Fazang says the principle is the mind, which is not only the "mind" of the subjective cognition, to which the "dust" stands in opposition, but also the "true mind," in which the whole "sole and true dharmadhatu" is manifested, a pure and perfectly harmonious state that transcends both subject and object.

According to the Avatamsaka Sect, "to become a Buddha" means getting rid of all absurd ideas and vain hopes, so that the source of one's "true mind" may manifest. Only when the illusions of all beings are gone may humans treat the world with their "original consciousness and true mind." Although the old still has the old look, such phenomena as the old differences, contradictions, conflicts, inequalities, and disharmonies now disappear, and a perfect and harmonious world comes into view. In this world, there are neither differences nor contradictions. In this world, all people, all things, and all relationships are mutually coordinated. In short, there is perfection, and there is no hindrance.

Since the philosophy of the Avatamsaka Sect is the quintessence of both Chinese and Indian Buddhist philosophies, among all the schools and sects of Buddhism in China, it became the school most possessed of theoretical system and depth. It is brilliantly characterized by its theoretical system, thinking route, formulation of topics, and application of categories. All these provided the ideological sources for the Neo-Confucianism of the Song and Ming dynasties, and especially for the Cheng-Zhu Idealist School.

The Chan Sect, which arose in the mid-Tang Period, is another typical example of Buddhist philosophy that sprang from Chinese soil. It exerted a particularly wide and profound influence upon the development of philosophy in the later feudal period. As a religious movement, it arose almost at the same time as the Avatamsaka Sect, and the two became one. Translations into Chinese of the sutras, scriptures, notes, comments, and commentaries on them became more numerous as time went by. By the time of Empress Wu (ca. 684–701) of the Tang Dynasty, there were 3,616 sutras in 4,841 volumes. Those who wanted to know something about Buddhism had first of all to be an expert or a scholar. In reaction to this, there arose an ideological trend to make the religion secular. The Chan Sect devised slogans such as "Your mind is the Buddha," "Perceive your nature, and you become a Buddha," "The moment you hear the word, you will attain sudden enlightenment." The Southern Chan School, in a bold way, undid the bondage of dogmas culled from the scriptures and religious ceremonies. Chan monks and congregations paid no attention to reading scriptures while worshiping the Buddha and sitting in meditation. The instruction to "point directly to the human mind" was a new, unsophisticated technique for teaching.

The Chan Sect is devoted in particular to Bodhidharma (ca. 460–534), who came to China in the reign of Emperor Wu (502–547). He advocated a new technique of dhyana, characterized by the parallelism of "entering Buddhism by understanding the principles" and "entering Buddhism by means of religious practices." The Chan Sect cultivated the essence of Buddhism in the genuine sense. In practice, the sect owes an obvious ideological debt to Daosheng, who lived in the Northern and Southern Dynasties period and advocated "entering Nirvana to acquire the Buddha nature" and "becoming a Buddha by sudden enlightenment." The Chan School inherits both these theories, further develops them, and builds up a unique system of Chinese Buddhist philosophy.

The process by which dhyana, originally a method of religious practice, became a religious school may be traced back to a monk named Hongren (601–674), who lived in the early years of the Tang. He opened the East Mountain Dharma Door in a monastery in Huangmei, Hubei Province. Hongren had converted to the belief of the *Diamond Sutra*. His disciple Shenxiu (605?–706) became a celebrated Chan master in the reign of Empress Wu, and was honored as the "Lord of the Law at the Two National Capitals of Chang'an and Luoyang, and the Teacher of Three Sovereigns." Very active at the time, Shenxiu headed the "Northern School" of the Chan movement. His disciple Huineng (638–713) was active mainly around Guangdong and headed the "Southern School," which was further developed by his disciple Shenhui (683–760). Chan soon spread all over the country.

The Chan Sect directed a series of "renovations" of Buddhist theories, merging traditional Chinese thought with Buddhism. As a result, Buddhism was further Sinicized and secularized. It shook off its traditional hair-splitting scholasticism and minute explanation of certain words and sentences. Buddhism turned from speculative reasoning to intuitive realization. With respect to theory, the Chan Sect focused on the ontology of mind, namely, the Thus-ness or the True Reality. With respect to practice, Chan adopted a new technique of cultivation, that is, "becoming a Buddha by sudden enlightenment." In this way, it upholds the banner of Chan as a formal Buddhist sect.

Chan ontology is encapsulated thusly: "The mind is the *bhutatathata* (true reality)." "Buddha nature" is the original nature by the attainment of which everybody may become a Buddha and is roughly equivalent to noumenon in Western philosophy. Buddha nature is the most fundamental problem for all schools and sects of Buddhism. Within the Chan Sect, Huineng's school tackled this problem with the most vigor, concluding that the "mind" is just the "thing-in-itself." Outside the "mind" there is nothing that may be called "thing-in-itself." Everything in the realistic world relies on the "mind." Huineng says, "When mental activity begins, the various things come into being. When mental activity ceases, the various things cease to exist. When there is not a single idea that springs up in the human mind, it is impossible to have the myriad ten thousand things." (*Platform Scripture of the Sixth Patriarch Huineng·Chapter 10: His Final Instruction*)

Huineng says, "Since the myriad things are right here in your mind, why don't you seek the True Reality in your own mind by way of sudden enlightenment?" As for the myriad things, whether they are in opposition to the human mind or complete and free depends on the mind itself. When one has any idea, opposition immediately comes into being, and the mind is bound to it. When not a single idea enters the mind, the opposition is immediately gone, and the mind becomes free. Freedom of mind is the presence of the noumenon, so by that time one has already become a Buddha.

"When you are mindless here and now, the thing-in-itself will appear all by itself." This is the Chan Sect ontology, from which is derived the methodology (the doctrine about getting rid of worldly sufferings) of "becoming a Buddha by sudden enlightenment."

Zhu Daosheng, who advocated the doctrine of "becoming a Buddha by sudden enlightenment," spoke of bhutatathata (true reality) and Buddha nature, namely, the absolute spiritual noumenon that is outside the human mind and stands in opposition to it.

Huineng's school of the Chan Sect inherits this mode of thinking, but transforms it into a certain state of mind that comes very naturally. This natural state cannot be acquired via any theory of knowledge, as all are bound by the sphere of logic, which always limits human cognition within oppositions such as right and wrong, good and evil, beautiful and ugly. In opposition, the human mind cannot be at liberty. So, only by sudden enlightenment can one become a Buddha. Because of this, some thinkers of the Chan Sect put forth a more radical view: Not only is the common people's cognition and judgment of reality "a surplus differentiation" or "turning the root and the trunk upside down," but also all the dogmas of Buddhism, once they are spoken, become rubbish. They say, "Any truth, once it is spoken, leaves traces of words. And traces of words are nothing but dross." So, we cannot help asking, what is "sudden enlightenment"? Sudden enlightenment is a concept that cannot be directly stipulated. Beyond words, it can only be described allegorically.

Sudden enlightenment includes two aspects: the total disappearance of all worldly fatigues and vain hopes, and the instant total incarnation of the noumenon of True Reality. Nevertheless, both in theory and practice the Chan Sect faces a contradiction: The unutterable dharma has to be uttered to preach Buddhism. To solve this contradiction, from the mid-Tang period on, impromptu methods of preaching Buddhism were created. Of these, some were famous: "the shout of the Linji Sect," "the stick of the Deshan Monk," "the cake of the Yunmen Sect," and "the tea of the Zhouzhou Monk"—threads of discourse by which all beings might conveniently understand Buddha's teachings. Yet once human beings understand Buddha's teachings, they must discard them immediately. From that time onwards the Chan Sect entered a more mysterious period of pondering over the thread of discourse and struggling to come up with witty and incisive remarks.

Of all Buddhist sects in China, the Chan had the greatest influence. In the later period of Chinese feudal society, both the Cheng-Zhu Principle School and the Lu-Wang Mind School directly take over important speculation materials from the Chan–Avatamsaka sects, which basically fused after the Tang Dynasty. Moreover, almost all aspects of Chinese culture in the later periods were profoundly influenced by the Chan school. In literature, in painting, and even in the national psychology we find its imprint. We may well say that without an understanding of the Chan teachings, nobody is able to know the Chinese people and Chinese culture in a truly comprehensive way.

The Chan Sect has a tendency toward extremist development, which leads it to self-contradiction and self-negation. By doing its best to shorten the distance between the Buddhist paradise and the human world, to put "Buddha" in the hearts of the people, and to proclaim "the common people are Buddha," Chan blurs the surrealist essence of Buddhism as a religion. And by emphasizing mysterious self-demonstration, sudden enlightenment, and self-experience, and by denying the authority of the Buddhist scriptures, Chan weakens the significance of the religious cultivation and teachings of Buddhism, and objectively lowers its social functions. Such is the Chan Sect that its methodology of advocating the "thread of discourse," "gong-an,"[1] and "witty and incisive remarks" led to internalization of the evaluation criteria. The mish-mash of methods and teachings espoused by the Chan Sect finally brought about the decline of Buddhism and its theories in China.

20.

Return to Confucian Orthodoxy: Han Yu and Li Ao

Han Yu (768-824) was a native of Nanyang County, Dengzhou Prefecture (Nanyang City, Henan Province). Since the Han clan had been influential in the prefecture of Changli, he was also called "Changli's Han Yu" or simply, "Han (of) Changli." He was a famous man of letters in the Tang Dynasty, who, together with others, championed the Classical Prose Movement. He was also a forerunner of Neo-Confucianism, which flourished in the Song and Ming dynasties. His writings were compiled into the *Collected Works of Han Changli*, of which the most important parts are *An Inquiry into Man*, *An Inquiry into the Way*, *An Inquiry into Human Nature,* and *An Inquiry into Ghosts*.

Li Ao (772–841), a native of Longxi (Wuwei County, Gansu Province), was a disciple of Han Yu and once served as a senior local official. His writings were compiled into the *Collected Works of the Reverend Li, the Literary Prince*, of which *The Recovery of Nature* best represents his philosophical thought.

In an effort to reassert the authority of Confucianism and combat the influence of Buddhism, which had enshrined a set of patriarchs who had transmitted Buddhist teachings, Han Yu matched them with a set of Confucian patriarchs who had done the same.

An Inquiry on Man sets out the general program of Han Yu's philosophical thought. In this essay, a generalization of the "Way" as the supreme category is made, which includes the Way of Heaven, the Way of

Earth, and the Way of Man. In his main philosophical essays, *An Inquiry into the Way*, the focus is on the Way of Man, which may be regarded as a supplement to and development of the general program.

The connotation of the "Way" is the feudal codes of ethics and morality rendered abstract: "When the Way of Heaven is in disorder, the sun, the moon and the stars cannot travel in their normal orbits. When the Way of Earth is in disorder, the grasses, trees, mountains and rivers cannot work smoothly. When the Way of Man is in disorder, the tribes living in the border regions, and the beasts and the birds cannot find proper expression for their feelings. Heaven is the lord of the sun, the moon and the stars. Earth is the lord of the grasses, trees, mountains and rivers. The nation living in the Central Kingdom is the lord of the tribes living in the border regions and of the beasts and the birds. When the lord is violent, he loses the Way to be the lord. Therefore, the saint extends the same treatment to all: He is kind to those near to him and elevates those far from him too." (*An Inquiry into Man*)

The Way upheld by Han Yu has shifted from the Mandate of Heaven, which is centered on the divine right of the ruler, to ethical norms, which are centered on moral principles.

When Han Yu discusses the Way of Man in *An Inquiry into Man*, he emphasizes the difference between Chinese people and those of other countries with an intent to combat the ideas of Buddhism and Taoism, for the former is a religion of a foreign people and the latter talks about immortal beings. He defines the concrete connotation of the Way as "humanity and righteousness":

"Humanity and righteousness are definite values, whereas the Way and virtue have no substance in themselves but depend on humanity and righteousness for it. . . . What I call the Way and virtue always involve both humanity and righteousness." (*An Inquiry into the Way*)

In his opinion, humanity lies on the inside, while righteousness is manifested in action, and to do something according to the principle of both humanity and righteousness is the "Way." Han Yu's concept of the Way does not match what Buddhists and Taoists mean by the term.

In Han Yu's opinion, Buddhism and Taoism preach the discarding of humanity and righteousness—and in so doing abolish the authority of father and monarch, in their world-renouncing way. Quite contrary to this, the Way Han Yu struggles to reach is the Confucian Way "sound both in theory and practice," namely, in the internal aspect, one learns from the saints—and in the external aspect, one helps the monarch rule the country well. Concretely speaking, in one's inner life one should "have rectitude of mind and propriety of intention"—and in social practice one should "run the government well and bring peace to the whole country."

> "The *Record* says, 'The ancients who wished to manifest their clear character to the world would first bring order to their states. Those who wished to bring order to their states would first regulate their families. Those who wished to regulate their families would first cultivate their personal lives. Those who wished to cultivate their personal lives would first rectify their minds. Those who wished to rectify their minds would first make their wills sincere.' Thus what the ancients meant by rectifying the mind and making the will sincere was to engage in activity (as against the principle of inaction of the Taoists and Buddhists)." (*An Inquiry into the Way*)

Han Yu constructs a Confucian "orthodoxy of the Way" to counter the Buddhist "orthodoxy of the patriarchs." "The Way of the former kings" started at "the very beginning" with Emperor Yao, and it was transmitted through his successors down to the Duke of Zhou, Confucius, and ending with Mencius (*An Inquiry into the Way*).

Therefore, Han Yu chooses to take up the great mission of transmitting and spreading the Confucian orthodoxy of the Way so that genuine Confucianism may be restored and carried forward.

In form, the Confucian orthodoxy of the Way advocated by Han Yu is nothing more than an imitation of the Buddhist orthodoxy of patriarchs. In theory, his theory of the orthodoxy of the Way lays more stress on symbolizing the Confucian stance, which is differentiated from Buddhism and Taoism, than on the systematic rectification of the Confucian orthodoxy of the Way per se. As far as function is concerned, his theory of the Confucian orthodoxy of the Way aroused the enthusiasm of Confucian scholars of later ages, and many actively opposed Buddhism and Taoism.

On the problem of human nature, in Han Yu's view, if one is endowed with inborn "humanity," one belongs to the superior grade. Without such "humanity," one belongs to the inferior grade. While the superior grade can be improved through education, the inferior nature can only be controlled; both grades are essentially unchangeable (Cf. *An Inquiry into the Way*).

Han Yu thinks society needs men of superior feelings (namely the saints), for they can start an undertaking and transmit the orthodoxy from generation to generation:

> "In the remote past there were more things that might do harm to man than nowadays. Fortunately, some saint emerged who taught the people the Way to live and to multiply. He became their ruler and their teacher, and drove away the snakes, wild birds, and beasts for them, so that the people might live in the middle region of the earth. When it was getting cold, he made clothes for them. When they were going hungry, he provided them with food. At that time, some people lived in the treetops, which was not very safe. Some people lived on the damp ground, and were prone to illness. The saint taught them how to build houses, and even palaces. He also taught them to make implements for everyday use. He taught them to do business so that each might make what the other lacked. He taught them medicine, so that they might avoid an early death. He taught them how to bury the dead and offer sacrifices to the ancestors, so that kindness and love might increase. He set up the rites, so that they might know who should go first and who next. He invented music, so that they might vent what had accumulated in their hearts. He administered them, so that they would not be lazy. He made laws, so that violence would be punished. Later, fraudulent conduct occurred among people, and the saint made tallies, seals, counterpoises, and weighing apparatuses, so that they might be true to their word. When struggles took place among the people, the saint taught them to build cities and to make weapons so that they might defend themselves. In short when any harm came, the saint averted them on behalf of the people; when disasters occurred, the saint cleared them up for the people. If in the remote past there had been no saint, mankind would have perished long ago." (*An Inquiry into Man*)

When Han Yu discusses the problem concretely, he shows his strong dissatisfaction with the behavior of man who, since he came to this world, has been breaking the great harmony of the yin and yang in the universe all the time. And he expresses his hope in a clear and definite way:

"If people would do less harm to the vital force and to yin and yang, it would be equal to doing a meritorious service to Heaven and Earth. But if such people propagate, they will surely become the enemy of Heaven and Earth." In this way, Han Yu protests against the typical approach of his time, that man should seek to conquer Nature. Instead, he maintains that man should live in harmony with Nature. In this, Han Yu's view coincides with the ecological philosophy that is in full bloom today.

With his theory of the Confucian orthodoxy of the Way, Han Yu strikes a blow at Buddhism and Taoism, with their patriarchs and immortals. He opposes the doctrine of renouncing this world by applying feudal ethics to the evaluation of religions. He points out that the spread of Buddhism and Taoism is detrimental to social production.

Nevertheless, his theory of the Confucian orthodoxy of the Way fails to touch the essence of Buddhism and Taoism. Careful examination shows us Han Yu even gets inspiration from these two religions. On the whole, no matter how many shortcomings may be found in his thought, in the history of the development of Chinese philosophy, Han Yu's theory of the Confucian orthodoxy of the Way is a vital link. It carries on the heritage of the past and opens up the future. By two routes, Han Yu solidifies his new theory. He renders natural laws as ethical ones, and renders feudal ethics as something *a priori*. Neo-Confucianism, which mounted the ideological stage in the Song Dynasty, came into being by taking advantage of Han Yu's theory.

Li Ao, faithful disciple and foremost exponent of Han Yu, inherited and developed Han Yu's theory of human nature. Similar to Han Yu, he thinks there are two aspects to human nature, one being man's nature, the other his feelings. Of these, man's nature is the main aspect, which expresses itself through feelings both derived from and dependent upon his nature.

As regards the origin of this "nature," he sees it as an inborn gift. As regards the good and the evil of "nature," Li Ao points out, "The nature of all people is originally good." (*The Recovery of Man's Nature· Part One*)

Be he a "saint" or a "vulgar person," his "nature" is equally good. In this aspect, he differs from Han Yu. For instance, Li Ao thinks that the nature of people of the superior grade is good, whereas the nature of people of the inferior grade is evil. But on some problems Han Yu is more thoroughgoing than Li Ao. This is revealed in *An Inquiry into Man*, where he thinks that only if an existence possesses "humanity," can it have the nature of goodness, no matter what it may be —the sun, moon and stars, or the grasses, trees, mountains, and rivers.

As Li Ao acknowledges that "the nature of all people is originally good," and that "feelings originate from the nature," we might expect him logically to conclude that everybody has good feelings. But in his opinion all feelings are evil. Why is this? According to his view, feelings are the activation of a person's nature. When vulgar people become active, abandoning the state of their original nature, which is silent and still, they are not able to keep the way of the mean any longer, so their feelings become evil. Therefore, only by returning to the state of "silence and stillness" can one recover the good state of one's original nature. Here, Li Ao is surely influenced by the theory of the Buddha-nature.

His theory of the opposition of man's nature and feelings, clearly Buddhist, is also the fountainhead of the doctrine of "maintaining Heavenly principles and eradicating human desires," one repeatedly discussed by Neo-Confucian philosophers of the Song and Ming dynasties.

The theories of human nature put forth by Li Ao and Han Yu are the same in that both are established on the basis of apriorism. Li Ao pursues the original nature of "purity," considering "purity" to be the basis of humanity and righteousness, deepening Han Yu's view that humanity and righteousness are the nature of man. According to Li Ao, anyone can become a saint by discarding feelings and recovering his or her true nature.

The mid-Tang period in which Han Yu and Li Ao lived saw Chinese Buddhism reach its zenith, and witnessed the emergence of a number of new and important sects. In this period, the fusion of elements of Buddhist, Taoist, and Confucian thought had a marked influence on Chinese philosophy. The beginning of such a fusion can be traced as far back as Sima Chengzhen (647–735), who founded the school of aristocratic Taoism. Bai Juyi (772–846), a leading Tang poet, claimed there were no fundamental differences between Confucianism and Buddhism (*The Complete Works of Bai Compiled in the Changqing Reign Period*).

In a more concrete way, Zongmi (780–841), an eminent Buddhist monk, linked the Confucius, Laozi, and Sakyamuni as supreme saints who founded different religions, any of which are suitable to follow (*Man in the Teachings of the Garland Sutra*).Han Yu went against the trend of the time by opposing both Buddhism and Taoism. His attacks on Buddhism as a foreign religion raised the ire of Emperor Xianzong; he barely escaped execution and was banished from court. In his defense of orthodox Confucianism, Han Yu borrowed much from both Buddhism and Taoism. As a result, he failed to carry his struggle against Buddhism to a satisfactory conclusion. His disciple Li Ao, both in his theoretical construction and concrete views, accepts even more from the Buddhist philosophy than his teacher.

Still, Han Yu is a great personage in Chinese history. The poet Su Shi (Su Dongpo, 1037–1101) praised him enthusiastically:

"He spearheaded a literary resurgence after a decline which had lasted for eight dynasties preceding the Tang Dynasty, and upheld the Way to save the whole country from being drowned in the foreign religion of Buddhism." (*Temple Inscription to Han the Literary Prince of Chaozhou*)

The Classical Prose Movement championed by Han Yu started a style of literature for a new era. It exerted a wide and profound influence upon the history of Chinese literature. In philosophy, he revived the theory of the Mandate of Heaven. By adopting the Buddhist practice of scriptural research, he ascertained the Confucian orthodoxy of the Way, and ushered Confucian thought into a period of systemization and genealogy. His system, known as Neo-Confucianism, formed the basis of the deification of Confucius and the adoption of the traditional ideas of Confucianism as the state creed in the following Song Dynasty. On the basis of Han Yu's thought, Li Ao went a step further by putting "the recovery of human nature" into the center of Neo-Confucianism.

21.

Atheism and Nature: Liu Zongyuan and Liu Yuxi

In the history of Chinese philosophy, Liu Zongyuan and Liu Yuxi are outstanding both for their contributions to theory and their practical efforts in political life to improve society. They challenged the theological world outlook centered on the Mandate of Heaven, and summed up the long-term controversy over the relationship between Heaven and Man, which had raged since pre-Qin times. They contributed a great deal to the development of atheism in China.

Liu Zongyuan (773–819) was a native of Yongji, Shanxi Province. Liu Yuxi (772–842) was a native of Luoyang. In the mid-Tang period, the earlier stage of Chinese feudalism was on the decline and various social contradictions became sharp. Both men were leading figures in the "Yongzhen Reform" movement, which started in the first year (805) of the Yongzhen reign of Tang Emperor Shunzong. This 146-day political movement—aimed to wrest power from the eunuchs and generals who had usurped it—was crushed. Reformers were either killed or banished from the court. Liu Zongyuan and Liu Yuxi, both banished, wrote their most important works during their long days in exile. Liu Zongyuan's writings were compiled into the *Collection of Liu from East of the River*; Liu Yuxi's writings, the *Collection of Liu, the Guest of the Crown Prince.*

Liu Zongyuan addressed the main problems of the ancient Chinese philosophers—the relationship between Heaven and Man, the origin and boundaries of the universe, and the foundation for the unification of the world. In Chinese, the word "universe" is pronounced "*yu-zhou*," space, which includes the six directions—east, west, north, south, Heaven (up) and Earth (down)—and "*zhou*," time, which includes the past, present, and future, a concept more expansive than the western term.

Early in the last years of the Warring States Period, Qu Yuan, great poet of the Chu State, raised these topics in his famous poem *Asking Heaven*. Liu Zongyuan wrote *Response to 'Asking Heaven,'* in which he clearly points out that material force is the origin of the universe.

> "There was a vast piece of darkness at the very beginning, so there is no reliable account of it. . . . Night follows day and day follows night. When Heaven and Earth began, there were comings and goings. In blindness, things were transforming. At that time there was only material force. Who knows the reason why?" (*Response to the 'Asking Heaven'*)

Liu Zongyuan probes into the laws for the movement of material force. The cause lies in the contradiction inside a substance itself. The whole of Nature is a material process in continuous motion. On this basis, Liu concludes that divine will does not dominate the phenomenal changes in Nature, nor is it relative to human affairs, refuting Han Yu's opinion that Heaven is able to reward good service and punish faults, and to reward good people and punish the wicked: "Heaven and Earth are two big fruits or melons. The material force is a big carbuncle. As for yin and yang, they are big plants or trees. Are they really able to give rewards for good service and punishment for evil deeds? The agent of a good service does it all by himself. The agent of an evil deed does it all by himself, too." (*A Discourse on Heaven*)

Hence, Heaven, Earth, and the material force have no will. Similar to melons, fruits, trees, and plants, in essence they belong to one and the same material existence. Man himself is the source of meritorious and evil deeds in human affairs; they are not the result of the interference of Heaven. To Liu, the legal system and behavior contrary to morals belong to the category of social phenomena. Natural and social phenomena occupy two separate spheres, and each follows its own laws to change and develop. These two sides cannot interfere with each other.

Liu's view breaks away from the theory that "Heaven and Man correspond to each other," first put forth by Dong Zhongshu in the Han Dynasty. This is also an inheritance and a development of Xunzi's admonition to "beware of the separation of Heaven from Man."

"Heaven and Man do not interfere with each other"—that sums up Liu Zongyuan's atheism. He claims that from ancient times to the present not one person could rule for long once he lost the virtue of benevolence or relied on auspicious omens. Furthermore, ancient scholars who expounded on the Mandate of Heaven did so to fool the common people. Such is Liu Zongyuan's continuation and development of the atheism initiated by Wang Chong (27–c. 97). He points out:

"Those who have enough strength ask for help from mankind, and those who have not enough strength ask for help from the gods." (*A Critique of the Remarks of Monarchs· Gods Have Fallen Down to the State of Shen*)

The Way, then, should not be sought in ghosts and spirits, nor in the Mandate of Heaven. Instead, it lies in appeasing the common people through virtuous rule and benevolent government, and in administering the country by choosing good and able men. In short, it lies in human beings.

Liu Zongyuan studied Buddhism for some thirty years, finding in it some ideas consonant with those in the *Book of Changes* and the *Analects*. For instance, he equated the Buddha-nature with the doctrine of "benevolence" in the *Analects*. However, he felt the Buddhist rejection of filial piety, "in order to reach thorough understanding," did not accord with "benevolence."

In various other philosophical systems, Liu Zongyuan found elements useful for administering the country—such as those of Taoism, Yang Zhu, Mo Di, Shen Buhai, Shang Yang, the Legalist school, and the Political Strategists—hence advocating that it is necessary to incorporate the strong points of diverse schools of thought. This not only enriches his ideological system of atheism but also carries forward the developmental history of Chinese philosophy.

Liu Yuxi and Liu Zongyuan were closely connected in both their thought and their political careers. When Liu Yuxi read Liu Zongyuan's philosophical essay titled *A Discourse on Heaven*, he felt that it did not probe deeply enough the relationship between Heaven and Man. So he wrote three articles under the general title *A Treatise on Heaven*. He brings into full play Liu Zongyuan's materialist world outlook, and engages in a profound discussion of a series of problems such as the formation of the myriad things in the universe and the relationship between Heaven and Man. He points out:

> "The turbid is the mother of the clear, and the heavy is the root of the light. When the Two Elementary Forms were fixed in their proper positions, they began to operate in a state of dependence on each other. Their breath became rain and dew, and their blowing became thunder and wind. Based on material force, things come into being, and are then divided into different kinds. Plants are called 'the living,' while the animals are called 'the worms.' Man as the head of 'the naked worms' is the most resourceful creature. He can overtake Heaven and utilize its advantages. On the other hand, he can establish the laws of human society. When these are broken, however, man will return to the very beginning." (*A Treatise on Heaven·Part Three*)

Nature produced man, and now man in return acts upon Nature with "human reason." Therefore, human society is unified in material Nature.

Liu Yuxi's demonstration of the material unification of the world is a criticism of both Metaphysics and Buddhism, which preaches the ontology of sunya (the void). He does his best to give a materialist explanation of formless space, saying:

"Does 'formless' mean space? Space is but that which is too small to see. Its body can receive the bodies of other things, its functioning is always dependent upon being, and its form follows the forms of matter." (*A Treatise on Heaven·Part Two*)

Liu Yuxi takes "space" as an existential form of a very slight and thin substance that may be examined by human intelligence. His views were praised by Liu Zongyuan, who said, "My friend, only you have seen that the so-called formless is of no constant shape. That is wonderful!" *(A Reply to 'A Treatise on Heaven' by Liu Yuxi)*

Liu Yuxi proposes that, "Heaven and Man alternatively overtake each other." He distinguishes two abilities, one being "the ability of Heaven," and the other "the ability of man," and expounds on their dialectical relationship.

"What Heaven can do is to create the myriad things. What man can do is to govern the myriad things." (*A Treatise on Heaven·Part One*)

"The Heavenly principle is creative, and it functions through the prevalence of the strong over the weak. The human principle is government according to law, and it functions through discrimination between right and wrong" (*Ibid*)

This adds to the view of the separation of Heaven and Man put forth by Liu Zongyuan, who says, "They are two things and no more."

Liu Yuxi affirms that "Man is then unable to do what Heaven can, nor can Heaven do what man is able to." (*A Treatise on Heaven·Part One*) On this premise, he says, "Because Heaven runs overtly without secrets, Man can positively overtake it." (*A Treatise on Heaven·Part Two*) Heaven does not have a will of its own, and is obedient to "the inevitable laws that the myriad things follow all the time." For this reason, Man can attempt to govern and organize society. Therefore, Liu Yuxi says, "What Man depends on to overtake Heaven is the legal system." (*A Treatise on Heaven·Part One*)

To demonstrate this point, he also attributes Man's original biological nature to the category of "Heaven." In his opinion, when Man leaves Heaven to act according to its own convenience, the result will be obvious—inevitably, the powerful side, Heaven, will be victorious. When man acts according to reason, the result will be equally obvious—inevitably, the reasonable side, Man, will be victorious. Liu Yuxi explains the phenomena in human society showing that "alternatively, Heaven and man overtake each other":

"Imagine a group of tourists going to the leafy suburbs. Now they want to take a rest under a tree or to have a drink at a spring. The man who first finds it must be the physically strongest among the tourists, although the others might be wiser and more virtuous. Does this not show that Heaven overtakes Man? Later they arrive in a town. Now they want to take a rest in a comfortable inn or enjoy a grand banquet. The man who first finds it must be the most sage and worthy among the tourists, although the others might be physically stronger. Does this not show that man overtakes Heaven?" (*A Treatise on Heaven·Part Two*)

He maintains that when there is a perfect legal system and a standard of right and wrong, "human reason" may be brought into play, even when people are living in the wilderness. But when the legal system is rotten, what takes effect is "Heavenly reason." He sees it is necessary to set up legislation based on the public judgment of right and wrong. When this is done, everybody will act within certain limitations. For man to overtake Heaven, any natural or biological attributes of man, when they run counter to the legal system, must be suppressed—a progressive idea at the time.

> "The human Way in a stable society is evident; hence people know why good fortune or disaster comes. Therefore, they neither bless nor blame Heaven. The human Way in a society in upheaval becomes unclear; hence people cannot know why good fortune or disaster comes. Therefore, they attribute all ills in human affairs to Heaven. This does not mean, however, that Heaven can really intervene in human affairs." (*A Treatise on Heaven·Part One*)

Here, Liu Yuxi discloses the social root cause of theism. He goes so deep into this sphere as to make a criticism of the privileged rule of feudalism.

Liu Yuxi lays a solid foundation for the systematic doctrine that "Heaven and Man alternately overtake each other, and make use of each other." It is a new generalization of the experiences undergone in the struggle for the correct means of production and achievements in the natural sciences and develops atheistic thought addressing the relationship between Heaven and Man.

In his masterpiece *A Treatise on Feudalism*, Liu Zongyuan puts forth a celebrated thesis on the emergence and development of the history of human society. The history of man is an objective process of natural development in which there is an innate "trend" independent of people's will. "Trend" refers to an objective and inevitable tendency, with which he attempts an atheistic explaination of the development of social history and political institutions.

In the first place, the appearance of feudalism (enfeoffment), characterized by a system of "investing nobles with hereditary titles and territories," is the result of the objective situation:

> "In the first stage, when man and the myriad things were created, everywhere was overgrown with grasses and bushes, deer and boars roamed at will, and human beings could not protect themselves against them. Human beings had neither fur nor feathers. But, as Xunzi says, man borrowed strength from the other beings for his own use. In this process there arose quarrels. When there was no end of quarrels they had to obey the one who could pass judgment on their quarrels. People submitted to the one who was wise, who punished those who did not accept his judgments. Gradually rulers and chiefs, laws and administration came into being. From these sprang petty officials in the townships, and then magistrate of counties, and then the feudal lords. And then there emerged leaders who governed several lords each, and then leaders who governed ten lords each. And finally there was the supreme ruler who was called the Son of Heaven. From the Son of Heaven down to petty officials, these leaders became convinced that their power stemmed from their personal virtues. So when they were dying they sought to hand on their positions to their sons. Therefore enfeoffment did not come from any divine arrangement, but was the result of the trend of history." (*A Treatise on Feudalism*)

In the second place, since enfeoffment was decided by the trend at the outset, it is impossible to halt its developmental process. While many evil consequences appeared, they, too, were not caused by subjective desire. Liu Zongyuan says, "Was it really because of the regulation of any saints that the situation became so? No, it was caused by the trend." (*A Treatise on Feudalism*) The developmental history of society is by no means the product of the will of any saints.

In the third place, the replacement of enfeoffment by the system of prefectures and counties is also decided by the "trend," and an inevitable result of an ever-developing situation. The root cause of the decline of the Zhou Dynasty lay in its failure to replace enfeoffment with the system of prefectures and counties, whereas when the first Qin Emperor unified the country, he immediately did exactly that.

Of course, the "trend" discussed by Liu Zongyuan is a kind of abstract necessity. His explanation of the appearance of enfeoffment and its replacement by the system of prefectures and counties still stands at a considerable distance from the materialist conception of history. Nevertheless, he affirms an inevitable tendency in the development of history, and he uses the concept of "trend" to explain the evolution of social and political systems. In this respect, he surpasses all his predecessors.

"The revolutionary nature of the Qin Dynasty lay in its changing of the old system for a new one. Rulers start from their own feelings, aiming at setting up their own authority and turning everybody and everything to their own use. But the view of the whole country as a public entity started with the Qin Dynasty." (*A Treatise on Feudalism*)

There are two sides here. One is the "public" that accords with the tendency of historical development. The other is the "selfish" that is the subjective feelings and desires of the First Qin Emperor. Liu Zongyuan not only makes a demarcation line between the two sides but also associates them. As he points out, not only did the "selfish" and subjective feelings and desires of the Emperor not hinder the objective effect of the "public" that accords with the tendency of historical development, it also accelerated the realization of the "public" trend that accords with the tendency of historical development.

Wang Fuzhi (1619-1692) agrees. He says, "The ruler of the Qin Dynasty abolished the marquises and set up the prefectural governors, but Heaven carried out a great cause for the majority of the people by means of his selfish desires." (*Discussions after Reading the Mirror of Universal History·Book 1*) George Wilhelm Friedrich Hegel (1770–1831) has a famous view, as follows: "The 'evil' is the form of the motive force of historical development which is expressed in it." Later, Friedrich Engels (1820–1895) absorbed the Hegelian view in a critical way. He accepted it and treated it as an important principle in his theories. And he points out as follows:

> "Ever since class oppositions came into being, it is man's wicked passions—covetous desire and the lust for power—that have become the levers of historical development. In this respect, the history of

feudalism and the bourgeoisie is a matchless and continuous demonstration." (*Ludwig Feuerbach and the End of the Classical German Philosophy*)

In his probe into the objectivity of the "trend" of history, Liu Zongyuan has already touched on the dialectics of historical movement, although he has a rather dim knowledge of it.

The world outlook of Liu Zongyuan and Liu Yuxi is original and in line with materialism, and their evolutional view of history is in line with atheism. These belong to the positive achievement of the development of philosophy and natural sciences in the earlier stage of feudal society in China. They also summarize the relationship between Heaven and Man first discussed in pre-Qin times.

But Liu Zongyuan and Liu Yuxi have unavoidable ideological limitations. Their materialist world outlook is at the stage of perceiving things directly through the senses. Their understanding of the objective laws of Nature and the initiative of Man takes abstract Man for the subject of practice. Their social and historical views restrict them to treating the attainment or loss of political power as a matter of whether or not the ruler practices benevolent government or carries out a strict legal system. This causes them to embrace an idealistic view of history despite having refuted the theological view of history.

PART III

Expansion and Transformation

(Northern Song Dynasty to Ming Dynasty, ca. 10th Century to 16th Century A.D.)

22.

The Rise of Neo-Confucianism

Neo-Confucianism emerged as the official ideology of the ruling classes of the Northern Song Dynasty onwards. In formation it is speculative, in tradition it takes Confucianism for its kernel, and it melds the philosophical doctrines of Buddhism and Taoism. Its major components are the doctrine of the "Great Ultimate" put forth by Zhou Dunyi, the doctrine of "patterns and numbers" put forth by Shao Yong, and the doctrine of "righteousness and principle" put forth by the two Cheng brothers—Cheng Hao and Cheng Yi.

Zhou Dunyi (1017–1073) was a native of Yingdao County, Daozhou Prefecture (Daoxian County, Hunan Province). In the reigns of emperors Renzong and Shenzong, when Zhou was a judicial magistrate in the Nan-an Military Prefecture, the two Cheng brothers went there to study under his guidance. Later, he assisted the governor of Hezhou Prefecture and "a great number of scholars followed him." There he met Wang Anshi, and "the two philosophers conversed day and night. When Wang Anshi returned home, he plunged into profound thinking so much so that he forgot to have meals and sleep." (*Life Chronicle of Master of the Stream of Waterfalls* by Du Zheng) In his later years, Zhou set up an academy, Book Hall of the Stream of Waterfalls, at the foot of the Lotus Flower Peak on Mount Lushan. He was called the Master of the Stream of Waterfalls and his doctrine the "Learning of the Stream of Waterfalls."

Zhou Dunyi was the founder of Neo-Confucianism. Merging elements of Confucianism, Taoism, and Buddhism into one doctrine, he transformed and synthesized ideological data from various sources, such as the Ultimate Nonbeing of the *Laozi*, the Great Ultimate of the *Commentaries on the Changes*, the idea of sincerity of the *Doctrine of Mean*, and the theories of yin and yang and the Five Elements. Thus he provided successors in this school with paradigms and patterns in line with cosmological ontology. Zhou Dunyi "pioneered" Neo-Confucianism, the Cheng brothers "expanded it," and Zhu Xi "epitomized" it. Zhou's extant philosophical works include *The Diagram of the Great Ultimate*, a revision of one of the Taoist diagrams, a 200-character treatise entitled *An Explanation of the Diagram of the Great Ultimate*, and *Penetrating the Book of Changes*. In these he discusses key issues. There is the ontological problem of "The Ultimate Nonbeing and also the Great Ultimate!" There is the problem of the view of activity and tranquility that "things cannot penetrate each other, but spirit works wonders with all things." There is the problem of the ethical view that "Regarding tranquility as fundamental, he establishes himself as the ultimate standard for man."

The variety and unification of the world constitute a complicated problem that aroused a long-term controversy in the history of Chinese philosophy. Via the question of the "one" and the "many," Zhou Dunyi once again brings it up:

> "The myriad things are created and transformed out of the two material forces and the Five Elements. These five elements are the basis of their differentiation, while the two material forces constitute their actuality. The two forces are fundamentally one. Consequently, the many are ultimately one, and the one is actually differentiated in the many. Of the one and the many, each has its own correct state of being. Of the great and the small, each has its definite function." (*Penetrating the Book of Changes· Chapter 22: Principle, Human Nature and Destiny*)

The "one" in Zhou Dunyi's vocabulary is the Ultimate Nonbeing mentioned in the *Laozi* or the Great Ultimate of the *Commentaries on the Changes*. Zhou here unifies the two philosophical categories, in essence merging Taoism with Confucianism, to form a new trend in philosophy.

Zhou Dunyi applies his "way of two reasonings" to illustrate the unified relationship of the "one" and the "many"—one, from the one to the many, from the thing-in-itself to the phenomena; two, from the phenomena to the thing-in-itself. The two are then combined:

> "When the reality of the Ultimate Nonbeing and the essence of yin and yang and the Five Elements come into mysterious union, integration ensues. The *qian* (Heaven) constitutes the male element, and the *kun* (Earth) constitutes the female element. The interaction of these two material forces engenders and transforms the myriad things. The myriad things produce and reproduce, resulting in an unending transformation." (*An Explanation of the Diagram of the Great Ultimate*)

Zhou here stipulates the original substance as an absolute entity, a practical existence but not a concrete thing. It originates in nonbeing, but it is not empty. This attempts to overcome the limitations of both Metaphysics and Buddhism, both of which take emptiness and nonbeing for their ontology. This sets a new ontological course for Song–Ming Neo-Confucianism.

By means of the Great Ultimate, within which "movement and tranquility alternate," Zhou explains how the two material forces of yin and yang come into being. They come from, or are derived from, the process in which the Great Ultimate moves by itself. Without it, no matter how "the essence of yin and yang and the Five Elements" may work, nothing can come into being, and the "mysterious union" can do nothing at all. The key lies in combining these two statements: "The myriad things produce and reproduce, resulting in an unending transformation," and "Things cannot penetrate each other, but spirit works wonders with all things." Thus, it follows that Zhou Dunyi sets the Ultimate Nonbeing (or the Great Ultimate) over the myriad things, the Five Elements, and the two material forces.

All Song Dynasty Neo-Confucian philosophers applied the theory of external cause to explain the relationship between principle and material force. The Cheng brothers inquire into "the reason there are yin and yang." Zhu Xi inquires into "the reason there are changes and intercommunication." Inspired by Zhou Dunyi's theory of the external cause, they all provide spiritual ontology with theoretical support for "the Way that is above any physical form."

The starting point of Zhou's treatise *An Explanation of the Diagram of the Great Ultimate* is the cosmological ontology epitomized in the phrase "The Ultimate Nonbeing and also the Great Ultimate." As for its terminal point, it is the feudal ethical view that "Regarding tranquility as fundamental, he establishes himself as the ultimate standard for man."

In the phrase "The Ultimate Nonbeing and also the Great Ultimate" there is a pattern of self-movement As a result of self-movement, there appears "man," who alone "receives the Five Elements in their highest excellence, and therefore he is most intelligent." (*An Explanation of the Diagram of the Great Ultimate*) Also, "the foundation of the multitude lies in one person." (*Penetrating the Book of Changes· Chapter 11: Harmony and Transformation*) Because this "one person" is possessed of the excellence of the multitude he is able to grasp the "Way of humanity and righteousness." And, "As the Way of Heaven operates, all things are in harmony. As the virtue of the sage-ruler is cultivated, all people are transformed. The great harmony and great transformation leave no trace, and no one knows how they come into being: This is called spirit." (*Ibid*) Such is the sage-ruler who rules society as the deputy of the Great Ultimate that works wonders with all things, and he "cultivates all things with humanity and sets all people right with righteousness." (*Ibid*) Zhou Dunyi sanctifies the Great Ultimate, and renders it into the absolute spirit that is formless, shapeless, supreme, and at the very beginning of all things.

In the second place, every move of the Great Ultimate, be it tranquil or active, holds the key to transforming all things. The series of links of the natural order such as the two material forces, the Five Elements, the four seasons, and so forth, are in mysterious union, and integration ensues. They engender and transform the myriad things endlessly. Corresponding to such a mysterious union are the order and ranks of feudal society. "Only when yin and yang operate according to order can they be in harmony. Then the ruler will truly be the minister, the father will truly be the father, the son will truly be the son, brothers will truly be brothers, and husband and wife will truly be husband and wife. All things must fulfill their principle before they can be in harmony." (*Penetrating the Book of Changes· Chapter 13: Ceremony and Music*)

In the third place, because man "receives the Five Elements in their highest excellence, and therefore he is most intelligent," he is always possessed of strong emotions and desires. "As abundance comes about, desires are aroused. People's feelings become dominant, and they are guided by advantages and disadvantages. Consequently they attack one another ceaselessly. There is a danger that they may destroy themselves, and human relations will be ruined." (*Penetrating the Book of Changes·Chapter 36: Punishment*)

To respond to such a situation, Zhou came up with a formula consisting of three words. The first word is "settlement." He says, "The sage settles these affairs by the principles of the Mean, correctness, humanity, and righteousness (for the way of the sage is none other than these four.)" (*An Explanation of the Diagram of the Great Ultimate*)

The next word is "fundament." That is to say, one should "regard tranquility as fundamental." This is because once people's desires are aroused and their feelings become dominant, the situation will be hard to control. In essence, it equals the exhortation to "eradicate human desires." Lastly,

there is "establishment." That is to say, it is necessary to establish sincerity, the noumenon of the universe, the original nature innate to everybody. "It is pure and perfectly good." (*Penetrating the Book of Changes·Chapter 1: Sincerity·Part One*) He says, "Sagehood is nothing but sincerity. It is the foundation of the five constant virtues (humanity, righteousness, propriety, wisdom and faithfulness) and the source of all activities." (*Penetrating the Book of Changes·Chapter 2: Sincerity·Part Two*) When everybody acts in accordance with the standards of feudal morality, sincerity is the result, and man will become the ultimate standard of everything.

Zhu Xi comments on Zhou Dunyi's doctrine of the Great Ultimate as follows: "He reasons out how the principle, the two material forces, and the Five Elements work by combining and separating, and how they embody the subtleness of the noumenon of the Way and the cardinal principles of ethics." (*Penetrating the Book of Changes·Preface*) His is an example of those philosophers of later generations who found inspiration in Zhou Dunyi's philosophy.

Shao Yong (1011–1077), native of Gongcheng County (near Mixian County, Henan Province), was given the posthumous title Kangjie. Unsuccessful in public life, partly as result of his opposition to Wang Anshi's reform efforts, Shao Yong lived in retirement in Luoyang.

He absorbed the theory of "*a priori* diagrams and numbers" (for example, the *Yellow River and Luoshui River Diagrams*) from Taoism, the theory of "cessation and contemplation" from Buddhism, and the principles of the Great Ultimate, "activity and tranquility," and "yin and yang" from the *Book of Changes*. Finally, he set up a gigantic system of diagram-number study, which "embraces the universe, and goes through all times from past to present."

His most important works are the *Supreme Principles Governing the World* and *A Collection of Earthenware Percussion Instruments*. In the *Supreme Principles Governing the World* two treatises represent his philosophical thought in a concentrated way: *Inner Chapters on the Observation of Things* and *Outer Chapters on the Observation of Things*.

Shao Yang's basic paradigm of the world is, "Spirit engenders number, number engenders form, and form engenders concrete things." (*Outer Chapters on the Observation of Things*) The spirit Shao Yong talks about generally does not refer to spirits such as God on High or to ghosts, but to the dominator of the "material force," which, hidden in Heaven and Earth, may freely go into and come out of the realm of life and death and existence and nonexistence. The myriad things originate in it, and return to it. To Shao Yong, The Great Ultimate, "the Way," and "the one" are aliases of "spirit."

Shao Yong uses patterns and numbers to explain the origin and development of the world.

When "one divides into two," there appear Heaven and Earth. When "two divide into four" and "four divide into eight," there appear the four heavenly bodies—sun, moon, stars, and zodiac spaces—and the four earthly bodies—water, fire, earth, and stone. By the movement of the sun, moon, stars, and planets, there appear summer, winter, day, and night. By the movement of water, fire, soil, and stone, there appear rain, wind, dew, and thunder. By the movement of summer, winter, day, and night, there appear the sexes, emotions, shapes, and bodies. By the movement of the rain, wind, dew, and thunder, there appear the birds, beasts, trees, and grasses. (*Inner Chapters on the Observation of Things*)

When all are put together, they equal "eight divide into sixteen"—

"the method of redoubling" in Cheng Hao's terminology. By moving step by step in this way and following the pattern, one may deduce the myriad things from the Great Ultimate and from "the one" to the "myriad." Therefore, both the history of the universe and the history of mankind may be governed.

As compared with Zhou Dunyi's formula that "the many are ultimately one, and the one is actually differentiated into the many," Shao Yong's proposition bears more significance. Therefore, Zhu Xi says, "Ever since the *Book of Changes* came into being, only Shao Kangjie has talked about a thing in such a uniform way." (*Classified Conversations of Zhu Xi·Book 100: About Shao's Books*) Shao Yong says, "If spirit is impeded spatially, it will not be able to effect transformation and will cease to be spirit. If Change had a definite, physical form, it would not be able to penetrate things, and would cease to be Change." (*Outer Chapters on the Observation of Things*) The "Great Ultimate" is veiled in mystery, whereas "things" are mechanical, fixed, stiff, rigid, stagnant. All things dwell in their established aspects and stick to fixed forms—making self-transformation impossible.

Shao Yong asserts that when one follows his diagram of prior existence, one may "get to know the climate of the sky, the geography of the earth, and the physical principles between the up and the down. One may also see through human affairs." (*Outer Chapters on the Observation of Things*) Therefore, his *a priori* determinism, clad in the garb of "objectivity" and "science," was far more influential as ideology.

On the whole, Shao Yong's *a priori* diagram-number study is an idealistic doctrine. Nevertheless, some modern scholars think the Circular Diagram of the Sixty-Four Hexagrams and the Diagram of the Placement of the Eight Trigrams have value as they stand the test of the binary system. Some scholars think Shao Yong also established the principle for determining the Chinese lunar calendar according to the twenty-four seasonal divisional points. Yet he failed to explain these series of numbers correctly. And, in a materialistic way, he regarded them as mysterious, even an expression of a transcendental order of existence. As a result, even his exceptional grasp of mathematics could not shake off the dominance of theology.

The final two contributors to Neo-Confucianism are the Cheng brothers.

Cheng Hao (1032–1085) served as a court official. Cheng Yi (1033–1107) also served as a senior official. When young, the two brothers were disciples of Zhou Dunyi. Later, they became famous scholars, known respectfully as "the two Chengs," their ideas basically in accordance with one another, their school the Luoyang School. They set up the theoretical system of Principle Learning.

Their discourse and works were compiled into the *Complete Works of the Two Chengs*, which includes *Surviving Works of the Two Chengs*, *Additional Works of the Two Chengs*, *Collection of Literary Works of Mingdao*, *Collection of Literary Works of Yichuan*, *Yichuan's Commentary on the Book of Changes*, *The Two Chengs' Explanations of the Classics,* and *Pure Words of the Two Chengs*. In the following discussion, when quotations are taken from these books, the general title *Complete Works of the Two Chengs* is omitted.

Cheng Hao says, "Although I learned some of my doctrines from others, the concept of *tian-li* (Heavenly Principle) came from my own contemplation." (*Additional Works of the Two Chengs·Book 12*) From the time of the Cheng brothers onward, Chinese thinkers formally took "Heavenly principle" as a basic category of philosophy. This laid a foundation for the Cheng–Zhu Rationalist School, the official philosophy of the later stage of feudal society.

The two Cheng brothers regard the "Heavenly principle" as the "practical principle." "It is simply a question of principle." (*Pure Words of the Two Chengs·Book 1*) Why do they prescribe the thing-in-itself in this way? They do so to emphasize that there really is a foundation for, substance in, and a function for the concept of the practical principle.

The ontology upheld by both Buddhism and Taoism ends in emptiness and extinction, and Shao Yong's study of priori diagrams and numbers degenerates into a mechanical gadget. In comparison, the two Cheng brothers' viewpoint that "Only the principle is true" is much more reasonable—because they hold that the thing-in-itself is an absolute body that is really existing and not a phenomenon, an original nonbeing instead of emptiness. As such, their study of righteousness and principle is a higher achievement than the thought of the Metaphysicians and Buddhists,and the study of diagrams and numbers. It also shows that the study of righteousness and principle is a kind of idealistic ontology.

The two Cheng brothers carry out their cognitive line centered on the principle by means of explaining that "extension of knowledge lies in the investigation of things," a proposition that first appears in the Confucian classic the *Great Learning*.

The Chengs discuss the relationship between the internal mind and external things. What does "*ge-wu* (investigating things)" mean? "The word *ge* means to investigate things to the utmost, and the word *wu* here means the principles hidden therein. So, *ge-wu* means to investigate the principles of things, and that is all." (*Surviving Works of the Two Chengs·Book 25*) Therefore, "to investigate things" is equal to "arriving at all the principles of things."

Where is the principle? "What is received by man and things from Heaven is called destiny. What is inherent in things is called principle. What man is endowed with is called nature, and as the master of the body it is called the mind." (*Surviving Works of the Two Chengs·Book 18*) The principles of Nature are identical with fate, which is irresistible. The principles of society are collectively termed "righteousness," which regulates man's behavior. The principle with which man is endowed is *a priori* human nature. The principle that dwells in the human body is the mind. Therefore, the principle is everything, and everything is no more than the principle. The principle is both outside the mind and within it. This is different from Zhu Xi's concepts of "the principles in things" and "the principles in one's own mind."

In this way, "The mind of one man is at one with the mind of Heaven and Earth. The principle of one thing is one with the principle of all things." (*Surviving Works of the Two Chengs·Book 2·Part 1*) And, "Principle and mind are one." (*Surviving Works of the Two Chengs·Book 5*) Here it is obvious that the two sides, namely, *a priori* principle and the subjective mind, have already become one.

Having concluded that everybody has the same mind, and that the human mind is governed by one principle, one can reason by analogy that, "to investigate things in order to understand principle to the utmost does not mean that it is necessary to investigate all the things in the world. One has only to investigate the principle behind one thing or one event to the utmost, and the principle behind other things or events can then be inferred." (*Surviving Works of the Two Chengs·Book 15*) Such inference means, in fact, judging things for oneself. Further, "Oneself is the measure, and the measure is oneself." (*Surviving Works of the Two Chengs·Book 15*)

In the second place, the Cheng brothers pay particular attention to the relationship between knowledge and action. They put knowledge first and action second: knowledge guides action. Once principles are understood, one can follow them and take action with enthusiasm. However, the Chengs exaggerate the function of knowledge, saying, "When one is hungry, one does not eat poisonous plants. People do not go into boiling water or try to walk on fire. This is exactly because they have knowledge." (*Surviving Works of the Two Chengs·Book 15*) They therefore conclude that "It is necessary to take knowledge for the foundation. Action is in the second place, and the order cannot be reversed." (*Pure Words·Book 2*)

Nevertheless, their concept of action does not refer to social practice but to personal behavior in the sphere of morality. When they advocate that people ought to learn more and to practice more, they mean that it is necessary to carry out the exhortations of the ancient sages and men of virtue, and follow their fine examples. Cheng Yi says, "The accumulation of knowledge increases in proportion to the extent that one engages in studying things. It is important to acquire more knowledge of the words and deeds of the ancient sages. By examining the traces they have left, you may find out how they behaved; by examining the works they have left to us you may find what their minds were like." (*Yichuan's Commentary on the Book of Changes·Hexagram Da Xu — The Great Taming Force*)

They pay particular attention to Confucius and Mencius. They speak highly of these two sages, saying, "Every sentence Confucius uttered came from his inborn mind. As for Mencius, every sentence referred to practical events." (*Surviving Works of the Two Chengs·Book 5*) For this reason, "Whenever one reads the *Analects* or the *Book of Mencius,* one should do one's best to ruminate over their remarks. It is important to keep in mind the words of the sages; one should never take them for merely discourse delivered at random. It is sufficient to have read only these two books, if one keeps them in one's heart all one's life, because they mean a great deal." (*Surviving Works of the Two Chengs·Book 22*) It is obvious that the knowledge obtained through hearing and seeing is not enough to guide one's actions, according to the Chengs; knowledge must also be acquired through reading the work of Confucius and Mencius.

In the third place, they discuss the relationship between pure principle and human desires. In their view, man has duality. One property of man is his transcendental nature. They say, "Nature is the same as principle." (*Surviving Works of the Two Chengs·Book 22·Part 1*) This refers to *a priori* nature. And what is contained in this concept is entirely equal to the principle that is contained in the vast expanse of Heaven. "Actions that come from moral nature are good. The sages, because such actions are good, called them humanity, righteousness, propriety, wisdom, and faithfulness." (*Surviving Works of the Two Chengs·Book 25*) This is the basis on which a human being may become a human being and a sage may become a sage. The other property of man is his natural endowments: "Some parts of the material force are clear, and some are turbid. Those who are endowed with the clear parts of the material force become the wise, whereas those who are endowed with the turbid parts of the material force become the foolish." (*Surviving Works of the Two Chengs·Book 18*) This is also the basis on which the wise may be differentiated from the foolish, and the good may be distinguished from the evil.

The duality of man causes contradictions and conflicts. This is because "When there is no heavenly principle, there must be selfish desires." (*Surviving Works of the Two Chengs·Book 15)* To "eradicate human desires and maintain the heavenly principles," the two Chengs pay particular attention to the self-cultivation of feudal morality. They say, "Self-cultivation requires seriousness." (*Surviving Works of the Two Chengs·Book 18*) People should concentrate closely on observing feudal ethics; even a single derivation from the latter is impermissible. As compared with Buddhist self-cultivation, this far better meets the demands of feudal rule.

The two Cheng brothers' theory of righteousness and principle is a kind of exquisite metaphysics that contains some ideological factors of dialectics.

For instance, regarding the problem of the relationship between the one and the two, they have some important ideas. They say, "According to the principle of Heaven and Earth and all things, nothing exists in isolation, but everything necessarily has its opposite." (*Surviving Works of the Two Chengs·Book 11*) And, "All the myriad things have their opposites." (*Ibid*) And "In the world there is nothing that does not have its opposite." (*Yichuan's Commentary on the Book of Changes·Book 3*)

Obviously, although they see that there are opposites in all things, they emphasize that these factors complement each other. Not only do the Chengs acknowledge that action and tranquility depend on each other and may be transformed into each other, but they emphasize that all things are in the process of everlasting movement. However, they regard the Three Cardinal Guides and Five Constant Virtues as eternal, never to be moved. So they say, "The father and sons, the ruler and ministers, are governed by the constant principles. Have you seen any movement between them?" (*Surviving Works of the Two Chengs·Book 2·Part 1*) And they say, "A hundred principles are right here; it is an obvious fact. When did Emperor Yao exhaust the way of being a sovereign and add something to the way of being a sovereign? When did Emperor Shun exhaust the way of being a son and add something to the way of being a son? Originally and at present, the principles are just the same." (*Ibid*) Therefore, in their opinion, only in ordinary things are there movement and changes. "Only in the way of the sages" is there "neither progress nor retrogress." (*Surviving Works of the Two Chengs·Book 25*) They then go on to urge: "When you can steadfastly stand your ground, you are a sage." (*Surviving Works of the Two Chengs·Book 6*) "Non-action" is the most fundamental principle and the highest standard of behavior and morality.

As regards the relationship between the constant and the change, a problem relative to the relationship between action and tranquility, the Chengs have several viewpoints. For example, they say, "Things will develop in the opposite direction when they become extreme." (*Surviving Works of the Two Chengs·Book 15*) And they say, "Affairs always reverse themselves after reaching an extreme." (*Yichuan's Commentary on the Book of Changes·Hexagram Da Xu—The Great Taming Force*) And, "It is quite natural that there are changes even in principles themselves." (*Pure Words of the Two Chengs·Book 1*) They even say, "Although there are things thick and firm as a mountain, they may assuredly be changed." (*Yichuan's Commentary on the Book of Changes·Book 3*) But the change they envisage is a return to the common principles. In their opinion, "When yang descends, it must then ascend. When yin ascends, it must then descend. Either coming or going, either contracting or expanding, all these are common principles." (*Yichuan's Commentary on the Book of Changes·Hexagram Fu— Returning*) By saying, "Things will develop in the opposite direction when they become extreme," they mean that everything ethical must return to the old orbit that yang is superior to yin. As we know, this is the fundamental principle of the stratified feudal system.

The Chengs expound on this as follows:

> "Of the things Heaven has produced, some are long and some are short, some are big and some are small. The superior men are those who have got the big things. How can they make the small things big? The Heavenly principle is like this. How can it be reversed?" (*Surviving Works of the Two Chengs·Book 11*). Clarification is of utmost importance. When asked, each man is superior with heavenly things.

> "When inferior men usurp a position, they may do their best to fulfill the duties of this position. Since they are, however, mean and low in temperament, they are not what ought to be at the higher levels. Therefore, sooner or later they will become pitiful creatures." (*Yichuan's Commentary on the Book of Changes·Book 3*)

That is to say, if either the small occupies the position of the big or the inferior occupies the position of the superior, this is contrary to rationality and is therefore abnormal. "Right in the relationship between father and son, and between ruler and minister, there is the fixed principle. Nobody who lives between Heaven and Earth, namely, in the world, can escape from it." (*Surviving Works of the Two Chengs·Book 5*) The ethical relations and the social order prescribed by the feudal system are manifestations of the "fixed principle." From this nobody can escape nor can alterations be made to it. This fixed principle is nothing but "the doctrine of the mean" that everybody must observe.

Such is their bold viewpoint denying any possibly qualitative changes. The Chengs' proposition that "the constant principle does not change" is identical to that of Sima Guang, who says, "The establishment cannot be changed." (*Commentaries on the Supreme Profound Principle·Chapter on Mysterious Unification*) These two propositions are used as the theoretical basis on which to prop up the old system and oppose the political reform carried out by Wang Anshi.

23.

Wang Anshi and the Material Force

Wang Anshi (1021–1086) was a native of Linchuan County in Jiangxi Province. He served as a provincial official until the year 1060, when he entered the imperial service of Emperor Shenzong of the Song Dynasty. Of great concern to him were the frequent peasant uprisings over the annexation of land., Full of reforming spirit and wishing to stabilize the order of feudal rule, he remarked, "In heavenly changes there is nothing to be feared; from ancestors there is nothing to be learned; and from gossip there is nothing to be concerned about." (*History of the Song Dynasty·Biography of Wang Anshi*) With the backing of Emperor Shenzong, he carried out a campaign of reform from top to bottom during the Xining reign (1068–1077). In the course of this, he had to battle opposition from a conservative clique of bureaucratic landlords headed by Sima Guang.

To gain support for his coming "new policies," Wang Anshi established a "new doctrine," with which he attempted to rejuvenate the classics. Dissatisfied with the old, arcane, hair-splitting annotations and commentaries done by scholars of the Han and Tang dynasties, he himself wrote commentaries on the Confucian classics, creating a "new doctrine" established to serve his "new policies." The Cheng brothers strongly opposed these policies.

When the Neo-Confucians introduced into Confucianism elements of Buddhism and Taoism, the principles of the Great Ultimate, yin and yang, and the theory of the Five Elements, producing and subduing one another had become ideological data from which almost all philosophers quoted. But there were fundamental divergences. For instance, is the Great Ultimate the principle or the material force? Is it a spiritual thing-in-itself or a material entity? These topics became the focus of controversy for philosophers of the Song–Ming period.

Zhou Dunyi put forth the ontology of the Great Ultimate before this period, and soon afterwards Li Gou (1001–1059) described the Great Ultimate as the nonbeing invisible as an object on the one hand, but a being heralded by its material force on the other—thus claiming material property in the primitively unified entity (*The Third Introduction to the Revised Diagrams of Changes*). Early in the Tang Dynasty, Liu Zongyuan put forth a theory on the transformation of the material forces: "In the blindness the things were transforming. At that time there was only the material force." (*Response to the "Asking Heaven"*) On this basis, Li Gou points out that only through the combination of yin and yang as two material forces can the Five Elements and the myriad things come into being. (*The First Introduction to the Revised Diagrams of Changes*) Wang Anshi followed Li Gou's materialist line to wage to demonstrate how the Great Ultimate produced the Five Elements and the myriad things.

In Wang Anshi's system, the supreme category is sometimes called the Great Ultimate, sometimes the Way, and sometimes Heaven. In his opinion, all three are the root cause of the myriad things in the world. What produced the myriad things is called material force. Therefore, the Great Ultimate and the Way have the same meaning in Wang Anshi's vocabulary. They both refer to the material "vital force" that fills the universe from time immemorial.

According to Wang Anshi, the Five Elements undergo a developmental process of cognition—from simple to complex and from abstract to concrete. At first, they are "five materials" which "the people use all alike; not one can be dispensed with." (*Zuo Commentary·Duke Xiang: 27th Year*) Shi Bo says, "So the former king made a hundred things by mixing earth with metal, wood, water, and fire." (*Conversations of the States·Book 16: Conversations of Zheng*)

From the view that yin and yang produce the Five Elements, Wang Anshi pushes the theory of the Five Elements to a new stage: "As for the Five Elements, when there are some changes in them, they take action and become ghosts and spirits, which come and go between Heaven and

Earth without end. They are called action-takers." (*Commentaries on the Great Norm*)

In the history of Chinese philosophy, Wang Anshi is the first to make a philosophical prescription for the actions of the Five Elements. For the first time also, he regards the Five Elements as the thing-in-itself that never stops flowing, comes and goes without end, has self-transformation, and is able to govern ghosts and spirits.

What spurs Wang Anshi to postulate the "new significance" of the Five Elements in a novel way? On the one hand he borrows from Confucius an old proposition that "the wise are active; the virtuous are tranquil." On the other, he uses a metaphor of "two merchants," of whom one is rich and the other is poor, to explain the economic causes of why one is active and the other is tranquil. In his opinion, "the reason the virtuous (merchant) is able to be tranquil" lies in the fact that he "has already become rich. The reason the wise (merchant) must be active lies in the fact that he has not." (*Collection of Literary Works by Wang Linchuan·The Virtuous and the Wise*) Wang Anshi emphasizes actions and upholds the active, whereas the Neo-Confucians emphasize tranquility. (*An Explanation of the Diagram of the Great Ultimate*). (*Penetrating the Book of Changes·Chapter 5: Caution about Actions*) The difference between Wang Anshi and the Neo-Confucians lies in social sources, which are, after all, decided by economic factors.

To Wang Anshi, the laws governing the development of things are established on the basis of contradictions (The Way stands in the two). As a result of the struggle of contradictions there appear new things ([The Way] establishes itself in the three). So then the Way actuates the things in the universe, which are represented by the Five Elements, to change in an endless way ([The Way] has changes in the five). All in all, everything has its opposite (its own antithesis). The various opposites are without limit. Therefore, we may make an analogy that there is nothing that is not in this situation. If one side is soft, the other side must be hard. If one side is dark, the other side must be bright. Not only are natural phenomena like this, so also are social phenomena. In society, when there is justice there must be evil; when there is good there must be bad; when there is ugliness there must be beauty; and when there is fortune there must be misfortune. This is true of the principles of "human nature and life" as well as of "morality and virtue." Similar to the other things in the universe, the Mandate of Heaven is in everlasting motion, and, what is more, the Mandate of Heaven contains its own opposite in itself. So not only does Wang Anshi think that in everything there are contradictory opposites, he also thinks that even in one and the same opposite are its own internal contradictions. So he says, "In the antithesis there are antitheses." (*Commentaries on the Great Norm*) In this way, the myriad things and affairs may change everlastingly and endlessly. He regards the boundless internal and external contradictions as the fundamental cause of things changing endlessly.

Not only does Wang Anshi see the unification of contradictions ("harmony") from a simple variation ("mixture"), he further sees the opposition of contradictions ("the two," "antithesis," "opposite") from the point of view of unification—in "opposites" there is "harmony." This differs from the viewpoint of the two Cheng brothers. Herein lies the important contribution Wang Anshi made to the development of naive dialectics.

In the *Commentaries on the Great Norm* Wang Anshi reflects upon "the Way and fate." What is the Way, and what is fate? He says, "The Way is that which the myriad things came from. Fate is that whose orders the myriad things must obey." The Way is the law all things must follow when they have any movements and changes whatsoever. And fate is the necessity all things must follow in the course of those movements and changes.

Wang Anshi's explanation of these contradictory relations is that things "produce and follow one another." Take, for example, wood, fire, metal, and water. They produce one another, and therefore spring, summer, autumn, and winter follow one another. This is the expression of mutual production following the seasons—the coming one prolongs the former one. (Cf. *Commentaries on the Great Norm*) The other relation concerns things "subduing and governing one another." Water, fire, metal, wood and earth are in conflict with one another, for there are contradictions among them. Therefore, people must be good at balancing them, so as to govern them well. This is the expression of mutual opposition and governing in respect of implements or other tangible things. (Cf. *Commentaries on the Great Norm*)

Wang applies the odd and even numbers of Heaven and Earth to explain the order of arrangement of the Five Elements in the *Great Norm*.

He adds "essence, spirit, masculine soul, feminine soul, and intention" to the Five Elements. Although he cannot get rid of the mystification of the far-fetched analogy of diagrams and numbers, he probes in a brand new way the contradictory relations among the Five Elements, which are characterized by "the odd and the even matching each other." On the one hand, "That which comes from an odd number must become an even number." On the other, "That which comes from an even number must become an odd number." Moreover, he maintains that the female must take initiative to match the male, while at the same time the male must take the initiative to match the female. So his theory is quite different from the old theory that the male is esteemed while the female is belittled, or that the female must unconditionally follow the male. (Cf. *Commentaries on the Great Norm*.)

Contrary to Zhou Dunyi's viewpoint that "things cannot penetrate each other, but spirit works wonders with all things," Wang Anshi thinks that things, represented by the Five Elements, are the most wonderful in transformation. Things possess the ability to "change," "transform," "follow," "reform," "change by following man's will," and so on. Take, for example, wood. "It becomes a fire when you burn it, and it becomes earth when it is rotten." In these two situations, qualitative changes take place. This is "change." He explains why the Five Elements are able to become the myriad things:

> "Roughly speaking, Heaven and Earth use the Five Elements in this way: They give water to things; they transform things with fire, they grow things such as wood; they make things with metal; they harmonize things with earth; they enliven things in a gentle way; and they transform things in a hard way. Therefore, a tree may be bent and water may be weak. Metal is hard and fire is violent. The violent and the hard may be adjusted so as to reach harmony, and thus the myriad things come into being. If there are only the bent and the weak and there is neither violence nor hard work, how can there be the establishment of things?" (*Commentaries on the Great Norm*)

So what enlivens and transforms things is not ghosts or spirits, but water and fire. It is not Heaven and Earth that create things, but wood and metal. Strength does not exist outside the things represented by the

Five Elements, it exists right inside the things represented by the Five Elements. The Five Elements possess the capability to be either hard or mild, and with such capability all things are produced. Balancing the hard side and the mild side is done by means of harmony. But in order to give free rein to harmony, "the violent and the hard must be adjusted so as to reach harmony." Without violence there cannot be any practical effect, despite the saying that "harmony truly produces things." This is because "metal is hard and fire is violent." To make iron, there must be a powerful fire in the furnace. To forge steel, there must be big hammers in the blacksmith's shop. This is Wang Anshi's criticism of Laozi and Zhou Dunyi. The former highly values the mild, and always adheres to the weak, while the latter advocates tranquility and is cautious of taking any action.

Wang Anshi wrote *Commentaries on the Great Norm* to deepen the naive dialectics contained in the primitive theory of the Five Elements. In this respect, he enriches the dialectical cognition of historical development by way of endowing some philosophical categories with "significance" on the basis that the Five Elements are always in motion.

Is change necessary? This is the first problem that the struggle for political reform must resolve. He points out, "That which has an affinity for changes is the Heavenly Way." (*Collection of Literary Works by Wang Linchuan·Meaning of the Yellow River Map and the Luoshui River Writing*) Changes are the Way, and apart from changes, the Way is impossible. On the one hand, Wang Anshi maintains that the fundamental principle of feudal rule should be well supported, and therefore says, "On condition that the foundation exists to keep constancy, the institution may be well maintained." On the other hand, he maintains that some concrete links of the feudal system should be reformed: "On condition that changes take place to fit in with the times, the government may still be run well." He says, "The middle way means that one should stand on the foundation but it does not mean one should follow the times. If one follows the times, it does not matter whether he takes the middle way or not, for constancy is not important; it is important that one acts according to circumstances." (*Commentaries on the Great Norm*) This is contrasted with the stand of the Neo-Confucians, who advocate the middle way, and say "it is necessary to avoid leaning to either side, and to change nothing."

Concerning the problem of whether or not to embrace change,

Wang Anshi directs his criticism at Sima Guang, whose "back to the ancients" doctrine states, "The laws laid down by the ancestors must not be changed." (*History of the Song Dynasty·Biography of Sima Guang*) Wang Anshi contends that the past and the present are quite different from each other: "In ancient times, the people practiced their own ways. This is not strange in that their ways were decided by the bygone times. At the present time, the people are practicing their own ways, too. This is not strange either in that their ways are decided by the coming times." (*Collection of Literary Works by Wang Linchuan·an Enquiry into the Doctrine*)

He further puts forth a theory that "the old and the new repel each other": "The old and the new repel each other, as decided by Heaven. Since there is silence and there is debate, so the old and the new repel each other, as decided by man." (*Collection of the Tortoise Hill· Wang Anshi's Explanation of the Origin of Chinese Characters*) Regarding this, Wang Anshi has two main ideas: First, the positive and the negative complete each other. Second, the strong and the weak are transformed into each other. He gives this explanation:

"Reaction is not the cause of action; it is actually a kind of motion, for the motion comes from the opposite. The weak is not the cause of the strong; it is actually a kind of strength, for this reason the weak can become strong." (Quoted by Jiao Hong, *Wing of the Book of Laozi*) In his opinion, as long as there is vitality, as long as an enterprise is assured of a future, even if it is in a situation in which "everybody hates it," the final victory is obtainable. Through hard struggle, "those who doggedly attack the fortified stronghold will win the battle." He hoped that his political reform would become "as powerful as storms and billows," so that "everything will be inspired by it and every form influenced by it." (*Wing of the Book of Laozi*)

But neither Wang Anshi's monism of the Way and the material force, nor his view of the development of contradictions is thoroughgoing. Although he lays stress on human effort, he acknowledges the Mandate of Heaven, and sometimes that "human efforts cannot match what Heaven mandates." (*Collection of Literary Works by Wang Linchuan·A Reply to the Question*) He acknowledges that things are moving and developing all the time, but emphasizes tranquility, saying, "Tranquility is the master of action." Accepting that in things there are contradictions and opposites, he maintains that one may meet no antagonism in the world as long as one forgets both oneself and other things. (*Annotations on the Laozi*) Wang Anshi's dilemma stems from the ideological contradiction between dialectics and metaphysics. This was decided by the duality of the reforming school of the landlord class, which he represented, and by the limitation of the philosophical heritage of his time, which he accepted.

24.

Zhang Zai: Metaphysics and the Great Void of the Universe

Zhang Zai (1020–1077) was a native of Chang'an. Since his family came from Hengqu Town, Meixian County in Shaanxi Province, he was also called Hengqu. For many years, he lectured in central Shaanxi, and founded a school called the Guan School of Thought. When Zhou Dunyi, Shao Yong, Cheng Hao, Cheng Yi, and others were learning from Buddhism and Taoism, building their respective systems, Zhang Zai criticized Buddhism and Taoism. He restored authority to the monism of the material force, creating a "theory of material force and transformation."

With respect to the distinguishing features of his thought and the academic style of the Guan School, they focused on researching reality and on learning in order to practice, an academic style quite different from that of the Cheng brothers, who spoke glibly about nature and principle. Their style exerted great influence on later scholars and developed into the practical basis of the thought of the Guan School.

Zhang Zai was deeply immersed in Buddhism and Taoism for many years, and felt qualified to criticize the world outlook of Buddhism. (*Academic Cases of the Song and Yuan Dynasties·Zhang Zai the Scholar*). In his anti-Buddhist stance, Zhang combined his philosophical thought with his knowledge of scientific practice to tackle the problem of Nature. In so doing, he presents the spirit of seeking truth from facts.

Zhang Zai restored the traditional concept of the "material force" and developed it. He made a thorough study of the *Book of Changes*, returning to the ancients. Based on this, he built his own theory on Nature, stating, "all things have form, and all forms are material force." (*Comments on the Book of Changes·Part Two*) His dialectics are expressed in the following: "In all actions there are internal causes, and no action is not actuated from the outside." (*Correcting Youthful Ignorance·Book 1·Part 2: The Three and the Two*) Combining his view on Nature and his dialectics, he says, "I know that the Great Vacuity is material force and that there is no such thing as nonbeing." In this, he stands opposed to Metaphysicists, Buddhists, and Neo-Confucians, whose proponents did their best to set up a noumenon that surpasses Nature and is above the material world. Zhang Zai vigorously refutes them. Among Zhang's main philosophical works are *Correcting Youthful Ignorance*, *Comments on the Book of Changes*, *Assembled Principles of Classical Learning,* and *Sayings of Master Zhang*. The Ming Dynasty saw the compilation of *The Complete Works of Master Zhang*.

In what is the world unified? This was the focus of the philosophical struggles of medieval times. Many thought the world was unified in the spiritual noumenon behind material phenomena. Sometimes they called it "nonbeing" or "vacuity," and sometimes "the Principle" or "the Great Ultimate." There were also philosophers who made great efforts to demonstrate its material unification.

Zhang Zai was crystal clear where the divergence lay. According to the Taoist view, the void produces material force and nonbeing produces being, while the Buddhists held phenomena (forms, things) and noumenon (nature, the void) are separated from each other and the objective world is an illusion. Zhang counters that the void and objects, and nonbeing and being, are in fact unified in the material force as the formless "void" and the visible "objects."

"Taoists and Buddhists regard the noumenon as the void," with no stipulations. And they do not consider the void material force. Furthermore, they take their own narrow consciousness for both the principal and subsidiary causes, from which Heaven and Earth come, and therefore regard the invisible void as sole reality and the visible world as illusion. What, then, is the root of their mistake? It lies in the fact that they do not understand that the visible 'brightness' and the invisible 'darkness' are the collection and dispersion of the material force. Yin and yang, the two basic material forces, always govern Heaven and Earth. This fundamental law applies to Heaven, Earth, and Man. It is foolish enough that the Taoists and Buddhists should concoct a noumenon that surpasses any forms whatsoever, but they go so far as to call it the 'void and nonbeing.' This is how Neo-Confucianism gets mixed up with Buddhism and Metaphysics ontologically. (*Correcting Youthful Ignorance·Book 1, Part 1: Great Harmony*)

Zhang Zai's disclosure was of great significance at that time. Zhou Dunyi put forth a theory of the Great Ultimate as "the subtlest of all things" because it is able to "engender yin and yang." Shao Yong established a paradigm of cosmology in which the formless spirit engenders "numbers," "diagrams," "implements," and the like. Sima Guang took for the starting point of his philosophy the proposition that "the myriad things originate from the void." In the Cheng brothers' view, the "creator" that formed and produced the myriad things in the universe is the metaphysical "Way" or "Principle," which is "still, silent, and traceless." All these ontological views are a kind of metaphysical speculation. In fact, they make such use of the duality of human cognition that the abstract loses contact with the concrete, and the general is divorced from the specific. Furthermore, they proclaim that the realistic world is only phenomena, whereas the abstract is the absolute and boundlessly real noumenon.

Zhang Zai cannot disclose the essence of metaphysical speculation, but, in accordance with his cognitive level, he points out that the root cause of the Metaphysicians' ontological mistake is the proposition that "vacuity is limitless, and material force is limited." As for the absolute void and illusionary reality, to which Buddhism devotes particular care, they are in fact also a mistake in ontology as the Buddhists "think that the production and annihilation of the universe are due to the elements of existence (dharma) created by the mind. They regard the small (human consciousness) as the cause of the great (reality), and the secondary as the cause of the fundamental." (*Correcting Youthful Ignorance·Book 4·Part 1: Enlarging One's Mind*)

After criticizing the Metaphysicians and Buddhists, Zhang Zai expounded on his own ontology, epitomized in the proposition that "the great void is the material force." The whole world is unified in the material force in its two existential states: the Great Vacuity, which is invisible, and the myriad things, which are visible.

"The Great Vacuity has no physical form. It is the original substance of material force. Its integration and disintegration are but objectifications caused by change." (*Correcting Youthful Ignorance·Book 1·Part 1: Great Harmony*)

> "As an entity, material force simply reverts to its original substance when it disintegrates and becomes formless. When it integrates and assumes form, it does not lose the eternal principle of Change. The Great Vacuity of necessity consists of material force. Material force of necessity integrates to become the myriad things. Things of necessity disintegrate and return to the Great Vacuity." (*Ibid*)

He says, "From the Great Vacuity, there is Heaven." (*Correcting Youthful Ignorance·Book 1, Part 1: Great Harmony*) "Heaven" refers to the totality of the universe, which is of unmeasured vastness. He says elsewhere that Heaven "is just material force in everlasting movement. By vibration, Heaven engenders the myriad things, and it is not concerned with showing any pity for the things." (*Comments on the Book of Changes·Part One*) Here "Heaven" refers to Nature, which has no consciousness.

The specific essence owned by either man or things changes with the integration and disintegration of the material force. In fact, the universal essence of both man and things is the innate essence of the material world, and therefore is eternal. So he says, "Only through fully developing one's nature can one realize that one possesses nothing in life and loses nothing at death." (*Correcting Youthful Ignorance·Book 3·Part 2: Enlightenment Resulting from Sincerity*) Such is Zhang Zai's doctrine of the deification of life. It is inferred that after death one's nature may exist independently. This idea inevitably falls into mysticism.

In Zhang Zai's opinion, "nature" is innate to the material force. Such being the case, then what is spirit? He says, "Spirit is the virtue of Heaven and transformation is the Way of Heaven. Virtue is the foundation of it, and the Way is the function of it. These two aspects are unified in the material force." (*Correcting Youthful Ignorance·Book 2·Part 2: Sprit and Transformation*)

Zhang Zai has two theories concerning material force, one being the theory of the transformation of material force as "one thing having two bodies," the other being the theory centered on material force as "the vacuity being material force." His outstanding contribution to philosophy is to use the theory of the transformation of material force to demonstrate his theory centered on material force.

With the monism of material force as his starting point, he says, "In everything there is a principle." And, "The principles are not made by man, for they are all innate in things." (*Sayings of Master Zhang*) Moreover, he never deviates from material force. He says, "Although material force in the universe integrates and disintegrates, and attracts and repels in a hundred ways, the principle according to which it operates has an order and is unerring." (*Correcting Youthful Ignorance·Book 1·Part 1: Great Harmony*)

Two points of creative development that Zhang Zai made of the dialectic thought of previous ages are: "When there is any movement there must be some subtle cause" and "Movement cannot be actuated by an external cause." Liu Zongyuan too referred to "self-movement," "self-stopping," "self-standing in opposition to each other," and "self-flowing." (*A Critique of Remarks of Monarchs*). But Zhang Zai's viewpoints are more concrete and more profound. What is more, Zhang Zai tackles the problem of internal and external relationships in a more definite way.

Regarding the relationship of the unity of opposites, which governs the internal contradictions of things, Zhang Zai puts forth his doctrine of "the one and the two." Between them, he says, there is a relationship that can never be cut apart.

Furthermore, he formulates "opposites," "opposition," "conflict," and suchlike categories to show how the antagonism of a contradiction serves as the agent by which the interaction of things may take place. He says, "As there are forms, there are their opposites. These opposites necessarily stand in opposition to what they do. Opposition leads to conflict, which will necessarily be reconciled and resolved." (*Correcting Youthful Ignorance·Book 1·Part 1: Great Harmony*) As a result of the struggle, a thing does not leap forward from the old quality to the new quality; it is a pity that the old quality once again returns to the old unity. The "reconciliation and resolution" seems to mean return to the vital force of the Great Harmony. And the vital force of the Great Harmony is nothing but the unity of yin and yang as opposites. Therefore, from the so-called "reconciliation and resolution" we may see that Zhang Zai fails to shake off the influence exerted by the theory of cycles. He cannot explain why the state of new quality will necessarily come into being, nor why the state of old quality will necessarily perish.

Zhang Zai›s dialectical thought expresses quite a number of fragments of brilliant ideas, especially when he strikes a blow against metaphysical speculation with his theory of the internal cause, which is based on the relationship of "the one and the two," which in turn is based on the theory that the material force can transform itself into myriads of concrete things. The dialectical thought of Zhang Zai is combined with naive materialism—the reason his dialectical ideas are so brilliant.

Zhang Zai breaks new ground in the sphere of the theory of knowledge, and he directs his research at the arguments used by the Buddhists. Of course, sometimes he takes a false step or follows a wrong path.

Zhang Zai affirms that human knowledge is a product of human nature.

> "Consciousness and knowledge emerge only when human nature is affected by contact with the external world." (*Correcting Youthful Ignorance·Book 1·Part 1: Great Harmony*)

> "Man has knowledge because human nature accepts what is seen and heard. Human knowledge comes from the combination of the internal mind and the external world." (*Correcting Youthful Ignorance·Book 4·Part 1: Enlarging One's Mind*)

Hence, the external world is the origin of perceptual knowledge. The reason perceptual knowledge is called "affected" lies in that its content comes from the objective world where content is ever-changing. "The mind varies and differs in a thousand ways because it is acted on by the external world in various ways." (*Correcting Youthful Ignorance·Book 1·Part 1: Great Harmony*) Here Zhang Zai persists in the epistemological principle that "when there is a thing there is knowledge of it. Here in a correct way he emphasizes that perceptual knowledge comes from the external world. Furthermore, he puts forth the proposition that when one truly desires to "combine the inside and the outside," one must exert every effort to make a thorough inquiry into the principle of things, as there is a limitation on perceptual knowledge.

"We have talked about how to make a thorough inquiry into things, but we have not yet talked about how to make a thorough inquiry into the principle. My only fear is that once one takes hearing and seeing for the mind, one will not be able to make a thorough inquiry into the mind. Originally one has no need to work with the mind at all; it is only when there are things that one works with the mind. But if one only takes hearing and seeing for the mind, my fear is that this will belittle the function of the mind. What the world is filled with are things. When one is limited within one's own hearing and seeing, how much can one accept from the world? So, how can one make a thorough inquiry into the things in the world? This is the reason I advocate making a thorough inquiry into the mind." (*Sayings of Master Zhang·Part Two*)

Zhang Zai›s difficulty here is that he does not understand the dialectical linkage between perceptual and rational knowledge. To oppose what he perceives as the Buddhist idea that the root cause of knowledge lies in the limitation of perception acquired by the sense organs, he—in a one-sided way—exaggerates the effectiveness and independence of rational thinking. Therefore, he ends up having two doctrines of knowledge by separating reason and perception.

In Zhang Zai's opinion, only "knowledge acquired by moral nature" can "unite itself with the mind of Heaven." By such knowledge one can "investigate the spirit to the utmost so as to know the transformations of Heaven." He says, "As is said in the *Book of Changes*, it is necessary to investigate the spirit to the utmost so as to know the transformations of Heaven. This is what the abundant virtue reaches when it is ripe. Nobody can reach such a spiritual realm by wisdom alone." (*Correcting Youthful Ignorance·Book 2·Part 2: Spirit and Transformation*) Such knowledge does not come from "what is heard and seen" or what comes from "the combination of the inside and the outside." Instead, it comes from one's personal cultivation of morality and virtue. The highest realm one may reach with such knowledge is "integrity with Heaven." (*Ibid*)

This is where the contradiction in Zhang Zai's thought lies. As far as knowledge is concerned, he sets relativity against limitation; as far as cognitive ability is concerned, he sets absoluteness against limitlessness. In his attempt to unite these contradictory pairs, he exerted his efforts on a wrong basis. He says, "Only those who fully develop their nature can unify the state of formlessness and unaffectedness, and the state of objectification and affectedness." (*Correcting Youthful Ignorance·Book 1·Part 1: Great Harmony*) On one side, there is the concrete state of "objectification and affectedness." On the other, there is the abstract state of "formlessness and unaffectedness." How can he unify these two sides? His answer is to "develop one's nature to the utmost." He says, "The sage, however, fully develops his nature, and does not allow what is seen or heard to fetter his mind. He considers everything in the world to be his own self. This is why Mencius said that when one exerts one's mind to the utmost, one can know nature and Heaven." (*Correcting Youthful Ignorance·Book 4·Part 1: Enlarging One's Mind*) Although Zhang Zai is different from Mencius in both starting point and destination, he has already fallen into mysticism, in just the same way as Mencius does when he says, "All things are already complete in us." (*The Book of Mencius, 13. 4*)

In the theory of knowledge, Zhang Zai loses his footing when he attempts to understand the cognitive route of Buddhism, which denies the existence of the objective world. He attributes such denial to the fact that Buddhists measure the vastness of the universe by means of the sense organs of man, of which the capacity of cognition is very limited. When they cannot understand thoroughly, he concludes, they absurdly regard the sun and the moon to be illusion or error. In this way, they deny the existence of the material world. Zhang Zai, however, goes to the other extreme. In his opinion, it is necessary to get into accord with the Heavenly mind by enlarging one's own mind. He urges people to grasp the whole boundless universe directly. As a result, one falls into the following situation: "Nature and the Heavenly way do not dwell in the difference that one is large and the other is small." (*Correcting Youthful Ignorance·Book 3·Part 2: Enlightenment Resulting from Sincerity*) "If so, the Way of both heaven and Earth may be put in a nutshell." (*Correcting Youthful Ignorance·Book 2·Part 1: The Heavenly Way*)

Zhang Zai sees the limitlessness of the material world as well as the limitedness of human knowledge. He opposes the Buddhists in that they use limited knowledge to deny the objective world, think that the cognition of the whole universe may be accomplished once and for all, and do not know that the cognition of the objective world is a limitlessly developmental process. In such a process, the opposites such as perceptive and rational, concrete and abstract, relative and absolute, are all united dialectically and deepened repeatedly. Therefore, man's cognition of them can only advance in a spiral way. This is the reason he advocates making a thorough inquiry into the spirit and transformation by exerting one's mind and nature to the utmost, and that one must put the Way of both Heaven and Earth in a nutshell. At first glance, it appears he has solved the complicated problem of knowledge, but he does it in a simplistic way.

Many thinkers of the ages succeeding the Northern Song Dynasty more or less drew inspiration from Zhang Zai. In the Song and Ming dynasties, the developmental routes of some philosophical schools of thought, which developed parallel to Neo-Confucianism, were all started by Zhang Zai, and summed up by Wang Fuzhi.

But, in the development of philosophy there is a long process from immature to mature. In the thought of Zhang Zai, famous for his "boldness in creating the Way," there are weak points, and some are serious indeed.

First, although Zhang Zai lays stress on the unity of the material world, he confuses to a certain degree the differences between material and spiritual phenomena. He says, "Heaven knows things not by means of ears, eyes, or the mind. But the principle by which Heaven knows greatly surpasses what is acquired by ears, eyes, and the mind of Man." (*Correcting Youthful Ignorance·Book 2·Part 1: The Heavenly Way*) He also says, "The sage has affections instead of secrets, just as the spirit of the heavenly Way has." (*Ibid*) Thus, he leaps from confusing the difference between spirit and matter to personalizing Heaven, and finally falls into mysticism.

Second, Zhang Zai sees the complexity of contradictory phenomena, which serves as the fountainhead of movement in the process of the material force becoming the myriad concrete things in Nature, but cannot give a scientific explanation for them. What is more, he regards the "spirit" innate in the transformation of material force as the "deified Heavenly Way," which is outside the "transformation of material force" and opposite to the "products of the transformation." He says, "Any visible material thing whatsoever has either size or weight. But spirit has neither size nor weight. Spirit is just spirit." (*Comments on the Book of Changes·Part Two*) In this way, he truly deifies "spirit," which governs yin and yang and is unfathomable.

Last, as far as the theory of human nature is concerned, Zhang Zai further divides abstract human nature into two—the "nature of personal disposition" and the "nature of Heaven and Earth." His "doctrine of personal disposition" was greatly appreciated by Zhu Xi, who commented, "With his personality he rendered service to the tradition started by the sages, with his doctrine he benefited the scholars of later ages." (*Classified Conversations of Zhu Xi*) As a result, Zhu Xi considers Zhang Zai, along with Zhou Dunyi, Shao Yong, Cheng Hao, and Cheng Yi, to be among the "Five Masters of the Northern Song Dynasty" and a founder of Neo-Confucianism.

25.

Zhu Xi: Cycles of Contradiction

Zhu Xi (1130–1200), born into a celebrated family of Confucian scholars, was attracted to the Yi-Luo School started by Cheng Hao and Cheng Yi. His birthplace, Fujian Province, is known as the Min region, and his school is called the Min School. He made an extensive study of the Confucian classics, as well as of history, literature, and other branches of learning. He wrote many books, among which his main philosophical works are *Collected Writings of Huian the Literary Prince* (121 volumes, including *Literary Works* in 100 volumes, *Supplementary Works* in 11 volumes, and *Additional Works* in 10 volumes), *Classified Conversations of Zhu Xi* (compiled by his disciples in 140 volumes), *Collected Commentaries on the Four Books*, *Commentary on an Explanation of the Diagram of the Great Ultimate*, *Commentary on the Western Inscription,* and *Commentary on Penetrating the Book of Changes*. He approved of the theory of the transformation of material force put forth by Zhang Zai. He inherited and developed the doctrine of the Great Ultimate put forth by Zhou Dunyi. He absorbed much from both the diagram-number studies put forth by Shao Yong and the studies of principle and righteousness put forth by the Chengs. WIth these as the foundation, he established the major philosophical system known as Neo-Confucianism. In the later stage of feudal society in China, Zhu Xi was a versatile philosopher who exercised far greater influence on the development of Chinese philosophy than any other thinker.

In the controversy with Buddhist nihilist ontology, the Cheng brothers maintained that "The vacuity is completely the principle" (*Surviving Works of the Two Chengs·Book 3*), while Zhang Zai held that "The vacuity is the material force." (*Correcting Youthful Ignorance·Book 1·Part 1: Great Harmony*) What attitude did Zhu Xi adopt?

Sometimes the principle Zhu discusses is "the original principle from which the myriad things come into being," and the material force is "the material attached to the principle that endows things with their physical forms." The emergence of both mankind and things is the result of the combination of the principle with the material. Such a view seems to be a dualist approach with the principle and the material in parallel. This shows that Zhu Xi synthesizes the two Cheng brothers' monism of the principle and Zhang Zai's monism of the material force.

Sometimes the principle he discusses means orderliness and arrangement of things, seeming to refer to law. As for the material force, it refers to physical form or material, namely, matter. He puts forth the view that "principle and the material force rely on each other," and "principle lies in the material force." Law and matter are interdependent, and law dwells in things themselves. He appears to maintain that the principle and the material force should be unified. His philosophical thought improves upon that of the two Cheng brothers and Zhang Zai by developing the former's monism of the principle and the latter's monism of the material force.

What is Zhu Xi's view on the relationship between principle and the material force? To answer this question it is necessary to do two things: one, grasp the fundamental tendency of his philosophy, and two, dissect the epistemological root cause of his philosophical thought.

The outstanding feature of Zhu Xi's philosophy lies in the cosmogony and the ontology of the universe. As far as cosmogony is concerned, he cites a large number of materials from the theory of the transformation of material force to explain how Heaven, Earth, and Man come into being, then develops his theory step by step. As far as ontology is concerned, he deliberately avoids or even refuses to give a direct and positive answer to the basic question, which comes into being first, the principle or the material force? Instead, he talks much about two formalized propositions: "Principle and material force rely on each other" and "Principle lies in material force." Nonetheless, "Principle is the fundamental" and "Principle plays the lead."

When summing up the experiences of theoretical speculation, Zhu Xi comes to see that there are theoretical weak points in demonstrating the thing-in-itself. Some scholars simply describe the thing-in-itself as "being" or a certain "thing or event" that can be seen or touched. In that case, it has been rendered "equal to a material thing" instead of being the absolute entity. Some scholars describe the thing-in-itself as "nonbeing." In that case, the thing-in-itself "has been rendered as emptiness and silence."

The above prescriptions have one thing in common: all are directed at setting up a noumenal world, abstract and silent, outside the phenomenal world, which is concrete and vivid. Simply put, they divide existence into two parts. This leads to a difficulty: In theory, there is no way to explain why "the myriad phenomena originate from one source." To overcome this weak point and get out of the theoretical dilemma, ontology is processed anew in Zhu Xi's theoretical system. He says as follows:

> "As regards the principle, it cannot be described as being; as regards thing or event, it cannot be described as nonbeing." (*Classified Conversations of Zhu Xi·Book 94*)

> "'The Ultimate of Nonbeing and also the Great Ultimate!' By this proposition we mean that there exists some entity that has no physical form but it truly has principle." (*Ibid*)

Principle is identified with the Ultimate of Nonbeing or the Great Ultimate. Zhu Xi differs from his predecessors in that the entity he talks about is neither a simple "being" nor a simple "nonbeing." Instead, it is a unity of both. When it serves as the abstract "Way or principle," because it has no physical form as things or events usually do, it cannot be called "being"; instead, it ought to be called "nonbeing." When it serves as conceptual existence, because it is "a principle as a practical being," it cannot be called "nonbeing"; instead, it ought to be called "being."

Zhu Xi processes the thing-in-itself into a purely logical existence to demonstrate that such an entity is abstract but real. As a purely logical conception, the thing-in-itself exists before any beings and after any nonbeings. It lies outside yin and yang, but it goes through yin and yang in the meantime. The thing-in-itself is neither prior nor posterior, neither interior nor exterior; it is an absolute entity that "goes through the whole and exists everywhere." Such an absolute entity is called the "Great Ultimate" or "Principle." (See *Commentary on an Explanation of the Diagram of the Great Ultimate*) As far as the philosophical essence is concerned, the principle is fundamental, while the material force and things are incidental. In Zhu Xi's ontology, two kinds of material force—the five elements and the myriad things—may be derived from the Principle or the Great Ultimate, and the myriad things may also return to the Principle. Now the essence of his philosophy is thus seen very clearly: Principle is fundamental, and material force is incidental. (See *Penetrating the Book of Changes·Commentary on Principle, Nature and Destiny*)

When Zhu Xi puts forth the proposition that "principle and material force rely on each other," what relationship is there between principle and material force? If the relationship between principle and material force is a parallel one, he must be a dualist. If he means a relationship between the principal and the subordinate when he puts forth the same proposition, he must be a monist. He says as follows:

> "The Great Ultimate is a term that can neither be separated from yin and yang nor mixed with yin and yang." (*Classified Conversations of Zhu Xi·Book 4*)

> "The Great Ultimate exists only in yin and yang, and cannot be separated from them. In the final analysis, however, the Great Ultimate is the Great Ultimate, and yin and yang are yin and yang." (*Classified Conversations of Zhu Xi·Book 8*)

Zhu Xi stresses that principle and material force rely on each other but are distinct. Only when "principle does not depart from material force" can the universal effectiveness of principle be guaranteed. However, only when "principle does not mix with material force" can the absolute supremacy of principle be guaranteed. His intent is to demonstrate that the relationship between principle and material force is that of principal and subordinate; it is not a parallel one:

> "What are called principle and material force are certainly two different entities. But considered from the standpoint of things, the two

> entities are merged one with the other, and cannot be separated, with each in a different place. However, this does not destroy the fact that the two entities are each entities in themselves. When considered from the standpoint of principle, before things existed, their principles of being already existed. Only their principles existed, however, and not yet the things themselves." (*Literary Works of Zhu Xi·A Reply to Liu Shuwen*)

When Zhu Xi says, "The principle and the material force rely on each other," he "considered [the problem] from the standpoint of things"—from the angle of cosmogony. In every particular thing, principle and material force are interdependent. But from the angle of ontology, he thinks that principle and material force depart from each other and differ from each other. Where does the difference lie? It lies in the fact that the principle is the genitor of the material force, and the principle is the dominator of the material force—a reliance in which the subordinate follows the principal.

To further understand Zhu Xi's thought we next ask, what is the essence of this proposition, "Principle lies in material force"?

There are two possibilities: one, principle "lies within" material force; two, principle "lies outside" material force. Which is Zhu Xi's meaning? He uses a metaphor to illustrate that he means the second possibility. He says that principle is to material force what a pearl is to water. Principle is as transparent as a bright pearl. When it falls into clear water, it is completely transparent both inside and outside. When it falls into turbid water, it is just as bright on the inside, although "it is no longer bright if seen from the outside." Therefore, "brightness" is the nature per se of the "bright pearl"; it does not depend on the transparency of water. When the water is clear, the pearl's brightness does not increase in the slightest, and when the water is turbid, its brightness does not decrease in the slightest either. The only difference is that sometimes the pearl seems to be bright and sometimes not bright, for the brightness of the outside of the pearl is conditioned by the degree of transparency of the water. Therefore, water is water per se, and a pearl is a pearl per se. In a like manner, the material force is the material force per se; the principle is the principle per se. When a pearl exists in water, its existence is the outside existence and by no means the inside existence. When principle exists in material force, its existence is also outside existence and by no means inside existence. (See *Classified Conversations of Zhu Xi·Book 4*) In Zhu Xi's opinion, principle exists outside material force. This is in direct contrast with Zhang Zai's statement that principle is "something innate in material force." (*Correcting Youthful Ignorance·Book 9·Part 2: Heaven Is My Father*) But if "principle and material force rely on each other" and "principle is in material force" which exists first, principle or material force? Zhu Xi says, "As far as the thing-in-itself is concerned, there is first principle and then there is material force." (*Questions and Answers on the Works of Mencius·Book 3*) He clearly affirms that principle comes first and material force second.

Thus it follows that "principle" exists as a variety of substance by itself, and at the same time as unity by itself. Because "the principle is partaken" there is the variety of things. Because "the principle is a single entity" there is the unity of things. Therefore, both the variety and unity of things are ultimately decided by "principle," which is not a law that the things themselves innately possess. In other words, principle is not "material generality." What is principle then? It is "abstract generality," which the myriad things take for their substance by partaking. In this way, Zhu Xi dissociates the generality, which dwells in the particularity and can exist only by means of the particularity, from the particularity. Then he renders it into the deified absolute, which overrides all the concrete things and dominates their changes.

In his opinion, "principle" is the thing-in-itself, and he applies it to explaining the fact that "The myriad things come from one source." So he says, "The myriad things are one and the same thing, and one and the same thing is the myriad things." (*Classified Conversations of Zhu Xi·Book 94*) He cites an example in order to illustrate his view:

> "When Man and things were produced, Heaven endowed them with the same principle. The only difference lies in that Man and things embody it in different ways. Take, for example, the water in a river. If you dip a ladle in it, you will get a ladleful of water. If you dip a bowl in it, you will get a bowlful of water. In like manner, you may get a pailful or a jarful of water. The quantity of water you get varies with the vessel you use. Principle varies in just the same manner." (*Classified Conversations of Zhu Xi·Book 4*)

Zhu Xi opposes the metaphysical view put forth by some idealists that "Principle contains the myriad things." When he explains how the hexagrams of the *Book of Changes* came into being, he reasons that if "principle contains the myriad things," there must be a tendency to acknowledge theoretically that the emergency of the myriad things is arranged once and for all, in other words, there is no process of development. If so, the function of the positive activities of the "principle" must be weakened by the simple theory that everything is decided all at once. On the other hand, "principle contains the myriad things" neglects the stages in the emergence of the myriad things. According to the old theory there must be a tendency to confuse theoretically the "posterior being" of the myriad things and the "prior being" of principle. If so, the absolute supremacy of the proposition that "principle is prior to the things" will be weakened. Only the viewpoint that "principle begets the myriad things" can solve the two problems involved, one being the ontological problem, the other being the problem of creation. On the one hand, it is ontologically necessary to use the stages of emergence to distinguish the "posterior emergence" of the myriad things from the "prior being" of principle. On the other hand, it is necessary cosmologically to use the internal contradictions and movements to explain the final cause of the creation of the myriad things. Only by so doing can his new theory pit itself against Zhang Zai's materialist theory of the internal cause that "the material cause begets the myriad things." According to Zhu Xi's viewpoint that "principle begets the myriad things," the "Two Elementary Forms," "Four Emblematic Symbols" and "Eight Trigrams" do not come into being all at once; instead, their emergence follows a successive order. The emergence and development of things are a process in which there are some objectively dialectical factors. (Cf. *Classified Conversations of Zhu Xi·Book 67*)

Based on this viewpoint, Zhu Xi thinks that in everything there are two contradictory relationships of interdependence, one being the externally reactive relationship, or more simply "external reaction," the other being the internally reactive relationship, or more simply "internal reaction." As for the external reaction, it means that one should treat yin and yang as "two kinds of material force." He cites an example, saying "There is a separate yin and a separate yang, and therefore the Two Elementary Forms are set up. Furthermore, such a fixed situation is formed as is called the four directions, which refer to Heaven, Earth, the top and the bottom." (*Classified Conversations of Zhu Xi·Book 65*) The world can only possess a fixed and unalterable outlook. As for internal reaction, it means that one should treat yin and yang as "one kind of material force." From one and the same yang, one can see the decline and growth of both yang and yin. And, likewise, from one and the same yin, one can see the decline and growth of both yin and yang. The world seen from this angle is not the world "in a fixed situation," which consists of yin and yang as two separate pieces. Instead, it is a world "in an ever-changing situation," in which both yin and yang are transforming themselves all the time. He describes it in this way: "One is action, the other is tranquility, and they are the roots for each other. So there is an ever-changing situation. For instance, winter and summer, going and coming, all belong to such a situation." (*Ibid*) Therefore, the so-called treatment of yin and yang "as kind of the material force" means that from "one" one should see "the two," or, from the unity one should see the opposites. This demands that from the seeming fixed and unalterable appearance one should find the internal movement of contradictions, which are constantly changing with either growth or decline. Such is his viewpoint that "in one thing there are two opposites." This is a development of Zhang Zai's view on contradiction, "In one thing there are two bodies."

But Zhu Xi thinks in this way: "One divides into two. At every stage of the development of things it is so, and will be so for ever. Everything is like this: one divides into two." (*Classified Conversations of Zhu Xi·Book 67*) Thus, he simplifies and combines the complicated contradictory movements in all objective things. As a result, he confines dialectics, which unfold objectively in many ways, in a metaphysical framework.

By making use of the theory that yin and yang are transformed into each other, Zhu Xi demonstrates that the principle begets the myriad things. Besides, he touches on the problem of the relationship between the gradual and sudden changes, which exist in the developmental process.

We now turn to Zhu Xi's theory of knowledge. How can we know "principle" as "a matter of course" that decides the development of things? This question is connected with the theory of knowledge. "By investigating things one may extend his knowledge," as expounded in the *Great Learning*, Zhu Xi probes some major theoretical problems in the sphere of epistemology. He opposes the Buddhist Chan Sect's proposition that "the mind is Buddha." He also opposes Lu Jiuyuan on the theory of introspection when the latter claims that "mind is principle." As one of his comments on the *Great Learning* goes, "Now I discuss how to investigate things and affairs instead of investigating principle to the utmost. If one discuss principle, it is hard to find the hint and clue, for there are things that sometimes seem to be separated from the principle. If you discuss things and affairs, naturally you will get to their principle. Therefore, you ought not to separate yourself from things and affairs." (*Classified Conversations of Zhu Xi·Book 15*) In short, principle "cannot be separated from" things or affairs. Likewise "to investigate principle to the utmost" cannot be separated from "investigating things and affairs." Such is the cognitive method Zhu Xi emphasizes, whose kernel is "Only by keeping in touch with things and affairs can one investigate their principle to the utmost." (*Syntactic and Semantic Analysis of the Great Learning·Additional Remarks to Chapter 5: Investigating the Principle of Things and Affairs*)

But as the target of knowledge, the "principle" he is going to investigate to the utmost is nothing but "reason without man." In other words, he regards self-consciousness as the target. When such reason "circulates" in things or affairs, it becomes "the principle dwelling in things or affairs." When such reason "circulates" in the human mind, it becomes the "principle dwelling in oneself." As for the relationship between grahaka (perceiver) and grahya (perceived), sometimes he puts "the principle dwelling in things or affairs" on "the opposite side to man." Thus he opposes the object to the subject. Sometimes, however, he combines "the principle dwelling in things or affairs" and "the principle dwelling in oneself" into one whole, saying, "All the principles that dwell in things or affairs are contained in the principle that dwells in oneself." (*Classified Conversations of Zhu Xi·Book 100*) Thus he postulates the unity of object and subject while regarding the subject as playing a dynamic role in reflecting and predicting the object. He goes so far as to say, "Mind embraces the myriad principles, and the myriad principles are included in one mind." (*Classified Conversations of Zhu Xi·Book 9*) Also, he says, "The perceived is the principle of the human mind. The perceiver has the spirit of material force," (*Classified Conversations of Zhu Xi·Book 5*) and, "The perceived is principle. Principle cannot separate itself from perception, and perception cannot separate itself from principle." (*Ibid*) In this way, he confuses two concepts, one being the human mind (the sense organs for cognition), which is able to reflect things, the other being the content of reflection, which is outside the human mind. Now the external principles that dwell in things or affairs are described as the internal principle that dwells in the human mind. According to this logic, the perceived and the perceiver are "inseparable," as also is the case with thought and thinker. What is more, "the principle" that man knows has already become "the principle of the human mind," and the perceived has already been included in the perceiver. Although there are great divergences between the Neo-Confucianism advocated by Zhu Xi and the Mind Learning advocated by Lu Jiuyuan as far as the cognitive method is concerned, we find that there exists no impassable chasm between them when we make a careful examination of their cognitive routes.

To sustain moral principles and ethics, Zhu Xi researches the relationship between knowledge and action. In his opinion, their relationship is like this: "With respect to order, knowledge comes first, and with respect to importance, action is more important." (*Classified Conversations of Zhu Xi·Book 9*) The knowledge he discusses in the main refers to the cognition of ethics and morality. The action he discusses in the main refers to practice in the sphere of ethics and morality. Because the cognition of ethics and morality serves as guidance to practice, it is just as he says—knowledge comes first. Because practice serves as the means to consolidate and to accomplish ethical cognition, therefore it is just as he says—action is more important. On the one hand, the effect that action has upon knowledge can only be realized through practice in the sphere of ethics and morality. For instance, "It is necessary for a son to have filial piety, and for a minister to have loyalty." When people have such cognition they have assuredly realized the rationality of ethics and morality. On the other hand, the effect knowledge has upon action lies in that people must have some cognition of ethics and morality. In case they have such cognition, whenever they meet with "their kinsfolk" they will be able to "act according to the principle of filial piety," and whenever they meet with their "monarch" they will be able to "act according to the principle of loyalty." In short, "whenever they meet with things and affairs, they will be able to act according to principle." (*Classified Conversations of Zhu Xi·Book 15*) In this way, human behavior may be guaranteed by "knowledge," and nobody may deviate from the common course prescribed by ethics and morality. Therefore, Zhu Xi's view of knowledge and action is an ethical and moral view.

Because of this, the main content of his theory of "investigating things and extending knowledge" is as follows: "In order to know the instruction of the sages and worthies we read their books. In order to know the principle of Nature we follow the instruction of the sages and worthies." (*Classified Conversations of Zhu Xi·Book 10*) But what is the essence of "the instruction of the sages and worthies"? In their books they "advocate the principles in the world which may serve the following generations." (*Classified Conversations of Zhu Xi·Book 67*) Zhu Xi establishes both the starting point and destination of his theory on the *a priori* principles of the sages and worthies. He reasons out his theory in two directions: One direction is from inside to outside. At first, the "already-known" principle must be applied to the relative thing. And then, "the sources" of the relative thing must be researched so that "the principle dwelling in the thing" may be "reasoned out." In other words, the a priori principles must be imposed on the objective things. This is called "the extension of knowledge." The other direction proceeds from outside to inside. At first, "the sources" of "the principle dwelling in a thing" must be "researched to the bottom." And then, you should proceed from outside to inside, namely, you return to your mind so as to seek for the "already-known" principle. As for the already-known principle, it will reach the ultimate degree of perfection after it is demonstrated by means of materials which have been collected beforehand in the subjective mind. This is called "the ultimacy of knowledge." Therefore, what is put yonder is the "already-known" principle, and what is put hither is also the "already-known" principle. Zhu Xi investigates continuously. But what he investigates is after all one and the same principle, which is already known:

> "Someone asked about the principle of knowing the new. Answer: The so-called new things are those that dwell in the old things, so they are old after all. When they are reviewed they may be applied to esteeming virtue and Nature. And then people may seek new ideas from them. To do so is to practice the Way and to engage in scholarship." (*Classified Conversations of Zhu Xi·Book 118*)

Such is Zhu Xi's advocacy of "reviewing the old and learning the new." As far as a method of study is concerned, it reflects certain objective laws on how to acquire knowledge. But his theory of knowledge accords with his world outlook. As there is no possibility of new things that may surpass the "already-known" principles appearing, in the theory of reflection there can be no possibility of any new knowledge that may surpass the "already-known" principles appearing either. Thus, it follows that there cannot be any development for the world, nor can there be any development for human knowledge either. Therefore, the theory that "principle begets the myriad things" has to end with the theory of cycles, i.e., "the fixed positions do not change." Likewise, the "investigation of things and extension of knowledge" has to end with the call to "review the old and learn the new," which is, however, essentially a certain kind of apriorism.

The Neo-Confucians of the Northern Song Dynasty used "the Imperial Ultimate" (Shao Yong) and "the Great Ultimate" (Zhou Dunyi) as the supreme categories, to shore up the feudal imperial system. And they proclaimed that social differences such as "superior and inferior, noble and humble" under feudal rule are "the fixed principle under Heaven." (the two Cheng brothers) On the other hand, rebellious peasants had their own ideal, that is, "Treat all people as equals in status and property!" They too regarded their ideal as "the Heavenly principle" and as "a matter of course." They regarded the feudal code that "divided people into the noble and the humble by laws" as "evil laws." And they proclaimed that these evil laws should be discarded, for this is also a matter of course. (See Xu Mengshen, *A Collection of the Treaties of Alliance in the Three Song Reigns 1117 to 1161*)

To demonstrate the "rationality" of feudal ethics, Zhu Xi makes use of the traditional doctrine of "natural endowment," which is decided by material force. The "rationality" of the differences in endowments is revealed by the doctrine that "principle is one, but its manifestations are many." Some people are sages and some are ordinary; some are clever and some are foolish—such are the qualitative differences. Some people are rich, and some are poor; some are noble and some are humble—such are the quantitative differences. Natural endowment is determined by the will of Heaven. But the so-called will of Heaven is in fact the will of the imperial court. He says, "The moment the imperial court appoints somebody to be an official, there must be many things which come up with him all at once." (*Classified Conversations of Zhu Xi·Book 4*) "When each person gets his own benefit, naturally the whole situation may reach harmony. If the ruler is in the position of the ministers and the ministers are in the position of the ruler, how can a harmonious situation be brought about?" (*Classified Conversations of Zhu Xi·Book 68*)

> "As for the demarcation line between noble and humble, and big and small, it is definitely not to be trespassed upon. They seem to be very disharmonious, but each category enjoys its own place. This is called harmony, and can never be surpassed by anything else!" (*Ibid*)

At last, he "finds" a Heavenly principle, "which can never be effaced." That is, "Disadvantage is in fact advantage," "Unsuitability is in fact suitability," "Disharmony is in fact a harmony." In short, "Whatever is irrational is rational." This is the essence of Zhu Xi's philosophy.

As for its theoretical sources, we may trace them back to the Huayan Sect of Buddhism. Its scholars apply the "principle" of "limitless divisibility" to remove the contradiction caused by "things" of "limited divisibility." Thereupon, all differences are "perfect and complete" in themselves so that they have already embodied "the boundless truth." (Cf. Fazang, *Huayan's View of Bodhi-Citta-Utpada*) And with this boundless truth, Zhu Xi gives a blessing to the ruling order of feudalism.

The dominating role of principle over Nature, in Zhu Xi's view, is illustrated in sayings such as the following: "Principle plays the lead, and material force follows," and "Principle and material force rely on each other." But in the sphere of human nature "material force" expresses itself as human desires that can "either withdraw into one's heart or develop into concrete actions." Human desires include feelings, consciousness, plans and measures, which dwell in the human mind at random. Even sages cannot avoid the troubles caused by human desires. He says, "It is true that the material force is begotten by principle. But once it comes into being, principle loses control of it." (*Classified Conversations of Zhu Xi·Book 4*)

What is to be done? Zhu Xi demonstrates the necessity of "discarding desires so as to restore principle." In his opinion, there is a duality in human nature. On the one hand, human nature refers to the "nature of the Mandate of Heaven," which includes "humanity, justice, propriety and wisdom." This is the so-called "Heavenly principle" or "goodness" Mencius talks about. On the other hand, human nature refers to the "nature of physical bodies," which includes "food, drink, and sex." This is the so-called "human desires" or the "evil" Xun Kuang talks about. These two aspects cannot coexist peacefully. He says, "Only man has the Heavenly principle and human desires at the same time. When this party advances, that party retreats; when that party advances this party retreats. Neither of these two parties can stand in the middle without making any advance or retreat." (*Classified Conversations of Zhu Xi·Book 13*) Such being the case, "When one is even not in its proper position, the Heavenly principle is cut off from that very event. When one moment is not connected in a proper way, the Heavenly principle is cut off from that very moment." (*Classified Conversations of Zhu Xi·Book 44*) For this reason, he denies that the "Heavenly principle" possesses the possibility to "expand" itself spontaneously. On the contrary, he emphasizes that only by "discarding human desires altogether" can one restore everything to the "Heavenly principle." (See the *Classified Conversations of Zhu Xi·Book 13*)

In the second place, he demonstrates the possibility of "discarding desires so as to restore principle." In his opinion, "As for the Nature, it is the principle of the mind. As for emotion, it is the activity of Nature. As for the mind, it is the master of both Nature and emotion." (*Classified Conversations of Zhu Xi·Book 5*) "Mind" possesses initiative for rational thinking, emotions and desires. In relation to the desires of the sense organs such as the ears and the eyes, it is called the "human mind." In relation to the "Heavenly principle," which includes "humanity, justice, propriety and wisdom," it is called the "moral mind." In fact, everybody shares this duality. "Everybody is just the same in that he or she has a physical form. Even the greatest sage and the lowest fool have a human mind. Therefore, they also have a moral mind." (*Syntactic and Semantic Analysis of the Doctrine of the Mean·Preface*) Such being the case, everybody has the possibility to change form good to evil and from evil to good. So, on the one hand, it is necessary to stifle desires and to hold fast to seriousness; on the other, it is necessary to nourish one's nature and extend one's knowledge by investigating things. And the best way is to combine these two aspects, and to do one's best to investigate the principles to the utmost. In this way, the human mind, which gets more and more dangerous as time passes, will cross over from danger to safety. Likewise, the moral mind, which gets fainter and fainter as time passes, will cross over from faintness to distinctness. At last, the moral mind will become the master of the body, and the human mind will always follow its directions in an emergency. (*Ibid*)

In short, as Zhu Xi emphasizes time and again: "Principle plays the lead and material forces follow." This proposition is a moral law, and, as such, is *a priori*. The development of this law undergoes a process full of twists and turns; sometimes principle and desire are mixed together, and sometimes principle and desire fight each other wantonly. Finally, the law is realized in ethical and moral practice, marked by the proposition that "the moral mind leads the way, and the human mind follows its directions."

When the "debate on principle and desires" is applied to the perspective of history, it expresses itself as the "debate on kings and despots." In Zhu Xi's opinion, in the three dynasties of Xia, Shang, and Zhou "The Heavenly principle circulated" in the minds of the emperors and kings, while in society all phenomena were filled with "light." Those were times of peace and prosperity, guided by the "kingly way." But in the later dynasties, the minds of the emperors and kings were filled with "the unavoidable desire of selfish interests," and in society all phenomena were filled with "darkness." Those were times of disorder and trouble, led by the "despotic way." With a great sigh, he points out, because the kingly way was lost and the orthodox tradition of Confucianism was interrupted, "In the past two thousand years, all people were blind, although everybody had a pair of eyes." And all people "fell into a pitch-dark basin of selfish interests so deep that they could not get out of it" and therefore they "tumbled in there." (*Literary Works of Zhu Xi·A Reply to Chen Tongfu*) Although the kingly way was lost, as a transcendental principle it remains. But if we desire to "bring it into full play" and enable it to "prevail everywhere," we must grasp it by the "great foundation" or the "key point." Zhu Xi says, "Of course, the so-called great foundation is nothing but the intentional calculation of the ruler. The so-called key point can only be detected by careful inference after the great foundation is established." (*Literary Works of Zhu Xi·A Reply to Zhang Jingfu*) Clearly, he takes the intention and calculation of emperors and kings for the "fundamental" motive force of history. And he always does his best to pull history back to the "time of peace and prosperity, which was guided by the kingly way." This is a retrogressive view of history, in line with idealism. Theoretically, this is completely in accordance with his developmental view that "Things always turn in cycles," and his theory of knowledge that stresses "reviewing the old and learning the new."

Zhu Xi praises his own philosophy, saying, "Wonderful theories dwell in seemingly trite talk, and flexible methods dwell in the rigid and unimaginative way of doing things." (*Literary Works of Zhu Xi·A Sealed Memorial to the Throne Written in 1188*) Emperor Kangxi of the Qing Dynasty once commented, "With his thought, he epitomizes the past scholarship interrupted for a thousand years and carries it forward. He enlightens the ignorant people by setting up the academic norm for ten thousand generations." (*Complete Works of Master Zhu·Preface*) In Zhu Xi's theory, four elements are combined. The first is the Heavenly principle, which is expressed in terms of ethics. The second is ethics, which is expressed in terms of philosophy. The third is the doctrine of "investigating things and extending knowledge." The fourth is the doctrine that "Principle takes charge of action and tranquility." And his combination of these is so exquisite that it meets the needs of social development in the later stage of feudalism. We may be so bold as to say that his philosophy is an essential link in the developmental chain from the philosophy of Zhang Zai to that of Wang Fuzhi.

26.

The Idealism of Lu Jiuyuan

In the later stage of feudalism in China, Neo-Confucianism split into two schools of thought—the Idealist and the Rationalist. Lu Jiuyuan combined the thought of the Si-Meng School of Confucianism with that of the Chan Sect of Buddhism. Then, influenced by Cheng Hao, who maintained that Heaven was the "principle" and the "mind," he set up the philosophical system of Idealism, which is centered on two points—"Mind is principle" and "The universe is my mind, and my mind is the universe." This school clashed with the Rationalist School of Zhu Xi, and heated controversy flared between the two during the Southern Song Dynasty. In the Ming Dynasty, Wang Shouren inherited and developed the thought of Lu Jiuyuan.

Lu Jiuyuan (1139–1193), a native of Jinxi County in Jiangxi Province, held several official posts in that locality. Later, he taught at Mount Yingtian, later known as Xiangshan, in the same province and therefore was called Master Xiangshan. After his death, his works were collected and compiled into the 36-volume *Complete Works of Lu Xiangshan.*

In ontology the philosophers of the Song-Mong Period all deal with the problem of explaining the variety and unification of things. The solution offered by

the Rationalist School of Zhu Xi is that "Principle begets things" and at the same time that "Principle leads material force"—forming an internal contradiction. Zhu Xi finds that it is very difficult to use his own theory to deal with the two Chengs' monism of principle and

Zhang Zai's monism of material force. Li Gong (1659–1733), a thinker of the Qing Dynasty, commented, "Master Zhu was now in a dilemma, and could not make a good case for his proposition." (*Later Collection of Li Gong*) On the one hand, Zhu Xi has to discuss the origin of the universe. This is a problem of ontology, and he says, "There was principle before there was material force." On the other hand, he has to discuss the way in which the universe is endowed with various attributes. This is a problem of cosmology, and he says, "There was first material force, and principle came into being to match it." Furthermore, he says, "When there is such a material force there is such a principle. When there is no such material force there is no such principle. The more material force there is, the more principle there is. The less material force there is, the less principle there is." (*Complete Works of Zhu Xi·Book 59: A Reply to Zhao Zhidao*) By saying this, Zhu Xi in fact goes against his own Rationalist system.

To deal with the problems in Zhu Xi's synthesis, his successors had to re-examine "principle," which had been separated from matter and made absolute. There are only two alternatives. One was to return Zhu Xi's "principle that is outside things" to the objective law innate in matter per se. This way is followed by Chen Liang and Ye Shi, saying "Principle is within things" and "Principle is in events." The other is to return Zhu Xi's "principle that is outside the mind" to the subjective law that is realized in self-consciousness. Lu Jiuyuan takes this route, saying, "What permeates the mind, emanates from it, and extends to fill the universe is nothing but principle." (*Complete Works of Lu Xiangshan·Book 34: Quotations·Part One*) Lu Jiuyuan replaces Zu Xhi's "monism of principle" with a monism of mind.

Lu Jiuyuan attempts to avoid the problem of principle and material force. Instead, he works hard at two problems, one being the relationship between mind and matter, the other being the relationship between mind and principle. In order to discuss these two problems properly, the key link is dealing with the opponent of "principle," that is, "material force." Zhu Xi regards "principle" as the "Way that is before physical form," and he regards "material force" as an "implement following physical form." According to such a view, principle is clearly set apart from material force. If you acknowledge the existence of "material force that is outside principle," it means that you have set up an opposite to principle or the Way. So, how does principle dominate material force? Or, how does the Way unify the implements? On the other hand, if you acknowledge the existence of the principle that is outside the material force and of the Way that is outside the implements, it means that the principle or the material force has already become a monster, "which surpasses the universe." And it is difficult to help such a monster settle down where "everything came after it" or to put the monster where "yin and yang dwell." This is because there is some distance between the "universe and the "outer-universe" and between "what is before the physical forms and what is after the physical forms." It is hard to describe them "directly and clearly." So Zhu Xi says, "Principle and material force are neither two separate things nor one mixture." He adds, "The Way and implements are either close to each other or far away from each other." He claims that these are two "wonderful propositions," which have been made "in a flexible way."

In Lu Jiuyuan's opinion, these are two thorny problems. To resolve these difficulties, he gives up the way of Zhu Xi, who simply introduces the material force into his theory. (Because in that way you have to permit the material force to play such an important role that it displaces the dominating role of principle.) Instead, Lu Jiuyuan makes material force as a kind of principle. By quoting from the *Commentaries on the Changes*, he refocuses on yin and yang. In his opinion, "One yin and one yang are what came before the physical forms" (*Complete Works of Lu Xiangshan·Book 2: To Zhu Yuanhui*) "The reason the *Book of Changes* may serve as the Way to guide people lies in that only one yin and one yang are discussed in it." (*Ibid*) In short, he regards both the "Way" and "implements" as one harmonious whole and "principle," and "material force" as one integrated mass. In this way, the "implements that came after physical form" have now been transformed into the "Way that came before physical form." The substantial material force has now been transformed into the spiritual principle. There are some thinkers who "only talk about material force," and never speak of "principle." Now, the thinkers have no need to discuss "material force," as "principle" alone remains.

This way out, of course, avoids the difficult problem of the relationship between principle and material force. But there is another problem which is even more difficult to solve. That is, how does principle beget things? Lu Jiuyuan resorts to the study of diagrams and numbers. But he disapproves of Shao Yong's method of "multiplying the former numbers." He says, "Although this method is strict, it runs against rational thinking." Lu Jiuyuan sets up a harmonious system of numbers more exquisite than that of Shao Yong and smoother in concrete application. In his opinion, some numbers are even, and some odd. The even numbers are "orderly," and the odd numbers are "disorderly." These two kinds of numbers play different roles. He says, "Only when things are disorderly there may be some changes, and therefore the odd numbers take the lead in the changes." With this view of the relationship between the odd and even numbers, he generalizes about phenomena being caused by the imbalance of contradictions and developments. Having found a law in odd numbers, he says, "The one is the beginning of the numbers, so we cannot say that there are any changes in it." The "one" is similar to Shao Yong's "Great Ultimate that does not move." It works according to the principle that "wherever there is the one there must be the two." Lu Jiuyuan says, "Wherever there is one thing, this very thing must have its top and bottom, right side and left side, fore part and after part, head and tail, front and back, outside and inside, exterior and interior." So, in one and the same thing there is contained the turning point for that very thing to change from one to two, from odd to even, from disorder to order, and from simple to complex. Moreover, "Wherever there is top and bottom, right side and left side, head and tail, fore part and after part, and outside and inside of one thing, there must be the middle of that very thing." As a result, he discovers this law: "The middle and the two ends become the three." Three is an important number, for "Heaven, Earth and Man constitute the three talents. The sun, the moon and the stars constitute the three Heavenly bodies. A trigram is made up of three strokes. A tripod has three legs." Moreover, three plus two is five, and "In the universe there are five elements, and on the earth there are five directions (namely, the four directions plus the center)." Five plus five is ten. And the numbers from one to ten may be divided into two groups. "One, three, five, seven and nine belong to the Heavenly numbers." These five numbers are called the "numbers of life" in that they are in charge of life. "Two, four, six, eight and ten belong to the Earthly numbers." These five numbers are called the "numbers of perfection." The numbers of life and the numbers of perfection match each other in an intricate and complex way, bringing about endless changes. As a result, "Numbers may change from one to three, and from three to five, and therefore the changes of numbers are without any end." (All the above quotations are from the *Complete Works of Lu Xiangshan·Book 21: Three and Five May Change in an Intricate and Complex Way*) But in the last analysis, that mysterious "one," which is "up to no terms of change," governs the myriad things, which are subject to countless changes. "One" is the beginning of "numbers," and, "Number is principle. If one does not know number, how can he understand principle?" (*Complete Works of Lu Xiangshan·Book 35: Quotations·Part Two*) Thus in Lu Jiuyuan's system, the material force is totally eliminated and the ever-changing numbers are so closely combined with the principle that they are as like as two peas in a pod. Material force as the opponent of principle has been discarded, and a new helper of principle has been invited, that is, number.

Once Lu Jiuyuan applies the ever-changing numbers to explaining absolute principle he gets rid of the bondage which he describes in the following terms: "Material force is strong, and principle is weak." He brings about a new situation in which principle has become the dominator of the world. He says as follows:

> 1. "This principle fills the universe.... This principle is very great. How can there be any limit to it?" (*Complete Works of Lu Xiangshan·Book 12: A Reply to Zhao Yongdao*)
>
> 2. "Heaven and earth are what they are because they follow this principle without partiality. Man coexists with Heaven and earth as the three ultimates. How can man be selfish and disobey principle?" (*Complete Works of Lu Xiangshan·Book 11: To Zhu Jidao*)

We may well recall the words of Zhu Xi, when he says, "[Principle] crosses the demarcation line between man and things, and between this and that. [Principle] surpasses the difference between life and death, and between the ancient and the modern." (*Collected Writings of Huian the Literary Prince·Book 41: A Reply to Liang Songqing*) Obviously, ontologically speaking, the "principle" discussed by Lu Jiuyuan is just the same as the principle discussed by Zhu Xi. In other words, it is the absolute thing-in-itself that surpasses the objective material world and that controls Nature and society. The only difference lies in the relationship between mind and principle. Zhu Xi distinguishes the general self-consciousness (mind) from the target-rendered self-consciousness (principle). So he acknowledges that exterior to the human mind there is a so-called "public principle." Lu Jiuyuan identifies principle simply with mind, and in his opinion: "The mind is principle." He says as follows:

1. "All men have this mind, and all minds are endowed with this principle. The mind is principle." (*Complete Works of Lu Xiangshan·Book 11: To Li Zai*)

2. "The mind is one, and principle is one. Perfect truth is reduced to a unity; the essential principle is never a duality. The mind and principle can never be separated into two." (*Complete Works of Lu Xiangshan·Book 1: To Zeng Zhaizhi*)

There is only one principle that governs the universe and the myriad things in it. There is only one principle that governs so many minds of all the people in the world. Obviously, principle and mind are definitely not the "one." But Lu Jiuyuan says that they are "reduced to a unity." Why does he say so? Obviously principle and mind stand on "two" sides. But Lu Jiuyuan says that there "is never a unity." Why does he say so? The grounds of Lu Jiuyuan's argument are as follows: "All men have this mind, and all minds are endowed with this principle." More or less, he has touched with the relationship between the reflector (mind) and the reflected (principle). It is true that the mind can reflect the principles, and the principles can be stored ("endowed") in the mind by rendering them into concepts. But Lu Jiuyuan exaggerates the initiative of human cognition, especially on the problem of the subject-object relationship (namely, the relationship between the mind and principle, and the relationship between the mind and things). On the one hand, Lu Jiuyuan thinks that the universe is limitless. So he says, "Man, Heaven, Earth and the myriad things are within the limitless." In other words, all these are limited existences. On the other hand, he thinks that the mind of a sage is able to grasp principle that is beyond any "limitation." In short, principle is limitless, as is mind. Therefore, he says as follows:

1. "There is only one mind. My mind, my friends' mind, the mind

of the sages of thousands of years ago, and the mind of the sages of thousands of years to come are all the same. The substance of the mind is infinite. If one can completely develop one's mind, one will become identified with Heaven." (*Complete Works of Lu Xiangshan·Book 35: Quotations·Part Two*)

2. "When sages appear in the East Sea, their mind is just the same, and principle is just the same. When sages appear in the West Sea, their mind is just the same, and principle is just the same. When sages appear in the South Sea and in the North Sea, their mind is just the same, and principle is just the same. Thousands of generations ago and thousands of generations to come, whenever sages have appeared or will appear, there is no difference in their mind, and there is no difference in principle, either." (*Complete Works of Lu Xiangshan·Book 36: A Chronicle of Lu Xiangshan's Life*)

With respect to the function of knowing the principle of things, "my mind," and "my friends' mind," and the mind of all sages in all places and all ages are just the same. In short, there is only "one mind." This thinking ability is the common characteristic of everybody's mind. By grasping such a common characteristic of the mind, Lu Jiuyuan emphasizes the subjective consciousness unique to man, and the cognitive activity which may "start working when the human mind is full [of perceptive data]." Thus he breaks through the "boundary" between subject and object. With one mind, man can understand the myriad principles. With one principle man can understand the myriad things and realizes how the universe is working. He says, "The affairs in the universe are my own affairs. My own affairs are affairs of the universe." (*Complete Works of Lu Xiangshan·Book22: Miscellaneous Writings*) And he says, "The universe is my mind, and my mind is the universe." (*Ibid*) This is his theory that Heaven and man are an integrated whole. Zhu Xi's theory based on principle has developed into Lu Jiuyuan's theory based on mind.

The controversy between Lu Jiuyuan and Zhu Xi was an academic argument which broke out between the two leading branches of Neo-Confucianism during the Southern Song Dynasty. Two debates in particular were vehement and concentrated on some crucial issues. The first debate took place in 1175. It is called the "Goose Lake Meeting" in the history of Chinese philosophy. Lu Zuqian, a friend of both schools, arranged the meeting at the Goose Lake Temple, located in Xinzhou (Shangrao City, Jiangxi Province). At the meeting, Lu Jiuyuan and his brother Lu Jiuling stood on one side, while Zhu Xi and his disciples stood on the other. They debated face to face on methods of scholarly research. The essence of their debate was to argue over certain epistemological problems. The second "meeting" was carried out through an exchange of letters between Zhu Xi and Lu Jiuyuan, in which they debated the Ultimate of Nonbeing and the Great Ultimate. The essence of their debate was a matter of ontology. These two debates, however, failed to find common ground.

The sticking point at the Goose Lake Meeting was Zhu Xi's insistence on "investigating things by investigating principle to the utmost." The two Lu brothers could not bring themselves to agree with him on this point. In Zhu Xi's opinion, "principle" is the supreme dominator of Heaven, Earth and the myriad things. Starting from this, he maintains that the purpose of cognition lies in "investigating the Heavenly principle to the utmost." In order to investigate the principle to the utmost, it is necessary to "investigate things to the utmost." In his view, on the one hand the human mind is able to know all things, and on the other hand all things in the world "are possessed of principle." Therefore, first of all, it is necessary to investigate the principle of each concrete thing, and then through "great efforts" people may naturally "come to understand the thorough meaning all of a sudden," namely, they may "have an insight into the Heavenly principle." The method of "investigating things" refers mainly to reading the books written by the sages. Lu Jiuyuan, however, starts from the premise that is epitomized in the phrase "mind is principle." In his view, Zhu Xi's way of "keeping contact with things so as to investigate principle to the utmost" is a cognitive route which is impracticable in that it is too incoherent and even hair-splitting. So he makes every effort to find an easy and direct method. His method consists of two parts: One is to persist in "genuine and personal concern, and self-examination"; the other is to "completely develop the original mind." As regards scholarly research, he thinks that the first step is to develop one's original mind. But Zhu Xi does not agree with him on this point, holding him up to ridicule:

> "The learning of Lu Zijing (namely, Lu Jiuyuan) dwells only on the mind alone.... If you come to know the mind, then the myriad laws will pour out, and therefore there is nothing to worry about.... So he fears nothing in Heaven or on Earth, and all the time he has been raising a hue and cry.... Just as the statement says, 'In heaven and on Earth, he prides himself upon his ability'." (*Classified Conversations of Zhu Xi·Book 124*)

Their divergence in epistemology became more and more vehement as time went by, and at last it developed into a controversy over ontology. Lu Jiuyuan and another brother Lu Jiushao expressed disagreement with "The Ultimate of Nonbeing and also the Great Ultimate." In their opinion, *An Explanation of the Diagram of the Great Ultimate* was not a work by Zhou Dunyi. Even if Zhou Dunyi wrote it himself, it was only the thought of the young Zhou Dunyi. They said he later changed his ideas, and never mentioned the "Ultimate of Nonbeing" any more. In the Lu brothers' view, "The Ultimate of Nonbeing" must not be given precedence over "The Great Ultimate." (Cf. *Complete Works of Lu Xiangshan·Book 2·To Zhu Yuanhui*) But in Zhu Xi's view, "The Ultimate of Nonbeing and also the Great Ultimate" means "That which has no form nevertheless has principle of one kind or another." And, what is more, if one refuses to use the concept of the "Ultimate of Nonbeing," the "Great Ultimate" will identify with a certain material object. In that case, the "Great Ultimate" cannot be great enough to be the foundation of the myriad things. In other words, as Zhu Xi emphasizes, the "Great Ultimate" is a spatially and temporally transcendental and absolute body that exists everywhere. Without any form, it is everywhere, and it penetrates everything. But in Lu Jiuyuan's view, this absolute body named the "Great Ultimate" is nothing but "mind." "The Great Ultimate" is the supreme category that marks the absolute body of "the mind as noumenon." Moreover, the "Great Ultimate" dwells in the mind. Therefore, it is quite enough to use only the concept of the "Great Ultimate." If any stress is laid on "The Ultimate of Nonbeing and also the Great Ultimate," one is bound to acknowledge that besides the "mind" or above the "mind" there is a supreme noumenon of one kind or another. "He [Zhu Xi] talks glibly. The more he talks, the more foolish he becomes. He is truly worthy of the statement: Easily he sets up his theory; vainly he has said so much. But what he has said may not hit home." (*Ibid*)

In practice, the argument over the "Ultimate of Nonbeing" and the "Great Ultimate" is nothing but a general expression of the different views on ontology within Neo-Confucianism. Zhu Xi makes "principle" the law of the universe, while Lu Jiuyuan, by means of alienation, returns "principle" to the "mind" in line with the subjective consciousness. For Zhu Xi, "principle" dwells either inside the mind or outside the mind. But in Lu Jiuyuan's opinion, the "Great Ultimate" is nothing but "principle," and the "mind" is nothing but "principle," too. Nobody can discuss the "Great Ultimate" apart from the "mind." Nobody can claim that above the "Great Ultimate" there is the "Ultimate of Nonbeing." In short, Lu Jiuyuan does not agree that outside the mind there is a noumenon that is "without any forms but with principle." In a clear-cut way, he proclaims that the mind is noumenon.

In their debate, both Lu Jiuyuan and Zhu Xi make a criticism of the crucial part of the opponent's argument on quite a number of issues. This was very helpful to the coming development of philosophical thinking, and helped the philosophers of the Ming and Qing dynasties to reconcile the differences between the Rationalist and Idealist schools in epistemology.

27.

Matter, Cause, and Contribution: Chen Liang and Ye Shi

Chen Liang (1143–1149) was a native of Yongkang County in Zhejiang Province. A famous scholar, he represented the "Yongkang School of Thought," and his works were compiled into the *Collection of Literary Works by Longchuan*. Ye Shi (1150–1223), a native of Yongjia County, Zhejiang Province, is the representative of the "Yongjia School of Thought." He left *Notes and Commentaries on Study*, *Collection of Literary Works by Shuixin*, and *Additional Collection of Literary Works by Shuixin*.

The doctrines of Chen Liang and Ye Shi are generally called "utilitarian." Such doctrines appeared as a result of the development of contradictions in the society, economy, and politics of the Southern Song Dynasty. The area around Jiangsu and Zhejiang provinces, where both lived, was the economic, political, and cultural center of Southern Song, and had a well-developed commodity economy. At that time, some landlords of the middle and lower social strata engaged in handicraft production and commerce, but their economic growth was hampered by the power of big landlords, big bureaucrats, and big merchants. Especially in the period when the whole country was split into north and south, ruled by the Jin and Southern Song dynasties, respectively, the small landlords and merchants suffered severely. The "school of cause and contribution," headed by Chen Liang and Ye Shi reflected the interests of these landlords in industry and business. Politically, they maintained that a reformation of domestic affairs must be carried out and an alliance to fight the Jin invaders must be set up. They also put forth views on economic reform. Chen Liang said, "Agriculture and industry should be treated equally." And Ye Shi said, "Aid should be given to merchants and traders." Ideologically they persisted in a line of "practical cause and contribution." As they waged a theoretical struggle against the uselessness and vanity of the orthodox Neo-Confucians, who "talk glibly about nature and life, and despise utility," their doctrines became an important link in the chain of the development of philosophy in the Song-Ming Period.

Zhu Xi describes Chen Liang's personality as follows: "Since he has put himself outside the laws and social norms, he disgusts Confucian scholars, who constantly talk about law and the rites." (*Collected Writings of Huian the Literary Prince·Book 36: To Chen Tongfu*) From the angle of the "doctrine of utility," Chen Liang had a controversy with Zhu Xi, who stuck to the "doctrines of righteousness and principle."

Zhu Xi puts the Way outside the implements, as if the Way is dangling but it is dangling in nowhere. Lu Jiuyuan puts principle in the mind. Chen Liang, starting from the principle of "practical cause and contribution," exposes the theoretical basis of the ontology advocated by Zhu Xi and Lu Jiuyuan, who "are always playing with the mind on the surface of formless gadgets" so that they may induce people to depart from the realistic world, pursuing the mysterious and invisible thing-in-itself that surpasses the realistic world. (Cf. *Collection of Literary Works by Longchuan·Book 19: To Ying Zhongshi*)

Does such a world of the thing-in-itself exist? Chen Liang gives a resolute and decisive answer to this question:

"As for what fills the universe, it is nothing but matter. As for what people deal with in everyday life, it is nothing but events. The emperors and kings of ancient times had unique characteristics. Why? They were unique in that they were aware of the historical facts of things and events." (*Collection of Literary Works by Longchuan·Book 10: Preface to My Opinions of the Classics*)

Chen Liang shows the spirit of seeking truth from facts, with which he opposes the theory of those Neo-Confucians. As he has affirmed the materialistic premise that "Everywhere, if there is something, it must be some substantial thing," the relation between the Way and things, which was turned upside down by the Neo-Confucians, is turned upside down once again. Chen Liang points out as follows:

> 1. "The Way does not exist outside the forms and the emanative material force, but functions permanently among things and events." (*Collection of Literary Works by Longchuan·Book 9: A Treatise on Endeavor to Practice the Way for Great Achievement*)
>
> 2. Since the Way is under Heaven, what can there be that is not material? There are one thousand ways and ten thousand routes. The principle of taking ways and routes is based on concrete events." (*Collection of Literary Works by Longchuan·Book 19: To Ying Zhongshi*)

"One thousand ways and ten thousand routes" refers to the diversity of things and events as well as the complexity of their movements and changes. By grasping this perplexing problem the Idealists may explain the world in a distorted way. For example, Cheng Yi says, "It is the Way that opens and closes." Zhu Xi says, "It is the Way that changes and transforms things." In short, they attempt to separate the spiritual Way from the realistic world, and then take it for the general root cause of the movements and changes of all things. They are fond of talking about the Way apart from material force. They are fond of putting the Way outside the implements. Opposing these two views, Chen Liang puts forth two views of his own. "There can be nothing that is not material, " and, "The principle of taking ways and routes is based on concrete events." The Way is useful only because it may serve as "the historical facts of things and events," and it "functions permanently among things and events." The Way "does not exist outside the forms and the emanative material force." Therefore, the demarcation line between the Idealist thinkers and the school of cause and contribution is very clear, although they both talk much about the Way. In the opinion of the Neo-Confucians, the Way is the absolute spirit that is pre-eminent above things, surpasses physical forms and dominates the myriad things. But the school of cause and contribution reduces the Way to being the objective law that is dependent on ("based on") things but does not function on things.

Liu Yuxi opposed the Buddhist and Metaphysical ontology, which is based on *sunya* (emptiness), by maintaining that the law ("number" and "potency") of things "is always dependent upon things." (*A Treatise on Heaven·Part Two*) But he did not take a step further to reveal the epistemological root cause of such ontology. It is indeed a theoretical weak point. Almost all the Neo-Confucian thinkers, such as Zhou Dunyi, Shao Yong, Cheng Hao, Cheng Yi, and Zhu Xi grasp this weak point, and then they put forth ontologies of various descriptions by cutting apart or turning upside down the relationships between the one and the many. Chen Liang is more or less aware of the root of these theories. He once had a dispute with Zhu Xi on the problem of whether one should "learn to be a man" or "learn to be a Confucian." In this dispute, he takes two propositions for his theoretical premise: "Everywhere, if there is something it must be some substantial thing," and, "There can be nothing that is not material." And he emphatically points out: "The so-called sages are sages only when they are among people. The so-called great people are great only when they are among people." (*Collection of Literary Works by Longchuan·Book 20: A Confidential Letter to Zhu Yuanhui*) He denies that there are any men who are "as perfect as beautiful wares of a generation." He then lifts the dispute to the level of the relationship between the one and the many, expressing expresses a new view, which is vivid and profound:

> "In my humble opinion, those who claim to preserve a unique scholarship which has been lost to others are deceiving ill-informed persons. A human being is a human being, and there is nothing more. Material force is material force, and there is nothing more. Talent is talent, and there is nothing more. Take, for example, gold, silver, copper, and iron. They are gold, silver, copper and iron, and nothing more. Some wares are fine, and some wares are coarse. The quality of a ware depends on how its material is refined. Apart from its original essence, not a single ware, even if it is an ordinary ware, can be made, not to mention men who are as perfect as beautiful wares of a generation." (*Collection of Literary Works by Longchuan·Book 20: A Confidential Letter to Zhu Yuanhui*)

The Way is a noumenon that has been sanctified by the Idealist scholars, in that they call it a "unique scholarship." (It is the "secret significance" of Ye Shi.) The Way is not mysterious, but present in the earliest and simplest abstraction. Take, for example, the proposition that

"Mr. X or Mr.Y is a man." This proposition itself is a general statement abstracted from a particular case. In this proposition is embodied the dialectical relationship that "The particular is the general." If this abstraction is used in a distorted way, the general may be removed from the particular, so that the general will become "a single existing thing" prior to any particular thing. In other words, the general will become the Way as the absolute spirit. Thus, the problem of the relationship between the one and the many is of methodological significance in the controversy about the relationship between the Way and things. Chen Liang sees this, and in a clear-cut way he generalizes the relationship between the one and the many into the relationship between "the general" and "this one." As he points out, the Way, which Zhu Xi and others had called "beautiful ware of a generation," is no more than "the general" abstracted ("made") from "this one." Therefore, he emphasizes that "A human being is a human being, and there is nothing more." With this, he denies that there are any "general" people. This embodies the thought of "the scholars of cause and contribution" who "take things for the fundamental." Zhu Xi exaggerates "the general"; Chen Liang emphasizes "this one." This sharp contrast is the essential contrast between the "doctrine of righteousness and principle" and the "doctrine of cause and contribution" as far as methodology is concerned.

In Chen Liang's view, the Way is not a single thing that spends itself in the air; instead the Way is historically in the developmental process of Heaven, Earth and Man. Apart from the movement of Heaven and Earth, apart from human action and creation, "where is the Way that is always working without any rest?" (*Ibid*) He says, "There are so many things in the world. Is there anything that does not embody the Way? The sun is shining brightly in the sky. It is brilliant everywhere. Of course, there are some people who close their eyes. When they open their eyes, they will see reality." (*Collection of Literary Works by Longchuan·Book 20: Postscript*) Of course, in the developmental process of history, people cannot avoid some temporary twists, turns or regressions. But the activities of man, which create history, can never be stopped by these setbacks. He says, "There is no end to the use of the 'mind,' for there is no cessation of its function. The texts of the 'laws' may not be perfect sometimes, but there is no oblivion of them." (*Collection of Literary Works by Longchuan·Book*

20: A Confidential Letter to Zhu Yuanhui) Although politics and the human mind are very complicated, he never has any fear of their cessation or oblivion. His view is clear: "Heaven and Earth move all the same, and people act all the same." (*Ibid*) He uses his view of movement and development to generalize history and to challenge the retrogressive view of history put forth by Zhu Xi, who values justice above material gains, esteems kings and despises despots, and lays more stress on the past than on the present.

Chen Liang warns Emperor Xiaozong, saying, "In the world, is there anything that is more important than the volition of the people and the destiny of the people?" (*Collection of Literary Works by Longchuan·Book 11: Answers Made in the Royal Court*) Although in a dim way he sees the will of the people and the life ("destiny") of the people, he cannot explain the laws and causes of historical development in a scientific way. He refutes Zhu Xi's theory that the "orthodox tradition of the Way" decides history, but at the same time he comes up with the mysterious theory that the "circulation of the material force" decides history. He rejects the view that "the present is not as good as the past," but he cannot get rid of the cyclical view of history that "the Heavenly Way changes every sixty years." (Cf. *Collection of Literary Works by Longchuan·Book 1: The First Letter to Emperor Xiaozong*) This is his historical limitation.

Ye Shi, enjoying equal popularity to Chen Liang, is another important thinker of the school of cause and contribution. His clashes with the Neo-Confucians led him to form an independent school, on a par with Zhu Xi's and Lu Jiuyuan's.

Ye Shi takes the same approach as Chen Liang. By grasping the key problem of the relationship between the Way and things, Ye Shi unfolds a debate with the Neo-Confucians. But he pays more attention to the philosophical heritage than Chen Liang does. In a critical way, he sums up the experiences of this heritage, draws lessons from it, and attempts to explore anew the relationship between the Way and things.

On the whole, the scholars of the Song Dynasty all accepted the formula devised by Zhou Dunyi, putting a spiritual thing-in-itself, which is defined as "the Ultimate of Nonbeing and also the Great Ultimate," above the material world, which is epitomized by the so-called "two material forces and five elements." They attribute the cause of the contradictory movement of things to an exterior force of one kind or another. Zhang Zai has two famous propositions: "If there is any movement there must be some subtle cause," and "Movements cannot be actuated by any external cause." His contribution lies in that he uses the transformational theory of material force to overcome the shortcoming of the primitive doctrine of the five elements, which maintains that a certain material object begets another material object. This may be seen clearly in the proposition that "Harmony truly produces things." Obviously, Zhang Zai cannot overcome the theoretical limitation of the doctrine of external cause. He distinguishes the "physical forms" from the "Great Void." In his view, the Great Void is a substantial entity, which may not only constitute the myriad things but also exist independently from the myriad things. Such a view is tinged with mysticism, for it seems to say that there can be some existence outside the material world. This is of course a theoretical defect, and Ye Shi seems to be dimly aware of it. Ye Shi uses the omnipresent "five elements" to generalize material phenomena, which are "as coarse as material objects," and spiritual phenomena, which are "as subtle as Nature and life." (Cf. *Notes and Commentaries on Study·Book 8*) He also uses the transformational theory of material force to explain these phenomena. Only by combining the contradictions between yin and yang, which is part of the transformational theory, with the substantial view of material objects, which is a part of the doctrine of the Five Elements, can one find the origin of the variety of things in their self-contradictory movement of "physical forms." (See *Additional Collection of Literary Works by Shuixin·Book 5: Writings Submitted to the Throne·About the Book of Changes*) Therefore, apart from the "physical forms" it is unnecessary to postulate any entities such as "the Great Ultimate," "the Ultimate of Nonbeing," "activity and tranquility," "men and women," "purity and vacuity," "the one and the great," and so forth. In this way, the theoretical difficulty raised by Zhang Zai may be overcome. He also refutes the so-called cosmogony put forth by Zhou Dunyi, who describes it as following the pattern: "Ultimate of Nonbeing (the Great Ultimate) → yin and yang → the five elements → the myriad things." Ye Shi develops a materialist conception of nature in line with the "school of cause and contribution," which "takes things as the fundamental."

Emphasis is placed by Ye Shi on the variety and unity of matter. In the world there is neither a spiritual noumenon such as "the Ultimate of

Nonbeing," "the Great Ultimate," nor substantial entities such as "purity and void," "the one and the great" and so forth. What fill the world are the boundless things with physical form of one kind or another. On the one hand, they are "one and the same, and in the meantime different." The materially monistic world expresses itself in material form, which includes the myriad things. Such a "difference" is the characteristic innate in matter in that it seems to be the "feeling" of the things rather than the embodiment of "principle." On the other hand, it is "different and at the same time one and the same." The variety of the physical forms is unified in the objective law of the movements and changes of matter. In other words, they are unified in the "principle of things" rather than in the "principle outside things." (Cf. *Additional Collection of Literary Works by Shuixin·Book 5: Writings Submitted to the Throne·About the Book of Poetry*) In this way, Ye Shi draws a line between his view of matter, which is based on "taking things for the fundamental," and the idealistic ontology, which is based on "taking principle for the fundamental."

He further explains why things are various and how they are unified in materiality by taking over the old proposition that "the golden mean is the Way" and developing the idea of contradictory unity contained in the other old proposition that "the one and the two complete each other." He thus explains the internal cause of the variety and unity of things. Both the movements of and changes in anything are caused by the interaction of the opposites in a contradiction within that very thing. "Everything has two sides instead of only one." In each and every thing two aspects contrary to each other are contained. "They succeed each other endlessly." Contradictory movements follow one another everlastingly. This view emphasizes the universality and eternality of contradictions, as Ye Shi inherits and develops the views of contradictory development put forth by Zhang Zai, who said, "The one and the two rely on each other," and by Wang Anshi, who said, "The new and the old repel each other." By the "golden mean," he attempts to grasp the objective law for everything, that is, the unity of opposites. On the one hand, "The Way originates from the one, but accomplishes itself in the two." "The ancient scholars, when talking about the Way, always discussed it in terms of the two." (*Additional Collection of Literary Works by Shuixin·Book 7: Writings Submitted to the Throne·About the Doctrine of the Mean*) According to the doctrine of the mean, one must first of all acknowledge that there are opposites in a unity. Ye Shi explains, "Heaven and Earth endow yin and yang with a great role. When the material force of yin and yang plays the role, there appear the four seasons, in which some things die off while other things are produced. Is there any benevolence in Heaven and Earth?" (*Notes and Commentaries on Study·Book 15*) The universal phenomenon in Nature is the opposition of yin and yang; this is their greatest function ("great role"). It is by yin and yang that "some things die off and other things are produced." Without death, there would be no life, and every life brings death. Heaven and Earth cannot be said to have humanity or inhumanity.

On the other hand, in any contradiction, no matter what it may be, there are both unity and opposition. If we see the opposition of a contradiction only while failing to see that the opposites are not associated with each other, we will exclude unity from the contradiction. And opposition repelling unity means a rigid opposition in which "no movement" may take place and "no transformation" may be realized either. Therefore, the doctrine of the mean may "benefit the opposites of a thing, and show the unity of the Way." (Cf. *Additional Collection of Literary Works by Shuixin·Book 7: Writings Submitted to the Throne·About the Doctrine of the Mean*) This demands that one should learn to grasp unity from opposition, so as to unify the two opposing aspects. Thus, the opposites may complete each other, and a transformation may be promoted. Only by doing so can an internally vigorous situation be brought about, in which some "subtle movements" or "mysterious changes" may take place. In the doctrine of the mean there is a traditional limitation: the unity of a contradiction is usually rendered absolute. Of course, Ye Shi cannot get rid of such a limitation, and he unavoidably moves to the theory of equilibrium. Nevertheless, he is aware that "it is necessary to benefit the opposites of a thing, and show the unity of the Way." He makes a study of how the opposites may be unified and enriches the dialectical idea that "Opposites are complementary." In the philosophical controversy over whether one should "take principle for the fundamental" or "take matter for the fundamental" he makes some new theoretical contributions.

In the third place, he redefines the "Great Ultimate." His view of a contradiction runs as follows: "The one and the two are complementary." And his conception of Nature runs as follows: "It is necessary to take matter for the fundamental." By applying his view of contradiction to demonstrate his concept of Nature, he restores the original idea of the "Great Ultimate." In the past, Taoist scholars worshipped the Great Way as something to symbolize "the mysterious significance of their canon." But now it becomes an attribute innate in matter. Ye Shi redefines the Great Ultimate in line with materialism. One should therefore search after the internal causes of the movements and changes of things from their interdependently contradictory relations. Ye Shi prepares the theoretical groundwork for the materialist view of the relationship between the Way and implements.

28.

Wang Shouren: Developing an Idealist World Outlook

Wang Shouren (1472–1582), native of Yuyao, Zhejiang Province, founded the Yangming Academy, and therefore his students—and later the common people—called him Mr. Yangming. He inherited Mencius' doctrine of "the innate knowledge of the good" and Lu Jiuyuan's view that "mind is the principle." At the same time, he criticized the Neo-Confucianism of Zhu Xi, and further developed the system of Idealism. Wang Shouren's works were compiled by his students under the title of *Complete Works of Wang Yangming*, in thirty-eight volumes. The two most important works are *Instructions for Practical Living* and *Inquiry into the Great Learning*.

The philosophical system of Wang Shouren is a comprehensive expression of Idealism. It is made up of three sets of doctrines: his world outlook that "There is no event outside the mind, and there is no principle outside the mind"; his theory of knowledge epitomized by "the extension of the innate knowledge of the good"; and his theory of motive generalized into the "unity of knowledge and action." Of these three, "the unity of knowledge and action" is the basic one, upon which he sets up his own all-embracing philosophical system. As he emphasizes, it is necessary to use an ethically and morally conscientious cultivation of personality to normalize people's actions, which has strong political overtones. As for the theoretical premise of the "unity of knowledge and action," it is centered on the mind, with "my mind" as the thing-in-itself of the universe. In previous ages, many thinkers put forth their views in a rather systematic way on the theory centered on the mind. For instance, in pre-Qin times the Zisi-Mencius School put forth the proposition: "Know the mind, know Nature and know Heaven." In the Tang Dynasty, the Chan Sect of Buddhism put forth the proposition: "Beget and destroy Heaven and Earth with the mental law." In the Southern Song Dynasty, Lu Jiuyuan put forth the proposition: "The universe is my mind and my mind is the universe." By lifting all these theoretical views to the height of basic issues of philosophy, Wang Shouren discusses the relations between the mind and things, and between the mind and principles.

Along a speculative route from inside to outside and from the mind to things, Wang examines basic issues of philosophy. In the first place, he takes as his point of departure the relationship between body and mind. In *Instructions for Practical Living (III)*, he puts forth a view that "there is no body without mind; there is no mind without body." It seems that here he affirms the interdependent relationship between body and mind. Nevertheless, from the angle of epistemology, he asks, "Without mind, how can one see, listen, speak and act?" That is, of the two parties, which is the dominator, and which is the dominated? The essence of the question is the relational problem of perceptual experience and rational thinking. It is an old problem, for in the history of Chinese philosophy there are many controversies about the "function of the ears and the eyes" and the "function of the mind." He raises the same question once again, to highlight the initiative of human knowledge. He claims that the mind is the dominator of the ears, eyes, mouth and body, namely, that the mind is the basis of all human knowledge. In Wang Shouren's opinion, it is not only possible to enable the sense organs to see, hear, speak and act by motivating the "will," it is also possible to orient seeing, hearing, speaking and acting by way of "knowledge" about "clear intelligence." These are the "practical situations" in which man can see, hear, speak and act. What governs the "practical situations" is the "original substance of the mind," which is the master of the whole body. Into the so-called "sincerity [is] on self-examination," which is an old proposition of Mencius, he pours an abundant content of ideas and perception, which is expressed by the "will of motivation" and the "knowledge of clear intelligence." By doing so, he prepares for the next step in his epistemology, namely, that knowledge comes from enlargement of the mind, which dominates all things.

In the second place, he makes a supposition that the mind may govern the sense organs and enable man to possess ideas and perceptive abilities. Starting from this supposition, he expands the initiative function of the mind step by step, so that he may discuss the relationship between the mind and things.

The first step is "No will is suspended in mid-air, for it must be in contact with things or events." (*Instructions for Practical Living (III)*) One ought not to discuss the will apart from things or events. The will, which is subjective, must be combined with things or events, which are objective. The second step is "The function of will must connect with certain things, and things are events." (*Instructions for Practical Living (II)·A Letter in Reply to Gu Dongqiao's Criticism*) For the process in which subject combines with object, it is necessary to grasp a key point, that is, once an idea or the perceptive ability is motivated, it must function on things or events. With each and every concrete thing, it is necessary to provide some subjective conditions to the will, such as "one's will functions on so-and-so," "one's will lies in so-and-so." If so, a "thing," no matter what it may be, cannot become a thing-in-itself which exists independently of the "will." Now the thing has become a target which is processed by the will: "Things are events." It is an appendix, which exists for me, having lost its objective independence.

The third step is "In case there is a will, there is a thing. In case there is no will, there is no thing. In this consideration, things are really functions of the will." (*Ibid*) Now his thought takes a step forward: A "thing" is not only the target processed by the "will," it is also the result of the function of the "will." By citing sounds, colors, tastes and so forth, the students of Wang Shouren raised the question: "Who distinguishes the sounds, colors, tastes, and so forth?" They imply that the objective is processed by the "will," and they draw the conclusion that "the sounds (colors, tastes, etc.) of the myriad things in the world only appear to exist because my mind is listening to them." (*Chronological Life of Wang Yangming*) In a like manner, they exaggerate the initiative of human cognition, so as to deny the objective independence of the target of human cognition. As a result, objective existence becomes an outgrowth of the subjective function.

Once the initiative, which is innate in human cognition, motivates that iota of "clear intelligence" in "my mind," there immediately appears the "wonderful function" of the "subtle correspondence between the two parties." (*Instructions for Practical Living (III)*) The moment the internal mind is stirred, the outside things send a corresponding echo back to it. In an instant, a perfect harmony or coincidence between the mind and things is realized: "Before you look at these flowers, they and your mind are in a state of silent vacancy. As you come to look at them, their colors at once show up clearly. From this you can know that these flowers are not external to your mind." (*Instructions for Practical Living (III)*) When you open your eyes, the flowers at once become clear. When you close your eyes, the flowers change their colors immediately. It seems that the same flowers are changing along with your sight.

Another example is "Who is going to look into the sublime if Heaven is deprived of my clear intelligence? Who is going to look into the depths if Earth is deprived of my clear intelligence?" (*Ibid*) Heaven itself is not high, but when somebody looks up to Heaven, it is high. Earth itself is not deep, but when somebody looks down at Earth, it is deep. Whether or not Heaven is high or Earth is deep depends on the man who contemplates them. There is a third example. When man's innate knowledge stops moving, both Heaven and Earth become chaotic. When man's innate knowledge functions in a subtle way, Heaven becomes fine and Earth becomes vivid. Along with each and every movement of innate knowledge there appear corresponding changes in Heaven and Earth. (*Ibid*)

Even in a single day, sometimes one's spiritual state is clear, and sometimes it is turbid. Even in a single day, sometimes one's motion swells, and sometimes it subsides. Such changes may lead the history of the world to great or dramatic changes. (*Ibid*)

Here lies the problem. "The innate knowledge of my mind" is always on the move. The "changeability" or "inconstancy" of "innate knowledge" is the ultimate motive force by which things and events are pushed forward to have endless and various changes. In this way, "Heaven, Earth and the myriad things are traveling in the emanation and functioning of my innate knowledge. How can there be any single thing that can surpass innate knowledge or become any obstacle to it?" (*Ibid*)

In the past, the scholars did not think so. For instance, Zhou Dunyi thought that things could be transformed by way of the self-movement of the Great Ultimate. Shao Yong reasoned that history is made by applying a hair-splitting series of numbers and diagrams to his theory. Zhu Xi emphasizes time and again that "principle takes the lead, and the material force follows it closely." But he is sometimes perplexed by the situation in which "material force is strong and principle is weak." Lu Jiuyuan first transforms material force into principle and then he explains this principle with numbers. But Wang Yangming finds a "direct and simple" solution. From Buddhism he finds a recipe, which runs, "Turn back just to your own mind." He recites a poem:

> Everybody has a compass in himself.
> The root of the myriad of changes is in the mind.
> Foolish scholars turn the business upside down,
> Looking for branches and leaves in a single tree.
>
> —*Four Poems on Innate Knowledge for My Students to Read*

The Great Ultimate is not in numbers and diagrams. It is not in righteousness or principle either. Then, where is it? It is in the "innate knowledge" of my mind. This is nothing but the spirit of the Creation, in correspondence with which one may be able to "produce Heaven and Earth, the ghosts, and the emperors as well." (*Instructions for Practical Living (III)*)

In short, "There is no event outside the mind." (*Instructions for Practical Living (I)*) Events are the result of "the innate knowledge that is emanating, functioning and going everywhere." Things exist and change nowhere but in the "subtle correspondence between the two parties that dominate innate knowledge." In this way, Wang Shouren explains the problem of the relationship between the mind and things.

Wang Shouren starts his demonstration by exaggerating the initiative of the mind. On the problem of the relation between mind and principle, he puts forth another proposition that "there is no principle outside the mind."

Although Zhu Xi emphasizes that, on the basis of the "mind," the subjective and the objective are unified, in order to objectify the "principle" he has to acknowledge that there exists the "principle in the things." So he demands that people "investigate the principle to the utmost" in "things and events." As for Wang Shouren, since he continues along the line of thought of Lu Jiuyuan, he thinks that Zhu Xi's practice is in fact "a division between mind and principle as two distinct things." Since Zhu Xi sets the subjective against the objective, it is only natural that he acknowledges that outside the mind there is the principle of Heaven, Earth and the myriad things which exist objectively because they are independent of Man's subjective will. In this way, the subjective is now "in charge of" the objective. Meanwhile, if the principles of loyalty and filial piety only exist in attendance on the ruler and the father, in my heart there must be no place to deposit loyalty and filial piety when the ruler and the father pass away. If so, there must be some loopholes in the consciousness of the ethical thought. For this reason, Wang puts forth the view that "the principles of things are not external to the mind. If one seeks the principles of things outside the mind, there will be no principles of things to be found." (*Instructions for Practical Living (II)·A Letter in Reply to Gu Dongqiao's Criticism*) He denies that outside the subjective mind there are "principles of things" which are objective. And he modifies Zhu Xi's idea of "mind and principle" into a proposition that "the mind is principle." Zhu Xi has a proposition that "One should possess all the principles so that one may meet with the myriad things." (*Syntactic and Semantic Analysis of the Great Learning*) Now, Wang changes it into another proposition that "The myriad things appear when all principles exist already." (*Instructions for Practical Living (I)*) A few changes in the wording show the dividing line between Principle Learning and Idealism as two ideological systems.

But, why is it that "principle in things" comes from "the mind in one's own mind"? Wang explains as follows:

> "Heaven and Earth exert their influences, and there ensue the transformation and production of all things. This is because the real principle is in circulation. The sages influence the minds of men, and the result is harmony and peace everywhere. This is because the supreme honesty has been discovered, leading to firm correctness. I have observed the principle by which Heaven and Earth exert their mutual influence and the way in which the sages influence the minds of men. The principle and the way are firm and correct, as a whole, and the myriad things are produced and peace is brought

about. Hence, we may see the whole situation of Heaven, Earth and the myriad things." (*Complete Works of Wang Yangming·Book 26: Thirteen Articles from My Assumption of the Five Classics*)

Herein appear the subtle causes of the mutual influence between Heaven and Earth, which exert their influences, and there ensue the transformation and production of all things. The sages influence the minds of men, and the result is harmony and peace everywhere. Such is the harmonious development of Nature and society. Not that Nature and society themselves are moving, but that "the real principle is in circulation." In the final analysis, this is nothing but the discovery of the supreme honesty. This is no more than the result of the mind of the sages, which works inside, affects outside, and embodies itself in things. In short, "The mind is principle," "The mind is the rites." Next, he reasons out a solution to the contradiction between mind and principles in things, and between principles in things and ethics. He says as follows:

1. "The so-called principle is orderliness of the mind. When the principle is embodied in attendance on one's parents, it becomes filial piety. When the principle is embodied in attendance on the ruler, it becomes loyalty. When the principle is embodied in attendance on one's friends, it becomes the honesty. There is an inexhaustible multitude of changes of principle. In short, all of them originate in the mind." (*Complete Works of Wang Yangming·Book 8: A Letter to Zhu Yangbo*)

2. "Compared to the tree, the mind with sincere filial piety is the root, whereas the offshoots are the leaves and branches. There must first be roots before there can be leaves and branches. One does not seek to find leaves and branches and then cultivate the root." (*Instructions for Practical Living (I)*)

Thus, he comes to see the wonderful development just as he sees the subtle causes. At first, "the orderliness of the mind" starts working, and then the morality of man appears. The whole situation is just like a tree. The former is the root from which leaves and branches may grow; the latter is the leaves and branches, which grow from the root. The root is nothing but the "innate knowledge of goodness," which is perfect by nature.

Wang Shouren combines two doctrines, one being the extension of knowledge, a doctrine found in the *Great Learning*, the other being the innate knowledge of goodness advocated by Mencius. He names his new doctrine the "extension of the innate knowledge of goodness." Solemnly, he declares, "I have delivered lectures all my life and what I have delivered are only the three characters *zhi-liang-zhi* (the extension of the innate knowledge of goodness)." (*Continuation of the Complete Works of Wang Yangming·Book 1: Two Letters in Handwriting to Adopted Son Zhengxian*)

Compared with Zhu Xi's exhortation to "extend knowledge by investigating things to the utmost," Wang Shouren's doctrine of the extension of the innate knowledge of goodness is possessed of noticeable features of Idealism.

29.

Wang Tingxiang and the Transformation of Material Force

Wang Tingxiang (1474–1544) was a native of Yifeng (present-day Lankao County, Henan Province). Wang was well accomplished in astronomy, biology and psychology. He held several important posts, such as Minister of War and the emperor's Censor on the Left.

Wang's scientific attainments and political experience led him to lay stress on "the practical knowledge of managing state affairs." His main works are preserved in the *Censor's Collection* and *Collected Works Kept in the Wang Family*. His main philosophical ideas are outlined in *Cautious Speeches* and *Statements of Grace*, the former being in thirteen volumes, and the latter in two. Also useful for studying Wang's ideas are his essays *A Debate on the Great Ultimate*, *A Debate on Zhang Zai's View of Principle and the Material Force* and *A Reply to He Baizhai's Theory of Creation*.

Wang Tingxiang is a materialist thinker. His basic attitude towards the doctrines in vogue in his time and the heritage from ancient times may be summed up as follows: "Those who follow the same way help each other; those who follow different ways stand apart." (*A Reply to He Baizhai's Theory of Creation*) He opposes the so-called attitude of "swallowing anything and everything uncritically." He advocates "a careful search" into sources and courses, and a distinction between right and wrong. In short, he advocates a critical spirit and a spirit of probing into the depths of things. (Cf. *A Debate on the Great Ultimate* and the *Statements of Grace*· (*I*)) Therefore, his criticism of Neo-Confucianism has a more self-awakening property than that of his contemporaries. Furthermore, he never directs his arguments at minor problems. In debate he is good at grasping the crucial problems. By examining the essence of different world outlooks, he discloses the internal connections between the Neo-Confucianism of the Song-Ming Period and the past schools of thought. In his opinion, the pre-Qin Taoist scholars took the Way for the foundation. The Metaphysical scholars of the Wei-Jin Period took "nonbeing" for the foundation. The Buddhist scholars of the Northern and Southern Dynasties and of the Sui-Tang Period took the "true nature" for the foundation. The scholars of Neo-Confucianism of the Song-Ming Period took "principle" for the foundation. Wang Tingxiang regarded all previous scholars as holding the same interest in fabricating a noumenon outside the material world. So their world outlook is diametrically opposite to the world outlook that takes "material force" for the foundation. (Cf. *Statements of Grace (I)*, and two essays titled *A Reply to He Baizhai's Theory of Creation* and *A Debate on Zhang Zai's View of Principle and the Material Force*)

Wang concentrates his argument on the relationship between principle and material force. He understands that the problem of their relationship is crucial to the philosophical controversy of his time. His solution is the restoration of material force: "Material force is the foundation of creation. There is something completely naive and vivid which is the substance of the Way. If there is life, there must be death. In like manner, if there is a beginning, there must be an end. That which fills up the universe is completely naive and completely invisible. Since there is nobody who has seen its beginning, how can there be anybody who will see its end? Confucian scholars know that material force is transformed, but they do not know that material force is the foundation. They have a long way to go before they can understand the Way." (*Cautious Speeches· The Substance of the Way*)

One of Wang Tingxiang's special contributions to Chinese philosophy was his transformation and restoration of some philosophical categories of the Neo-Confucians as part of his development of the monism of material force. His main ideas are as follows: "Vital force" is the "original moment of creation and transformation." This is his starting point. Then he infers that the "Great Ultimate" is not "the highest form of principle," as Zhu Xi assumed; instead, it is "the highest form of material force." In like manner, the Great Void is not the "pure and open world of principle," as Zhu Xi also assumed. Instead, it is the form in which matter exists. He explains this, saying, "Wherever there is a void there must be material force. The void cannot get away from material force, and material force cannot get away from the void." Neither "being" nor "nonbeing" any longer belongs to a pair of categories used to distinguish between the limitedness of the phenomenal world and the limitlessness of the noumenal world. Now they are a pair of categories used to illustrate how everything is undergoing changes in an everlasting process, growing out of nothing, returning to nothing, circulating all the time, and always moving. Thus, it follows that "principle" is not such a "spiritual Absolute" as described by Zhu Xi in the statement, "After there is this principle, there can be this material force." Quite the contrary. It is an objective law (the possession of material force). The "implements" are correspondingly no longer the so-called "implements after physical form," which are governed by principle and lie in secondary place. Quite the contrary; they are the concrete forms (the completion of the material force) in which the material entities exist. As for "yin and yang," they are no longer the carrier of the spiritual Absolute discussed by Zhu Xi, who describes this metaphorically, saying, principle is to yin and yang what a horseman is to a horse. Instead, yin and yang are the internal motive force for "going and coming," "extension and recoil," and the other forms of restless movement of the material world per se. (Cf. *Cautious Speeches·The Substance of the Way*, and *A Debate on the Great Ultimate*)

In short, categories such as "Great Ultimate," "Great Void," "being and nonbeing," "principle and the implements," "yin and yang," and so on are the "expressions of the myriad goodness and the supreme virtues" which the Neo-Confucians had applied to generalize the absolute noumenon. But now Wang Tingxiang uses them to describe the variety of the "transformation of the material force" from multiple aspects, although he calls them the "expressions of the myriad goodness and the supreme virtues," as before. Thus, he develops them into a forceful weapon by which he may defend the monism of material force and refute the theory which treated principle as the basic unit. As for the theoretical basis of Wang Tingxiang's doctrine of categories, it is as follows: "Outside and inside Heaven, there is nothing but material force. Inside the Earth, there is noting but material force. All things are made of material force, no matter what they may be, visible or invisible. And this is the universal rule for all the entities of creation." (*Cautious Speeches·the Substance of the Way*) He claims that what fills the universe is material force, not principle. Material force is the basic unit. Wang Tingxiang thus further develops the view put forth by Zhang Zai, who says, "Therefore I know that the Great Vacuity is the material force, and that there is no so-called nonbeing."

Wang Tingxiang thinks that Taoism, Metaphysics, Buddhism and Neo-Confucianism all share idealist ontology, which is confused and incoherent. According to Taoists, "*The Way* begets Heaven and the earth." According to the Metaphysicists, "Nonbeing begets all beings." According to Buddhism, "The *sunya* (emptiness) begets material force." And according to Neo-Confucianism, "Principle begets material force." All of them follow the same line of thought, that is, they "set up another thing to dominate it (i.e. material force)." Of these views, the most influential one is that of the Neo-Confucians, and therefore he directs his criticism at them, and he closely examines the grounds on which they put forth their view that "Principle begets material force." And then, starting from the theory of taking material force as the basic unit, he supplies a clear and affirmative answer for the origin of the universe.

While Wang denies the principle that serves as the spiritual entity, he affirms the principle that serves as the law governing the transformation of material force. He thinks that matter is preserved forever:

> "There are integration and separation in material force, but not appearance and disappearance. The beginning of rain or water is the transformation of material force. When material force gains warmth from fire it becomes vapor again. The emergence of grass and trees is the condensation of material force. When material force gains heat from fire, it becomes smoke again. Judging from the shape or form, it seems that there is a difference between being and nonbeing. Although it enters and leaves the Great Void, material force never decreases even one iota." (*Cautious Speeches· The Substance of the Way*)

If we examine things from their states of movement, we see that there is a difference between integration and separation, and between transformation and condensation. If we examine things from their concrete forms of existence, we see that there is a difference between rain and water, and between grass and trees. But all these are the result of material force, which is always in transformation. This is the discussion of the eternality of material force from its movement and changes. At the same time, he thinks that the theory of principle does not hold water. The Neo-Confucians had long since rendered principle a cipher, which had neither substance nor place. But principle does exist as a conception, which reflects some historical features and the laws of things. In this sense, it is an objective existence. Therefore, on some occasions principle is "suitable," and when such occasions pass by principle becomes "rotten" accordingly. Thus it follows that the absolute principle, which "may not be discussed in terms of being and nonbeing," demonstrates its nonexistence. And objective principle, which "may be discussed in terms of being and nonbeing," demonstrates its past existence in the same way. (Cf. *Statements of Grace (II)*) Essentially, the changing nature and variety of principle are decided by the motional states of material force. Wang Tingxiang says:

> "The primordial emanative material force keeps producing the multitude of beings between Heaven and Earth. Since it has both the aspect of constancy and that of variety, the multitude of beings cannot be the same. Thus, in considering the identity of the emanative material force, principle is equally identical; in consideration of the ten thousand varieties of the emanative material force, there should be ten thousand principles. Nevertheless, the Neo-Confucians mention only the identity of principle while neglecting the ten thousand varieties of it. Heaven has the principle of Heaven; Earth has the principle of Earth; Man has the principle of Man; things have the principles of things; obscurity has the principle of obscurity; and the manifest has the principle of the manifest. All these principles differ from one another. From the aspect of identity, they are all transformations of the emanative material force. Things originate in an identical source. From the aspect of difference, the emanative material force has a hundred ways of development. As the saying goes, 'The small virtues move like rivers.' Each principle possesses its respective nature." (*Statements of Grace (I)*)

Obviously, Wang Tingxiang differs from Zhu Xi, who discusses the relationship between principle and the material force by starting from the standpoint that principle determines material force. In Zhu Xi's opinion, if there is one principle, there is one material force; if there are ten thousand principles, then there are ten thousand material forces. In this way, Wang Tingxiang restored to principle the status of a law governing changes innate to material force. This is monism of material force.

Wang Tingxiang develops the view concerning a contradiction put forth by Zhang Zai, who says, "One thing has two bodies." Thus, he supplies a new theoretical basis for the view that "The vital force is the foundation of creation." He says as follows:

> "The yin and yang are the vital force. At the first stage when the vital force has a body, the body itself is turbid, and cannot be separated. Therefore, in the things which the vital force produces by transformation, there are yin and yang, which cannot be separated either." (*A Reply to He Baizhai's Theory of Creation*)

That is to say, vital force is the unity of yin and yang as two material forces opposite to each other. And the myriad things, which are produced by the vital force, also possess a contradictory nature the same as yin and yang. So Wang Tingxiang says, "Yin and yang are the bellows *[1] of creation." (*Cautious Speeches·The Substance of the Way*) He applies the developments and changes of yin and yang as two contradictory forces to analyzing the origin of natural phenomena such as the wind, thunder, clouds and water. Between yin and yang there is a developmental tendency of contradiction. Each of the two parties must be in one situation, that is, either "controlling" or "subduing," either "overriding" or "underlying." In other words, each governs the other; each replaces the other. In things of the so-called yin category, the true situation is only that yin prevails over yang, instead of there being purely yin. In things of the so-called yang category, the true situation is that yang prevails over yin, instead of there being purely yang. Therefore, nothing has a simple identity of pure yin or pure yang. Everything is in a state of contradic-

---

★ [1]How Heaven and Earth are like a bellows! While vacuous, it is never exhausted. When active, it produces even more. — *Laozi,·Chapter 5*

tory unity, in which yin and yang are interlocked with each other. (Cf. *Cautious Speeches· The Movement of the Hexagram Qian — The Creative*, and *A Reply to He Baizhai's Theory of Creation*)

It is from the analysis of the contradictions contained in concrete things that he vaguely conjectures that there must a universal law that governs the contradictory movement of everything. So he puts forth the view that "sometimes one material force prevails over another, so that it takes charge of a thing." (*A Reply to He Baizhai's Theory of Creation*) And he says, "In the combination of yin and yang, sometimes one party prevails over the other, just as in a house one is the master, while the other is the guest. The prevailing party is always in charge of a thing in which two parties dwell together." (*Cautious Speeches· The Movement of the Hexagram Qian — The Creative*) In other words, yin and yang as two opposites are not always in balance. The reason why things may change lies in that the imbalance of the contradictory development brings about a situation in which the master and the guest exchange places. In this way, he puts new content into Zhang Zai's doctrine that "one thing has two bodies." And he transforms Zhou Dunyi's theory by transferring the subtle key to governing the activity and tranquility of things from the "Great Ultimate" to the lively and vivid transformational movements of material force. What is more, in so doing he takes away the foundation of Zhou Dunyi's theory that "the Great Ultimate begets yin and yang through activity and tranquility."

In this way, on the basis of a world outlook which combines "material force as the basic unit" with "material force in transformation," Wang makes a powerful criticism of the various schools and superstitious thoughts of religions.

Although Wang Tingxiang emphasizes that knowledge must be based on the direct experience of "seeing and hearing," he is not a narrow empiricist. In his opinion, "The reason why sages and worthy men had knowledge lies in that they combined thinking with seeing and hearing." (*Statements of Grace (I)*) That is to say, only by the synthesis of reason ("thought") and perception ("seeing and hearing") can knowledge be formed. While he opposes apriorism, in a particular way he points out that the limitations of knowledge gained from seeing and hearing may lead people into falsehood. Wang Tingxiang regards Zhu Xi saying, "You may perceive the intention of sages and worthy men by reading their works" (*Classified Conversations of Zhu Xi·Book 9*) as a kind of preconception, which is an obstruction to the formation of knowledge gained from "personal experience." In order to get rid of such an obstruction, Lu Jiuyuan recommends "reducing the burden." But Wang Tingxiang says, "As for direct knowledge gained from the ears and eyes, when it is used well it may enlarge the human mind, but when it is used ill it may restrain the human mind." (*Cautious Speeches·Seeing and Hearing*) How can we enlarge our mind and expand our information? In Wang Tingxiang's opinion, we should lay stress on the role that rational thinking plays in the process of forming knowledge. Since things are connected with one another by certain categories, by way of "analogy" we may have "a thorough understanding" of the principle of things. By tracing the analogies between things we may find their mutual relations, and may infer and judge. This is the so-called method of "understanding by innuendo."

Here is an example: From the phenomenon that "the rocks of the mountain are slanting," we may infer that "in ancient times they were once under water." Here is another example: From the situation that "between the mountains there is a valley," we may infer that "this was caused by a watercourse which scoured downwards." Here is a third example: From a plain we may infer that rivers poured across the earth and the accumulated earth gradually became a plain. (Cf. *Cautious Speeches·The Movement of the Hexagram Qian — The Creative*) On one side there are materials from "seeing and hearing," while on the other side there is the process of "thinking and considering." These two sides ought to be combined with each other, and a long-term accumulation ought to be made. It is possible to expand human knowledge in width and depth as well. In width, human knowledge may make "a thorough inquiry into Heaven and Earth." In depth, human knowledge may make "a thorough inquiry into hair-splitting affairs." (Cf. *Statements of Grace (I)*, and *Cautious Speeches·Great Concentration*) Especially under the guidance of rational knowledge, one must be able to look far ahead and aim high. Wang says, "I let my mind soar above creation, I let my body touch the realistic situation of the myriad things. I seek the middle, correct and sincere principle to the utmost, and then I grasp it tightly. My hearing, my seeing and the philosophers of the past are nothing but the constituents of my great synthesis." (*Cautious Speeches·Seeing and Hearing*) Such is his idea of synthesizing personal experience gained from seeing and hearing (great synthesis). His aim is to understand the universe thoroughly. He absorbs and transforms Zhang Zai's doctrine of "enlarging the mind" and Zhu Xi's doctrine of "investigating principle to the utmost." And he develops his epistemology in line with materialism.

But rational knowledge must undergo a test in which "it is examined carefully through common things and daily affairs so that it may be thoroughly understood." In other words, whether or not one has a thorough understanding depends on the test of practice. In order to explain this, Wang uses a metaphor of a man who "learns boating within a closed room." He directs his forceful satire and profound criticism at the Neo-Confucians, who talk and guess groundlessly. Although they have never experienced any "perils of storms and billows," they are eager to discuss "the skill of rowing a boat" by shutting themselves up. When they go out to practice, the wind and the rushing water will foil them. In addition, whirlpools will disturb their wisdom, the boat will turn upside down, and they will get a soaking. If they sail on big rivers or oceans, they will be buried beneath the waves. (*A Critical Analysis of Learning for Shilong Academy*) Therefore, it will not do if one only hears with one's ears and talks with one's mouth; one must "make efforts in practice and have experiences with persons." (*To Xue Juncai (II)*) Why? "Those who are fond of nothing but vain talk will lose opportunities and be short of measures. This is because in the world there are so many things and events changing without an end that no amount of discussions can exhaust them. Those who adhere to nothing but the mind will perform no meritorious services at all. This is because the mind is so subtle and insubstantial a thing that nobody may use it to make himself thoroughly familiar with events and opportunities." (*To Xue Juncai (II)*)

Things and events are always changing. And what is more, the cause of their changes cannot be easily found, nor can the key point of their changes easily be grasped. Without practical experience, it is very difficult for anybody to realize the secret and subtle parts of the things and events. When a complex event occurs, one will panic, and "lose opportunities and be short of measures." In an emergency, one will be frightened, and one will "perform no meritorious services at all." In short, neither the Heavenly principle nor innate knowledge is effective. What we should do is follow the developmental law of knowledge honestly and sincerely.

We must exert great efforts in the three aspects of "observing," "thinking," and "acting," and do our best to examine the real situation.

> "The practical situation of things and events must be tested by personal experience. If you believe hearsay only, you will become perplexed. The essence of things and principles should accord with correct thinking. If you rely on memory only, you will become careless. The fine point of things and opportunities can be seen only in action. If you merely talk bombastically, you will become shallow." (*Cautious Speeches·Seeing and Hearing*)

By way of practical contact, one may see the "real situation of things and events" with one's own eyes. By way of thinking, one may have a thorough understanding of the "essence of things and principles." By way of practicing what one preaches, one may grasp the "fine points of things and opportunities." Only in this way can knowledge become continuously deeper and deeper. The subjective will be in accordance with the objective step by step. Such is Wang Tingxiang's epistemological formula of "observing thinking acting." This is a criticism and negation of Zhu Xi and Wang Shouren. The former says, "Knowledge comes first, and action second," and the latter says, "Knowledge and action are one." Thus Wang Tingxiang prepared a theoretical premise for the thinkers who were active at the turn of the Ming and Qing dynasties to make a historical summary of the relationship between knowledge and activity.

PART IV

Coming to Terms: Decline, Crisis, and Stabilization

(Ming Dynasty to Contemporary China, ca 17th Century to 20th Century A.D.)

30.

Heterodoxy and the Opposition to Neo-Confucianism

Li Zhi (1527-1602) was a native of Jinjiang County, Quanzhou Prefecture, Fujian Province. He was a thinker of the early enlightenment in China.

Li Zhi's life span included the Jiajing (1522-1566) and Wanli (1573-1620) reign periods of the Ming Dynasty. This was a time when the old feudal society underwent profound economic changes accompanied by social crises. By that time, the germination of new relations of production, namely, relations of production with some capitalist ingredients, had appeared in some areas and in some lines of business, especially in the textiles industry of southeast China. A group of industrial laborers and small industrialists and businessmen had appeared. But these new social productive forces were constrained by the traditional feudal privileges of the dynastic order. Thus, the last stage of the Ming Dynasty was characterized by exacerbation of class contradictions, which culminated in the Great Peasant Uprising led by Li Zicheng and Zhang Xianzhong, which finally overthrew the dynasty.

Against this background arose the Taizhou School of philosophy, which had great appeal for ordinary people. It opposed the dogmatic Neo-Confucianism of Zhu Xi, and transformed the Heavenly Principle and the theory of innate knowledge into "a daily learning," which "foolish men and stupid women could understand and put into practice." At this stage it had not yet gotten rid of the traditional influence of feudal ethics, but later it became more down-to-earth. "Every day the common people used it as the correct way." "Lo and behold, it seemed that the street was thronged with sages." "Heaven and earth have been overturned." "The Confucian ethical code cannot control the situation any longer." This caused consternation in ruling circles: "They worried deeply about it, as if another Yellow Turbans revolt and the five-bushels-of-rice sect of Taoism might arise again." (The above quotations are all from the *Academic Cases of Ming Confucians·A Preface to the Taizhou School of Thought* and from the *Historical Materials of Yanzhou* compiled by Wang Shizhen) Not surprisingly, the Taizhou School was soon suppressed.

Li Zhi was the inheritor and developer of the Taizhou School. His doctrines were labeled "heterodox" by the "orthodox" Neo-Confucians. Undismayed, Li took a clear-cut stand, and never hid his "heterodox" views.

His *Book Which Risks Burning* and *Sequel to the Book Which Risks Burning* are full of "excited and indignant words." They record debates in which he engaged with Neo-Confucians. In them, Li purports to expose the defects and fallacies of the *Analects* and the *Mencius*. His "heterodoxy" also extends to history in his magnum opus, the *Hidden Book*, and the *Sequel to the Hidden Book*. In the first, he gives completely different evaluations of more than 800 historical personages who lived from the Warring States Period to the fall of the Yuan Dynasty. The second work is a collection of commentaries on some prominent figures of the Ming Dynasty.

Li Zhi was fond of putting forth unusual views. "He likes to spring surprises on people in his criticism of the Song Dynasty Neo-Confucian scholars." (This is a comment on Li Zhi made by Shen Zan, who compiled *Fragmental Series of the Late Affairs*) He dismissed domestic discipline, tutorial admonishment and the prohibitions of officialdom, so revered by the Neo-Confucians, as mere ropes to bind human nature. His rebellious character reflected the struggle against feudal rule which was being waged by the people of both the countryside and the newly burgeoning cities of his day. Springing from a merchant family, Li Zhi is naturally filled with sympathy for the class of traders and townspeople. He hates the falsehood of the sanctimonious Neo-Confucians, and he admires "plowmen and traders" for "matching word to deed." Such an ideological stance has its roots in the changes that were taking place in the late Ming Dynasty, and expresses itself as an acute struggle between "heterodoxy" and "orthodoxy." Thus, Li Zhi is quite different from Wang Shouren, who in form opposes Zhu Xi's Neo-Confucianism but in essence supports the ideology of feudalism. Li Zhi puts himself "right in the battle array." He holds high "the banner of justice." He has "righteousness in his mind." (*Sequel to the Book Which Risks Burning·To Zhou Youshan*)

Li attacks the Neo-Confucian scholars of the Song-Ming Period for turning Confucian thought into eternal and immutable dogma. The feudal rulers treated the Neo-Confucians' annotations on the Four Books and the Five Classics as the "authorized versions." Boldly, Li attacks this cultural autocracy as follows:

> "Other people regard Confucius as a great sage, and I regard him as a great sage, too. The other people regard Laozi and Buddha as heterodox, and I regard them as heterodox, too. But in fact nobody really understands what a great sage is or what heterodoxy means.... The Confucian scholars first imagined, and then told people what they had imagined. Then, fathers and teachers followed them, and recited their instructions. The young fellows, since they were ignorant, followed them, too. And then ten thousand mouths were reciting the same words, so they became universally believed. This has been the situation for the past several thousand years, but nobody knows the true situation." (*Sequel to the Book Which Risks Burning·Inscription on the Portrait of Confucius in the Zhifo Monastery*)

Facing Confucian authority, people can do nothing but believe blindly, as if their ears and eyes were entirely stopped up. Although several thousand years have passed, they follow the same pattern, obeying the ancient instructions and uttering the same dogmas. As a result, although Confucius passed away ages ago, Confucian thought still dominates men's minds. "In the past, there have appeared many things except right and wrong," Li says, adding, "There is neither a fixed standard nor a fixed conclusion when it comes to right and wrong." He goes on:

> "As for right and wrong concerning people, at first there is no fixed standard. As for comments on whether people are right or wrong, since it is a human activity, there can be no fixed conclusion. Since there is no fixed standard, this may be right and that

may be wrong, and as a result this and that may run parallel. Since there is no fixed conclusion, this may be affirmed and that may be denied, and as a result this and that may run parallel, too." (*Hidden Book·A Front Treatise to the General Catalog of the Biographies of Centuries*)

Here, Li fails to deal with the relationship between relative truth and absolute truth in a dialectical way, but he does pose the question of the relativity of truth. He uses the relativity of right and wrong to oppose the Confucian dogma, rendering right and wrong into an absolute conception. He upholds the principle that two ideas may coexist, and they may contend freely with each other to create the conditions in which new ideas may develop. He uses the skeptical and critical spirit of "turning upside down the right and wrong of a myriad generations" to oppose the blind fideism of "taking the Confucian standards of right and wrong as one's own standards of right and wrong." In this way, he aims at the vulnerable point in Neo-Confucian theory which supported political absolutism.

In his opinion, the six major Confucian classics, the *Analects* and the *Mencius* were nothing but fragmental notes which "have a beginning but no end," and which "gain the back and lose the front." The words and deeds of Confucius and Mencius recorded in these books are no more than personal opinions, similar to "medicines given to whoever is ill and recipes written at various times." Li accepts that they may "treat the head when the head aches, and treat the foot when the foot hurts." But they cannot be "regarded as the supreme theory for all ages," because, for one thing, in later ages there appeared many "high-sounding and impractical disciples," who embezzled recipes from the sages, gave fake medicines, and pretended to treat diseases. Thus, these classics became the "sham of Neo-Confucianism and a hotbed of sanctimonious men." (*Book Which Risks Burning·On Childlike Innocence*) In a figurative and energetic way he reveals the fraudulent nature of the Neo-Confucians, who deify the words of the "sages" in order to monopolize public opinion.

He particularly hates the cultural monopoly which prevailed at that time. "Everybody takes the Confucian standards of right and wrong as his own standards of right and wrong," while all the other schools of thought "have no right to set up their own standards of right and wrong." For this reason, he criticizes a narrow-minded view of Mencius, who said, "But what I wish to do is to learn to be like Confucius." (*Mencius·Gongsun Chou (I)*) Li says as follows:

> "Everyone created by Heaven has his own role to play, and it is unnecessary to study Confucius to complete oneself. If one had to wait for Confucius to come along to complete oneself, there would have been no people in remote antiquity. But in the remote antiquity there was Confucius. Confucius was a human being, wasn't he?" (*Hidden Book·In Reply to Censor Geng Dingxiang*)

With the claim that "there is neither a fixed standard nor fixed conclusion concerning right and wrong," his main aim is to undermine the cultural monopoly of the Neo-Confucians and break the fetters with which the Confucian classics bound the minds of the people of his day.

Diverging from the orthodox schools, he affirms that the First Emperor of the Qin Dynasty was "a great emperor of all the ages," and that Wu Zetian was a "wise empress," because she had the ability to appreciate a person's character and capability, and knew how to care for talented people and cultivate them. Thereby he refutes Zhu Xi's theory of historical retrogression, which claimed that the Han and Tang dynasties were not as good as the remote "three ages." He praises the uprising led by Chen Sheng and Wu Guang, saying, "Two ignorant persons initiated a peasant uprising. This was an unprecedented great event." As for the leaders of the peasant rebels who lived by the marshes of Liangshanpo, they were all "energetic, worthy, loyal and righteous heroes." In contrast to them, the feudal rulers who suppressed the Liangshanpo Uprising were "robbers." To a certain degree, he affirms that peasant uprisings have a just cause. And he has sympathy for Zhuo Wenjun and Sima Xiangru, who married the partner of their own choice. He says, "Similar sounds echo each other. Like attracts like.... A young man seeks a girl's love, just as a male phoenix seeks its mate. Wherein lie the grounds for accusation?" Li commends the action of Hongfu, a legendary figure who was bold enough to defy the authority of her parents, and married for love, a scandalous step according to feudal ethics, which sanctioned only marriages arranged by go-betweens and approved by the young person's parents.

Starting from an abstract and generalized view of man, Li opposes the view of innate determinism which decrees social stratification. In his opinion, everybody has the same cognitive ability, moral consciousness and material needs, and therefore all men are equal in these respects. What is more, he opposes the view that men are superior to women, which was deeply rooted in feudal society. He demonstrates this equality from the angle of the human ability to know things. He says as follows:

> "Therefore, we may say that there are men and women in the same conception of man, but we may not say that there are male views and female views in the same conception of view. There is no such rule, is there? We may say that some views are all long-term and some views are all shortsighted, but we may not say that men's views are all long-term and women's views are all shortsighted. There is no such rule, is there?" (*Book Which Risks Burning·A Letter to Rebuke Those Who Regard Women's Practice of the Way as a Shortsighted View*)

He adds, "Everybody in the world has the inborn ability to know things." (*Book Which Risks Burning·In Reply to Zhou Xiyan*) He goes on to conclude that since both men and women are human beings who may possess "views" of one kind or another, all men and women may "practice the Way." The quality of a view or the skill of a practice is mainly decided by the subjective efforts of man but not by the physiological differences of individual human beings.

In Li's view, if women who are bound by feudal ethics and rites are brave enough to ignore the "vulgar words," and if they are brave enough to "practice religion," their views must be much more advanced than those men who are fettered by feudal ethics and rites. In the Zhifo Monastery, where he had lived for a long time, there was such a group of such women. Because of this, the feudal rulers of the day accused him of cajoling women. "He allured some scholars and wives and daughters of good families into the monastery, where they mixed together and expounded the texts of Buddhism." (*History of the Ming Dynasty·Book 216: Biography of Cai Yizhong*)

Starting from the view that everybody has "virtues," he opposes the stand of the Neo-Confucians that only the sages have virtues, while ordinary people have no virtues at all. He says as follows:

> "Do just as your nature prompts you to do, and this is enough. You should not regard the sages as supermen. Emperors Yao and Shun were the same as those who are hurrying on with their journey. The sages are the same as the ordinary people." (*Literary Works of Li Zhi·A Bright Lamp for the Ancients*)

All the so-called "orthodox" schools have in common the problem of human nature. That is, they attribute the "original goodness of human nature" to the sages, while attributing "the realistic evilness of human feelings" to the common people. What is more, "to worship moral character" is a holy undertaking of the sages, and the sages are high up and beyond reach. As we may well remember, Wang Shouren puts forth a view that everybody is possessed of innate knowledge and every street is thronged with sages. In other words, it is "simple, direct and easy" to overcome all worldly thoughts and enter sainthood. Nevertheless, he still regards the sages as the ultimate standard, and he demands that ordinary people emulate them. Li Zhi, however, denies that there is an impassable demarcation line between the sages and ordinary people. In his opinion, the sages and ordinary people are equals in that both of them possess "moral character." The actions of sages and those of ordinary people are common in "acting from the will," and it is very hard to tell which is better. Therefore, "worshiping moral character" is not an action peculiar to the sages, and the sages' actions are not mysterious, either. "When Emperor Yao yielded the throne to Emperor Shun, this great event was accomplished amid glasses of wine. King Tang and King Wen dealt with state affairs as if they were playing chess." (*Literary Works of Li Zhi·A Bright Lamp for the Ancients*)

Since that the human body per se is a material entity, Li Zhi boldly puts forth his view that it is necessary to treat the ruler and the common people as equals:

> "As the sage knows, the body of a common person is just the same as his own body, as he is a human being, too. Therefore, from the emperor down to the lowest commoner, everybody is the same as far as the body is concerned." (*Ibid*)

By this, Li means that everybody has the same physical constitution, ruled by the laws of life and death. Such being the case, everybody has the same material demands. In this respect, everybody without exception is the same. He draws the conclusion that, "the common people are by no means inferior to the nobility; and the nobility is by no means superior to the common people." (*Series of Li Zhi·Annotation on the Laozi*)

Li oppose the prejudices held by the feudal "orthodox" schools such as those relating to relations between men and women, between the sages and ordinary people, between the ruler and the people, etc. However, he does not understand man's social and class character, and he fails to acknowledge the social foundation on which the differences in feudal society came into being. This is because he was ideologically limited by the times in which he lived. But with his two famous theories — that people are born equal and that there is no fixed standard of right and wrong — he attacks the feudal code of ethics. This reflects the heterodox tendency which is one of the epochal features of philosophy in the late Ming Dynasty.

By maintaining that all people have the same instincts, and are therefore born equal, Li opposes the feudal hierarchical system. At the same time, he insists that different people have different personalities, and therefore he opposes the Confucian code of ethics by advocating the liberation of the individual personality. His views are diametrically opposed to those of Gen Tiantai, a representative of the feudal orthodox school in Huang'an County,* and there was a heated controversy between them. In Gen Tiantai's opinion, the sage had supreme status in the hierarchy of human relations, while Li held that the sage was an unliberated individual.

As regards the root cause and irrationality of feudal ethics, Li says, "The rule of a gentleman is based on his own body. The rule of a supreme man is based on the whole people. Since a gentleman bases his rule on his own body, he must run the country just as he treats his own body. Since a supreme man bases his rule on the whole people, he must rule the country just as he deals with the whole people." (*Book Which Risks Burning·On the Government*) In other words, there are two ways to

---

* Huang'an is now the Hong'an County in Hubei Province. Gen Dingxiang he went by the alias Tiantai. He had been a friend of Li Zhi, but later he became hostile to Li .

run a country, one being in accordance with the wishes of the people, the other being in accordance with the ruler's own will. To be in accordance with the wishes of the people means to adopt the principle of "autonomous rule." To be in accordance with the ruler's will means to follow the feudal code of ethics. The former represents the will and interests of the whole people; the latter represents the will and interests of the ruler only. Therefore, all the "complicated regulations and ordinances" and all the "penalties, laws and codes" are nothing but fetters imposed on the people, which serve only one purpose, that is, to consolidate feudal rule and to prevent deviations arising among the people.

Li has a particular hatred of hypocrisy. The feudal ethical code was in essence life-destroying and smothered "childlike innocence." As soon as a person "loses his sincere heart," he will become a fellow with a "hypocritical personality." "Since one's personal experiences increase with each passing day, one's knowledge also increases with each passing day. In addition, a good reputation is attractive to everybody. And everybody is bound to do his best to spread his good reputation if he has one. As a result, it is easy to lose one's childlike innocence. Similarly, a bad reputation is repulsive to everybody, and everybody is bound to do his best to cover up his bad reputation if he has one. As a result, it is easy to lose one's childlike innocence. Both personal experience and knowledge may come from one's extensive reading and a deep study of principles." (*Book Which Risks Burning· On Childlike Innocence*)

Li's theory of childlike innocence has its origin in Wang Shouren's theory of innate knowledge, but he means exactly the opposite of what Wang Shouren does. Wang's innate knowledge is righteousness and principle. Whether or not anything is in accordance with the Heavenly principle depends on innate knowledge. But for Li, both righteousness and principle constitute a blindfold for childlike innocence. The more righteousness and principle are instilled into one's mind, the more of one's childlike innocence one will lose. In order to distinguish childlike innocence from innate knowledge, he defines the former as the "sincere heart." "Childlike innocence is the sincere heart. If you do not approve of childlike innocence, this means that you do not approve of the sincere heart. Childlike innocence is as far away as possible from falsehood, and absolutely sincere. It is the original mind from which gushed forth the first idea. If anybody loses his childlike innocence, he loses his sincerity.

When a person loses his sincere heart, he loses his true personality." (*Book Which Risks Burning·On Childlike Innocence*)

In other words, childlike innocence is like the pure heart of a newborn babe, which has never been sullied by righteousness or principle. Although the original mind is very pure, once it is invaded by the Neo-Confucians doctrine of righteousness and principle, the "disappearance of sincerity" takes place immediately. Li demands that everybody revert to his "sincere heart," and have a "true personality." He calls for the awakening of "the original mind from which gushed forth the first idea." This is a self-awakening of the individual personality, which shifts restlessly under the heavy weight of feudal rites and ethics. And he boldly puts forth the demand that people should break through the "prohibitions of feudal regulations." This is a demand for the individual personality to be liberated from all feudal fetters. "A man of noble character uses the people to rule the people; he never dares to use himself to rule the people. The people ought to enjoy autonomous rule, because when society first emerged it was so. If the people can enjoy autonomous rule, evils will stop before they are prohibited.... Once the people are ruled by the people, the prohibitions of the feudal regulations will be totally useless." (*Literary Works of Li Zhi·A Bright Lamp for the Ancients*)

Objectively speaking, his demands for the rejection of the feudal regulations and the people ruling the people reflect the aspirations of the newly emerging bourgeois class of his day.

In the last stage of the Ming Dynasty, the new economic factors, which had just begun to germinate, and the narrow relations of production, which served as the foundation of feudal society, came into conflict. This adds some new content to the controversy over the relationship between principle and desire, in the course of which Li fiercely attacked feudal ethics and rites.

Li stands in diametrical opposition to the demand of the Neo-Confucians, which runs, "Eradicate human desires, and maintain the Heavenly principles." Li's view of "the human relations and the innate principles of things," runs, "Everybody must have food and clothing." About this, he says as follows:

"Apart from food and clothing, there is no room to discuss the so-called human relations and the innate principles of things." (*Book Which Risks Burning·In Reply to Deng Shiyang*)

Moreover, a good ruler must listen to the people carefully, and observe their conditions:

"All worldly affairs related to the people's livelihood and production are their common interests, and therefore they study them in common, understand them in common, and discuss them in common. These are truly intimate words.... The reason why I like to observe the people's conditions lies in that I want to know the intimate words they common people say in their everyday life." (*Book Which Risks Burning·In Reply to Deng Shiyang*)

The voices which reflect "the people's livelihood and production" are "intimate words" and "good words," which sound the kindest and the sweetest to Li. The Neo-Confucians' preaching consists of "vicious remarks," being "in opposition to the common people's desires."

To discredit the Neo-Confucians, who set up "the mind of the Way" outside "the mind of the people," Li asserts that "without the private property, there would be no mind at all." "Private property is the mind of the people. Only after one has private property can one's true mind appear. Without private property, there would be no mind at all. If those who farm the land keep the autumn harvest as their private property, they will put all their efforts into farming the land. If those who manage the houses may have what are accumulated in the barns, they will put all their efforts into managing the houses.... This is in accordance with the natural principles." (*Hidden Book·A Treatise on the Confucian Ministers of Virtue and Achievement*)

Thus it can be seen clearly that the "sincere heart," which stands in opposition to the "hypocritical heart," is by no means abstract "childlike innocence." Instead, it refers to the "private mind," with which the new social stratum of the bourgeoisie may pursue their "freedom of private property." In like manner, the "true personality," which stands in opposition to the "hypocritical personality," refers to those who "farm their land diligently" and those who "run their business earnestly." Their desire to develop the private economy is an aspect of the "natural principles" and an irresistible tendency of development. Thus, Li played a progressive role in the movement to destroy the feudal relations of production within the historical scope of his day. Nevertheless, his view is established on an egoistic theory of human nature and deserves serious criticism.

Li boldly puts forth a view of the "private mind," analyses the words and deeds of the sanctimonious scholars of Neo-Confucianism Accordingly: "They practice Neo-Confucianism in appearance, but they seek personal gain in their hearts. They clothe themselves in Confucian garments, but when they act they are just like dirty curs and greedy swine." It is because in reality they fear the people's aspirations as "terrible poisons and sharp daggers" that they pretend to oppose material desires with glib words, while in practice they seek high positions and handsome incomes, and they lead the most decadent and dissolute lives.

Li suffered for his views. Because he championed the sufficient supply of food and clothing for the common people, calling this demand of theirs "intimate words" and "good words," he had to give up his position and salary, left his family, drifted from place to place, and lived in poverty. In the last stage of the Ming Dynasty, when peasant uprisings broke out frequently, Li used his pen and tongue as weapons, taking an active part in the struggle against the feudal rule of the day. This shows that Li was an enlightenment thinker with a sturdy character.

The philosophical thought of Li Zhi is somewhat complicated. So, when we attempt to bring to light the developmental process of his thought, it is useful to consider the historical conditions of his day at the same time. Only in this way can we see clearly what the main tendency in his thought is and where the social root causes of his ideological contradictions lie.

We should note the singular features of Li's character. "From childhood he was too stubborn to be tamed. He had no faith in scholarship, in Taoism, in celestial beings or in Buddhism. The moment he saw a Taoist priest or a Buddhist monk he was nauseated. And he was especially averse to Neo-Confucian scholars." (*Postscript to the Chronological Biography of Wang Yangming*, which is an appendix to the *Collected Writings of Wang Yangming on Neo-Confucianism*) Thus the virulence of his diatribes against those three trends of thought is not surprising. In his criticism of Zhu Xi's theory of the Great Ultimate, he says:

"At the very beginning of the creation of man, there were merely two material forces. Man and woman are two kinds of life, and there is no difference between the so-called one and the principle. How can there be the Great Ultimate? Judging from the present situation, I have to ask about the so-called one. What the devil is it? As for the so-called principle, where the devil is it? As for the Great Ultimate, what the devil does it refer to?" (*Book Which Risks Burning·On Husband and Wife*)

"Therefore when I investigate the beginning of things to the utmost, I see that husband and wife are the origin of creation. So I mention husband and wife as the only two parties. I have never discussed the one, and I have never discussed principle, either. Now that the one has been excluded from my discussion, how can I discuss nonbeing? Now that nonbeing has been excluded from my discussion, how can I discuss the non-existence of nonbeing?" (*Ibid*)

Obviously, when he researches into the origin of the universe ("investigate the beginning of things to the utmost"), he discusses things "in terms of the two but not the one." Here he does not use dualism to oppose Zhu Xi's monism of material force. Instead, he adopts the then prevalent view of material force as the basic unit, and he uses the contradictions and changes of "yin and yang as two material forces" to illustrate "the origin of creation" of all things. Furthermore, he uses it to refute the monism of principle as advocated by Zhu Xi, to refute the Metaphysical theory that nonbeing begets beings, and to refute the Buddhist theory of *sunya* (emptiness).

However, despite his attacks on Taoism and Buddhism, he finally shaved his head and became a Buddhist monk. During this transition, some changes happened to his world outlook, too. It changed from emphasis on "human relations and innate knowledge of things" to cognition of "the absolute void," from "the existence of things" to the cognition of "the non-existence of things," from "the mountains, rives and the vast land" to seeking "the ultimate source pure and clear." The progress of his epistemology in the end led him to withdraw from the real world. We can find a hint of this in the following words:

"Without mountains, rivers and the vast land there would be no ultimate source pure and clear. Therefore, we may say that mountains, rivers and the vast land are the ultimate source pure and clear. Without mountains, rivers and the vast land, the ultimate source pure and clear becomes a pile of rubbish or something lifeless, which cuts off the world from the *sunya*. If so, it is no longer the mother of the myriad things. It is not worth a farthing, is it?" (*Book Which Risks Burning·Questions about Avalokitesvara·Answer to Self-Confidence*)

Then, what is "the ultimate source pure and clear"? He explains, "When you look at it, you see nothing. When you listen to it, you hear nothing. You have a strong desire to look at it, but you can see nothing. You have a strong desire to listen to it, but you can hear nothing. It is just like the hair of tortoises and horns of rabbits — it exists in name but not in reality. It does not exist in reality, but we may say that it is very pure and clear." (*Ibid*) Such being the case, "the ultimate source pure and clear" is a kind of original substance that exists only in the spiritual realm. When he says, "Mountains, rivers and the vast land are the ultimate source pure and clear," he attempts to demonstrate two points. First, "the ultimate source pure and clear" is the "mother of the myriad things." Second, the existence of "mountains, rivers and the vast land" is evidence for "the ultimate source pure and clear." The evidence tells us the reason why "the ultimate source pure and clear" is not "a pile of rubbish." Therefore, he takes "the ultimate source pure and clear" for the primary premise, and the "mountains, rivers and the vast land" for the secondary premise.

Li's thought changes abruptly, his stance is shifted from sturdily criticizing reality to escapism. Finally he finds refuge in the Chan Sect of Buddhism. Why does he do so?

First, we should cast light on the social root cause of Li's ideological contradictions, starting with the epochal features of the later stage of the Ming Dynasty. In this stage feudal society had already started its process of collapse, with the anti-feudal movements waged by the broad masses of the peasants and the newly rising social stratum of the townspeople gaining momentum. But feudal ethics and ways of thought were still prevalent, and had not yet been replaced by new ways of thinking. Li describes this mental confusion thus: "In the mind, there are stored many queer events which are beyond description. In the throat, there are many disgusting things to be vomited out, but they won't come out. And in the mouth there are many words longing to be spoken out loud, but one cannot tell what they are." These new factors "have accumulated too long to be prevented from gushing out all of a sudden." Once they break out, "they will cry out madly, and shed tears bitterly without ceasing." The situation is like a newborn baby who has just been born of feudalism, waving its small feet and hands. When the baby raises its first cry, its voice is naturally very clear. Such a cry seems to contain many "pearls and gems," which shed ideological brilliance "as beautiful as the shifting pink clouds in the sky." (The above quotations are all from the *Book Which Risks Burning·Fragmentary Argumentations.*) Nevertheless, he is a newborn baby after all and is not physically well developed yet, so he cannot deal with the complexities of ideological struggle. When he plunges himself into the theoretical struggle against the Neo-Confucianism of Zhu Xi, he is bound to look for an ideological weapon. Since a hungry baby is not choosy, he picks up a weapon at random. With his Idealism as a weapon Wang Shouren wages a formal struggle against Zhu Xi. Many years later, when Li Zhi recalled the period of the epochal transition in his thought, he said, "I had just reached the age of forty, and Li Fengyang and Xu Yongjian, two of my friends, told me of the views of Mr. Longxi (namely, Wang Ji), and they showed me the books of Mr. Wang Yangming. So I came to know that those who had attained the highest state of spiritual enlightenment would not die, in that they were the same as the true Buddha and true immortals. Although I was very stubborn, I was convinced by them." (*Postscript to the Chronological Biography of Wang Yangming*) It is obvious that there were two factors at work in the transition of Li Zhi. One was the immaturity of his theoretical development, and the other was the influence of his friends.

We should also take into account the class origin from which the contradictions of his philosophical thought sprang. To do so, we must examine the historical position and the class characteristics of the landlord class at that time, to which Li belonged. Li's thought reflects the ideological outlook and the class characteristics of the intellectuals of the landlord class during that period of turmoil, when feudalism was beginning to decline, and the differences between the old and the new were becoming distinct, as described in the adage "The new and the old have not yet merged -- the granary is nearly empty but the new crop is not yet ripe." He does his best to "fight his way forward from within the stronghold" of the age-old feudal ideology. But, the umbilical cord of tradition cannot be severed all of a sudden. While he "pins his ambition on solving the problem of food and clothing," placing particular stress on realistic problems: "To feed and to clothe are the core of human relations and the innate principles of things." On the other hand, his view of material desire belongs to the "morality of the well-fed and the well-clad." This shows that he has not yet cast off the moral consciousness of the feudal scholar-officials. So he puts forth another view: "You must not confine yourself merely to human relations and the innate knowledge of things as they are." Instead, "it is necessary to know the absolute void from the angle of human relations and the innate knowledge of things." Here we see a process in which he dissociates himself from "human relations and the innate knowledge of things," and dwells in "the absolute void," changing his stance from criticism of reality to escape from reality.

The conditions of class and ideological struggle of his day compelled him in the end to take a wrong path. From his practical experience, he saw that history was filled with "the principle of perverse acts and backwaters." (These words come from an annotation made by Hong Fu to Jiao Hong's *The Wings of the Laozi·Book 1*) He also concluded that history was filled with "junctures at which disadvantages and advantages are interrelated." (*Book Risks Burning·To Jiao Ruohou*) So he believes that "during a period in which nothing can be done, there must be a situation in which something can be done." (*The Ninth Revision of the Inquiry into the Book of Changes*) Since his heterodox thought faces a situation in which he has to "fight a huge army of hundreds and thousands of enemies every day," he fails to find a social force that is able effectively to combat the feudal tradition. His only allies are a handful of like-minded friends: "Even I myself cannot explain the situation which I find myself in. I have particular regard for some good friends. Whenever I have them, I am happy. Whenever I lose them, I become sad." (*Book Which Risks Burning·In Reply to Zhou Youshan*)

When he could not find any "good friends," he had to resort to the "soul and spirit," so that he might find some way to extricate himself from his predicament: "Bodhisattva's wisdom sheds light on the other shore of un-attainability." (*Book Which Risks Burning·An Outline of My Mental Sutra*)

In this way, this thinker, who had been accused of "extremely heterodox sins," was much vexed by the pressure of feudal mores in the later stage of the Ming Dynasty, when "the day was very dark and the night was even darker." His life was filled with arduous struggles. Limited by the times he lived in and the class he belonged to, he finally embraced the illusion of "the other shore." But his cause was carried on by another group of thinkers, who belonged to the enlightenment period of the history of Chinese philosophy, namely the intersectional period of the Ming and Qing dynasties. The newcomers opened up a fresh outlook.

31.

Huang Zongxi's Historical Philosophy of the Enlightenment

In the *Academic Cases of Ming Confucians·The Case of the Donglin Clique*, there is a passage which eulogizes the Donglin partisans for their lofty ideals and national integrity: "In the past few decades, the brave saw their wives and children burnt to ashes, the weak saw their thatched cottages reduced to ruins. The prevalence of loyalty and righteousness had surpassed that of past dynasties. This was because the influence of the Donglin Clique was still surviving at that time. The Donglin Clique is composed of teachers and friends we can resort to for advice, who once filled this great hall. Cold as the wind was, their blood was hot. With their blood, they purged the world." This is Huang Zongxi's appraisal of his ideological forerunners. It is also an extraordinary high opinion he formed of himself.

During the last years of the Ming Dynasty, against a background of unrest and rebellion, the the Donglin Clique and then the Fushe Association appeared in succession to the Taizhou School of Thought. Progressive literati and officials gave lectures in academies or formed associations. This served as a cloak under which "they commented on the political situation and the power of the imperial court, and they evaluated various personages who were active then." (*History of the Ming Dynasty·Book 231: Biography of Gu Xiancheng*) "They preserved the ancient academies only for the purpose of using them to solve practical problems." (*An Outline History of the Fushe Association*) The political and ideological struggle against powerful officials exerted a direct influence on the development of the early enlightenment trends in the period of the intersection of the Ming and Qing dynasties.

Huang Zongxi (1610-1695) was a native ofYuyao County, Zhejiang Province. His father was Huang Zunsu, a leading figure in the Donglin Clique. From his early youth, he followed his father, and afterwards he himself became the leader of the Fushe Association. He carried on a prolonged struggle against the surviving supporters of the eunuchs' faction, and became famous all over the country.

After the fall of the Ming Dynasty, as Manchu troops entered northern China through the Shanhaiguan Pass, Huang Zongxi joined the resistance to the invaders by organizing the "Loyal-to-the-Age Battalion." After the Ming loyalists were defeated, Huang wandered as an exile. He once lived on the Zhoushan Archipelago, at that time a group of remote and impoverished islands off the coast of Zhejiang Province. Later, he went to Japan, and lived there until 1656. He finally settled in his hometown, where he devoted himself to scholarly pursuits. In 1667, he revived the Zhengren Academy, where he gave lectures and did research.

Huang began to summarize the experiences of the Donglin Clique and the Fushe Association, which had struggled against the forces of feudalism. As he did so, he developed his thoughts on social reform. In 1662 (the first year of Emperor Kangxi's reign of the Qing Dynasty), he finished writing a brilliant book entitled *Obscuration Awaiting Inquiries*. This book amply reflects the political, economic and cultural views of the reformers among the landlord class, and therefore it may be called a manifesto of Chinese civil rights in the 17th century.

Huang was a very erudite scholar who had many original views concerning the Confucian classics, history, literature, the calendar and mathematics. His major works are *Academic Cases of Ming Confucians* and *Academic Cases of the Song and Yuan Dynasties*. The latter was completed by Huang Baijia (1643- ?), his son, and a student, Quan Zuwang (1705-1755).

Huang grew up in the turmoil of the peasant wars in the last years of the Ming Dynasty, and was much influenced by the anti-feudal ideas of the Donglin Clique. He sympathized with the resistance to the Manchu rulers in the early years of the Qing Dynasty. Therefore, his criticism of feudal absolutism is filled with a militant spirit, reflecting the Zeitgeist of the day.

Huang draws a lesson from the fate of his own ethnic group, the Han people, which fell under the yoke of the Manchus in his lifetime. When doing so, he pays special attention to the problems of political reform. In his preface to his *Obscuration Awaiting Inquiries*, he writes as follows: "Although I am rather old, I may as well live as Viscount Ji, who was asked about the root cause of the failure and subjugation from which his people suffered. Although the obscuration has only just been illuminated, and the brightness has not yet been totally recovered, how can I hide the secret of the event, and not tell the inquirer? "He believed firmly that the brightness or darkness, the order or disorder of society could be reversed. "Obscuration" (*ming-yi*) is one of the 64 hexagrams in the *Book of Changes*. Hexagram 36, *Ming Yi*, means the darkening of light. The lower part is a trigram, (*li*), meaning fire, and its upper part is also a trigram, (*kun*), meaning earth. Under the dark and gloomy earth there hides a live coal that can start a new fire.

To probe into the root cause of the rise and fall of societies, Huang extensively adopts the method of historical comparison in this book. He directs his study at social reality, putting forth his ideas about social reform. The book criticizes absolute monarchy and the feudal system.

The feudal ruler was described by the upholders of Confucian norms as "he who occupies the center of the world," "he who epitomizes the world's virtues," and "he that fixes the supreme standard." (Zhu Xi, *A Debate on the Supreme Principle*) But Huang begs to differ. He says, "The greatest evil-doer in the whole country is the emperor. People all over the country nurse strong hatred for their monarch, they regard him as the foe or robber, and they called him the autocrat." (*An Inquiry into the Monarch*) Why is it so? By utilizing the contradictions between the ruler and the common people, he discloses the root cause. "Such is the ruler … he regards the world as his private property, which he may bequeath to his children and grandchildren. It is private property that the ruling family may enjoy endlessly." (*An Inquiry into the Monarch*)

> "Therefore, before he obtains the world, he tries every means to get it. He plunges the people into an abyss of misery, and he breaks up families everywhere. He does all these things in order to enlarge his private property. What a tragic picture it is!… After he obtains the

world, he breaks the people's bones and sucks out the marrow.... He regards all this as a matter of course." (*Ibid*)

In short, the ruler enjoys all the world's good things, and the common people suffer all the world's ills. The feudal rulers do not care whether the people live or die, and they regard "a mass impoverishment" as "a small problem of no importance." In the meantime they regard the property created by the people as their private property. The feudal ruler "regards the world as something that is in his bag." (*An Inquiry into the Subject*) Therefore, it stands to reason that the people should adopt a hostile attitude towards such rulers and the bureaucrats who serve them. By pointing out the realistic interests and contradictions between the ruler and the people, Huang explodes the myth endorsed by the Neo-Confucians that "Heaven begets the people, and sets up a ruler for them," and "The ruler teaches the people how to live and how to help each other.".

He goes on to disclose the contradiction between "the laws of the whole country" and "the laws of the ruler's own family," making a profound criticism of the feudal privileges and laws.

In the early years of the feudal system, soon after it had replaced slavery, Han Fei, an ideological representative of the newly rising landlord class, stated clearly that the essence of the policies, laws and decrees, which are made by the ruler, are "made in order that the people of the whole country may follow them." But later, when feudal rule was firmly established, the stress was on the role of the rites and music: "The rites are the distillation of 'order,' and music is the distillation of 'harmony'." (*Additional Works of the Two Chengs*·*Book 18*) Here, the realistic contradictions which arise from differences of social strata and class antagonism, are covered up under the theory that contradictions maybe reconciled. At the same time, ideological backing for feudalism is sought beyond social reality, viz, "The three cardinal guides may be found in Heaven." Meanwhile, the Metaphysicists say, "The Confucian ethical code originates in Nature." The Buddhists chant, "The noble and humble come from one's karma." The Neo-Confucians claim that "human relations are connected with the Heavenly principle." All these statements serve one "fixed heavenly principle as hard as iron," that is, that the ranks and rights of the ruling order of feudalism must all be safeguarded. Huang rips the ideological and philosophical masks from these theories, pointing out sharply that they serve merely to justify the privileges of the feudal hierarchical system. "After a ruler obtains the world, a problem then immediately arises, namely, that his good fortune on the throne will not last as long as he wishes, and his children and grandchildren may lose the throne. So he thinks about what laws he can make in order that he or his descendants may prevent trouble before it comes. It is a pity that the laws he makes are the law of one family, and not the laws of the whole country." (*An Inquiry into the Law*)

Further, he says:

> "The laws of the later ages serve as a strongbox in which the ruler may store the world.... All the people know full well where that strongbox is. Whenever I think of the strongbox, I become timid, and every day I worry if there is anything wrong with the strongbox. Therefore, the laws have to be made very carefully. But the more careful the laws are the more disorders appear, as the laws are the hotbed of disorder. Therefore, the so-called laws promote illegality." (*An Inquiry into the Law*)

Using "the law of one family," the ruler monopolizes all the "fortunes and interests" in the world by putting them in his personal "strongbox." On the other hand, the people concentrate their hatred on the "strongbox." As a result, the finer the net of justice is, the more doubts and fears there are; the wider the net of justice is, the heavier disasters and misfortunes are. In the long run, the laws made to control disorder become the root cause of disorders; and the ruler who used to be the lawmaker becomes the object of the law's strictures. From the antagonism of interests between the ruler and the ruled, Huang sees the social roots whence spring the "laws of illegality" and the "disorder of the world." This is a rather profound cognition. Nevertheless, he thinks there is the "law of the whole country," which is in opposition to the "laws of illegality." So he harbors the illusion that the "law of one family" can be substituted by the "law of the whole country." He imagines that this may protect the people's interests. But, of course this was absolutely impossible under the exploitative system of Huang's day.

In the third place, Huang puts forth the political principle that "The whole country is the master, while the ruler is only a guest."

Throughout the prolonged period of feudal rule, the dominant class exploited and suppressed the people cruelly, demanding that the people must "stifle their anger and overcome their desires" so that they may be "contented in poverty and devoted to things spiritual." The Neo-Confucians denied that the people had the right to live well, exhorting them to "eradicate human desires and maintain the Heavenly principles!" In opposition to this, Huang claimed that "Everybody has the right to have property of his own, and everybody has the right to make a profit for himself!" That is to say, he regards the satisfaction of personal interests as man's universal right. In essence, he agrees with Li Zhi, who regards "food and clothing" as the basis of "human relations and the innate knowledge of things." This reflects the utilitarianism of the townspeople, an emerging social stratum striving for equal rights. But, under feudal absolutism "the people all over the country neither have their own property nor are they allowed to make profits for themselves." It is necessary to abolish the monarchical system of feudalism to restore such rights to the people:

> "If there were no monarch, everybody would have the right to own property, and everybody would have the right to make profits for himself." (*An Inquiry into the Monarch*)

The relationship between the ruler and the people in the remote past was different from that in later ages.

> "In ancient times, the whole country was the master, while the ruler was only a guest. Whatever a ruler did was for the benefit of the people all over the country. But now, the ruler has become the master, while the people are the guests. Nowadays, there are many people who have neither land nor shelter. Why is this so? It is only because there is a ruler over them." (*An Inquiry into the Monarch*)

Referring back to the golden age of the primitive commune, Huang protests against the reality of monarchical absolutism. The ruler in his ideal "must take the myriad people in the world for his business. His diligence must be ten thousand times that of the people." A good ruler can never be a public enemy.

In the fourth place, Huang analyzes the relationship between the monarch and his officials. The monarch and his officials must work together for the benefit of the people. Their relationship is like that between a teacher and his friends, and not like that between a master and his servants:

"To govern a country is similar to hauling a huge log of wood. When the pullers in front cry, 'Heave-ho!' the pullers in the rear respond with the same 'Heave-ho!' The monarch and his ministers are like people pulling a huge log of wood." (*An Inquiry into the Subject*)

"Officials who work for the ruler only and not for the benefit of the people are no more than the concubines and servants of the ruler. Officials who work for the benefit of the people are either the teachers or friends of the ruler." (*Ibid*)

Defending his own career as an official, Huang says, "The reason I became an official was to serve the people, not only the ruler." (*An Inquiry into the Subject*) Furthermore, he says, "Order and disorder in the nation do not lie in the rise and fall of the fortunes of the ruling family, but in the weal and woe of the masses of the people." (*Ibid*)

It is in the condition — "weal and woe" — of the people as a whole that we can discern whether a political measure of one kind or another is appropriate or not. Thus he devises the following formula: The people are the main body of the state, not an appendix to the ruler; the ruler is a guest, not the master; and the ministers work for the people, not for the ruler. Thus, Huang's view of society is imbued with the spirit of democracy.

In order to realize the principle that "The whole people are the master, while the ruler is only a guest," Huang sums up historical experiences, criticizes reality, and designs a blueprint for the future, a new, uncompromising plan for social reform. It is necessary to limit the monarchical power, and to set up a body, which he calls a "school" (namely, a parliament) where the people may discuss state affairs:

"It must be guaranteed that all policies and political measures are made in the parliament.... All the things that the ruler affirms are not necessarily correct, and all the things that the ruler denies are not necessarily wrong. If there is a parliament, the ruler will not dare to decide everything according to his own will; instead every important matter will be decided in the parliament." (*The School*)

The concrete procedures are as follows: At the level of the country, there will be the "Imperial College," which will correspond to the parliament. In the Imperial College there will be a "Libation Officer," who will correspond to the presiding officer or the speaker in the parliaments of many Western countries. The emperor should be supervised by the libation officer. The libation officer will have the power to make direct criticisms of the imperial court and state affairs. In prefectures or counties there must be similar schools, overseen by a school officer. The local schools must supervise the officials and functionaries of the relevant prefecture or county. The school officer of a prefecture or county will have the power to change wrong decisions, and he may dismiss the officials and functionaries of the prefecture or county when necessary.

This proposal is a direct challenge to the traditional idea that "the common people have no right to discuss state affairs." It is also an affirmation of the experience of political struggles waged by the Donglin Clique and the Fushe Association. In the *Academic Cases of Ming Confucians·Academic Case of the Donglin Clique*, he makes an extremely high evaluation of "the purely political criticism" made by the Donglin Clique, identifying it as "the supreme workshop for state affairs." He treats the "purely political criticism" made by the reformers of the landlord class as the expression of the people's will. He placed his hopes in it as a force blocking the reactionary policies and perverse acts of the ruling class, so as to save the state from failure and destruction. In fact, at the most it could only promote the suffrage of the petty landlords and the townspeople by limiting the privileges of the monarch and big bureaucrats. The democratic germination of Huang is brilliant, but it is tinged with some illusionary factors and feudal dregs. The next step in Huang's plan for social reform was a redistribution of farmland according to the number of persons in a family.

In the last years of the Ming Dynasty, the ownership of land was highly concentrated. One-tenth of the total farmland was occupied by garrison troops, and government land occupied three-tenths of the total. The manors of the influential landlords and powerful gentry each occupied several thousand acres of land. The minor landlords and peasants possessed only small stretches of farmland. Huang desired the restoration of the ancient "nine squares" system of landholding. The concrete procedures are like this: In the first place, "it is necessary to measure all the farmland in the country." (*The Land System·(III)*) In the second place, "it is necessary to distribute the existing land to the people. The government should grant each and every household fifty *mu* (8.2 acres) of fields." (*The Land System·(II)*) In this way, he hoped to see a reversal of the over-concentration of land. Such a system would be the foundation for the growth of a small-peasant economy. This would spur the germination of capitalism. Although such a plan was impractical during that period, it reveals the irrationality of land ownership under feudalism. Obviously, Huang was influenced by the demand for a fair distribution of land raised by the peasant rebels in the later years of the Ming Dynasty.

From the middle of the Ming period, industry and commerce with early capitalist features appeared in the coastal regions of Southeast China. For fear that these features might destroy the foundations of the feudal economy, rulers began to carry out a policy "of upholding the fundamental professions by suppressing the incidental ones." This policy brought about a steady decline in the economy. Standing on the side of the urban freemen, Huang demands that all obstacles to the development of industry and commerce must be swept away. For the first time in the history of China, he raises the slogan, "Industry and commerce are fundamental!" In his opinion, "Industry has a history going back to the sage kings, and commerce drives traders to travel with their wares. So it is clear that both industry and commerce are both fundamental." (*Finance and Planning·(III)*) In order to promote the development of industry and commerce, Huang advocates reform of the monetary system, reorganization of the market and enlargement of trade. "Throughout the country, there should always be a multitude of properties and materials circulating without end." (*Finance and Planning·(II)*) If this were the case, agriculture, handicrafts and commerce would all develop rapidly. Such an idea reflects the demand of the peasants and the townspeople as a newly rising social stratum, and is in accordance with the demands brought about by the germination of capitalism.

Moreover, it is necessary to abolish the civil-service examination system, and to advocate "real scholarship."

Huang particularly attacks two social practices of the day, one being the decadent style of study which prevailed in the late Ming Dynasty, with scholars indulging in empty talk about nature and principle, the other being the imperial examination system which stifled the emergence of talented people:

> "The participants in the imperial examination know clearly that the reason why they studied was not to attain wisdom but to attain a lucrative official post. There are mediocre and presumptuous persons who stick to the accepted formulae and conventions necessary for success in the imperial examination, and with these they judge scholarship ancient and modern. If there is one single word running against the classics, they are shocked, and gaze at each other, saying, 'This is a departure from the classics,' or 'This goes against the old precepts.' And the annotations or re-annotations of the classics become fixed standards by which people test the order and disorder of past dynasties, and the merits and demerits of historical figures. Obviously such fixed standards are nothing but shallow and blind sayings making people unwilling to probe and ponder facts." (*Definitive Edition of the Writings of Nanlei·Preface to the Collected Writings of Yun Zhongsheng*)

In addition, he censures the Confucian scholars of his times for their cultivated ignorance:

> "The learning of Confucian scholars should endow them with the ability to rule the country. But they indulge in perusing classical quotations. By adding one or two quotations to the Yi-Lo school of thought, they place themselves in the ranks of Confucian scholars.... They prattle, 'In order to enable the people to live, the Great Ultimate must be set up. In order to know Heaven and Earth, the mind must be cultivated. In order to guarantee rule for a myriad generations, national peace and order must be maintained.' This is of course nothing more than empty talk, but they use it as the theory for dealing with state affairs. When a national crisis appears, and the day for devoting oneself to the country comes, they can say nothing, but stand with their mouths agape. They do not know what to do, as

if they were sitting in the clouds and mists." (*Sequence to the Definitive Edition of the Writings of Nanlei·An Epitaph to Wu Bianyu the Imperial Compiler*)

From the Song Dynasty onward, Confucian scholars were obsessed with the imperial examination system. Concentrating on nature and principle, they ignored practical problems. As a result, social problems raged unchecked. Before the middle of the Ming Dynasty, Chinese science and technology occupied an advanced place in the world. But because of the stagnation of the economy and the intellectual bondage of the imperial examination system, from the late Ming period the natural and technological sciences of our country began to fall behind. Bearing in mind the need to develop agriculture, handicrafts, and especially the cause of national defense, Huang encourages people to study the "unique scholarship," which refers to the natural and technological sciences: "The so-called unique scholarship refers to calendar calculation, temperament, surveying, meteorology, firearms, water conservancy and suchlike sciences. If there are people who are talented in these spheres, the prefectures and counties must recommend them to the imperial court. The central government should then examine them, and if they are found to have truly made discoveries or inventions, they should be appointed as technological officers. If they are not so ingenious, they must resign from office, and go home." (*On How to Enlist Talented People·(II)*)

Huang himself did much research into the "unique scholarship," and wrote works on astronomy, the calendar, meteorology, geometry, geography and other sciences. Unfortunately, most of these works have been lost.

Neo-Confucianism, of course, staunchly upheld the imperial examination system, and had little regard for the "unique scholarship." Huang's reaction to this was to advocate the complete liquidation of Neo-Confucianism.

In his attacks on Neo-Confucianism, Huang follows the philosophical line of Liu Zongzhou (1578-1645), his teacher. Although Huang opposes Zhu Xi's monism of principle, he attempts to reconcile the contradiction between monism of material force and monism of the mind. As a result, he generally hovers between the two. What is more, his thought is tinged with pantheism.

The relationship between principle and material force is an important issue which the philosophers of the Song-Ming Period debated endlessly. Huang firmly opposes the Cheng-Zhu school of Neo-Confucianism, and he readily agrees with Liu Zongzhou, who says, "Nothing can be the foundation of principle apart from material force." (*Academic Cases of Ming Confucians·Academic Case of Liu Zongzhou*) Huang concurs, and says that "the age-old doubt" is "instantly dispelled." (*Sequence to the Definitive Edition of the Writings of Nanlei·Preface to the Collected Writings of Liu Jishan My Beloved Teacher*)

Huang also praises Luo Qinshun (1465-1547), a philosopher of the mid-Ming period, as putting forth a correct view on the relationship between principle and material force: 1. "Mr. Luo Qinshun discusses principle and material force in quite accurate terms. In his opinion, throughout the universe and in times ancient and modern, ultimate existence is nothing but material force." (*Academic Cases of Ming Confucians·Academic Cases of Various Confucian Scholars·Part Two (I)*)

> 2. "That which goes through a multitude of things which are entangled with one another is principle. That which arranges everything properly and logically is principle. That which exists but nobody knows the whys and wherefores of it is principle. It is not the case that there is another kind of original substance which exists over there, but that the universe exists by depending on material force, and the universe moves by attaching itself to material force, too." (*Ibid*)

He affirms that principle is not "another kind of original substance which exists over there." Furtermore, principle is only the law that material force follows when changing and moving:

> "Principle and material force are terms made up by people. Their movement, which includes emergence, disappearance, rise and fall, is called material force. The law governing their movement, which includes emergence, disappearance, rise and fall, is called principle. They are one thing, yet have two names; they are not two things, yet they have one body." (*Academic Cases of Ming Confucians·Academic Cases of Various Confucian Scholars·Part One (II)*)

Huang denies that principle is an original substance that exists independently outside material force, stipulating: "The great creation is always in circulation, and it is only material force that fills up the great creation." (*Definitive Edition of the Writings of Nanlei·A Letter to Discuss Scholarship with Friends*) Material force is the common original substance of the myriad things. This is in conrast to the theory that holds principle to be the basic factor behind the myriad things.

The Neo-Confucians try their best to reverse the relationship between "the Way" (the general) and the "implements" (the individuals). In their opinion, "the Way," which comes before physical form, produces the implements, which come after physical form. This means that they regard "the Way," which is invisible and rather abstract, as the original substance of the myriad things in the universe. But Huang agrees with Liu Zongzhou when he says, "Only when the implements exist can principle exist. Apart from the implements, the Way can be found nowhere." (*Sequence to the Definitive Edition of the Writings of Nanlei·A Preface to the Collected Writings of Liu Jishan My Beloved Teacher*) That is, he affirms that "the Way" is only the internal law of things, so it cannot exist independently apart from the existence of concrete things and events.

Furthermore, he points out that the ontology of Zhu Xi is in accordance with that of Buddhism. Zhu Xi says, "Principle is fundamental, and material force is incidental," and Buddhist scholars say, "Bhava (being, existence) is prior to Heaven and Earth," and "Sakyamuni (Buddha) is the master of all phenomena." Huang points out the following:

> "Approximately my idea is as follows. Apart from material force, there is no foundation for principle, and apart from mind, there is no foundation for Nature. Some Buddhists say, 'Bahva is prior to Heaven and Earth, /The formless ones are all in silence./Sakyamuni is the master of things, /He never withers although the seasons change.' This is evidently a theoretical mistake. However, Confucian scholars say, 'Principle begets material force.' As a proverb goes, 'A miss is as good as mile.' So what is the difference between them?" (*Academic Cases of Ming Confucians·Academic Case of Liu Zongzhou*)

The common essence between the views of Zhu Xi and the Buddhists is revealed, one being that "principle begets material force," and the other being that "nonbeing begets being." After that, Huang criticizes another Buddhist view, that "three realms originate in the mind." In his opinion, apart from the material force which is the origin of all things in the universe there can be neither mind nor disposition: "Buddhist scholars say that they understand mind and see disposition. And they think that nonbeing can beget material force.... They seek mind and disposition apart from material force. But I really do not know what mind they have already understood and what disposition they have already seen!" (*On the Book of Mencius the Great Master·Chapter of the Noble Spirit*)

Huang accepts monism with material force as its basic unit, which was expounded by Zhang Zai, Wang Tingxiang and some other thinkers who lived after them.

But since Huang is not free from the influence of the Neo-Confucianism of Wang Shouren, he has some confused ideas in respect to the relationship between mind and material force. For instance, he says, "Ambition is the essentially bright part of material force," and "Knowledge is the spiritual part of material force." (*On the Book of Mencius the Great Master·Chapter of the Noble Spirit*) He confuses the difference between matter and spirit. Since he treats spiritualized material force as a medium in his inference, he draws the conclusion that "I circulate with one and the same material force as Heaven, Earth and the myriad things, and there is nothing that obstructs me from material force. Therefore, the principle of the human mind is the same as the principle of Heaven, Earth and the myriad things." (*Academic Cases of Ming Confucians·Academic Case of the Wang School in the Jiangxi Area (VII)*) Regarding the relationship between mind and things, he writes:

> "What fills up Heaven and Earth is the mind. Since the mind changes constantly and unpredictably, it has to have various manifestations.... Therefore, investigating things to the utmost means investigating the various manifestations of the mind, not investigating the various manifestations of the myriad things." (*Academic Cases of Ming Confucians·Author's Preface*)

The "various manifestations of the myriad things" are objective, but they can be reflected by the subjective mind by means of man's correct cognition, and such reflection is the "various manifestations of this mind."

The human mind plays a role in governing things, but if you exaggerate such a role excessively, you will draw a wrong conclusion. For instance, you may think that the variety of things comes from the mind, which is "changing constantly and unpredictably." And you may think that only by "investigating the principle to the utmost" in your "head," will you be able to know the "various manifestations of the myriad things." If so, you will inevitably glide into a series of wrong ideas, for instance, "Mind is things," "Mind is principle," "Mind is material force," and so on.

Once Huang exaggerates the initiative role of mind to such a degree that it can create everything, he has gone over to pantheism. He says, "Material force has never been ineffective. Wherever material force goes, there is mind. At the beginning, there is the mind in one's head. And, what is more, there is the material force in one's head before anything else exists there." (Cf. *Academic Case of Xue Dong'an*, and *Academic Case of the Hedong School of Thought*. Both of them are in the *Academic Cases of Ming Confucians*) Huang affirms that "Mind is material force," and that "Material force is mind." This is the pantheistic coloring of his thought.

In the course of his critique of Neo-Confucianism, Huang compiled the *Academic Cases of the Song and Yuan Dynasties*, and he himself wrote the definite edition of the *Academic Cases of Ming Confucians*. In doing so, he created a precedent for other scholars to compose and compile works of intellectual history in a systematic way. These two books stand as landmarks in the progress of academic history. Huang was able to make such a valuable contribution because he adopted a critical attitude when he researched the philosophical history of the Song, Yuan and Ming dynasties. What pushed the reformist trends forward were of course the class contradictions and the class struggles of the day, and not the ideas, which emerged in the early stage of the enlightenment movement in the intersectional period of the Ming and Qing dynasties. But it is truly amazing that Huang's thought and work should play an active role in the political movement which took place more than 200 years later. Today, those who discuss the history of political reform in China usually connect two books. One is the *Obscuration Awaiting Inquiries* by Huang Zongxi, and the other is *An Investigation into Confucius' Institutional Reforms* by Kang Youwei (1858-1927). Both borrow the language of ancient precedents in spreading the voice of a new era.

32.

Fang Yizhi's Doctrine of Contradiction

Along with the emergence of the sprouts of capitalism in the intersectional period of the Ming and Qing dynasties, there was an upsurge in interest in the natural sciences in China. And, what is more, there appeared a trend of synthetic research, as quite a few scholars tried to understand both ancient and modern ideas, to combine Chinese and Western scholarship, and to link philosophy with the natural sciences. Fang Yizhi, as a scholar particularly versatile and fond of deep thinking, was an outstanding representative of such a tendency.

Fang Yizhi (1611-1671) was also called the Fool of Mount Fushan, the Herb Field and the Polar Pill. He had about a dozen such nicknames, which sound strange or even eccentric. He was a native of Tongcheng County, Anhui Province. In his early years he witnessed social crises, and plunged into reform activities. Together with Chen Zhenhui (1604-1656), Wu Yingji (1594-1645), Hou Fangyu (1618-1654) and other progressive scholars, he "followed the footprints of the members of the Donglin Clique and became head of the Fushe Association." (Cf. Lu Jianzeng, *Collected Accounts of the Old Days*) "In his early years he was already popular throughout the country." (Wang Fuzhi, *Factual Record of the Yongli Reign·A Biography of Fang Yizhi*) In the Chongzhen reign period (1628-1644) he became a palace graduate and then he served as a compiler in the Imperial Academy. When his father Fang Kongzhao was sentenced to death on a charge trumped up by a clique of eunuchs, he wrote directly to the emperor, and his father was reprieved. Now, unutterable sadness filled Fang Yizhi's heart. He wrote a poem criticizing the conspirators, of which some lines run as follows:

I once carried my essays to the capital,
But the dukes and ministers refused to read them.
When tigers and wolves attacked the palace,
They sat watching, like cranes in beautiful plumage.

When the peasant rebel Li Zicheng overthrew the Ming Dynasty, he asked Fang Yizhi to remain in office and serve him, but the latter fled south to join the Ming remnants. In exile, he and Wang Fuzhi became bosom friends. When the Qing Dynasty conquered the whole of the southern region, Fang Yizhi disguised himself as a monk. But he was finally tracked down, and died as he was being escorted under arrest.

Fang Yizhi was noted as a very learned man. "At the age of fifteen he could recite by heart the main paragraphs from the classics, histories, and works of the philosophers." (*Biographies of the Venerated Old People in Tongcheng·A Biography of Fang Yizhi*) He studied and researched many fields, including astronomy, meteorology, rituals, mathematics, phonology, philology, painting, medicine, music and martial arts. "He wrote books which amounted to half a million words." (*Ibid*) In his early years, he became fascinated by the natural sciences, and studied both the traditional Chinese and Western natural sciences. His scientific works include the *General Encyclopedia*, and *A Primary Study on the Reasons of Things*. Wang Fuzhi praised him, saying, "The old man Mizhi and his son engaged in the learning of substantial investigations. This is truly a practical meritorious service based on working hard and thinking deeply. Probably physics means an investigation into the reasons of things using only the things themselves as data. This can only be done by substantial investigation." (*Scratching My Head, I Ask*) In his later years he occupied himself with studying philosophy, and he wrote many books on the subject, of which the most famous ones are *Pitch Pipe and Potter's Wheel*, *Changes and Other Questions* and *Consistency and Catechism*.

Fang Yizhi had extensive knowledge of the natural sciences, and he attempted to combine his research into the philosophical world outlook and methodology with new developments in the sciences. He draws new philosophical conclusions from the new achievements in the natural sciences while using the natural sciences as a new weapon to refute Neo-Confucianism, which advocated "discarding things to talk about principles."

He divides the whole of learning into three departments, namely, "substantial investigations," "principles of government" and "penetrating comprehension." By substantial investigations he refers to the natural sciences. By principles of government he refers to socio-politics, and by penetrating comprehension he refers to philosophical principles. He says, "Matters have their respective reasons for existence and transformation. Making concrete surveys of matters is called substantial investigation. No matter whether they are as great as the whole universe or as small as a blade of grass, a tree, a fly, or a worm, it is necessary to classify their characters, to find their likes and dislikes, and to discuss their generalities and differences." (*A Primary Study on the Reasons of Things·Self-Preface*) In other words, substantial investigation includes macro-study of the evolution of the whole universe and micro-study of the classification of concrete things such as tiny plants and insects. It is necessary to examine the original nature and mutual relations of organisms. It is also necessary to find the cause-effect relationships among things and the objective laws dictating their changes.

The so-called "penetrating comprehension" takes the developmental moment and internal essence hidden in the myriad things for its target. Here is Fang Yizhi's explanation of this: "Let us go wider to discuss Heaven and Earth. They are both matter.... Exploring deeply the origin of matters from its stillness to its response is called penetrating comprehension of the essence." (*A Primary Study of the Reasons of Things·Self-Preface*) When people take a comprehensive view of things, they may perceive various phenomena, they may go deeply into the imperceptible moment of subtle changes innate to the things, into the universal essence, and into the internal laws. This is the task of philosophical study, in Fang's view.

Concerning the relationship between "substantial investigations" and "penetrating comprehension," Fang puts forth two viewpoints.

His first viewpoint is as follows: "The substantial investigations are the learning in which the penetrating comprehension of the essence dwells." The concrete knowledge gained by learning through substantial investigations contains the principles the "penetrating comprehension" seeks. "Penetrating comprehension" cannot stray from "substantial investigations"; quite the contrary, it must be based on "substantial investigations." If one neglects substantial investigations to talk abstractly about penetrating comprehension, what one says is only empty talk, although one may think oneself too profound to be understood.

His second viewpoint runs as follows: "Penetrating comprehension shields the shortcomings of substantial investigations." (*Quotations from a Buddhist Who Called Himself a Fool of Wisdom· To Zhonglu*, hereafter abbreviated as *Quotations*.) In other words, penetrating comprehension may help people overcome the limitations and one-sidedness of various experimental subjects. Sciences must be guided by philosophy so that the natural laws may be disclosed.

Accordingly, he correctly evaluates the Western knowledge of the natural sciences which the Jesuits had introduced into China. He says as follows:

> "During the Wanli reign period (1573-1620), the theories of the Far West (namely, Europe) began to be introduced into China. They are good at substantial investigations but ignore the importance of penetrating comprehension of the essence. As viewed by wise intellectuals, however, these theories of substantial investigations are imperfect." (*A Primary Study of the Reasons of Things· Self-Preface*)

He acknowledges that the Western natural sciences introduced into China at that time have something to recommend them, but he thinks that they are far from perfect. The theological world outlook of the Catholic Church, the guiding ideology of the Jesuits, he especially considers rather clumsy and not worthy of being regarded as penetrating comprehension.

At the same time, Fang despised the feudal "principles of government" espoused by the Neo-Confucians. He scoffed at their pathetically meager knowledge of science, and concluded that "their theories are as short-lived as mere delusions." (*Quotations· To Zhonglu*)

Fang takes the standpoint of scientific philosophy, which is epitomized as "making substantial investigations a medium of penetrating comprehension," for his own guidance. He advocates a down-to-earth attitude as a new style of study. "Seek deeply for the causes," he urges: "I once had some friends who were engaged in the traditional Chinese experimental sciences, so I desired to grasp their experimental arts very much. Whenever I met with some queer things I wanted to know their names. Doubtlessly, things must have reasons for their existence. I would have doubts time and time again, so I made up my mind to seek deeply for the causes." (Cf. Qian Chengzhi's *Preface* to Fang Yizhi's *General Encyclopedia*)

If there is a need "to seek deeply for the causes," there must be a need "to check" the thing being studied. Fang attempts to distinguish one thing from another by experiment and evidence. Fang Zhongtong, his eldest son, records this description of him: "Such is my old father.... Every time he hears of something, he must jot it down and put it in the relevant category. His manner of compilation is just like that in such books as the *Book of Mountains and Seas* and the *Map of the White Lake*, which are by anonymous authors, the *Natural History* by Zhang Hua, the *Natural History* by Li Shi, *The Master Who Embraces Simplicity* by Ge Hong and the *Compendium of Materia Medica* by Li Shizhen. He collected data from a multitude of folks, and he found that some data lacked evidence and some failed the test of experimentation. It is particularly important to make substantial investigations, so he only put the accurate data in his book." (*A Primary Study of the Reasons of Things·Compilation, Intention and Introduction*)

As we know, the *General Encyclopedia* and *A Primary Study of the Reasons of Things*, two of Fang's representative works, are written in this way. In these books there is a reliable record of the scientific knowledge available in his day, including details of astronomy, physics, the calendar, geography, meteorology, physiology, pharmacology, mineralogy, botany and zoology. He examines data both ancient and modern, both Western and Chinese. His works reflect the scientific spirit of early modern times in China.

Further, Fang rejects the traditional attitude of scholars, who accepted the words of the ancients unquestioningly. He says, "By investigating the ancient facts I decide the present situation. One cannot put one's unequivocal trust in the ancients.... We have the fine writings left to us by the ancients.... I am able to collect the wisdom accumulated over a thousand generations, even if I shut myself behind closed doors, and I am able to examine them carefully." (*General Encyclopedia· The Beginning of the Book (I)*) He once planned to invite experts in various fields to compile a book to be titled *Comprehensive Physics*. This would discuss the reasons of things, and would cover both the "Heavenly ways" and "human affairs," which were to be put respectively in the categories of "the reasons of things" and "the reasons of character." As it turned out, the times were not propitious for the carrying out of Fang's great project. But history advances in a zigzag way. By the reigns of Kangxi (1662-1722) and Yongzheng (1723-1735), the situation had changed. Despite a literary inquisition and cultural autocracy, these two emperors organized a group of scholars who compiled 10,000 volumes of valuable documents in a series titled *Collection of Books Ancient and Modern*.

Relying on his abundant knowledge of natural sciences, Fang established his natural philosophy of "fire and material force" as a basic unity. He attempts to combine the unity of matter in the world with the eternality of material movement. Fang affirms that the whole universe is a unified existence of matter:

> "Matter is omnipresent in the space between Heaven and Earth.... The sages invented utensils, and made use of them in order to satisfy human life, and they cultivated their minds both outside and inside. Utensils are, of course, matter, and the mind is also matter. Let us go deeper, and discuss human nature and destiny; they are both matter. Let us go wider, and discuss Heaven and Earth; they are both matter, too." (*A Primary Study of the Reasons of Things· Self-Preface*)

Here he defines all phenomena in the world as "matter," so as to emphasize objectivity. Thus, he fundamentally denies the subjective and arbitrary manner of discourse, namely, that "one may discard things to talk about principles." (*A Primary Study on the Reasons of Things· Pandect*) Furthermore, he analyzes the unified foundation of "matter" which is omnipresent in the space between Heaven and Earth. Inheriting the philosophical theory of monism of material force, Fang pays great attention to developing the world outlook that "both the void and the substantial are material force." He elaborates:

"All things are made up of material force. As for the void, it is substantial because it is filled with material force." (*A Primary Study of the Reasons of Things·Book One*)

Although material force is unified, it may be represented mainly in four states when it exhibits itself. Furthermore, Fang analyzes these four states of material force: "When the gas of material is condensed, it assumes some shape. When material force is inspired, it sends out lights. When the aperture of material force vibrates, it produces sounds. Essentially, all these are one and the same material force. And there is much material force which has not yet been condensed, inspired or vibrated. Here I only take the four subtleties as examples. They are gas, shapes, lights and sounds." (*A Primary Study of the Reasons of Things·Book One*)

This is his doctrine of the "four subtleties," which is based on the "learning of substantial investigations." The four subtleties are concepts of the natural philosophy which prevailed at that time. The essence of the subtleties is a preliminary generalization of the states of material movement, which are discussed in physics. But Fang takes them for his starting point, from which he demonstrates that "material force" per se, which exists as the origin of matter, or the primitive substance, is eternal and unchangeable. He says, "When I examine their practical situation, I find that in the world all the visible and tangible things will decay one day or another. Only material force will not decay." (*Pitch Pipe and Potter's Wheel·The Origin of the World*) Material force is possessed of many states, which may change into one another, and that material force per se, since it exists as the origin of matter, is "immortal," and "indestructible," and therefore it permeates both the void and the substantial.

Fang advances along the traditional thought of the monism of material force. He seeks the internal root cause of material force, which moves ceaselessly and transforms itself into the myriad things. So he formulates a special category of philosophy, that is, "fire." This "fire" is a material element which permeates space, and moves eternally. It is the internal root cause of "material force," which moves ceaselessly and transforms itself into the myriad things.

It was an important hypothesis in the development of physiology and physics in China to use fire to illustrate movement as an attribute of all material phenomena. This hypothesis was discussed heatedly in the Jin-Yuan period and a long time after that. For instance, Zhu Zhenheng (1281-1358), one of the four experts on medicine in the Yuan Dynasty, claimed that "Heaven is always in motion. Man is also always in motion. This is because they are both made of fire." *Records Official and Unofficial* is a book written by Fang Dazhen, the grandfather of Fang Yizhi. In this book there is a passage, which runs as follows: "The whole of space is filled with fire. The vitality of all the things is also fire." *A Hidden Old Man's Drafts* is a book written by Fang Kongzhao, father of Fang Yizhi. In this book there are two passages, one of which runs as follows: "The whole of space is filled with fire." The other passage runs as follows: "The light in the space between Heaven and Earth is the fire of the sun." And the Buddhist abbot who initiated Fang Yizhi into the monk-hood says, "The old man has a doctrine that among the five elements fire is particularly esteemed. This is because the four elements of metal, wood, water and earth have substantial forms; only fire has no body, for it is visible when it attaches itself to something else. My sect uses this doctrine to instruct our disciples." (Cf. *Quotations·Book Two*)

Fang Yizhi inherits the thoughts of these scholastic forerunners, and develops them in the orientation of philosophy. On the one hand, he makes a comparative study of the different thoughts in the world, and he comes to see the differences among them. For instance, "The Chinese people talk about the five elements of metal, wood, water, fire and earth. The Western peoples talk about the four elements of water, fire, earth and air. The Indian people talk about the *catur-mahabhuta* (literally, the four great beings) of earth, water, fire and wind. Shao Yong once discussed water, fire, earth and stone, but he omitted wood." Having made such a comparative study, Fang Yizhi thinks that the doctrine of the five elements should be transformed into a doctrine of yin and yang as two elements. He points out, "As it says in the *Book of Changes*, 'the successive movement of yin and yang constitutes what is called the Way.' Is there an application of the two? So we may just as well use water and fire as the two elements. And we may just as well call these two elements the void form of material force and the substantial form." (*A Primary Study of the Reasons of Things·Book One*)

Fang Yizhi characterizes the fundamental features of fire: "The inside of fire is inactive, while the outside of fire is active. So action results from a combination of the inside and the outside." Here he endorses a medical theory prevalent in his time, i.e. that there is "the ruler's fire" and there is "the ministers' fire," which are opposite to each other. Fire per se is a unity of contradictions, in which "The ruler and his ministers are combined, for they are following the same Way." In other words, this unity contains the two contradictory aspects. One refers to the ruler, and the other refers to the ministers. One refers to yin (inactive), and the other refers to yang (active). One refers to the master, and the other refers to the followers. Because of the interaction of these two aspects, there appear physical movement and life movement in Nature. Thus is formed the internal source of the self-movement of matter.

Fang Yizhi does not think that "fire" exists outside "material force." As he emphasizes, "Yang is in command of both yin and yang," and "fire is in command of both water and fire." "Fire" is one of most fundamental attributes of the constituents of "material force." "Fire" can act only by attaching itself to something else, and is hidden in "material force." In other words, fire is the source of motive force, which is innate to the self-movement of matter. In Fang Yizhi's philosophical system, the two viewpoints are closely combined: "Fire takes the initiative" and "Material force transforms itself into the myriad things." He posits inside of matter the root cause of material movement.

On the basis of his insistence on substantial investigation, Fang unifies "fire," which marks all substantial entities, and "material force," which marks the eternal movement of matter. Thus he establishes his natural philosophy in line with monism of "the fire and material force," thereby contributing to the doctrine of the monism of material force in traditional Chinese philosophy.

The theory of the monism of material force appeared quite early in the history of Chinese philosophy. Wang Chong of the Eastern Han Dynasty was the first to systematically expound it, and it was later distorted and attacked by the Metaphysicists and Buddhists. Quite a few philosophers, for instance, Liu Zongyuan and Liu Yuxi of the Tang Dynasty, and Zhang Zai and Wang Anshi of the Northern Song Dynasty, exerted efforts to restore the authority of the monism of material force, and each contributed something to it. But in the Song and Ming dynasties, and for a long time afterwards, the theory was opposed by such claims as "Mind is principle," "Heaven is principle," "Principle is fundamental, while material force is incidental," and "Principle takes the lead in activity and tranquility." During the intersectional period of the Ming and Qing dynasties, on the basis of the development of science, Fang Yizhi, Wang Fuzhi and others elucidated the monism of the material force in a new way under the new historical conditions as part of their attack on Neo-Confucianism. Fang considered "material force" to be a unified substantial entity which constitutes the myriad things in the universe. He replenished the category with the characteristics of "fire," claiming that "the vitality of all things is of the nature of fire," and "all movements are caused by fire." These ideas endow the principle that substance and movement are unified with a scientific foundation. Of course Fang's demonstration is still a rough one; it does not surpass the level of direct observation, and sometimes falls into confusion of speculation. Especially in the *Pitch Pipe and Potter's Wheel* and some other works written in his later years there are some suggestions of mysticism. There is amazing similarity between his demonstrative method and that of Denis Diderot (1713-1784), Paul-Henri Dietrich Baron d'Holbach (1723-1789) and suchlike famous thinkers of 18th century France who demonstrate the self-movement of matter. Baron d'Holbach says, "In Nature, fire as an element is almost the fountain of all the motive forces. It is the second source, which ferments and enlivens the mass." (*Système de la Nature, Part One*) And Denis Diderot writes, "As far as objects per se are concerned, according to some philosophers, they are of neither action nor force. This is a terrible mistake.... You so firmly imagine that matters are still. Can you imagine that 'fire' is still? In Nature, everything has its peculiar activity, just as that mass which you call 'fire' does. In that mass which you call 'fire,' every molecule has its original nature and peculiar activity." (*Principes Philosophiques sur la Matière et le Mouvement*)

Fang claims that matter and movement are unified, and on the basis of this principle, he further examines the origin of the motion and the related laws of the myriad things in the universe. In this way, he pushes the ancient dialectics to a new stage.

In the first place, he develops the theory of "the constant and the variable," which is an old topic in Chinese philosophy. In his analysis, the emergence, destruction and changes of the myriad things are an endless process. The things in the world are either in continuous variation or in endless transformation. He affirms and quotes the view of Deng Yuanxi (1527-1593), a scholar of the Ming Dynasty:

> "In the world the difference of the soil is not great, but the vegetation is quite different. And what is more, in the world one country is our motherland — China — and the others are foreign countries. High mountains and great rivers separate the countries in the world. There must have been numerous strange and even absurd events which happened in these countries. Who can record all of them? What did not exist in ancient times may appear today. Who can say that they are not new creatures? What is familiar to everybody today may disappear in future. Who can predict that it will not disappear?" (*A Primary Study on the Reasons of Things· Pandect*)

That is to say, new things are created ceaselessly, and old things are destroyed continuously. This is a general law of the universe. Further, he points out, "In the ever-changing things there exists something that does not change." As far as the changes of things are concerned, there are some constant rules man may follow. These constant rules dwell in the changes. He quotes from *A Hidden Old Man's Drafts* by Fang Kongzhao:

> "Is there any termination to the changes? Will one thing return to itself when it changes to the utmost? Only those who are as wise as deities can answer these questions.... Man may reason out the law hidden in things which are changing, but in the ever-changing things there exists something that does not change. There are some people who do not know that there is a difference between the constant and the variable, but they want to be in charge of a country. When such people are in charge of a country, they cannot run the country well even if they adopt the rites formulated by Duke Zhou. When such people treat patients, they will kill the patients with medicines even if they have perused the *Materia Medica* of Shen Nong[*1]." (*A Primary Study of the Reasons of Things· Pandect*)

---

* Shen Nong (literally, Divine Peasant) is the legendary ruler in ancient China supposed to have introduced agriculture and herbal medicine, also called Yandi or

The unification of the constant and the variable are equated with the supreme principle. On the one hand, he affirms the constant law, saying, "In the ever-changing things there exists something that does not change." He demands that people grasp the constant rules of the changes of things. On the other hand, he opposes any fixed models, saying, "There are some people who do not know that there is a difference between the constant and the variable, but they want to be in charge of a country." Such people refuse to probe concrete situations, and they regard the general laws as dogma. In his opinion, people should pay attention to the changes of the myriad things in the universe. "One should always grasp the law of the constant and the variable. That way, one will never be confused." (*A Primary Study of the Reasons of Things·Pandect*)

In the second place, he puts forth this principle: "Having made an examination of the whole world and the whole of history, I find that in everything there are two factors opposed to each other." He claims that the cause of the changes of anything lies in the contradictory nature within that very thing. In his opinion, fire, which constitutes the myriad things, is not the only case in which there are "two poles," one being like "the ruler," the other being like "the ministers." This is the case with the myriad things in the world. There are changes in the myriad things only because the internal contradictory sides "oppose each other and rely on each other at the same time." The unity of opposites governs everything: "When water and fire cooperate in the human body, one lives well. When they do not cooperate in the human body, one falls ill. They are mutual causes, aren't they? ...Because the four seasons are in motion, rain, dew, frost and snow appear. In spring plants grow, and in autumn they wither. Good luck and ill luck exist by relying on each other. So do misery and happiness. Death and birth are subtle. What will die must live before death. What grows rapidly must die soon. The inactive sinks down, and the active floats up. Their principles are as different as ice and charcoal. But in the inactive lurks the active, and in the active lies the inactive. When the inactive reaches its height, it must be the active's turn. When the active reaches its height, it must be the inactive's turn. If there is unity there must be the opposite, and the opposite forms the foundation of unity." (*Pitch Pipe and Potter's Wheel·Opposite Causes*)

Fire Emperor.

From Nature to society, and from the movement of the four seasons to the life and death of man, all things in the universe are expressions of universality, as shown in the following law of contradiction: "If there is unity there must be opposites." And therefore he says, "Two opposite things are bound to meet each other; everything is the unity of the opposites. Things opposite to each other are the causes of each other. Only because of opposites can anything be accomplished." (*Pitch Pipe and Potter's Wheel· Three Superficial Characteristics*)

In the third place, he affirms that the basic relationship of both sides in a contradiction is "to save each other, to subdue each other and yet also to complement each other." Both sides of a contradiction rely on and struggle against each other, while complementing each other:

> "I once talked about the supreme principle of the world. What constitute causes for each other must be utterly opposite to each other.... I say that things opposite to each other are the causes of each other. This is because they save each other, subdue each other and yet also complement each other." (*Pitch Pipe and Potter's Wheel· Opposite Causes*)

He cites a series of antithetical categories to disclose this relationship of the two sides in a contradiction. By "saving each other," he means the combination, condensation and unification of opposites. By "subduing each other," he means that the two sides of a contradiction are in such a situation as one side is always going to pin down the other side. By "complementing each other," he means that the two sides of a contradiction form a new unity after a series of struggles, and from that time on they begin a new process of saving each other and subduing each other. Fang calls this relationship "the supreme principle of the world." He takes medicine as an example of the relationship. On some occasions, two medicines whose properties are diametrically opposite to each other may bring about an unexpectedly good effect in the course of treatment in that they have saved each other and subdued each other. (Cf. *A Primary Study of the Reasons for Things· Pandect of Drug Properties*)

In most cases the things in the Nature are similar: "Things that harm each other nurture each other at the same time. Things that oppose each other go hand in hand with each other." (*Pitch Pipe and Potter's*

Wheel·Opposite Causes) The correct attitude to such phenomena displaying that "opposites complement each other" is to regard them as the embodiment of "the supreme principle," and there is no need to be surprised at them at all.

Another example is the bow, which alternates tension with relaxation when it works Only by the alternation of tension with relaxation can the force of a bow be brought about and can the arrow be shot. If there is only tension but no relaxation, or, if there is only relaxation but no tension, a bow cannot function.

In Fang's opinion, in society there exist two forces that oppose each other and at the same time complement each other. The safety of and danger to a country and order and disorder in a society also embody the principle that opposites are the cause of the existence of each other:

> "Only because of wars and hardships can virtuous persons be cultivated. Therefore, I say that what is in peril may turn out to be in safety, what is in destruction may turn out to be in existence, and what is in toil may turn out to be at ease, and what is in distortion may turn out to be in extension." (*Pitch Pipe and Potter's Wheel·Opposite Causes*)

The above is one definite and universal principle that Fang discovers from his extensive observation of natural and social phenomena. As the myriad things in the world, each have two antithetical ends, he affirms the universality of contradictions. Further, he affirms that in both sides of a contradiction there are both identity and militancy, reaching complementarity by saving each other and subduing each other. "In order to take, one must first give; in order to stand at the front, one must first stand at the back." He dwells on this time and again.

In his great efforts to find the general law that governs the contradictory movement of things, Fang comes up with the concepts of "combination," "connection" and "subtlety":

> "Combination refers to two things combining into one whole. Connection refers to one thing connecting with another in a corresponding way.... Subtlety refers to something subtle and dan-

gerous. Subtlety is the beginning of adaptability in tactics and the commencement of any change." (*Pitch Pipe and Potter's Wheel·Three Superficial Characteristics*)

By "combination," he means the identity of opposites. By "connection," he means situations in which contradictions promote the transformation of things. By "subtlety," he means the source of motive force that runs through the process of transformation. Here, though in a vague way, he seems to realize that it is the internal contradictions that propel things to undergo transformations in a continuous way. In the meantime, negativity is the internal motive force that runs through such a transformational process, namely, the process in which new things replace old ones.

Fang discloses the contradictory movement of objective things, but he is influenced by the speculative manner of the so-called "three dogmas in one mind" of the Buddhist Tiantai School, especially when he deals with man's subjective attitude toward objective contradictions. He divides man's knowledge of and attitude toward objective contradictions into the three levels of "obedience," "effacement" and "synthesis." By "obedience," he means the normal cognition to which people are in obedience. At this level, people affirm the differences and oppositions that exist objectively. By "effacement," he means a further cognition in which people wipe out all the differences and oppositions. By "synthesis," he means a blending of the above two types of cognition. Only by uniting "obedience," "effacement" and "synthesis" can one acquire supreme knowledge. In practice, he tries to reconcile opposition in principle between dialectical thinking, which affirms contradictions, and metaphysics, which effaces contradictions. As a result, by means of "a subjective application of conceptual flexibility" he ends up embracing relativism and sophistry.

Although Fang catches sight of the struggle of opposites, he refuses to acknowledge that the militancy dwells in the identity. Despite his emphasis on the significance of the identity of contradictions, he fails to distinguish the concrete identity from the abstract identity. And in abstract speculation he sometimes understands the "one" in the proposition that "two combine into one," as the "great one," which is another concept in the proposition that "two may be transformed into one." In the "great one" there are no oppositions at all. Although he asserts that "no-opposition is in opposition" and "absolute opposition is in relative opposition," he does not mean that the absolute dwells in the relative, but that it is necessary to seek an absolute unity which surpasses or even cancels oppositions altogether. Where is such an absolute unity? It soars above oppositions. Thus, he adopts a metaphysical viewpoint which cancels contradictions. In Fang's opinion, above yin and yang there is a so-called "genuine yang," and above being and nonbeing, there is a so-called "great nonbeing." "genuine yang," the "great nonbeing" and suchlike may be called either "super-yin-yang," or "super-being-nonbeing," or "no-yin-yang," or "no-being-nonbeing." In fact, the so-called "genuine yang" and "great nonbeing" without any contradictions do not exist. They are but a realm of "no-opposition" which is fabricated in the course of metaphysical speculation. So the dialectical brilliance which shone forth from his philosophical system suffers. This is the limitation of his thought, which has much to do with his class stance and his becoming a monk in his later years.

Fang's naïve dialectics led him to postulate that in the cognitive process "There may well be contradictions." And he analyzes a series of contradictions which appear in the cognitive process. In doing so, he makes a new contribution to the development of epistemology.

The essence of man's cognitive activity is "a mutual investigation of the mind and things." In other words, there occurs an interaction between the thinking organ (the mind) and the target of cognition (things). Here, he means the mind and not the heart, to which traditional Chinese philosophers attributed the function of thought. In fact, Fang was the first scholar to point out in no uncertain terms that man's thinking organ is not the heart but the brain. He says, "Some are wise, and some are foolish, this depends on the clearness or muddiness of their brains." (*A Primary Study of the Reasons of Things·Book Three*) And he says, "After a person is born, he immediately begins to store knowledge by means of his brains" (*Ibid*)

According to Fang's terminology, the activity of knowing the objective world is figuratively called "a study of Heaven and Earth." He says, "Since man is between Heaven and Earth, man should make a study of Heaven and Earth." (*Pitch Pipe and Potter's Wheel·The Marvelous and the Mediocre*) In his view, in the "learning" process there is a need for "communication between perception and enlightenment." Perception refers to the acquisition of perceptual materials by means of the sense organs in contact with the outside world. Enlightenment refers to the processing of perceptual materials by means of rational thinking. Only by "communication between perception and enlightenment" can man obtain genuine knowledge. In addition, one must apply one's knowledge to practice and thereby put one's knowledge to the test:

> "To learn anything means having communication between perception and enlightenment. Recitation, review, and practice in person of what one has learned must be combined." (*General Encyclopedia·Book One*)

Since man's mind is "able to communicate between man and Heaven, Earth and the myriad things," man can obtain knowledge of the principle hidden in them, the laws of things. Nevertheless, man's knowledge must start from objective practice in order to find "what things follow," namely, the laws that are innate in objective things.

Fang suggests that in the cognitive process it is necessary to carry out the cognitive principle that "there may well be contradictions." In such a principle lurks the naïve dialectics of cognition. His theory of knowledge differentiated from the "words to set up a religion," which refers to the Neo-Confucianism of the Song and Ming dynasties. Within the framework of the "words to set up a religion," every means is used to cover contradictions and to extinguish struggles, and the Neo-Confucians use a metaphysical approach to deal with the ever-changing world, for they are in fear of all contradictions. According to the enlightenment thinkers, the world is filled with contradictions, and if the world is to be known and reflected upon truthfully, it is necessary to recognize these contradictions. This is the difference in principle between dialectics and metaphysics as two distinctive world outlooks and methodologies.

Fang analyzes a series of contradictions in the cognitive process by starting from the principle that "There may well be contradictions."

In the first place, in order to reach a thorough understanding, he discusses the unity of "versatility" and "consistency."

In Fang's opinion, when people know the things in the outside world, versatility and consistency constitute a unity of opposites. "Versatility" refers to the abundant conceptual knowledge acquired from the outside world. "Consistency" refers to the general principles drawn from empirical materials, namely, the objective laws by which man may grasp the meanings of things: Both sides are in opposition to each other, but at the same time they complement each other. Over-emphasis on either side or negligence of either side must bring about defects in human cognition.

> 1. "Here the so-called 'one' refers to the one that dwells in the many. Here the so-called 'many' refers to the many that dwell in the one. Outside the one there would be no many, and outside the many there would be no one. This is what true consistency means." (*Consistency and Catechism*)
>
> 2. "There is versatility which is cut off from consistency. Such versatility is of course a defect. There is consistency which is cut off from versatility. Such consistency is of course a defect, too." (*Ibid*)

Overemphasis on plentiful knowledge means a mere grasp of the various superficial phenomena of things. If so, it is inevitable to neglect their common character and to catch at trifles instead of at the essence. But if there is overemphasis on the common character or general principle of things and a divorce from the concrete expressions of things, there can only be a seeming abstraction of things. If so, one's cognition of things will be irrelevant to them. The above two tendencies are serious defects in human cognition. The correct way to know things is to recognize that "the one and the many are combined together." This demands that we should combine versatility, namely, a comprehensive observation of the presentation, with consistency, namely, a correct abstraction of the essence. This is Fang's method for scientific research.

In the second place, in order to reach a thorough understanding, he discusses the unity of "the part" and "the whole." Both in academic studies and in learning skills one should try one's best to specialize in one's sphere. Namely, one should concentrate on a certain subject or a certain aspect, so as to master it. But as far as one's scope of knowledge is concerned, the wider and more comprehensive, the better. Fang reconciles the tension between these two ideals by saying, "If you study only a part of a subject you had better specialize in it," and "If your scope of knowledge is small you had better have a comprehensive command of it." Overemphasis on versatility and comprehension leads to shallowness and superficiality, as it does not benefit specialization and essentiality. Overemphasis on specialization and essentiality leads to a peephole view, for it is not beneficial to versatility and comprehension. "Non-partiality means non-specialization." (*Pitch Pipe and Potter's Wheel·The Part and the Whole*) That is to say, partiality is necessary. If one can deeply dissect a sparrow, one's knowledge of sparrows may become more systematic and more comprehensive. Even if one's scope of knowledge is small, one's understanding becomes comprehensive automatically. Even if one's knowledge is partial, one's understanding will not be partial.

In the third place, he talks about the unity of "commonality" and "uniqueness."

The common character is called "commonality," and the individual character "uniqueness." He points out that the relationship between the two parties is like this: "Each thing has its own principle, and all the things have their common principle. The latter is called the Heavenly principle.... People are different in their intellectual capacities; some are clever, some are foolish. This is called uniqueness. But, as for their common character, they are one and the same. Commonality dwells in uniqueness." (*Herein-Hide-I Veranda's Suitable Compilation·Nature and Reason*)

This uniqueness varies with different people and things, but commonality is one and the same with everybody and everything. "Commonality dwells in uniqueness" is an important principle in Fang's epistemology. His statement that "Substantial investigations are the learning in which the penetrating comprehension of the essence dwells" is a concrete application of such cognitive dialectics.

In the fourth place, in order to reach a thorough understanding, he discusses the relationship between two propositions, The first, "The ancient and the modern accumulate a great deal of knowledge by their wisdom." The other, "Successors excel their predecessors."

From ancient times to the present day, human knowledge accumulates in a continuous way. The knowledge of any individual increases by accumulation, too. From small increments comes abundance. He says,

"Blue is extracted from the indigo plant, but is bluer than the latter," and "The latecomers become wiser than their predecessors." He says as follows:

> "The ancient and the present accumulate a great deal of knowledge by their wisdom. But I live in an era posterior to that of my forerunners. So, by investigating the ancient facts I decide the present situation. Nevertheless, one cannot have unquestioning belief in the ancients.... Living in modern times, we have the beautiful writings left to us by the ancients, which have been carefully debated by a group of talented scholars. I am able to collect the wisdom accumulated over a thousand generations, even if I shut myself behind my door. (*General Encyclopedia·Book's Beginning (I)*)
>
> And further:
>
> "Kapok, machine-finished paper, wood block printing, folding fans and others were perfected in successive ages, and so we may think that successors excel their predecessors through increased intelligence. If so, the principles discovered in later ages cannot be regarded as things that run counter to the laws of the former kings.... I demonstrate real principles with real facts, and I demonstrate former principles with later principles." (*Pitch Pipe and Potter's Wheel·Enlarging the Belief*)

Starting by summing up the experiences of scientific practice, Fang applies dialectics to the theory of knowledge. As a result, he resolves a series of contradictions in epistemology which had baffled his forerunners. This is very significant in directing people's cognitive activities. It is also an important contribution he made to the development of the ancient theory of knowledge.

33.

Knowledge and Action: Wang Fuzhi and a Critical Evaluation of Neo-Confucianism

Wang Fuzhi (1619-1692), styled Ernong, had the secondary names of Jiangzhai, which means "Ginger Studio," and Chuanshan, which means "Boat Mountain," for near the village where he lived there was a rocky hill in the shape of an inverted boat. A native of Hengyang County, Hunan Province, Wang Fuzhi was born into a landlord family which had come down in the world. In 1648 Wang Fuzhi organized an army to fight the Manchu invaders, in a vain effort to restore the Ming Dynasty. After serving the last Ming emperor, Yongli (Zhu Youlang, 1647-1661), in his exile in southern China, as a minor official, Wang Fuzhi fled court intrigue to retire to his native place. There, he devoted himself to philosophical speculation, and wrote over 100 works on philosophy and history in some 400 volumes. The most prominent of these books are the *Outer Commentary on the Book of Changes*, *A Deduction from the Laozi*, and the *Yellow Book*, a political treatise in which he summed up the lessons of the fall of the Ming Dynasty and expounded his views on social reform. His son Wang Yu recorded his father's last years as follows:

> "He lived in seclusion, engaged in academic research. He often opened the small windows and lit a solitary lamp to read the Thirteen Classics and the Twenty-One Histories as well as the surviv-

ing works by Zhang Zai and Zhu Xi. Despite hunger, cold and danger, he never desisted from study. (*A Brief Biography of Revered Jiangzhai*)

On his deathbed, he wrote his own epitaph. It reads, "Mine was not a heroic career predestined from birth, but I harbored disillusionment with the world, as Liu Yueshi did. Mine was not a brilliant scholarly career, but I carried on the orthodox doctrine, as Zhang Hengqu did."* He, in fact, regarded the subjugation of the Han ethnic group by the Manchus as an inevitable result of the debilitation of the nation due to the ideology of Neo-Confucianism. Therefore, he emphasized that Neo-Confucianism, since it had wrecked the country and ruined the people, must submit to the judgment of history.

Wang Fuzhi inherited and developed Zhang Zai's theory of the transformation of material force in the new historical conditions. By applying "substantial investigation" to his research, he made an analysis of the problem of the relationship between principle and material force in a comparatively profound way. Thus, he grasped firmly the relationship between the Way and implemented as a crucial problem that permeated both epistemology and ontology. Around this crucial problem, he unfolded his demonstration concerning the material unity of the world and its laws of development.

By tackling the relationship between being and nonbeing and that between the void and the substantial, Wang Fuzhi discusses the material unity of the world. He develops Zhang Zai's view that "since the great void is material force, there is no nonbeing." And he definitely affirms the monist principle of material force by affirming that "the great void is material force":

1. "The great void which man sees is material force but not the void. The void contains material force, and material force fills the void.

---

* This is from Wang Fuzhi's *Self-Inscription of the Tombstone*. Cf. *Anthology of Wang Chuanshan, Book 1* (Beijing: Zhonghuashuju Press, 1962), p. 116. Liu Yueshi is the style of Liu Kun (270– 318 AD), a heroic general of the Jin Dynasty, who resisted against the invaders firmly. Cf. *History of Jin·Book 62: Biography of Liu Kun*. Zhang Hengqu is the style of Zhang Zai (1020-1077), a famous thinker of the Northern Song Dynasty, who has been thoroughly discussed in this book. Cf. Chapter 24.

There has never been so-called 'nonbeing' at all." (*Notes on Master Zhang's Correcting Youthful Ignorance·Great Harmony*)

2. "Two kinds of material force, yin and yang, fill up the great void. Apart from them, there is nothing else." (*Ibid*)

The void, which everybody sees, is one form in which material force exists. Apart from material force, there is simply nothing in the universe at all. In this way, he stipulates the universality and limitlessness of material force. And further, material force, which exists objectively, may gather together and spread out; material force is possessed of neither birth nor death. "Its emergence is not the creation of being, and its disappearance is not the destruction of nonbeing, either. It follows the natural principle of yin and yang." (*Inner Commentary on the Book of Changes·Book 5*) He cites some practical examples in order to illustrate that matter may neither be born nor wiped out. One example is a cart of charcoal. When the charcoal is burnt, it seems that it has been wiped out. But the actual situation is not so. "Wood results in wood, water results in water, earth results in earth, and the only difference lies in that they are too tiny to be seen. Although we do not know whither it flies, it finally enters the earth." (*Notes on Master Zhang's Correcting Youthful Ignorance·Great Harmony*) He points out emphatically: "Since what are visible are so, how can the subtly invisible things be not so?" (*Ibid*) That is, charcoal, mercury and the other changeable forms are "variants of the material force," which can be neither created nor destroyed. In this way, he stipulates the eternality and indestructibility of "material force."

Wang Fuzhi does not regard "material force" as something concrete; instead, he attempts to make a higher generalization of material existence from the angle of philosophy. By using the category of "real being," he further stipulates the most essential attribution of "material force" as objective reality, stating:

"As for the term honesty, it means real being. As for real being, it means the being that may be shared by the whole world. Whoever has eyes may see it, and whoever has ears may hear it." (*Elaboration on the Meaning of the Book of History·Book 3*)

Here, all objective things are described as "real being" and "honesty." This shows that all things belong to the category of objective existence. In this way, he discloses the most fundamental attribution of material force. Therefore, in Wang Fuzhi's terminology, "honesty" and "real being" are the supreme abstraction:

> "As for 'honesty,' it is a word which has no antonym.... Whenever we use the word 'honesty,' we understand that it is a word which is at the highest peak of our vocabulary. No other word whatsoever can replace it or explain it. No other word whatsoever can be its antonym, either." (*Discussions after Reading the Great Collection of the Commentaries on the Four Books·Book 9*)

Wang Fuzhi makes a philosophical abstraction of "material force," but on a higher plane than the categorization of "material force" of Zhang Zai and Wang Tingxiang. He attempts to surpass the idea of concrete objects by borrowing categories such as "honesty," "real being" and so forth. His expression of the generally objective reality of matter marks progress in epistemology in China.

On the problem of the relationship between principle and material force, Wang Fuzhi stresses that "principle relies on material force." This is in direct contradiction to the claims of the Neo-Confucians that "principle leads material force" and "principle begets material force."

The Neo-Confucians separated the general from the individual in the cognitive process, and looked at the problem in isolation. Then, they regarded the general as something separated from concrete things. At last, they go even farther by expanding this general entity into "a deified absolute." After their elaborate processing, such a general entity becomes an absolute spiritual noumenon from which everything may derive. Thus, the idea of "principle" drawn from objective things has been exaggerated into the dominator of the world. By using the duality of the process in which man know matter and its laws, they describe the general abstraction as a spiritual noumenon which surpasses all concrete things. As a result, they put forth a theory centered on principle as the basic unit, which may be epitomized as either "Principle is the fundamental while material force is the incidental," or "Principle begets material force."

Wang Fuzhi, however, maintains, "As for material force, it is what principle relies on." (*Record of Thoughts and Questionings·Inner Chapter*) That is to say, principle depends on material force. And he says, "Outside material force there is no principle; if there is any, it must be fictitious and solitary." (*Discussions after Reading the Great Collection of the Commentaries on the Four Books·Book 10*) Principle is made manifest in material force:

> "At bottom, principle is not a finished product that can be grasped. It is invisible. The details and order of material force is principle that is visible. Therefore, the first time there is any principle is when it is seen in material force. After principle has thus been found, it of course appears to be a tendency. We see principle only in the necessary aspects of tendencies." (*Discussions after Reading the Great Collection of the Commentaries on the Four Books·Book 9*)

Material force is the substantial noumenon which brings about new changes every day. The objective necessity innate to the process of its changes is called "principle." As for principle, it is invisible, but it cannot exist independently. It cannot separate itself from the substantial noumenon — material force — either. In the view of Wang Fuzhi, the relationship between principle and material force, which was an old topic debated as early as in the Song Dynasty and for a long time thereafter, is the relationship between the substantial noumenon, which exists objectively, and its laws, which are innate in its movement and changes. Both sides can never be split apart. In this way, he thoroughly rebukes the ideological fraud of "empty talk of nature and principle" carried out by the Neo-Confucians, who "discard material force to talk about principles." Thus, he leads people ideologically back to the objective and realistic world.

On the problem of the relationship between the Way and implements, Wang Fuzhi puts forward two propositions: "The world consists only of concrete things," and "The Way is rightly in the implements." He criticizes the Neo-Confucians, who "talk about the Way apart from the implements."

There is a proposition in the *Commentaries on the Changes* (*Ten Wings*), which reads as follows: "What exists before physical form is called the Way. What exists after physical form is called a concrete thing."

But the Neo-Confucians distorted this. In their opinion, theoretically the "Way," as the general principle, is the foundation of concrete things ("implements"). In practice, they attempt to take the "Way," which serves as the core of the cardinal guides and constant virtues of feudalism, for the divine principle, which exists and will always remain the same.

Wang Fuzhi continues to regard the Way and implements as a pair of antithetical categories. By the "Way," he means the common essence or universal law of things. By "implements," he means concrete things, which are individual and special. In his view, both sides are unified, and they can never be separated from each other:

"Taken together, these two sides are one thing. Taken apart, what exists before physical form is called the Way; what exists after physical form is called implements. Everything is made up of one yin and one yang. If we make a thorough study of the implements, we find that the Way is rightly in the implements." (*Record of Thoughts and Questionings·Inner Chapter*)

This is a return to the original condition, because he restores the problem of the Way and refers to the unified material world. By saying that "the Way is in the implements," he draws a demarcation line with the Neo-Confucians, whose scholars "discard the implements to talk about the Way." Then he puts forth a topic for discussion: "In the world nothing is more important than implements." He discusses this topic carefully:

> "The world consists only of concrete things (namely, "implements," similarly hereafter). The Way is the Way of concrete things, but concrete things may not be called concrete things of the Way. Few people are capable of saying that without a concrete thing there cannot be its Way, but it is certainly true. In the period of wilderness and chaos, there was no Way to bow to or yield a throne. At the time of Yao and Shun, there was no Way to pity the suffering people and punish their sinful rulers. During the Han and Tang dynasties there were no Ways as we have today, and there will be many Ways in future years which we do not have now." (*Outer Commentary on the Book of Changes·Book 5*)

In the first place, the interrelation between the Way and the implements is a relative association. Because the Way and the implements work upon each other in this way, when they are "taken together, these two sides are one thing." They are two aspects of one and the same thing, and no hard and fast line can be drawn between the two. The so-called "before physical form" and "after physical form" refer to some special target, and therefore we must not separate them. Thus, Wang Fuzhi forcefully criticizes and rebukes Zhu Xi's view that "the Way is prior to the implements."

In the second place, "The world consists only of concrete things (i.e. implements)." This means that all things in the universe are concrete existences. Whatever events and things there are, they must each be possessed of a special essence. In the meantime, they are possessed of a common essence as one and the same category of things. We can only say, "The Way is in the implements," or "The Way is the Way of the implements." This is because the general is only a part or an aspect of the essence of the particular. So we must not say, "The implements are the implements of the Way." This is because the particular cannot be completely put into the general. He says, "Without a concrete thing there cannot be its Way." This means that the general can only exist in the particular, it can only exist by means of the particular, and without the particular there cannot be the general.

In the third place, he rejects the so-called views that "without the Way there cannot be its concrete things," and that "principle is prior to the events." The experience of mankind demonstrates that at first there appeared individual implements and events, and then people might draw some general laws or principles from them. He says, "Before bows and arrows existed, there was no Way of archery. Before chariots and horses existed, there was no Way to drive them." (*Outer Commentary on the Book of Changes·Book 5*) Along with the development of human society, newly born events and things emerge constantly. And there are many potentially new laws and new principles concerning the new things and new systems, which do not exist now but will appear in the future. Thus, he denies the Neo-Confucian speculations of the two Cheng brothers and Zhu Xi and also the dogma that "the cardinal guides and constant virtues will exist throughout the ages," which they repeatedly attempted to demonstrate.

In the fourth place, he gives hiis starting point and principle for reasoning: "During the Han and Tang dynasties there were no Ways as we have them today, and there will be many in future years which we do not have now." From this statement, the conclusion is that the "Way" can only vary with the changing times. If one obstinately clings to the "Way" of the Han and Tang dynasties, one will get nowhere, for such a "Way" absolutely unworkable. One should renew one's ideas and keep pace with the times. This is the political conclusion which the enlightenment thinkers living in the intersectional period of the Ming and Qing dynasties strove to reach.

By means of his conception of the Way and the implements, Wang Fuzhi demonstrates the dialectical association between the general and the particular in a plain way. He has already touched on the general process of human cognition, which always proceeds from the particular to the general, and he has also already touched on the developmental process of human cognition, which proceeds from the general to the particular. Wang Fuzhi's conception of the Way and the implements is valuable in its theoretical depth and critical sharpness. It shook the foundations of the idealist ontology formed before his time, and had a tremendous impact on the enlightenment of Chinese philosophy in early modern times.

We next turn to Wang Fuzhi's view of dialectical development. In Wang Fuzhi's opinion, matter and movement cannot be separated from each other, and all the things in the universe move and change ceaselessly. He says as follows:

"The great void is originally in motion. It enters into motion with its original motion, so it is neither in inertia nor adherent to a fixed position.... Without a heart there would be neither pulse nor creation. The tendency is that it cannot keep its original outlook, so it is unnecessary to depend on its original outlook before there is a birth of things." (*Outer Commentary on the Book of Changes·Book 6*)

The material world is in a state of self-movement every hour and moment, and movement is an attribution innate in the material world. He rebukes Zhou Dunyi and Zhu Xi for their preaching of the "Great Ultimate," which they claimed to be immovable. He emphasizes that yin, yang, activity and tranquility are all implications of the Great Ultimate. (*Notes on Master Zhang's Correcting Youthful Ignorance·Great Harmony*) That is to say, he regards yin, yang, activity and tranquility as the internal vigorous development innate in the self-movement of the material world. Thus, he denies the external cause put forth by Zhou Dunyi, Shao Yong, the two Cheng brothers and Zhu Xi.

Further, Wang Fuzhi expounds on the relationship between movement and inertia. He affirms that movement is absolute, while inertia is relative. He says as follows:

> "The movement of the Great Ultimate begets yang (i.e. the positive material force), which is the movement of movement. The inertia of the Great Ultimate begets yin (i.e. the negative material force), which is the inertia of movement. If there is only inertia and no movement as if the movement has been cancelled already, how can yin (i.e. the negative force) be brought about?" (*Record of Thoughts and Questionings·Inner Chapter*)

The universe is the motional process in which the changes of yin and yang contain the two states of activity and tranquility. Activity is the movement of the dynamic state, and tranquility is the movement of the static state. Therefore, Wang Fuzhi says, "Tranquility is the static activity, and it is by no means motionless." (*Record of Thoughts and Questionings·Inner Chapter*) And he says, "Both movement and inertia are movement. The change from movement to inertia is also a kind of movement." (*Discussion after Reading the Great Collection of Commentaries on the Four Books·Chapter 10*) Denying that the universe is inert, he affirms that inertia is relative and temporary, and that movement is absolute and eternal. He points out, "In inertia is contained movement, and in movement there is inertia." (*Record of Thoughts and Questionings·Outer Chapter*) With respect to the process, movement and inertia are in mutual permeation and transformation. As far as a particular stage is concerned, "movement has its own function, and inertia has it own quality." (*Notes on Master Zhang's Correcting Youthful Ignorance·Great Harmony*) When he affirms the absoluteness of movement, Wang Fuzhi does not ignore the effect of inertia. Relative inertia and balance are the fundamental condition in which matter becomes divided and forms "the myriad phenomena and the ego." They are also necessary links in the process of material movement. Wang's inquiry into the dialectical association of movement and inertia proceeds in a deeper way than other scholars. As a result, he denies the theory of tranquility which was preached by the Neo-Confucian thinkers of the Song and Ming dynasties.

Further, Wang expounds the view that "transformation brings about daily renewal." All things are changing and being renewed all the time. There has never been anything that is eternal and uncheangeable. He categorizes daily renewals into two types, one being the accumulation of quantity, the other being the renovation of quality. In everything there is quantative change on the basis of the present quality; this is "internal accomplishment," which comes into being spontaneously. Although the quality of things undergoes small changes, the essence does not change. When things develop to a certain degree they will "disintegrate and perish," i.e., they will change into other things. This is "exterior genesis." Since new things emerge in an endless stream, a boundlessly abundant world results.

The universe is boundless both in space and in time, and the myriad things are always in transformation and changes. Inside a thing there is the formation of new factors. Outside a thing there is the formation of new things. The world alters from day to day. The myriad things of the world are abundant in both species and states. This is the developmental view of the universe which Wang Fuzhi unfolds.

We now proceed to Wang Fuzhi's view of contradictions. Wang Fuzhi develops Zhang Zai's two views — "One thing has two bodies" and "Movements cannot be actuated by external causes" — by stressing internal cause and opposing the theory of external cause: "There are a myriad of changes in the world, but they may all be attributed to the two ends." (*A Deduction from the Laozi*) By "the two ends" he means the opposites contained in everything. Changes in things originate from mutual friction and mutual agitation, which exist within things. He disagrees with the *Book of Changes* that the hexagram *Qian* (The Creative) is the first of the eight trigrams. Rather, *Qian* (the Creative) and *Kun* (the Receptive), or yin and yang, are opposites. Neither has priority. Both sides come into being simultaneously, and both exist simultaneously. "*Qian* and *Kun* were set up at the same time; neither side had priority." Of both sides of a contradiction, one side cannot exist without the other. He says, "There is not a single day when there is only *Qian* and not *Kun*. Likewise, there is not a single day on which there is only *Kun* and not *Qian*." (*Outer Commentary on the Book of Changes·Book 6*) And he says, "As for yin and yang, neither of the two material forces circulates alone in the universe." (*Outer Commentary on the Book of Changes·Book 7*) Everything whatsoever is a unity of opposites.

Wang Fuzhi analyses the essential relationship of the opposites in a contradiction. The opposites in a contradiction "stand side by side while being in opposition to each other," and "they seem to be two things quite different from each other." This relationship may be described with the statement, "By severing the one there appear the two." Both sides of a contradiction "rely on each other and depart from each other." Hence, "By combining the two there appears the one." These two relationships cannot be treated in isolation, and on this point he says, "As I have said, by combining the two there appears the one. And I have also said, by cutting apart the one there appear the two. The former statement is a characteristic innate to the latter statement." (*Outer Commentary on the Book of Changes·Book 5*) He also says, "If there is not the one, there cannot be the two." (*Notes on Master Zhang's Correcting Youthful Ignorance·Great Harmony*)

In a comparative way, he emphasizes the significance of identity. The stress of research should be on the relationship that the antithetical things which "rely on each other do not necessarily oppose each other." He cites the example of inhalation and exhalation, which are the two sides of a contradiction. In discussing the *Treatise of Remarks on the Trigrams*, a chapter of the *Book of Changes*, he says, "If there is exhalation there must be inhalation, and if there is inhalation there must be exhalation. When they are combined there is breath. They rely on each other, but they do not necessarily oppose each other." (*Outer Commentary on the Book of Changes·Book 7*) The hard and the mild are in opposition, and the dry and the wet are in opposition, too. But, "The dry plus the dry is the broken but not the hard. The wet plus the wet is fluid but not the mild. If opposite functions of a thing are combined into a harmony, they will carry forward the thing to a new stage. If so, all things may communicate with one another." (*Ibid*) Whoever regards opposites as "a boundary line distinctly dividing them" is totally wrong.

Further, Wang Fuzhi maintains that in opposites there is identity. "In the opposite side dwell non-opposite factors," and "A gentleman is ready to see the opposites." What if one is good at seeing the common source from a number of different offshoots! What if one is good at hearing the harmonious canto from a multitude of sounds! This shows that one has the ability to know and to grasp the unity in differences or contradictions. If so, one must be able to treat contradictions in an objective way. One will be "ready to see the opposites." And one will be able to "make good use of them." Wang directs his spearhead of criticism at the "mediocre persons" who refuse to recognize contradictions, and at the "madmen" who obstinately stick to the contradictory side only. In his opinion, the correct attitude is to look squarely at contradictions. But this is not enough; one must do one's best to treat opposites readily so that one may make good use of them. (*Outer Commentary on the Book of Changes·Book 7*)

In addition, he expounds the principle that both sides of a contradiction will change into their opposites under given circumstances. He denies that there are "such things as are in a distinct dissection or in a diametrical opposition." Without exception opposites must undergo a mutual transformation. Things may be noble or humble, superior or inferior, existing or perished, but all these may be mutually transformed, for there has never been a fixed situation in which the things are immutable. We ought not to treat the opposites of a thing in an isolated, static and one-sided way.

Wang Fuzhi notices the struggle of the aspects of a contradiction. It is an objective, inevitable and innate phenomenon that the two contradictory aspects of a thing struggle against each other. There is no need to make a fuss about it. The correct attitude is "to defy their struggles." (*Outer Commentary on the Book of Changes·Book 4*) And he says as follows:

> "For yin and yang always communicate with each other; they are not necessarily compelling each other. To compel each other is not their common state. All of a sudden, yang compels yin, and thunder rolls; all of a sudden, yin compels yang, and the wind blows. These are variations of the communication." (*Outer Commentary on the Book of Changes·Book 7*)

The mutual communication between yin and yang is the constant state, whereas their mutual coercion and vehement struggle are abnormal states. Wang Fuzhi clearly acknowledges that there is a struggle among the aspects of a contradiction, and that vehement changes in a thing will be aroused through such a struggle.

And further, he uses the view of the struggle among the aspects of a contradiction to explain social phenomena. He acknowledges that "the despotic and influential families who have annexed farmland" and "the small people who have become destitute and homeless" are the two polarized strata of society. These two strata are diametrically opposed to each other. He says, "Those who have already amassed a large fortune are getting richer day by day; and those who have been deprived of their living are getting poorer day by day." (*Extensive Commentary on the Book of Poetry*·Book 4) As for the rulers, "they expose the common people to mortal danger, and therefore the common people look upon them as mortal enemies." (*Discussions after Reading The Mirror of Universal History*·Book 20) "When treasures are amassed in the upper strata, complaints must circulate in the lower strata." (*Ibid*) "When the common people are poverty-stricken, how can you forbid them not to rise in arms?" (*Ibid*) In his opinion, not all the vehement struggles occurring in social and political life are bad, for they may bring forth good results. The intensification of a contradiction must trigger a series of violent struggles. Since violent contradictions cannot be dissolved, the only way out is for one side to overthrow the other. As Wang Fuzhi says, "After the old situation is overthrown, there is great joy." There is struggle between the opposites of a contradiction, and this struggle promotes the transformation of the contradiction. Therefore, the situation may change from "stagnation" to "joy." (Cf. *A Discussion of the Song Dynasty*·Book 8) This is a most revolutionary idea, which emerged in the early period of the ideological trend of enlightenment in China.

Wang Fuzhi knows that the myriad things in the universe are changing all the time, and that these changes follow a universal law. People ought to grasp the conventional practice (the constant) of the changes of things so that they may promote these changes (the variable). He combines these two aspects into one proposition, which runs, "I cope with the variable by sticking to the constant." One should "do one's best to treat the constant with a constant attitude and to treat the variable with a variable attitude." If one does so, one will not be thrown into a panic when facing an emergency situation: "A thing usually dwells in its constant state. As for the symbol, it is the most constant factor of all. A thing usually moves in its variable state. As for the number, it is the most variable factor of all. A superior man should do his best to treat the constant with a constant attitude and to treat the variable with a variable attitude. If he is able to do so, his position will become stable. The constant may be used to govern the variable, and the variable may be used to chasten the constant. If one understands the above principle, one will be crowned with success." (*Outer Commentary on the Book of Changes·Book 5*)

Why must we know the relationship between the constant and the variable? First, we must grasp the objective necessity of the changes of things. Wang says, "As for the gain or loss of a given thing, even if it is as tiny as a fine hair or speck of dust, I believe that it will come sooner or later." When any abnormality occurs in an event or object, one should not panic. "When he acts, he is unfazed by the abnormality." In this way, "he can live a life of ease and leisure, even if great changes take place." In other words he already knows the inevitable course of things, and so he is able to face emergencies in a calm manner: "A superior man chastens the constant so that he may handle incidents properly. He will not be overjoyed by unexpected fortunes, and he will not be surprised at any unexpected calamities. He can live a life of ease and leisure even if great changes take place." (*Outer Commentary on the Book of Changes·Book 5*)

According to Wang Fuzhi, "The sages manage the variable situations with the constant principle. This is because in variable situations there is something constant. Therefore, they are well prepared against whatever calamities that may happen." He opposes the attitude assumed by quite a few people who swim with the stream. As regards historical incidents, he points out, "One should think over the relevant variable factors, so that one may know how to govern the constant spirit." One should try to be a man who "cannot be confused by the upheavals of the world." One must not be "an inconsistent man" who will become "terribly frightened by a fly or a butterfly." (*Waiting for the Answer*) And, "I cope with the variable by sticking to the constant. In the midst of changes, you must not lose your constant stance. If you can do this, you will become great and constant when these incidents pass over." (*Outer Commentary on the Book of Changes·Book 7*)

In Wang Fuzhi's dialectics there is a theoretical contribution with which he has greatly surpassed his forerunners either in the view of activity and tranquility, or in the view of contradiction, or in the view of the constant and the variable. Nevertheless, he exaggerates the significance and effect of the identity of contradiction, so much so that he renders absolute the identity of contradiction.

Wang Fuzhi's epistemology and his criticisms of Song-Ming period Neo-Confucianist and Buddhist epistemology is the next topic for examination. Wang Fuzhi transforms two Buddhist categories, one being *grahya* (Sanskrit, literally the seizer, namely, the perceiver), the other being *grahaka* (Sanskrit, literally the seized, namely, the perceived). He affirms that *grahya* (perceiver) is the knowing ability possessed by the agent of cognition, and the *grahaka* (the perceived) is the object of cognition. He clearly distinguishes between subject and object, and cognitive ability, which is subjective, from cognitive target, which is objective: "Thus I call what is to be used '*grahaka*,' because it must have its own body in reality. When there is what is to be used on one side, there must be those who wait to use what is to be used on the other side. I call those who wait to use what is to be used '*grahya*,' because it must have its own function in reality. Body waits for function, and therefore, because of the '*grahaka*,' the '*grahya*' may display its role in a full way. What is function? Function means what is applied to the body, and therefore the '*grahya*' must go hand in hand with the '*grahaka*.'" (*Elaboration on the Meaning of the Book of History·Book 5*)

Here, he affirms that both the "*grahaka*" and the "*grahya*" exist in reality. The "*grahaka*" must "have its own body in reality," otherwise it cannot be the target of cognition. In like manner, the "*grahya*" must "have its own function in reality," otherwise it cannot give full scope to the function of cognition. From his point of view, then, Buddhists confuse subject with object and turn the relationship between body and function upside down. As regards the relationship between the "*grahya*" and the "*grahaka*," he sums up his idea into two points: On the one hand, any object whatever must accept the effect of subject before it becomes a target ("I call what is to be used '*grahaka*'"). Nevertheless, subjective cognition cannot be formed until one subjective target or another touches it off ("Because of the '*grahaka*,' the '*grahya*' may display its role in a full way"). In short, the objective target is primary. On the other hand, he says, "Function means what is applied to the body, and therefore the '*grahya*' must go hand in hand with the '*grahaka*.'" As far as cognitive activity is concerned, subject should act on object. Nevertheless any correct cognition whatever must be in accordance with the objective target. In short, subject is only a copy of object. These express the basic principle of his theory of reflection. Based on the above two points, he profoundly criticizes the erroneous essence of the idealism advocated by Lu Xiangshan and Wang Yangming, who both follow the conventional doctrines of Buddhism. Their error lies herein: At first, they "remove *grahaka* so that they may enter *grahya*." And then they "take *grahya* for *grahaka*." They attribute object to subject, or, they use subject to devour object.

Wang Fuzhi's criticism of idealism does not mean that he simply gives it up. He stipulates the cognitive target as "what is to be used," and afterwards he stipulates man's cognitive ability as "that which exerts something successfully upon the circumstances." In other words, he notices that man's cognition is possessed of such initiative as to "exert something successfully upon the circumstances." He takes over some speculative ideas from Buddhism and transforms them. And, what is more, he distinguishes his theory of knowledge from the abstract initiative exaggerated by Lu Xiangshan and Wang Yangming in their Idealism.

Therefore, as regards the relationship between *grahya* and *grahaka* or between ego and things, he persists in two points. First, he persists in the principle of the theory of reflection. Second, he opposes the passive ideas of the theory of reflection; for example, "A mirror is hung up so as to reflect things." One should pay attention to two aspects in the cognitive process, one being the "coming of the things," the other being the "going of the mind." One must give full scope to the active effect of the latter as well. Only by doing so can one reflect the outside object as it is. (*Elaboration on the Meaning of the Book of History·Book 1*) According to Wang Fuzhi's analysis, cognitive activity is the result of the mind "having intercourse with things." He uses sight as an example:

> "There is something right here, and I pass by it time and again. Sometimes I see it, and sometimes I do not see it. I fail to see it, not because it does not come to me, but because I do not go to it. In all cases, my mind must first cause me to look at it, and then my eyes may have intercourse with that very thing. Otherwise, things remain things as they are, no matter how splendid they may be, be they beautiful brocade or figured silk; no matter how alluring as they may be, be they beautiful Xishi or pretty Maoqiang. They cannot enter

my mind before I examine them carefully." (*Elaboration on the Meaning of the Book of History·Book 1*)

Here, he notices that either exaggeration or effacement of the subjective initiative may lead to the pitfall of fallacy. Thus, he sublimates the Lu-Wang idealism at a thinking level which is even higher than that of his forerunners.

Wang Fuzhi also directs his criticism at the *a priori* theory of paradigm advocated by the two Cheng brothers and Zhu Xi. The latter says, "A myriad of changes does not exceed my patriarch." Wang Fuzhi advances the principle that "It is necessary to investigate the principle to the utmost by touching the things." He opposes the rationalist stipulation that "Mind contains the myriad principles," writing:

"Everything has its original function, and everything has its natural law. This is what we call 'principle.' Therefore, what man must know and follow is just this 'principle.' Apart from what man cannot know or follow, there is no 'principle' at all." (*Explanation of the Meaning of the Four Books·Book 8*)

The "principle" is objective and knowable, and therefore it can serve as the guidance for human actions. The "principle" may dwell in the mind. Nevertheless the real situation is neither "Outside the mind there is no principle," nor "Mind contains the myriad of principles." The real situation can only be like this: "One may use one's mind to seek the principle." Wang Fuzhi puts forth a cognitive principle that "It is true that by contacting things man can investigate principle to the utmost; it is not true that by setting up principle man may restrict things." To seek relevant principles from objective things and their relations is the correct route by which man knows the world, and Wang Fuzhi generalizes it as, "by contacting things man investigates principle to the utmost." To restrict or to stipulate the changes and developments of objective things by concocting one structure or another according to some *a priori* principle is a wrong route by which some people imagine they can know the world. Wang Fuzhi warns, "by setting up principle man restricts things." It is true that Wang Fuzhi criticizes rationalism, but he does not sink into the pitfall of empiricism. Quite the contrary, he pays full attention to the function of rational thinking. By emphasizing the "unique function" played by "the mind as an organ," which is distinct from the "eyes and ears," he gives full scope to the function of abstract thinking played by "the mind as an organ." "Color and sound act respectively on the eyes and ears, so on seeing and hearing one immediately knows what they are. Even if one goes further to probe into them they are no more than color and sound. Things cover color and sound, but the covers may be exhausted in the things. How can they be compared with the mind? The more one thinks with the mind, the more one increases one's knowledge. Mind can grasp all the details which things are already possessed of, including both the exterior and interior details of the things. As for what things are not yet possessed of in exteriority, the mind can make them appear vividly, as if they have clear forms and overt actions." (*Discussions after Reading the Great Collection of Commentaries on the Four Books·Book 10*)

Wang Fuzhi transforms some traditional categories in antithesis, for example, the investigation of things to the utmost versus the extension of knowledge, extensively studying all learning versus keeping oneself under the restraint of the rules of propriety, and so forth. In so doing, he expands on some dialectical ideas of cognitive movement.:

> "On the whole, the function of 'the investigation of things to the utmost' lies in the fact that the mind as an organ and the eyes and ears are used together, and learning and studying take the lead, while thinking and speculation serve as aids. What one thinks over and speculates on falls into the scope of learning. As for the function of 'the extension of knowledge,' it lies precisely in the mind as an organ. In this case, thinking and speculation take the lead, while learning and studying serve as aids. What one learns and studies are used to dispel the doubts that arise in one's thinking and speculation. The extension of knowledge depends on investigating things to the utmost, so one should use one's ears and eyes to aid the function of the mind, so that the mind may act on some basis. The ears and eyes cannot take over the function of the mind, and the mind can never be laid aside." (*Discussions after Reading the Great Collection of Commentaries on the Four Books·Book 1*)

At the perceptual stage of cognition, man relies mainly on the perceptive activity of the sense organs such as the ears and eyes ("learning and studying take the lead"), but this does not mean that one can break away from the mind's function of thinking and speculation as an organ ("thinking and speculation serve as aids"). At the stage of abstract thinking, man relies mainly on the speculative function of the mind as an organ ("thinking and speculation take the lead"), but this does not mean that one can break away from the perceptive materials, which serve as the basis of cognition ("learning and studying serve as aids"). This is because what one learns and studies is the foundation upon which one may "dispel the doubts that arise in one's thinking and speculation." In the process of human cognition, the perceptual stage and the rational stage are distinct from each other but associated with each other. In short, the relationship between these two stages is a dialectical unity. What is more, as he points out, if one investigates things to the utmost but one cuts oneself off from the extension of knowledge, one will be perplexed by phenomena. As a result, one will "sap his spirit seeking pleasures." If one extends one's knowledge but one cuts oneself off from investigating things to the utmost, one will merely indulge in daydreams. As a result, one will "lose one's ambition and take to evil ways." Therefore, the cognitive process ought to be a harmonious combination of "extensively studying all learning" and "keeping oneself under the restraint of the rules of propriety." "Extensively study of all learning is one aspect of cognition. Keeping oneself under the restraint of the rules of propriety is the other aspect of cognition. These two aspects ought to cooperate with each other, so that a good job of cognition may be accomplished. Once you have extensively studied all learning you should keep yourself under the restraint of the rules of propriety. In learning dwell the rules of propriety, so one may use the rules of propriety to find evidence of learning. As for the rules of propriety, they are the Heavenly principle and the natural laws." (*Discussions after Reading the Great Collection of Commentaries on the Four Books·Book 6*)

"Extensively studying all learning" demands that one should come into contact with the exterior phenomena of individual things in an extensive way. In so doing, one can obtain an abundance of perceptual knowledge. As for "keeping oneself under the restraint of the rules of propriety," one should first generalize and synthesize different kinds of knowledge, and then sum them up into theoretical cognition. In so doing, one can find the objective laws (the natural laws). When these two aspects "cooperate with each other," people's cognition will be continuously enhanced. As Wang Fuzhi says, "The more extensively one studies the more youthful one's thought becomes." And he says, "Learning depends on accumulation. Since old knowledge and new knowledge complement each other, one can renew one's old knowledge." He emphasizes time and again: "Once you have extensively studied all learning you had better keep yourself under the restraint of the rules of propriety." "One should renew one's knowledge every day, and make achievements in new realms." He refutes Zhu Xi, who says, "One may suddenly see the whole thing in a clear light." And, "I hope I will be suddenly enlightened some day." Wang Fuzhi dismisses this as sinking into the abyss of Buddhist mysticism. (*Ibid*)

On the problem of the relationship between knowledge and action, the Neo-Confucians of the Song and Ming dynasties "argued back and forth, and could not agree with one another." The idealism advocated by Lu Xiangshan and Wang Yangming maintains that "knowledge and action are one." Ostensibly, they attach importance to action, but virtually they confuse knowledge with action by effacing the difference between them. Wang Fuzhi criticizes them, saying, "They negate action in order to attribute everything to knowledge." The scholars who follow the Cheng-Zhu Neo-Confucianist School oppose the proposition that "knowledge and action are one"; instead they put forth another proposition that "knowledge is ahead of action." In fact, they sever the connection between knowledge and action. Wang Fuzhi adds this criticism, "By overemphasizing knowledge, they abolish action." And, "Deviating from action, they glibly advocate knowledge." (*Elaboration on the Meaning of the Book of History·Book 3*)

Wang Fuzhi's view on the relationship between knowledge and action is centered on two propositions; one being that "Knowledge and action help each other to play their roles," the other being that "When knowledge and action advance together, success will be achieved." He writes:

> "Knowledge and action aid each other's role. Each side may play a role by itself, and each side may exert its own effect. Therefore, both sides may aid each other in playing their roles. Since both sides may

play a role for mutual benefit, I know quite well that they must be examined as two sides distinct from each other. Things of the same nature do not aid each other, and things of opposite natures are on harmonious terms. Therefore, they can work together. This is a rule, which has already been proved." (*Syntactic and Semantic Analysis of the Book of Rites·Book 31*)

He affirms that of knowledge and action each side has its own function or effect, and therefore they cannot be confused. He posits "knowledge and action are one" but are distinct from each other, so they can aid each other in playing their respective roles. In the concrete activities of human cognition, knowledge and action cannot be clearly separated from each other. This is because in knowledge there is action, and in action there is knowledge. So he says, "From beginning to end knowledge and action do not depart from each other." (*Discussions after Reading the Great Collection of Commentaries on the Four Books·Book 3*) In order to learn to play chess you must have a game of chess with somebody. Hence, when we handle any affair, we do not proceed in this order: "After you have finished knowing an affair well, you begin to handle the affair." (*Ibid, Book 1*) Wang Fuzhi ridicules Zhu Xi and others who propose "knowledge first and action second." Knowledge and action aid each other and this constitutes a developmental process which repeats itself in endless cycles. Wang describes the process, saying, "From knowledge, we know what action we are taking. From action, we know that in action we make use of our knowledge. We should say, 'When knowledge and action advance together success will be achieved'." (*Ibid, Book 4*) In action, people deepen their knowledge; those without knowledge may acquire it, and people with superficial knowledge may acquire profound knowledge. "They are getting better qualified day by day and their progress is without end." (*Record of Thoughts and Questionings·Inner Chapter*) Knowledge and action advance together, as a process; cognition depends continuously on the basis of practice, and subject becomes gradually in accord with object. Although knowledge and action advance together, this does not mean that both sides are in parallel with each other. As Wang Fuzhi firmly believes, action is the guiding aspect of the cognitive process in that action plays a decisive role in the development of knowledge:

> "As for knowledge, of course it takes action for its function. But as for action, quite the contrary: It does not take knowledge for its function. If you act, you are able to know the effect of knowledge. If you know, you are not able to acquire the effect of action.... Action can connote knowledge, but knowledge is not able to connote action." (*Elaboration on the Meaning of the Book of History·Book 3*)

All knowledge must be tested by action, for in action the effect of knowledge may be embodied. Action can contain knowledge, but knowledge cannot replace action. Action is superior to knowledge, knowledge is subordinate to action, and action is the basis of knowledge. Besides all these, he emphasizes that "so-called knowledge is not true knowledge at all. You must put it into practice with great efforts; only then will you be able to have true knowledge." (*Ibid, Book 13*). From such a conclusion, Wang Fuzhi profoundly discloses the common root of idealism and Neo-Confucianism. His criticism is expounded in the following passage:

> "Deviating from action, they glibly advocate knowledge. The lower-ranking scholars of these schools can do nothing more than explain the words of the ancient books. Their job is just the same as making toys of articles and words, and they make the toys in a clumsy way. The higher-ranking scholars of these schools usually sit with their eyes closed in a self-important manner, as if they have already dissolved the mind and become isolated from things. It is true that some of them succeed in something in scholarship, but quite a number of them fail so tragically that they betray the Way, and fall into a trance. They are robbers following a way of heterodox learning. The crux of the problem is right here!" (*Elaboration on the Meaning of the Book of History·Book 3*)

In the Song-Ming time, and for a long period after that, a decadent style of study was in vogue. Some scholars withdrew from society and lived in solitude to pursue scholarship, while others indulged in abstract discussions. In Wang Fuzhi's opinion, the scholars who advocated heterodox learning, including the two Cheng brothers, Zhu Xi, Lu Xiangshan and Wang Yangming, encouraged such a style of study. The pernicious influence of Song-Ming Neo-Confucianism led to this situation: "The minds of the people were befogged, and social customs became extravagant." Later, this became the root of the failure and destruction of the whole nation. Wang exerted great efforts to expose and criticize the Song-Ming Neo-Confucians from the angle of epistemology. He did so by erecting a political motive force on such a cognitive foundation.

On the problem of the relationship between Heaven and Man, Wang maintains that "It is with human efforts that Heaven is created." Man is able to engage in "the great cause of assisting Heaven," transforming Nature and administering society. If man is going to "assist Heaven," man must "make a thorough inquiry into Heaven." Man should temper himself conscientiously so that he may fully develop his capacity to know and transform the objective world.

Wang Fuzhi emphasizes that in many cases the objective necessity of historical development is realized through the subjective activity of some individual historical personalities, which is a contingent factor. For instance, when the First Emperor of the Qin Dynasty instituted the system of prefectures and counties, his motive was to treat the country as his family property, but in practice he did a good thing by rendering the whole country "one big community." Wang says, "The First Emperor of Qin dismissed the marquises and appointed prefects in order to make the country his family property, but Heaven carried out its great impartiality through the private intention of the emperor." (*Discussions after Reading The Mirror of Universal History·Book 1*) In addition, he points out that the peasant uprisings in previous dynasties played a role historically in overthrowing feudal rule and in opening a way to social progress, even though they failed altogether. The tendency of historical development does not depend on the subjective will of any individual personalities. Wang Fuzhi explains how contradictions work in the process of historical development in societies rent by conflict, and his exposition is even clearer than that of Liu Zongyuan. He touches on such dialectics of historical movement as are expounded by Friedrich Engels: "Since class antagonism came into being, it is the evil lusts of man, namely, the covetous desire and the lust for power, that have become a lever of historical development."

Wang Fuzhi regards "Heaven," which "combines principle and situation into one whole," as the decisive force which dominates the development of history. He guesses that in the course of historical development the will and struggles of the people play a role. He takes over Liu Zongyuan's doctrine on the motive force of history to the effect that "Heaven wills that people shall live." And he claims that "Heaven is the reason why all human beings are born alike." He says as follows:

> "What can proceed with its work for a thousand years but not change its nature is the human race or Heaven. So there is the saying, 'What Heaven sees is from what the people see.' To go against this principle is to trespass against Heaven. Only after getting rid of what runs against the principle or Heaven can one's mind be at peace.... People know how to discipline Heaven with the principle, but they do not know that what dwells in Heaven is the principle. People know how to control Heaven with the principle, but they do not know that the reason why all human beings are born alike lies in Heaven." (*Discussions after Reading The Mirror of Universal History·Book 19*)

He calls the objective motive force of historical development "Heaven," and he attributes to "Heaven" "the reason why all human beings are born alike." That is to say, he attributes to Heaven an objective force that is able to see and hear. He fundamentally negates the theological view of history, and he attempts to negate the heroic conception of history, too. He persists in the progressive view of history that "On the people's stance one ponders over Heaven," affirming that the broad masses of the people are a force of historical development which is not to be neglected. He sees that the demands of the majority of the people are reasonable, for the people are wise. If anybody wishes to push history forward, he must value the will of the people, he must experience the life of the people, and he must observe what the people support and what they oppose. This is both a development of and a return to the view, held previously by Xun Kuang and Jia Yi for instance, that the people should be valued. Furthermore, Wang analyzes the problem of human nature, putting forth the view that "Heavenly principle dwells in human desires." In this way, he replenishes the conception of "the people's Heaven," which is generalized as "the reason why all human beings are born alike," with some realistically material content. He says, "The satisfaction of everybody's human desires is the great impartiality of the Heavenly principle." (*Discussions after Reading the Great Collection of Commentaries on the Four Books·Book 4*) And, "Just as we can see human desires everywhere, we can see Heavenly principle everywhere." (*Ibid, Book 8*) In short, he regards the satisfaction of the people's desire for material comforts as a problem which is closely related to the development of society and history:

> "The satisfaction of everybody's human desires is the great impartiality of Heavenly principle. In the great impartiality of Heavenly principle there is no difference from human desires. (Author's note: This view of mine is simple but profound.... If one seeks truth from this point, one will neither fall into the category of the vulgar Confucian scholars nor be counted as one of the heterodox thinkers.)" (*Discussions after Reading the Great Collection of Commentaries on the Four Books·Book 4*)

Wang rebuffs the various false theories of asceticism advocated by the Neo-Confucian scholars of the Song and Ming dynasties, such as "Separate yourself from human desires so that you may talk about Heaven," "To get rid of desires is to contribute to principle," and so on. Rather, the desires for "food, drink and sex," common to all humans, are not the source of all evil. (Cf. *Extensive Commentary on the Book of Poetry ·Book 2*) Wang thinks that the advancement of man's social life is pushed forward by the rational desires common to every member of the human race. To satisfy the people's material desires so that the people may proceed in production and life normally is the "Heavenly principle" which those who "undertake the task given by the people of the whole country" ought to obey.

In a class society this is, of course, only an illusion. Nevertheless, starting with this goal, he puts forth a set of suggestions for reforming society, for instance, "Divide all wealth under Heaven equally," and "Treat all people under heaven impartially." He says as follows:

> "When farmland is divided up, there must be people in want of wild land that can be divided among them. When the population increases, there must be people in want of food to appease their hunger. People with empty stomachs easily hatch resentment, so

> that even a little vibration of air immediately moves them. In such a situation, once a man raises the standard of revolt, all people under Heaven will flock to him. Corrupt officials and degenerates spoil the country. When the country is spoiled by them, witches will appear and spread rumors. Although the imperial court tries to wipe them out, how can such a task be accomplished? Therefore, he that administers the country must divide all the wealth under Heaven equally." (*Extensive Commentary on the Book of Poetry·Book 4*)

Here, a prism is made according to the thought of the reformers who come from the landlord class. With such a prism, he refracts the egalitarian demands of the peasant revolutions of his day. He designs a concrete plan of reform, with the division of all land among the peasants so that "the able-bodied ones may farm their land." (*A Nightmare*) As a result, "everybody can have his own land, and thus the land will be equally divided." (*A Discussion of the Song Dynasty·Book 12*) If the annexation of land by powerful families is prevented, the over-concentration of land in the hands of the few may be avoided, and, as a result, peasant revolt may be averted. This is in practice a demand for economic reform. He substitutes the "country of the public" for the "country of one family." And he emphasizes, "All under Heaven is by no means the private property of one family." (*Discussions after Reading the Great Collection of Commentaries on the Four Books·Origin of the Book*, which is at the end of the last chapter) As for tyrants, in his opinion, it is quite right to call on the people to abolish them. He points out, "Change our common lord. Kill these officials. We do so in order that we may give vent to our resentment." (*Ibid*, *Book 27*) He opposes the bureaucratic landlords' monopoly of political power and the autocratic monarchy. This is his demand for political reform.

Wang Fuzhi's historical and political theories contain the germ of humanism and democratic thought. Such a germ was covered by somber clouds for more than 100 years, but in the last stage of the Qing Dynasty it played a unique role of ferment for the democratic trends of early modern times.

Wang Fuzhi's philosophy is a product of the special historical conditions of 17th-century China. It reflects the essence of the Zeitgeist of the intersectional period of the Ming and Qing dynasties.

It is a powerful driving force in the sphere of ideology to try to find the truth that may help people rejuvenate the nation. Being actuated by such a driving force, Wang contributed a great deal to various aspects of philosophy by synthesizing research into both natural history and the history of mankind. Such is Wang who "discards what has outlived its time to develop the new in a particular way," and finally he founded a brand new system of philosophy.

In the aspect of ontology, he applied his new theoretical creation to philosophical research. In a more definite way, he stipulates a series of philosophically antithetical categories such the material force and principle, the Way and implements, being and nonbeing, foundation and function, the void and the substantial, activity and tranquility, the constant and the variable, the one and the two, and so forth and explains their relations. His philosophy further reflects the violent changes and contradictory connections in the social life of his day. He also generalizes the scientific achievements in the newly rising learning of "substantial investigations." And his philosophy ruminates on the ideologically abundant materials hidden in the two systems of the *Book of Changes* and of the *Laozi*. As a result, the dialectical thinking which permeates the theoretical system of his naïve materialism achieves the highest point that it was capable of reaching in feudal society.

In the aspect of epistemology and methodology, he examines and arduously criticizes three spheres, the first being the Lao-Zhuang Learning, which belongs to the system of Metaphysics, the second being the Dharmalaksana School and the Chan School, which belong to Buddhism, the third being self-awakening, initiative and suchlike problems, which belong to the Neo-Confucianism and the idealism of the Song and Ming dynasties. His working method is epitomized as follows: "He enters their strongholds, plunders all therein, reveals their strong points, and at last he finds their shortcomings." He reveals in a profound way the dialectics of the cognitive movement. As a result, on the kernel problems of the philosophical *Weltanschauung*, he sums up and consequently disposes of the Neo-Confucianism of the Song and Ming dynasties.

In the aspect of historical philosophy, by adopting the historical view that "principle and situation combine into one whole," he attempts to probe into the laws and motive force of historical development. In so doing, he reveals some of the objective dialectics in the historical process.

On the basis of his scientific attitude of seeking truth from facts and the critical spirit of historicism, he gets rid of the theological view of history. He was the first to reject the superstitious interpretation of history, shaking the theoretical foundation of the doctrine of "back to the ancients."

Due to these contributions, Wang's philosophy occupies a glorious place in the history of development of Chinese philosophy. The appearance of Wang's philosophical system marks the end of the absolute philosophy of the whole medieval period. His philosophical system provides us with an example of the theoretical height and historical form which the philosophy of feudal times was able to reach. It is, after all, a product of the 17th century. Four factors seriously limit his thought, one being the subjective stance of the reform party of the landlord class, the second being the objective motive force of the peasant wars and national struggles against feudalism and oppression, and the third being the narrowness of the small-peasant economy and handicraft production, the fourth being consequently the backward level of general sciences. Therefore, his thought inevitably possesses duality. It contains an ideological spearhead that "The new breaks through the old." And yet, his philosophy has not yet cast off the heavy fetters of feudal ideology. The contradictions contained in Wang Fuzhi's philosophy are a mirror for the epochal contradictions of 17th-century China.

Because of the ideological features caused by the concrete characteristics of the contradictory development of Chinese society in the past 300 years, Wang Fuzhi's thought became one of the important sources of the enlightenment trend in early modern times although it was revived only after the suffocating cultural absolutism of the Qing Dynasty, which lasted nearly two centuries. His historical and social ideas especially exerted an active and extensive influence upon the patriotic reformist movement toward the end of the 19th century, and upon the anti-Qing revolutionary movement which broke out at the beginning of the 20th century. Tan Sitong, a radical in the Reform Movement of 1898, takes Wang for his own direct forerunner in thought. He praises him in a poetical line: "Thunder that awakens Heaven and Earth." (*Six Quatrains on Art·Quatrain 2*) And he says, "The wonderful doctrine of Master Wang, who is a native of Hengyang, ... comes into being after a silence of 500 years. It is truly a learning that communicates between Heaven and Man." (*Benevolence Studies·Part Two*) Politically, he affirms

Wang, saying, "Mr. Chuanshan (referring to Wang Fuzhi) is the only personality who lived in the early Qing Dynasty whose learning is a subtle doctrine that can spark civil rights." (*A Letter to Ouyang Banjiang, My Master*) Liang Qichao was another reformer who praised Wang: "In the early Qing Dynasty there were some great masters, for example, Huang Lizhou (Huang Zongxi), Gu Tinglin (Gu Yanwu), Zhu Shunshui (Zhu Zhiyu) and Wang Chuanshan (Wang Fuzhi).... In the past 200 years and more, everybody was blind to the views of these masters. By now, their ideas stirred so many young fellows, as if a current of electricity had hit their heartstrings. Their hearts are now throbbing." (*An Academic History of China in the Past 300 Years*) Zhang Taiyan says, "Toward the end of the Qing Dynasty some eminent Confucian scholars with firm convictions rose in revolt against the authorities, and they made some achievements in the great cause of regaining possession of last territory. They all drew spiritual nourishment from Wang Fuzhi." (*Preface to the Surviving Works of Wang Fuzhi*) These words, although they are somewhat exaggerated, indeed reflect the pearls of truth contained in Wang Fuzhi's thought, which has undergone the test of time and emits inextinguishable rays in the new historical conditions.

34.

Practical Learning: New Ideological Trends in the Philosophies of Yan Yuan and Dai Zhen

The philosophical enlightenment of the Ming and Qing dynasties (1368-1911) centered on opposing the doctrines of Neo-Confucianism. In order to break the intellectual fetters of feudalism formed in the Song and Ming dynasties, the enlightenment underwent an arduous and twisted course of ideological struggles. First of all, Li Zhi was murdered for his heterodox views. The Donglin Clique was suppressed for introducing state affairs into their lectures. Despite this unfavorable climate, a generation of scholars represented by Fang Yizhi and Huang Zongxi advanced bravely in a pioneering spirit in many spheres of learning. Finally, Wang Fuzhi made a thorough critique of Neo-Confucianism. Intellectual stagnation then set in. Zhang Taiyan (1863-1936) says, "In the Qing Dynasty, no flowers of Neo-Confucianism remained, because the relevant talks had been exhausted." (*A Book of Urgent Words·Confucian Scholars of the Qing Dynasty*) Such an ideological trend failed to find a new world although it criticized the old world. It did not and could not provide the nation with the intellectual approach of modern times, either.

Therefore, philosophy remained hampered by the thinking of feudal times, and feudal absolutism was strengthened. Intellectuals were cramped by the reactionary cultural policies of a literary inquisition, "imperial compilations" and "authorized editions" and so on. On the other hand, along with the revival and growth of the seeds of capitalism, various enlightenment trends under the cloak of going back to the ancients continuously came into the open. These trends began to break through the theoretical structure of the feudal ideology, as reflected in the philosophical thoughts of Yan Yuan and Dai Zhen. Zhang Taiyan commented, "In the decaying and disordered times there were two great Confucian scholars, one being Yan Yuan, and the other being Dai Zhen.... Although they followed different doctrines, their academic roots may be traced back to the great masters of the late Zhou Dynasty. So, as compared with the Confucian scholars of the Song Dynasty in their views there are more genuine personal realizations." (*Recorded Essays· Collection of Sayings (I)*) They were both known as scholars "going back to the ancients," but they fiercely attacked Song-Ming Neo-Confucianism. Regarding problems such as the debate about righteousness and interests, and that about principle and desires, they show distinctly the consciousness of the new urbanites, who balked at feudalism. As regards the cognitive line and thinking method, Yan Yuan emphasized "exercise and action" instead of "pure mediation," and he advocated "practical learning." In short, in his theories there was a tendency of materialist empiricism. Dai Zhen emphasized "mental knowledge" and he called attention to "differentiated principles." He brought forth the proposition that "Bright spirit mirrors things," and advocated "a careful analysis of all details." In short, in his theories there was a tendency of materialist rationalism.

Yan Yuan (1635-1704) had two styles, one being Yizhi, and the other being Hunran, but he called himself Xizhai (literally, Practice Studio). He was a native of Boye County, in present-day Hebei Province. He was born into a poor family, and while a baby he was adopted by another family with the surname Zhu. He was put to farm work. In his reminiscences he wrote, "I plowed the land and irrigated the garden." Later, he practiced medicine and taught some disciples. He never took an official post. His major works are the *Four Preservations*, *Correction of Wrong Interpretations of the Four Books*, *Commentaries on Classified Conversations of Zhu Xi*, and *Records and Remainders of Xizhai*. Li Gong (1659-1733) was the eldest disciple of Yan Yuan. He inherited Yan Yuan's thought, and publicized it energetically, with the result that his name is linked to that of his master in the designation Yan-Li School of Thought.

Yan Yuan's ideological development reflected the rise and fall of the ideological trends of the day. When he was young he practiced Taoism, later espousing the Lu-Wang version of Neo-Confucianism, and then switching to the Cheng-Zhu version. He followed strictly all the directions laid out in the *Family Rituals* by Zhu Xi. He gradually came to the conclusion that "to think is not as good as to learn, and to learn must be combined with some exercise." (*A Chronological Biography of Xizhai·Part One*) And he declared, "What era is it now? People all over the land are dreaming and in confusion. As for the scholars, they can do nothing but follow either the Cheng-Zhu School or the Lu-Wang School." (*Records and Remainders of Xizhai·A Letter to Qian Xiaocheng*) He vigorously combated the intellectual legacies of the two Cheng brothers, Zhu Xi, Lu Xiangshan and Wang Yangming. In his late years, he presided over the Zhangnan Academy, where four disciplines, namely, literature, military affairs, classics and history, and arts and crafts, were taught. The latter discipline comprised "hydrogen science," "fire science," engineering, and "images and numbers" (geometry and mathematics). So Yan Yuan's thought matured at the stage at which he embraced the empirical sciences.

In his *Preservation of Human Nature*, Yan Yuan maintains that yin and yang, the two kinds of material force, circulate throughout the universe, and transform themselves into the myriad things. Material force, of which yin and yang are the substantial nature, is the foundation of the universe. As for "principle," it can do nothing but rely on material force. He criticizes the doctrine that "Principle comes before events": "If there were no material force which is substantial, to what could principle be attached?" (*Preservation of Human Nature·Book 1*)

And he takes further steps to demonstrate the idea that "Body and nature are *advaya* (Sanskrit: not of two kinds)." The so-called "human nature" is embodied in the human body, which is possessed of both physiological and psychological qualities. The Neo-Confucian scholars divided the single human nature into "the nature of the Mandate of Heaven" and "the nature of physical substance," and they treated the first as good and the second as evil, the two being in perpetual opposition. This is an utter fallacy, according to Yan Yuan:

"Without physical substance there is no material of which any nature can be made up. Without physical substance there is no material in which any nature can be seen. Therefore it is fruitless to distinguish the nature of the Mandate of Heaven from the nature of physical substance." (*Preservation of Human Nature·Book 1*)

The sense organs, which are visible and tangible, are substantial entities, so they are the basis of all senses. As for "nature" and "principle," they are no more than their effects or functions. The Confucian scholars of the Song Dynasty severed the relationship between foundation and function, their intention being to deny the actually existing forms and bodies. Yan Yuan's criticism of this is as follows:

> "Since they have acknowledged that body has no function at all, the principle they talk about is no more than empty principle. The Buddhists are just like the Confucian scholars of the Song Dynasty who talked about 'the empty.' The Confucian scholars of the Song Dynasty were just like the Buddhists who talk about 'the principle.' Between them, the difference cannot be wider than an inch." (*Commentaries on Classified Conversations of Zhu Xi*)

There is no essential difference between Neo-Confucianism and Buddhism.

In Yan Yuan's opinion, the relationship between man's consciousness, including the thinking function, and his physical body is that the former depends on the latter, and therefore these two sides cannot be separated from each other. This is called "Body and nature are *advaya* (not of two kinds)." (*Correction of Wrong Interpretations of the Four Books·Book 6*) It is a typical fallacy of Buddhism to sever the body from its nature. Buddhists vainly hope to cancel the physical body, so as to concentrate the mind on cultivating one's "original nature." But Yan Yuan points out: "At every turn, Zhu Xi talks about the physical nature being disorganized and evil." In fact, this idea originates in Buddhism, and leads people astray. The result of such a pursuit is to despise the body and adore the spirit. Paying excessive attention to the mind saps the will to make progress. "Buddha neglects the body, saying that it is a hindrance. The ears have to take in many sounds; the eyes have to take in many colors, the mouth and nose have to take in many tastes and smells; the mind and will have to take in many events and things. As a result, it is impossible for one to go without let or hindrance. Therefore, he regards his own ears, eyes, mouth and nose as robbers. In his opinion, only after one dies or perishes can one get rid of the burden of the body. So he talks about "parinirvana" and "nirvana." ...In short, he harbors illusion." (*Preservation of Human Beings·Book 1*)

Such is the practice of Buddhism, which treats "emptiness and silence" as the supreme realm of human nature. This is no more than regarding "illusionary nature" as true nature. But in fact, "If there are to be ears and eyes there must be hearing and watching.... Since there is no way to deprive anybody of ears and eyes, how can there be anybody who is empty in his nature? ...Since there is no way to take the functions of hearing and watching away from the ears and the eyes, how can there be anybody who is able to be completely silent?" (*Ibid*) As a result, "The more one talks about the principle of emptiness and silence, the more muddleheaded one will become. The more wonderfully one practices in emptiness and silence, the more absurd one will become." (*Ibid*) When the two Cheng brothers, Zhu Xi, Lu Xiangshan and Wang Yangming talked about human nature as something empty, they were following in the footsteps of the Buddhist Chan sect.

Yan Yuan's view is contrary to this, as mentioned above. He maintains that it is necessary to give ample scope to the function of the sense organs, which are visible and tangible. He says,

> "The eye can thoroughly see the colors of all directions, as is helpful for enlarging the nature of my eyes.... The ear can thoroughly hear the sounds of all directions, as is helpful for expanding the nature of my ears. This is a rule which is suitable for the mouth, nose, hands, feet, heart and mind, for they are all in a similar situation.... Therefore, the rites and music in riotous profusion may give the amplest scope to the ears and the eyes. They do not satisfy the desires." (*Preservation of Human Beings·Book 1*)

According to him, if there is such a foundation there must be a correspondent function. What is more, he thinks that it is possible to trace from a given function back to the correspondent foundation. This is a fundamental negation of feudal asceticism.

There is a fallacy that "Principle is good, while material force is disorganized and evil," which is a typical view of the problem of human nature preached by the scholars of Neo-Confucianism. In order to rebuke this fallacy, Yan Yuan asserts that foundation accords with function. In answer to the question why man commits evil, he points out, "If you say that material force is evil, this is equal to saying that principle is evil, too. If you say that principle is good, this is equal to saying that material force is good, too." (*Preservation of Human Beings·Book 1*) Why does man do evil? He explains, "Any misfortune originates from hidden matters. It becomes evil because the evildoers have fallen into a bad habit." (*Ibid, Book 2*) That is to say, the root cause of evil is, after all, the circumstances, which are not innate to any individual. The evildoer falls into the bad habit step by step; he or she is by no means a bad person endowed with innate bad qualities. In short, the evilness of human nature has nothing to do with a person's inborn temperament. The reason why some people do evil lies in the fact that they have "misused" their sense organs, which are visible and tangible. "Through one's ears one hears evil sounds, and through one's eyes one sees evil colors. This is neither the fault of the ears and eyes nor the fault of the faculties of hearing and seeing. These faults come from misuse, when one misuses one's emotions. Misuse is evil right from the start, for all misuse is evil. Since there are hidden matters, there are misuses. Without hidden matters, there are no misuses. Bad habits come first, and misuses come second. Without bad habits, there can be no misuses." (*Ibid*)

How should one prevent such misuses? Yan Yuan explains:

> "A hundred parts of my body exert the functions of my nature. When one part is not efficacious, one function is out of use. The myriad things in the world are the objects to which my nature may adopt measures to know them respectively. When one thing is not in its normal order, a measure which my nature adopts must be in an abnormal order correspondingly. The body and the world are an organic whole, so they must function in coordination." (*Preservation of Human Beings·Book 1*)

In order that the various organs of the body may develop normally, there must be some concrete measures by which one may temper one's nature to experience the myriad things and events. Therefore, one must do one's best to come into contact with things and events, so that one may really understand the practical situation. Only when one identifies oneself with the external things and events can the body's organs function normally. In other words, it is necessary to combine the cultivation of one's personality with the accomplishment of one's cause. In this way, one may treat objective things correctly in practical life, one may avoid temptation arising from evil tendencies, and one may prevent the misuse of one's organs. As a result, one may revert to goodness and keep oneself away from evil. In Yan Yuan's opinion, so-called human nature is nothing but the nature of a person's temperament. And the nature of human temperament is to revert to human physiology. In essence, he regards man as an abstract natural person. His efforts show that he attempts to get rid of the nature of righteousness and principle, and that he inclines toward the thinking mode of early modern times. However, he has some shortcomings. For instance, he retains the traditional theory of the original goodness of human nature, and he emphasizes that it is necessary to adjust, or at least to influence human nature by reading the *Book of Poetry*, the *Book of History*, the *Book of Rites* and the *Book of Music*. Nevertheless, he maintains that foundation accords with function, and that body and nature are not of two kinds. He underscores the importance of early education. He comes to see the influence of the surroundings on man, and the action of man on his surroundings. If man is diligent, human nature will improve.

In his *Preservation of Learning*, Yan Yuan points out that the two Cheng brothers and Zhu Xi are mistaken in substituting book knowledge for action, and Wang Yangming and Lu Xiangshan, by taking subjective perception for action, make another error. They are wrong because they all put knowledge above action. They not only depart from true knowledge, they indulge in deep meditation and empty talk, and as a result they bring misfortune to the country and the people. He discloses that such a style of study is superficial, boastful and impractical. Therefore, he says, the Neo-Confucianism of the two Cheng brothers and Zhu Xi, and the version advocated by Wang Yangming and Lu Xiangshan both tend to "kill the people." "If the learning of Wang Yangming is subdued and the learning of Zhu Xi prevails, how can the people not perish? If the learning of Zhu Xi is subdued and the learning of Wang Yangming acts alone, how can the people not perish? At present, there is neither a scholar in the whole country nor a sage within a circumference of one thousand *li*. The ministers of the imperial court do not discuss the state affairs, and in the countryside folks do not follow good customs. In one word, the people are living in destitution. Whose fault is this? Every time I think of such a society and such a nation, I cannot help shedding tears." (*Records and Remainders of Xizhai·Book 6*)

In order to put right existing evils, Yan Yuan grasps tightly the proposition first appearing in *Great Learning* that "Extension of knowledge lies in the investigation of things," and he endows it with a new explanation. In doing so he expounds his unique idea of the problem of knowledge and action. What are "things"? How should man "investigate" them? According to Zhu Xi's explanation, "to investigate" is "to arrive in," and "To investigate things means a thorough study of the principle that dwells in everything," (*Syntactic and Semantic Analysis of the Great Learning*), since he firmly believes that Heaven, Earth and the myriad things are the embodiment of principle, he demands that in dealing with things and events one should first understand the principle which is an existence prior to Heaven, Earth, and the myriad things.

According to Wang Shouren's explanation, "to investigate" means "to put in good order," and therefore, "to investigate things" means "to put things in good order." Since he maintains that outside the mind there is nothing, he demands that one should extend one's innately good knowledge by exterminating evil and following good.

To the one and the same proposition that "Extension of knowledge lies in the investigation of things," Yan Yuan gives a new explanation:

> "As for the word 'investigate' in 'investigating things,' according to Wang Yangming and his school, it means 'to put in good order,' according to Zhu Xi and his school, it means 'to arrive in,' and according to the Confucian scholars of the Han Dynasty, it means 'to come.' It seems to me that these explanations are not perfectly exact.... In my opinion, it means 'to kill' just as 'to kill ferocious beasts with one's hands,' which is a phrase common in historical records, or as 'to kill somebody with one's bare hands,' which is a phrase describing how a murderer kills somebody by hitting him with a fist. You must learn something by touching the very thing: This was the teaching of Confucius when he urged his disciples to learn the six

classic arts of rites, music, archery, riding, writing and arithmetic." (*Records and Remainders of Xizhai·Book 6*)

The so-called "investigating" demands that one must exert all possible efforts on the external things just as one would when fighting a ferocious beast. In that case, one must raise one's fist to beat the beast to death. Therefore, Yan Yuan compares the "investigation of things" with "a murderer carrying out his task." (*A Record of Words and Deeds·Part One*) In other words, he demands that intention be translated into action. Below is his explanation of the proposition that "Extension of knowledge lies in the investigation of things":

> "Nowadays, scholars who talk about the extension of knowledge do nothing but read, discuss and speculate. They do not know how to extend their own knowledge, but the secret of extending true knowledge does not lie in these affairs.... For instance, if you are going to know music, you will remain ignorant of it no matter how many times you read, discuss and speculate about musical scores. You must play the musical instruments with your hands or mouth, and you must sing and dance by yourself. In short, you must personally take a hand in making it before you can know something about music. To know music in this way is to follow a correct way. This is my explanation. Investigate things first, and extend knowledge afterwards." (*Correction of Wrong Interpretations of the Four Books·Book 1*)

Yan Yuan first affirms that "things" are objective and independent of the sense organs of man. If you wish to acquire some knowledge, you can see nothing if you do not use your eyes to watch everything, even if "your eyes are bright." In like manner, you cannot attain any knowledge if you do not come into contact with external things by using your sense organs, even if "your mind is intelligent." Only personal involvement can make one familiar with music. Otherwise, "you will remain ignorant of it no matter how many times you read, discuss and speculate about musical scores." As Yan Yuan explains "investigating" as "a murderer carrying out his task," his theory is a sharp contrast to those of the two Cheng brothers, Zhu Xi, Lu Xiangshan and Wang Yangming. There are two stresses in Yan Yuan's theory of knowledge, one being that knowledge relies on action, the other being that knowledge may promote action. Thus, he demands that people earnestly transform their objective surroundings. Man is richly endowed by Nature with all the attributes of Heaven and Earth; he is the paragon of the animals, able to know the myriad things. Yan Yuan emphasizes the continuous self-renewal of man, advocating "activity" and repelling "tranquility." "Zhou Dunyi, the two Cheng brothers, Zhu Xi and Shao Yong could do nothing but sit still, and talk or write nonsense. In short, they did not act. As a result, talents have been frittered away, the Holy Way has died out, and the country has degenerated! Yet I am emboldened to say as follows: When a physical body acts, the body will become strong. When a family acts, the family will become strong. When a country acts, the country will become strong. When the whole world acts, the whole world will become strong." (*A Record of Words and Deeds·Part Two*)

Yan Yuan's views are a heavy blow at Neo-Confucianism, and by them he adds some new content to the epistemology of ancient Chinese philosophy.

Yan Yuan claims that the destruction of the Ming Dynasty was caused by a decadent style of study, which originated from the practice of idly chattering about mind and nature. The scholars of the day "regarded those who manage state affairs as rough squires or vulgar officials, and regarded those who work in the sphere of the economy as utilitarian fellows or miscellaneous despots." (*Commentaries on Classified Conversations of Zhu Xi*) In short, they looked down on the people who engaged in practical occupations. The scholars of the day were fond of sitting and reading, and engaging in empty talk and empty writing. Therefore, "The whole country became an empty game." (*Correction of Wrong Interpretations of the Four Books·Book 6*) As a result, "the misfortunes brought about by empty talk are far greater than those brought about by the burning of books and burying scholars alive in the Qin Dynasty." (*Preservation of Learning·Book 1*) The malpractices have a long history, from the Han to the Song Dynasty, and Yan Yuan bitterly rebukes Confucian scholars for focusing on reading and useless controversy to the detriment of the national economy and the people's livelihood.

In order to advocate a new style of study aimed at preparing students to manage state affairs and improving the practical application of knowledge, Yan Yuan compares those who read mechanically to persons who are taking arsenic. Full of grief and indignation he says, "I used to be a scholar who took arsenic. I have exhausted my strength mentally and physically. I have suffered a great deal from reading mechanically." This is because to read mechanically not only exhausts one's energy but also blunts one's brains. He says, "The more you read, the more perplexed you become. When you examine any event, you will find that you have no judgment at all. When you deal with economic affairs, you will find that you are simply incompetent." (*Commentaries on Classified Conversations of Zhu Xi*)

As an educator, Yan Yuan does not totally exclude the role which reading plays. Directing his criticism only at current evils, he opposes desperate reading, mechanical reading and the reading of useless books. His aim is to oppose the rigid way of thinking and the neglect of cause and contribution: "The following is applicable to both teachers and students: Of praise, only ten or twenty percent is to be given to those who teach and read, and eighty or ninety percent to those who practice and act." (*Preservation of Learning·Book 1*) The reason is "because what are discussed in the Four Books, the other classics and historical books belong to either the ultimate principles of human affairs or the way to attend to business. Nevertheless, quite a number of scholars can do nothing but read classics and histories, or at most make textual criticism of them. They imagine that they are seeking the ultimate principles and the way to attend to business. But in fact there are ten thousand *li* between them and the truth." (*Ibid*, *Book 3*) In other words, the contents of the ancient books are at most the experiences of the ancients. If you deal with the present by citing the past, believing that the way to govern the country and rule the people is contained in the ancient books, you have already missed the point by a thousand *li*, for you are ignorant of the times. Some of the Neo-Confucian scholars substitute the reading of classics and histories for a profession, some of them substitute the annotation of ancient books for a livelihood, and some of them naively believe that this is the only way to find the ultimate principles and the only way to attend to business. As a result, there is a still greater distance between them and the truth. In short, books are at most tourist handbooks or maps. The secret of reaching any desired goal is nothing but practical action. To read blindly will bring about poor results. "If scholars all over the country do nothing but read, write or sit still, people will refuse to be genuine scholars, farmers, artisans or merchants." (*Records and Remnants of Xizhai·Book 9*) As a result, the nation will be in peril, and the people will be in peril, too. Therefore, Yan Yuan advises, "We must concentrate our efforts on practice and action and not on bookish knowledge only." (*A Record of Words and Deeds·Part Two*)

In Yan Yuan's view, "the empty" must be replaced by "the practical." The subjects he advocates are called "practical literature," and the learning method is called "practical learning" or "learning and action." The actions he advocates are called "practical action." The cause and contribution he advocates are called "practical application." The nature and body he advocates are called "practical body." In short, he plans to substitute "learning, practice, action and ability" for the "lecture, reading, writing and narration" preached by the Neo-Confucians. He says, "I prefer the practical ones, even if they seem to be partial and small, to the empty ones, even if they seem to be whole and great." (*Preservation of Learning·Book 1*)

The "practical learning" advocated by Yan Yuan demands that people should grasp practical skills needed to do practical jobs. With such skills, they may become talented enough to be able to deal with the affairs of everyday life. Although the subjects he advocates come clad in the ancient costume of the "six arts" of "rites, music, archery, riding, writing and arithmetic," they reflect the new demands of his times. He says, "Be versatile! Military affairs, agriculture, monetary affairs, grain management, water conservancy, fire control, engineering, astronomy and geography are all important subjects which you must study hard." (*Correction of Wrong Interpretations of the Four Books·Book 2*) These were the subjects taught at the Zhangnan Academy, over which Yan Yuan presided for a while. He demanded that every student must be useful and talented enough to govern the country, attend to business, and correct the current evils. Therefore, he laid stress on not only "learning" and "action" but also on training the "ability" of the students. He says, "Every student must become weak and meager if he does nothing but sits still in his study all day long. If so, he will be laughed at by soldiers and farmers." (*Preservation of Learning·Book 3*) And he says, "Both the farmer who grows good crops or the merchant who collect goods and makes money have a certain amount of experience, patience and courage. Only when they are possessed of these qualities can they establish themselves." (*Correction of Wrong Interpretations of the Four Books·Book 3*)

At the age of fifty-nine, Yan Yuan said, "One day, I failed to practice the six arts. When I think of it, I feel very ashamed of myself. This is because my style is Xizhai (literally, Practice Studio)." (*A Chronological Biography of Xizhai·Part Two*) Even at the age of sixty-two, he continued to preside over the Zhangnan Academy, and taught his disciples himself. "He taught his disciples to dance, he raised a big stone dumbbell for physical exercise, and sometimes he sang loudly and heartily." (*Ibid*) This serves to show that he was full of enthusiasm in advocating practical learning. No wonder in "Elegiac Address to Xizhai," Li Gong, one of his disciples, said, "After I, a humble person named Li Gong, became his disciple, I began to know discretion in conduct, critical examination of myself, the rites, music, archery, riding, writing and arithmetic. I also got to know the current economic situation and the economic situations of a hundred generations. I dare not be unworthy of my teacher!" (*A Chronological Biography of Shugu·Book 3*)

To sum up, the most outstanding feature of Yan Yuan's philosophical thought is the emphasis on "the practical" in opposition to "the empty," practical action over all empty talk. Therefore, by his new explanation of "investigating things," he gives a forceful rebuttal to the apriorism of the Cheng-Zhu and Lu-Wang schools of thought. The "exercises and action, which he advocates and the new style of study centered on "practical learning" reflected the demand of the times and exerted a great influence on the ideological and cultural circles of his day, as well as of coming ages. All of these ought to be historically affirmed. It is a pity that he identifies human nature with the physiological temperament of the natural person. It is also a pity that when he emphasizes action he sometimes ignores knowledge. Thus, he neglects rational thinking, and also neglects the dialectics of cognitive movement.Dai Zhen (1723-1777) was a native of Xiuning County (present-day Tunxi City in Anhui Province). He was born into the family of a small merchant. While young, he followed his father, who was a wandering peddler. Later, he became a student of Jiang Yong (1681-1762), and gradually became well versed in classics, history, scripture, phonology, textual criticism, astronomy and the calendar. He started a new school of thought, namely, the Anhui School of Plain

Learning, which witnessed its prime in the Qianlong (1736-1795) and Jiaqing (1796-1820) reigns of the Qing Dynasty. Having an aversion to the prevailing Song learning, which was a variety of Confucian scholarship that opposed the Han learning, Dai Zhen failed the imperial examinations several times. He taught professionally for most of his life. In his later years, he became a compilation official in the Hall of the Four Branches of Literature, in charge of books of astronomy, mathematics, geography and the like. He was an outstanding expert on textual criticism, a natural scientist, and a thinker of the enlightenment in 18th-century China.

Apart from monographs on the natural sciences, scripture, phonology and textual criticism, Dai Zhen wrote a number of books on philosophy. In his early years, he wrote *On the Nature of Goodness*, in which he uses the Confucian classics to give free rein to his own philosophical thought. Since he laid stress on the problem of human nature, this book is also a work on ethics. He wrote the *Introduction* to the book after its completion, in which he not only discusses human nature, he also probes a series of problems concerning the conception of nature and the theory of knowledge. His views are antagonistic to those of the two Cheng brothers and Zhu Xi, which were dominant at that time. Later, he revised the *Introduction*, and enlarged it into a new book titled *Commentary on the Meanings of Terms in the Book of Mencius* (Hereinafter, the *Commentary*). He once declared, "Of all the books I have written the *Commentary on the Meanings of Terms in the Book of Mencius* is the one into which I poured my greatest efforts. This book serves to rectify the mind of man. My contemporaries, be they righteous or evil, miscall their personal opinions 'principles,' and I think that they are misleading the people. Therefore, it was necessary to write the *Commentary on the Meanings of Terms in the Book of Mencius*." (*A Chronicle of Dai Dongyuan's Life*)

The *Commentary on the Meanings of Terms in the Book of Mencius* is a masterpiece in which categories such as the Way, principle, nature, life and so forth are explained in a new way. In his explanation Dai Zhen voiced many new opinions unthought of by his predecessors, and thus he made a distinctive contribution to philosophy.

Dai Zhen lived in a period in which the Chinese feudal system was deteriorating day by day, and the urban class was on the rise. As a result, the contradiction between the absolute rule of feudalism and the engenderment of capitalism became more acute all the time. The only response from the rulers of the Qing Dynasty was to borrow theoretical weapons from Song-Ming Neo-Confucianism, centering on "the debate on principle and desires," which was in essence the doctrine "maintaining the Heavenly principles and eradicating human desires." The rulers of the day used this doctrine to suppress revolts, attributing the latter to the pursuit of human desires in neglect of the "Heavenly principles," in essence the cannibalistic ethics of feudal society.

Dai Zhen directed his criticism at the Neo-Confucians, who poured out a lot of preposterous views on the problem of principle and desire, developing a set of theories on the properties of the natural person. He first affirms these properties, saying, "From the time of man's appearance, he has desires, emotions and knowledge. These are the three components of human nature, based on blood, vital force, mind and intelligence." (*Commentary·Part Three*) Once one is possessed of life, one naturally has various desires and feelings with which one seeks to live. Dai Zhen formulates the content of human nature into the desires, emotions and knowledge innate to blood, vital force, mind and intelligence. He says, "Man has feelings such as pleasure, anger, sorrow and joy. Man has desires for sounds, colors, smells and tastes. Man has knowledge of the right and the wrong, beauty and ugliness. All of them are rooted in human nature and originate in Nature." (*Introduction·Part One*) All these properties come from human nature, and their manifestation is quite natural. Following Wang Fuzhi, he transforms Mencius' theory on the "original goodness of human nature." On the problem of principle and desire, he puts forth a new view, which runs as follows:

> "Principle is something in which desire dwells." (*Commentary·Part One*)

He cites some examples to illustrate his idea. When one sees a child about to fall into a well, one runs to save the child at once. Such a deed comes from his kindheartedness, and it is in accordance with "principle." Nevertheless, such kindheartedness is still rooted in desire. This is because everybody has the instinct to hope for life and to fear death. Such being the case, one is able to have vigilance and sympathy when one sees a child about to fall into a well. It is not that there is another conception of kindheartedness which has been stored in the human mind in advance. On this analogy, feelings such as those of shame and dislike, of approval and disapproval, and of modesty and complaisance, which are discussed by Mencius, are nothing but social and ethical concepts, which are formed by Nature and are the original properties of man.

Dai Zhen goes a step further by putting forth the two categories of "Nature" and "necessity." They illustrate the relationship between the natural properties of man and the social norms. "Desires are the natural properties of blood and vital force.... Starting from the natural properties of blood and vital force, one may examine the necessary course of their development, which is called rites and righteousness. The natural and the necessary are not two notions.... To let things take their natural course may sometimes bring about evil. In that case, the natural will be lost. Once the natural is lost, it is non-natural. Therefore, things must return to necessity so that they can truly take their natural course." (*Commentary·Part One*)

He takes human desires for the natural, and the Heavenly principle for the necessary. In his opinion, these two sides are distinct from one another but they cannot be separated. He objects to the view of the Neo-Confucians, who separate "the Heavenly principle" from "human desires," setting one side against the other. Adamant that principle and desires are unified, he points out, "The way to give birth to and to bring up children lies in desires. The way to interact and communicate with one another lies in emotions. When these two ways are in accordance with Nature, all the affairs of the world are accomplished." (*On the Nature of Goodness·Part One*) Only when there is the desire to live on, and only when there are external things which may cause various responses, can one give free rein to one's natural instincts and accomplish various causes in the world. Otherwise, if one follows blindly the empty talk of the Neo-Confucians, quibbling about nature, life, righteousness and principle, which is designed to extinguish human desires, one's heart will be like dead ashes. When one is utterly dissipated, one can accomplish nothing.

In Dai Zhen's opinion, some teachings of Neo-Confucianism of the two Cheng brothers and Zhu Xi are truly harmful, for instance, "The Heavenly principle and human desires cannot stand side by side," and "Maintain the Heavenly principle, and eradicate human desires." He claims that "they completely take their own opinions for principle, and bring misfortunes to the whole country. As a result, the debate on principle and desire becomes nothing more than an instrument to kill people." (*Commentary·Part Three*) Bitterly and indignantly, he says as follows:

> "The superior blame the inferior because of principle, the old blame the young because of principle, and the noble blame the humble because of principle. Even if their blames are put wrongly, they say their blames are put smoothly. When the inferior, the young and the humble argue about something on the basis of reason, even if their arguments are made appropriately, they say that their arguments are made adversely.... When somebody is put to death in accordance with the law, perhaps people may feel pity for him. When somebody dies because of principle, who will feel pity for him?" (*Commentary·Part One*)

Obviously the "principle" the Neo-Confucians talk about has already become an instrument by which the superior, the old and the noble may satisfy their selfish desires. In the meantime, the inferior, the young and the humble are blamed and suppressed by the so-called "principle." And, what is more, their reasonable demands cannot be guaranteed. In short, such a "debate on principle and desire" becomes a reactionary instrument by which the inferior, the young and the humble are slaughtered. The so-called "principle" is the politics and ethics of feudalism, which is a gentle knife with which the reactionaries murder the people without spilling blood. He says, "Cruel officials use the law to kill people, the latter-day Confucian scholars use principle to kill people. Step by step, they shunt aside the law to talk about principle. But once a person is put to death, there is no way to rescue him." (*A Letter to So-and-So*)

According to the *County Annals of Xiuning*, in Xiuning, the native place of Dai Zhen, the population in his day was some 65,000, but in the period from the early years of the Qing Dynasty, which was founded in 1644, to the Daoguang reign period (1821-1851), the number of women who kept their "chastity," namely widowhood, and who "heroically" killed themselves after their husbands' death amounted to more than 2,000. In those years, when a woman's husband passed away, she was expected by some to follow him through suicide. And there were even examples of betrothed girls who committed suicide when their fiancés died. This was how, according to Dai Zhen, the Neo-Confucians kill people with "principle."

The "debate on principle and desire" is rooted in the doctrines of Buddhism and Taoism. "Because there is a physical body, there are, of course, desires. They seek something outside the physical body. They equate death with life, and they discard emotions and desires altogether. Their spirit may be at peace, they say." (*On the Nature of Goodness·Part Two*) Both Buddhism and Taoism advocate the giving up of emotions and desires in order that one may seek an obscure state free from all thought. The doctrinal foundation of the Neo-Confucians is nothing but the religious theory that the spirit is above the physical body. Herein lies their mistake: They do not know that only when man's natural instincts and desire to live on are satisfied on a normal way can man really return to Nature.

Dai Zhen takes a step further to disclose the fallacy of the Neo-Confucians in a more profound way. Their preaching is designed to satisfy the selfish desires of the rulers. He points out, "The Taoists preach 'long life and eternal sight.' The Buddhists preach the 'non-reality of birth and extinction.' They seek nothing but selfish gain." (*Commentary·Part Three*) And he repeatedly emphasizes, "The Way of the sage and worthy person lies not in 'no desires' but in 'unselfishness.' They use 'unselfishness' to regulate the emotions of all the people in the world, so that they can satisfy the desires of all the people in the world." (*Ibid*) Indignantly, he denounces the feudal rulers, "who are so unbridled in cupidity that they are no different from bandits and invaders," and argues that revolt is a necessary response to bad rulers:

> "In order to satisfy his personal cupidity, the ruler does not care whether the people live or die. The people have to revolt. The people are compelled to do so by the ruler who sits on high. The origin of all the disturbances is at the top of the country." (*On the Nature of Goodness·Part Three*)

Dai Zhen puts forth his own version of the ideal society. In his opinion, in the ideal society, everybody will know how to infer others' emotions and desires according to his own emotions and desires. As a result, in dealing with all affairs, everybody will be just and unselfish, and nobody will use his subjective prejudices to deal with his relations with others. In this way, "If one uses one's own emotions to infer others' emotions, everything will be handled in a just way. Such is the case." (*Commentary·Part One*) A ruler must be good at "observing the people's conditions and satisfying the people's desires," so that he may "spend happy days with the people." Since a good ruler must apply benevolent policies toward the people, he must "commutate penalties and alleviate taxes." In this way, everybody can live well. As for each household, "Every man should wait on and support his parents, and every man should be able to support his wife and children." As for society as a whole, "The dweller finds that his barn is full of grain, and the traveler finds that his bag is full of food. Within, there is no unmarried woman pining for a husband; without, there is no unmarried man pining for a wife. In this way, a good situation may be brought about in which a benevolent government following the 'kingly way' administers well a merry land." (*Ibid*) Such is Dai Zhen's view on principle and desire and his fantasy of the ideal society. In his views and fantasy he expresses, although in a dim way, his longing for a rational realm of equality and fraternity.

In Dai Zhen's concept of society, "Principle exists in material force." This is established on the foundation of his outlook on Nature. Thus, he criticizes the viewpoints of the Cheng-Zhu school of Neo-Confucianism, such as "Principle comes before material force," "Principle is present in every event," and so on. He lays stress on the new explanation of the "Way" by differentiating the "Way" from "principle." And, further, he puts forth a new philosophical category, called the "principle of differentiation."

He says, "The Way is something on which the people walk. Material force transforms and circulates. Continuously, material force reproduces things in endless succession. Therefore, it is called the Way." (*Commentary·Part Two*) And he says, "Yin and yang and the Five Elements are the substance of the Way." (*Ibid*) The "Way" is not a substance at all; one must take yin and yang and the Five Elements for the substance of the Way. The so-called "Way" is only an expression of the process in which the material force of yin and yang and the Five Elements transform and circulate, and continuously reproduce things in endless succession. It is worth noting that he adopts the view of scholars of the Han Dynasty who interpreted the "Way" as "walking." He does so in order to oppose the view of the Cheng-Zhu school of Neo-Confucianism, which takes "principle" for substance, and which maintains that principle comes before material force. Therefore, he comes up with a new explanation of the relationship between the "implements" and the "Way." He discusses in detail a famous proposition in the *Book of Changes·Appended Remarks*: "What is above physical form is called the Way, and what is below physical form is called the implement." In his opinion, "above physical form" should mean "antecedent to material form" and "below physical form" should mean "subsequent to material form." Therefore, "above physical form" and "below physical form" are terms which are used to illustrate the different states or different stages of the transformation and circulation of material force. When "yin and yang have not assumed any physical form," the transformation of material force is described as above physical form. Only the "substantially visible" implements can be described as being below physical form. It is thus clear that Dai Zhen refutes the tenet of the Cheng-Zhu School that above the transformation of the yin and yang material forces there is another existence, which is called the "Way."

The reason why the Neo-Confucians insist that the "Way" begets the "implements" is because they want to demonstrate that "principle" begets "material force." He says, "Just as Master Zhu says, yin and yang are the material forces, they are below physical form. Therefore, a yin plus a yang constitutes principle. The Way is the nomination of principle." (*Commentary·Part Two*) "Material force" is below physical form, and "principle is above physical form. Only when there is "principle" can there be "material force." And "principle" is the "Way," which belongs to another kind of existence in that it is independent of the two material forces of yin and yang. In fact, here Zhu Xi makes two mistakes in logic. At first, he confuses the Way with principle. And then he "debates the problem of principle and material force" on the false premise that both the Way and principle belong to substance. After pointing out these mistakes, Dai Zhen concludes: "In fact, Zhu Xi has already lost the nomination of the Way." (*Ibid*)

Dai Zhen holds high esteem for Zhang Zai in that "he never takes principle for another kind of thing." (*Commentary·Part One*) In the first part of the *Introduction* he makes a profound analysis: Both the "Way" and "principle" are "empty terms" in that they are no more than abstract conceptions of necessity, laws and the essential attributes of objective things and events. As regards the conceptions per se, there is the Way in a broad sense, and there is the Way in a narrow sense, too; there is principle in a broad sense, and there is principle in a narrow sense, too. In short, "The Way as a general term governs unification and the principle as a specific term governs separation." Since the "Way" refers to the fundamental law of both Nature and human affairs, in Nature it is embodied as the "Heavenly way," and in human affairs it is embodied as the "human way." Quite the contrary, principle is a qualitative conception which is used to differentiate one thing from another, and it can only be the principle of differentiation, the specific characteristic , essence or law, of things and events.

In the history of Chinese philosophy, it was Han Fei who first distinguished the "Way" from "principle," and treated them as two distinct conceptions. He thought that "principle" was the difference among things and events. By "principle," Han Fei referred only to the differences of things and events in their external forms, such as size, length, color and shape. He had not yet endowed "principle" with the significance of the intrinsically qualitative attributes of concrete things and events. At a level of theoretical thinking much higher than that of Han Fei, Dai Zhen returns to Han Fei and innovates. Every objective thing or event has its intrinsically qualitative attributes. A general conception forms after these attributes are reflected in the human mind. Therefore, between the intrinsically qualitative attributes and the conception that reflects these attributes, there are differences, for instance, the difference between ego and things, the difference between subject and object, and so on. Nevertheless, there are some organic connections between them, too. In this way, he uncovers the cause of theoretical thinking of the Cheng-Zhu scholars, who talk about conceptions by cutting off the connections with concrete things and events, but who afterwards venerate and enlarge these conceptions so much that they say that these conceptions are the origin of the myriad things and events, and finally put forth their doctrine that "Principle is one, but its manifestations are many."

Dai Zhen's conception of nature is, of course, limited by the times in which he lived. For instance, when he discusses every category of things, he solidifies the qualitative stipulations. Once a category of things comes into being, "it remains so throughout the ages," and there is no addition of new qualities at all. He cannot draw a strictly clear demarcation between necessity, the laws of Nature and the ethical norms of human society. Thus, he attributes humanity and propriety, which belong to the category of ethics, to the "order of Heaven and Earth." (*Commentary·Part Three*)

In order to understand the specific principle, namely, the intrinsically qualitative attributes, one must concern oneself with two points: First, one should seek the thing per se, which has already been brought into one's scope of attention. Second, of that very thing one must "make an analysis in a very careful or even minute way." Of course, in order to know a thing or event, the sense organs must first be applied to the thing or event. This is the first step in the cognitive process. In order to "make an analysis in a very careful or even minute way," one must depend on rational thinking. He says, "When the sense organs such as the ears, eyes, nose and mouth come into contact with outside things, the mind opens up to the law of the outside things." (*On the Nature of Goodness·Part Two*) Man is possessed of the ability of theoretical thinking, by which, and by which alone, man is clearly and fundamentally distinct from the other animals. He says, "Animals and plants can do nothing but follow Nature, whereas man is able to be aware of necessity. Right here lies the difference between man and animals and plants." (*Introduction·Part Two*)

Man's "ears, eyes and a hundred other organs" are able to "bring all things and events to the mind," and "the mind is able to reach principle and righteousness." Such being the case, in order to realize human cognition it is of paramount importance to depend on the synthesizing role which the mind plays, although each of the five organs of the human body may play its own role. This is a cognitive capacity unique to man, which Dai Zhen calls "deity."

The meaning of the word "deity" in Dai Zhen's vocabulary is quite different from that of the same word in Zhu Xi's works. The former emphasizes that the "deity" of man refers to man's thinking capacity per se. He says, "The deity is similar to the mind. It means the storage capacity of the mind, which acquires knowledge from elsewhere." (*Commentary·Part One*) This is a criticism directed at Zhu Xi, who is particularly fond of the idealistic factors of Mencius. When Zhu Xi comments on the *Mencius*, he says, "The mind is the deity of man, and therefore it is possessed of all the principles by which man can deal with the myriad events." (*Commentaries on the Mencius·Book XIII (I)·Exhaustion of the Mind*) Thus he parts from the Cheng-Zhu scholars, who preach that "the principles are in one mind." At the same time, he defies the Lu-Wang scholars, who preach that "mind is principle."

Dai Zhen lays particular stress on the process of arduous study. In his opinion, "Only by means of study can one make up what one lacks and increase one's wisdom." (*Commentary·Part One*) This is the only way to become wiser than before and finally enter the stage of "deity." And the rational light of such "deity" may illuminate the myriad things and events. By such a light, man can obtain knowledge of principle, which governs all things and events. In his opinion, one can assuredly enlarge one's vision through study even if one is a fool. If one is willing to learn, "one is bound to improve one's wisdom, I am sure."

Dai Zhen, in his theory of knowledge, lays stress on the role of the rational light in illuminating things. He says as follows:

> "As far as things and events are concerned, it is not the case that outside the things and events there are any principles. As is said, 'If there is a thing, there must be the law of that thing.' And people use the law to rectify the corresponding thing. That is all there is to it. As far as the human mind is concerned, it is not the case that there is a principle of one kind or another with which the mind has been endowed. The deity of the mind is enough to know the unchangeable laws of all things and events." (*Commentary·Part One*)

As regards objective things and events, it is not the case that there are some "principles" apart from things and events. In case there is a thing or event, there must be a law innate to that thing or event. When we measure or distinguish the attributes of a thing, the only correct way is to apply the innate law to the thing or event itself. As regards man's capacity for thinking, it is originally innate to man. It is not the same thing as what the Neo-Confucians mean when they say, "Principle is received from Heaven, and it is Heaven that endows the human mind with principle." The role of man's deity lies precisely in that with which man can know the necessity and law of things and events.

Why is there error in man's knowledge? In Dai Zhen's opinion, this is because the mind fails to reach the "deity" as there are "hoodwinks" of one kind or another in the mind. He says, "If there are hoodwinks in the mind, the mind cannot obtain proper information about things and events. Such being the case, how can the mind grasp principle?" (*Ibid*) Only when the hoodwinks are removed can the deity illuminate things and events, and reach the concept of principle. In order to remove the hoodwinks, it is necessary to concentrate on study. If one does so, one may progress from being ignorant to becoming informed, and from being informed to becoming wise. He highly praises Master Xun's view when the latter says, "[A gentleman] recites and enumerates his studies so that he will be familiar with them, and ponders over them and searches into them in order to fully penetrate their meaning." (*Xunzi·Book 1: An Exhortation to Learning*) Master Xun also says, "If you accumulate enough good to make your inner power whole, a divine clarity of intelligence will be naturally acquired, and a sage-like mind will be fully realized." (*Ibid*) As regards knowledge and action, Dai Zhen maintains that action comes first and knowledge follows. In his view, in order to remove hoodwinks from the mind, the correct way is to lay stress on knowledge first. He says, "If one intends to remove selfishness, it is a failure to follow the holy learning if one does not remove hoodwinks. If one intends to lay stress on action, it is a failure to follow the holy learning if one does not lay stress on knowledge first." (*Commentary·Part Three*) By advocating that people should lay stress on action on condition that they lay stress on knowledge first, he clearly displays a tendency toward rationalism.

When Dai Zhen discusses the standard of the truth, he first distinguishes the truth of objective things and events from the subjective opinions of individuals in order to demonstrate that the Neo-Confucians pass their personal opinions off as the principle of the things and events. His retorts: "Only what all men's minds similarly approve can be called 'principle' or 'righteousness.' What all men's minds have not yet similarly approved can only be called 'opinions,' for they are neither principle nor righteousness. As for what one man approves, if it is approved by the people of the whole world for all ages, it can be called 'similar approval of all men's minds.'" (*Commentary·Part One*) The so-called "similar approval of all men's minds" is in opposition to personal opinions. It is perfect knowledge which issues from the examination of both the fundamental and the incidental. He takes such knowledge to be the criterion for testing truth, and with this criterion he fights against the prejudices and arbitrary ideas of the Neo-Confucians of his day. The positive significance of such a view should be affirmed, even though he does not understand the decisive role which social practice plays in the process of cognition. All in all, his "similar approval of all men's minds" cannot solve the problems of how to distinguish truth from falsehood and right from wrong, although in it there is a positive aspect, that is, the concentration of the wisdom of the masses. Moreover, his "similar approval of all men's minds" echoes a similar concept deduced by Mencius. This is because it is a view which advocates testing knowledge by knowledge, when everything remains within the scope of subjectivity. Second, he regards "principle and righteousness" as something that is approved by the people of the whole world for all time, who say, "these are unchangeable matters." Once again, he fixes the notion of cognition, and once again he negates the necessity that the people must continuously develop their cognition. These two points constitute the fundamental limitations of his theory of knowledge.

In short, the rationalistic spirit in Dai Zhen's philosophy and some metaphysical features in his world outlook and methodology mark the coming to an end of Chinese philosophy of the medieval age, either in the form of arbitrary "opinions" or in the form of directly perceived "truth." A new stage of philosophy characteristic of early modern times will rise up to replace the old one. Such is the philosophy of the coming stage, established on the foundation of the natural sciences and characterized by metaphysical methods.

35.

From the Opium War to the Taiping Rebellion

After the Qing period of the "Prosperous Reigns of Kangxi,Yongzheng and Qianlong emperors" came to an end which lasted for more than a century (1662-1795), serious social unrest arose in China, as the old feudal system was on the verge of collapse and the seeds of capitalism, which had been choked and suppressed in the historical backflows of the Ming and Qing dynasties, once again germinated. In the meantime, Western capitalist countries started hammering on the tightly closed gate of China, with the intention of exploiting the country's huge and untapped markets, to the extent of smuggling in large amounts of opium. These factors finally led to the First Opium War launched by the British in 1840. From then on, the history of China entered a new epoch in which the feudal society began to turn into a semi-colonial, semi-feudal society.

Nevertheless, as Karl Marx pointed out, the importation of opium into China "failed to play a part of hypnosis; instead it played a part of awakening." The rapid changes in Chinese society and the extremely serious crises of the Chinese nation awakened many patriotic intellectuals, and stimulated them to open their eyes to the whole world. They underwent all kinds of hardships to seek the truth that might save the country and the people from the impending danger. The question, "In which direction should China go?" hotly debated in China's intellectual circles gave birth to three different schools of thought.

The first centered on the management of state affairs. This trend of thought emerged among the reformers within the landlord class. The second was the revolutionary ideology of the Taiping Tianguo (Heavenly Kingdom of Great Peace), which appeared in the form of theology and represented the interests of the peasant class. The third was the thought of early reformism, which reflected the preliminary development of capitalism. Although these ideologies failed to form complete systems of their own, they all absorbed elements of Western culture, and they all challenged the old traditions. Their importance lies in the fact that they heralded the advent of Chinese philosophy of modern times.

Gong Zizhen and Wei Yuan were representative of the reformers within the landlord class. The hallmarks of this school of thought were patriotism and the demand for modernization. They lived in a transient period, in which the ancient Chinese civilization was in transit to its form in early modern times. Pushed by the tide of the times, they got rid of the bonds of the prevailing Song-Ming Neo-Confucianism, which was fond of empty talk, and the fashionable Qing textual criticism, which was far removed from practice. They advocated research into the management of state affairs in such fields as politics, economics and other practical subjects. They borrowed ideological data from the Confucian classics, and transformed these data into new ideas, such as "reforming the ways" and "changing the ancient ways," which appropriately reflected the trends of the times. Thus they became the inaugurators of the new ideological trends in China in modern times. Gong Zizhen and Wei Yuan were bosom friends. And, what is more, they had a similar style of study and similar ambitions, so their contemporaries habitually called them "Gong-Wei."

Gong Zizhen (1792-1841) was a native of Renhe County (near Hangzhou, Zhejiang Province). In his childhood he was taught by his grandfather-in-law Duan Yucai (1735-1815), a famous expert on textual criticism, philology and the critical interpretation of ancient texts. In his youth, he studied under Liu Fenglu (1776-1829), a scholar of the Confucian classics. But his horizons were wider than the traditional texts, and he paid attention to the problem of the management of state affairs. His works include *On Enlightened Monarchy and Good Ministers*, *A Paper Completed in 1815-1816*, *My View of Embryo Completed in 1812-*

1813, *On the Equalization of Riches*, *Patriarch and Agriculture* and *Miscellaneous Poems Written in 1839*. In these poems and essays, he exposes the long-standing abuses of the feudal system, castigates the decadent landlord class and calls for social reforms. He associated with a group of noble-minded patriots, including Lin Zexu, Wei Yuan and Huang Juezi, with whom he formed the reforming school within the landlord class, which was active in the middle of the 19th century. They campaigned against the importation of opium to China and called for resistance to the encroachment upon Chinese sovereignty of the Western capitalist countries. In 1839, carrying an imperial edict, when Lin Zexu went to Guangzhou to ban the opium trade there, Gong Zizhen wrote an article titled "To Revered Lin of Houguan, the Imperial Envoy," in which he put forth ten suggestions about the banning of opium. He hoped that by banning the opium trade there would appear a new situation in China in which "The price of silver would be stable, material resources reliable, and the public feeling calm." In short, he expressed the zeal of an ardent patriot. But although he was determined to dedicate himself to the service of his country, Gong Zizhen never rose high in the civil service, and died of illness at the age of forty-eight. Some time later, his writings were compiled into the *Complete Works of Gong Zizhen*.

Borrowing ideological data from the *Spring and Autumn Annals with Commentaries by Gongyang Gao*, Gong Zizhen reveals the serious crises with which the Qing Dynasty was faced in his time. When Dong Zhongshu of the Western Han Dynasty studied the *Spring and Autumn Annals with Commentaries by Gongyang Gao*, he divided the Spring and Autumn Period (770-467 BC) into three stages. The first stage was "the age which people know from legends"; the second stage was "the age about which people heard from others' lips"; And the third stage was "the age which people have seen with their own eyes." Later, in the Eastern Han Dynasty, when He Xiu wrote the *Explanation of the Spring and Autumn Annals with Commentaries by Gongyang Gao*, he renamed the three stages "the turbulent age of separatist forces," "the age of peace" and "the age of peace and prosperity." In Gong Zizhen's view, the history of each dynasty may be divided into three stages, namely, "the age of peace and prosperity," "the age of decadence," and "the age of turbulence." He considered that the Qing Dynasty in his day had passed its "age of peace and prosperity" and entered its "age of decadence." He describes the situation in the following lines: "Now the sun is declining in the west, and a mournful breeze has sprung up." He pointed out that the antagonism between the rich and the poor was becoming more and more serious as time passed. He says, "From the capital to the four directions, the general situation is like this: The rich households have become poor, and in the poor households starvation reigns." (*A Proposal to Set up Provinces in the Western Regions*) He also says, "The poor become bankrupt day by day, and the rich become opulent day by day." (*On the Equalization of Riches*) At that time, along with the intensification of social contradictions, there appeared the acute antagonism between "the imperial capital" and "the people who live in the mountains." The "imperial capital" refers to the feudal rulers of the day. Gong Zizhen describes them as fatuous and shameless, enmeshed in intrigue, oppressing and exploiting the masses of the people, and getting more and more decadent all the time. As for "the people who live in the mountains," who stood in opposition to the rulers, Gong Zizhen does not illustrate and perhaps he could not illustrate the properties of such a social force. But he has a premonition of the coming events when he says, "The people who live in the mountains will utter a great shout. Heaven and Earth will ring bells and beat drums for them, and a divine personage will stir up the waves for them." (*Esteem to the Helmets*) Their strength will be like a mighty and irresistible storm, he warns, in the midst of which the Qing Dynasty will be overthrown.

In the second place, Gong Zizhen further analyzes the causes for which the Qing Dynasty was doomed to decline. In his opinion, this was the evil consequence of a series of feudal practices which the Qing Dynasty followed unquestioningly. The main pillar of backwardness was the civil service examination system. This examination focused exclusively on knowledge of the classical *Four Books* of Confucianism. For centuries, scholars had trodden the same path of grinding, narrow study in order to pass the civil service examination, which was virtually the only way to achieve wealth and power. This resulted in a scramble to climb the social ladder, and led to rampant corruption and wrongdoing, to the detriment of independent thought and honorable ambition. (*Discourse on Politics*) The second major flaw in the governmental system was promotion according to status. It took thirty to forty years to reach the highest ranks of the civil service, counting from the first day of being a junior official, and promotion was strictly according to seniority.

As a result, officials tended to be over-cautious, afraid to make a mistake. They were indecisive, and lacked vitality. Outstanding young officials languished in lowly positions. The third drawback in the governmental system, according to Gong Zizhen, was absolute monarchy. "All affairs under Heaven, be they trivial or important, are handled according to one and the same rigid convention." (*On Enlightened Monarchy and Good Ministers·Part Four*) These were the feudal bonds that strangled talent, led to the decadence of the ruling class, and brought the Qing Dynasty face to face with serious crises. The only way out, Gong Zizhen urged, was for the Qing Dynasty rulers "to reform the ways." (*On Enlightened Monarchy and Good Ministers·Part Four*) He says as follows:

> "From ancient times to the present, every law has been revised time and again, for, as the accumulation of forces brings about new situations, every instance of events may be changed, and every social practice may be improved." (*A Letter to the Grand Secretary*)

Along with social developments, the ruling systems and methods must also be changed. Gong Zizhen says as follows:

> "The laws of one ancestor cannot avoid having defects and the discussion of a thousand men can sweep the country. It is much better to have conscientious self-reform than to be reformed by other people forcibly, isn't it?" (*A Paper Completed in 1815-1816·Part Seven*)

In Gong's view, no ruling system can be eternally unchangeable, and the ruler turns a deaf ear to public opinion at his peril. If a ruler does not carry out reforms himself, he will bring about unexpected and cataclysmic changes which may sweep him from the throne. This idea of "self-reform" expresses the conflicting attitudes of the reformers within the landlord class. On the one hand, they wanted political reforms, but on the other they feared an uprising by the masses of the people. Nevertheless, Gong Zizhen was the first thinker to articulate in an unequivocal manner the need for political reform in China in early modern times.

Still, Gong Zizhen cannot find the realistic forces which would guide the "reform." On this problem, he expresses himself in a contradictory manner. He sees the strength of the masses of the people, which "sages" of all sorts shunned. He affirms that the masses of the people play the major part in creating the world. In his opinion, "Heaven and Earth were created by man, by the masses of the people, not by any sages." (*My View of Embryo Completed in 1812-1813·Part One*) He further points out, "The dominator of the masses of the people is neither the Way nor the Great Ultimate, but the masses of the people under the name of Ego." (*Ibid*) That is, the dominator of the masses of the people is neither the mysterious "Heavenly Way" nor the fashionable "Great Ultimate," but the subjectivity of the masses of the people. However, he exaggerates man's subjective spiritual strength. In his opinion, "To avenge a great insult, to treat a great disease, to solve a great difficulty, to make a great plan, to learn a great Way, all depend on mental power." (*My View of Embryo Completed in 1812-1813·Part Four*) He attributes the force which changes reality to "mental power." Gong Zizhen pays great attention to "ego" and "mental power," showing that he emphasizes the importance of man and affirms the value of man. His views played an active and enlightening part in the struggle to criticize the feudal autocracy. His stress on "mental power" is a part of Gong Zizhen's thought which is influenced by Buddhist philosophy, and leads him to exaggerate the function of the subjective spirit. The journey from his call to "reform the ways" to his superstitious belief in "mental power" was typical of that followed by many progressive thinkers of early modern times who failed to find the objective forces with which to change reality.

Wei Yuan (1794-1857) was a native of Shaoyang County, Hunan Province. While young, he studied under Liu Fenglu, a famous expert on the Confucian classics. Later, he became an assistant to various civil and military governors, and in these positions he became involved in planning the transportation of grain by water to the capital, water conservancy, salt administration and suchlike practical affairs. This background gave him an insight into the management of state affairs and led him to compile the *Statecraft Essays of the Present Dynasty*. He was a close friend of Gong Zizhen and Lin Zexu, and shared their sense of the urgency to resist the encroachments of the Western capitalist countries. During the two opium wars, Wei Yuan became an aide to Yu Qian, governor-general of Jiangnan and Jiangxi provinces, and he himself experienced battles against the British invaders. The humiliation of the Qing Dynasty in the opium wars spurred Wei to write the *Histories of Holy Warriors*, in which he describes the military achievements of the early Qing Dynasty, with a view to arousing the dormant patriotic spirit of the Chinese people. Commissioned by Lin Zexu, he wrote the *Maps and Records of the Island Countries*, the first systematic introduction in Chinese to the history, geography, politics, economies and cultures of the rest of the world. This book played a great part in helping the Chinese people understand the West. And, what is more important, in the 1850s it became known in Japan, which was on the verge of a social revolution that would open up and modernize that country.

Wei Yuan's main work of philosophy is the *Silent Goblet*. Taking cognizance of the deepening of the various social contradictions at home and abroad, he treats this situation as philosophical problem. He says, "Nothing in the world exists just by itself, and everything in the world has its opposite." In other words, everything is a unity of opposites. But the opposites are not balanced, and so he says, "Of opposites, one must be the main one, while the other must be the subsidiary one. Only in this way can each of the opposites exist together." (*Silent Goblet· On Learning· Part Ten*) Such being the case, the opposites struggle against each other, and they turn into each other. He calls such a contradictory movement "adversity," and, in his opinion, it is in contradictions and struggles that the things develop. Therefore, he says, "In adverse circumstances there is a long life. In favorable circumstances there is early death. Adverse circumstances may turn one into a sage, and favorable circumstances may turn one into a madman. If grasses and plants have never had to bear frost and snow, they cannot have a firm life. If men have not gone through miseries, they cannot become wise." (*Silent Goblet· On Government· Part Two*) Everything will turn into its opposite when it reaches its apex: "The apex of summer does not beget summer but begets coldness, and the apex of winter does not beget winter but begets hotness. When one thing is inflected extremely, it will stretch out violently, when a bird has been prostrate on the ground for a long time, it will fly up at full speed." (*Silent Goblet· On Learning· Part Seven*) Wei pays much attention to the initiative of man in the process of the conversion of a contradiction: "Man will conquer Nature. Man may turn a rich, noble and long life into a poor, humble and short life. Man may also turn a poor, humble and short life into a rich, noble and long life." (*Silent Goblet· On Learning· Part Eight*)

Under the guidance of such a dialectic view of contradiction, Wei elaborates on his thought of "changing the ancient ways." He says as follows:

> "Back in the three dynasties of Xia, Shang and Zhou, Heaven was obviously different from today's Heaven, Earth was obviously different from today's Earth, the people were obviously different from today's people, and the things were obviously different from today's things." (*Silent Goblet·On Government·Part Five*)

Since Heaven, Earth, people and things are continuously changing in daily transformation from old to new, the social system can of course be no exception to this general rule. He points out, "Shoes are not necessarily of the same style, but nevertheless they are expected to fit the feet. Governments are not necessarily of the same style, but nevertheless they are expected to benefit the people." (*Silent Goblet·On Government·Part Five*) And he says, "The more completely the changes are carried out, the more convenience the people may enjoy." (*Ibid*) In the Qing Dynasty of his day so many evils have been accumulated that the governmental system has to be changed. But, by his call to "change the ancient ways" Wei does not mean the overthrow of the feudal system. For, in the meantime he also emphasizes, "What remains unchanged is only the Way." (*Silent Goblet·On Government·Part Five*) In other words, in his opinion, the feudal system and its associated superstitions cannot be changed even a little bit. Right here we may see his serious limitations as a representative of the reformers within the landlord class.

On the basis of such a naively dialectic view of contradiction, Wei puts forth an outstanding solution for the problem of how to treat Western culture: "Learn advanced technologies from the foreign countries to subdue the foreign countries." (*Maps and Records of the Island Countries·Preface*) He is an outstanding patriot, but, in his view, resisting the foreign insults equals neither cutting off China from the outside world nor parochial arrogance. Instead, it is highly necessary to understand the West, learn from the West, and absorb the strong points of the West. Only by doing so can the Western invaders be defeated. In his opinion, it is worthwhile for the Chinese to learn earnestly from the West either in respect of urgent needs such as warships, cannons and military arts or in respect of long-term needs such as industrial technology. Confidently, he predicts that by learning from the West the Chinese nation will be able to keep up with the West. He says, "The current tendencies in society are getting more and more open with each passing day. And more and more wisdom is brought into play with each passing day. Very soon I shall see that the Nation of the Eastern Seas is similar to the nations of the Western Seas." (*Maps and Records of the Island Countries·Book 2*)

The urgency of learning the correct way to manage state affairs is also reflected in his theory of knowledge. And this constitutes his view of knowledge and action, which lays stress on practice:

> "Only after you have come to some place can you know something about that place. Only after you have practiced something can you know how difficult that thing is. How can it be that without going to some place one can know something about that place?" (*Silent Goblet·On Learning·Part Two*)

In his opinion, only by practice can one acquire knowledge. In order that he might get to know something about the West, he himself once went to Hong Kong and Macao, which had been invaded and occupied by Western countries at that time, to investigate Western culture. In his view, such sages as are believed to have knowledge by birth have never existed at all. This is a materialist idea according to Wei Yuan's theory of knowledge.

Nevertheless, when Wei probes the role that rational thinking plays, he once again puts forth a view which is contradictory to the above-mentioned ideas. In his opinion, "a thorough enlightenment of the mental sources leads me to understand that the myriad things are originally in my mind. This is the great knowledge and the great awakening." (*Silent Goblet·On Learning·Part Two*) In this, he is similar to Gong Zizhen, for he exaggerates the function of the "mind" in the same way.

The contributions and limitations in the thoughts of Gong Zizhen and Wei Yuan characterize the ideology of the forerunners of enlightenment in China of early modern times in a typical way. These constitute the beginning of the contradictory movement in Chinese philosophy in early modern times, which exerted a wide and profound influence upon the development of Chinese philosophy in the coming periods. In Liang Qichao's opinion, both Gong Zizhen and Wei Yuan played an important part in liberating thought in the late Qing Dynasty. He says, "The germination and sprouts of all the new thoughts must be traced back to Gong Zizhen and Wei Yuan." (*A General Tendency in the Changes of Chinese Academic Ideas*)

Following the two opium wars, Western countries speeded up their expansion in China, while the Qing Dynasty intensified its oppression and exploitation of the people. These two trajectories combined stirred up all kinds of social contradictions, and directly led to the eruption of the Taiping Rebellion in 1851. This was a major peasant uprising which dealt a heavy blow to the decadent and declining Qing Dynasty, but at the same time it made an outstanding contribution to the ideological development of China in modern times. Hong Xiuquan and Hong Ren'gan, the two leaders of the revolutionary movement of the Taiping Heavenly Kingdom belong to the category of advanced Chinese intellectuals of early modern times who turned to the West for inspiration in their quest to save their country and people. Their ideas constitute a major link in the developmental chain of Chinese philosophy in early modern times.

Hong Xiuquan (1814-1864) was a native of Huaxian County, Guangdong Province. He was born into a peasant family, and later became a teacher at an old-style private school in the countryside. Having failed several times in the civil service examinations, he gave up all hope of an official career, and turned to the newly introduced Western Christianity for solace. The God Worshipping Society, which he set up in 1843, had all the outward trappings of Christianity together with a messianic vision of a peasant revolution which would overthrow the Qing Dynasty and set up the "Heavenly Kingdom of Great Peace (Taiping Tianguo)." In the period 1846-1848, Hong published his ideas in a series of poems and essays, including *A Song on the Origin of the Way and Salvation*, *A Sermon on the Origin of the Way and Awakening*, *A Sermon on the Origin of the Way and Consciousness* and *The Great Peaceful Heaven and Sun*. In these writings he formed a comparatively complete system of theological thought.

In the first place, Hong asserts that the "Heavenly God" is the sole genuine deity, and all the people in the world are children of this god. "They were born because all of them have been endowed with the monist vitality of the Heavenly God." Therefore, "all the people in the world are members of the same family, and all mortals are brothers." However, those who oppose the Heavenly God are "Yama monsters, which are old snakes, spirits and ghosts, which are adept at changing into other monstrous forms and bringing constant calamities upon mankind. They bewitch mortals, and take their souls away from them." (*A Sermon on the Origin of the Way and Consciousness*) Thus it is clear that the "Heavenly God" and the "Yama monsters" are extremely antagonistic to each other, symbolizing the struggle between the upright and bright forces and the evil and dark forces, or, in more concrete terms, representing the class antagonism between the Chinese peasants and their feudal rulers. Hong preached that in the final fierce struggle, the "Heavenly God" would defeat the "Yama monsters." The world will change from disorder to order, from darkness to brightness, from "an absurd, perverse, thoughtless and treacherous society" to "a fair, peaceful, just and upright society." (*A Sermon on the Origin of the Way and Awakening*) In consequence, he called on the broad masses of the people to wipe out the monsters. He says, "All mortals, all our brothers and sisters ought to wipe out the monsters. We are anxious that our action might come too late." (*A Sermon on the Origin of the Way and Consciousness*) Essentially, this is a call for class struggle to overthrow the Qing Dynasty.

In the second place, Hong maintains that all objects of worship except for the "Heavenly God" must be overthrown. This leads him to condemn Confucius, the icon of centuries of feudal orthodoxy. He pointed to the Confucian doctrines as the root cause of all the evils and crimes of the feudal rulers. He says, "I have investigated the reason why the monsters make trouble. I find that there are many mistakes in the books by which Confucius teaches the people." And he invented the following fable: "One day, the Heavenly God blamed Confucius for the fact that he had misguided some people. And he ordered the angels to whip Confucius. The so-called sage knelt down before the Heavenly Brother named Christ, and begged for mercy time and again. But this did not save him from a whipping" (*The Great Peaceful Heaven and Sun*).

Hong is remarkable for putting forth the idea that "The Heavenly Kingdom is near, because the Heavenly Kingdom is right here in the mortal world." (*Notes to the Authorized Edicts of the Late Heavenly King*) And he urged the masses of the people to rise up in arms and establish the "Heavenly Kingdom of Great Peace (*Taiping Tianguo*)." In 1853, at the head of a massive peasant uprising, Hong established the capital of his Heavenly Kingdom in Nanjing. One of his first acts was to issue the *Heavenly Land System* — a blueprint for an earthly paradise. In the new order, the feudal land tenure system was completely abolished, and, "All the fields under Heaven are plowed by all the people under Heaven." The farmland was distributed to every household on a per capita basis. As for the harvest, except for that portion used for food, all had to be handed over to the national treasury. Special food requirements, such as were needed for festivals and celebrations were doled out from the national treasury. "If there is farmland, it is plowed by the people; if there is rice, it is enjoyed by the people; if there are clothes, they are worn by the people; if there is money, it is used by the people. In short, in everything everybody is equal, so everybody dresses warmly and eats his or her fill" (*Heavenly Land System*). These ideas are essentially those of Utopian socialism based on the natural economy of small-scale agricultural production. They are the consummate generalization of the economic demands put forth by peasant rebels of the previous millennia.

Hong's thought played the major role in sparking and guiding the revolutionary movement of the Taiping Heavenly Kingdom. Zeng Guofan (1811-1882), the leading ideologist of the landlord class at that time and a military commander who played a major role in the suppression of the Taiping Heavenly Kingdom, wrote, "The rites, righteousness, human relations, odes, classics, codes and laws which have existed for several thousand years were thrown away and swept clean in a single day [by the Taipings]! This is not only a great calamity which has befallen our Qing Dynasty but also a blasphemy against the Confucian ethical code, which has been in existence ever since the world was created." (*A Denunciation for Suppressing the Bandits in Guangdong*) This quotation highlights the alarm felt by the feudal ruling class of the Qing Dynasty at the Taipings' challenge to all aspects of traditional society. However, there were bourgeois reformers who admired the Taiping doctrines, and took the revolutionary road themselves. The most notable of these were Sun Yat-sen and Zhang Taiyan. Both praised Hong's revolutionary spirit, and Sun Yat-sen once claimed to be a successor of Hong. Zhang Taiyan said,

"I have observed Mr. Hong carefully. He raised an army for a just cause. Among his foremost opponents were Zeng Guofan and Li Hongzhang, both base persons with a mild appearance and a treacherous heart." (*The Revolutionary Army·Preface*)

Nevertheless, in Hong's ideas of peasant revolution there are serious limitations. First, it is couched in the form of theology and strongly tinged with religious feeling. Since he sublimates the strength of the peasant revolution into the dominant power of the supreme Heavenly God, his thought was unable to guide the revolutionary movement of the broad masses in a correct way. Second, although Hong aimed at overthrowing the dark rule of the Qing Dynasty and its ages-old feudal system, he himself was not free of feudal consciousness. For instance, his new "earthly paradise" would be ruled by Hong as emperor, and in fact would be nothing more than a kind of agricultural Utopian socialism, in which the small producers, having wiped out exploitation, oppression and private ownership, would live and work on the basis of absolute egalitarianism. These were the flaws in the ideology of the Taiping Heavenly Kingdom, which finally led to its downfall.

Hong Ren'gan (1822-1864) was a younger brother of Hong Xiuquan. He was one of the first members of the God Worshipping Society. Later, he fled to Hong Kong to escape government persecution. There he came into contact with aspects of Western science and culture, and so acquired a better understanding of the outside world than most of his contemporaries. Such being the case, he finally became an intellectual of early modern times, contributing new ideas. In 1859, having undergone all kinds of hardships, he arrived in Nanking (now Nanjing) and became one of the important leaders at the late stage of the Taiping Heavenly Kingdom. In order to rejuvenate the revolutionary cause of the Taipings, Hong Ren'gan wrote the *New Guide to Government*, and presented it to Hong Xiuquan. In this book, he put forth a complete plan for social reforms, which had some capitalist elements to them. The *New Guide to Government* can be considered a concentrated embodiment of Hong Ren'gan's thought.

In the first place, in the *New Guide to Government* he urges the setting up of a modern-type economy, in which capitalist industry and commerce are developed. He says that it is necessary "to start construction of land and water transportation," and to manufacture and operate railways and ships; in short, modern communications. He also advises his brother, the "Heavenly King," to permit private businessmen to prospect for and extract minerals. To him, it is necessary to develop a modern mining industry. And he advocates "encouraging suitable persons to invent and create, and to permit them to sell their inventions or manufactures." That is, it is necessary to develop modern industrial arts and technologies. He also points out the need for a banking system which would issue paper money. Even more remarkable, he was ahead of his time in recommending the setting up of a free press so that "current affairs and daily events or incidents may be reported." When public opinion is reflected in freely circulating newspapers, "what is going on at higher levels may be made known to lower levels, and vice versa, so that the higher may not plot against the lower." In the field of judicial institutions, he maintains, it is necessary to combine "the use of personnel" with "the search for ideas and plans." Attention must be paid to the selection of people with excellent talents and to the establishment of a legal system so that "both sides may support each other." In his opinion, "The inappropriate use of personnel may destroy the laws. Inappropriate ideas and plans may bring harm to the people."

In the *New Guide to Government*, he advocates the construction of a modern civilization by reforming traditional ideas, consciousness, customs and habits. For instance, it is necessary to "demolish temples, monasteries and other places of worship." As for the properties of these institutions, they may be used for building hospitals. In this way, "the people may be saved from superstitious ways and enter the bright kingdom." He resolutely opposes superstitious practices such as the use of "the eight yin-yang diagrams" and for fortune-telling, and geomantic practices which may obstruct the exploitation of minerals. He points out, "In the big mountains and deep recesses there are usually ores of gold, silver, copper, iron, tin, coal and suchlike useful minerals, which are of great benefit to the livelihood of the people and the economy of the country. But people frequently talk about evil omens if the land is disturbed, so that precious minerals remain unexploited. The people have not used them up till now. I have to ask everybody to think over the question. Between geomancy and minerals, which is beneficial to the people? Geomancy is a doubtful mass of superstition, but it remains as solidly believed as before. It is truly a great pity!"

In short, the ideological features of the *New Guide to Government* lie in "destroying what is old and establishing in its place the new order of things." With great efforts, the author depicts "a new Heaven, a new Earth and a new world," by which he means the spread of capitalism as it had developed in early modern times. For the same purpose, Hong Ren'gan wrote an essay titled, *Elites Returning to Truth*, in which he philosophically demonstrates the objective necessity of transforming the old into the new. He says, "The clouds are so pure, and the moon is so bright. When spring comes, the mountains become beautifully lush. Only by washing can filth be cleaned away. Only by reforming can things be renewed." In his view, "destroying what is old and establishing in its place the new order of things" is the objective law of the myriad things in the universe, and this law is irresistible. The people are able to change the old things and create a new world through revolutions and changes.

Hong Ren'gan was a loyal and steadfast leader of the revolutionary movement of the Taiping Heavenly Kingdom, and was also an advanced thinker who first advocated the spread of capitalist civilization in China in early modern times. In his masterpiece *New Guide to Government* he attempts to break through the ideological limitations of the old type of revolutionary movement waged by the peasants. He aims at leading the Taiping Heavenly Kingdom from the goal of agricultural Utopian socialism, to capitalism and modernization. Therefore, in respect of seeking truth from the West, he is more advanced than Hong Xiuquan by a big step.

In 1864 the Qing Dynasty suppressed the Taiping revolution. After that, a new polarization emerged within the ruling class. There appeared a group of people devoted to "new policies for self-improvement," called the *yangwu* (foreign affairs) faction. Under the stimulus of foreign contacts and new policies, some of the country's bureaucrats, landlords and merchants began to engage in modern industry and commerce, laying the foundations of national capitalism in China. Reflecting this trend in the ideological sphere, there appeared a group of intellectuals who raised new demands for reforms. These demands reflected the interests and wishes of the emergent national bourgeoisie. On the basis of these factors, the ideological trend of reformism flourished from the 1870s to the 1890s. Among the reformists, Wang Tao (1828-1897), Xue Fucheng

(1838-1894), Ma Jianzhong (1845-1900), Zheng Guanying (1842-1921) and He Qi (1859-1914) were the representatives.

Wang Tao, styled Zhongtao, was a native of Suzhou, Jiangsu Province. In his early years, he worked as a compiler and proofreader at the Ink Sea Publishing House, which was run by British missionaries. He visited Britain, France and some other countries. Later, he fled to Hong Kong because of his pro-Taiping sympathies. There, he founded a newspaper called the *Circulation Daily*, through which he propagated reforms and self-improvement for China. Among his works the *Outer Chapters of Taoyuan's Anthology* is the best known.

Wang Tao had a better understanding of Western capitalism than most of his contemporaries. Having examined the ancient and present societies and cultures of the West and China, he points out, "The reason why the people have to change the ancient in order to have a better understanding of the present lies in the urgency of the situation." (*Outer Chapters of Taoyuan's Anthology·Political Reform·Part One*) Change is an inevitable tendency of historical development. He maintains that China underwent its first great change when the Qin Dynasty unified the Warring States. Its second great change was occurring in his own time. If Confucius had been living in modern times, he would have followed the changes of the times, too.

What exactly does Wang Tao mean when he says, "Change the ancient in order to have a better understanding of the present"?

In the sphere of the economy he opposes the *yangwu* faction, which monopolized the new-type industry and commerce of the day. He demands that national capital should be cultivated and developed. Various sources of profit, for instance, those which come from the natural resources of the mountains and rivers, the profits from the labor of the workers who operate the machines, and the profits from trade, must "all return to the common people." Only in this way can the development of the nation's industry and commerce be guaranteed. He says, "When the people's livelihood is sufficient, the prestige of the country will rise naturally. After that, we can pursue every great cause." (*Outer Chapters of Taoyuan's Anthology·An Addition to the Proposal of Wiping Out Rickets and Other Chronic Diseases*)

In the field of politics he advocates "a joint government of both the monarch and the people," by which he means a constitutional monarchy. He opposes leadership by an emperor or king, because only a ruler as wise as the sage kings Yao and Shun can ensure a long period of stability. Likewise, it is not a good thing for "the people to take the lead," because, in such a case it would be difficult to unify the legal system, as people are of different minds. So he proposes, "The best way is a joint government of both the monarch and the people. Then the top level and the lower levels will be in harmony. The sufferings of the common people will be known by the top level, and the kindness and grace of the monarch will reach the common people." (*Outer Chapters of Taoyuan's Anthology·Emphasis of the People·Part Two*)

As far as culture is concerned, he lays stress on learning modern sciences (namely, the investigation of the physical world) from the West. He yearned for "a prosperous development in China of scholarship, technology and industry." (*Rambling Notes Written While Wandering Abroad·Frequent Opening of Grand Banquets*) When traveling in Europe he visited the World Expo in Paris and Oxford University in England. He gave high praise to Britain's progress in natural sciences, saying, "Britain lays stress on the branches of practical learning, such as astronomy, geography, electricity, firearms, meteorology, optics and chemistry." (*Rambling Notes Written While Wandering Abroad·Creation of Wonders*) Confidently he predicts, "I am sure China is able to change its backwardness and surpass the Western nations in one hundred years. It is not a difficult thing, I think." (*A Proposal for the Curriculum of the Scientific Academy*)

Nevertheless, Wang Tao cautions that the reforms he advocates should be restricted to the sphere of "implements" and not extended to the "Way." What needs to be changed is only the concrete contents of economy, culture and politics. As for the cardinal guides and constant virtues of feudalism, which were established on the basis of the doctrines of Confucius and Mencius, they must not be tampered with: "As for the implements, they may be obtained from the Western countries. But as for the Way, we must persist in this, as it is our own. This is because the doctrines of Confucius and Mencius must remain unchanged for ten thousand generations." (*Outer Chapters of Taoyuan's Anthology*) Wang Tao's theory of the relationship between the Way and implements reflects the contradictory characteristics of the Chinese national bourgeoisie, which was beginning to take shape at that time.

Zheng Guanying (1842-1921) was a native of Xiangshan County (present-day Zhongshan County), Guangdong Province. In his early years, he worked for shipping companies in Shanghai. Later, he started his own business, which was managed in a modern way, and thus became one of China's first national capitalists. In the 1880s, the top state officials Li Hongzhang and Sheng Xuanhuai commissioned Zheng to build up China's industries, and in succession he held the posts of director-general of the Shanghai Machine-Weaving Bureau, Shanghai Merchants Steam Navigation Company, Shanghai Telegraph Bureau and Hanyang Iron and Steel Mill. Deeply involved in the study of Western-type modernization, he came to see clearly that China was facing a severe national crisis. It was his earnest belief that national rejuvenation was to be found in learning from the West. Following the Sino-French Wars of 1883-1885, Zheng was cast into profound melancholy: "Indignantly I resent yonder nation's demands, profoundly I have pity for the Chinese court's misjudgment." He wrote a book titled *Frightening Words for a Prosperous Age,* in which he expounds his reform theories:, "In my book titled *Frightening Words for a Prosperous Age,* I raise a cry of warning to wake up the people in political circles. I hope that they may come to know how to love the country and protect the people." (*Sequel to Frightening Words for a Prosperous Age·Book 4*)

Zheng urged the adoption of capitalism and a constitutional monarchy with a parliament. After examining the systems of some of the countries in the West, he draws the following conclusion: "As for the Western countries, the origin of their politics and economies does not merely lie in their warships and cannons; instead it lies in the fact that the upper and lower chambers work in concert, and their education is highly developed." (*Frightening Words for a Prosperous Age·Author's Preface*) In his opinion, although the Western countries are different from China in respect of national conditions, there is also the distinction between foundation and function, between the fundamental and the incidental. And he says, "There, talented people are cultivated in schools and colleges. Politics are discussed in the parliaments. The monarch and the people constitute one body. The top level and the lower levels work with one heart. They tend to deal with concrete matters relating to work, and they refrain from empty talk. They act only after a careful plan is made. These are the foundation. As for steamships, cannons, rifles, naval ships, railways and electric wires, they are the function." (*Ibid*) "Foundation" means the representative system based on the democracy of Western capitalism and its guiding thought, whereas "function" means the scientific and technological achievements of the West in modern times and material civilization. In his view, both sides are inseparable. If we desire to learn from the Western countries, we should not only learn the "function," which is marked by "warships and cannons," the "foundation," which is marked by "the one body of the monarch and the people." It is not enough to pay attention to the manufacture of guns and cannons, to the construction of railroads, to the exploration of minerals, and so on. If we refuse to reform the political system, we can never have a real grasp of the strong points of the Western countries. He correspondingly rebukes the feudal diehards as they hate and suppress "Western learning." Additionally, he points out that there are some defects in the "new policies for self-improvement" advocated by the *yangwu* faction. It is true that the *yangwu* faction has learned something of the Western "function," but the *yangwu* faction has not yet understood anything of the Western "foundation." Zheng attributed the strength of the Western capitalist countries to parliamentary democratic system in which "political affairs are discussed in public." This guarantees the transmission of the ruler's orders from above, and at the same time the transmission of the people's will from below. As a consequence, it is possible for "collective purposes to form a fortress." (*Frightening Words for a Prosperous Age·Parliaments·Part One*) In the second place, the parliaments are in charge of the "promotion and demotion of all officials." (*Frightening Words for a Prosperous Age·Local Administration·Part One*) In the West, "Everybody is allowed to display his talents fully, the soil is put to the best use, there is a smooth flow of goods," and this results in those countries becoming rich and their military forces efficient. (*Frightening Words for a Prosperous Age·Author's Preface*) It is necessary for China to set up a parliament and to reform its politics, because they are the basis on which the national power and influence may be enhanced and foreign aggression resisted. He urges that the following situation be brought about: "The top level and the lower levels work with one heart. The monarch and the people become one body. Then we will have no worries that hostile countries and foreign forces may insult us. Is that not right?" (*Frightening Words for a Prosperous Age·Parliaments·Part One*)

These reformist ideas of Zheng are more progressive than Wang Tao's. Nevertheless, Zheng also fails to cast off the bonds of the traditional theory of the relationship between the Way and implements. Although he maintains that it is necessary to learn the foundations of Western capitalism, he thinks that such learning cannot replace the doctrines of Confucius and Mencius, which are the core of Chinese tradition. He persists in the view that the implements may be changed if necessary, whereas the Way cannot be changed even a little bit. He says as follows:

> "The Way is the fundamental, and the implements are the incidental. The implements can be changed, but the Way cannot be changed. We must be clear that politics is indeed changeable, and that is the way we can make our country rich. But no shifts in politics can be compared with the importance of the classics of Confucius and Mencius, which contain the constant guiding principles for us." (*Frightening Words for a Prosperous Age·A Reading Guide*)

Of course, when Zheng says, "The implements can be changed, but the Way cannot be changed," he does not mean the same thing as the proposition, "Heaven changeth not, likewise the Way changeth not." His thought is not just in accordance with the proposition which the ruling class of feudalism had preached for a long time. He has no intention of propping up the political system of feudalism. Instead, he hopes that the Chinese political system may be transformed according to the outlook of the bourgeoisie in modern times. Zheng's view on the relationship between the Way and implements reflects the duality of the Chinese national bourgeoisie at the early stage of its growth. Such a duality pushes Zheng into an ideological contradiction. He has to reform the political system of feudalism while sustaining the cardinal guides and constant virtues which serve such a system.

Zheng's thought exerted a direct influence on the Reform Movement of 1889. What is more, it played a great part in enlightening Chinese intellectuals in the coming years. In fact, the young Mao Zedong himself was fond of reading *Frightening Words for a Prosperous Age*.

36.

The Philosophy of Enlightenment in the Reform Movement of 1898

By the end of the 19th century, major capitalist countries had entered the stage of imperialism. After the Sino-Japanese War of 1894-1895, the big imperialist powers intensified their exports of capital to China, controlling the railways, grabbing land concessions and manipulating the central finance and customs departments. In fact, they divided large parts of China among themselves, regarding them as their own spheres of influence. China was facing a national crisis, in which its whole territory would soon be carved up among the imperialist powers. In such a grim situation, as a newly rising class, the national bourgeoisie of China came upon the political stage. And in 1898 its leading spirits started the Reform Movement. This was a patriotic movement for saving the nation from extinction, but it was also a movement of ideological emancipation, in which enlightened thinkers emerged from among the bourgeois reformers. They turned to the West to find ways to save the country and the people. They propagated the new culture of the Western bourgeoisie, and they opposed the old culture of Chinese feudalism. Thus, there appeared an acute struggle between the "new learning" and the "old learning," and between "Western learning" and "Chinese learning." The reformers learned from Western natural sciences and Western philosophy. With this foundation, they tentatively formed a modern philosophical world outlook with Chinese characteristics. The representatives of the enlightenment movement included Kang Youwei, Tan Sitong and Yan Fu.

Although the Reform Movement of 1898 fizzled out and its adherents were executed or fled into exile, enlightenment thought marked the beginning of a new stage in the history of Chinese philosophy, which accelerated the great awakening of the Chinese nation.

Kang Youwei (1858-1927) was a native of Nanhai County, Guangdong Province, who held the honorific title "Master Nanhai." In his early years he studied Neo-Confucianism and Idealism. Visits to Hong Kong and Shanghai gave him glimpses of Western modernization. He was struck by the contrast between capitalist advances and inventions, and the grim situation of China. He devoted himself to an extensive study of the Western knowledge of natural sciences and the humanities. Clashes between China and France in 1883-1895 caused Kang Youwei to adopt an outlook of passionate patriotism. Although he was a scholar by training and nature, he took an active part in the political struggle aimed at changing the feudal system, and soon became a leader of the enlightenment movement. The ten years from 1888 to 1898 were the golden age of Kang Youwei's political and academic activities. He submitted seven written statements to the emperor with suggestions for reforms, launching the Reform Movement. He also wrote two books, laying the groundwork for doing away with the fetishes and superstitions of traditional feudalism. One was *An Investigation into the Classics Forged in the New Learning Period*, and the other was *An Investigation into Confucius' Institutional Reforms*. In the former, he declares that the Confucian classics are forged canons, and in the latter he claims that Confucius was a reformer who "carried out reforms under the cloak of ancient conventions." In his opinion, the reason why Confucius wrote the *Spring and Autumn Annals* was that he desired to propagate the idea of the evolution of the three ages. These two books shored up the movement for political reform among intellectuals. During this period he also wrote *Outer and Inner Chapters*, *Lectures on the Heavens* and *Book of Great Unity*. In doing so, he formed a world outlook based on the philosophy of modern times. In June 1898, Emperor Guangxu accepted the necessity of reform, and appointed Kang Youwei as a Part-Time Secretary in the Ministry of Foreign Affairs, namely an adviser to the emperor. Kang wrote many memorials to the throne, and was regarded as the ideological leader of the reform movement. But a hundred days later, in a palace coup, diehard conservatives headed by Empress Dowager Cixi suppressed the reform movement, and Kang had to flee abroad. During his exile, he continued to dream about bringing about a constitutional monarchy for China. He founded the Party to Preserve the Emperor, gradually becoming conservative in his thinking and opposing the bourgeois democratic revolution. After the Revolution of 1911, Kang returned to China. He attacked democracy and the republican system, and advocated worshipping Confucius and reading the classics. Besides, he had a hand in Zhang Xun's intrigues aiming at restoration of the imperial system. Kang's final transformation was from being a conservative to becoming a reactionary.

The most fundamental category of Kang's philosophy is "origination." He says, "Origination is the foundation of the myriad things. Man and Heaven partake of the same origination." (*Dong Zhongshu's Doctrines of the Spring and Autumn Annals·Book 6·Part One*) In his opinion, both the natural world and man have "origination" as their foundation. He explains, "Origination is the material force." (*Ibid*) In his vocabulary, "origination" means "the material force of origination." It is the primordial base from which Heaven and Earth are formed. Nevertheless, Kang does not simply take over the traditional theory of "material force"; instead, he tries to endow his doctrine of "the material force of origination" with new content taken from the modern natural sciences.

Kang accepts the nebular hypothesis which was put forth by Immanuel Kant (1724-1804) in his *Allgemeine Naturgeschichte zu einer Theorie des Himmels* and Pierre-Simon de Laplace (1749-1827) in his *Exposition du système du Monde*. Kang applies the nebular hypothesis to explaining the category of "the material force of origination." In his view, the so-called nebula is nothing but "gas." According to the nebular hypothesis, he says, "Before the various heavenly bodies were created, they were visible or invisible gases, which were floating in the universe, and whose molecules attracted one another." (*Lectures on the Heavens·Book 2*) He continues: "As the gases accumulated over a long period of time, they became Heaven. After a long term of interaction, heat and gravity appeared, as did light and electricity. These were the result of changes in the primordial base. In like manner, the sun appeared. The sun begot the Earth, and the Earth begot the myriad things." (*Outer and Inner Chapters·Principle and Material Force*) Such is Kang's doctrine of the "nebula-material force of origination," by which he makes a materialist explanation of the evolution of the universe.

In accordance with this doctrine, he criticizes Zhu Xi's ideas. For instance, Zhu Xi says, "There is first principle and then there is material force." (*Questions and Answers on the Works of Mencius·Book 3*) And he says, "There is this principle, which begets this material force afterwards." (*Classified Conversations of Zhu Xi·Book 1*) In Kang's opinion, "everything originates from material force. After there is the material force, there is principle. What begets human beings and the myriad things is material force." (*Oral Accounts of the Thatched Hall Surrounded by Ten Thousand Trees*) And he says, "Master Zhu Xi once said, 'Principle exists before material force.' This view is wrong." (*Ibid*)

But Kang fails to explain the cause of material movement in a correct way, because he has only a superficial knowledge of the natural sciences developed in modern times. In his opinion, the reason why "the material force of origination" is able to attract, absorb and collect lies in that it has some "consciousness," and in that there exists a "god" that is possessed of spiritual properties. In other words, "the material force of origination" is also a kind of "knowing force" or "spiritual force." Such a "knowing force" or "spiritual force" is similar to "electricity." It is changing all the time and in an unpredictable way, and it is a force penetrating everywhere. He says, "The knowing force is the soul. It is similar to electricity. The knowing force exists in everything." (*Commentary on the Evolutions of Rites*) He says, "Everything has electricity, and everything has spirit. Light and electricity are able to convey everything, and the spiritual force is able to perceive everything." (*Book of Great Unity·Section A*) In his view, the so-called "knowing force" or "spiritual force" is nothing but "electricity that has perception." (*Ibid*) This leads to the theory that everything material is possessed of consciousness. But this cannot explain the relationship between matter and spirit in a correct way.

With such a fundamental error, Kang goes so far as to confuse substantial entity with spiritual phenomenon. In his opinion, "The mind that cannot bear to see the suffering of others is humanity. It is electricity. It is ether. Everyone has it." (*Subtle Meaning of the Book of Mencius·Book 1*) Thus he draws the following conclusion: "All things in the world and I are one uniformity, and there is no demarcation line between the two sides." Later, he says, "All things in the world are my own self and my own self is all things in the world." (*Commentary on the Doctrine of the Mean*) In short, he exaggerates the role of subjective spirit.

In Kang's opinion, "the mind that cannot bear to see the suffering of others" innate to man is "humanity" or the "humane heart," which is able to grow up to be or develop into the myriad things. He describes such a mind: "It is the seat of all transformations, the root of all things, the source of all things, the seed that will become the tree reaching up to the sky, the drop of water that will become the great sea." (*Subtle Meaning of the Book of Mencius·Book 1*) And further, he emphasizes that the benevolent governmental measures of the bourgeoisie may be realized by enlarging "the mind that cannot bear to see the suffering of others." So he says, "All benevolent governmental measures proceed from the mind that cannot bear to see the suffering of others." (*Ibid*) He attributes all that is morally praiseworth to the humane mind: "Man's feeling of love, human civilization, the progress of mankind, down to Great Peace and Great Unity all originate in this mind." (*Ibid*) Previously, he took "origination" for the foundation of his theory, but now he takes "humanity" for the foundation. In this transformation, his doctrine of "the material force of origination" stumbles into the pitfall of idealism. Kang Youwei's philosophy gives much importance to the idea of "comprehensive reform." He reaches back as far as the *Book of Changes* for "changes and reforms" while at the same time accepting some of the achievements of the modern natural sciences. Reminding us that "the Heavenly Way values change," he says as follows:

> "This is because reform accords with the Heavenly Way. The Heavenly Way would not work if there were only day and no night or only winter and no summer. Heaven embraces change, and therefore Heaven continues to exist. Out of volcanoes flows gold. Seas change into mulberry fields, and mulberry fields into seas. Mount Liyang changes into a lake. The Earth embraces change, and therefore the Earth continues to exist. So also is the case with Man. In the process in which one person grows up to be an able-bodied man from a small child, changes take place in his figure, his complexion, his mood and his appearance. These changes happen to

everybody all the time." (*Memorial to the Throne about the Reforms of Peter the Great of Russia*)

Heaven, Earth and mankind undergo everlasting changes. There is nothing in this world that is eternally fixed, or unchangeable, or has eternally one and the same outlook. In his view, such changes are not merely quantitative ones; instead, they mean qualitative change in which the new qualities replace the old ones. The new superseding the old is an irresistible law. He says, "When a thing is new, it is powerful. When a thing is old, it is decrepit. When a thing is new, it is fresh. When a thing is old, it is rotten. When a thing is new, it is vigorous. When a thing is old, it is stiff. When a thing is new, it is communicable. When a thing is old, it is stagnant. This is the principle of all things." (*The Sixth Letter to the Qing Emperor*) Why do all things develop or change? In his opinion, this is because everything is made up of opposites. Antagonism and struggle of the opposites of a thing promote its change and development:

"Everything can be fixed in one. Only when there is the unification of opposites can there be the existence of a thing. Everything can be separated into two. Only when there is the struggle of opposites can there be any progress." (*Commentary on the Analects·Book 3*)

With such dialectical ideas, Kang assaults the traditional view that had remained the same for the previous 2,000 years, that is, "Heaven changeth not, likewise the Way changeth not." He also breaks through the limitation of the reformist view that appeared in the early stage of the reform movement, that "the implements may be changed, but the Way may not be changed." Thus, he provides the bourgeoisie with a theoretical weapon for the launch of political reforms.

Starting from this point, Kang concentrates on expounding on the problems concerning the evolution and reform of social systems:

> "The laws have accumulated over a long period of time, and so evils must have accumulated among them as thick as brambles. No law should remain the same for a hundred years." (*The Sixth Letter to the Qing Emperor*)

There can be no such thing as "rules handed down from our ancestors," which claim to be unchangeable for ten thousand generations.

All social systems ought to change along with the times, which change continuously. In his opinion, great changes had already taken place in Chinese society even before his time. For China, a vast empire with an especially long history, the only way out was to carry out comprehensive reforms in line with the development of the times. He says, "Political reform makes the country strong; conservation will destroy it." (*The Sixth Letter to the Qing Emperor*) He also says, "A comprehensive reform will make the country powerful; a small reform cannot avoid destroying the country." This comprehensive reform should be fourfold: "Reformation of the implements," "reformation of the events," "reformation of the government" and "reformation of the laws." The first refers to "purchasing warships and other types of military equipment," or it learning advanced technologies from the West. As for the "reformation of events," it refers to "setting up post offices and exploring mines," or developing modern-type industry and commerce. As for the "reformation of government," it refers to "changing the official system and holding general elections," or instituting the political system of capitalism. As for the "reformation of the laws," it refers to "following the example of the Meiji Reform in Japan," or changing the feudal system into the capitalist system. (Cf. *An Investigation of the Japanese Reform·Book 7*)

In Kang's view, since the opium wars there had appeared many advanced personages who advocated reforms. But it is a pity that all of them failed to put forth any plan for "comprehensive reform." Especially, they failed to point out the fundamental problem of the reform, which was to change the feudal system. He says as follows:

"If there is to be political reform, there must be reforms in the systems and laws. Otherwise it will not be political reform in the true sense." (*Chronological Autobiography of Kang Youwei Alias Nanhai*)

Only by persisting in comprehensive reform and in changing the old feudal system into a capitalist system can China embark on the developmental road to capitalism. This is a far more audacious plan than those of other enlightenment thinkers of his time, in that this plan surpasses the ideals of the reformers within the landlord class. Kang's ideas caused a sensation, and accelerated the process in which the Chinese nation started to waken.

Stressing comprehensive reform, Kang makes full use of the ideological data concerning the "evolution of three ages" from the *Spring and Autumn Annals with Commentaries by Gongyang Gao*. And on this basis he puts forth his ideal of great unity.

To recap, the "three ages" are "the age which people know from legends," "the age which people have heard from others" and "the age which people have seen with their own eyes." These three ages refer to three historical phases — the "age of disorder," the "age of rising peace" and the "age of great peace." And these three historical ages proceed in an orderly way and step by step, namely, from the "age of disorder" to the "age of rising peace," and then from the "age of rising peace" to the "age of great peace." The progress of mankind follows such a gradual order, as does the development of civilization. Progress and development can only be realized step by step. For instance, viewed from the angle of the degree of civilization, the age of disorder is a historical phase in which culture and education have not yet appeared; the age of rising peace is a when culture and education appear gradually; and only in the age of great peace can man enter upon a phase in which culture and education are perfect. (Cf. *Dong Zhongshu's Doctrines of the Spring and Autumn Annals·Book 2*) Viewed from the angle of social positions, the age of disorder is a historical phase in which women have to depend on men; the age of rising peace is a phase in which women's rights gradually attracted the attention of the people; only by the age of great peace can man enter a historical phase in which everybody is independent, men and women are equal, and people marry whom they will. (Cf. *An Investigation of the Subtle and Profound Language of the Spring and Autumn Annals*) Viewed from the angle of the political system, the age of disorder is a historical phase in which the ruler ruled absolutely; the age of rising peace is a phase in which constitutional monarchy was adopted; and the age of great peace is a phase in which democracy and republics are realized.

According to the characteristics of civilization of these three historical phases, Kang also calls the age of rising peace "the age of small peace," and the age of great peace "the age of great unity." In his opinion, for the previous 2,000 years China had been in a constant state of disorder. Through political reform, a constitutional monarchy may be realized. Only by that time can China leave the age of disorder and enter the age of rising peace. Only when its society has matured will China enter upon the ideal society of great peace.

The society of "great peace" is the only ideal state for man to strive for. In his masterpiece, titled *Book of Great Unity*, Kang describes his ideal state. In the society of great peace, there is democracy and a republic. "All people are equal. There are neither ministers nor concubines nor slaves. There are neither monarchs nor presidents. There are neither religious founders nor a pope." In the society of great peace, there are no states nor armies nor punishments. There is only one "public government" in the world. All the members of the legislative assembly are to be elected by the people. "The power to decide every major issue resides in the public." There is public ownership of the means of production: "All sectors of industry, agriculture and commerce must belong to the public." Machines are used extensively in all trades, and all trades are administered according to the methods of modern science and technology. "New principles are discovered every day, and new machines are invented every day. New technologies are adopted every day. There is no limit to creation. And man's new scope for creation is beyond imagination." In daily life, everybody's needs are satisfied to the fullest, whether for clothing, food, shelter or transportation. Society takes care of everybody's birth, death, illness and old age. "A job which an able-bodied man used to need a whole day to finish can now be finished in only three to four hours or in one to two hours. The rest of the time is to be used in either reading or touring or playing games." In Kang's opinion, seeking happiness and avoiding suffering are parts of the original nature of all human beings. Only in the society of great unity can great progress in politics, economy and life be made and all human beings be saved from the various kinds of sufferings created by past generations, enabled to live a happy and free life. In short, only in this way can the original nature of man be realized in a genuine way.

In accordance with his historical view of the "evolution of the three ages," Kang affirms that human society follows a process from lower to higher. He discloses the historical necessity that there must be a transition from feudal society to the capitalist society. He describes an ideal future society, which is possessed of an advanced material civilization and an advanced spiritual civilization, and, what is more, which is filled with humanist spirit. Thus he makes an important contribution to the development of Chinese philosophy in the early modern period. His ideal of "great unity" is an important achievement of the advanced thinkers of the Chinese bourgeoisie, who once turned to the West to seek truth. The ideal of "great unity" greatly surpasses the agricultural utopian socialism espoused by Hong Xiuquan. Nevertheless, in Kang's view of history there are serious limitations. In the first place, he fails to explain that the development of human society must follow objective laws. Instead, he adheres to the evolution of the three ages as an evolutionary pattern described by Confucius. In the second place, he fails to explain that the motive force of historical development is the broad masses of the people. Instead, he attributes social progress to "the mind that cannot bear to see the suffering of others" of the sages. In the third place, he fails to explain that "leaps forward" play an important role in the transition to different stages of historical progress. Instead, he divides each of the three ages into several minor stages. In his opinion, between these minor stages there cannot be any "skipping over the normal order" or any "leaps forward." Social progress can only "proceed in a fixed and orderly way, and step by step"; it can only be realized slowly or in a reformist way, bit by bit. He regards the society of "great unity" as an unachievable target or a matter to be left to the dim distant future. (Cf. *Commentary on the Evolution of the Rites·Preface*) Therefore, Kang's ideal of "great unity" is also utopian. As Mao Zedong says, "Kang Youwei wrote the *Book of Great Unity*, but he did not and could not find the way to achieve Great Unity." (*On the People's Democratic Dictatorship*)

Tan Sitong (1865-1898), styled Fusheng, was also known by the alias Zhuangfei. He was a native of Liuyang County, Hunan Province. In his early youth Confucianism influenced him in a rather profound way, and he was at first antagonistic toward the "Western learning." But China's defeat in the Sino-Japanese War of 1894-1895 shocked him out of his complacency. In 1895, he became acquainted with Liang Qichao (1873-1929), a disciple of Kang Youwei. Liang introduced him to Kang's thought. In 1896, Tan finished writing a book titled *Philosophy of Humanity*, which was a watershed in his thought, in that he changed from advocating "Chinese learning" to advocating "Western learning." Later, he organized the Society of the South in Hunan, and launched the *Hunan Newspaper*. He was active in propagating political reform, soon becoming the most radical of the young reformists associated with the Reform Movement of 1898. In that year, Tan was summoned to Beijing by Emperor Guangxu to serve as one of the secretaries of the Grand Council to supervise the reform. The feudal diehards, headed by Empress Dowager Cixi, suppressed the Reform Movement when the military forces of Yuan Shikai failed to intervene. At this juncture, Tan was advised to flee, but he refused, saying, "So far, all the political reforms of other countries have succeeded only in shedding blood. In China today I have never heard that anybody has shed blood for reform. This is the reason why my country is not prosperous. I am willing to be the first to shed blood for reform!" (Lang Qichao, *Biography of Tan Sitong*) Empress Dowager Cixi snatched back the reins of power by putting Emperor Guangxu under house arrest. At her order, Tan and some other reformers were arrested. Soon after that Tan was executed, together with Yang Rui, Lin Xu, Liu Guangdi, Kang Guangren and Yang Shenxiu, who are known in history as the "Six Gentlemen of 1898." Of the history of the bourgeois reform movement Tan wrote a page with his own blood.

Tan's main philosophical work is the *Philosophy of Humanity*. His philosophy is characterized by a confusion of the old and the new. His ideas are somewhat spotty and even contradictory. This is because, first, his thought underwent a rapid change from "Chinese learning" to "Western learning"; second, his thought was influenced by various ideas of different times and different countries; and, third, there was not enough time for him to reflect upon these influences.

The basic categories of Tan's concept of nature are "ether" and "humanity." In order to construct a new philosophical concept of nature, he exerts great efforts to combine these two categories, which are extremely different from each other in both background and content.

An important concept in classical physics, "ether" is a hypothetical medium, once believed to be a kind of substance but different from substantial particles, and which was thought to fill space. In the 19th century, physicists universally believed that "ether" was the medium of light, electricity and magnetism. It was thought to possess elasticity, and might be compressed and diffused evenly throughout space. The "ether" hypothesis was not abandoned until in the early 20th century, when Albert Einstein (1879-1955) formulated the special theory of relativity.

The "ether" theory was introduced to China in the last years of the 19th century, and influenced some advanced Chinese thinkers. For instance, Kang Youwei once said, "The mind that cannot bear to see the suffering of others is humanity. It is electricity. It is ether." (*Subtle Meaning of the Book of Mencius·Book 1*) Tan went a step forward by taking "ether" for a new concept of substance, in order that he might establish his own idea of Nature.

In his understanding, "ether" is the "origin of the primordial substances." The so-called primordial substances are the chemical elements: "There are sixty-four primordial substances, which are different from one another. As for their origin, there is only one origin of the primordial substances, and that is 'ether'." (*Philosophy of Humanity*)

"Ether" is the fundamental substance, indestructible, uncreated and penetrating everywhere. The reason why light, sound, air and electricity may vibrate and spread in the manner of water waves, and why material particles and the myriad things may adhere and congeal, the heavenly bodies of various stellar clusters in the universe may attract one another but not scatter apart lies in the existence of "ether." In short, the world is unified in "ether": "Throughout the realms of elements of existence (dharmas), empty space, and sentient beings, there is something supremely refined and subtle which makes everything adhere, penetrates everything and connects everything, so that all is permeated by it. The eye cannot see its color, the ear cannot hear its sound, and the mouth and nose cannot perceive its flavor and fragrance. There is no name for it, but we shall call it ether. The realms of elements of existence (dharmas), empty space and sentient beings all issue from it." (*Philosophy of Humanity*)

In this way, in respect to the material unification of the world, Tan makes an explanation which is characterized by the approach of the natural sciences of early modern times.

Nevertheless, Tan blurs the division between substance and spirit. In his view, "ether" permeates everything as electricity does, and the "brain nerves" are also possessed of an electrical feature. Therefore, the function of "ether" is very great. "When it functions, it becomes waves, forces, particles and brain nerves." (*On Ether*) On this basis, he equates the material "ether" with the spiritual "humanity": "Penetration is the first significance of humanity. Ether is electricity, and ether is the power of the brain. As I have pointed out, all of them have the function to penetrate." (*Philosophy of Humanity*) In short, "ether" may be called "humanity" (Cf. *On Ether*), and "humanity" is the origin of the universe. He says, "Humanity is the origin of Heaven, Earth and the myriad things. Therefore, ether is mind-only and consciousness-only." (*Philosophy of Humanity*) The power of the brain is inestimable and beyond compare. He says, "Big as Heaven and Earth are, the brain can establish them, destroy them and transform them. The brain is able to do anything it pleases." (*To Ouyang Zhonghu*) Thus, he turns from the materialistic theory of "ether" to the idealistic theory of "the power of the brain."

The reason why such a contradiction may emerge in Tan's concept of nature lies in his theory of ideological root cause and class root cause. As far as ideological root cause is concerned, Tan was influenced in his early years by the materialism of Zhang Zai and Wang Fuzhi. Later, he studied Buddhism under the guidance of Yang Jiahui, a famous scholar of Buddhism in the early modern times, and was influenced by his idealism. In addition, Tan was deeply influenced by Kang Youwei, and attempted to combine materialism and idealism. As far as his class root cause is concerned, on the one hand he was eager to break the bonds of feudalism, while on the other he realized that China's national bourgeoisie was still weak, so he deeply felt that he had no strength to save China from its desperate situation. As a result, he could do nothing but resort to "the power of the brain" in the hope that he might realize his social ideal in this way.

Tan's theory of knowledge is likewise characterized by contradiction. He maintains a materialistic theory of perception, but he falls into the pitfall of a mystical theory of sudden enlightenment.

Tan starts from the relationship between concept and objective being, and he points out that knowledge originates in "objective being," not in "concept." He says as follows:

"What ears and eyes come into contact with is nothing but objective being. What mouth and nose take in is nothing but objective being. What hands take hold of or feet follow is nothing but objective being. Everything we are faced with is objective being." (*Ten Articles on Governing Affairs Written in Zhuangfei Tower·A Debate about Objective Being*)

All the objects that people contact with their sense organs are objectively realistic things and events, and all perceptual experiences arising therefrom become sources of human knowledge. In other words, knowledge must start with "objective being"; it cannot start with "concept." This is the materialistic theory of perception.

Going forward from here, Tan firmly opposes "taking a name for an ethical code." He vehemently criticizes the cardinal guides and constant virtues propagated for centuries by feudal rulers: "When they take a name for an ethical code, their ethical code has already become the predicate of an actuality but not an actuality per se. Besides, men give names, and not vice versa. Since the top level governs the lower levels, the lower levels have to follow the top level. Because of this, the disasters and poisons brought about by the three cardinal guides and the five constant virtues of the past thousands of years have become more terrible." (*Philosophy of Humanity*)

It is a mistake to use a "name" as an *a priori* dogma eternally unchangeable. Whereas the relationship between concept and objective being has been turned upside down, the three cardinal guides and the five constant virtues are made an instrument to oppress the people or fetters to confine their thoughts. "The ruler uses a name [referring to status] to fetter his ministers. The officials use various names to shackle the common people. A father uses a name to oppress his sons. A husband uses a name to confine his wife to the household." (*Philosophy of Humanity*) Tan also says, "Since there is a name [of a crime], the mouths of the people are closed, and they cannot express freely what they want to say. What is more, the minds of the people are confined, and they dare not think freely." (*Ibid*) These ideas are a loud cry by a bourgeois thinker attacking feudal obscurantism, and they played an important role in enlightening the people in those days.

Nevertheless, when Tan goes further, and probes whether the subject is able to reflect the object of cognition correctly or not, he once again doubts the reliability of the conceptual experiences in general. In his opinion, there is a limitation to man's sense organs. When man applies his eyes, ears, nose, tongue and body to contacting external things, what he acquires are only the colors, sounds, smells and senses of touch, so he cannot get fundamental knowledge of the boundless world. Therefore, in order to know the boundless world, the only way out is to depend on the method of "immediate attainment of enlightenment," which is advocated by the Chan Sect of Buddhism. In his view, this method is simple and easy to apply: "It is unnecessary to watch with the eyes, to listen with the ears, to taste with the tongue, to touch with any part of body, or to think with the mind." (*Philosophy of Humanity*) He rejects the ordinary routes of perceptual and rational knowledge altogether, and advocates mystical intuition. From here, he concludes that knowledge is more important and more fundamental than action.

There are several root causes of the contradiction in Tan's theory of knowledge. First, there is an epistemological root cause. He fails to understand that there is a dialectical relationship between perception and cognition, between knowledge and practice, and between absoluteness and relativity. Second, there is a class root cause. This reflects the duality of the national bourgeoisie of China, and the duality is fully exposed in its struggle against feudalism.

In Tan's view of history there is also a contradiction. On the one hand, he affirms that society changes and becomes a new society with each passing day, and therefore he advocates that it is necessary to carry out social reforms in a comparatively intense way. On the other hand, he envisages the smoothing — and even the abolition — of contradictions, in the hope that he may break through all the snares and traps of feudalism.

Tan's view of history is deeply influenced by Wang Fuzhi's thought. He inherits Wang's idea that "The transformations of Heaven and Earth bring about daily renewal." (Wang Fuzhi, *Outer Commentary on the Book of Changes·Book 6*) In Tan's opinion, "daily renovation" is the universal law by which the myriad things change and develop. He says as follows:

> "If Heaven does not renew itself, how can it produce things? If the Earth does not renew itself, how can it revolve? If the sun and moon do not renew themselves, how can they be bright? And if the four seasons do not renew themselves, how can there be the cold and warm seasons? If grasses and plants do not renew themselves, there will be no bumper harvest. If blood and vital force do not renew themselves, the main and collateral channels will be clogged up. If ether does not renew itself, all the elements of existence in the three realms (the threefold world of sensuous desire, of form, and of formless world of pure spirit, that is, our world) will become extinct." (*Philosophy of Humanity*)

Without the new superseding the old, there can be no existence of the universe. He also accepts Wang Fuzhi's idea that "Without a concrete thing there cannot be its Way." (Wang Fuzhi, *Outer Commentary on the Book of Changes·Book 5*) In Tan's opinion, the "Way" should change and develop along with the "implements." He says, "The Way is the function, and the implements are the foundation. Only after the foundation is set up can the function come into play. As long as the implements exist, the Way will not become extinct." (*A Booklet Written in the Tower of the Worried Mind*) He also says, "As long as our discussion of the Way is carried out together with that of the implements, it is certain that the role which the implements of the world play will be great. When the implements have already changed, how can the Way refuse to change?" (*Ibid*) Here, the "implements" refers to society, and the "Way" refers to the social system. Now that society decides the system, it is quite natural that along with the development of society the system, no matter what it may be, should change or be changed. Wang Fuzhi once said, "In the Han and Tang dynasties there was not today's Way. Today, there is not the Way of Han and Tang dynasties." Tan interprets Wang Fuzhi to mean, "The laws must change with the times." (*A Booklet Written in the Tower of the Worried Mind*)

Based on such a view of history, Tan energetically advocates constitutional reform and modernization. He launches a violent assault against the feudal absolute monarchy in China. He points out:

> 1. "The system of government for the past two thousand years has been just the same as that of the Qin Dynasty, and all the monarchs have been robber barons." (*Philosophy of Humanity*)
>
> 2. "The relation between the monarch and the ministers in the past two thousand years was especially dark and irrational. Although there is no humane principle in such a relationship, it has been handed down to the present time. And it is getting darker and darker, and more and more irrational with each passing day." (*Ibid*)

The feudal ruler regards the whole country as his personal possessions. He treats the common people as dogs and horses which are always at his beck and call, and he uses the cardinal guides, constant virtues and ethical codes to fetter the minds of the broad masses of the people.

"He takes their wisdom, their wealth, their power and their lives for his private property. And he returns foolishness, poverty, weakness and death to the common people. Since the feudal rulers used all kinds of means to oppress the people and they had no idea how to resist foreign invasions, China was always in the position of being beaten and suffering failures. "Foreign invasions are getting more and more serious. The navy has failed, and the fleet has become ashes. Strategic advantages have been seized by the foreign invaders. The foreign invaders have entered our hallway. Our interests are being encroached upon, and our territory is about to be carved up. The people are at their last extremity. Our country, our creed and our race will soon be extinct!" In short, China is at a crossroads. The country has to be reformed. "Only by political reform can she be saved." Facing such a situation, Tan demands, "Change the present system! Abolish the monarchy! Advocate democracy! Turn inequality into equality!" He demands that the absolute monarchy of feudalism be abolished, and that a capitalist system of democracy and equality should be set up. This is the most radical thought of democracy in the reform movement of the bourgeoisie. (Cf. *Philosophy of Humanity*)

Tan sees that the agent of historical development lies in the contradictory nature inside things and events. The opposites of things are like this: "There is identity, and there is difference. Because of the difference, both sides attack each other. Because of the identity, both sides embrace each other." (*Philosophy of Humanity*) It is the "difference and identity, attacking and embracing" that cause things to change and develop. Therefore, when Tan advocates political reform, he maintains that it is necessary to use violence to overthrow the rule of the feudal diehards:

> "In China today, only when the conflicts between the new and the old parties cause blood to flow everywhere can there be some hope of rejuvenation." (*To Ouyang Zhonghu*)

This is a clear expression of the courage of Tan, who dared to break through all the snares and traps of feudalism. In the struggle, he himself became a brave fighter, and finally sacrificed his young life to the cause of political reform.

Tan says, "Antagonism originates from this side and that side, and both sides originate from my own self." The contradictions in things do not exist objectively; instead, they are something additional made by the subjective mind when it postulates things. As long as the subjective mind expels the contradictions, the contradictions in things will disappear. "Antagonism is indestructible by others; only by itself can it be destroyed." (*Philosophy of Humanity*) Thus, he regards "the power of the brain" as the decisive force in historical development:

> "When the *mano-vijnana* (perception of mind) is broken, the *atma-samjna* (self-ideation) is expelled. When the *atma-samjna* is expelled, differences and identity become extinct. When differences and identity become extinct, equality appears." (*Philosophy of Humanity*)

As long as people are able to do away with subjective prejudices, contradictions will disappear or be eliminated, and equality will be realized. Thus, it clearly follows that Tan's "breaking through all snares and traps of feudalism" has to resort to "the power of the brain," which is his ultimate weapon:

> "If there is the genuine ability to break through, there are of course neither snares nor traps at all. If there is genuine existence of snares and traps, it is quite normal to speak of breaking through. Therefore, I say, 'breaking through all snares and traps' means that nobody has ever broken through any snares or traps." (*Philosophy of Humanity*)

In other words, breaking through all snares and traps is a criticism which was made merely in the sphere of subjectivity; it was by no means practical struggle. The weakness of the Chinese national bourgeoisie, which was exposed in the struggle against feudalism, renders this fighter, who stepped forward bravely from the ranks of the reformers, incapable of realizing his ambition to break through all snares and traps of feudalism.

Yan Fu (1853-1921), whose original name was Yan Zongguang and alias was Youling, was a native of Houguan County (present-day Minhou County), Fujian Province. In 1867, he was admitted to the Fuzhou Naval Academy, which had been founded by the "Western learning" or "Westernization" faction. There, he systematically studied modern science and technology. After graduation, he held a post in the navy. In 1877, the Qing government sent him to study in England, where he came into contact with Western culture and academic thought in an extensive way, and was influenced profoundly. When he returned to China, he took up several posts in the Northern Fleet, including Chief Instructor and Director-General. He sat the imperial examination several times, but failed every time. China's defeat in the Sino-Japanese War of 1894-1895 was a moment of awakening for Yan. He published some political essays, including "On the Necessity of Political Reform," "An Inquiry into Power," "A Critique of Han Yu," and "A Resolute Idea to Save the Nation from Extinction." In these essays, he propagated reform, and called on the broad masses of the people to save the nation from extinction. He translated the *Evolution and Ethics* by Thomas Henry Huxley (1825-1895) into Chinese, and thereby propagated the Darwinian theory of evolution, which was summarized as "survival of the fittest in the course of natural selection." His translations played a tremendous part in encouraging the Chinese people to carry out reforms to rejuvenate the country with their own efforts. They included *An Inquiry into the Nature and Causes of the Wealth of Nations* by Adam Smith (1723-1790), *System of Logic* and *On Liberty* by John Stuart Mill (1806-1873), *L'Esprit des Lois* by Baron de La Brède et de Montesquieu (Charles-Louis Secondat, 1689-1755), *The Study of Sociology* by Herbert Spencer (1820-1903), *A Short History of Politics* by Edward Jenks (1861-1939), and *A Primer of Logic* by William Stanley Jevons (1835-1882). By translating these famous works into Chinese, he introduced Western theories of philosophy, logic, sociology and economics to China. To these translations Yan attached a large number of translator's comments, commentaries and notes, in which he compared the ideological features of the Chinese and Western cultures. Thereby, he started a common practice as a style of study for a whole generation. After the failure of the Reform Movement of 1898, Yan gradually became conservative in his thought, advocating worshipping Confucius and reading the classics. Following the Revolution of 1911 he supported Yuan Shikai's attempt to restore the imperial system.

Yan's concept of Nature was established on the basis of the modern natural sciences, different from the naive materialism of ancient China.

Yan lays particular stress on the modern Western natural sciences.

Of the Western natural sciences, he judges mathematics, logic, mechanics and chemistry to be the most important. This is because mathematics and logic provide man with the tools to know the myriad things, and mechanics helps man know the constructional details inside things, the mechanics of movement and the association of cause and effect. He holds in particular esteem the work of Nicolaus Copernicus (1473-1543), Sir Isaac Newton (1642-1727) and Charles Darwin (1809-1882). In his opinion, the first law of motion of Newtonian mechanics is the result of "careful meditation upon the past thousands of years." (Translator's Preface to *Evolution and Ethics*) And he praises Darwinian evolution highly, saying, "The theory of evolution enables us to find everything fresh and new, and it reforms the mind." (*An Inquiry into Power*) He honors Darwin above Newton.

On the basis of the modern natural sciences, Yan gives an explanation of the material unification of the world:

> "I take Heaven, Earth, man, birds, beasts, insects, grasses and trees as a whole, and I attempt to understand thoroughly the general principle which governs them all. I find that they all originate in one material force, and it is this material force that evolves into the myriad things." (*An Inquiry into Power*)

Both the universe and the myriad things in the universe originate and are unified in "material force," which is fundamentally substantial. Nevertheless, he is quite different from the materialist philosophers of ancient China, who regarded "material force" as an "isolated Great Void." Instead, he thinks that material force is nothing but the "ether" discussed in classical physics: "The so-called material force is a substance in which there are mass point, loving force and refusing force. Its weight may be calculated, and its motion may be felt." (*An Introduction to Logic*, Section 30)

He attempts to define "material force" from the angle of classical mechanics, giving new content to an old philosophical category. Material force is a basic material entity in which there are mass point, attractive force ("loving force") and repelling force ("refusing force"). On this basis, Yan takes a step forward. According to the theory of Newtonian mechanics, he demonstrates that the evolution of the universe lies in the material and motional properties of matter per se:

"In the great universe, matter and force work upon each other. Without matter there would be no force, and without force there would be no matter." (Translator's Preface to *Evolution and Ethics*)

Here, the term "matter" refers to mass point, and in the extensive sense it refers to matter in general. The term "force" refers to two things. First, it refers to the fact that in any mass point there is both attractive force ("loving force") and repelling force ("refusing force"). Second, it refers to the energy produced by all mechanical movements, or, in the extensive sense, it refers to movement in general. In his view, matter and movement are unified. Without matter there would be no movement. In like manner, without movement there would be no matter, for matter cannot show its existence. The whole universe is the matter of movement and the movement of matter. "Evolution is matter changing itself." (*Comments on the Book of Master Zhuang·Notes to On the Uniformity of All Things*)

Yan goes on to demonstrate the form in which the universe evolves. He writes:

> "As for evolution, it is like this. In an entirely harmonious way the mass points gather together, and in a penetrating way the mass points send out forces." (Editor's Notes to "Generalization," *Evolution and Ethics*)

There are two forms of evolution of the universe. One form is "in an entirely harmonious way the mass points gather together." In the process in which mass points attract one another, they form various objects under the action of the force of attraction. The other form is "in a penetrating way the mass points send out forces." When the mass points are getting together, they produce heat, light, sound and movement, releasing energy. By means of these two forms, all things in the universe are transformed from the simple to the complicated, from the fluid to the congealed, and from the chaotic to the definite. Take, for example, the sun. In the beginning, there was the nebula. And then its mass points attracted one another in the course of movement, gradually forming the sun and the eight planets (at that time, Pluto had not yet been discovered). Again, in Yan's opinion, animals and plants come from such an evolution, too; they represent the different developmental stages of evolution. According to the Darwinian theory, he points out that "living organisms come from the same origin, but in different forms. From worms, fish, birds and beasts to man there is a chain of evolution." (Editor's Notes to "Examination of the Changes," *Evolution and Ethics*)

These ideas of Yan show his effort to apply modern natural science to illustrate the various forms of movement. Yan's scientific conception of nature is in opposition to the idea of a creator or god, as taught by various religions. He says, "All creatures are set up on one and the same foundation, and they move with a great force. The reason why the myriad things assume their present appearances lies in themselves, and there has never been any Creator at all. Since Charles Darwin put forth his theory of evolution, people have become aware of the fact that man is only one link in the chain of evolution, and that even now man continues to evolve. It is inconceivable that some creator, as religions maintain, made man out of nothing but dust." (Editor's Notes to "Examination of the Changes," *Evolution and Ethics*) In addition, Yan's scientific conception of nature overcomes the contradiction in the philosophy of Kang Youwei and Tan Sitong, who confused "material force" with "humanity" or equated "ether" with "mental force." In the history of Chinese philosophy, Yan's thought is the first modern system of philosophy in the real sense.

Starting from his concept of nature, Yan puts forth some ideas in line with British empiricist philosophy.

In the first place, Yan inherits the doctrine of the "blank tablet (tabula rasa)" from John Locke (1632-1704), who discussed this in *An Essay Concerning Human Understanding* (1690). In his opinion, human knowledge comes from perceptual experiences:

> "Wisdom grows on one foundation, the mind is a blank tablet, and experiences are the colors. Nothing can be designated as intuitive knowledge." (Editor's Notes to Chapter 6, Part 2, J. S. Mill's *System of Logic*)

In other words, the mind of man is just like a sheet of white paper, which is waiting for practical experiences to paint it with various colors. This is the only source of any kind of wisdom. As for so-called "intuitive knowledge," it has never existed. In his view, all science and knowledge are summaries of practical experiences. Even though the knowledge in question is as abstract as mathematical axioms, it must come from experience, too. Then, how do men acquire knowledge from practical experience? "First, the sense organs come into contact with things. And then the nerves send messages to the brain, where consciousness forms. And then ideas are formed from consciousness." (Editor's Notes to the "Generalization," *Evolution and Ethic*)

When sense organs touch objective things, man acquires conceptual experiences. When nerves convey conceptual experiences to the brain, man gains knowledge. This is a materialist line of cognition -- from things to the senses, and further to form thinking.

On these grounds, Yan criticizes apriorism. He points out, "There is the Western term "*a priori*." It means ignoring the examination of facts, proceeding from causes to effects, and putting forth a generalizing doctrine in advance, and suchlike methods of reasoning." (Editor's Interposed Remark to Chapter 4, Part 2, J. S. Mill's *System of Logic*) Apriorism is in opposition to the materialist line of cognition in that the former maintains that knowledge exists before things and conceptions. In this way, he discloses the essence of apriorism. Moreover, he mentions Lu-Wang Neo-Confucianism is a typical example of apriorism. "As for the essence of the doctrines of Lu Xiangshan and Wang Yangming, they advocate learning from one's own mind, and there is nothing more. They think themselves smart fellows who know all the wide world's affairs without having to step outside the gate. But herein lies the question: Is it true that the wide world's affairs are in accordance with their knowledge? Or, if they are quite different from each other, how can they know the true situation? They fail to answer this question." (*A Resolute Idea for Saving the Nation from Extinction*)

The essence of the Lu-Wang Neo-Confucianism lies in exaggeration of the function of the "mind." According to Lu Xiangshan and Wang Yangming, knowledge is begotten in the mind automatically. They fail to pay attention to the key point that all knowledge must accord with practice; so their doctrines are essentially the same as apriorism, which was in vogue in the West.

In the second place, Yan lays stress on Western logic, and especially the inductive logic of Bacon. In his opinion, this is a scientific way to grasp truth. As he points out, this is the reason why the sciences were developed in the West in modern times, and why there emerged so many new theories in the West. He says, "Their methods or ways are no more than two, one being 'abstracting from the inside,' the other being 'abstracting from the outside.'" (Cf. *The Approach to and Functions of Western Learning*) By "abstracting from the inside," he means the inductive method. He says, "It means knowing the whole thing by examining the indirect parts, and having a comprehensive understanding by taking hold of the subtle places." In other words, in order to know things correctly, it is necessary to deduce the universal law of such a category of things or phenomena by proceeding from a particular thing or phenomenon. By "abstracting from the outside," he means the deductive method. He says, "It means starting from axioms to pass judgment on various things, and proceeding from the known cases to the unknown things." In order to grasp things correctly, it is necessary to infer various unknown things according to some known axioms. These two methods are of paramount importance for investigating things to the utmost. (Cf. Translator's Preface to *Evolution and Ethics*) In Yan's opinion, induction and deduction complement each other. But, after he makes a comparison of these two methods, he draws the conclusion that "The method of abstracting from the inside is more important." (*A Primer of Logic*, Section 108) Before proceeding in any deductive reasoning, it is necessary to start from practical experience, to infer a general law from particular instances, and then to draw a conclusion. Otherwise, one may fall into the pitfall of apriorism. In the main, it is necessary to rely on the inductive method to acquire new knowledge. Besides, he emphasizes that any theory or laws obtained using the logical method must be tested in practice. He points out, "It is necessary to commit all principles and laws to the test of things and events, so that one can debate each principle and set up each law. No principle or law can be taken for granted before it is put to the test." (*A Resolute Idea for Saving the Nation from Extinction*)

In the third place, starting from the substantial learning of abstracting from the inside, Yan makes a vehement criticism of the "old learning," namely, the traditional academics of China's feudal society. As he points out, since Western learning lays stress on "substantial investigation and abstracting from the inside," it is characterized by "accurateness" and "usefulness." He says, "Since Western learning is detailed and accurate, more and more of Nature's secrets are revealed to the Western people with each passing day, and the minds of the Western people are getting more and more enlightened with each passing day, too. All the strong points of Western learning may be attributed to one word — usefulness. This is the key." (Editor's Notes to Chapter 4, Part 2, J. S. Mill's *System of Logic*) But the Chinese "old learning" is quite the contrary, with its imperial examinations, eight-part essays, hair-splitting textual criticism, and Song-Ming Neo-Confucianism, which were completely divorced from practice. One can never discover any truth or acquire any knowledge with such an ossified way of thinking, no matter how hard one tries. He says, "In one word, the old learning is useless, because it is unsubstantial. The old learning brings about misfortunes, first to academics and then to the country." (*A Resolute Idea for Saving the Nation from Extinction*) Iin order to save the nation from subjugation and ensure its survival, it is necessary to adopt Western learning. But what way should be taken to do so? At that time, Zhang Zhidong (1837-1909), a representative of the "Western learning" faction, raised the slogan. "Chinese learning as the basis, Western learning for application." His main points are as follows:

> "The Three Cardinal Guides and the Five Constant Virtues are the supreme teachings of China, which have been handed down from the times of the sages, so they are the origin of rites and politics. They stress the importance of the five human relations and clarify the origin of the one hundred professions. They have been in circulation for several thousand years, and nobody has ever raised any objections to them. The reason why the sages remain revered and China remains China lies right here." (*An Exhortation to Learning*)

The reason why Zhang Zhidong advocates emulating Western learning is that he wishes to shore up the feudal system, which he calls the "basis." Yan opposes the slogan "Chinese learning as the basis, Western learning for application." In his opinion, the "basis" and the "application" should be a unity. He illustrates with a cow and a horse. A cow and a horse have different bodies and different applications. We cannot take a cow's body for a horse's application; likewise, we cannot take a horse's body for a cow's application. He says, "Therefore, in Chinese learning there is both the basis and application of the Chinese learning, and in Western learning there is both the basis and application of the Western learning." (*Letter to the Editor of the Foreign Affairs Newspaper*) Zhang Zhidong took "Western learning" only for an appendix to the feudal system.

In the fourth place, Yan points out that conceptual experiences restrict the cognitive activities. In his opinion, man's cognition cannot surpass the scope of his conceptual experiences, and therefore what people know is only the phenomena of experience. Human knowledge cannot surpass the noumenon of experience. He says, "The noumenon of the myriad things is unknowable. What is knowable is only perception." (Editor's Notes to Chapter 3, Part 1, J. S. Mill's *System of Logic*) In this way, he proceeds from empiricism to a criticism of the ontology of traditional Chinese philosophy. The categories, which are discussed in traditional philosophy such as "the beginning of Heaven and Earth, the true dominator of creation, and the noumenon of the myriad things," should be regarded as "inconceivable principles." It is unnecessary to discuss them, and the way ahead for philosophy lies along a scientific and pragmatic road.

Evolution and Ethics exerted the widest influence in China among the many books Yan translated from English into Chinese. He praises highly the Darwinian theory of evolution, which he applies to human history.

Darwinian evolution may be generalized into two points, one being "competition between things" and the other being "natural selection." (Editor's Notes to the "Examination of the Changes," *Evolution and Ethics*) He says, "As for competition between things, it means that things compete for their own existence. As for natural selection, it means that Nature selects the best species for survival." (*An Inquiry into Power*) In his view, the survival of the fittest is not only the law by which living organisms evolve, but also the law by which human society develops. He says as follows:

> "Charles Darwin says that things compete for their own existence, and only the fittest survive. This is just as true with politics and religion as it is with animals and plants." (*An Inquiry into Power*)

That is to say, countries and peoples are also locked in a perennial and violent competition for existence. "That which advances will exist and spread. That which does not advance will fall sick and die out." (Editor's Notes to the "Fundamental Purport," *Evolution and Ethics*)

Yan's theory of "survival of the fittest in the course of natural selection" was greatly influenced by the social Darwinism of Herbert Spencer. He praises highly Spencer's *System of Synthetic Philosophy*, saying, "He sets up a unified theory by citing examples from Heaven, Earth, Man, the formed and vital force, the nature of the mind, animals and plants. His theory is especially incisive and all-round." (Editor's Notes to the "Examination of the Changes," *Evolution and Ethics*) Nevertheless, Yan does not agree with Spencer on "leaving things to the mercy of Nature." This is because he believes that, in essence, such a view means that the weak will become easy prey to the strong. Instead, he agrees with Thomas Huxley that it is important to "conquer Nature." This is because in such a view human efforts are emphasized. Yan regards the evolution of man as a struggle in which man takes the initiative against his surroundings, both natural and social. "In order to ensure its survival, mankind must exert its physical strength and intelligence in struggling against that which hinders its existence. In the struggle, the losing side retreats day by day, while the winning side gets stronger and stronger with each passing day. The reason why one side triumphs lies in that it is stronger than the other side in wisdom, qualities and strength." (Editor's Notes to the "Fundamental Purport," *Evolution and Ethics*)

Yan proceeds to probe this issue from the angle of comparative culture. He analyzes the factors which caused the West to become powerful, and China to become weak. "The Chinese people leave themselves to predestination, while the Western peoples rely on human capacities. The Chinese people love the things of the past, and despise the things of the present, whereas the Western peoples work hard at the things of the present so that they may surpass the things of the past. The Chinese people think it quite normal that an orderly dynasty is followed by a disordered dynasty, and a prosperous society is followed by a degenerate society, whereas the Western peoples think that the ultimate goal of academics, politics and education is to pursue boundless progress day after day, to keep prosperity from decline and to prevent the orderly society from sinking into disorder." (*On the Necessity of Political Reform*)

Through such a comparison, Yan penetratingly discloses the backwardness and decadence of China's feudal system. He energetically advocates "the development of human initiative," "the development of human intelligence" and "the renewal of the people's view of virtue." He says, "The national make-up must be cleaned and reformed, so that it may be in accordance with the social changes taking place at present." (*An Inquiry into Power*)

The so-called "cleaning and reforming the national make-up" and political reform must concentrate on one important point, that is, it is urgently necessary to change the absolute monarchy of feudalism into the democratic system of capitalism. He points out that the relationship between the monarch and the people in China's feudal society is nothing more than the monarch's cruel exploitation and the slavery of the masses of the people. The absolute monarchy of feudalism initiated by the First Emperor of the Qin Dynasty, which rules all the land, continually brings terrible misfortunes to the masses of the Chinese people. So he vehemently attacks this system. He says as follows:

> 1. "Since the Qin Dynasty, all the monarchs of China have been those who were more ruthless than others. They were the most capable of deluding the populace by trickery and robbing them by force or guile." (*A Critique of Han Yu*)
>
> 2. "Since the Qin Dynasty, among the rulers there have been differences of tolerance and cruelty, but they have had one feature in common, that is, they treated our people as either slaves or prisoners." (*An Inquiry into Power*)

In *A Critique of Han Yu*, he criticizes Han Yu's historical view that the sages decide the direction of history. Singling out Han Yu's statement that "If the common people refuse to support their superiors by producing millet, rice, hemp and silk, by making implements and wares, and by managing commerce and transportation, they must be put to death" (*An Inquiry into the Way*), Yan says, "Han Yu fails to see that all the monarchs since the Qin Dynasty have been robbers who usurped the country." (Cf. *A Critique of Han Yu*) More concretely, he says:

> "The common people are, originally speaking, the true masters of all under Heaven." (*A Critique of Han Yu*)

In Yan's opinion, the masses of the people, and the masses of the people alone, are the genuine masters of society; the kings, marquises, generals and ministers ought to be the public servants of society. And he maintains that the absolute feudal monarchy should be abolished.

"Esteem the people, and revolt against the ruler." This is Yan's battle cry, based on the theory of "the innate rights of man." He emphasizes, "The people's liberty is bestowed upon them by Heaven." (*A Critique of Han Yu*) And he says, "A person values his freedom; a country values its independence." (*An Inquiry into Power*) In his view, freedom is a sacred right innate to everybody. Freedom is the fundamental condition on which a human being can be a human being. Democracy is only the embodiment of freedom and depends on it: "We should take freedom as the base, and democracy for application." (*An Inquiry into Power*)

There is freedom before there is democracy. This is of great significance for the emerging anti-feudal trend of thought. It is the first time in the history of Chinese philosophy that this sublimation of freedom into democracy has been formulated. Yan explains:

> 'Freedom' is a term for which the Chinese sages and worthies of the past had a deep awe, so they never set it up as a canon to teach the people." (*On the Necessity of Political Reform*)

However, his theory of "innate rights" was derived from the Western enlightenment movement as it reached China. He asserts that "everybody has his own freedom." (*On the Necessity of Political Reform*) This indeed plays an important part in ideological emancipation.

Yan helped to introduce Western learning to China, and he formulated his own philosophical framework for it. In the ideological and cultural circles of China of the day, he played an important role in emancipating people's thoughts and in opening the social atmosphere at the turn of the 19th and 20th centuries. He accelerated the awakening of Chinese intellectuals as well as of the broad masses of the people. Especially, he put forth an evolutionary view of history, i.e., that "the fittest survives in the course of natural selection." This view stimulated a great fervor of patriotism among the Chinese people who were then marching towards self-improvement and independence. Yan's views provided the bourgeois reformers with a spiritual weapon for the carrying out of political reform. He exerted a profound influence upon the philosophical thought of those reformers. Yan was the first to set up a modern system of philosophy in the history of Chinese philosophy. He translated and introduced works on empiricism and logic, which were the two branches representative of modern learning in the West. With these activities, he forcefully accelerated the transformation of traditional Chinese philosophy into a modern philosophy. Yan did a good pioneering job of synthesizing Western and Chinese philosophies, and in the process he influenced many people who were actuated by high ideals. Among them were Sun Yat-sen and Zhang Taiyan, two representatives of the Chinese bourgeois revolution. In addition, modern thinkers such as Hu Shi, Lu Xun and the young Mao Zedong learned from Yan's translations of *Evolution and Ethics* and other works of Western philosophy.

37.

Philosophical Banners in the Xinhai Revolution of 1911

The failure of the Reform Movement of 1898 dashed the hopes of the bourgeoisie, who had sought to set up a constitutional monarchy. The suppression in 1901 of the peasant struggle carried out under the name of the Boxer Rebellion sounded the death-knell of the old-type peasant revolutions. It was in such historical conditions that the revolutionaries among the Chinese bourgeoisie came to the forefront of political struggle at the turn of the 19th and 20th centuries. In 1894, Sun Yat-sen (Sun Zhongshan) founded the China Revival Society, which was China's first modern revolutionary organization. In 1904, the Chinese Nation Revival Society was founded under the sponsorship of Huang Xing, Chen Tianhua, Song Jiaoren and others. In the same year, the Restoration Society was founded under the sponsorship of Cai Yuanpei, Zhang Taiyan and others. In 1905, the China Revolutionary League was formed as an umbrella organization for all these groups, at the suggestion of Sun. The revolutionary program reads: "Drive out the Tartars (i.e. the Qing Dynasty) and revive the Chinese nation, establish a republic and equalize landed property." The League led a series of armed anti-Qing uprisings, until finally, in the Revolution of 1911, the reactionary and decadent rule of the Qing Dynasty was overthrown, and a bourgeois republic was founded. In the decade preceding the Revolution of 1911, on the ideological front the revolutionaries among the bourgeoisie waged an intense ideological struggle against feudal obscurantism and the bourgeois reformists, who wanted to set up a constitutional monarchy.

After the failure of the Reform Movement of 1898, the reformist school of the bourgeoisie, headed by Kang Youwei and Liang Qichao, continued to cherish the illusion of a reformed monarchy. As a result, they turned into a conservative school that opposed the bourgeois-democratic revolution. Kang Youwei published a series of essays, among which the most famous was titled *A Reply to the Chinese Merchants of North and South America on the Reason Why China Can Only Have a Constitutional Monarchy and Not a Revolution* (It is also entitled *A Retort to the Revolution*). In his opinion, the only way out for China was to carry out reform little by little, with the aim of setting up a constitutional monarchy; revolution was out of the question, not to mention the establishment of a republic. He said, "Evolution entails gradual advance, as does benefiting the people. The sages themselves had no alternative in these spheres. Even if they desired rapid advance, it was impossible." (*Commentary on the Analects·Book* 7) Leaps forward and revolutionary changes lead nowhere. He states baldly: "Revolution leads to the destruction of a country." The reason is that, "in order to start a revolution, you must make use of the mob. How can a country be governed in coalition with the mob? Sooner or later you yourself will perish; the only difference is that you perish with your family and your country." (*On the French Revolution*) In 1902, Liang Qichao founded the *Journal of the Renovated People*, in which he published a series of essays opposing the idea of democratic revolution. Unequivocally, he points out, "China today must say a definite no to a constitutional republic. Enlightened absolutism is what China needs today." (*On Enlightened Absolutism*)

The revolutionaries headed by Sun Yat-sen waged a relentless ideological struggle against the reformists. Sun declared, "Only two choices lie before us — revolution or the protection of the emperor." (*To My Dear Countrymen*) He called on the revolutionaries to draw a strict line of demarcation line between themselves and the reformists. Zhang Taiyan published an essay titled *Rebuttal of Kang Youwei's A Retort to the Revolution*. He pointed out, "When axioms are not clear, the revolution may make them clear. When old customs linger, the revolution may get rid of them. Revolution is not a mere purgative. It is a good dose of medicine." In 1905, the China Revolutionary League published its own official organ, the *People's Journal*, in Japan. The *People's Journal* took a clear-cut stand and carried on open polemics with the *Journal of the Renovated People* published by the reformists. The *People's Journal* promoted the development of the democratic-revolutionary thought of the bourgeoisie by advocating revolution and opposing protection of the emperor. From this revolutionary ideological tide emerged a group of young thinkers and propagandists, including Zou Rong and Chen Tianhua.

Zou Rong (1885-1905) was a native of Baxian County, Sichuan Province (present-day Banan District, Chongqing Municipality). At the age of seventeen, he went to study in Japan, where he took part in the patriotic movements organized by other Chinese students in Japan. When he returned to China, he joined a patriotic society, and in 1903 he published the book entitled *The Revolutionary Army*, which advocated revolution. He was thrown into jail, where he died of disease. In *The Revolutionary Army*, Zou Rong takes "the theory of natural rights" for the basis of the revolution. According to him, man enjoys equality and liberty by birth. It is only because of feudal absolutism that the people do not enjoy equality and liberty, and the country has been turned into the private property of the rulers. He says, "We must make joint efforts to drive out the alien race that rules us, and we must kill the monarch that imposes absolutism upon us, so that the innate rights of man may be restored to us." In his view, revolution plays an important role in historical development. Revolution "gets rid of corruption, and preserve goodness." Revolution can "bring man from the barbarian state to the civilized state." And revolution "enables everybody to enjoy the happy state of equality and liberty." Therefore, China's only way out lies in revolution. He appeals to his countrymen thus:

> 1. "If this China of ours is to get rid of the Manchu bondage, we have to make revolution. If this China of ours is to have independence, we have to make revolution. If this China of ours is to stand side by side with the world powers, we have to make revolution. If this China of ours is to endure in the new world of the 20th century, so we have to make revolution. If this China of ours is to become a famous country and the Chinese people are to be the masters of their own lives, we have to make revolution." (*The Revolutionary Army*)

> 2. "How lofty the revolution is! How splendid the revolution is!" (*Ibid*)

Zou's these ideas contributed to the leap forward from the reformist thought of the bourgeoisie to the revolutionary thought of the bourgeoisie.

Chen Tianhua (1875-1905) was a native of Xinhua County, Hunan Province. In 1903 he went to study in Japan. Together with Huang Xing and others, he organized the Chinese Nation Revival Society. In order to propagate the revolutionary thought of this group, he wrote *Alarm Bell*, *Sudden Awakening* and suchlike progressive works. When the China Revolutionary League was founded, he held the post of secretary, and edited the League's *People's Journal*. To protest a crackdown on Chinese students' political activities, Chen Tianhua jumped into the sea and drowned, leaving behind his manifesto titled, *Suicide Note*. Chen Tianhua was among the first of the bourgeois revolutionaries to point out that imperialism was a ferocious foe of the Chinese people, and therefore the anti-Qing struggle had to be combined with the anti-imperialist struggle. He analyzed the serious crisis that faced China at that time as follows:

> "Russia surrounds us in three directions in the north. England, via trade relations, concocts an insidious scheme against us. France has already occupied Guangzhou, and is casting greedy eyes on Guangxi and Guizhou. Germany has already occupied Jiaozhou, and is looking to expand her influence in eastern China. Modernized Japan has already taken Taiwan, and is preparing to invade Fujian. The USA is, of course, no exception to this gangsterish scheme, and is also going to join those who are carving up our territory." (*Sudden Awakening*)

Because of the aggression of the imperialist powers, the beautiful mountains and rivers of China have become "a world in which wolves are eating the sheep," the Chinese people have become "cows and lambs in the pens of foreigners," and the whole of China is faced with "the misfortune of being carved up." (*Sudden Awakening*) He blames the decadent rule of the Qing Dynasty for this perilous state of affairs. The rulers of the Qing Dynasty have always treated the Chinese people as cattle and sheep. Now these same rulers have presented these cattle and sheep as a gift to the imperialist powers, and the latter may kill, cut up and cook these cattle and sheep at will. The conclusion he draws is as follows:

> "Now that we have made up our minds to oppose foreign aggression, we must pay special attention to revolution and independence, we must not support the monarchy by any means." (*Sudden Awakening*)

Accompanied by the development of democratic revolutionary thought, new philosophical thoughts soon took root and sprouted. The democratic revolutionaries among the bourgeoisie began to notice the relationship between materialism and the democratic revolution, and plunged into making propaganda for materialism, and even atheism. For instance, in 1903 an essay titled "On the Doctrines of Two Great Thinkers (Diderot and La Mettrie) of Materialism" was published in the Continent, a leading intellectual magazine of the day. In this essay, the doctrines of Denis Diderot (1713-1784) and Julien Offray La Mettrie (1709-1751), two materialist philosophers of 18th century France, were introduced to the Chinese reader. The essay's argument is that it was the enlightening role played by materialism that enabled the downtrodden masses of the French people to escape the snares and traps of religion to struggle for truth. And their struggle led to the French Revolution of 1789, and to the establishment of the French republic. The essay is also a criticism of the theist thought of "immortal souls." Human ability to perceive and to think does not come from the "soul," but is a product of the brain, which itself is a part of the human body, which is material. The essay poses the question: "Why is the human brain possessed of thinking capacity? This is because it is specially formed and constructed, and on the cerebral cortex there are many folds."

While propagating materialism and atheism, the revolutionaries launched violent assaults on the traditional Chinese theory of the Mandate of Heaven. For example, in 1903 in an essay titled "Revolution in Heaven" published in the first collection of the *Compilation of the National Dailies*, the Confucian doctrine of the Mandate of Heaven was criticized. In the author's opinion, this doctrine "holds in esteem the unknowable Heavenly Way, and distresses the current and urgent issue of the Human Way. The root cause of the mistakes China has made in the past several thousand years is right here." In like manner, the author disagrees with Laozi's view that the Heavenly Way does nothing but let things take their own course. In his opinion, the theories of "inaction" and "letting things take their own natural course" are the cause of "fatigue and weakness in man," for by adhering to them man loses his aggressive spirit. Therefore, the author advocates "making a revolution in Heaven" and "replacing Heaven." The author affirms the strength of man, saying, "Heaven needs to be transformed. The reason why we must make a revolution in Heaven lies not in man's subjective desire but in that which refuses to let it slip away. Only when Heaven is transformed can the other transformation be carried out." Here we see there are two tasks, one being to do away with the theory of the Mandate of Heaven, and the other being to carry out the democratic revolution. And now these two tasks are combined. The author points out that only by expunging from the minds of the people the ideas of the Mandate of Heaven and "divine right" can the revolution in the other respects be carried out smoothly.

Among the bourgeois revolutionary thinkers, Zhang Taiyan and Sun Yat-sen made the greatest philosophical contributions. Their theories constituted the ideological banner for the Revolution of 1911.

Zhang Taiyan (1869-1936) was a native of Yuhang County, Zhejiang Province. In his early years, he studied under Yu Yue (1821-1907), a leading scholar of traditional Chinese studies. The influence of Yu Yue naturally led Zhang to research the early Confucian manuscripts. But the outbreak of the Sino-Japanese War of 1894-1895 awakened him to the seriousness of the national crisis, and he threw himself into the Reform Movement. The rout of the reformers of 1898 brought him to the realization that only a violent revolution could bring China into the modern world. In 1902, he went to Japan, where he became a close friend of Sun Yat-sen. Upon his return to China, he revised his *A Book of Urgent Words*, incorporating his newly-found democratic revolutionary thought. In 1903, he published an essay titled "Rebuke of Kang Youwei's Debate on Revolution." He wrote a preface to the *Revolutionary Army* by Zou Rong, in which he praises that book as a "masterpiece which serves as the harbinger of an army fighting a just war." Imprisoned for sedition, in 1904 Zhang managed to found the Restoration Society, a revolutionary organization, in collaboration with Cai Yuanpei and other revolutionaries. Released in 1906, Zhang went to Japan for a second time, where he became editor-in-chief of the *People's Journal*. He took a clear-cut stand in this journal against the reformists. In 1908, the Japanese government banned the *People's Journal*. Zhang returned to China following the Revolution of 1911. His views became more conservative. He put forth the slogan, "Now that the revolutionary army has risen up, the revolutionary party should disappear by itself." He opposed Yuan Shikai's attempt to restore the monarchy, and became a member of Sun Yat-sen's provisional government in Guangzhou. Later, he separated himself from the democratic-revolutionary movement, and concentrated on academic activities. After the September 18th Incident of 1931, Zhang Taiyan urged that strong resistance be put up against Japanese aggression, and publicly condemned Chiang Kai-shek's policy of non-resistance.

The course of development of Zhang Taiyan's philosophical thought may be roughly divided into two periods. In his early years, he studied the modern natural sciences. He was profoundly influenced by the theory of evolution, and he opposed religious ideas, especially the theological theory of the creation. These ideas are reflected in *A Book of Urgent Words* and essays such as "A Theory of Watching Heaven" and "On Germs." From 1906, when he was in Japan and editing the *People's Journal*, he began to doubt the scientific theory of evolution, and advocated the establishment of a new religion of atheism. In the *People's Journal* he published a series of essays, including "On the Evolution of Both Sides," "On Atheism," "The Morality of the Revolution," "On the Establishment of Religion," "On the Non-self of Man," "On Five Nonbeings" and "On the Four Perplexities," which reflect the changes in his philosophical thought.

In his early years, Zhang inherited the materialist tradition of ancient China, while at the same time actively learning from the natural sciences of the West. He persisted in a materialist line in his conception of nature and theory of knowledge.

As regards his concept of nature, Zhang first makes a new elaboration of Heaven, which is an ancient topic in Chinese intellectual history. First, he opposes the deification of Heaven as the creator of the myriad things. Second, he is different from the naive materialists of ancient times who "regarded Heaven as accumulated material force." (*A Book of Urgent*

Words·On Heaven) Instead, he bases his theory on modern astronomical knowledge. He says as follows:

> "It is the Great Potter's wheel that makes the myriad things. All kinds of material force are governed in their own ways. The moon is governed by the earth, the earth is governed by the sun, and the sun is governed by the stars. They move and change, they rotate and revolve, because each of them plays an important part by itself. Where is the necessity for their attendance on Providence?" (*A Theory of Watching Heaven*)

In other words, Nature is just like the potter's wheel, which turns round and round all the time. Nature expresses itself in the mutual attraction among the moon, the earth, the sun and the stars. There exists no "providence" that dominates the myriad things. He says, "The birth and death, and the growth and extinction of the myriad things are caused up by the light and heat of the sun. They have nothing to do with 'providence'." (*A Theory on Watching Heaven*) Therefore, Zhang firmly opposes religious or theological theories of the creation of the world, declaring, "As for Heaven and God, there have never been any such entities." (*A Book of Urgent Words·On Heaven*) In his opinion, the eulogies and allusions to, and the scolding of Heaven of the ancients were completely foolish actions.

In addition to this, Zhang thinks that "ether" is the original foundation of the myriad things in the universe. He criticizes Tan Sitong for obscuring the demarcation line between matter and spirit, and for understanding "ether" as "humanity" and "mental force." Zhang emphasizes that "ether" is a kind of material entity. In his opinion, "ether has a form, albeit very tiny." And "ether" is the medium through which light travels. Because the light has different colors, the movement of ether is sometimes fast and sometimes slow. Therefore, "ether" is not "mental force," and "we cannot say it has no form." ("On Germs") In addition, Zhang thinks that "ether" is constituted of "elements" (atoms). An atom is not a thing that is unintelligible. Quite the contrary, an atom "possesses a form, and is measurable. The size of an atom can be expressed in terms of a molecule being divided into fifty million parts." Every atom possesses the forces of attraction and repulsion, "for this reason, various elements have to disperse into their individual state, and afterwards have to unite and integrate."The myriad things in the world are formed up of various atoms. He writes:

> "Atoms are the very beginning of all things, although there are plenty of variations." ("On Germs")

The myriad things originate in "atoms" and "ether." The latter is even tinier than an atom. In this way, Zhang gives a materialist explanation of the problem of the unification of the world.

Pointing out the basis on which a "cell" emerges and develops, he says as follows:

> "As for all things in the world, each and every one of them originates from cells. Cells are more or less spherical. In a cell there is the nucleus, which is spherical, too. The nucleus is filled with liquid, which is called cytoplasm. There are two kinds of cytoplasm, one being chromatic and the other being achromatic. A group of cells makes up protoplasm, which is similar to protein and called by Thomas Huxley 'the origin of life.' But protein has no capacity for either assimilation or multiplication, whereas protoplasm has." ("On Germs")

Here, the basis of his argument is the knowledge of biology of modern times, with which he makes an analysis of the structure of the cell. By such an analysis, he points out that the material basis of life is the "protoplasm," which consists of "protein." The protoplasm possesses the function of the new superseding the old and the function of self-reproduction. The movement of life organisms come from this, and develops from this too. Therefore, he firmly opposes the theory that a deity created life. In his opinion, "life is neither given nor dominated by any deities." (*The Revised Manuscript of "On Germs"*)

Furthermore, Zhang describes the human spirit as the characteristics innate to the human body, maintaining that the spirit cannot exist independently of the human body. He says as follows:

> "As soon as a person dies, the nitrogen, oxygen, carbon, hydrogen,

salt, iron, phosphorus and calcium of which the body consists will return to original nature of motion and rest, and the nature of man will thereby perish." ("On Germs")

In his opinion, as soon as a man dies, his body dissolves and returns to its original elements; there can be no independent existence of the spirit. With his knowledge of modern science, he augments the ancient Chinese theory on the extinction of the spirit.

As regards the theory of knowledge, Zhang inherits and develops Xun Kuang's materialist approach to epistemology, advocating materialist rationalism.

In the first place, Zhang thinks that human knowledge comes from perceptual experiences. He often refers to John Locke's theory of the *tabula rasa*. He says, "The spirit of man is like a blank sheet of paper." (*A Book of Urgent Words· Wang Yangming's Learning*) In order to know the world, the sense organs must come into contact with objective targets. "Different colors, such as the yellow, red, green and black, and different dimensions, such as length and width, vary from eye to eye. Different musical notes, voices, cries and sounds vary from ear to ear. Different tastes, such as sour, sweet, pungent, salty, bitter, astringent and suchlike, vary from tongue to tongue. Different smells, such as fragrant, stinking, fishy, gamy and suchlike, vary from nose to nose. Different tactile sensations, such as warm, cold, wet, smooth, thorny, hard, dense, dry and sleek, vary from hand to hand. All these are common to each member of mankind." (*A Book of Urgent Words·An Open Speech*)

The differences of things in form, color, sound, taste, smell, temperature, moisture and sense of touch are distinguished by means of the eyes, ears, mouth, nose and body, respectively. Since everybody has the same sense organs, everybody may obtain the same perceptual experiences of the same external things. In addition to this, he emphasizes that outside things exist independently from any human perceptual experience. For instance, with the correct sense of sight one can distinguish various colors. But if there is something wrong with the eyes, one may perhaps mistake the light of fire for blue. If a given sense organ is defective, we cannot say that changes of one kind or another have happened to any outside thing per se. In short, he persists in the materialist theory of reflection, by which the route of cognition is from things to perceptions.

In the second place, Zhang thinks that the knowledge obtained merely from the sense organs is very limited, and therefore such perceptual knowledge needs to be raised to the level of rational knowledge. According to him, as far as man's perception of outside things, either in depth or in width, is concerned, his sense organs are limited indeed. What is more, there are some objective targets which cannot be directly perceived by the human sense organs: "As for the vibration of sounds, the lowest frequency is 16 Hz and the highest frequency is 38,000 Hz. The hearing ability cannot catch such frequencies. The light and heat of the red sun, and the light and heat of the blazing lightning are too powerful for the human sense of sight to catch." (*A Book of Urgent Words·An Open Speech*) Infra- and ultrasound waves are beyond the capacity of human hearing ability. The real light and heat of the sun and the lightning are not visible to the human eye. Therefore, Zhang holds a critical attitude towards Yan Yuan's empiricist tendency, although he approves of Yan Yuan's epistemological approach, which lays stress on perceptual experience. He says, "I feel regret about his learning only in that it is centered on material objects. He maintains that each and every material object must be studied. He seldom uses any abstract conceptions." (*A Book of Urgent Words·Yan Yuan's Learning*) In his opinion, the limitation of Yan Yuan is that he fails to lay stress on theoretical thinking. In this respect, he appreciates Xun Kuang very much, for the latter lays stress on reason, and persists in the materialist theory of knowledge, saying, "The mind has the function of collecting the knowledge of the senses." He explicates further:

> "The human sense organs acquire information about different things, and combine that information into words. Then, various comparisons and classifications are made in order to weigh different things accurately. At last, a great general term may be established. Nevertheless, comparison cannot go so far as to surpass the ready-made ultimate. A comparison must be within the domain of the human imagination." (*A Book of Urgent Words·Open Speech*)

In other words, human cognition must first rely on the sense organs. It is through the sense organs that man obtains perceptual experiences, which are in accordance with the objective targets. And then, by means of reasoning ("comparisons and classifications"), some universal concepts ("great general terms") may be arrived at, which are different from concrete perceptions. Although such universal conceptions are different from concrete perceptions, there is after all a common standard ("ready-made ultimate"), which cannot be fabricated subjectively. By means of rational cognition man can understand and grasp the special things and events in a more profound way. Hence, rational cognition can direct people's practical activities in a more efficient way. As Zhang points out, if you have the knowledge of mathematics, you may count objects well; if you have the knowledge of music, you may play a piano well. In short, with the necessary knowledge beforehand one may get twofold results with half the effort. There are many opposite examples, too. If you calculate without using signs, you cannot count clearly; if you learn to play a piano without a musical score, you cannot learn to play the piano well. In short, without the necessary knowledge beforehand, one will get half the results with double the effort, or even no result.

On the basis of the materialist theory of reflection, Zhang emphasizes the importance of rational knowledge, and thereby he deepens the theory of knowledge. But in the meantime he has a tendency to overvalue the function of rational knowledge and devalue the function of perceptual knowledge.

Since Zhang early accepted Yan Fu's evolutional thought of "survival of the fittest in the course of natural selection," he was able to start from modern knowledge of the natural sciences in his examination of Nature. He points out that Nature has undergone a developmental and evolutionary process from the inorganic circle to the organic circle, and from life organisms of lower degrees to life organisms of higher degrees. In his view, not only is there a process of "survival of the fittest in the course of natural selection" in Nature, but there is also one in human society. He says, "If material objects have their own will, they will assuredly strive against Heaven and Earth. For this reason, the myriad things have continued to change from ancient times to the present. They change and change, and eventually change into man. Such being the case, how can they stop changing?" (*A Book of Urgent Words·Inquiry into Changes*)

In Zhang's opinion, the evolution of mankind does not equal the evolution of nature, in that human evolution is characterized by tools of production, or "implements" in his vocabulary. He says, "Men strive against one another by means of implements." In a concrete way he discusses the relationship between the improvement of implements in ancient society and the consequent social development. In the Age of the Fiery Emperor, people "used stones as weapons," and cut down trees to build palaces and houses. In the Age of the Yellow Emperor, people "used jade for weapons," and cut down trees to build palaces and houses. In the Age of the Great Yu, people "used copper for weapons, "and cut through hills, dug canals, dredged rivers and leveled the land. In later ages, people "made iron weapons," expelled the wild beasts and changed the courses of the rivers. In these endeavors man displayed strength with which to conquer nature. Therefore, by the material used to make implements we can distinguish one age from another. These implements are the marks of different stages of the development of human society. (Cf. *A Book of Urgent Words·Inquiry into Changes*)

Such a view of historical evolution implies that the evolution of mankind is not a passive process which merely fits in with nature; instead it is an active process, which conquers the nature. Although we usually say "natural selection," in fact the agent of evolution is "man" rather than "Nature." Therefore, according to Zhang, it is necessary to use "human power" to replace the "Mandate of Heaven." He emphasizes, "As far as bringing order out of chaos is concerned, the key lies not in whether or not there is such a thing as the Mandate of Heaven but in whether or not human power is great enough." (*Refutation of Kang Youwei's Debate on the Revolution*) How is mankind expected to use "human power" to overcome the "Mandate of Heaven"? He says, "The best way is to be gregarious and to define the class divisions clearly. If mankind can do so, it can establish its independence of the other species." ("On Germs") He develops Xun Kuang's thought of the necessity of class divisions being clearly defined. (*Xunzi·Chapter 9: On the Regulations of a King*) As long as people can be gregarious, as long as they can rely on the strength of society, they are able to take their fate in their own hands and achieve their desires. Then, "human power" will assuredly conquer the "Mandate of Heaven."

Starting from this viewpoint, in line with the theory of evolution, Zhang energetically advocates a revolution to overthrow the Qing Dynasty. In his opinion, this would play an important role in the evolution of Chinese society. He says, "Look at the present official circles! Everywhere there are tiny worms, molds and viruses, which are so rampant. Since the revolution of the common people has not been victorious, how such a pestilential atmosphere be swept away?" (*A Speech Delivered on the Anniversary of the People's Journal*) And he says, "When axioms are not clear, the revolution may make them clear. When old customs linger, the revolution may get rid of them. A revolution is not simply a violent remedy like a medicinal purgative. A revolution is a good dose of medicine which reduces ailments and reinforces the health." (*Refutation of Kang Youwei's Debate on the Revolution)* Of course, there are some shortcomings in Zhang s revolutionary thought. On many occasions he confuses the democratic revolution, which opposes the feudal rule of the Qing Dynasty, with the "racial revolution," which aims at replacing Manchu political power with the political power of the Han people.

In 1906, Zhang went to Japan for the second time, which provided him with a chance to see with his own eyes many aspects of the negative effects brought about by the development of capitalism, especially the various miseries imposed on the broad masses of the laboring people. He feels that the evolution of mankind is by no means a simple process, with the ideal realm as the goal. In his view, it is true that the replacement of the feudal system by the capitalist system is a kind of progress, but in capitalist countries the worship of the feudal nobility has changed into the worship of capital. He says, "The rich merchants and big traders never sit at the same table with the poor people or take the same bus as they do." (*On the Evolution of Both Sides*) In the field of foreign relations, capitalist countries launch aggressive wars, and enslave weak and small nations, especially after they enter the imperialist stage. He says, "There is one thing that imperialism never forgets even in sleep and at meals. That is, to plunder and to kill. It grinds its teeth and sucks blood. Even if the resulting wastelands extend over thousands of miles, imperialism thinks that it is quite normal." (*On Five Nonbeings*) His reflections on these social contradictions raise serious doubts in his mind with respect to the scientific theory of evolution. In his opinion, the movement of human society is different from the movement of Nature, in that the latter tends to become perfect and happy, while the former has two possibilities. On the one hand, it can become perfect and happy, but on the other it can go in the opposite direction. In view of this, he puts forth a theory of "the evolution of both sides," by which he emphasizes the simultaneous evolution and development of both sides of human society, such as good and evil, bitterness and happiness, and so forth: "The reason why evolution is called evolution lies in the simultaneous advance of both sides rather than the advance of any single side. The sole exception is the evolution of the intelligence. As far as morality is concerned, there is the evolution of good and there is also the evolution of evil. As far as livelihood is concerned, there is the evolution of happiness and there is also the evolution of misery. The general situation is the evolution of both sides, just as the shadow follows the body, and the demons follow the monsters." (*On the Evolution of Both Sides*)

In other words, the progress of morality and livelihood is different from that of knowledge. In morality, both goodness and evil develop at the same time; in livelihood, both happiness and misery develop at the same time, too. Along with the progress of knowledge, morality may degenerate at an ever-faster pace. Along with the progress of material civilization, miseries may increase in everyday life. Thus it follows that he expresses a pessimistic attitude toward the prospect of human evolution. In his opinion, "It is true that evolution is beyond reproach; however, the function of evolution is not recommendable." (*On the Evolution of Both Sides*)

What is the way out for mankind? Where is the future of the revolution? Zhang says, "First, it is necessary to use religion to stimulate confidence and to enhance morality among the people. Second, it is necessary to use the quintessence of Chinese culture, lay stress on our racial characteristics and strengthen patriotic enthusiasm." (*Collection of Speeches*) That is to say, in order to enhance morality and to push forward the revolution, he attempts to seek a kind of religious or spiritual force which is outside knowledge and material civilization.

In the search for a spiritual force which may enhance morality and push forward the revolution outside the realms of knowledge and material civilization, Zhang, in his later years, set up a philosophical system aimed at elevating self-consciousness by absorbing the ideological data of Buddhism, Immanuel Kant (1724-1804), Johann Gottlieb Fichte (1762-1814) and Arthur Schopenhauer (1788-1860).

The basic category of the philosophical system set up by Zhang in his later years is "consciousness," or "*alaya-vijnana*" (storage consciousness), preached by the Consciousness-Only School of Buddhism. "Storage consciousness" is the origin of the "*sadvijnana*" (six perceptions) — *caksur-vijnana* (sight-perception), *strotra-vijnana* (ear-perception), *ghrana-vijnana* (smell-perception), *jihva-vijnana* (tongue-perception), *kaya-vijnana* (touch-perception) and *mano-vijnana* (mind of mind). In his opinion, "There is nothing at all except *alaya-vijnana*." (*On the Establishment of the Religion*) In other words, all things in the world, including human perceptions and human consciousness, are derived from the *alaya-vijnana*. In his view, the *alaya-vijnana* is the same as Kant's "Urbildesgedanke" (or, the *a priori* thinking form) and Schopenhauer's proposition that "the world lies in the motivation of the idea." The *alaya-vijnana* contains and prescribes everything in the real world. He says as follows:

> "The *alaya-vijnana* comes from the no-beginning. In it, there are realms as varied as millet and corn, which have been got together. In these various realms, there are the phenomena of the twelve categories, the phenomena of the corporeal and the void, and the phenomena of the three periods, namely, the past, the present and the future. Even the six perceptions are contained in the *alaya-vijnana*. Since in it there is the foundation of everything, it has neither beginning nor end nor interruption." (*On the Establishment of the Religion*)

In other words, if there is anything that really exists in the world or merely in the human mind, be it Kant's twelve categories* or the objective phenomena or time of existence ("the phenomena of the corporeal and the void," "the phenomena of the three periods, namely, the past, the present and the future") or the perceptions or consciousness ("the six perceptions"), it has long since been contained in the *alaya-vijinana*, which

---

* Immanuel Kant's passion for system led him to a fourfold division with three categories in each. Under quantity we have unity, plurality, and totality; under quality we get reality, negation, and limitation; under relation we have inherence and subsistence, causation and dependence, and reciprocity between agent and patient; under modality we have possibility, existence, and necessity. — Cf. Immanuel Kant, *Prolegomena to Any Future Metaphysics* (1783), §21.

is just like the seeds of maize. And from these seeds of maize comes a boundlessly abundant world. In Zhang's opinion, the *alaya-vijnana* is the "real ego." He says, "The so-called 'real ego' is the *alaya-vijnana*." (*On Non-self of Man*) And he says, "Whosoever talks about the mind should rightly talks about the *vijnana*." (*On the Four Perplexities*) In this way, he constructs a philosophical system centered on the *alaya-vijnana*, which elevates the self-consciousness.

Starting at this point, Zhang opposes materialism on the one hand and theism on the other, and he advocates the establishment of a new religion of atheism. In the first place, he fundamentally denies the existence of the objective world. In his opinion, the objective world is no more than a fantasy of the subjective consciousness. He says, "The universe is not essential. People imagine that there is a universe in order to have something to meditate on." (*On the Establishment of the Religion*) As we know, materialists think, "There is nothing except things." But Zhang thinks that their argument is untenable. He says, "Even scientists who research into matters are not materialists in the true sense." The reason is very clear: "Those who talk about science cannot be divorced from the laws of cause and effect. As for cause and effect, it is not a thing; it is one of the primitive conceptions. If one admits that there is cause and effect, it means that there are some other entities besides matter." (*On the Four Perplexities*) In the second place, in like manner he denies the existence of any deity. He points out, "This very mind is real, and this very god is fantastic." We cannot "take this fantastic phenomenon for the noumenon." (*On the Establishment of the Religion*) In his view, self-consciousness (namely, the "*alaya-vijnana*") is the only real existence. Outside the *alaya-vijnana*, all kinds of ghosts, spirits and gods are sheer fantasy. Anyone who takes these fantastic concoctions for real existence is completely wrong. He objects to Christianity, which is established on the worship of God. In his opinion, "In order that all people may be equal to one another, it is necessary to do away with all theistic religions." (*On Atheism*) In the third place, he advocates the establishment of a new religion of atheism. The new religion "does not depend on anything else" but "on valuing one's own mind." The new religion "does not take any ghost or spirit for its founder." (*A Reply to Tiezheng*) In his opinion, the new religion aims at carrying on and promoting self-consciousness, and at enhancing revolutionary morality. Believing in the new religion, the revolutionary partisans have self-respect, and are dauntless and not afraid of any sacrifices. Each may proceed in revolutionary struggles by relying on his own subjective spirit as an independent individual. They have no need to rely on any outside forces. And, furthermore, by believing in this new religion, people may set up an ideal world of "five nonbeings" — no government, no villages, no human race, no living creatures, and no world altogether. (Cf. *On Five Nonbeings*) Thus a thin religious veil covers the democratic-revolutionary thought of Zhang.

There are both epistemological root cause and social root cause for the philosophical thought of Zhang in his later years, which elevates self-consciousness. The epistemological root cause is connected with the rationalist character of the philosophical thought of his early years. The social root cause in a profound way reflects the fact that the revolutionaries among the Chinese bourgeoisie had separated themselves from the broad masses of the people, and they lacked the practical strength to carry forward the revolution. Zhang was stuck in the same dilemma. Holding up the democratic-revolutionary banner to engage in a heated controversy with the bourgeois reformists, he had to resort to the subjective spirit so that he might make efforts to transform the old religious belief into a revolutionary weapon. Fundamentally speaking, the contradiction in his thought was decided by the times in which he lived and the class of which he was a representative.

Sun Yat-sen (1866-1925) was originally named Sun Wen. Yat-sen was his alias. Later, for the sake of convenience in the course of his revolutionary activities, he changed his name to Sun Zhongshan, the name by which he is universally known today. He was born into a peasant family in Xiangshan County (present-day Zhongshan City), Guangdong Province. While still very young, he went to Honolulu with his elder brother, where he attended school. It was at that time that he began to come into contact with Western society. Later he studied at the new College of Medicine in Hong Kong for five years. After graduation, he practiced medicine in Macao, Guangzhou and other places. The crisis of the Chinese nation at the end of the 19th century aroused patriotic zeal in the mind of Sun. In 1894, he wrote a letter to Li Hongzhang, Minister of the Northern Sea and Foreign Trade of the Qing Dynasty, proposing a plan for political reform and the salvation of China. In the letter, he said,

"A good government should be able to make the best possible use of men, be able to turn land resources to best account, be able to let all things serve their proper purpose, and be able to facilitate commodity interflow." (*A Letter to Li Hongzhang*) When his advice was ignored, Sun determined that the only way to save China from subjugation by foreign powers and ensure her survival was to overthrow the Qing Dynasty by means of revolution. In 1894, he founded China Revival Society in Honolulu, the first revolutionary association in the modern history of China. Sun's revolutionary manifesto included a call to "Drive out the Tartars (meaning the Qing Dynasty) and revive the Chinese nation, and establish a federal government." He threw himself into preparations for an armed uprising. In 1905, he founded the China Revolutionary League, the program of which included the equalization of landed property. In the *Foreword to the People's Journal*, he enunciated his famous Three Principles of the People, viz, "The principle of nationalism," "The principle of the people's rights" and "The principle of the people's livelihood." The first principle entailed the overthrow of the Qing Dynasty and opposition to imperialist oppression of China. The second involved the abolition of the feudal monarchy and its replacement by a constitutional, democratic government. The third principle was based on an age-old call of the peasants for the right to own land. The Three Principles of the People laid the ideological foundation for the eventual success of the democratic revolution led by the Chinese bourgeoisie.

Sun Yat-sen organized armed uprisings again and again. All ended in failure, until a spontaneous insurrection sparked the Revolution of 1911, which finally put an end to over 2,000 years of despotism. A bourgeois democratic republic was established. On January 1, 1911, Sun Yat-sen assumed the office of the Provisional President of the Republic of China, in Nanjing. His ambition to change China into a modern bourgeois republic was thwarted, however, first by Yuan Shikai, a senior general of the erstwhile Qing Dynasty, who briefly restored the monarchy with himself as emperor, and Duan Qirui, who aspired to rule the country relying on the forces of the warlord generals.

Pondering the failure of the revolution, from 1917 to 1919 Sun Yat-sen wrote extensively. During this period, he finished his magnum opus *The Program of the Construction of the Nation*. This work is divided into three parts, namely, *The Doctrine of Sun Wen*, *A Plan for Industry*, and

The Preliminary Democracy. In this work he expounds his theories and plans for building a bourgeois democratic republic in the three aspects of philosophy, economics and politics. Of these three parts, the *Doctrine of Sun Wen* is Sun's main philosophical work. In it, he constructs a unique philosophical system by summing up the experiences and lessons of his forerunners in the democratic revolution and by absorbing the achievements of modern Western natural and social sciences. He attempts to elucidate the developmental road of the Chinese democratic revolution. But it was only after the October Revolution in Russia in 1917 and the May Fourth Movement of 1919, and with the help of the Chinese communists, that Sun Yat-sen was able to see clearly the way for the salvation of China. He stated, "As for the revolution, in future we have to learn from Russia; otherwise we will not be able to achieve anything." (*A Letter to Chiang Kai-shek*) In 1924, Sun presided over the First National Congress of the Chinese Nationalist Party (Kuomintang, or KMT), at which he reorganized the party, expounded upon the Three Principles of the People and put forth the Three Great Policies: uniting with Russia, uniting with the Communists, and assisting the workers and peasants. Thus he developed the Old Three Principles of the People into the New Three Principles of the People. It was clear that the new principles were basically in accordance with the political program for that stage of the democratic revolution put forth by the Chinese Communist Party. So they constituted the political foundation of the first period of cooperation between the KMT and CCP (1923-1927). Consequently, the Great Revolution of 1924-1927 started.

In March 1925, Sun passed away in Beijing. Immediately before his death, he announced, "The revolution has not yet succeeded, and all comrades must continue to make the utmost efforts." Mao Zedong paid fitting tribute to Sun when he said, "He exhausted his life's energies in order to transform China. He truly bent his back to the task until his dying day." (*In Commemoration of Dr. Sun Yat-sen*)

Sun Yat-sen absorbed the achievements of modern natural sciences, especially the Darwinian theory of evolution, and gave a materialist explanation of the problems of the origin of Nature and the evolution of the universe.

Sun says, since Charles Darwin's *On the Origin of Species by Means of Natural Selection* was published, "People have become suddenly clear-minded about the theory of evolution." Since ancient times, many people of wisdom have puzzled over the question, "Of what are Heaven, Earth and the myriad things made up?" But none of them could come up with a correct explanation. Charles Darwin was the first person to discover the truth that the world and the myriad things in it are the results of evolution. On the basis of the principle of evolution, Sun divides the development of the universe into three stages. The first stage is "the period of the evolution of matter," which refers to the origin of the universe and its formation. The next stage is "the period of the evolution of species," which refers to the stage of the emergence and development of life organisms. The last stage is "the period of the evolution of man," which refers to the stage of the emergence and development of mankind. (Cf. *The Doctrine of Sun Wen·Chapter 4*) The universe is a natural process the basis of which is the evolution of matter.

Sun's provides a materialist explanation of the origin and formation of the universe:

> "During the primeval period, the Great Ultimate (i.e., the "ether") moved, and produced electrons. The electrons congealed, and produced the elements. The elements combined, and produced matter. Different kinds of matter got together, and produced the Earth. This was the first stage of the evolution of the world." (*The Doctrine of Sun Wen·Chapter 4*)

He adopts the term "Great Ultimate," a category in ancient Chinese philosophy, to translate the Western concept of "ether." "Ether" is the primitive material from which the electrons, the elements and even the Earth were produced. In his view, "ether" is without any spiritual properties. Life and spiritual things appeared only after the Earth came into being. Sun, in his theory of evolution, overcomes the defect of Tan Sitong, who confuses "ether" with "benevolence" and "mental force."

Sun also gives a materialist explanation of the emergence and development of revolution. According to his doctrine, the development of the natural sciences demonstrates that life organisms came into being only after a long period of evolution of the Earth: "All species, from the smallest to the largest, from the simplest to the most complicated, according to the laws of struggle for existence, natural selection, and the survival of the fittest, were already in existence when man appeared on the Earth. Thousands of years passed before mankind acquired human nature." (*The Doctrine of Sun Wen·Chapter 4*) What is the starting point of life, which evolves from a lower level to a higher level, and of the life organisms, which evolve from simple forms to complicated forms? Sun puts forth a category, which is called the "living atom," equal to the cell of modern biology. The "living atoms" are the basic units of the structures and functions of all living things. Every cell is an independent unit of life, and many cells constitute a unified life organism. He says, "Research done by modern scientists shows that the material of which human beings and all living things are composed is nothing other than cells, namely, living atoms." (*The Doctrine of Sun Wen·Chapter 4*) His thought constitutes a scientific and materialist explanation of the origin and evolution of species, and it is also a negation of the theory that some deity created the world. Nevertheless, limited by the level of the biology of the day, Sun mistakenly thinks that "the living atom has perception." That is, every cell has perception and even consciousness:

> "According to the knowledge of sciences that we have today, the living atom is something that has perceptions, soul and intelligence. It is able to act and to think. It is able to have ideas and to make plans." (*The Doctrine of Sun Wen·Chapter 1*)

He agrees with Mencius that "living atoms" have "intuitive knowledge and innate ability." In this, he confuses the cell's reaction to stimuli with the consciousness of the human brain, which is a kind of special matter. In short, his doctrine of the living atoms is inclined towards hylozoism. Such being the case, Sun is not a thoroughgoing materialist when he discusses the relationship between matter and consciousness. He uses two categories from traditional Chinese philosophy, namely, the base and application, to explain the relationship between matter and consciousness. "In the human body there are five organs and several hundred bones. They constitute the base of a human being, and they belong to matter. A man is able to speak and act. Speech and action belong to the application, which is actuated by the human spirit. Both sides help each other, and they cannot be separated from each other." Here, he affirms that matter decides spirit, and that the spirit has the initiative. On the other hand, he says, "Whatever does not belong to matter belongs to spirit." (*The Spiritual Education of the Servicemen*)

Obviously, he does not understand that spiritual phenomena are attributions of the human brain. Therefore, he sometimes exaggerates the function of the spirit. He says, "As for the mind, it is the ultimate source of the myriad things." (*The Doctrine of Sun Wen·The Author's Preface*)

In the third place, Sun makes a materialist explanation of the emergence and development of mankind. In his opinion, man has evolved from animals. He says, "In the first period of mankind's existence, man was in no way distinguishable from animals. Thousands of years passed before mankind acquired human nature." (*The Doctrine of Sun Wen·Chapter 4*) He refutes the Christian doctrine that the world was made by God in six days. He attacked the theories of divine creation and the Mandate of Heaven as fictions concocted to serve the feudal ruling class. He points out as follows:

> 1. "Those who occupy the positions of emperors or kings in many cases forge "heaven's will" as a guarantee for their interests. They say that the special positions they occupy were awarded to them by Heaven. Therefore, if the people dare to oppose them, it means that the people oppose Heaven." (*The Principle of the People's Rights·Lecture 3*)
>
> 2. "Today's worldwide trends obviously spell the end for 'divine right' and the power of monarchs." (*The Principle of the People's Rights·Lecture 1*)

While combining the struggle against "divine right" with the struggle against monarchical power, he combines the advocacy of science with the advocacy of democracy. He firmly believes that science will defeat "divine right," and that democracy will remove monarchical power. This is the general tendency of the development of the history, and it is irresistible.

All his life, Sun was a conscientious thinker, "who adopted himself to the trends of the world, and who met the needs of the people and the society." (*The Doctrine of Sun Wen·Chapter 8*) From beginning to end, he stood in the forefront of the tide of the times. All his life, he advocated the progressive theory of the evolution of the universe.

Sun's view on knowledge and action is the essential part of the whole system of his philosophy. By summing up the experiences of and drawing lessons from China's democratic revolution, in a modern hermeneutical way he makes a new interpretation of the views of knowledge and action of the Chinese philosophical tradition. He puts forth a unique theory: "To know is difficult, but to do is easy."

First of all, Sun gives a novel elaboration of the relationship between knowledge and action. He does not agree with Zhu Xi's contention that "Knowledge goes before action" and Wang Shouren's dictum, "Knowledge and action should go hand in hand." Sun thinks that the relationship between knowledge and action develops along with the evolution of society. "The evolution of the world and mankind can be divided into three periods. The first period is from the primeval state to that of civilization; this is the period of action without knowledge. The second period is from a lower civilization to a higher civilization; this is the period of action before knowledge. The third period refers to the stage in which the sciences have already been developed; this is the period of knowledge before action." (*The Doctrine of Sun Wen·Chapter 5*)

Sun's three stages imply that the development of human knowledge is a process going from ignorance to knowledge, from a little knowledge to a great deal of knowledge, and from spontaneous knowledge to conscious knowledge. The so-called "action without knowledge" means that man takes practice for the starting point of cognition: "All the progress of mankind originates in action without knowledge. This is a natural law, and it does not change along with the invention of the sciences. Therefore, the first step in the development of mankind is one of action without knowledge." (*The Doctrine of Sun Wen·Chapter 7*)

In his view, practice goes before any knowledge. Despite the progress made in science, this situation remains unchanged. The so-called "action before knowledge" means that man acquires knowledge by means of practice. "The ancients acquired their knowledge in a painstaking way. Perhaps at the very beginning they might have spent hundreds or even thousands of years in taking action before they came to form some knowledge. Perhaps there might have been thousands of people who made extraordinarily persistent and painstaking efforts and underwent numerous trials before they came to form some knowledge." (*The Doctrine of Sun Wen·Chapter 5*)

Sun provides various examples from Chinese history to show this:

> "In ancient China there was Suiren, a legendary ruler, who first got fire from wood by friction. We should like to ask, if he had not rubbed the wood, how could he have got fire from it? Shennong, also a legendary ruler, discovered medicines by tasting herbs with his own tongue. We should like to ask, if he had not tasted the herbs with his own tongue, how could he have known the nature of the medicines?" (*To Know Is Difficult But to Do Is Easy*)

Thus it is clear that knowledge develops in the course of practice. "Knowledge before action" means that people use true knowledge to direct their practice. This happens only after man enters the era of well-developed science. It is necessary to use science to direct the people's practice. He says, "Opinions come from knowledge. Proper arrangement comes from opinions. In accordance with proper arrangement, a good plan may be made. With a good plan, people may make efforts to realize their goals." If we act in this way, we may avoid mistakes and yield twice the result with half the effort. Therefore, in his opinion, "If we seek true knowledge through scientific laws, we shall never meet with any difficulties in our actions." And "With knowledge one must be able to act, and with knowledge it is easier for one to take action." (*The Doctrine of Sun Wen·Chapter 5*) Based on the three stages of the development of the relationship between knowledge and action, Sun recapitulates the relationship between knowledge and action as follows: "From action we seek knowledge, and with knowledge we proceed in action." (*The Doctrine of Sun Wen·Chapter 5*) Here he emphasizes that action plays a decisive role in the acquisition of knowledge, and at the same time he affirms that knowledge plays an initiative role in action.

Sun's theory that "To know is difficult, but to do is easy" is a direct refutation of a traditional mindset in China, i.e., that "To know is not difficult, but to act is truly difficult." This, he considers, has exerted a terribly negative influence upon the Chinese people. The reason why quite a number of revolutionaries lost faith in the revolutionary cause in the period of difficulties in the aftermath of the Revolution of 1911 lies in the fact that they have been obsessed with the idea that "To know is easy but to do is difficult." Therefore, on the one hand they paid no attention to the role of revolutionary theory, and on the other, they lacked the courage to plunge themselves into the practical struggle. To remedy this situation, Sun stands the maxim on its head:

> "To act is not difficult, but to know is truly difficult." (*To Know Is Difficult But to Do Is Easy*)

In his view, the acquisition of theoretical knowledge is much more difficult than proceeding in practice. In order to illustrate this point, he cites ten examples, which are food and drink, expenditure, composition, house building, shipbuilding, city construction, canal digging, electronics, chemistry and evolution. In the case of food and drink, it is the most universal and easiest thing in the daily life of everybody. Even newborn babies receive nourishment in the form of the mother's milk. But to acquire knowledge of nourishment, cooking and hygiene, is not at all easy. For centuries, many experts have spent their lives mulling these spheres earnestly, but nobody has yet thoroughly resolved these problems. To spend money on something is another example. It is an indispensable thing in daily life. In civilized, society money is absolutely necessary for the purchase of clothing, food, shelter and transportation. But it is very difficult to have a thorough understanding of the theory of money. Sun says: "Until you have a comprehensive survey of the evolution of human culture, until you have a detailed examination of the sources and changes of finance and trade, you will not be able to understand the function of money. Until you research into economics, make a detailed examination of the history of industry and commerce, the banking system, the evolution of the monetary system, you will not be able to understand the function of money."

Sun maintains that there is practice before there is knowledge. And he urges people to act because it is very clear that "without knowledge one is able to act all the same. In action, one may get to know what one does not know." (*The Doctrine of Sun Wen·Chapter 7*) At the same time, he says, "To know is difficult." In his opinion, scientific knowledge, which is a summary of practice, is very valuable. We must pay full attention to the guiding role of scientific knowledge upon practice. "Those who are able to know must be able to act." (*The Doctrine of Sun Wen·Chapter 6*) Therefore, Sun Yat-sen demands that all the members of the revolutionary party must boldly take part in practice, meanwhile being attentive to the revolutionary theories and methods, so that the revolutionaries may be clear about the goal of their struggle and be confident of winning the final victory. After he developed the Old Three Principles of the People into the New Three Principles of the People, he emphasized even more earnestly that it was necessary to follow the example of the Russian Revolution. Revolutionary practice should be directed by a revolutionary theory. He says, "From now on, if we make revolution, we must first seek knowledge. After we have gained knowledge, we will start to take action. If we take action after we have gained knowledge, our success will be naturally as great as that obtained in Russia." (*Speech to KMT Representatives from Various Provinces and Mongolia*)

By a deep-going elaboration of the relationship between knowledge and action, Sun develops and enriches the traditional categories in Chinese philosophy of "knowledge" and "action." The ancient Chinese philosophers' understanding of the relationship between knowledge and action was in most cases restricted to the knowledge and practice of feudal ethics. As for the "knowledge" talked by Sun, it refers to scientific knowledge and the theory of the bourgeois democratic revolution. Such knowledge and theory reflect objective things and events correctly, because they are formed when people apply science and rational thinking to their activities. As for the "action" talked by Sun, it includes productive activities, scientific experiments and the struggles of the bourgeois democratic revolution. Thus, his view of knowledge and action possesses the brand-new features of modern times in that it has already broken through the narrowness of the ancient Chinese view of knowledge and action.

Sun's view of knowledge and action possesses great significance both in theory and in practice. Nevertheless, in his thought there are some limitations. First, in a mechanical way he divides the relationship between knowledge and action into three stages, separating the relationship between knowledge and action. Furthermore, he infers his view of "the divisions of knowledge and action" from the social division of labor. He thinks that the more the sciences develop, the more people separate knowledge from action. He says, "Those who know do not necessarily act, and those who act do not necessarily know." (*The Doctrine of Sun Wen·Chapter 5*) It seems that only practical men may act, while theorists, scientists and revolutionists should be content merely to "know." Second, in his theory that "To know is difficult, but to do is easy" there is a tendency to exaggerate the role of theory and to despise the significance of practice. He even goes so far as to say, "Most of the civilization and progress in the world is the product of propaganda." *(Propaganda Creates Social Strength*)

When Sun explains the new version of the Three Principles of the People, he puts forth a historical view of the people's livelihood, as follows:

"The people's livelihood is nothing but the peoples' life. It means the existence of society, the means of livelihood of the nationals, and the life of the masses." (*The Principle of the People's Livelihood·Lecture 1*)

In his view, "the people's livelihood" includes both the economic life of society and the demands of mankind for its existence. Since mankind continuously seeks existence, and demands that the economy should be developed, society evolves continuously. In this way, the problem of the people's livelihood becomes "the crux of history" and "the primitive motive force of social evolution." (*The Principle of the People's Livelihood·Lecture 1*)

Sun sees many problems in the people's livelihood. The problem of food and clothing of the broad masses of the Chinese people is worth the fullest notice. He says, "To feed the people is the first important task of the people's livelihood. To clothe the people is the second important task of the people's livelihood." In order to solve the problem of the people's livelihood, "We must ensure that the four hundred million people of China may have their demands for food and clothing satisfied." (*The Principle of the People's Livelihood·Lecture 4*) In order to seek the route and method for the solution of such an important problem, he concentrates on the two areas, the economy and politics. In respect to the economy, Sun postulates two measures. The first measure is the "equalization of landed property." The second measure is the "control of capital." By the first, he means that the government should collect land taxes according to the current price of the land and purchases land at current prices in order to gradually abolish the monopoly of the land wielded by the landed aristocracy, that is, "The land should be distributed to all the tillers." (*The Principle of the People's Livelihood·Lecture 3*) By the second, he means that the government should administer the banks, railways, navigation lines and suchlike large-scale enterprises and monopoly enterprises, so that "the private capitalist system cannot manipulate the people's livelihood and the national economy." (*Declaration of the First Congress of the Chinese Nationalist Party*) With respect to politics, Sun maintains that the country should take an independent stand, keep the initiative in its hands, oppose imperialist aggression, and nurture the development of the national economy. He says, "In order that the problem of the people's livelihood may be thoroughly solved, we must first turn our hand to politics. It is urgently necessary to refute all the unequal treaties and to regain control of the customs, which have been under foreign administration for quite a long time. Only by so doing can we increase taxes according to our own wishes and protect our own products, thereby stemming the flow of foreign goods into our markets. Then, the industry of our country will grow naturally." (*The Principle of the People's Livelihood·Lecture 4*) In Sun's opinion, these measures are the main content of the principle of the people's livelihood. He explains its essence like this: "We must ensure that everybody can make his livelihood with equal status. Only then will the four hundred million Chinese people be able to enjoy a happy life." (*Speech at the Peasants' Get-Together in Guangzhou*) Full of confidence, he predicts that, so long as his principle of the people's livelihood is put into practice, China will be able to catch up with the advanced countries of Europe and America in near future. "China will become a peaceful and happy country and a cheerful land." (*Speech at the Commemoration Meeting on the Anniversary of the First Guangdong Women's Normal School*)

And Sun points out, the solution to the problem of the people's livelihood is closely connected with the political one of the people becoming the masters of their own affairs. He says, "When everybody's mind is inclined towards the republic, China will permit no emperor, and China will become prosperous and powerful." (*Speech at the Commemoration Meeting on the Anniversary of the First Guangdong Women's Normal School*) He proclaims, "The Republic of China today is the family property of all of us, so everyone of us is the master of this family property." Only by taking the people for the masters in this way can the broad masses of the people enjoy equal status economically. Only by so doing can China build itself up. Therefore, he calls for "arousing the masses" and "assisting the peasants and workers."

Sun strives to find the fundamental agent of history in social and economic life. He lays stress on the fundamentally material interests of the masses of the people. He maintains that officials should work for the happiness of the people, and he hopes that China will be built up into a democratic and civilized modern country. This shows that he embraces a great ambition as a herald of the revolution. His historical view of the people's livelihood he inherits from a democratic idea which sprouted in ancient China, to the effect that "when the way of virtue and justice prevails, the whole world will be one community." He also embraces and develops the vision of utopian socialism described by Hong Xiuquan and Kang Youwei in modern times. And what is more important, he accepts the influence of the materialist conception of history in line with Marxism, so he makes an important breakthrough in the development of the Chinese philosophy of history. Nevertheless, Sun is not a Marxist, and therefore there is a separation between the historical view of the people's livelihood and the materialist conception of history. In the first place, Sun's category of "the people's livelihood" lacks the concrete content of society and history. He overemphasizes man's desire for existence, and he fails to see the fact that it is the mode of production that decides the level of development of society. In the second place, since Sun does not understand the decisive role of the mode of production, he cannot understand the profound root cause of the class struggle. On the one hand he shows great indignation toward the exploitation of the peasants by the landlords, and of the workers by the capitalists. On the other, he thinks that class struggle is a kind of "disease" occurring in the course of social evolution. And he thinks that the remedy for class struggle is to substitute "the principle of mutual aid" for "the competitive principle." In his opinion, "The foundations of the evolution of mankind are quite different from the basic principles of the evolution of other creatures. Among the latter, the struggle for existence was the law, whereas men were guided by the principle of mutual aid. Society and the sciences are the concrete expression of this mutual aid. Morality, love, friendship and justice, all these are forms of expressing mutual aid. Mankind develops and progresses only on the condition that it obeys these fundamental laws. Otherwise, it perishes." (*The Doctrine of Sun Wen·Chapter 4*) Furthermore, he thinks, "The Chinese are altogether poor people. None of them is a tycoon. Among them, there is only the difference between big poverty and small poverty." (*The Principle of the People's Livelihood·Lecture 2*) Such a social contradiction can be solved only by "the equalization of landed property" and "the control of capital." It is absolutely unnecessary to wage class struggle or violent revolution. He says, "We are talking about the principle of the people's livelihood. Although we revere Marx's learning very much, we cannot apply Marxist ways to the practice here in China. Today, it is quite enough for us to follow the intention of Marx, but we cannot use Marxist ways." (*The Principle of the People's Livelihood·Lecture 2*) In the third place, although Sun has sincere sympathy for the broad masses of the people, and he wholeheartedly plunges himself into the transformation of China, his discourse is burdened with the serious limitation of the heroic conception of history. In his opinion, according to the natural gifts of various individuals, mankind may be divided into three categories, namely, "people who have foresight," "people who know afterwards," and "people who do not know." As for the "people who have foresight," they are extremely intelligent. "Mankind achieves progress and civilization only on the condition of finding the ways and means in advance, and thereupon proceeding in many great causes." As for the "people who know afterwards," they are at a lower rank of intelligence and capability. "They themselves cannot create or invent; they can only follow other people and imitate them." As for the "people who do not know," they are at an even lower rank of intelligence and capability. "They know nothing even if they are taught by somebody else. They can do nothing but follow the directions of other people." As a result, "The people in the first rank are inventors. The people in the second rank are propagandists. The people in the third rank are activists." (*The Principle of the People's Livelihood·Lecture 5*) Here, the "people who have foresight" refers to the bourgeoisie and petty-bourgeoisie, and their intellectuals. The "people who do not know" refers to the workers and peasants — the broad masses of the people. In this way, by distinguishing between natural gifts and between the capability for knowledge and action, when he proceeds to the next step, it is quite natural that he debases the role that the broad masses of the people play in pushing forward the wheel of history.

Sun Yat-sen was a great revolutionary and thinker of the bourgeois democratic revolution. His philosophical activities reflected the great historical progress of the Chinese democratic revolution, which underwent a great revolutionary transition from the old democratic revolution to the new democratic revolution. His philosophy contains contributions and limitations as well, both of which were products of history.

When Sun passed away, his philosophy was developed in two opposite directions.

On the one hand, the ideological representatives of the Chinese comprador bourgeoisie distorted Sun's ideas by discarding the democratic and materialist essence of his thought, giving full play to the defects in his theories. By so doing, they set up an ideological system in opposition to Marxist philosophy. For example, Dai Jitao (1890-1949) put forth a "philosophy of the people's livelihood," in which he fits the category of "the people's livelihood" into the body of transmitted orthodox teachings of Confucius and Mencius. He says, "The people's livelihood is the expression of the great virtue of the universe. Benevolence and charity constitute the foundation of the philosophy of the people's livelihood." (*Foundation of Sun Wen's Philosophy*) Again, Chen Lifu (1900-2001) put forth a "theory of life organisms." According to him, the "living atom" is "the noumenal attributions of the universe." (*The Principle of Life*) He says, "The whole universe is constituted of atoms which have life, and therefore everything in the universe has life." (*Theory of Life Organism*) Chiang Kai-shek, Sun's political successor, stipulated a "philosophy of arduous action," in which he distorts the idea that "to know is difficult, but to do is easy." He says, "From ancient to modern times in the whole universe there is only one key word, namely, 'action,' which can create everything." He adds, "People who know afterwards and people who do not know should do only one thing. That is, they should only follow people of foresight. In this way, they may save much precious time, and complete the revolution in time." (*A First-hand Account of the Stages in Researching the Revolutionary Philosophy*) In fact, this is propaganda for the obscurantist philosophy that the broad masses of the people should obey their rulers, preached by Chiang Kai-shek and his clique.

On the other hand, the Chinese Marxists inherited and developed the materialist and democratic essence of Sun's philosophy. They combined the theory of knowledge in line with dialectic materialism with the practice of the Chinese revolution. Under the guidance of such a world outlook and theory of knowledge, the Chinese people achieved victory in the democratic revolution. As Mao Zedong pointed out, "(Sun Yat-sen) left us many beneficial things politically. The modern Chinese people, excluding a handful of reactionary elements, are all successors to Dr. Sun Yat-sen's revolutionary cause." And he further points out, "Like many other great historical personages who stood in the forefront while directing the trend of the times, Dr. Sun Yat-sen had his own defects. This must be explained in the light of historical conditions. The people should understand him, and not make excessive demands of the forerunners." (*In Commemoration of Dr. Sun Yat-sen*)

38.

The Fusion of Chinese and Western Philosophies After the May Fourth Movement

Although the Revolution of 1911 overthrew the feudal monarchy which had lasted for 2,000 years, and established the Republic of China, it failed to accomplish the task of the Chinese democratic revolution, and especially it failed to accomplish the task of wiping out feudalism in the ideological and cultural spheres. In such a situation, a batch of progressive intellectuals represented by Chen Duxiu (1880-1942), Hu Shi (1891-1962), Li Dazhao (1889-1927), Lu Xun (1880-1936), Wu Yu (1871-1949) and Qian Xuantong (1887-1939) launched the New Culture Movement. Holding high the twin banners of "science" and "democracy," they violently attacked China's traditional feudal ideology and culture on an unprecedented scale.

In September 1915, the magazine *Youth*, under Chen Duxiu's general editorship, started publication in Shanghai (In 1916 the magazine changed its name to *La Jeunesse*, or *New Youth*), which marked the commencement of the New Culture Movement. In the first issue of *Youth*, Chen Duxiu published an article titled "An Address Given Respectfully to Youth," in which he first raised the watchwords "science" and "democracy." He asserted, "If our compatriots are going to get rid of the age of barbarism, if our compatriots feel ashamed of being under-civilized people, we must exert ourselves to catch up with the advanced nations, and we should lay equal stress on science and democracy." He called on youth "to cut a piece of iron with a trenchant edge, and to cut a tangled skein of jute with a sharp knife." He called on them to give full play to such a spirit, so as to emancipate their thinking, break through all snares and traps, and struggle against the ideology and culture of feudalism. "Even if they are part of the legacy bequeathed to us by our ancestors, instructions provided by the sages and worthies, that which is advocated by the government, and that which is worshipped by society, they are not worth a cent." Li Dazhao also published essays in *New Youth*, of which the most famous was "Youthfulness." He called on young people to "break through the snares and traps of history, and destroy the jails of the cliché doctrines." He encouraged young people to struggle for a youthful new China: "We young people must swear an solemn oath to the whole of society, to make our determination clear. Our determination does not lie in having a glib tongue to demonstrate that the white-haired old China will not perish. Our determination lies in promoting a movement to bring forth the rebirth of a youthful new China. Whether or not this generation of ours will have a foothold in the world does not lie in the prolongation of the meager existence of white-haired old China, but in the reincarnation or resurrection of the youthful new China." ("Youthfulness")

Soon after the New Culture Movement arose, it directed its critical spearhead at the moral principles, cardinal guides and constant virtues of China's traditional feudal society. A loud cry was raised: "Down with the 'Confucian shop'!" This showed the determination of a generation who desired to break completely with Confucius and his followers. Chen Duxiu published an essay titled "1916," in which he condemns the Three Cardinal Guides:

> "The Confucian doctrine of the Three Cardinal Guides is the great foundation of all the moral principles and political measures. According to the first cardinal guide, that 'the ruler guides the subject,' the common people become an appendix to the monarch, and they have no independent personality at all. According to the second cardinal guide, that 'the father guides the son,' children become an appendix to their father, and they have no independent personality at all. And according to the third cardinal guide, that 'the husband guides the wife,' the wife becomes an appendix to her husband, and

> she has no independent personality at all. Now let us examine the men and women in the world. We find that they are either subjects or children or wives, but none of them has an independent personality of his or her own. This queer phenomenon is brought about by the doctrine of the Three Cardinal Guides. And from this doctrine there have appeared quite a number of moral terms that are treated as golden laws and precious rules — loyalty, filial piety, chastity and so on. They are not moral principles which instruct people to consider others in one's own place. They are nothing more than slave morality which causes one to put oneself willingly under the yoke of others."

Lu Xun published a famous short story titled, *A Madman's Diary*, in which he mercilessly discloses that the essence of feudal ethics is to destroy man. Adopting the tone of a madman, he says, "I opened a history book, and checked. This history book had no ages or dates. On each page there were several words written in a poor hand. They were 'Humanity, Justice and Morality.' Anyhow, I could not go to sleep, so I stared at these words for a good while. Then I saw these words clearly, and they read, 'Eat the flesh of human beings!'" Wu Yu also pointed out the negative influence of Confucian thought upon the development of Chinese culture. He says, "Confucius was, of course, a great personage in his day. But if one adheres to his doctrines and uses them to direct the whole world and the later ages, one will obstruct the development of culture. To do so is to fan the flame of absolutism. We have to launch an assault against those who dare to do so. It is the historical situation that makes such a demand on us." (*To Chen Duxiu*) These ideas exerted a tremendous influence upon the society of Wu Yu's time, as if they had opened the ears of the deaf and the eyes of the blind.

Of course, the New Culture Movement in its initial stage belonged to the old-type enlightenment movement of the bourgeoisie. Nevertheless, since it launched a bold attack against feudal ideology and culture on an unprecedented scale, its historical achievement was great. As the pace of the movement accelerated, all kinds of Western philosophical trends rushed into China, including Marxism. In 1917, the October Revolution was victorious, and in 1919, the May Fourth Movement broke out in China. These two great events brought advanced thinkers among the

Chinese people quickly to Marxism. It was in this period that Li Dazhao, Chen Duxiu and other advocators of the New Culture Movement began to accept and propagate Marxism. Accordingly, the New Culture Movement broke away from the old-type enlightenment movement of the bourgeoisie in China, as its ideological and cultural content was in line with the new democratic movement.

In the course of the New Culture Movement, there arose a long-term controversy on "the problem of the Eastern and Western cultures" around the central topic: "Where should China go?" The commencement of this controversy lies in a dispute which broke out in 1915 between Chen Duxiu, who was then the editor-in-chief of *New Youth*, and Cangfu (the penname of Du Yaquan, 1873-1933), who was the editor-in-chief of *East* magazine. Before long, the dispute involved several hundred people, some 1,000 essays and dozens of monographs. By the early 1920s, the participants had divided into three major factions.

One faction was represented by Hu Shi, Jiang Menglin (1886-1964), Luo Jialun (1897-1969), Ding Wenjiang (1887-1936) and Wu Zhihui (1866-1953). The scholars of this school affirmed the value of Western science and democracy. They claimed that it was necessary to thoroughly do away with traditional Chinese culture, and take the road of "wholesale Westernization." This was the only way to transform China, which "falls behind the other countries in all things," and to help her enter the family of nations.

Another faction was represented by Du Yaquan (1873-1933), Zhang Shizhao (1882-1973), Liang Shuming (1893-1988) and Liang Qichao (1873-1929). In their opinion, the World War I of 1914-1918 marked the complete bankruptcy of the Western theory that "Science can achieve anything." It was urgent to save Western material civilization by means of Eastern spiritual civilization. They emphasized that Eastern culture possesses values that cannot be replaced by any in Western culture. Therefore, it was necessary to reexamine the doctrine of Confucius and adopt the Confucian school to modern needs.

The third faction was represented by Chen Duxiu (1880-1942), Li Dazhao (1889-1927) and Qu Qiubai (1899-1935). The scholars of this school began to use the materialist conception of history of Marxism to analyze Chinese society and the general world situation. They maintained that it is necessary to have a double retrospection covering traditional Chinese culture and modern world culture. They categorically affirmed that only socialism can save China.

The two major representatives of the "wholesale Westernization" school were Hu Shi, who advocated a philosophy of pragmatism, and Liang Shuming, who advocated "philosophy of life." We shall discuss the dissemination and development of Marxist historical materialism in the next chapter.

Hu Shi (1891-1962) was a native of Jixi County, Anhui Province. He was one of the scholars who exerted the greatest influence on Chinese society in the modern period. In his early years, Hu Shi studied in the US under John Dewey (1859-1952), a leading philosopher of pragmatism. When he returned to China, he became a professor at Peking University. At the early stage of the New Culture Movement, he published a number of essays, including "My Humble Opinion of the Literary Reform and Ibsenism," in the magazine *New Youth*. In these essays he advocated a revolution in literature and the liberation of the personality. He played an active part in the struggle against feudal ideology and culture, becoming one of the leading personages in the New Culture Movement. Hu Shi devoted his life to political reform, advocating the establishment of a democratic political regime in China. During the anti-Japanese War, he served as Chinese ambassador to the US, and contributed greatly to the work of winning international support for the Chinese people's resistance to Japanese aggression. In 1946, he took up the post of president of Peking University. In 1948 he returned to the US, and from there went to Taiwan in 1957, where he assumed the office of president of the Academia Sinica. Hu Shi left his mark in many fields, including philosophy, literature and history. His main philosophical treatises are *Experimentalism*, *Problems and Doctrines*, *Preface to the Sciences and Outlook on Life*, *Which Way Shall We Take?* and *Introduction to My Own Thought*. On the history of philosophy, he wrote *An Outline of the History of Chinese Philosophy (1)*, *A Discourse on Confucianism*, *A History of Pre-Qin Logic* and *A Draft History of Chinese Thought in Ancient and Medieval Times*. Of these works, *An Outline of the History of Chinese Philosophy (1)* is worth special notice. This book was written on the eve of the May Fourth Movement of 1919. It was the first work to use the views and methods of modern times to investigate the history of Chinese philosophy, and, as such, it was a pioneering work, marking the emergence of the study of the history of Chinese philosophy as an independent discipline.

After Dewey, Hu Shi was most influenced by the thought of Thomas Henry Huxley (1825-1895). In his view, Huxley was the representative of neo-pragmatism in its "age of destruction." In this age, the goal was to free man's thought from the fetters of religious absolutism. Hu Shi considered Dewey to be the representative of neo-pragmatism in its "age of construction." In this age the goal was to use human thought as a tool for the transformation of society and the education of the people. He lays some emphasis on absorbing and carrying forward John Dewey's pragmatist philosophy, which is centered on instrumentalism. "All thoughts, knowledge and experiences are instruments for life, and they constitute the foundation of life." (*John Dewey's Philosophy*, Lecture 1) And Hu says, "All truths, all academic endeavors, all methods of education in the world, as well as the adages of the sages and worthies, the golden laws and precious rules, and all the unquestionable ideas are nothing more than instruments." (*Ibid*) In his view, the crucial part of Dewey's pragmatist philosophy is the scientific method. That is to say, only "the methods used in the scientific laboratory" can constitute the foundation on which people may discuss the problems of truth, knowledge, morality and education. Following this line of thinking, Hu Shi's pragmatist philosophy centers on the problems of methodology and the conception of truth.

Hu Shi takes "agnosticism" as the method with which to abolish the old ways of thought. The most important contribution made by Huxley, who is noted for advocating the theory of evolution, lies in his methodology of "agnosticism": "According to Huxley, people can put their belief only in knowledge supported by the amplest evidence. Whatever lacks ample evidence can only be left as a matter for future consideration, and people cannot put any belief in it. This is the key point of agnosticism." (*Evolutionism and Agnosticism*)

Starting from this point, Hu maintains that it is necessary to use the attitude of "agnosticism" to weigh all the words of the sages and worthies, all the old histories and legends, all customs and systems, and all the standards used to distinguish right from wrong. In short, it is well to boldly doubt and energetically criticize traditional culture. Especially in the work of research into the science of history, Hu Shi urges, "Prove it with facts!" In effect, he is calling upon researchers to "revaluate everything." He breaks the fetters of the feudal conception of historical science, and lays a foundation for the application of modern methods to historical research. In the process, he attacks Liang Shuming for advocating a revival of the Confucian teachings in order that the Chinese culture might be rejuvenated. Hu Shi points out that this is a cultural philosophy which is totally subjective and arbitrary. He says, "In future, science and democracy will prevail in both China and India." (*After Reading Liang Shuming's The Cultures of the East and the West and Their Philosophies*) There is no doubt that Hu Shi's ideas played an active part in transforming the cultural-psychological structure of traditional Chinese culture.

Hu Shi was famous for saying "Be bold when you raise a hypothesis, and be careful in verifying it." He embraced Dewey's method of establishing a new theory or a new doctrine by dividing the thinking process into five procedures, as follows:

First, it is necessary to set the starting point of thought. This is the realm of perplexity and difficulty.
Second, it is necessary to find where the point of perplexity and difficulty is.
Third, it is necessary to put forth various hypotheses to solve the point of perplexity and difficult.
Fourth, it is necessary to foresee the various results each hypothesis may bring about so as to find which hypothesis is suitable for solving the point of perplexity and difficulty.
Fifth, it is necessary to verify whether such a solution is reliable or not.

Of these five steps, the first two involve setting forth a problem, the third step involves putting forth a hypothesis, and the last two involve the verification or falsification of the hypothesis. Sometimes Hu Shi simplifies the five-step method into a two-step method.:

"There are two important parts of the scientific method, one being the putting forth of a hypothesis, the other being the carrying out of an experiment. Without a hypothesis, an experiment is superfluous." (*How Did the Qing Scholars Pursue Their Studies?*)

Further, he generalizes this idea into two pentameter lines: "Be bold when you raise a hypothesis, /And be careful when you verify it." (*An*

Introduction to My Own Thought) Here, Hu Shi lays stress on the importance of the two links in any scientific discovery, one being to put forward a hypothesis, the other being to apply various experimental means to verify the hypothesis. To a certain degree, he encourages and supports ideological liberty and the spirit of exploration, while opposing the morbid psychology of submitting to ideological "authority."

Hu Shi's statement that "experiences are life" is a typical assertion of empiricism. And he says, "The useful is the truth." Therefore, in his theory of the scientific method there is a tendency to render everything subjectively. He points out, "Experiences are indeed all the intercourse which a living man has when he is confronted with his natural and social surroundings." The result is very clear: "Experiences are life, and life is a way of dealing with the surroundings." And it is quite logical that "in dealing with man's surroundings, the role which thought plays is the most important. Thought is an instrument for dealing with the surroundings." (*Experimentalism*) It follows that experiences include all human activities. Nevertheless of all human activities, the principal part is "the creative activity of thinking." (*The World Philosophy of the Past Fifty Years*) Any hypothesis whatsoever comes from experience and grows out of one's subjective mind. Furthermore, Hu proposes a standard by which people may test whether or not a hypothesis is true. The touchstone is whether or not such a theory is useful when it serves as an instrument. According to Hu Shi, truth "is nothing more than an artificial hypothesis which may be applied to illustrating things and phenomena. When it brings about a satisfactory explanation, it is true. When it fails to bring about a satisfying explanation, it is false. In the latter case, it is necessary to look for another hypothesis to replace the old one." Thus he denies the objectivity and absoluteness of truth. Instead, he thinks that truth is but a hypothesis for man's convenience, and that it is an instrument changing continuously, with which people may deal with their surroundings. In his view, any truth whatsoever is subjective and relative. He says, "The absolute truth is in suspension in midair, abstract, indistinct, and groundless. Therefore, it is beyond verification." (Cf. *Experimentalism*) Thus it is clear that in these precepts "Be bold when you raise a hypothesis," and "And be careful when you verify it," there is a tendency of rendering everything subjectively.

Hu Shi's pragmatist philosophy played a positive role in criticizing

China's traditional feudal culture and in breaking away from the traditional mode of thinking. On the other hand, it exerted a certain negative influence by opposing the dissemination of Marxism. In July 1919, Hu Shi published an essay titled "Research More Problems, Talk about Fewer 'Isms'!" Dealing with the "controversy on problems and isms." he says, "Of course, all kinds of isms and all scientific principles deserve research. Nevertheless, we can only put forth some hypothetical views; we cannot regard them as dogmas with unquestionable values." (*The Third Essay on Problems and "Isms"*) Therefore, "It is the easiest thing to indulge in empty talk about the 'isms,' which are pleasant to the ear. It is something that a kitten or a puppy is able to do. It is something that a parrot or a gramophone is able to do." In his opinion, to disseminate Marxism in China would be no more than "daydreaming, which deceives oneself and others." Only by researching concrete problems can people find the way out for China: "All the valuable ideas are found by tackling this or that concrete problem." (Cf. "Research More Problems, Talk about Fewer 'Isms'!") In addition, Hu Shi applies the pragmatist methodology and concept of truth to guiding historical research. In so doing, he sets up his multi-element conception of history, attributing the causes of social movements to various factors, and he negates the basic premise of historical materialism that the mode of production is the decisive factor behind historical changes. "The causes of historical facts are usually many-sided. Therefore, although we extend the warmest welcome to the 'economic conception of history,' and treat it as an important instrument for historical research, we at the same time have to acknowledge that thoughts, knowledge and suchlike mental things are 'objective causes' as well, which may also 'change society, explain history and dominate the outlook of life.'" (*A Reply to Mr. Chen Duxiu*)

Such ideas of Hu Shi were scathingly criticized by the Marxist thinkers of the day in China, including Li Dazhao, Chen Duxiu and Qu Qiubai.

On the problem of culture, Hu Shi maintains that China should take the road of "wholesale Westernization." In his later works he uses the term "full globalization" to replace the old term of "wholesale Westernization." In this respect, he notices the great inertia of traditional Chinese culture. So he maintains that great efforts must be devoted to introducing and accepting modern Western culture in order that the Chinese people may overcome the weak points of their traditional culture. However, he falls into the trap of blindly eulogizing modern Western civilization, and renouncing traditional Chinese culture wholesale. He goes so far so to say, "We fall behind other countries in all things — in material and political culture and even in the sphere of morality. And what is more, we fall behind other countries with respect to knowledge, literature, music and even with respect to our physical constitutions we fall behind other countries." (*Introduction to My Own Thought*) This is obviously a nihilist attitude toward Chinese culture, and shows that Hu Shi had already lost self-confidence in his own nationality. It is quite natural that afterwards he came in for severe criticism from the "Eastern Culture School of Thought."

Liang Shuming (1893-1988), originally named Liang Huanding, was a native of Guilin, Guangxi Province. In his early years, he was a professor at Peking University. Later, he resigned from the professorship and engaged in the "rural construction" movement. He first worked at the Henan Village Administration College, and then he himself founded the Shandong Institute of Rural Construction. His idea of "rural construction" involved the spreading of education in the countryside and modernizing the ways of thinking of the peasants. During the War of Resistance against Japanese Aggression (1937-1945), he advocated cooperation between the KMT and Communist Party of China (CPC). In 1940, he took part in the founding of the China Democratic League of Political Organizations, which was later reorganized into the China Democratic League. When the People's Republic of China was founded in 1949, he was first a member of the Chinese People's Political Consultative Conference and then a member of its standing committee. His major works are *The Cultures of the East and the West and Their Philosophies*, *An Introduction to Indian Philosophy*, *The Last Consciousness of the Self-salvation Movement of the Chinese Nation*, *Theories of Rural Construction*, *The Essentials of Chinese Culture*, and *Human Mind and Human Life*.

Different from the philosophy of Hu Shi, which lays emphasis on scientific methods, Liang's philosophy is a kind of cultural philosophy. Its ideological origin consists mainly of three elements. One is the Lu-Wang Neo-Confucianism, together with the thought of the Taizhou School, which is a branch of the former. Another is the philosophical thought of

Henri Bergson (1859-1941), and the third is the philosophical thought of the Consciousness-Only Sect of Buddhism. The main content of his philosophical thought is to demonstrate the identity of the "life organism," "life" and "the human mind" with the "universe" through a comparative study of Eastern and Western cultures. He advanced a theory of the life of the universe and one of intuitive knowledge.

First, Liang postulates that the universe is a life organism, and the so-called universe is life. He says as follows:

> 1. "The universe is a great life organism. Both the evolution of the life organism and the evolution of human society are the unfolding and expression of this great life organism. What is more, the latter naturally comes from the power of the former." (*Reading Notes from Striving for Humanity-cultivating Studio*)
>
> 2. "All things in the universe are life, and are life alone. In the very beginning there was no universe at all. Life is continuous, and therefore it seems that the universe is an eternal existence." (*The Cultures of the East and the West and Their Philosophies*)

In other words, the universe is the uninterrupted duration of life organisms and the eternal movement of life. Without the succession of life organisms and the life of mankind, there would be neither existence nor development of the universe. And Liang also thinks that the relationship between life organism and life is that between the foundation and application. Life organisms constitute the foundation of life, and life is the application of life organisms. Therefore, the essence of the universe is life organism. When one understands the concept of life organism, one naturally understands the universe.

Moreover, the kernel of life organisms, which dwell in the universe, is the theory that the mind and the myriad things are one, as the latter dwell in the human mind. He says as follows:

> "The universe is a great life organism. When one understands the life organism, one naturally understands the universe. Although there are expressions in all places, there is one place where the kernel of the great life organism of the universe dwells. This place is 'man.' Life

is alive, and in the universe, the greatest living thing is the human mind. If one can have a true understanding of the human mind, one will naturally reach a true understanding of life organisms in the universe." (*Fundamental Concepts of John Dewey's Pedagogy*)

The kernel of life organisms is the human mind, namely, the subjective consciousness of man. Such being the case, the universe is active, not passive, and it is alive, not dead. As for the great life organism, it is a kind of "great need or great desire — the inexhaustible desire." (*The Cultures of the East and the West and Their Philosophies*) This "great desire" is the free activity of the mind, and it is an impulse of the life instinct. This is clearly volitionism.

From volitionism, Liang finally goes to egotism. In his opinion, only the "ego" has real existence in the world. According to him, in the universe there are merely two "egos," one being "the ego before this very instant" or "the already-existing ego," the other being "the ego of the present" or "the desire at the present," which people call "mind" or the "spirit." "The ego of the present" always demands forward-going activity, while "the ego before this very instant" is always a hindrance. The development of the universe is a compound of the efforts and struggle of "the ego of the present," which continuously overcomes "the ego before this very instant." (*The Cultures of the East and the West and Their Philosophies*)

In his view of the unification of Heaven and Man, and of the unification of the mind and the myriad things there is no difference between the subject and the object, or between the *grahya* and *grahaka*: "Man's life organism was from the start combined with the great life organism of the universe. They constitute a whole body, and between them there is no gap. They are not in any opposition. The relationship between both sides is by no means that between the *grahya* and *grahaka*." (*A Morning Talk·The Differences between the East and the West*)

Therefore, any cognition of the universe is in essence the self-inspection, self-demonstration, self-examination and self-consciousness of the human mind. Such a self-cognition of the noumenon of the universe cannot depend on any sense or intelligence; quite the contrary, it must depend on the intuition. Science researches into the outside substance, and the means it uses to do so is the human intelligence. Religion seeks the lifeless noumenon, and the means it uses to do so is the human senses. But metaphysics (namely, philosophy), in its probe into the internal life organism of the universe, uses intuition to do so. Only by means of intuition can one realize the human mind and know the true aspect of the life organism of the universe. He says, "What the intuition knows is a kind of significant spirit, a tendency or inclination." (*The Cultures of the East and the West and Their Philosophies*) He also says, "The moment when one has intuition is the moment when one feels that one is living. At that moment, all things have become one whole, in which there is neither subject nor object. Intuition may thus be called the absolute." (*Ibid*) In order to know or grasp the noumenon of the life organism of the universe as a "great desire," one must enter the metaphysical realm, in which subject and object become one harmonious whole. In such a realm, one can realize the human mind, which is dynamic, integrated and profound.

Liang's theories of the life organism of the universe and of intuitive cognition are in line with subjective idealism. However, they contain some rational factors. For instance, he raises a series of important philosophical problems, such as the initiative of the subjective consciousness, the function of the intuitive consciousness and the value of the life impulse. And from these problems he draws some positive conclusions. For instance, starting from the idea that the great life organism of the universe is a "great desire," he puts forth a view on principle and desires which is in opposition to asceticism. In his opinion, "The Confucian school of thought praises life. Since all the instincts such as hunger and thirst and even sexual intercourse between man and woman come from Nature, the Confucian school does not expel them. Quite the contrary, if we can deal with them suitably, human life will become full of vitality and wonderful." (*The Cultures of the East and the West and Their Philosophies*)

On the problem of culture, according to the differences of desires, Liang divides the cultures of mankind into three types, which are quite different from one another. The first is Occidental culture, which "takes the forward-going demands of the desires for its fundamental spirit." The second is Chinese culture, which "takes self-harmonious and impartial desires for its fundamental spirit." The third is Indian culture, which "takes the bending-back and backward-going demands of desires for its fundamental spirit." Since the fundamental spirits of these three cultures are different from one another, the peoples brought up in these three cultures naturally adopt different attitudes toward life. The peoples living in the Occidental culture, which harbors "forward-going demands," adopt a "hard-struggle attitude." The people living in the Chinese culture, which "follows the changes, seeks harmony and persists in the mean in accordance with the people's own ideas," adopt a "retrospective attitude which calls for resignation to one's situation." The people living in the Indian culture, which "bends back to demand everything," adopt "an attitude of turning one's back on all current problems and demands." And their thinking structures are different, too. The peoples living in the Occidental culture pay attention to researching into the outside substance, and the instrument they use is intelligence. The people living in the Chinese culture pay attention to researching into the internal life organisms, and the instrument they use is intuition. The people living in the Indian culture pay attention to researching into the lifeless noumenon, and the instrument they use is *pratyaksa* (namely, the senses). In Liang's view, these three cultures represent the three stages in the development of human culture, too. The first stage is the Occidental culture, the second stage is the Chinese culture, and the third stage is the Indian culture. The Occidental culture "shows many innate defects, and inflicts untold sufferings on itself. In the past, people thought that it was very good in many aspects, but now people find that is not good in many aspects. Now the ideological circles of the West are already raising a clear demand that their consistent attitude toward life should be changed. And in their demand there is a tendency which urges the people to follow the road of China and the road of Confucius." (*The Cultures of the East and the West and Their Philosophies*) Here, Liang senses that there will soon be a great change and a great rejuvenation of the Chinese culture under the impact of the Occidental culture. Therefore, there is a need to comprehend the value of the traditional Chinese culture once again. He says as follows:

> "The reason why my nation cannot seek to prevail over the other nations in the world today has already been decided objectively by the course of history. Meanwhile, in like manner, it has already been decided by history that my nation has been bequeathed a great mission to start the future culture of the whole world. The so-called national consciousness refers to consciousness of this point,

I think." (*The Last Consciousness of the Self-salvation Movement of the Chinese Nation*)

We may say that this is another kind of national consciousness by which people may distinguish "the school of the Eastern culture" from "the school of the Western culture." Nevertheless, Liang exaggerates the defects and evils which have appeared in the development of the Western culture. He assumes that the culture of mankind will inevitably develop from the Occidental culture, which upholds science, to the Chinese culture, which esteems Confucianism, and then to the Indian culture, which emphasizes religion. What is more, he even thinks that all these stages are decided by the desires. Thus he falls into the pitfall of an idealist conception of history and culture. These thoughts of Liang were criticized both by Marxists such as Chen Duxiu and Qu Qiubai and by non-Marxists such as Hu Shi. The latter points out that Liang's concept of culture is "a subjective philosophy of culture" and "a subjective doctrine of the transmigration of culture." (*After Reading Liang Shuming's The Cultures of the East and the West and Their Philosophies*)

"The controversy between science and metaphysics" (also called "the controversy between science and the outlook on life") raged in 1923 and 1924, launched by Zhang Junmai and Ding Wenjiang. Zhang Junmai (1887-1969) was a native of Baoshan County, Jiangsu Province (Now a part of Shanghai Municipality). He studied first in Japan and then in Germany. He researched the philosophies of Rudolf Christoph Eucken (1846-1926) and Henri Bergson. When he came back to China, he taught at Yanjing and Peking universities. In 1932, in collaboration with Zhang Dongsun and others, he prepared to establish the National Social Party (The name was changed to Democratic Social Party in 1946), of which he was chairman for a time. The party's ideology was that of National Socialism. In 1940, he helped organize the China Democratic League of Political Organizations (later known as the China Democratic League), and became a member of its standing committee. He opposed any compromise with Japan, and demanded that democracy be realized in China. In 1946, he withdrew from the China Democratic League and joined the KMT. In 1949, he left China to live overseas. Ding Wenjiang (1887-1936) was a native of Taixing County, Jiangsu Province. He studied zoology and geology in Britain in his early years, becoming a leading geologist upon his return to China. As a professor at Peking University he assumed the post of the general secretary of the Academia Sinica. His thought was greatly influence by Machism. In 1923, Zhang Junmai delivered a speech under the title, "The Outlook on Life." Soon after that, Ding Wenjiang published an essay titled, "Metaphysics and Science," in which he criticized Zhang Junmai, touching off a fierce controversy between them and involving Liang Qichao, Hu Shi, Wu Zhihui and Wang Xinggong. The essays dealing with the controversy were afterwards collected into volumes under the titles *Science and the Outlook on Life* and *The Controversy over the Outlook on Life*. Originally, the controversy was between the "school of science," which upheld Machism and pragmatism, and the "school of metaphysics," which upheld the philosophies of Eucken and Bergson. But shortly after its commencement, Marxists including Chen Duxiu, Qu Qiubai and Deng Zhongxia (1894-1933) joined in, bringing about a triangular dispute between the "school of science," the "school of metaphysics," and the "school of historical materialism."

The focus of "the controversy between science and metaphysic" is the various relationships between science and philosophy (outlook on life), between material civilization and spiritual civilization, between the law of causality and free will, and so on.

Zhang Junmai attributes the eruption of World War I to highly developed science and material civilization. Modern Western science can only be applied to outward-going probes and can only make achievements in material civilization. It cannot, unfortunately, contribute to spiritual civilization. As a result, modern Western science finally brought the whole of Europe into a crisis. If we want to build spiritual civilization, we must lay stress on philosophy and the outlook on life. This is because the outlook on life is possessed of features different from those of science:First, science is objective, whereas the outlook on life is subjective.

Second, science is dominated by the logical method, whereas the outlook on life originates in intuition.

Third, science solves problems by analyzing them, whereas the outlook on life solves problems in a synthetic manner.

Fourth, science is subject to the domination of the law of causality, whereas the outlook on life originates in the singleness of personality.

Fifth, science originates in the phenomena of the targets, whereas the outlook on life originates in free will.

Therefore, he draws a conclusion, saying, "No matter how developed science may be, it can do nothing to solve any problem related to the outlook on life." In his view, all the scholars of Confucianism and Neo-Confucianism laid stress on the cultivation of the inner life. They adopted an inward-going attitude to probe into the problems of the outlook on life. As a result, in these ages China achieved a highly developed spiritual civilization, unique in the world. He urged the many people who were engaged in constructing a new culture for China to take this point as the key position. At the same time, he held that it was urgent and highly necessary to mend or save Western material civilization, which was beset by various crises. (Cf. "The Outlook on Life")

Ding Wenjiang criticizes these views of Zhang Junmai. He thinks that science should not be held responsible for the European cultural crises brought about by World War I. He says, "Those who are responsible for the war are politicians and educators. But the majority of these two kinds of people do not engage in science." And he points out, "Science is not outward-going. And, what is more, it is the best instrument of education and cultivation. This is because science demands that people seek truth every day and eradicate preconceived ideas constantly. This endows those who study science with an ability to seek truth, and with sincerity to love truth." In his view, scientific methods are omnipotent. By means of science, people are able to examine everything in the world. Citing Hu Shi, he says, "When we observe the demands of our era, we have to recognize that the greatest responsibility and most pressing demand of mankind today are the application of the scientific method to the problems of human life." As for the Confucian stress on cultivation of the inner life, it is merely empty talk about nature and principle. It is a "religion without belief" and a "philosophy without methodology." He maintains that no spiritual civilization can be created purely by the cultivation of the inner life. Only when there is a certain degree of material civilization can a highly developed spiritual civilization of one kind or another be created. He lashes out at the school of metaphysics, saying, "They are unwilling to acknowledge the so-called economic concept of history. I would not mind this, but they have forgotten the old adage that 'when people are adequately fed and clad, they learn the rites and etiquette.

When the granaries are full, people learn the meaning of honor and disgrace.' How can I tolerate this?" (*Metaphysics and Sciences — A Comment on Zhang Junmai's The Outlook on Life*)

In the second place, as for the relationship between the law of causality and free will, which is a frequent actor in human affairs, Zhang Junmai thinks that the law of causality is only applicable to material phenomena; it cannot explain any spiritual phenomena. He says, "The general motive force of human life is the impulse of the living organism. In respect to psychology, it is self-awakening which changes all the time. In respect to time, it is duration which is uninterrupted." (*A Preface to the Controversy on the Outlook on Life*) As regards "the impulse of the living organism," it is purely free will. "There is absolutely no measurement for it. And it cannot be explained by the law of causality, either." (*On the Outlook on Life and Science · My Second Article Simultaneously Serving as a Reply to Mr. Ding Zaijun*) In his view, all historical phenomena, be they monarchy or democracy or capitalism or socialism, are altogether created by free will in a free way. In these phenomena there is no law at all. Ding Wenjiang and Hu Shi hold another view. They believe that the outlook on life cannot surpass science at all. The changes of moral conceptions may be found out in a scientific way of one kind or another. Therefore, there is a great dharma of causality, which dominates everything in man's life.

Judging from this, it is very clear that the so-called "controversy between science and metaphysics" is in fact a deep-going development of the "controversy on the problems between the Eastern and Western cultures." Both sides of the controversy put forth some ideas, which are rational and highly suggestive. For instance, the school of science opposes the school of metaphysics on the grounds that the latter propagates the Neo-Confucianism of the Song and Ming dynasties. The former points out that the achievements of material civilization depend on the development of science. Such a view contains some materialist factors.

On the whole, these two schools object to the application of historical materialism to the problem of explaining history and human life. In Zhang Junmai's opinion, the general motive force of history is the absolutely free "impulsion of the living organism." In other words, he thinks that spirit controls matter. As for "the great dharma of causality" talked about by Ding Wenjiang and Hu Shi, it is by no means an objective and inevitable law, but a hypothesis which has yet to be proved, and which has been made subjectively on the foundation of scientific common sense. In Hu Shi's opinion, mankind "may use its wisdom in order that it may create new causes to seek for new effects." (*A Preface to Science and the Outlook on Life*) And he says, "Thoughts, knowledge, opinions and education may also change society, explain history and dominate the outlook on life." (*A Reply to Mr. Chen Duxiu*)

Marxists, including Chen Duxiu, Qu Qiubai and Deng Zhongxia criticized both the school of science and the school of metaphysics. Chen Duxiu safeguards the materialist conception of history, pointing out, "We believe that only objective material causes may change society, explain the history, and dominate the outlook on life." (*A Preface to Science and the Outlook on Life*) He criticizes Hu Shi's multi-element conception of history, and points out that Hu Shi's mistakes lie in juxtaposing the material causes with the mental causes, and that in such a multi-element conception of history there is inevitably a loophole that can be used by Zhang Junmai, who advocated an idealistic conception of history. He lashes out at Zhang Junmai, who uses the theory of a spiritual agent to explain history. He points out, "In the changeable phenomena of society they only see the later stage, in which thoughts have evolved into facts, and at the same time they forget the earlier stage, in which facts have created the background for thoughts. This is the common and central mistake made by various schools of idealism." (*A Reply to Zhang Junmai and Liang Qichao*) Qu Qiubai propagates a theory on the relationship between freedom and necessity according to Marxist philosophy. So he provides a correct answer to the core problem of the controversy, that is, the relationship between the law of causality and free will. He says, "Social phenomena are made by man, but man's will and action are governed by the law of causality. If man can get a thorough understanding of these laws of causality, man's will and action will be in accordance with practice in an even better way, and man will obtain more freedom than before. By that time, man will be able to begin realizing his own rational ideals." In other words, on the one hand, the material conception of history acknowledges man's will and its function, and, on the other, the law of causality in the final analysis governs man's will. Marxists acknowledge that in social phenomena there are laws which can be known by man, but they are by no means fatalists. If people can get to know the inevitable law of causality, they will get the "freedom" to apply this law to explain concrete historical phenomena. So how can people get to know the law of causality? Qu Qiubai points out, "When we research the laws of social phenomena, we must first of all seek the ultimate cause of society; we cannot take any personal motives or the motives of the masses for the only factor causing social phenomena. We must seek the factors of these factors." And he himself renders the above into another version, which runs as follows: "The ultimate motive force of social development lies in the essence of society, which refers to nothing but the economy." (Cf. *The World of Freedom and the World of Necessity*)

The Marxists' criticism of both the school of science and Neo-Confucianism centers on the fundamental mistake of these two schools concerning the problem of the concept of history. Nevertheless, at that time they were unable to provide a Marxist answer to a series of valuable questions about culture, science and human life, which were put forth by those two schools.

After the New Culture Movement, Eastern and Western cultures and the relative philosophies underwent both conflicts and fusion as well. In the 1930s, these problems came to a head. It was in this decade that Japanese imperialism launched a war of aggression against China, and the very existence of the Chinese nation was at stake. In such conditions, the second period of cooperation between the KMT and the CPC came into being, and a salvation movement against Japan's invasion swept the nation. The issue of national rejuvenation gripped the minds of philosophers, and a group of non-Marxist scholars set up various philosophical systems in the 1930s and 1940s, which combined Eastern and Western philosophical thought. The representatives of this movement were Xiong Shili, Feng Youlan, Jin Yuelin and He Lin. While these four scholars differed in temperament, experience, knowledge, academic tradition and mode of thought, and that their philosophical systems possess different features, there are many similarities and common characteristics among them in that they emerged from the same cultural background and they faced the same epochal themes. They all had a rather profound understanding of both Eastern and Western cultures, which they attempted to combine. They probed the problems of man and culture both ontologically and epistemologically. Their efforts reflected the thinking of the Chinese national bourgeoisie under the new epochal conditions on a common topic, that is, how China was to catch up with the modern trends. Nevertheless, at that time they did not know Marxism, so it was quite natural that they made quite a few of mistakes when they pondered the problems relevant to the road to the modernization of China. All in all, they failed to solve this major topic of the era.

Xiong Shili (1885-1968) was a native of Huanggang County, Hubei Province. In his youth, he joined revolutionary organizations working for the overthrow of the Qing Dynasty. During the Revolution of 1911, he served as staff officer to the military governor of Hubei Province. Later, following Sun Yat-sen, he took part in the movement to uphold the constitution. Thereafter, he abandoned politics to concentrate on the study of philosophy, becoming a professor at Peking University. After the founding of the People's Republic of China in 1949, he was a representative to the first four Chinese People's Political Consultative Conferences. His academic career took him from Confucianism to Buddhism, and then from Buddhism back to Confucianism. He collected ideological data extensively from various schools of thought ancient and modern, native and foreign. He once said, "The six classics are notes for my own learning." His philosophical system is called "a new theory of consciousness-only." Among his main philosophical works are *A New Theory of Consciousness-Only*, *A Refutation of A New Theory of Consciousness-Only*, *Quotations and Essentials from Xiong Shili*, *A Thorough Explanation of Buddhist Terms*, *How Should We Read the Classics? An Inquiry into Confucianism*, *A Theory of Foundation and Application*, *A Chapter on the Enlightenment of the Mind* and *An Elaboration of Qian and Kun*. *A New Theory of Consciousness-Only*, Xiong's most important work, was published in two versions; the version published in the 1930s was written in classical Chinese, and the version published in the 1940s was written in the vernacular. There are three basic propositions in Xiong Shili's philosophy: First, "Foundation and application are not two things"; second, "To close and to open constitute changes"; and third, "One must turn back to oneself in order to find self-knowledge."

He criticizes modern Western philosophy for separating noumenon from phenomenon. He points out that in the history of philosophy there have arisen many theories of noumenon, which have one and the same fatal defect: "On the whole, they take noumenon for something external, for something that is apart from the mind, and seek for noumenon in the outside by means of reason. Each of these theories sets up a kind of noumenon fabricated at random." (*A New Theory of Consciousness-Only (Vernacular Version),* Chapter 1) In his view, all the past theories on noumenon — be it the theory of spiritual entity in line with idealistic monism, or the theory of material entity in line with materialist monism, or dualism or pluralism — there are two big mistakes in the grounds on which the various theories are set up. First, these theories separate noumenon from phenomena, or foundation from application. Second, these theories cut off the absolute from the relative, and treat them as two things. Xiong Shili criticizes these two big mistakes. As regards the first mistake, he says as follows:

> 1. "The entity is the entity of phenomenon. We cannot presume that the entity is an independent existence divorced from phenomenon." (*An Elaboration on Qian and Kun*, Section 2)
>
> 2. "Since there is the entity, there must be some function relevant to it. Without application, there would be no foundation at all." (*Ibid*)

In other words, noumenon is phenomenon, or function. These three cannot be separated from one another. As regards the second big mistake, Xiong Shili points out, "The absolute is the relative, and the relative is the absolute. An absolute that is an independent existence apart from the relative can never exist." (*A Chapter on the Enlightenment of the Mind*) We cannot set up an absolute entity, spiritual or material, apart from the relative world of phenomena. Such is Xiong Shili's theory that foundation and application, or the absolute and the relative, are not two things. He often uses the metaphor of "the sea and bubbles" to illustrate his theory. As he points out, the water of the great sea cannot exist apart from the bubbles; the water of the great sea is the very body of the bubbles. The water of the great sea is the noumenon, the innate ceaseless rolling is the function, and the bubbles are the phenomenon of the water of the great sea, which is ceaselessly rolling. Xiong Shili calls this "the theory of monist entity," with which he opposes both the theory of spiritual entity in line with idealistic monism and the theory of material entity in line with materialist monism. On the one hand, he opposes the theory that noumenon is regarded as the Creator. In his opinion, "the spirit of Heaven and Earth" talked about by Zhuang Zhou, "the absolute spirit" talked about by Hegel, and suchlike idealistically monist entities, are in fact the "Heavenly God," which should be denied. On the other hand, he firmly denies the conception of matter in line with materialist monism. He vehemently refutes the argument that spirit is a product of matter. He says as follows:

> "Idealistic monism is not a reliable theory. As for the materialist monism, how can it be explained as a logically reasonable theory? As for the movement of matter, the differentiation of matter, the analysis of matter, the transformation of matter, the formation of matter, the leading of matter — all of them depend on vitality, which must be enriched continuously and permanently, and the mind, the function of which is to create freely and boundlessly. But nowadays, some people emphasize one side and set up a theory of materialist monism. According to this theory, matter plays the leading role in life, while mind is reduced to a lower rank, as a mere byproduct of matter. They fail to see the many facts indicating that mind plays a leading role in matter." (*An Elaboration on Qian and Kun*, Section 2)

Therefore, in Xiong Shili's view, noumenon is complicated and not simple. Because inside matter there are neither the properties of matter merely nor the properties of spirit merely, noumenon is possessed of properties and functions which are opposite to each other. Therefore, noumenon contains the moment of movement, which leads to the development and changes of the universe. What is more, because noumenon cannot separate itself from phenomena, such moment of movement exists in the myriad things and man himself. The myriad things and man have the capacity to emerge of themselves, to reproduce themselves, and to create everything.

Starting from the proposition that "foundation and application are not two things," Xiong Shili logically infers that "to close and to open constitute changes." "To close and to open" refers to two functions inside noumenon, which are opposite to each other and in the meantime complete each other. "To close" refers to the function of assimilating and collecting substance for the sake of forming concrete things. Because of its active assimilation and contraction, the material world was formed. "To open" refers to the function of things actively unfolding. Because of its initiative, the material world is pushed forward, and changes and develops continuously. By merely depending on closing and opening by turns, which are opposite to each other and in the meantime complete each other, the noumenon keeps its continuous movement. Starting from this point, Xiong Shili also nominates "to close" as the "thing," and in like manner he nominates "to open" as the "mind." The "mind" and the "thing" are the two sides of noumenon, one being the foundation, and the other being the application. They are not two independent entities. Nevertheless, the "mind" and the "thing" are not placed on a par with each other. He says, "The opening contains the closing, and the closing is dependent on the opening." (*A New Theory of Consciousness-Only (Vernacular Version)*, Chapter 4) The "mind" is similar to the seed, which is hidden up in the "thing." The mind leads the universe in the development from inorganic matter to organic matter, and then to higher animals, and finally to mankind. It is the "mind" that pushes the universe forward continuously, and it is also the "mind" that enables the universe to change without end. From this we may see the kernel of the problem very clearly: the capacity to create everything, which is innate to the myriad things and man, is nothing but the "opening," namely, the "mind." In Xiong's view, the true dominator of the universe is neither the absolute spirit, which is divorced from phenomena, nor matter, which is rigid, dead and passive. The true dominator of the universe is the subjective spirit, that is, "the original mind," which is active and lively, inexhaustibly creative, and never fixed in one place but forever existing everywhere. Therefore, he makes two statements. He says, "Noumenon is not something that is apart from mind and dwells outside." And, "The original mind alone is the noumenon that my physical body and the myriad things in the world possess simultaneously." (*A New Theory of Consciousness-Only (Vernacular Version)*, Chapter 1) In this way, Xiong Shili inherits the methodology of Mencius and Wang Shouren. As we may remember, Mencius says, "All things are already complete in us." And Wang Shouren says, "Wherever your intention is, there is the thing." Thus Xiong Shili exaggerates the function of the mind.

"Foundation and application are not two things" and "To close and to open constitute changes" may be reformulated as "Apart from the mind, there is no *visaya* (dominion)," and "One must turn back to oneself in order to find self-knowledge." In his opinion, on one side there is the subject of knowledge, which is called the "mind," and on the other there is the object of knowledge, which is called "*visaya* (dominion)." Both sides constitute a contradictory unity. He says as follows:

> "We only acknowledge that the mind and the dominion are the two sides of a unity. We cannot acknowledge that the dominion exists independent from the mind." (*A New Theory of Consciousness-Only (Vernacular Version)*, Chapter 2)

Only by giving play to the initiative of the subject of cognition, only by putting the objectively existing things into the cognitive activity of the subject, can the cognitive target be formed.

Apart from the cognitive subject, there can be no cognitive target at all. The mind and the dominion are closely combined, and they cannot be separated. The only difference between the mind and the dominion lies in that the former is the active part and the latter is the passive part. That being so, how can we know "the original mind," which exists as the noumenon of the universe? According to Xiong Shili's, it is necessary to adopt the intuitive method of inner experience, which is called "meditation in darkness, demonstration and realization by inner experience," or more simply, "One must turn back to oneself in order to find self-knowledge." He draws a demarcation line between science and philosophy. Science lies in "differentiated observation of the universe," and involves people being in the outside world and researching various concrete things. Science demands that people apply strictly logical thinking to their jobs. Meanwhile, philosophy lies in a synthetic observation of the universe, researching the noumenon of the universe, namely, "the original mind." Philosophy demands that people turn back to themselves, and engage in introspection. Philosophy can only be pursued by means of intuition, which surpasses any logic, and gets rid of any hindrance of language. He says as follows:

> 1. "Noumenon is the original mind. It is not anything exterior to my mind. It permits no search of the outside. It is important to turn

back to oneself in order to get a self-demonstration." (*A New Theory of Consciousness-Only (Vernacular Version)*, Appendix)

2. "The mind and things are combined into one in a dark and profound way. It is a realm in which the mind and things are fused well, and there is no discrimination between *grahya* and *grahaka*, or between the internal and the external. This is called demonstration and realization, in which there can be no fabricated differences whatsoever, because such a realm is true knowledge." (*A New Theory of Consciousness-Only (Vernacular Version)*, Chapter 7)

Only by means of such a "good fusion of mind and things," by such an "indiscrimination between subject and object," namely, by intuition and sudden enlightenment, can people reach a true knowledge of the noumenon of the universe, namely, "the original mind."

Science and philosophy have their own respective spheres and methods of knowledge. In *Xiong's* view, it is necessary for the mankind to recognize Nature through logical thinking. This is because mankind wants its knowledge to be "more accurate, more detailed, more correct and more distinct, so that it may get real knowledge of physical things." Further, mankind wants to "manipulate, transform, change, fabricate, conquer and make good use of the myriad things." Moreover, mankind wants to apply intuition, namely, the method suggested by the proposition that "One must turn back to oneself in order to find self-knowledge." Xiong Shili elaborates on this by saying, "If mankind is to ponder human life, it has to probe into the root cause of the universe, in order that it may explain where human life starts, what the best way is to cultivate human life and what the best termination of human life is." (*A Chapter on the Enlightenment of the Mind*) Both science and philosophy have their own values existing independently. Science and philosophy may complete each other, so we cannot emphasize one at the expense of the other. With this division between science and philosophy, Xiong Shili overcomes the defects incurred by the simplistic approach of the Chinese philosophers of early modern times, who directly introduced the categories and methods of Western science into Chinese philosophy without any refinement. Thus, Xiong Shili makes a new *aufhaben* of the controversy over the relationship between "science and the outlook on life," affirming the function of intuitive cognition.

Xiong 's emphasis on the principle of subjectivity is the product of his philosophical meditation after the failure of the Revolution of 1911. In his opinion, the reason why the Revolution of 1911 failed at last lies in that the bourgeoisie, which occupied the leading position of the revolution, lacked self-confidence. In the last analysis, the bourgeoisie failed to give full play to its subjective initiative. Therefore, in his own philosophy he emphasizes, and even exaggerates, subjectivity. The next representative of the non-Marxist movement is

Feng Youlan (1895-1990), who was a native of Tanghe County, Henan Province. In 1918 he graduated from Peking University, having specialized in Chinese philosophy. In 1919 he went to the US, and in 1924 the University of Columbia conferred on him the title of Doctor of Philosophy. When he came back to China, he taught at Zhongshan University, Guangdong University, Yenching University, Tsinghua University and Southwest Associated University. After the founding of the People's Republic of China in 1949, he became a professors at Peking University. He was a member of the Second, Third and Fourth Chinese People's Political Consultative Conferences, a member of the standing committee of the Sixth, Seventh Chinese People's Political Consultative Conferences, and a representative to the Fourth National People's Congress. Among his main philosophical works are *A Conception of Life*, *A History of Chinese Philosophy*, *A New Treatise on Neo-Confucianism*, *China's Road to Freedom* (also titled *A New Treatise on Things*), *A New Treatise on the Way of Living* (also titled *A New Admonition to the World*), *A New Treatise on the Nature of Man, The Spirit of Chinese Philosophy* (also titled *A New Inquiry into the Way*), *A New Treatise on the Methodology of Metaphysics* (also titled *New Words on Knowledge*), *A Short History of Chinese Philosophy*, *The First Draft on the Science of Historical Data for the History of Chinese Philosophy*, *A New Edition of A History of Chinese Philosophy*, *My Memoirs* (also titled *Autobiography of the Master of the Hall of Three Pines*) and *An Anthology of Academic Essays from the Hall of Three Pines.*

Feng Youlan was the leading Chinese philosopher and expert on the history of philosophy in modern times. In his more than seventy years studying philosophy, the central problem of his research was the philosophies behind Eastern and Western cultures. He says as follows:

"I am living in a period full of contradictions and struggles among different cultures. How can I understand such contradictions? How should I deal with such struggles? And how should I stand up in the whirlpool of such contradictions and struggles? I am faced with these and suchlike perplexing problems. I have to answer them." (*An Anthology of Academic Essays from the Hall of Three Pines*, Author's Preface)

In the process of solving these problems, Feng's cognition undergoes three stages. In the first stage, he uses the characteristics of geographical regions to explain the differences in cultures. In his opinion, the cultural differences are nothing but the differences between the East and the West. In the second stage, he uses the characteristics of history and times to explain the cultural differences. The cultural differences are nothing but the differences between ancient times and modern times. In the third stage, he uses social developments to explain the cultural differences. Only by judging from the social types can China's road to modernization be correctly pointed out. The way out for China lies in the transformation of its socio-economic formation from the type of ancient society, whose basic unit was the individual family, to the type of the modern society, whose basic unity is the whole of society. The key to realizing such a transformation is the industrial revolution. In this way, he sees the universal law governing the development of both human culture and human thought. And he sees the possibility of the mutual completion and future fusion between the cultures and philosophies of the East and the West. Based on such cognition, during the War of Resistance against Japanese Aggression he wrote six books under the general title of "the books written during the period in which the rejuvenation of the Chinese nation fermented." (They are also called the "Six Books of Fermentation.") They are *A New Treatise on Neo-Confucianism*, *China's Road to Freedom*, *A New Treatise on the Way of Living*, *A New Treatise on the Nature of Man*, *The Spirit of Chinese Philosophy* and *A New Treatise on the Methodology of Metaphysics*. In these books, by combining Cheng-Zhu Neo-Confucianism and new realism, he sets up a system of "New Neo-Confucianism." According to him, although his "New Neo-Confucianism" is a continuation of the Neo-Confucianism of the Song and Ming dynasties, it is a "completely new" system of philosophy.

A New Treatise on Neo-Confucianism is the general program of this

"New Neo-Confucianism." In it, the author discusses the problem of noumenon, the relationships between common phases and particular phases, and the relationship between the general and the individual. As for *China's Road to Freedom*, it was designed to explain social problems on the basis of such a discussion. He attempts to disclose the road along which China may go towards modernization in the hope that the relations between common and particular phases and between the general and the individual may be well explained. In the process of learning from the West, China ought not to discard the features of her own culture but ought to take a road of industrial revolution in which China can realize the transformation of its socio-economic formation from the type of ancient society, the basic unit of which was the individual family, to the type of modern society, the basic unity of which is the whole of society.

If we say that *A New Treatise on Neo-Confucianism* discusses noumenon, and that *China's Road to Freedom* discusses society, we may as well say that *A New Treatise on the Nature of Man* discusses human life. In that work, he divides human life into four stages.

The first stage of human life is "the natural stage," in which a person is a member of society, without self-awakening and devoted entirely to selfish interests.

The second stage of human life is "the utilitarian stage," in which a person is a member of society, is possessed of self-awakening, but who is still devoted to selfish interests.

The third stage of human life is "the stage of morality," in which a person is a member of society, is possessed of self-awakening and is devoted to the public interest.

The fourth stage is "the stage of Heaven and Earth," in which a person is a member of the universe, is possessed of self-awakening and who is devoted to the public interest.

Of these four stages, the highest stage of human life is "the stage of Heaven and the earth," for it is the stage in which a person may acquire the fullest freedom to become a sage. People should make efforts to free themselves from "the natural state" and "the utilitarian state." They should promote themselves first to "the stage of morality" and then to "the stage of universe."

In the *Spirit of Chinese Philosophy*, Feng Yulan elaborates on the position that the system of the "New Neo-Confucianism" occupies in the history of Chinese philosophy. Such a system inherits the orthodox tradition of the Neo-Confucianism of the Song and Ming dynasties on the one hand, and starts a new tradition on the other. This is because such a system plays a part in promoting the spiritual realm of man. In *A New Treatise on the Methodology of Metaphysics*, he discusses the methodology of the system of the "New Neo-Confucianism." One of the important features of philosophy lies in that it thinks about the unthinkable and speaks the unspeakable. In order to realize such a goal, both a "negative method" and a "positive method" are needed. What is the negative method? The mode of reasoning of the Buddhist Chan Sect is an example of the negative method. It refuses to say what the unspeakable is, and only says what the unspeakable is not. What is the positive method? It means the application of theoretical contemplation to think the unthinkable and to speak the unspeakable. Below, then, is a brief introduction to the system of the "New Neo-Confucianism":

In the first place, the author of *A New Treatise on Neo-Confucianism* distinguishes philosophy from science. The target of science is "the extremity of reality," while that of philosophy is "the extremity of being." He says, "The extremity of being is different from the extremity of reality. The extremity of being refers to whatever may be called 'being,' so it may also be called 'originality.' The extremity of reality refers to all that really exist as facts, so it may also be called Nature." The so-called "extremity of being" refers to "the world of principle" which exists logically prior to all objective things and events. The so-called "extremity of reality" refers to "the world of implements," which marks the existence of all objective things and events. "The extremity of reality" cannot be divorced from "the extremity of being," but "the extremity of being" may exist in the absence of "the extremity of reality." "The extremity of being" is more fundamental and more extensive than "the extremity of reality." Philosophy must go though "the extremity of reality" in order to reach "the extremity of being." But once philosophy reaches "the extremity of being," it may discard "the extremity of reality" and concentrate on "the extremity of being." Science lays emphasis on "the extremity of reality," and so it can provide man with positive knowledge, while philosophy lays emphasis on "the extremity of being," and so it can promote the spiritual realm of man to a new level.

In the second place, when the author of *A New Treatise on Neo-*

Confucianism probes "the extremity of being," his discussion is on the problem of the relationship between the general phase and the particular phase. This is nothing but the relationship between generality and particularity. In order to illustrate this relationship, Feng inherits and develops the categories of "principle" and "material force" of Neo-Confucianism upheld by the two Cheng brothers and Zhu Xi. In his opinion, the "principle" of Cheng-Zhu Neo-Confucianism is one which may explain why each and every sort of thing or event is just so. Such a "principle" refers to the common phase of things and events. As for "the material force" of the Cheng-Zhu Neo-Confucianism, it refers to the general material basis of the concrete world. And when "the material force" combines with "the principle," there appear realistic and concrete things, namely, the implements, which are the particular phase of individual things and events. As for each and every concrete thing or event, it is a particular phase which also possesses the attributions of a certain sort of thing or event, the nature of which is decided by the common phase. Therefore, in each and every thing or event there is a contradiction between the common phase and the particular phase. But the common phase does not dwell in the particular phase, for it is an existence more fundamental and more extensive than the particular phase, and logically it is a "world of principle" prior to the particular phase. In this way, Feng divides the world into two, one being "the world of implements," the other being "the world of principle." As for their relationship, "the world of implements" is the embodiment of "the world of the principle," and "the world of principle" is the basis of "the world of implements." By way of illustration, he points out, "Before there were any aircraft, there was the principle of the aircraft." Thus he draws a conclusion very similar to that of the scholars of the Cheng-Zhu Neo-Confucian School, that is, "The principle is prior to the things," and, "The principle is above the things."

In the third place, when the author of *A New Treatise on Neo-Confucianism* emphasizes the independent existence of "principle," he points out that "without material force, principle has nowhere to adhere to." Feng calls "material force" "the absolute material." According to him, "material force" is not matter, as discussed by science or materialism but the general basis of matter, from which all the concrete attributions of matter have been taken away. Therefore, "material force" is indescribable, unspeakable and inconceivable. Thus, he makes the scope of "material force" even more abstract. Nevertheless, when "principle" and "material force" are combined to produce practical things and events, "principle" is the formal cause and plays the leading role, while material force is the material cause, which is passive. In Feng's view, as far as the relationship between "principle" and "material force" is concerned, it is the former that plays the leading role, and the latter only serves as something to which "principle" may attach itself.

By starting from the separation of the common phase from the particular phase, Feng separates perceptual knowledge from rational knowledge. He thinks that perception and thinking (logical analysis) have their respective targets. Perception cannot know the common phase, but it can know the particular phase. Thought cannot know the particular phase, but it can know the common phase. In his view, knowledge of the common phase is more profound than knowledge of the particular phase. On important task of philosophy is to know the common phase.

Now let us summarize his New Neo-Confucianism. In his probe into the relationship between the common phase and the particular phase, Feng emphasizes the position of the common phase as being of active significance. He thereby highlights the problem of the relationship between the specific quality of Chinese culture and the common quality characterized by the development of human culture as a whole. This reflects the demand of the Chinese national bourgeoisie which sought a road of modernization along which it could merge into one organic whole with the international society. But he goes so far as to separate the common phase from the particular phase, and the generality from the particularity. In doing so, he postulates a "world of principle," which is divorced from all concrete things. In his opinion, "The world of principle is logically prior to the world of reality." (*The Spirit of Chinese Philosophy*) And he says, "The principle transcends both time and space." (*A New Treatise on Neo-Confucianism*) This inevitably leads him to a position of objective idealism. It was on this point that some Marxist thinkers, including Chen Jiakang, Du Guoxiang and Hu Sheng, criticized the system of "New Neo-Confucianism" the moment it was proclaimed. Chen Jiakang profoundly analyzes the speculative structure of the objective idealism into which Feng falls. He points out, "Mr. Feng attempts to set up a universe in his own mind, which is quite different from the real universe. In order to set up such a universe in his mind, Mr. Feng separates principle from material force. He extracts principle from reality and takes it for the law by which the universe develops. At the same time, he separates things from material force. He extracts material force from reality, and takes it for the foundation on which the universe is set up. In other words, he takes it for the materials with which the universe is made up." (*Principle and Material Force*) In short, "Master Feng is ignorant of separation, and so does not know of combination. He is ignorant of principle, and so does not know of things." (*Things and Principle*) After Feng accepted Marxism following the establishment of New China in 1949, he changed his views: "As regards the relationship between the common phase and the particular phase, the correct answer should be: 'Principle dwells in things.' In other words, 'the common phase dwells in the particular phase.'" (*My Memoirs*, Chapter 6)

Our third representative of the non-Marxist philosophical movement is Jin Yuelin (1895-1984). He was a native of Changsha City, Hunan Province. In 1914, he graduated from the Tsinghua School, the predecessor of Tsinghua University in Beijing. Later he studied in the US and earned a Ph.D from Columbia University in 1920. He then traveled and studied in Europe, including a stint doing research at Cambridge University in England. In his early years he studied politics, but his aspirations and interest shifted to philosophy during his time at Cambridge, where he was influenced by the thoughts of David Hume (1711-1776) and Bertrand Russell (1872-1970). In 1925, he returned to China, and taught first at Tsinghua University and then at Southwest Associated University. After the founding of the People's Republic of China, he became a professor at Peking University, and later a research fellow at the Institute of Philosophy of the Chinese Academy of Social Sciences. He was a member of the Second, Third, Fourth, Fifth and Sixth Chinese People's Political Consultative Conferences. Among his main works there are *Logic*, *A Treatise on the Way* and *A Treatise on Knowledge*. In addition, Jin was the editor of *Formal Logic*, China's first textbook of logic, published in the 1960s and extensively used in colleges and universities.

Jin made a great contribution to the dissemination of modern epistemology and logic in China. In his masterpiece *Logic*, which was published in 1937, he systematically introduced deductive logic and mathematical logic from the West to China, and made profound investigations into some fundamental theoretical problems of logic. As a result, he exerted a profound and extensive influence upon Chinese intellectuals. At the same time, Jin had a profound understanding of traditional Chinese philosophy. *A Treatise on the Way*, published in 1940, combines neo-realism, the Taoist thought of Laozi and Zhuangzi, and the Neo-Confucianism of the two Cheng brothers and Zhu Xi, establishing an ontological system centered on "the Way" that he regarded as the supreme category. In the 1940s, he completed his magnum opus, titled, *A Treatise on Knowledge*.* By sublimating British empiricism and neo-realism, he set up an epistemological system of his own. Jin's ideological entire system of philosophy is contained in three books — *A Treatise on the Way*, which discusses ontology, *A Treatise on Knowledge*, which discusses the theory of knowledge, and *Logic*, which discusses methodology. After 1949, Jin transformed himself into a Marxist, joining the CPC in 1956. Here we will give a brief introduction to his ontological thought, contained in *A Treatise on the Way*.

Similar to Xiong Shili, Jin affirms in *A Treatise on the Way* that the realistic world is a boundless progress of movement and changes, like a river that never stops flowing. He affirms the emergences, extinctions, changes and motions of the myriad things in the realistic world. As for Xiong Shili's philosophy, it lays tress on the motive force of the movement and changes in the realistic world, so it takes "original mind" for the supreme category, and it probes the relationship between "mind" and "things." Jin's philosophy is different from that of Xiong Shili in that it lays stress on researching the complicated and confused connections of the realistic world and the laws of movements and changes. It takes "the Way," which is a central topic in traditional Chinese philosophy, for the supreme category. It examines the relationship between the common phase and the particular phase:

> "The Way is the highest concept or the supreme realm of philosophy." (*A Treatise on the Way*, Chapter 1)

He considers "the Way" to be the general progress and the general law

---

* The book was finished in 1942, but it was lost in an air raid alarm. So he had to rewrite it and the second draft was completed in 1948. In 1983 *A Treatise on Knowledge* was formally published.

of the whole realistic world, and at the same time it is the process and law of the changes, motions, emergences and extinctions of the myriad things and myriad events in the realistic world. He says, "We can discuss the Way as an organic whole, and we can also discuss the Way part by part." (*A Treatise on the Way*, Introduction) In other words, the Way always exists in every concrete thing or event. He says, "Each and every one of the myriad existences has its own Way." (*A Treatise on the Way*, Introduction) Every concrete thing and event contains a contradiction between the common phase and the particular phase. Jin emphasizes that the particular phase depends on the common phase, and the common phase expresses itself as the particular phase. Therefore, the common phase is universal, and possesses typicality and perfection. In the developmental process of the realistic world, every particular phase will gradually reach an even fuller expression of the common phase.

Nevertheless, Jin points out that a concrete thing or event cannot be made up only of the common phase and the particular phase. A particular thing or event is by no means an accumulation of common phases. No matter how hard you may pile up common phases, you can never produce any particular thing or event. In like manner, a particular thing or event is by no means an accumulation of particular phases, either. The cominbation of particular phases never produces any particular thing or event. Thus it is clear that "In any particular thing or event there are elements that do not belong fundamentally to any phases at all." (*A Treatise on the Way*, Introduction) Therefore, by transforming the categories of "principle" and "material force" of Cheng-Zhu Neo-Confucianism and the Aristotelian categories of "form" and "matter," Jin puts forth the categories of "mode" and "energy" to illustrate this problem. "Mode" is similar to "principle" or "form," and "energy" is similar to "material force" or "matter."

"Energy" is an element which dwells in concrete things and events but it does not belong to any phase, and "energy" is the material out of which all concrete things are made. He says, "It is the material which constitutes the similarities of the myriad things and events; it is not reason which explains the similarities of the myriad things and events. Reason cannot explain the essential essence of the myriad things." (*A Treatise on the Way*, Introduction) For instance, an electron is not "energy." No matter how small an electron may be, it is a kind of thing. Each and every electron has its own "energy." In a tiny thing — for example, the electron — or in a huge thing — for example, the universe — there is "energy" of its own. The energy has neither size nor properties. It is an object which is inconceivable and unimaginable. But man can grasp energy in experiences in a broad sense. Then we cannot help asking why Jin chooses the word "energy" to express the idea of "material" or "material force,"? This is because the word "energy" may indirectly convey the connotations of being alive and busy instead of being dead and tranquil. And the word "energy" (*neng*) may help people think of the word "possibility" (*keneng*).

"Possibility" refers to "the 'frame' or 'form' which may exist, but which may not possess any 'energy'." (*A Treatise on the Way*, Introduction) It corresponds roughly to logical possibility in our ordinary vocabulary. This possibility contains two parts, one being "realistic common phase," the other being "empty conception." The former is the "frame" or "form" into which the "energy" may be put, for example, the common phase of "red," "green," and so on. The latter is the "frame" or "form" which may exist but which may not possess any energy, for example, the appellation of a kind of thing or event such as "dragon," and "superman." Jin explains his idea, saying, "Although the common phase is the possibility, the possibility is by no means the common phase. Although possibility may possess energy, it may also possess no energy." (*A Treatise on the Way*, Chapter 1) Jin puts forth another idea. If we extract all the possibilities and arrange them together, they constitute the "mode." He says, "The mode is the possibilities which are all-inclusive and which may be extracted." (*A Treatise on the Way*, Chapter 1)

Then we cannot help asking what relationship is there between the "mode" and the "possibility"? In Jin's opinion, the "mode" is the pure form which is unitary and which keeps its tranquility all the time. Energy is the pure material, which is varied and which keeps its activity all the time. Neither side has a beginning or ending. We should take them up at the same time, for we cannot say which is early and which is late. And they cannot be separated from each other. He says,

"If there is energy, there can be mode. If there is mode there can be energy" (*A Treatise on the Way*, Chapter 1), and

> "There is no mode that has no energy, and there is no energy that has no mode" (*Ibid*).

Since the "mode" is the possibilities which are all-inclusive and which may be extracted, it has neither inside nor outside. The "energy" cannot escape from the possibilities that dwell in the "mode." But the possibilities of the energy are not unitary, so there is both going out and coming in. The so-called "going out" refers to running out of a certain scope of possibility. For example, when we say, "Nowadays there are no dinosaurs," this means that "energy" has run out of the possibility of "dinosaur." The so-called "coming in" refers to putting in a certain scope of possibility. For example, when we say, "There is a person," this means that "energy" has put in the possible scope of "person." The process in which such "energy" goes out of and comes into the "mode" is the very process by which concrete things and events or kinds of things and events appear and disappear. When "energy" comes into the possibility, a thing or event appears. When "energy" goes out of the possibility, a thing or event disappears. The development and changes of the realistic world unfold by means of such a "mode-energy" relationship.

Therefore, Jin draws a conclusion, which runs as follows:

> "The Way is mode-energy." (*A Treatise on the Way*, Chapter 1)
>
> "The Way" is nothing but the logically evolutionary process of "mode-energy." It is a continuous process in which energy and possibility come into the realistic world, and in the realistic world they continue to go forward and never stop their evolution: "What dwells in mode has energy, so it exists for the sake of the Way." (*A Treatise on the Way*, Chapter 1)

On this basis, Jin further explorees the problem of the relationship between necessity and contingency, by which the realistic world develops and changes. Since "mode" contains all the possibilities, "energy" cannot run out of the possibility of "mode," and therefore either appearance or extinction or changes or motions of any particular phase must abide by the "mode." The "mode" is the correlation between possibility and possibility. This is called "pure reason," which is the common law the myriad things, the myriad events and even the whole realistic world must abide by. In addition, between common phase and common phase there is also a correlation. This is called the "innate principle," or the "principle," and is what the myriad things and the myriad events must abide by. What is more, there are various correlations which may exist between common phases, between possibilities, and between common phases and possibilities. These various correlations constitute a related network of complicated and confused "principle." Nevertheless, there is contingency in the appearance and disappearance of particular phases. Such appearance and disappearance are called "potentiality." Therefore, the changes and motions of any concrete thing or event depend upon two aspects — the "principle," which is the correlation between common phases, and the "potentiality," which is the appearance and disappearance of particular phases. Jin expresses this relationship as follows:

> "Although the principle is innate, the potentiality may not be a necessity." (*A Treatise on the Way*, Chapter 8)

In this way, Jin discloses the relationship between generality and particularity, necessity and contingency of the development and changes in the realistic world. Affirming the commonness and necessity of the realistic world, he also affirms the particularity and contingency of the realistic world.

Jin uses the phrase "The Ultimate of Nonbeing and also the Great Ultimate" to illustrate the motional process of the universe. The so-called "Ultimate of Nonbeing" refers to the chaotic state in which the principle has not yet become apparent, and in which the potentiality has not yet been realized. It is the limit of the bygone boundlessness. The so-called "Great Ultimate" refers to the greatest accomplishment of the realistic world's development. It is the limit of the future boundlessness. The so-called "Ultimate of Nonbeing and also the Great Ultimate" refers to the realistic world's developmental course, which is boundless in time and space, without beginning or end, and which moves like a river flowing forward continuously. In such a process, all things irrational and imperfect will be gradually cleared away, the particular phase will try its best to express itself as the common phase, and the "potentiality" will strive to reach the "principle." As a result, man will reach the realm of the Great Ultimate, which is the truest, the best, the most beautiful and the most perfect state.

Here it will be useful to make a comparative study of Jin and Feng.

Jin's *A Treatise on the Way* was completed at almost the same time as Feng's *A New Treatise on Neo-Confucianism*. These two scholars often exchanged views, and influenced each other. Moreover, the main purports of the two books are almost the same. They both affirm the principle of objective idealism that logically the common phase is prior to the particular phase. But with respect to the concrete relationship between the common phase and the particular phase, they have different views. Directly and candidly, Feng divides the world into two worlds, one being "the world of principle," and the other being "the world of implements." Jin puts forth a view that "the correlation of the common phase dwells potentially in the circle of individuals." (*A Treatise on the Way*, Chapter 3) He attempts to unify the common phase and the particular phase, and he further develops this attempt in *A Treatise on Knowledge*.

In the first place, he clearly points out that knowledge comes from objective reality and sense-experience:

> "This is a proposition that 'there are outside things.' This is also a proposition that 'there are sense organs.' These two propositions give us the true sense in the same way. These two propositions are simultaneously needed in the theory of knowledge." (*A Treatise on Knowledge*, Chapter 2)

He emphasizes that there are two features at the starting point of any knowledge. On the one hand, one must affirm that there are sense-experiences; on the other, one must affirm that the senses reflect objective reality. He calls the particular phase of objective things and events which presents itself in normal perception, to be "the Given." He points out, "The Given has a position in two aspects. It is the content, and at the same time it is the object. As far as the content is concerned, it is a presentation. As far as the object is concerned, it is a part of the outside thing that has the nature of being an object or simply of the outside thing per se." (*A Treatise on Knowledge*, Chapter 3) In other words, "the Given" is the most fundamental material of any knowledge. Starting from this point, he criticizes the various brands of sensationalism preached by George Berkeley (1685-1753), David Hume (1711-1776), Immanuel Kant (1724-1804), and Bertrand Russell (1872-1970).

In the second place, he points out that any idea has a double function — the function of description and the function of standardization. An "idea" is the common phase which the subject extracts out of "the given." Once the "ideas" are formed, the knowledge uses these ideas to describe "the given" and to standardize "the given." He thus explains consciousness:

> "Knowledge and experience entail using 'the gained' to govern 'the given.' When one uses an idea, which comes from 'the given,' to govern 'the given,' one will have consciousness." (*A Treatise on Knowledge*, Chapter 8)

In this way, the development of knowledge is promoted. Here, he criticizes the mechanical theory of reflection, so his thought contains some dialectical factors. We may call Jin's theory of knowledge fundamentally materialistic. It is the most outstanding achievement obtained by a non-Marxist philosopher in this sphere.

The final representative of non-Marxist thought is He Lin (1902-1992), a native of Jintang County, Sichuan Province. In 1919, he entered the Tsinghua School, the predecessor of Tsinghua University. From 1926 to 1931, he studied in the United States and Germany, gaining an M.Phil. from Harvard University. Returning to China, he taught at Peking University. After the founding of the People's Republic in 1949, he became a research fellow at the Institute of Philosophy of the Chinese Academy of Social Sciences. He was a member of the Fourth, Fifth and Sixth Chinese People's Political Consultative Conferences. During the period He Lin studied abroad, Josiah Royce (1855-1916), a Neo-Hegelian in the US, influenced him, and he did research into the philosophies of Benedict Spinoza (1632-1677), Immanuel Kant (1724-1804) and Georg Hegel (1770-1831). In the 1930s and 1940s, he set up a philosophical system of his own by combining the philosophy of rationalism from Plato and Aristotle to Kant and Hegel, Neo-Hegelianism, voluntarism, and Song-Ming Neo-Confucianism. After 1949, he accepted Marxism, and made a great contribution to philosophy by translating the Hegelian philosophy and introducing it to China. In 1982, he joined the CPC at the age of eighty. Among his main works are *A Brief Explanation of Early Modern Idealism*, *Chinese Philosophy Today*, *Culture and Human Life*,

Speeches on Modern Western Philosophy and *Speeches on Hegelian Philosophy*. Among his translations are *Essentials of Hegelian Philosophy* compiled by Josiah Royce, *Ethica in Ordine Geometrico Demonstrata (Ethics)* and *Tractus de Intellectus Emendatione (On the Improvement of the Intellect)* by Spinoza, and *Encyclopedia of the Philosophical Sciences in Outline*, *The Phenomenology of the Mind* and *Lectures on the History of Philosophy* by Hegel. *A Brief Explanation of Early Modern Idealism*, which was published in 1942, is regarded as the representative work on He Lin's philosophical system.

He Lin attempts to take Immanuel Kant for a starting point so that he may set up a major system of philosophy which surpasses both materialism and idealism, subjective idealism and objective idealism, scientific philosophy and humanistic philosophy, and which includes a theory of universe, theory of knowledge and theory of human life. The kernel of this philosophy is "Mind is principle."

In He Lin's judgment, the defect of traditional Chinese philosophy lies in the fact that it lacks a kind of subject that may start from the noumenon and enter the phenomenal world. As for the spirit of such a subject, it may be explained by phrases. One phrase is from Spinoza, and runs, "Think by definition." Another phrase is from Kant, and runs, "Learn by principle." In his opinion, the logical mind, which serves as the target of philosophy, is different from the psychological mind, which serves as the target of science, in that in essence it is free and independent. He Lin says as follows:

> "The mind, in a logical sense, is an idealized spiritual principle which surpasses all experiences. It is the only subject of experiences, actions, knowledge and evaluation. This mind is the governor of experiences, the dominator of actions, the organizer of knowledge and the judge of values. The reason why Nature and human life may be understood, and may be possessed of any significance, order and value, lies in this mind. It is the mind in the proposition that 'Mind is principle'." (*A Brief Explanation of Early Modern Idealism*, Chapter 1)

This "logical mind" is the dominator of all the conscious activities of man and the agent that endows Nature and human life with value. It is a rational subject that is possessed of gigantic initiative.

He Lin regards the "logical mind" as the mind of the subject that governs knowledge, nature, principle, and human life as well. He says, "As regards the origin and limit of knowledge, the philosophy which stresses that 'Mind is principle' belongs to the realm of idealism. As regards the target of cognition and the foundation of self-development, such a philosophy belongs to the doctrine of original nature. As regards the orientation and destination of actions, such a philosophy belongs to the doctrine of high aspiration." According to He Lin, "original nature" is a common phase extracted from the whole storehouse of abundant objective data. Therefore, it is universal and concrete at the same time. In other words, it is the so-called "principle." Such being the case, "Idealism is the doctrine of original nature." He maintains that "in order to seek true freedom, we have to put a lofty ideal in front of us, and treat it as the benchmark of our freedom." In his view, the lofty ideal is the key demarcation between man and animals: "The doctrine of high aspiration represents the fundamental spirit of the movements in early modern times which aimed at freedom." (Cf. *A Brief Explanation of Early Modern Idealism*, Chapter 1)

With respect to the relationship between the mind and things, He Lin is close to Xiong Shili. He explains the unequal relationship between the mind and things:

> "The mind and things are always parallel to each other, and they constitute the two sides of the same entity. The mind is the dominant part, and things are the instrumental part. The mind is the foundation of things, and things are the application of the mind. The mind is the essence of things, and things are the expression of the mind." (*A Brief Explanation of Early Modern Idealism*, Chapter 1)

In the domain of science it is necessary to explain the things by the things, to explain the mind by the mind. Here the premise is the doctrine that the mind and the things are parallel to each other.

In the domain of philosophy, it is necessary to emphasize that the mind dominates the things. He says, "The mind is the foundation and the things are the application. The mind is the master, and things are the followers. This is the genuine view of idealistic philosophy." (*A Reply to Mr. Xie Youwei on His Three Points of Criticism*) The mind is logically prior to things. Form, significance and value are decided by the mind. It is quite impossible to discuss things by discarding the mind. He says, "So-called matter must be matter that has already been cogitated." (*Chinese Philosophy Today*) And he says, "Its color and appearance are the result of the exaggeration of consciousness. And the reason why its significance, order and value possess objectivity lies in the fact that in the subject of such cognition and evaluation there is an objective, inevitable and universal category of cognition or standard of evaluation." And he says, "If we talk about anything apart from the mind, the thing is just complete darkness which has neither color nor appearance nor significance nor value. In other words, there is nothing at all." (*A Brief Explanation of Early Modern Idealism*, Chapter 1) He Lin sees that objective things around human beings are stamped or branded by human beings with their subjective activities. He Lin sees that the value of things "comes from the relationship in which people treat outside things which may meet their needs."*[1] Nevertheless, he exaggerates the role that the subject plays. And, further, he denies the objective reality of the material world, which he interprets as the product of the subject of man. In this way, he falls into the abyss of subjective idealism.

Starting from the theory of the subject that "Mind is principle," He Lin further probes the methods of cognition, and sums up the controversy over cognitive methods waged between Hu Shi and Liang Shuming. In his opinion, in both the scientific method, which Hu Shi advocates, and the intuitive method, which Liang Shuming upholds, there are historical grounds and existing values. The textual critics of the Qing Dynasty applied the scientific method to their researches, but the Neo-Confucian scholars, whether of the Lu-Wang school, which stressed "extension of good knowledge," or of the Cheng-Zhu school, which stressed "extension of knowledge by investigation of things," applied the intuitive method to their researches. He Lin extends the analysis of intuition:

> "Intuition is a kind of experience, and it is also a kind of method. When I say that intuition is a kind of experience, I mean that it is, in an extensive sense, an attitude toward life, a spiritual world,

* Cf. *Complete Works of Marx and Engels*, Beijing: The People's Publishing House, Chinese edition, volume 19, p. 406.

> an experience of coincidence with the deity, a revelation from inspiration, a sudden enlightenment or a spur of the moment in the aspect of knowledge, and suchlike. When I say that intuition is a kind of method, I mean that it is a kind of function or technology which may help us know the truth and grasp reality." (*A Brief Explanation of Early Modern Idealism*, Chapter 4)

Hence, "There are three things no philosophers should lack — formal analysis and inference, the speculative method of contradictions, and the method of intuition." (*A Brief Explanation of Early Modern Idealism*, Chapter 4)

In cognitive activities, what position does the intuitive method occupy? In order to answer this question, He Lin inherits and transforms the thought of Kant, who divides cognition into the three stages of *sthetik* (sensibility), *Verstand* (understanding) and *Vernunft* (reason). In He Lin's system, the three stages are "pre-intellectual intuition," "analysis of the intellect" and "post-intellectual intuition." In the stage of "pre-intellectual intuition," man undergoes chaotic experiences but does not acquire knowledge in the true sense. This stage corresponds to the stage of *sthetik* (sensibility) in Kant's system. In the stage of "analysis of the intellect," man acquires scientific knowledge. This stage corresponds to the stage of *Verstand* (understanding) in Kant's system. In the stage of "post-intellectual intuition," man acquires philosophical knowledge. This stage corresponds to the stage of *Vernunft* (reason) in Kant's system. As regards "pre-intellectual intuition," He Lin points out, "It means that people first use the intuitive method to grasp the entirety, so as to probe the details of the target. And then people use intellect to analyze the entirety to elaborate the details of the target." As regards "post-intellectual intuition," He Lin points out, "It means that people first engage in research into different parts, and in the analysis and dissection of trivial affairs. After long-term accumulation, people may gradually acquire and then use intuitive ability. With the help of intuition, people may get a peep into entirety so as to see the significance hidden in the target." And, further, He Lin reasons, "Thus, it clearly follows that both intuition and intellect represent different stages or different aspects of one and the same progress of human thinking. There is no fundamental conflict between intuition and intellect." And he says, "No philosopher who in the main adopts the intuitive method will spurn the methods of formal logic and dialectical speculation. In like manner, no philosopher who in the main adopts the intellectual method will spurn the methods of intuition and dialectic speculation." (*A Brief Explanation of Early Modern Idealism*, Chapter 4)

Among the modern philosophers, He Lin's analysis of intuition is more profound and careful than those of Liang Shuming, Xiong Shili and Feng Youlan. In fact, He Lin regards intuition, as well as intellect, as cognitive methods.

Starting from the stipulation that "Mind is principle," He Lin responds to the problem of the relationship between knowledge and action by putting forth a "natural theory of the unity of knowledge and action."

In He Lin's opinion, Wang Shouren's theory on "the unity of knowledge and action" indeed has factual grounds and a theoretical foundation. Nevertheless, such a theory is an "evaluation of the unity of knowledge and action" focused on how knowledge and action are governed by their ethical values. Therefore, when people formulate the categories of "knowledge" and "action" according to such a theory, they are in fact adopting a dualist approach to knowledge and action. With respect to an activity in which there is a high degree of knowledge but a low degree of action, they only treat it as "knowledge" alone. An activity in which there is a high degree of action but a low degree of knowledge is treated as "action" alone. "In fact, they divide knowledge and action into two different things, and then they make efforts to combine knowledge and action into a unity."

To overcome this dualist tendency and to exercise control over "the evaluation theory of the unity of knowledge and action,", He Lin puts forth the "natural theory on the unity of knowledge and action." This theory owes much to the legacy of Spinoza, who maintained that mind and body are parallel to each other, and of Thomas Hill Green (1836-1882), a British Neo-Hegelian philosopher, who held that knowledge and action are parallel to each other. In He Lin's opinion, "Knowledge is the activity of consciousness. Action is the activity of physiology." These two activities take place at the same time, and as far as time is concerned we cannot say which takes place first and which takes place second. He points out, "We cannot say that knowledge is prior to action, and we cannot say that knowledge is posterior to action, either." He further explains, "All actions contain the function of consciousness, and all knowledge contains the function of physiology. Knowledge and action are always in a unity and parallel to each other. Knowledge and action always work together as two sides of the same unity, one being the psychological side, and the other being the physiological side."

He traces the natural theory on the unity of knowledge and action to the thought of the two Cheng brothers, Zhu Xi and Wang Shouren, who "all demonstrated the development of knowledge and action as a central problem." For centuries, there have been two opposing views on the relationship between knowledge and action. One view is that "knowledge is the principal, while action is the subordinate." The contradictory view holds that "action is the principal, while knowledge is the subordinate." He Lin affirms the first view, and opposes the second:

> "The natural theory on the unity of knowledge and action holds that knowledge and action take place at the same time, and they are parallel to each other. They cannot decide each other. Nevertheless, we may say that there is an internal decision or logical decision. In other words, knowledge is the internal motive force of action, and knowledge has the logical priority over action." (*A Brief Explanation of Early Modern Idealism*, Chapter 3)

This standpoint is one of subjective idealism.

Such is his "natural theory on the unity of knowledge and action," which completely denies that practice plays a decisive role in the acquisition of knowledge. It is thus clear that he attempts to use an idealistic theory that psychology and physiology are combined into one to replace the view of dialectic materialism that knowledge and action are unified. As compared with Sun Yat-sen's thoughts that "Action comes first, and knowledge second," and that "Knowledge is difficult, but action is easy," He Lin has slipped back ideologically. Nevertheless, He Lin made a careful elaboration of the relationship between knowledge and action theoretically and he finally set up a system which possesses a certain sense of early modern times. This is indeed significant in the history of epistemology. After 1949, He Lin gradually accepted Marxism, and came to understand that knowledge and action are unified on the basis of practice. From then on, he made new elaborations of many major problems concerning the relationship between knowledge and action.

39.

The Dissemination and Development of Marxist Philosophy in China

The victory of the October Revolution in Russia in 1917 and the eruption of the May Fourth Movement in China in 1919 drove a batch of advanced intellectuals, who immersed themselves in the New Culture Movement, to reflect on both traditional Chinese culture and modern Western culture. They came to regard Marxism as the only doctrine that could save the Chinese nation, and sought to integrate Marxism with the specific conditions of China.

The integration of Marxism with the labor movement in China brought about the birth of the Communist Party of China (CPC). After severe struggles lasting decades, and paying a heavy price in blood, the Chinese Communists finally brought about the victory of the democratic revolution, and founded the People's Republic of China. In the course of this historic development, Marxist philosophy witnessed extensive dissemination and important development in China. There appeared a large number of Marxist thinkers and philosophers, and Mao Zedong Thought came into being.

In 1899, the names of Karl Marx and Friedrich Engels first became known to the Chinese people, when Timothy Richard (1845-1919), a commissioner of the Baptist Church of Great Britain, published his abridged translation of *Social Evolution* by the British sociologist Benjamin Kidd in the *Bulletin of All Nations*, a newspaper run by the Christian Literature Society for China. Later, Liang Qichao (1873-1929) gave a brief introduction to Marx and Marxism in essays. In 1902, in the *Journal of the Renovated People*, he published an essay titled "Doctrines by Kidd the Revolutionary of Evolutionary Theory," in which he says, "Marx is a German native, and a leading authority on socialism." After the establishment of the China Revolutionary League, Zhu Zhixin (1885-1920), a radical bourgeois revolutionary, published "Brief Biographies of German Social Revolutionaries" in the *People's Journal*. In the article he gives a comparatively detailed introduction to the ideas and activities of Marx and Engels to the Chinese reader for the first time. He explains, "They are the leaders of the communists all over the world. At the request of the International Communist League, they wrote and published the *Manifesto of the Communist Party*." Zhu also gives a brief introduction to the main ideas of the *Manifesto*. He later made an abridged translation of the ten points of the program of the *Manifesto of the Communist Party (II)*. In the coming years, many essays, concerning Marx and Engels, were published in the *People's Journal*. And after the Revolution of 1911, a large number of articles on Marxism were published in various periodicals and newspapers in China.

Nevertheless, the inspiration of the October Revolution accelerated the movement against imperialism and feudalism in China among many intellectuals who had become involved with the New Culture Movement. They began to accept and propagate Marxism, engaging in many important controversies on major issues. For instance, between them and Hu Shi there was the "controversy over problems and isms." Between them and Liang Qichao and Zhang Dongsun there was the "controversy over socialism." With Huang Lingshuang and Ou Shengbai there was the "controversy over anarchism." Through these controversies, the ideological front of Marxism was enlarged. After the establishment of the CPC in 1921 and during the revolutionary years from 1924 to 1927, there was extensive dissemination of Marxism and preliminary research into its application to Chinese conditions. Li Dazhao, Chen Duxiu, Li Da, Qu Qiubai, Mao Zedong, Cai Hesen, Deng Zhongxia, Zhou Enlai, Yun Daiying and others played important roles in promoting its dissemination. Li Dazhao, Chen Duxiu, Li Da and Qu Qiubai especially made large contributions to the spread of and research into the materialist concept of history. Their activities had a great influence on Chinese intellectual circles.

Li Dazhao (1889-1927) was a native of Leting County, Hebei Province. In his early years, he studied in Japan. Returning to China in 1916, he immediately took part in the New Culture Movement. He became a professor at Peking University, and at the same time was the director of its library. In addition, he was one of the editors of *Youth* Magazine. Following the October Revolution of 1917, he began research into that revolution, and came to accept Marxism. In 1918, he published three essays in succession, titled, "A Comparative View of the French and Russian Revolutions," "The Victory of the Common People," and "The Victory of Bolshevism," respectively. He points out, "The Russian Revolution of 1917 was the herald for the world revolution in the 20th century. The future globe will be a world full of red banners!" Together with Chen Duxiu and others, he founded a magazine called *Weekly Commentaries*, in which many articles on Marxism were published. These activities show that at that time Li began to undergo an ideological change from being a revolutionary democrat to being a communist, and one of the first batch of Marxist thinkers in China. In 1919, he took part in the May Fourth Movement. He engaged in the "controversy on problems and isms," in which he rebutted Hu Shi for his reformist call to "research more problems, talk about fewer isms." Thus, he enlarged the influence of Marxism. In 1920, he set up a communist group in Beijing, and so he can be regarded as one of the founders of the CPC. After the formal establishment of the CPC, he was its leader in north China and launched labor movements. In 1924, he took part in the First National Congress of the Chinese Nationalist Party (Kuomintang, or KMT), during which he helped Sun Yat-sen reorganize that party and promoted the establishment of the united front between the KMT and the CPC. In 1927, Zhang Zuolin, the warlord who controlled northeast China and Beijing, had Li arrested and executed.

In the years immediately following the May Fourth Movement, while engaged in arduous political struggles, Li contributed greatly to the theoretical progress of the Chinese Communists, especially in the propagation of the materialist concept on history.

Among his main philosophical works are *My View of Marxism*, *Ma-*

terial Changes and Moral Changes, *An Economic Explanation of the Ideological Changes in Early-Modern China*, *Karl Marx's Philosophy of History and Heinrich Rickert's Philosophy of History*, *The Value of the Materialist Concept of History in the Modern Historical Sciences*, *Historical Science and Philosophy*, and *Essentials of Historical Science*.

Li gives a general explanation of the basic ideas and their significance of the materialist concept of history and a criticism of the various idealist concepts of history. He teaches people how to use the new materialist point of view to understand the specific conditions of Chinese society and to seek the road to the Chinese revolution.

In the first place, in a comparatively intact and systematic way he explains the basic ideas of the materialist concept of history. He says as follows:

> "The summation of the social and relations of production of mankind constitutes the structure of the society and economy. This is the fundamental structure of society. In society, there are political, legal, ethical, philosophical and suchlike spiritual structures, which keep changing all the time. And all spiritual structures of society will change along with the structural changes of the economy. We may regard these spiritual structures as superficial structures. And superficial structures are in most cases dependent on the fundamental structure. Changes in the fundamental structure are brought about by internal causes, which are the supreme agents of the evolution of the fundamental cause. The supreme agent is productivity." (*My View of Marxism*)

And he expounds on the relationship between social organization and productivity:

> "Whenever there is a change in productivity, there must be a corresponding change in social organization. Social organization is productivity. And productivity is similar to cloth, silk, beans and millet in that it is one of the products which the mankind has ever produced according to a certain degree of productivity. Stone mortar operated by hand produced the society of feudal princes. The steam engine and flour-milling machine produced capitalist

society. Productivity exists within a certain social organization. At first the social organization promotes the growth of productivity, but as time goes by productivity may become so powerful that the social organization cannot match its growth, but ends up hindering it. Nevertheless, despite the fact that the social organization limits and even hinders the growth of productivity, the latter continues developing without ceasing. The greater the strength of the development, the sharper the conflicts between the development and the social organization, which cannot fit in with the development any longer, will be. As a result, the old social organization cannot avoid a total collapse. This is social revolution. After that, a new social organization will arise to replace the old one. And when productivity outgrows that new social organization, the collapse of the latter will be just as unavoidable." (*My View of Marxism*)

In this way, he correctly explains the decisive role which productivity plays in social relations, as the economic basis affects the superstructure. As he points out, productivity is the fundamental agent of social development and social revolution. So we say that in a comparatively intact and systematic way he introduces the basic ideas of the materialist concept of history to China.

In the second place, Li points out the immense significance of the materialist concept of history. The materialist concept of history demands that people seek to understand the laws of society and history through economic relations. In this way, "the science of history is elevated to the same status as the natural sciences, and this opens up a new era for historians." (*Karl Marx's Philosophy of History and Heinrich Rickert's Philosophy of History*) The materialist concept of history is different from the traditional theological concept of history and the rational concept of history. The key point in the materialist concept of history is that "all bygone history was created by the same human power as exists in us but not by this great man or that wise man. It was not a favor from God, either." (*The Value of the Materialist Concept of History in the Modern Historical Sciences*) And this is "the outlook on life with which people may rouse themselves to strive to be strong." According to such a new concept of history and according to such a new outlook on life, "We should experience a self-awakening of our efforts, we should unite as one, and we should create a new history for the life of the common people all over the world." (*Ibid*)

In the third place, Li emphasizes that it is highly necessary to apply the materialist concept of history to analyzing the practical conditions of China in order to determine, why the political and economic situation of the country is in such poor shape and to find a way to free China from the oppression of the imperialist powers (Cf. *This Past Week*). He explains the cause of changes in Chinese ideology in early modern times according to the materialist concept of history. Since ancient times China has been a country whose economic foundation is agriculture and whose social foundation is the clan system. For over 2,000 years, the feudal ethics and rites of Confucianism have dominated the mentality of the Chinese people. And the "cardinal guides" and "constant virtues" as specified in the feudal ethical code are nothing but the products of such a cultural foundation. But as world history enters modern times and the agricultural economy of the Eastern countries is oppressed by the industrial economy of the Western countries, the latter has shaken the former to its very foundations. Now the system of big clans is collapsing, and all kinds of new ideological trends are appearing, undermining the dominant position of the "cardinal guides" and "constant virtues" and all the rest of the Confucian system. Li is adamant that the new ideological trend can never be stemmed. "This is because new thoughts emerge to fit in with the new state of the economy and to meet the new needs of the society. They are not a sheer concoction from the mind of a few young fellows." (*An Economic Explanation of the Ideological Changes in Early-Modern China*)

Although Li's research into the materialist concept of history is just a preliminary effort, it is a call to advanced intellectuals to accept, study and apply the materialist concept of history. Therefore, we may say that Li indeed played an enlightening and pioneering role in the dissemination of Marxist philosophy in China.

Chen Duxiu (1880-1942) was a native of Huaining County (present-day Anqing City), Anhui Province. Chen also studied in Japan. When he returned to China, he took part in the Revolution of 1911 and the struggle against Yuan Shikai, who had seized the fruits of the Revolution. In 1915, Chen started a publication entitled *Youth* Magazine in Shanghai. The title was changed to *La Jeunesse* the following year. As the editor-in-chief of this popular magazine, Chen became the leader of the New Culture Movement. In 1918, in collaboration with Li Dazhao and other progressive thinkers, he started another magazine, titled *Weekly Commentaries*, in which a number of advocates of the New Culture Movement propagated Marxism. After the May Fourth Movement of 1919, Chen began to embrace Marxism. In 1920, together with Li Da and other Chinese Marxists, he helped with the preparatory work for founding the CPC, and moreover was elected the first general secretary of the Party. In the "controversy between science and metaphysics" of 1923-1924, he defended, from the standpoint of Marxism, the materialist concept of history against Hu Shi and Zhang Junmai. During the revolutionary ferment of the years of 1924-1927, he made the serious mistake of Right opportunism, and at the August Seventh Conference of the CPC in 1927, the Party dismissed him from the post of general secretary. He then became an important member of the opposition faction within the Party, and was subsequently expelled.

Among Chen's main philosophical works are *A Message Addressed Respectfully to Youth*, *The Last Consciousness of My People*, *The Way of Confucius and the Life of Modern Times*, *A Discussion on Socialism*, *Doctrines of Karl Marx*, *Foreword to Science and Outlook on Life*, *A Reply to Zhang Junmai and the Revered Mr. Liang Qichao*, *The Bourgeois Revolution and the Revolutionary Bourgeoisie*, and *The Chinese Nationalist Revolution and Classes in Chinese Society*.

Chen's principal contribution to the dissemination of Marxist philosophy was that he criticized non-Marxist thought, and explained and safeguarded the materialist concept of history. When he took part in the "controversy between science and metaphysics," he refuted the multi-element concept of history preached by Hu Shi, stressing the interrelations between social existence and social consciousness.

Chen Duxiu declares that the materialist concept of history does not deny the existence of mental phenomena such as thoughts, cultures, religions, morality and education. "But it assigns such mental phenomena to the realm of the superstructure, which rests on the foundation of the economy; mental phenomena can not be the foundation." (*Reply to Mr. Hu Shizhi*) And he says, "Thoughts, knowledge, speech and education are of course important instruments for promoting social progress. Nevertheless, we cannot say that they are able to change society, to explain history, or to dominate man's outlook on life. In short, they are not in an equal position with the economy." (*Ibid*) Social existence decides social consciousness, but social consciousness does not reflect social existence in a passive way. Instead, there exists a certain reaction in social consciousness when it reflects social existence, and such a reaction must depend on social existence, for social existence is the basis of social consciousness. However, Chen tended to look down on the masses, whom he described as "a tray of loose sand, and a swarm of foolish creatures." He fails to see the great historical role the broad masses of the people may play. When he analyzes the class structure of Chinese society, he puts forth a odd view, saying, "The peasants live scattered in the countryside, so it is difficult to concentrate their strength. Their cultural level is rather low, and their life requirements are simple, too. Therefore, they are prone to conservatism. Since China has a large territory, it is easy for the peasants to move here and there, and when they suffer from hardships, it is easy to appease them. That is why it is difficult for the peasants to take part in the revolutionary movement." (*The Chinese Nationalist Revolution and Classes in Chinese Society*) He also says, "In China, industry is still in its infancy. The working class in China is not only infantile in quantity, it is also infantile in quality." (*Ibid*) Accordingly, the bourgeoisie should be endowed with the leadership of the democratic revolution. This stand led him into the pitfall of Right opportunism.

Our next Marxist thinker is Qu Qiubai (1899-1935), a native of Changzhou City, Jiangsu Province. In 1920, he visited the Soviet Union as a journalist, and there he embraced Marxism. In 1922, he joined the CPC, and quickly rose to become one of its leaders. He was the editor in succession of *La Jeunesse*, *The Guide* and *The Vanguard*, which were publications of the CPC Central Committee. He published a large number of essays, in which he propagated Marxism and dwelt on the problems of the Chinese revolution. In 1927, he presided over the August Seventh Conference, at which Chen Duxiu's Right opportunism was condemned. At the same conference, the Party determined to wage armed struggle against the rule of the Kuomintang. In the period from the winter of 1927 to the spring of 1928, when he presided over the work of the CPC Central committee, he made a mistake of putschism. In 1930, Qu presided over the Third Plenary Session of the Sixth Central Committee of the CPC, which put a stop to the previous line of Left adventurism. Later, under attack from Wang Ming and his cohorts, Qu was expelled from the Central Committee, and devoted himself to cultural work for the revolution. In 1933, he entered the central revolutionary base in Jiangxi Province, where he served as the commissar of people's education in the Democratic Government of Workers and Peasants of the Chinese Soviet Republic. In 1935, he was captured by Kuomintang troops and executed.

Among Qu's main philosophical works are *An Introduction to Social Philosophy*, *Modern Sociology*, *An Introduction to the Social Sciences* and *An Introduction to the World Outlook of Materialism*.

Qu translated "dialectics" into "mutual dialectics." In his opinion, the philosophy of Marxism contains materialism and the materialist concept of history, which are both in line with the "mutual dialectics." As he carries on vigorous propaganda of the materialist concept of history, he lays stress on disseminating materialist dialectics.

According to Qu, if one thinks over any philosophical question, one will immediately meet with a series of questions on the relations between ego and non-ego, between cognition and essence, and between soul and Nature. And the answers to these questions will differ depending on whether one takes an idealistic point of view or a materialistic one. Materialism takes objective reality for the starting point, while idealism takes the subjective imagination for the starting point. Furthermore, he points out that idealism is associated always with religion of one kind or another. For instance, the so-called "absolute spirit" originates from the "conception of the soul" via a long period of "distillation." Quite the contrary, materialism is always associated with science. This is because when one examines Nature from a scientific point of view, one cannot use "acts of spirits of one kind or another" to explain the various phenomena of Nature; what one should do is investigate the laws of the various phenomena of Nature. He says, "Spiritual phenomena originate in material phenomena, and matter may be examined in a practical way. This is materialism." (*An Introduction to Social Philosophy*)

Starting from this point, Qu further emphasizes that Marxist philosophy is the unification of materialism and dialectics:

"The foundation of the world outlook of Marxism lies in dialecti-

> cal materialism. The term dialectical materialism itself tells us that Marxist materialism is a synthesis of both materialism and dialectics. And thus clearly it follows that it is the integrity of these two doctrines, which are at their highest stage of development and evolution." (*An Introduction to the World Outlook of Materialism*)

In this way, he specifies the essential distinction between Marxist philosophy and all the philosophical thoughts of bygone ages. And he introduces the basic principles of materialist dialectics to the Chinese reader: "The foundation of the universe is the movement of matter. And the fundamental nature of this movement is contradiction. This means the negation of the negation, and the mutual change of both quantity and quality." (*An Introduction to Social Philosophy*) And he links contradiction that is characteristic of matter to the rise of material phoneomena: "Without any mutual changes in the contradiction, there would be no movement. Without movement, there would be no life organisms or other phenomena." (*Ibid*) Herein he introduces some important laws of materialist dialectics to the Chinese reader, including the law of the unity of opposites, the law of quantitative change and qualitative change, and the law of the negation of the negation, as well as the role of contradiction in the developmental movement of things.

As regards the theory of knowledge, Qu propagates a cognitive line of materialist dialectics, that is, all cognition is from thing to perception and then to thought. He points out as follows:

> "Any thought, no matter what it may be, is by no means the creation or imagination of a single individual. All our knowledge comes from experience of outside things. Even if our knowledge is about arithmetic, which seems to be purely abstract, it is after all a reflection of the realistic world. This is because abstract arithmetic is also established in external space and time, which constitute its target. In other words, it is by no means created by the mind out of nothing." (*An Introduction to Social Philosophy*)

Therefore, any correct cognition lies in "pure investigation into external things and events. When people are faced with the various phenomena, it is necessary to look for their material causes, namely, the objective and practical causes. They must not explain the phenomena of the universe or society according to any subjective, idealistic, or psychological causes." (*An Introduction to the World Outlook of Materialism*) Any explanation of Nature, society or history must be established on the basis of objective practice; it can never be established on the basis of subjective imagination.

Qu was the first Marxist philosopher in China to treat dialectical materialism and historical materialism as a strict and integrated system when he introduced them to China. His introduction of the basic theories of materialist dialectics was the start of the dissemination of dialectical materialism in China, and he played an important role in inspiring the advanced Chinese intellectuals. Thanks to Qu's diligent work in the theoretical sphere, China's advanced intellectuals began to grasp Marxist philosophy and the concept of materialism, and apply this new knowledge in a practical way.

Li Dazhao, Chen Duxiu, Li Da, Qu Qiubai and others assisted in the early stage of the dissemination of Marxist philosophy in China, and thus started a revolutionary change in the development of Chinese philosophy. Their dissemination and development of Marxist philosophy in China was connected with the democratic revolution led by the CPC. As a result, Marxist philosophy is possessed of vitality and influence much greater than the other philosophies which were advocated during the same period. Of course, in the early stage of the dissemination of Marxist philosophy there were quite a few examples of immaturity — especially on the problem of how Marxism could be integrated with the concrete and specific conditions of the Chinese revolution. Such immaturity in theory was one of the causes of the failure of the Democratic Revolution in China from 1924 to 1927.

After the failure of the Democratic Revolution in China in 1927, there arose an extremely grim situation on the philosophical front. Chen Duxiu was criticized for Right opportunism. The CPC found itself alone in the armed struggle against Kuomintang rule, but it creatively opened up the revolutionary way of "using the rural areas to encircle the cities." In such a new revolutionary situation, how to understand the nature of Chinese society accurately and how to scientifically analyze the various contradictions in the Chinese revolutionary movement their changes, and development became urgent and important tasks for the Chinese Marxists. This meant that they had to formulate the line, strategy and policies for the Party. On the other hand, the Kuomintang's Rightists, represented by Chiang Kai-shek, waged a frenzied war of encirclement and suppression of Marxism when they ended the period of Kuomintang-Communist cooperation and set up a counter-revolutionary dictatorship. Chen Lifu and Chiang Kai-shek gave full play to the defects of the philosophical thought of Sun Yat-sen. They put forth a "theory of life organisms" and a "philosophy of arduous action," respectively, so that they might combat Marxist philosophy and consolidate their counter-revolutionary rule.

Chen Lifu maintains that "all things in the universe have life, and in all kinds of existence there is both matter and spirit." (*A Theory of Life Organism*, Part One) He effaces the essence of the unity of the world, that is, that the world is a unity in that it is matter. And he interprets the essence of the universe as "a long flow of life organisms." As for Chiang Kai-shek, he advocates both the theory that "Knowledge and action are one," which was put forth by Wang Shouren, and the theory that "To know is difficult, and to do is easy," which was put forth by Sun Yat-sen. He maintains that both belong to "a philosophy that emphasizes action." (*The Importance of the Revolutionary Philosophy*) His logic runs as follows: If stress is laid only on the theory that "To know is difficult, and to do is easy," ordinary people will not uphold the "Three Principles of the People." What is more, "When they hear someone talking about materialism, they will follow him at once." (*A First-hand Account of the Stages in Researching the Revolutionary Philosophy*) Therefore, the only way out is to discard knowledge and to take arduous action. "Only by so doing can the national spirit innate to the Chinese nation be rejuvenated and the character of the whole nation be cultivated successfully." (*The Importance of the Revolutionary Philosophy*) In short, he assiduously propagates a set of obscurantist philosophical tenets, demanding that the people submit to his dictatorship.

Therefore, breaking through the encirclement and suppression of Marxism waged by the Chiang Kai-shek clique and clearly showing the orientation in which the Chinese people could advance ideologically became urgent tasks for the Chinese Marxists at that time.

Under the leadership of the CPC, Marxist workers in the fields of philosophy and other social sciences undertook this task. Since 1928, a number of revolutionary periodicals began to publish articles propagating materialist dialectics. In the 1930s, an ideological movement arose engaging in vigorous propaganda and research into materialist dialectics. In 1930, under the leadership of the CPC, the League of Chinese Social Scientists, called the "Social League" for short, was founded. According to its working principle, the "Social League" aimed at "researching and introducing Marxist theories, and disseminating these theories among the ordinary people." Quite a number of theoretical fighters for Marxism, including Li Da, Li Yimang, Wu Liping, Xu Deheng, Guo Moruo, Hou Wailu, Yang Dongchun, He Sijing, Ke Bainian and Qian Yishi, despite living in conditions of "white terror," worked very hard and successfully to translate, research and propagate Marxist theory. In the 1930s, all the classical works of Marxist philosophy were translated into Chinese and published. They were *The Poverty of Philosophy* (1847) by Karl Marx, *Anti-Dunring* (1878) by Friedrich Engels, *The Capital* (1867) by Karl Marx, *The Dialectics of Nature* (1886) by Friedrich Engels, *Ludwig Feuerbach and the Outcome of German Classical Philosophy* (1886) by Friedrich Engels and *Materialism and Empiriocriticism* (1909) by Vladimir Ilyich Lenin. In addition, works on Marxist theory written by Soviet theoreticians were also translated and introduced to the Chinese reader, for instance, *A Course of Dialectics and Materialism* by Shirokov and others, and *An Outline of the New Philosophy* and *Dialectical Materialism and Historical Materialism* by Mark Borisovich Mitin (1901-1989). The translation and publication of these works played an important role in promoting the dissemination and development of Marxist philosophy in China, especially of dialectical materialism.

Also on the ideological front, Marxists carried on a fierce struggle against the various ideological trends which attacked dialectical materialism. Of these struggles, the most important one was "the controversy on dialectical materialism," which was carried on from 1930 to 1936. It was also called "the controversy on philosophy" or "the controversy between dialectical materialism and anti-dialectical materialism." The controversy was in the main waged against the ideas of Zhang Dongsun and Ye Qing.

Zhang Dongsun (1886-1973) was generally regarded as a native of Yuhang County (present-day Yuhang County), Zhejiang Province. In his early years he went to study in Japan. After the Revolution of 1911, he worked as the secretary of the Ministry of Internal Affairs in the Nanjing Provisional Government. In 1934, in collaboration with Zhang Junmai and others, he organized a political party — the National Social Party, which changed its name to the Democratic Socialist Party in 1946. After the founding of the People's Republic of China, he held posts in the Central People's Government. Early in the period of the May Fourth Movement, he advocated so-called guild socialism, launching a "debate on socialism" with Marxists including Li Dazhao, Chen Duxiu and Li Da. In the 1930s, from the viewpoint of Neo-Kantianism, he opposed dialectical materialism in his works *The Theory of Knowledge*, *A Retelling of the Multi-element Theory of Knowledge* and *A General Examination of Dialectical Materialism*.

He confuses the dialectical materialism of Marxism with the idealistic dialectics of Hegel. He wrote, "Marx has nothing new in this respect, but according to his own words, he has turned upside down the Hegelian dialectics, and that's all." (*A General Examination of Dialectical Materialism*) In this way, by negating Hegelian dialectics he negates Marxist dialectics and attacks materialist dialectics, saying, "It is so mistaken that no remedy can save it." (*Ibid*) In addition to this, he puts forth a "multi-element theory of knowledge." Knowledge is not the product of actions but a "combined product" of sensitive phases, gestalts and other *a priori* forms assumed by people. He says, "Apart from the sensitive phases, there is no knowledge at all. In like manner, apart from the gestalts, there is no knowledge at all. Apart from assumptions, there is no knowledge at all. That's all." (*The Theory of Knowledge*) Apart from phenomena, it is absolutely impossible for man to know the noumenon of things, and it is absolutely impossible for man to know the subject of knowledge. Therefore, he attacks the materialist line of Lenin's theory of knowledge, saying, "It is sheer nonsense; a lot of fuss and nothing more." (*A General Examination of Dialectical Materialism*)

Ye Qing (1896-1981), originally named Ren Zhuoxuan, was a native of Nanchong City, Sichuan Province. He was an early member of the CPC. In 1928, he was arrested by the Kuomintang, and forced to betray the revolution. After that, he wrote a large number of works in which he distorted Marxism under the signboard of Marxism. After the War of Resistance against Japanese Aggression began, he sought refuge with the Kuomintang. He held many posts in the Kuomintang administration, for instance, secretary of the central committee of the Three Principles of the People's Youth League and deputy minister of propaganda. In 1949, he went to Taiwan. In the 1930s, Ye Qing wrote several philosophical works, including *Whither Philosophy?*, *A Criticism of Zhang Dongsun's Philosophy*, *Concerning Matter — Spirit — Matter* and *Theory and Practice*.

Outwardly in these works, Ye Qing criticizes the philosophical thought of Zhang Dongsun. In practice, he embraces a strong objection to materialist dialectics and maintains that mankind's cognition of the world develops from religion to philosophy, and then to the science. Therefore, Hegel reached the summit of philosophy long ago. He says, "It is hard to say if there has been anything worth being called philosophy since Hegel." (*Whither Philosophy?*) And he says, "It is a pity that Karl Marx dabbled in science, politics and practice." (*Ibid*) Ye Qing's theory is designed to put a full stop to philosophy. In addition, he distorts the Marxist theory of knowledge by confusing the concept of practice of Marxist philosophy with the concept of practice of classical German philosophy. In his opinion, practice is a category specifically innate to idealist philosophies. Furthermore, he distorts the relationship between knowledge and practice, viewing it as a parallel relationship. According to him, as far as the formation of theory is concerned, "Fact is the mother of thought." And as far as the function of theory is concerned, "Thought is the mother of fact." He says, "When facts act on the thinking process, there emerge theories. When theory acts on practice, there emerge facts." (*Theory and Practice*) "In the former situation, the formula is 'practice — theory.' In the latter situation, the formula is 'theory — practice.'" (*Ibid*) In fact, he equates practice with the knowledge, and he even goes so far as to say, "Knowledge is practice, and practice is knowledge." (*Ibid*)

Although Ye Qing and Zhang Dongsun were at loggerheads on the correct way to oppose materialist dialectics and on the relationship between knowledge and practice, they had much in common. Marxists such as Ai Siqi (1910-1966), Deng Yunte (Deng Tuo, 1912-1966) and Shen Zhiyuan (1902-1965) launched a forceful counterattack, correctly and clearly expounding the essence and characteristics of materialist dialectics and refuting the theory that philosophy had reached its apex with Hegel. Ai Siqi writes, "The new materialism was established immediately after the Hegelian philosophy. Only by inheriting the important legacy of Hegel's thought, and by criticizing and transforming his philosophy was such an epoch-making new philosophy constructed." (*On the Reversion of Hegelian Philosophy*) And he describes the features of the new materialism by saying, "The new materialism does not disperse philosophy into various departments of science. It enables philosophy to keep its own independent sphere, and to have its own target. That target is the most universal and most general law of the development of the world, namely, the general law of the movement and changes of Nature, society and the thinking of mankind." (*Several Philosophical Problems*)

Li Da and Ai Siqi probably made the greatest contributions in this regard.

Ai Siqi, originally named Li Shengxuan, was a native of Tengchong, Yunnan Province. In his early years, he twice went to Japan to study. There he encountered Marxism. Upon his return to China in 1931, he plunged into the work of propagating and researching Marxist philosophy. In 1935, he joined the CPC, and in 1937, he went to the revolutionary base at Yan'an. For a considerable length of time after that he engaged in the work of philosophical dissemination and philosophical education for the CPC. He achieved remarkable success, and was the author of several authoritative works. In the movement to promote materialist dialectics, which unfolded in the 1930s, this young philosopher not only made an energetic refutation of the philosophical theories of Zhang Dongsun and Ye Qing, he also reflected in his *Popular Philosophy* some new achievements made in Marxist philosophy both home and abroad from contemporary sources. In popular and lively language, he made a comparatively systematic explanation of the fundamental principles of materialist dialectics from the three aspects of ontology, epistemology and methodology.

In *Popular Philosophy*, he often cites simple examples from daily life to illustrate the abstruse principles of the materialist dialectics. For instance, when he discusses the relationship between knowledge and practice, he cites the example of the similarity in appearance of the contemporary cinema comedian Charlie Chaplin (1889-1977) and the German Nazi leader Adolf Hitler (1889-1945). In order to acquire correct knowledge, one must raise one's perceptual knowledge to the level of rational knowledge. And in the process, one must test and rectify one's knowledge in the course of practice, and reach the unification of subject and object:

> "We must go from the perceptional to the rational, and from the rational to the practical. And then we must go from the practical to the new rational, and further to the even newer rational. Such a process is boundless in succession and circulation. Nevertheless, every time there is a circulation, our knowledge becomes more abundant than before. Therefore, such a circulation is spiral circulation and not circular circulation. It keeps developing eternally and it makes progress eternally. It won't stop anywhere in the original cycle." (*Popular Philosophy*)

He explains the relationship between knowledge and practice in a comparatively accurate way, effectively refuting the distortion of this problem made by Zhang Dongsun and Ye Qing. *Popular Philosophy* helped popularize materialist dialectics and in helping the broad masses of the people, especially young intellectuals, acquire the knowledge of Marxist philosophy.

In the meantime, Li Da (1890–1966) finished writing his opus magnum, *An Outline of Sociology*. In this work, which is in the form of a textbook, he makes a profound and complete elaboration of the philosophical system of Marxism, especially its materialist dialectics and historical materialism. *An Outline of Sociology* possessed great significance both in respect of the author's deep-going research into materialist dialectics and in respect of helping the Chinese revolutionaries, who were all eager to get a better understanding of Marxist philosophy. We may say that the *Popular Philosophy* and *An Outline of Sociology* represent theoretical achievements from two different sides of the movement to promote knowledge of materialist dialectics.

The campaign to promote knowledge of materialist dialectics in the 1930s was an enlightenment movement led by the CPC. This movement pushed forward the dissemination of Marxist philosophy in China, promoted the awakening of the broad masses of the people, and laid the theoretical groundwork for the systematic formation of Mao Zedong Thought. Such a movement was an indispensable link in the integration of Marxism with the Chinese revolution. Of course, not having access to the KMT-controlled areas, the philosophical and social workers of Marxism were not able to have a direct and comprehensive understanding of the practical conditions of the Chinese revolutionary war and of the line struggle around such a problem within the leading group of the CPC. It was difficult for them to put forth a set of theoretical principles of the highest universality concerning the Chinese revolution. History was waiting for a great man to accomplish such a task. Mao Zedong, who meditated upon this problem for the long period in which he underwent the Long March and lived in a cave in Northern Shaanxi, accomplished this task gradually.

At the same time as the movement to promote knowledge of materialist dialectics got underway, the materialist concept of history also underwent an even more profound development in the course of intensive ideological struggle. From the late 1920s to the mid-1930s, there was an intensive controversy among Chinese Marxists between the "new vitality faction" and the "motive force faction." The controversy focused on the nature of Chinese society.

The representative of the "new vitality faction" was Tao Xisheng (1899-1988). In 1928, in the magazine *New Vitality* he published an essay titled, "Exactly What Kind of Society Is Chinese Society?" And in 1929, he published a book titled *Analysis of the History of Chinese Society*. In his opinion, during the Xia and Shang dynasties, China was made up of primitive tribes. The society of the Zhou Dynasty belongs to that of feudal society. During the Qin, Han and following dynasties, Chinese society changed gradually. When China entered the Ming and Qing dynasties, the nature of its society belonged to that of commercial capitalism. And after the two opium wars (1840-1842 and 1856), China became a capitalist society. Tao Xisheng maintains that China did not undergo the stage of slave society, and it is quite natural that post-opium-war China did not belong to the stage of semi-feudal and semi-colonial society. Thus he draws out the following conclusions: There is no general and objective law that governs the development of human society; the materialist concept of history is not applicable to China; and the program and line of the democratic revolution led by the CPC is the result from "a random deduction from the conclusions drawn by some European and American scholars who dissected European society." Closely following in his footsteps, Zhou Fohai, Gongsun Yuzhi (Gu Mengyu) and others also published essays in the magazine *New Vitality*, in which they energetically preached these views. Thus, the "new vitality faction" was formed. Soon after, a group of Trotskyites, including Ren Shu, Yan Ling-feng, Wang Yichang and Li Ji formed around the magazine *Motive Force*. Thus, the "motive force" faction was formed. These two factions acted in cooperation with each other.

Under the difficult and perilous conditions of the "white terror," Marxists in China put up an extremely brave struggle on the theoretical front in order to fight against these ideological trends, which opposed the materialist concept of history. Their extremely brave struggle promoted the integration of the materialist concept of history in the specific conditions of Chinese society. In this respect, Guo Moruo, Lu Zhenyu, Wang Xuewen and others made outstanding contributions.

Guo Moruo (1892-1978), whose school name was Kaizhen and whose many pennames included Moruo and Guo Dingtang, was a native of Leshan City, Sichuan Province. In 1930, he published *Research into Ancient Chinese Society*. Applying the materialist concept of history to guide his research into ancient Chinese history, Guo concretely explains how ancient Chinese society gradually developed from the primitive commune to the slave system. He demonstrates that in the ancient times in China there did exist the stage of slave society by investigating the economic basis and the superstructure of that time. Guo points out, "The development of the human race is more or less the same, whether the race be brown, yellow, black or white. So also is the case with society, in that society is made up of human beings." (*Research into Ancient Chinese Society,* Author's Preface) And he says, "The Chinese people are neither deities nor monkeys. The society made up of Chinese ought not to be any different from any other society whatsoever." (*Ibid*) He affirms that the development of Chinese society is in accordance with the general law of the development of human society as disclosed by Marxism, and he refutes the view that "Marxism does not conform to the national conditions of China."

Lu Zhenyu (1900-1982), who had many aliases, including Chenguang, He Minhun and Liu Gang, was a native of Wugang County (now a part of Shaoyang City), Hunan Province. In 1934 he published *Research into Chinese Society at the Prehistoric Stage*. He points out, "Historical materialism is not only a sharp weapon with which we may dissect human society but also the only correct methodology of historical science. As long as we grasp this sharp weapon when we dissect the process of the development of Chinese society, all the problems will be easily solved."

(*Research into Chinese Society at the Prehistoric Stage*) In his opinion, Chinese society has already gone through the stages of primitive society, slave society and feudal society. Therefore, "the present stage of Chinese society is, of course, that of a semi-colonial and semi-feudal society." In 1937, Lu published *A History of Political Ideas in China*, in which he analyzes and sums up the development of the philosophical ideas and political ideas which have appeared in China from the Shang Dynasty to the pre-opium war years. Since it was the first monograph in which the author uses Marxism to sum up the history of the development of Chinese philosophy, this book exerted an important influence upon the process in which research into Chinese philosophy became more scientific.

Having covered some of the contributors to the spread of Marxism in the 1930s, we now shift our attention to Li Da. Li Da (1890-1966) was a native of Lingling County, Hunan Province. In his early years he studied in Japan. There, he took part in the movement organized by patriotic Chinese students. In 1918, the *Agreement on Taking Joint Action against the Enemy*, which was in essence a treacherous treaty, was signed in secret between the Chinese government of the day, which was under the control of a warlord named Duan Qirui (1865-1936), and the Japanese government. The Chinese students in Japan opposed the agreement, and went out on strike with Li Da at their head. In fact, he and some other Chinese students, including Xu Dehang, returned home to express their opposition to the treaty. Back in Beijing, they presented a petition to the government of Duan. But because they did not mobilize the masses fully and they lacked the experience of engaging in mass struggles, their attempt ended in failure. From this failure, Li absorbed some lessons, of which the key one was only by learning from the fine example of the October Revolution can China be saved. He then went to Japan for a second time to pursue his studies, but this time he concentrated on the research into Marxism. As a result, he emerged as one of the first batch of Chinese Marxists.

Following the eruption of the May Fourth Movement, Li wrote a number of progressive essays, including "What Is Socialism?" And he translated several relevant books into Chinese, including *An Explanation of the Materialist Conception of History*. He sent his essays and translations to China by mail, where they were published. Thus began his work of the dissemination of Marxism in China. In 1920, he returned to China, and worked in Shanghai with Chen Duxiu and others for the establishment of the CPC. In order to criticize the revisionism of the Second International (1889-1914), the pseudo-socialism advocated by Liang Qichao and his clique, and the anarchism that was then in vogue, he wrote a series of essays, including *Return to Karl Marx*, *A Discussion of Socialism and a Question for Mr. Liang Qichao* and *A Dissection of Anarchism*. In 1921, he attended the First National Congress of the CPC as a representative of the Shanghai Communist Group. At the congress, he was made director of the publicity department of the CPC Central Committee. In 1923, Li and Chen Duxiu had a heated dispute on the problem of Kuomintang-Communist cooperation. Li went on to produce a number of monographs covering a wide range of disciplines, including *Modern Sociology*, *An Outline of Sociology*, *An Outline of Economics*, *A History of Social Evolution*, *An Introduction to Monetary Science* and *An Outline of Jurisprudence*.

After the founding of the People's Republic, Li was the president of Hunan University until November 1952, and president of Wuhan University from November 1952 to August 1966, when he passed away. During this period he wrote *An Explanation of On Practice*, *An Explanation of On Contradiction*, and a number of articles on the philosophical thought of Mao Zedong. In 1956, he began work to reestablish the department of philosophy at Wuhan University, and edited *An Outline of Dialectical Materialism*. Li was one of the first to warn against the "Left" errors which the CPC made in the late 1950s. At the beginning of 1966, he criticized the contention by Lin Biao (1907-1971) that "Mao Zedong Thought is the summit of Marxism-Leninism of the contemporary era." He pointed out that such a formulation was not in accordance with dialectics. Because of this, as soon as the "cultural revolution" started he was persecuted and he died with his name un-cleared. Li left us many spiritual treasures of great value through his philosophical activities, which lasted for half a century. Both in the early stage of the dissemination of Marxist philosophy in China and in the movement to promote the knowledge of materialist dialectics in the 1930s, he made outstanding contributions. His works *Modern Sociology* and *An Outline of Sociology* represent his philosophical achievements in these two periods, respectively.

Early in the period of the May Fourth Movement, Li began to propagate the materialist conception of history. When he lived in Japan, he translated *An Explanation of the Materialist Concept of History* into Chinese. In 1922, at the invitation of Mao Zedong, who was in charge of the work of the CPC in Hunan Province, he delivered lectures on the materialist concept of history at the Hunan Self-study University. After several years of diligent work, he published *Modern Sociology* in 1926, a monograph in which he systematically elucidates the materialist concept of history. In this book, Li first explains the essential difference between the materialist concept of history and the various pre-Marxist concepts, such as the theory of the social contract, the theory of biological society, the theory of psychological society, and so on. Next, he elaborates on the structure, origin and development of society, and he discloses the general laws of how productive power decides the relations of production and how the economic foundation decides the superstructure. He then examines the family, the tribe, the class, and the state, one by one. At last, he dwells on the task and the future of the Chinese revolution in the imperialist era as well as the relations between the Chinese revolution and the world revolution. This was the most comprehensive and systematic discussion of the materialist concept of history since the latter was introduced into China.

The author explicates the materialist concept of history by integrating the aspects of materialism and dialectics. Throughout the book, the author emphasizes the fact that productive power plays the decisive role: "The progress of social life is the productive progress of the various materials, which is decided totally by technology and productive power. In the productive progress of materials, there is both spirit and culture. Both spirit and culture are products of the relations of production. They develop as the productive power develops, and they change as the relations of production change. The progress of society is the progress of the productive power." And he says, "Social organizations of one kind or another can never be overthrown unless there is absolutely no room for all the productive forces to develop within these organizations. In like manner, newborn higher productive forces of one kind or another can never be realized unless the material conditions of their existence have already been formed as an embryo within the womb of the old society."

Li Da also explains how the relations of production and the social superstructure may affect the economic base. In the first place, the relations of production exert an important influence on the development of the productive forces. This is especially so in modern society, in which industry and the world market are developing by leaps and bounds. "When the productive forces are within the relations of production of capitalist society, they cannot develop, because they are hindered. When they are kept as they are, they become cannibal monsters. If they are placed in rational relations of production, they will find a good arena in which to bring into full play their original nature, which is always eager to develop. In that case, the relations of production can become a faithful servant for mankind."

Therefore, "to change the relations of production so as to develop the productive forces is an inevitable procedure in social evolution. This is also the reason why there must be revolutions in modern society." In the second place, the superstructure may exert an influence upon the productive forces and the relations of production: "In the process in which man makes progress, human thoughts indeed play a very great part." Socialism is the tool in the liberation of the working class: "Karl Marx formulated the doctrine of socialism, which has become an instrument with which the working class, now oppressed, is making a social revolution." Marxism plays an important role in pushing forward both social changes and social development. Starting from such a view of the fundamental contradictions and progress of society, Li stipulates that social revolution ought to include both an economic revolution and a political revolution. He says, "The economic revolution is the change of the social base. The political revolution is the change of the superstructure." And what is more, "both sides must go hand in hand with each other. Only in this way can the social revolution be accomplished." In other words, the realization of the social revolution depends on two conditions. First, there must be adequate surroundings that are materially mature. Second, there must be adequate efforts of the human agent that is fully self-awakened. He says, "A person cannot wholly depend on his own efforts if he really desires to change society. He cannot relax the efforts he may make to influence society by just waiting for the natural change of the society tranquilly, either." At last, he calls on the people, saying, "We live in the world today, and we are human beings today, so we should carefully inspect the trends of society, and we should carefully examine the spirit of the times, so that we may create our own history and promote social progress."

The author uses the materialist concept of history to analyze Chinese society, answering some major and urgent questions concerning the Chinese revolution. In a definite and clear way, Li points out that since China is a semi-feudal and semi-colonial country the target for the Chinese revolution at the current stage is imperialism and the feudal ruling class. Concerning the leadership of the revolution, he says, "Who will lead the movement of the national revolution? Ought it truly to be the bourgeoisie? Or, ought it, in the final analysis, to be the proletariat?" in his opinion, the leadership of China's democratic revolution can only be the proletariat and its political party — the CPC. This is because "although the workers, the peasants and the other proletarians suffer oppression from imperialism and its deputies simultaneously with the petty bourgeoisie, their anguish is much keener than that of the petty bourgeoisie. Therefore, their revolutionary spirit is extremely high." Thus, he makes a forceful condemnation of Chen Duxiu's mistake. Chen failed to see the great role which the broad masses of workers and peasants would play in leading the revolution, and entrusted that role to the bourgeoisie. Li's argumentation shows that, in understanding and grasping the materialist concept of history, the Marxists of China had reached a rather profound level.

Modern Sociology represents the supreme theoretical achievement obtained by the Chinese Communists at the early stage of the dissemination of Marxist philosophy in China. This very influential book circulated extensively among the revolutionaries of the day. When the revolution of 1927 failed, the Kuomintang authorities ordered the arrest of Li one the grounds that he "wrote a book titled *Modern Sociology*, in which he vigorously propagates turning the country red." Nevertheless, Li went on to write another book along the same lines, titled *Elementary Knowledge of Society* in 1929, further developing the main ideas of *Modern Sociology*. In this book, he puts forth a "systematic view of society." He says, "Society is a system which includes all the constant interrelations among the members of mankind. In this system, all the constant interrelations take economic constant interrelations for the foundation." He devotes a whole chapter to "the way out for China." He adds, "China is a semi-colonial, semi-feudal society. Therefore, the Chinese revolution, which aims at the continuance of China's existence, must be carried out on two fronts, involving the repulsion of imperialism by a national revolution and the wiping out of the feudal remnants by a democratic revolution. And in the future the Chinese revolution will converge with the trend of social evolution all over the world in a mighty torrent."

From the late 1920s, Li began to lay special stress on the propagation of and research into materialist dialectics. His philosophical activity in this period may be divided into two stages. In the first stage, he concentrated on translating foreign books on materialist dialectics into Chinese. Among them are *The World Outlook in Modern Times* by August Thalheimer (1884-1948), *The Foundation of Marxist Philosophy* (in collaboration with another translator) by Kawakami Hajime (1874-1946), *The Social Sciences: Theory and Practice* by Ivan Kapitonovich Luppol (1896-1943) and *A Course of Dialectics and Materialism* by Shirokov and other theoreticians of the USSR. Through these translations, he introduced materialist dialectics to the Chinese people. In the second stage, he continued his researches into the Marxist classics, extensively absorbing the achievements in this field made abroad. He then wrote *An Outline of Sociology*. This book was first published in 1935, followed by a revised edition in 1937.

In the form of a textbook, *An Outline of Sociology* gives an integrated and profound elucidation of the philosophical system of Marxism, namely, materialist dialectics and historical materialism. Li points out that materialist dialectics and historical materialism are an inseparable whole, and neither part can be dispensed with. The one and only scientific method of the materialist concept of history is that of materialist dialectics. Only by applying materialist dialectics to observation of social and historical phenomena can man know the essence and laws of these phenomena. Li spends nearly half of the book making a systematic elucidation of the principles of materialist dialectics. He takes the history of epistemology as the point of departure to emphasize that materialist dialectics is by no means the product of any individual genius but the synthesis of man's struggle to understand the world born of social practice. He then gives a comprehensive discussion of the laws and categories of materialist dialectics, and points out that the law of the unity of opposites is the fundamental law of materialist dialectics. Finally, he examines the relations between dialectics and the theory of knowledge, as well as the relations between dialectics and logic. His argumentation of the theory of knowledge is the cream of the whole book. It is worth particular mention that he makes a systematic and profound elucidation of the relationship between knowledge and practice. As we know, such a relationship constitutes a problem which has to be settled urgently.

In *An Outline of Sociology*, Li dwells on the relationship between knowledge and practice by laying stress on the following four aspects.

In the first place, the author systematically elucidates the decisive role of practice upon knowledge. He points out that dialectical materialism is the "materialism of practice." "Such is the materialism of practice. From the moment practice is been introduced into materialism, it causes changes in the content of the philosophy of the bygone ages." (*An Outline of Sociology*, Part 1, Chapter 1)

The essential difference between the epistemology of dialectical materialism and the epistemology of metaphysical materialism lies in the understanding of practice as a category. So also is the case with the essential difference between the epistemology of dialectical materialism and the epistemology of idealism. According to the former, one sees knowledge as the reflection of objective reality in the mind of people, but one cannot understand the moment of practice in the process in which knowledge emerges and develops. The epistemology of idealism lays stress on the conception of practice, but it interprets practice as something abstract and spiritual. The epistemology of dialectical materialism is the only doctrine according to which practice is a category of history and society; practice is human activities realistic and perceptual; and practice is the material production and social struggles which have been developing throughout history. Practice is superior to knowledge. "[Practice] is the starting point and source of knowledge. And it is the standard of truth." (*An Outline of Sociology*, Part 1, Chapter 1) Only in this way can the whole developmental history of human knowledge be understood and explained correctly.

In the second place, Li systematically elucidates the impact of knowledge on practice. Human consciousness is by no means like the surface of a mirror, which is senseless. It does not reflect the targets in front of it in the same pattern and according to a certain unchangeable law. Reflections of the outside things in human consciousness are a kind of initiative reflection. In practice, through which man transforms Nature and changes society, if people understood the developmental laws of Nature and society, they could transform Nature and change society more efficiently and more actively. Any practice, when it is divorced from the guidance of correct knowledge, can only be a blind and foolish action. He emphasizes as follows:

> 1. "Practice not only demonstrates the truth of knowledge, it also changes the world in an active way according to the truthfulness of the knowledge." (*An Outline of Sociology*, Part 1, Chapter 4)
>
> 2. "If people do not research into the laws concerning the realistic nature of society, they will be unable to understand the unity between the theory of society and the practice of society. In that case, they will be unable to transform society. "(*An Outline of Sociology*, Part 2, Chapter 1)

As for the correct theory which may guide the Chinese revolutionaries in transforming China, in his opinion it is Marxism and Marxism alone. In the "Preface" to the fourth edition of *An Outline of Sociology*, he writes, "In order to proceed in the work of struggle efficiently, in order to accomplish the great cause of national liberation, the fighters must arm their minds with the scientific world outlook and scientific concept of history. They must apply the scientific method to knowing newborn social phenomena, and to solving new problems they encounter in practice. In short, it must guide our practice."

In the third place, Li emphasizes that knowledge and practice must be unified. Time and again, he points out that, "practice and knowledge are so unified that neither may be dispensed with." (*An Outline of Sociology*, Part 1, Chapter 4) Practice is the foundation of knowledge, and knowledge is the guidance of practice. This is especially so in the activities of social and historical practice:

> "Social theory and social practice are so unified that neither may be dispensed with. In social theory there are elements of social practice, and in the social practice there are elements of social theory. Social theory may be obtained from social practice, and social practice may

be guided by social theory. Social theory which lacks social practice is no more than empty theory, and social practice which lacks social theory is no more than blind practice." (*An Outline of Sociology*, Part 2, Chapter 1)

Only on the basis of the unification of theory and practice can the materialist concept of history reflect the developmental laws of society, predict the future of society, and direct the people to advance from the realm of necessity to the realm of freedom.

In the fourth place, Li generalizes the above analyses and renders his main ideas into a general formula of the cognitive process, as follows:

"'Practice → direct concreteness → abstract thinking → concreteness of the medium → practice.' This development takes the form of circular movement." (*An Outline of Sociology*, Part 1, Chapter 4)

Of these links of the formula, cognitive development may be divided into two stages. In the first stage, man's cognition proceeds on the basis of social practice. When the relations and developments of the objective world act upon the subject, perceptions and presentations are formed. In this way, human thought, which is just as active and self-initiating as practice, is now connected with the objective world. In other words, human cognition proceeds from direct concreteness to abstract thinking. In the second stage, man proceeds in the process of abstract thinking, using the connections and movements of conceptions to reflect the developmental process of the objective world. The process goes from phenomena to essence, from contingency to necessity, from form to content, and from cause to result. In such a process, the real situation of the development of the objective world is revealed more and more clearly, and finally the human mind can reach synthetic cognition. In this way, the objective world may be represented concretely in human thinking. In other words, human cognition proceeds from the abstractness to the concreteness of mediums. Although the concreteness of mediums may explain the laws and tendency of the development of the objective world, whether this explanation is correct or not remains an unsettled problem, which can only be finally demonstrated in practice. Practice not only demonstrates the truthfulness of knowledge, it also actively changes the objective world according to the truthfulness of that knowledge. In this way, knowledge returns from the sphere of thinking to the sphere of practice. It starts at practice and ends at practice. Therefore, we may say, "The movement of knowledge is a circular movement." Li emphasizes this as follows:

> "Such a circular movement is not the circulation of metaphysics but the development of dialectics. Knowledge develops along with the development of the objective world. Knowledge develops along with the development of social practice. In the historical process of social practice, new contradictions, new interrelations, new attributes and new aspects are revealed continuously. And these new contradictions, interrelations, attributes and aspects intrude into man's consciousness continuously. Then new contradictions between the subject and the object are formed. Thus, a new round of movement of knowledge is promoted. It is in this way that knowledge advances. Knowledge then begins to reflect a new developmental stage of the objective world. And at this new stage man is able to grasp the objective world more profoundly and more concretely. Therefore, at this new stage social practice will go a step further, and be able to change the objective world more actively and with more initiative. In short, the circular movement of knowledge is a historical developmental process. It is also a developmental process from relative truth to absolute truth." (*An Outline of Sociology*, Part 1, Chapter 4)

An Outline of Sociology occupies an important position in the development of Marxist philosophy in China. By the time of its publication, nearly twenty years had passed since Li Dazhao first introduced the materialist concept of history to China and Qu Qiubai had first introduced materialist dialectics to China. Li Da's magnum opus elucidated Marxist philosophy, namely, materialist dialectics and historical materialism, for the first time, accurately, completely, systematically and strictly. It provided the Chinese Communists and revolutionary youth with an excellent textbook with which to study and grasp Marxist philosophy. Not only that, *An Outline of Sociology* is also a wholesale exposure and criticism of the various ideological trends of the 1930s which were in opposition to materialist dialectics. Mao Zedong called *An Outline of Sociology* "the first textbook of Marxist-Leninist philosophy written by one of us Chinese." Of course, limited by the circumstances of the day, there are some deficiencies in the book. For instance, the author fails to combine his philosophical discussion directly with the specific and practical conditions of the Chinese revolution. In addition, he fails to distinguish formal logic from metaphysics. These deficiencies were overcome in *An Outline of Dialectical Materialism*, which was published later under Li's editorship.

The dissemination and development of Marxist philosophy in China underwent an arduous process -- from the dissemination of the materialist concept of history in China in the early years to the movement of materialist dialectics in the 1930s, from a preliminary introduction of some theories into China to an accurate, complete and systematic elucidation of Marxism, and from the acceptance of the general principles of Marxism to the gradual combination of Marxism with the concrete practice of the Chinese revolution. In the late 1930s, a philosophical system of Sinicized Marxism at last emerged, that is, Mao Zedong's philosophical thought.

Mao Zedong (1893-1976) was a native of Xiangtan County (now Xiangtan City), Hunan Province. While a teenager, he was inspired by *Frightening Words to a Prosperous Age* by Zheng Guanying (1842-1921) and the *Journal of the Renovated People* under the editorship of Liang Qichao (1873-1929). In 1911, he went to Changsha, capital of Hunan, to pursue his studies. In the nationwide revolutionary ferment of the day, he supported Sun Yat-sen, and joined the Western-style army which was the main force of the uprisings in the Revolution of 1911. Disillusioned by Yuan Shikai's coup, Mao threw himself back into his studies in order to find the road for liberating the Chinese people. In 1912, he systematically read the Western books translated by Yan Fu (1853-1921), which brought him into contact with Western philosophical thought and modern political doctrines. In 1913, he was admitted to the First Normal School of Hunan Province, where he made a wide-ranging study of philosophy under the guidance of Yang Changji and he was particularly impressed by the ideas of Kant. It was in this period that he formed his philosophical world outlook of dualism of the mind and things, which is imbued with dialectical factors. In 1915, under the influence of *La Jeunesse*, he became a democrat, favoring revolution to overthrow the warlords and resist the encroachments of imperialism. In 1918, he founded the Association of the Renovated People, the aim of which was to "transform China and the world."

In 1918 Mao went to Beijing for the first time, where he became acquainted with Li Dazhao and Chen Duxiu, who introduced him to Marxism. When the May Fourth Movement broke out, he led the student movement of Hunan Province. He founded the *Xiangjiang River Review*, and published essays, including "The Great Union of the Common People," in which he hailed the victory of the October Revolution. He maintained that the broad masses of the people must unite to strike down the bureaucrats, warlords, aristocrats and capitalists. And he maintained that the common people should be the masters of their own destiny. This shows that there was a rapid change in orientation to Marxism in the thought of the young Mao Zedong. At the end of 1919, he returned to Beijing. This time, he read the *Manifesto of the Communist Party* and many other books which introduced Marxism to the Chinese reader. These works gave him a comparatively systematic understanding of the fundamental principles of Marxism. and he gradually transformed his own world outlook. In January 1921, at the conference to greet the New Year which was held by the Association of the Renovated People, he advocated the adoption of the "dictatorship of the proletariat." In a letter to Cai Hesen, he states, "The materialist concept of history is the foundation of the philosophy of our Party." This indicates that by 1921 Mao had already changed from being a revolutionary democrat to being a Marxist, from a man upholding dualism of the mind and things to a man upholding historical materialism. From that time on, Mao followed the road of seeking the integration of Marxism with the concrete practice of the Chinese revolution.

In the revolutionary period of 1924-1927, Mao published two essays in succession, one being the *Analysis of Classes in Chinese Society*, the other being the *Report on an Investigation of the Peasant Movement in Hunan*. In these two essays, in a comparatively successful way he applied the Marxist materialist concept of history to analyzing the practical conditions of the Chinese revolution, and on this basis he formulated the line and policies of the Communist Party of China. Mao's philosophical thought matured following the failure of the revolution in 1927. These years witnessed arduous revolutionary struggles carried out by the Chinese Communists, and were marked with two great treatises written by Mao, viz., *On Practice* and *On Contradiction*.

In what conditions was the philosophical thought of Mao formed?

In the first place, Mao's philosophical thought is the philosophical generalization of the practice and experiences of the Chinese revolution. When the revolutionary movement failed in 1927, the CPC carried out armed struggle against the Kuomintang's rule. The Chinese Communists, mainly represented by Mao, made efforts to combine the universal principles of Marxism with the concrete practice of China, which was a semi-feudal, semi-colonial country of huge size in the East. And they creatively opened a revolutionary way, which may be epitomized as the formula of "using the rural areas to encircle the cities." Along the way, armed forces of the Chinese people were founded and revolutionary base areas were set up in the countryside. In coordination with the people's struggles, which were carried out in the area of the Kuomintang's rule, the Chinese Communists continuously pushed the revolution forward. But in the late 1920s and early 1930s, a tendency of dogmatism prevailed both in the international communist movement as well as in the CPC. This tendency greatly harmed the party and the revolutionary cause, and for a time it put the Chinese revolution in an almost hopeless situation. Mao waged an arduous struggle against this tendency. In 1930, he wrote a philosophical essay titled, *Oppose Book Worship*, in which he writes:

> 1. "Of course we should study Marxist books, but this study must be integrated with our country's actual conditions. We need books, but we must overcome book worship, which is divorced from the actual situation." (*Oppose Book Worship*)
>
> 2. "Victory in China's revolutionary struggle will depend on the Chinese comrades' understanding of Chinese conditions." (*Ibid*)
>
> 3. "Without investigating the actual situation, there is bound to be an idealist appraisal of class forces and idealist guidance in work, resulting either in opportunism or in putchism." (*Ibid*)

For the first time, he clearly advances a rule that the universal principles of Marxism must be integrated with the practice of the Chinese revolution, and he makes a philosophical generalization of the rule. Thus, he puts forth a materialist line of epistemology, which opposes the inner-Party tendency of dogmatism. Nevertheless, since the revolutionary at that time was carried out in grim and even cruel conditions, it was quite natural that Mao Zedong had to seek a solution to such a problem amid fierce struggles on the political and military front; he was unable to concentrate his attention on philosophical research. This situation lasted for a long time.

In January 1935, the political bureau of the CPC Central Committee, which was in the middle of the Long March, held an enlarged meeting in Zunyi, Guizhou Province. The Zunyi Meeting spelt the end of the domination of the "Left" opportunist line in the CPC Central Committee, and established Mao's leadership of the whole Party. Mao led the Chinese Workers and Peasants Red Army, which had accomplished the Long March and succeeded in reaching northern Shaanxi in October1935. From that time on, he began to sum up the historical experiences of the Party from the angle of theory. In 1936, he wrote a treatise titled *Problems of Strategy in China's Revolutionary War*, in which he systematically summed up the lessons of the battles of the Chinese revolution. He criticized dogmatic mistakes made in military affairs, disclosed the law of China's revolutionary war, and especially dwelt on the relations between the subjective and the objective, practice and knowledge, the general and the particular, and the whole and the part. This is a military treatise but in it there is abundant philosophical thought. With this treatise he pushed forward the philosophical thoughts discussed in *Oppose Book Worship*. On this basis, Mao Zedong made a further sublimation of the experiences in the revolutionary practice of China. In 1937, he finished writing two treatises on philosophy, *On Practice* and *On Contradiction*. In these two works, he elucidated the ideological system of his own philosophy.

In the second place, Mao Zedong's philosophical thought is a scientific summing up of the movement of the materialist dialectics of the 1930s. Following the failure of 1927, for a rather long time Mao Zedong and other revolutionary leaders were engaged in political and military work in difficult and isolated surroundings in the countryside, and he was unable to concentrate his energy on philosophical research. This task was undertaken by a large number of Marxist workers in philosophy and the other social sciences who lived under the Kuomintang's rule. Thus was formed the movement of the materialist dialectics of the 1930s, which made an important contribution to the dissemination and development of Marxist philosophy. This laid an objective theoretical groundwork for Mao's philosophical research, which was carried out in the late 1930s. When Mao arrived in northern Shaanxi, he consolidated his research. First, he read carefully the Chinese translations of the main philosophical works by the classical writers of Marxism. Second, he paid great attention to philosophical works by the scholars of the USSR and other foreign countries, which had been completely or partly translated into Chinese. For instance, he repeatedly read *A Course of Dialectics and Materialism*, written by Shirokov and other theoreticians of the USSR and translated into Chinese by Li Da and others. In the margins of the pages of this book, he wrote a large number of comments. Third, he attached great importance to the theoretical achievements made by Chinese Marxist philosophers. He especially held in esteem those written by Li Da and Ai Siqi. At a meeting held in Yan'an, Mao said, "Comrade Li Da sent me a copy of *An Outline of Sociology* by mail. I have read this book ten times from cover to cover."*[1] And he recommended this book to the Yan'an Association of New Philosophy and to the Chinese People's Anti-Japanese Military and Political University. He read with absorbing interest *Philosophy and Life* by Ai Siqi, and compiled *Extracts from Ai Siqi's Philosophy and Life*. He said, "This book benefited me a great deal." (*A Letter to Ai Siqi*) In the two treatises *On Practice* and *On Contradiction*, Mao sums up the theoretical fruits of the movement to disseminate materialist dialectics together with practical experiences of the revolutionary war. In clarifying these two aspects, he pays particular attention to making a more profound and more accurate elucidation of the theory of knowledge.

In the third place, Mao's philosophical thought is a critical inheritance of the traditional philosophy of China. The dissemination and development of Marxist philosophy and the formation of Mao's philosophical thought constituted a revolutionary turning point in the development of Chinese philosophy. Nevertheless, Mao did not simply discard the whole legacy of the philosophy of the bygone ages. Instead, he inherited this legacy critically. Being good at applying the Marxist method, and having a good grounding in Chinese culture, Mao greatly enriched

---

* The quotation is from Guo Huaruo, *Fragments from the Memoirs of My Working by Chairman Mao's Side — In Commemoration of the Eighty-Fifth Birthday of Chairman Mao.*

his own philosophical thought by absorbing nutrition from the Chinese philosophy of ancient and early modern times. First and foremost, he directly inherited and deepened some important categories and ideas of traditional Chinese philosophy. For example, he points out that there are two levels of significance in a celebrated dictum from the *Sunzi*, which runs, "Know the enemy and know yourself, and you can fight a hundred battles with no danger of defeat." (*Sunzi·Chapter 3: Attack by Stratagem*) Mao says, "There is a saying in the book of Sun Wu Tzu, the great military scientist of ancient China, 'Know the enemy and know yourself, and you can fight a hundred battles with no danger of defeat,' which refers both to the stage of learning and to the stage of application, both to knowing the law of the development of objective reality and to deciding on our own action in accordance with these laws in order to overcome the enemy facing us." (*Problems of Strategy in China's Revolutionary War*, Chapter 1: How to Study War, Section 4: The Important Thing Is to Be Good at Learning) In this way, he gives a dialectical materialist explanation of the process of human cognition. Another example: He gives a new explanation of the ancient proposition that "things that oppose each other also complement each other." This proposition means that "things that are opposed to each other have identity." He explains:

> "We Chinese often say, 'Things that oppose each other also complement each other.' That is, things opposed to each other have identity. This saying is dialectical, and contrary to metaphysics. 'Oppose each other' refers to the mutual exclusion or the struggle of two contradictory aspects. 'Complement each other' means that in given conditions the two contradictory aspects unite, and achieve identity. Yet struggle is inherent in identity, and without struggle there can be no identity." (*On Contradiction*, Part V: The Identity and Struggle of the Aspects of a Contradiction)

Mao goes a step further. He sums up and advances research into some important philosophical problems which constitute the basic topics in the history of traditional Chinese philosophy. For instance, in the history of Chinese philosophy there was a long-term controversy on the relationship between knowledge and action. Xun Kuang (c. 298-238 BC) first put forth an idea on the relationship between knowledge and action.

He says, "Knowing it is not as good as putting it into practice. Learning reaches its terminus when it is fully put into practice." (*Xunzi·Chapter 8: The Teaching of the Ru*) Afterward, there appeared various views on the relationship between knowledge and action. Zhu Xi (1130-1200) put forth a view on this relationship, which is usually generalized as follows: "Knowledge goes first, and action afterwards." Wang Shouren (1472-1528) stressed that "Knowledge and action are one." Wang Fuzhi (1619-1692) said, "Action is able to connote knowledge, but knowledge is not able to connote action." (*Elaboration on the Meanings of the Book of History·Book 3*) Sun Yat-sen maintained, "To act is not difficult, but to know is truly difficult." (*To Know Is Difficult But to Do Is Easy*) By the 1930s, among the various schools of philosophy a fierce controversy raged over the central problem of knowledge and practice. In the course of this controversy, Li Da and Ai Siqi made important contributions to disseminating the theory of knowledge in line with materialist dialectics. In his treatise *On Practice*, Mao makes a profound summing up of all the controversies in the history of philosophy. By elucidating the view of dialectical materialism that knowledge and action are unified, Mao gives a Marxist answer to the question of the relationship between knowledge and action. Therefore, Mao's philosophical thought is closely connected both with the traditional philosophy and traditional culture of China. It criticizes and inherits Chinese tradition at the same time, and it is a new chapter in the development of the Chinese philosophy.

In *On Practice* and *On Contradiction*, Mao makes a philosophical generalization about the historical experiences of the integration of the universal principles of Marxism with the concrete practice of the Chinese revolution. And he systematically discusses the theory of knowledge and dialectics according to Marxism. In doing so, he provides the Chinese Communists and the revolutionary people with a scientific world outlook and methodology.

In *On Practice*, Mao discloses the dependency of knowledge on practice by means of carefully examining the cognitive process and cognitive laws. And he puts forth a general formula for the development of knowledge, which is based on practice:

> "Discover the truth through practice, and again through practice verify and develop the truth. Start from perceptual knowledge, and

actively develop it into rational knowledge; then start from rational knowledge and actively guide revolutionary practice to change both the subjective and the objective world. Practice, knowledge, again practice, and again knowledge. This form repeats itself in endless cycles, and with each cycle the content of practice and knowledge rises to a higher level." (*On Practice*)

In Mao's view, this general formula expresses the whole of the dialectical-materialist theory of knowledge, and the dialectical-materialist theory of the unity of knowledge and action. Thus, materialistically and dialectically are decided the relationship between the subjective and the objective, and the relationship between knowledge and practice. At the level of the theory of knowledge, Mao provides a philosophical foundation for the integration of the universal principles of Marxism with the concrete practice of the Chinese revolution.

Mao further unfolds in *On Contradiction* the various levels of the law of the unity of opposites by probing into the dialectical connection between the universality and individuality of the contradiction of the things. In this way, he provides a philosophical methodology for realizing such integration:

> "According to dialectical materialism, contradiction is present in all processes of objectively existing things and of subjective thought, and permeates all these processes from beginning to end; this is the universality and absoluteness of contradiction. Each contradiction and each of its aspects have their respective characteristics; this is the particularity and relativity of contradiction. In given conditions, opposites possess identity, and consequently can coexist in a single entity and can transform themselves into each other; this again is the particularity and relativity of contradiction. But the struggle of opposites is ceaseless; it goes on both when the opposites are coexisting and when they are transforming themselves into each other, and becomes especially conspicuous when they are transforming themselves into one another; this again is the universality and absoluteness of contradiction. In studying the particularity and relativity of contradiction, we must pay attention to the distinction between the principal contradiction and the non-principal contradictions and to

> the distinction between the principal aspect and the non-principal aspect of a contradiction. In studying the universality of contradiction and the struggle of opposites in contradiction, we must pay attention to the distinction between the different forms of struggle. Otherwise, we shall make mistakes." (*On Contradiction*, Part VII: Conclusion)

If the Chinese Communists truly grasp such a methodology, they will do a good job of grasping the theory of Marxism. Mao claims, "If, through study, we achieve a real understanding of the essentials explained above, we shall be able to demolish dogmatist ideas which are contrary to the basic principles of Marxism-Leninism and detrimental to our revolutionary cause, and our comrades with practical experience will be able to organize their experiences into principles, and avoid repeating empiricist errors." (*On Contradiction*, Part VII: Conclusion)

Under the guidance of Mao's philosophical thought, the Marxists of China indeed made efforts to integrate the universal principles of Marxism with the concrete practice of the Chinese revolution. They devoted themselves to creative work in military struggles, in Party building, and in ideological and theoretical work. They led the Chinese people to win the great victory of the democratic revolution. The formation of Mao's philosophical thought was an accomplishment of great importance in the development of Chinese philosophy in modern times. And what is more, it has exerted a great influence upon the philosophical thought of China in the historical period of socialism.

List of Works Cited

Academic Cases of Ming Confucians (Huang Zongxi)
Academic Cases of the Song and Yuan Dynasties (Huang Zongxi)
An Academic History of China in the Past 300 Years (Liang Qichao)
Additional Collection of Literary Works by Shuixin (Ye Shi)
Additional Works of the Two Chengs (Cheng Hao, Cheng Yi)
After Reading Liang Shuming's The Cultures of the East and the West and Their Philosophies (Hu Shi)
The Aim of the Garland Sutra (Fazang)
Analects
Annotations on the Laozi
An Anthology of Academic Essays from the Hall of Three Pines (Feng Youlan)
Anthology of Ji Kang
Apocryphal Treatise on the Changes: a Penetration of the Laws of Qian
The Approach to and Functions of Western Learning (Yan Fu)
Asking Heaven (Qu Yuan)
Assembled Principles of Classical Learning (Zhang Zai)

The Balanced Discussion
The Balanced Inquiries
Benevolence Studies (Tan Sitong)
The Biographies of Eminent Monks
Biographies of the Venerated Old People in Tongcheng
Biography of Tan Sitong (Lang Qichao)
Biography of Wang Bi
Blaming the Qin
Book of Changes (*Yi Ching, I Ching*)
Book of Diverse Crafts
Book of Great Unity (Kang Youwei)
Book of History
Book of Lord Shang
Book of Mozi
Book of Music
Book of Poetry
Book of Rites

Book of Songs
Book of the Yellow Emperor
A Book of Urgent Words (Zhang Taiyan)
Book Which Risks Burning (Li Zhi)
A Booklet Written in the Tower of the Worried Mind (Tan Sitong)
A Brief Biography of Revered Jiangzhai (Wang Yu)
A Brief Explanation of Early Modern Idealism (He Lin)

Cautious Speeches (Wang Tingxiang)
Censor's Collection (Wang Tingxiang)
A Chapter on the Enlightenment of the Mind (Xiong Shili)
China's Road to Freedom (Feng Youlan)
Chinese Philosophy Today (He Lin)
A Chronicle of Dai Dongyuan's Life
Chronological Autobiography of Kang Youwei Alias Nanhai (Kang Youwei)
A Chronological Biography of Xizhai (Yan Yuan)
Classified Conversations of Zhu Xi (Zhu Xi)
Collected Commentaries on the Four Books
Collected Works Kept in the Wang Family (Wang Tingxiang)
Collected Works of Han Changli (Han Yu)
Collected Works of the Reverend Li, the Literary Prince
Collected Writings of Huian the Literary Prince (Zhu Xi)
Collected Writings of Wang Yangming on Neo-Confucianism
A Collection of Earthenware Percussion Instruments
A Collection of Expositions of Truth (Sengyou)
Collection of Literary Works by Longchuan (Chen Liang)
Collection of Literary Works by Shuixin (Ye Shi)
Collection of Literary Works by Wang Linchuan (Wang Anshi)
Collection of Literary Works of Mingdao
Collection of Literary Works of Yichuan
Collection of Liu from East of the River (Liu Zongyuan)
Collection of Liu, the Guest of the Crown Prince (Liu Yuxi)
Collection of Seng Zhao's Treatises
Collection of Speeches (Zhang Taiyan)
Collection of the Tortoise Hill (Yang Shi)
Commentaries on Classified Conversations of Zhu Xi (Yan Yuan)

Commentaries on the Changes (also known as *The Ten Wings of the Book of Changes*)
Commentaries on the Great Norm (Wang Anshi)
Commentaries on the Supreme Profound Principle (Sima Guang)
Commentary on an Explanation of the Diagram of the Great Ultimate (Zhu Xi)
Commentary on Penetrating the Book of Changes)
Commentary on the Analects (Kang Youwei)
Commentary on the Book of Changes (Wang Bi)
Commentary on the Doctrine of the Mean (Kang Youwei)
Commentary on the Evolutions of Rites (Kang Youwei)
Commentary on the Laozi (Wang Bi)
Commentary on the Liezi (He Yan)
Commentary on the Meanings of Terms in the Book of Mencius (Dai Zhen)
Commentary on the Mhyamika Sastra (Benwu)
Commentary on the Western Inscription
Comments on the Book of Changes (Zhang Zai)
Comments on the Book of Master Zhuang (Yan Fu)
The Complete Works of Bai Compiled in the Changqing Reign Period (Bai Juyi)
Complete Works of Gong Zizhen
Complete Works of Lu Xiangshan (Lu Jiuyuan)
Complete Works of the Two Chengs
Complete Works of Wang Yangming (Wang Shouren)
Comprehensive Discussions at White Tiger Hall
The Controversy over the Outlook on Life (Zhang Junmai)
Conversations of the States
Correcting Youthful Ignorance (Zhang Zai)
Correction of Wrong Interpretations of the Four Books (Yan Yuan)
A Critical Analysis of Learning for Shilong Academy (Wang Tingxiang)
A Critique of Han Yu (Yan Fu)
A Critique of the Remarks of Monarchs (Liu Zongyuan)
The Cultures of the East and the West and Their Philosophies (Liang Shuming)

A Debate on the Great Ultimate (Wang Tingxiang)
A Debate on the Supreme Principle (Zhu Xi)
A Debate on Zhang Zai's View of Principle and the Material Force (Wang Tingxiang)
A Deduction from the Laozi (Wang Fuzhi)
Definitive Edition of the Writings of Nanlei (Huang Zongxi)
A Denunciation for Suppressing the Bandits in Guangdong (Zeng Guofan)
The Diagram of the Great Ultimate (Zhou Dunyi)
Diamond Sutra
A Discourse on Heaven (Liu Zongyuan)
A Discourse on Peace and Security (Jia Yi)
Discourse on Politics (Gong Zizhen)
Discussions after Reading the Great Collection of Commentaries on the Four Books (Wang Fuzhi)
Discussions after Reading the Mirror of Universal History (Wang Fuzhi)
The Doctrine of Sun Wen (Sun Yat-sen)
Dong Zhongshu's Doctrines of the Spring and Autumn Annals (Kang Youwei)

An Economic Explanation of the Ideological Changes in Early-Modern China (Li Dazhao)
An Elaboration of Qian and Kun (Xiong Shili)
Elaboration on the Meaning of the Book of History (Wang Fuzhi)
Elementary Knowledge of Society (Li Da)
Elites Returning to Truth (Hong Ren'gan)
Elucidation of the Laozi with Parables
Emphasizing Nonbeing (Yue Gang)
The Emptiness of the Unreal (Seng Zhao)
Esteem to the Helmets (Gong Zizhen)
Evolution and Agnosticism (Hu Shi)
Exalting Being (Yue Gang)
An Exhortation to Learning Zhang Zhidong
Experimentalism (Hu Shi)
An Explanation of the Diagram of the Great Ultimate (Zhou Dunyi)
Explanation of the Laozi (Han Fei)

Explanation of the Spring and Autumn Annals with Commentaries by Gongyang Gao (He Xiu)
Extensive Commentary on the Book of Poetry (Wang Fuzhi)

Factual Record of the Yongli Reign (Wang Fuzhi)
Fangguang Jing (*The Scripture of the Shedding of the Light of the Buddha*) – translation of
Mahaprajnaparamita Sutra
Finance and Planning (Huang Zongxi)
A First-hand Account of the Stages in Researching the Revolutionary Philosophy (Chiang Kai-shek)
The First Introduction to the Revised Diagrams of Changes (Li Gou)
Foundation of Sun Wen's Philosophy (Dai Jitao)
Four Poems on Innate Knowledge for My Students to Read (Wang Shouren)
Four Preservations (Yan Yuan)
Fragmental Series of the Late Affairs (Shen Zan)
Frightening Words for a Prosperous Age (Zheng Guanying)
Fundamental Concepts of John Dewey's Pedagogy (Liang Shuming)

Garland Sutra
The Garland Sutra Shows Bodhi-Citta (Fazang)
General Encyclopedia (Fang Yizhi)
A General Examination of Dialectical Materialism (Zhang Dongsun)
A General Tendency in the Changes of Chinese Academic Ideas (Liang Qichao)
Gongsun Longzi (*Book of Master Gongsun Long*)
Great Learning
The Great Master's Maxim (Ji Kang)
The Great Peaceful Heaven and Sun (Hong Xiuquan)
Great Policy (Jia Yi)
Guanzi

Han Feizi
Herein-Hide-I Veranda's Suitable Compilation
Heshanggong's Interpretation of the Laozi
Hidden Book (Li Zhi)

A Hidden Old Man's Drafts (Fang Kongzhao)
Historical Materials of Yanzhou
A History of Chinese Philosophy (Feng Youlan)
History of Han
History of Jin
History of the Ming Dynasty
The History of the Eastern Han Dynasty
History of the Song Dynasty
How Did the Qing Scholars Pursue Their Studies? (Hu Shi)
Huainanzi
Huang-Lao Silk Manuscript
Huayan's View of the Buddhist Schools and Sects (Fazang)

The Immutability of Things (Seng Zhao)
The Importance of the Revolutionary Philosophy (Chiang Kai-shek)
In Commemoration of Dr. Sun Yat-sen (Mao Zedong)
Inner Commentary on the Book of Changes (Wang Fuzhi)
An Inquiry into Man (Han Yu)
An Inquiry into Power (Yan Fu)
Inquiry into the Great Learning (Wang Shouren)
An Inquiry into the Law (Huang Zongxi)
An Inquiry into the Way (Han Yu)
An Inquiry into the Monarch (Huang Zongxi)
An Inquiry into the Subject (Huang Zongxi)
Instructions for Practical Living (Wang Shouren)
An Introduction to Indian Philosophy (Liang Shuming)
An Introduction to Logic (Yan Fu)
Introduction to My Own Thought (Hu Shi)
An Introduction to Social Philosophy (Qu Qiubai)
An Introduction to the World Outlook of Materialism (Qu Qiubai)
An Investigation into Confucius' Institutional Reforms (Kang Youwei)
An Investigation into the Classics Forged in the New Learning Period Kang Youwei
An Investigation of the Japanese Reform (Kang Youwei)

Jia Yi's New Book
Jie Lao (*Explanation of the Laozi*) (Han Fei)
John Dewey's Philosophy (Hu Shi)

Karl Marx's Philosophy of History and Heinrich Rickert's Philosophy of History (Li Dazhao)

The Land System (Huang Zongxi)
Laozi (*Tao Te Ching*, *The Canon of Tao and Te*, or *The Classic of the Way and Virtue*)
The Last Consciousness of the Self-salvation Movement of the Chinese Nation (Liang Shuming)
Later Collection of Li Gong
Lectures on the Heavens (Kang Youwei)
A Letter to Ai Siqi (Mao Zedong)
A Letter to Chiang Kai-shek (Sun Yat-sen)
A Letter to Li Hongzhang (Sun Yat-sen)
A Letter to Ouyang Banjiang, My Master (Tan Sitong)
A Letter to So-and-So (Dai Zhen)
Letter to the Editor of the Foreign Affairs Newspaper (Yan Fu)
Life Chronicle of Master of the Stream of Waterfalls (Du Zheng)
Literary Works of Li Zhi
Literary Works of Zhu Xi
Logic (Jin Yuelin)
Lu's Spring and Autumn Annals (Lu Buwei)
Luxuriant Dew of the Spring and Autumn Annals (Dong Zhongshu)

A Madman's Diary (Lu Xun)
Mahayana-Sraddhotpada-Sastra
Man in the Teachings of the Garland Sutra (Zongmi)
Maps and Records of the Island Countries (Wei Yuan)
The Master Who Embraces Simplicity (Ge Hong)
Mathematical Classic on the Gnomon
Memorial to the Throne about the Reforms of Peter the Great of Russia (Kang Youwei)
Mencius

Metaphysics and Sciences — A Comment on Zhang Junmai's The Outlook on Life (Ding Wenjiang)
Miscellaneous Poems Written in 1839 (Gong Zizhen)
Modern Sociology (Li Da)
A Morning Talk (Liang Shuming)
Mozi
My Memoirs (Feng Youlan)
My View of Embryo Completed in 1812-1813 (Gong Zizhen)
My View of Marxism (Li Dazhao)

New Guide to Government (Hong Ren'gan)
A New Theory of Consciousness-Only (Xiong Shili)
A New Treatise (Lu Gu)
A New Treatise on Neo-Confucianism (Feng Youlan)
A New Treatise on the Methodology of Metaphysics (Feng Youlan)
A New Treatise on the Nature of Man (Feng Youlan)
"1916" (Chen Duxiu)
The Ninth Revision of the Inquiry into the Book of Changes (Li Zhi)
Notes and Commentaries on Study (Ye Shi)
Notes on Master Zhang's Correcting Youthful Ignorance (Wang Fuzhi)
Notes on the Observation Door to the Dharmadhatu of the Avatamsaka Sect (Zongmi)
Notes to the Authorized Edicts of the Late Heavenly King (Hong Xiuquan)

Notes to the Vimalakirtinirdessa Sutra (Zhu Daosheng)

Obscuration Awaiting Inquiries (Huang Zongxi)
Of the Nature of Things (Yang Quan)
On Atheism (Zhang Taiyan)
On Contradiction (Mao Zedong)
On Enlightened Absolutism (Liang Qichao)
On Enlightened Monarchy and Good Ministers (Gong Zizhen)
On Ether (Tan Sitong)
On Five Nonbeings (Zhang Taiyan)
"On Germs" (Zhang Taiyan)
On How to Enlist Talented People (Huang Zongxi)
On Non-self of Man (Zhang Taiyan)

Preservation of Learning (Yan Yuan)
A Primary Study on the Reasons of Things (Fang Yizhi)
A Primer of Logic (Yan Fu)
Principle and Material Force (Chen Jiakang)
The Principle of the People's Livelihood (Sun Yat-sen)
The Principle of the People's Rights (Sun Yat-sen)
Problems of Strategy in China's Revolutionary War (Mao Zedong)
The Program of the Construction of the Nation (Sun Yat-sen)
Propaganda Creates Social Strength (Sun Yat-sen)
A Proposal for the Curriculum of the Scientific Academy (Wang Tao)
A Proposal to Set up Provinces in the Western Regions (Gong Zizhen)
Pure Words of the Two Chengs

Questions and Answers on the Works of Mencius (Zhu Xi)
Quotations from a Buddhist Who Called Himself a Fool of Wisdom (Fang Yizhi)

Rambling Notes from a Cottage (Fang Yizhi)
Rambling Notes Written While Wandering Abroad (Wang Tao)
Reading Notes from Striving for Humanity-cultivating Studio (Liang Shuming)
Rebuttal of Kang Youwei's A Retort to the Revolution (Zhang Taiyan)
Record of Thoughts and Questionings (Wang Fuzhi)
A Record of Words and Deeds (Yan Yuan)
Recorded Essays (Zhang Taiyan)
Records and Remainders of Xizhai (Yan Yuan)
Records of the Historian (Sima Qian)
Records Official and Unofficial (Fang Dazhen)
The Recovery of Man's Nature (Li Ao)
A Reply to 'A Treatise on Heaven' by Liu Yuxi (Liu Zongyuan)
A Reply to He Baizhai's Theory of Creation (Wang Tianxiang)
A Reply to Mr. Chen Duxiu (Hu Shi)
Reply to Mr. Hu Shizhi (Chen Duxiu)
A Reply to Mr. Xie Youwei on His Three Points of Criticism (He Lin)
A Reply to the Chinese Merchants of North and South America on the Reason Why China Can Only Have a Constitutional Monarchy and Not a Revolution (also entitled *A Retort to the Revolution*) (Kang Youwei)

A Reply to Tiezheng (Zhang Taiyan)
A Reply to Zhang Junmai and Liang Qichao (Chen Duxiu)
Research into Ancient Chinese Society (Guo Moruo)
Research into Chinese Society at the Prehistoric Stage (Lu Zhenyu)
A Resolute Idea for Saving the Nation from Extinction (Yan Fu)
Response to 'Asking Heaven' (Liu Zongyuan)
The Revised Manuscript of "On Germs" (Zhang Taiyan)
The Revolutionary Army (Zou Rong)

Sayings of Master Zhang (Zhang Zai)
The School (Huang Zongxi)
Science and the Outlook on Life (Zhang Junmai)
Scratching My Head, I Ask (Wang Fuzhi)
Sequel to Frightening Words for a Prosperous Age (Zheng Guanying)
Sequel to the Book Which Risks Burning (Li Zhi)
Sequel to the Hidden Book (Li Zhi)
Sequence to the Definitive Edition of the Writings of Nanlei (Huang Zongxi)
Series of Li Zhi
A Sermon on the Origin of the Way and Awakening (Hong Xiuquan)
A Sermon on the Origin of the Way and Consciousness (Hong Xiuquan)
Several Philosophical Problems (Ai Siqi)
Silent Goblet (Wei Yuan)
Simple Exemplification of the Subtle Implications of the Laozi (Wang Bi)
The Sixth Letter to the Qing Emperor (Kang Youwei)
Six Quatrains on Art (Tan Sitong)
A Song on the Origin of the Way and Salvation (Hong Xiuquan)
Speech at the Commemoration Meeting on the Anniversary of the First Guangdong Women's Normal School (Sun Yat-sen)
Speech at the Peasants' Get-Together in Guangzhou (Sun Yat-sen)
A Speech Delivered on the Anniversary of the People's Journal (Zhang Taiyan)
Speech to KMT Representatives from Various Provinces and Mongolia (Sun Yat-sen)
Spirit of Chinese Philosophy (Feng Youlan)
Spring and Autumn Annals
Spring and Autumn Annals with Commentaries by Gongyang Gao
The Star Classics of Messieurs Gan and Shi

Statecraft Essays of the Present Dynasty (Wei Yuan)
Statements of Grace (Wang Tingxiang)
Subtle Meaning of the Book of Mencius (Kang Youwei)
Sudden Awakening (Chen Tianhua)
Sunzi (*The Art of War*)
Supreme Principles Governing the World (Shao Yong)
Surviving Works of the Two Chengs
Syntactic and Semantic Analysis of the Book of Rites (Wang Fuzhi)
Syntactic and Semantic Analysis of the Great Learning (Zhu Xi)

Temple Inscription to Han the Literary Prince of Chaozhou (Su Shi)
The Two Chengs' Explanations of the Classics
The Theory of Knowledge (Zhang Dongsun)
Theory and Practice (Ye Qing)
A Theory of Life Organism (Chen Lifu)
"A Theory of Watching Heaven" (Zhang Taiyan)
Things and Principle (Chen Jiakang)
The Third Essay on Problems and "Isms" (Hu Shi)
The Third Introduction to the Revised Diagrams of Changes (Li Gou)
This Past Week (Li Dazhao)
To Chen Duxiu (Wu Yu)
To Know Is Difficult But to Do Is Easy (Sun Yat-sen)
To My Dear Countrymen (Sun Yat-sen)
To Ouyang Zhonghu (Tan Sitong)
To Xue Juncai (Wang Tingxiang)
A Treatise on Feudalism (Liu Zongyuan)
A Treatise on Heaven (Liu Yuxi)
Treatise on How to Beware of Courage (Ji Kang)
Treatise on How to Reach Zhuangzi (Ruan Ji)

Treatise on Keeping Good Health (Ji Kang)
A Treatise on Knowledge (Jin Yuelin)
Treatise on the Extinction of the Soul (Fan Zhen)
A Treatise on the Major Ideas of the Six Schools (Sima Tan)
Treatise on the Nameless (He Yan)
A Treatise on the Way (Jin Yuelin)
Treatise on Why Sound Has Neither Sorrow nor Joy (Ji Kang)

Under Heaven (Zhuang Zhou)

The Value of the Materialist Concept of History in the Modern Historical Sciences (Li Dazhao)
Vimalakirtinirdesa Sutra
Vimalakirti-Nirdesa-Sutra

Waiting for the Answer (Wang Fuzhi)
Whither Philosophy? (Ye Qing)
Wing of the Book of Laozi (Jiao Hong)
The World of Freedom and the World of Necessity (Qu Qiubai)
The World Philosophy of the Past Fifty Years (Hu Shi)

Xunzi (*The Book of Master Xun*)

Yellow Book (Wang Fuzhi)
Yichuan's Commentary on the Book of Changes
"Youthfulness" (Li Dazhao)
Yu Lao (*Elucidation of the Laozi with Parables*) (Han Fei)

Zhuangzi (Chuang Tzu)
Zuo Commentary

Index

C

L

N

O

U

V

W

X

Y

Z